# BUSINESS COMMUNICATION
## SECOND EDITION

**Meenakshi Raman**
*Former Professor and Head*
*Department of Humanities and Management*
*BITS Pilani, K K Birla Goa Campus*

**Prakash Singh**
*Associate Professor and Area Chairman*
*Finance and Accounting*
*Indian Institute of Management*
*Lucknow*

# OXFORD
UNIVERSITY PRESS

Oxford University Press is a department of the University of Oxford.
It furthers the University's objective of excellence in research, scholarship,
and education by publishing worldwide. Oxford is a registered trademark of
Oxford University Press in the UK and in certain other countries.

Published in India by
Oxford University Press
22 Workspace, 2nd Floor, 1/22 Asaf Ali Road, New Delhi 110 002

© Oxford University Press 2006, 2012

The moral rights of the author/s have been asserted.

First Edition published in 2006
Second Edition published in 2012
18th impression 2023

All rights reserved. No part of this publication may be reproduced, stored in
a retrieval system, or transmitted, in any form or by any means, without the
prior permission in writing of Oxford University Press, or as expressly permitted
by law, by licence, or under terms agreed with the appropriate reprographics
rights organization. Enquiries concerning reproduction outside the scope of the
above should be sent to the Rights Department, Oxford University Press, at the
address above.

You must not circulate this book in any other form
and you must impose this same condition on any acquirer.

ISBN-13: 978-0-19-807705-3
ISBN-10: 0-19-807705-X

Typeset in Garamond
by Star Compugraphics, Delhi 110 096
Printed in India by Rakmo Press, New Delhi 110 020

For product information and current price, please visit www.india.oup.com

Third-Party website addresses mentioned in this book are provided
by Oxford University Press in good faith and for information only.
Oxford University Press disclaims any responsibility for the material contained therein.

# Preface to the Second Edition

Effective and efficient communication is central to doing successful business. The evolution of communication over the years has turned it to a much specialized domain worth studying. Be it our daily lives or business contexts, the need for effective communication is one aspect that can hardly be ignored. The importance of communication has only increased over the years and present day communication necessitates the knowledge of various aspects—both linguistic and technological.

The coming together of technology and communication has indeed helped communication transcend to new heights. Nowadays, one can communicate through various media and thus the channels of communication have grown manifold. The need of the hour is to understand the various characteristics of technology-enabled communication. Moreover, globalization has further added to the need to communicate effectively, especially in the organizational context. With multinational companies operating across continents, there has emerged a pressing need to comprehend not only linguistic differences but also cultural differences. The second edition of *Business Communication* focuses on these aspects of communication with special reference to cross-cultural communication. This edition includes new chapters, cases, and additional features that facilitate easy learning, quick comprehension, and long-term retention. The book is designed to cater to the syllabi requirements of management students and help professionals in communicating effectively—both verbally and non-verbally—at the workplace. The book also features a new chapter on résumé writing and career building—aspects that are of paramount importance to students readying for their careers in management.

The practical aspects of business communication are presented through lively and pedagogically effective examples interspersed throughout the text and end-of-chapter material. Students will be assisted in understanding business communication terminology through several sidebars. The practical examples and cases included in each chapter would facilitate the learners to assess their understanding and apply the concepts of business communication in real-time business contexts.

## Key Features

- Contains cases and examples in the key areas of business communication
- Provides end-chapter exercises with concept review and critical thinking questions and interesting classroom activities and field projects

## New to the Second Edition

- Two new chapters on cross-cultural communication and résumés
- New sections, such as interpersonal communication, communication styles, fluency development strategies, types of interviews, video conferencing, and teleconferencing
- New features, such as business communication insights and communication tools
- Appendices on transitional words and phrases, impact words, interview questions, common usage errors, commonly misspelt words, and British and American vocabulary
- New figures and photographs

## Organization of Content

The content of the book has been organized into four parts and six appendices. Each part of the book presents both the theoretical and practical aspects of business communication.

Part I (Chapters 1 to 4) introduces those aspects of communication essential for getting insights into the foundations of communicating for business purposes. It includes an extensive chapter on cross-cultural aspects of globalized business environment and also on using appropriate technologies for business communication.

Part II (Chapters 5 to 9) deals with an important aspect of organizational communication, namely writing business messages and documents. Besides introducing the elements of effective business writing, this part of the book includes a chapter on instructions, which is very rare to find in any book of this kind. The newly included chapter on career building and résumé writing would not only catch the attention of the readers, but also prove to be immensely useful for them.

Part III (Chapters 10 to 16) elaborates on the various forms of oral communication that interest most readers and are also much in demand in the academic and professional world. Here again, the chapters on conversations and team briefing are seldom found in other books on business communication. The guidelines on presentations, public speaking, meetings, and interviews would prove to be valuable tools for the readers in enhancing their oral communication skills.

Part IV (Chapters 17 to 21), the last part of the book, focuses on specific communication needs of organizations. For instance, it explains the communication strategies for various functions, such as marketing, HR, and finance, at the workplace. Chapters on ethics and persuasive strategies enhance the appeal of the book by making it more comprehensive in almost all aspects of business communication.

A set of six new appendices have been added at the end of the book. Readers will find the interview questions included in Appendix A quite useful. Appendix B presents a list of words that can help create a positive impact on the interviewers during an interview. While Appendix C exhibits some transitional words and phrases, Appendix D shows the difference between British and American vocabulary. Appendices E and F present some common usage errors and commonly misspelt words, which will also help students as well as aspiring professionals.

**Meenakshi Raman**
**Prakash Singh**

---

### Praise for the First Edition

*The book deals with all aspects of the course contents.*

—Dr Rajendra Prasad Sharma, IIFT, Kolkata Campus

# Acknowledgements

We are grateful to the administration of BITS Pilani and the Indian Institute of Management, Lucknow, under whose aegis we were provided an environment conducive to the completion of this edition. The editorial team at Oxford University Press deserves our special thanks for initiating and accomplishing the process of revision. We appreciate the constructive suggestions given by the reviewers to add new topics and update the first edition so as to suit the needs of a diverse population of students and professionals. Meenakshi Raman would like to acknowledge the help provided by Mr G. Gyanesh, her colleague at the Goa Campus, in preparing the new chapter on career building and résumé writing.

At the home front, we sincerely acknowledge the support and encouragement we got from our family members in successfully completing this revision.

We sincerely hope that this revised edition, with its updated, comprehensive coverage of all aspects and types of business communication, will prove to be highly useful to the readers in enhancing the effectiveness of their communication. Any suggestions for improvement are welcome.

**Meenakshi Raman**
**Prakash Singh**

# Preface to the First Edition

The need to communicate is universal and transcends the notions of language, location, and lifestyle. People transmit and exchange their ideas, facts, feelings, or courses of action for personal or professional purposes. While the term 'personal communication' refers to *exchanging personal messages*, the term 'business communication' denotes the *process of sending and receiving business messages*.

An organization being a group of people working together to achieve a common goal, communication plays a significant role in the process of its formation and continuance. A group of people working together must interact in order to share their needs, thoughts, plans, expertise, opinions, and so on. Communication is the means by which information is shared, activities are coordinated, and decisions are implemented. Whether it is an academic institution or business organization, communicating formal and technical messages is vital for its progress, prosperity, and sustenance. The various oral and written forms of communication, such as presentations, briefings, meetings, interviews, conversations, seminars, conferences, discussions, instructions, reports, proposals, letters, advertisements, and so on, not only enable people to come together and share their ideas at various workplaces but also enable organizations to progress and prosper.

Good communication skills are basic to successful management. Today, the reputation of an organization, an industry, or a nation depends on the quality and quantity of information they transmit and exchange. Gone are the days when information dissemination used to be the function of a specific group in an organization. With the phenomenal advancement in technology, accessing and sharing of information has now become a common function and communication has assumed more importance than ever before. This makes it necessary for business organizations to reorient themselves towards a better understanding of the process of transmitting and receiving information effectively and efficiently through oral and written media.

The educational institutions offering management programmes play a significant part in inculcating the much-needed managerial skills in their students—the aspiring managers. There is no denying the fact that acquiring knowledge of the various managerial functions is important, but it is important to realize that developing business communication skills is central to carrying out all these functions effectively. Taking cognizance of this fact, all academic institutions offering undergraduate and postgraduate programmes in management have included business communication as a part of their curriculum.

Business communication is evolving at a rapid pace with the introduction of new network-based collaborative technologies. These technologies and tools are making real-time communication a reality, which can improve employee productivity and deliver tremendous returns for employers. As a result of global competition and restructuring, we are witnessing dramatic changes in work environments. Information is now exchanged via email and voicemail; meetings are conducted through teleconferencing and video conferencing; business presentations are made with the use of sophisticated presentation software; shopping is offered online; and customer information is collected and products are promoted using the Internet.

Because of the various phenomenal changes in the business environment, recruiters now look for students with good computer-cum-communication skills. To thrive in this new world of work, management students must be flexible and willing to continually learn new skills that supplement the basic skills they acquire as students. Probably, the most important basic skill for managers in the new environment is the ability to communicate effectively, which means being able to exchange information and ideas effectively in speech and writing. As they climb higher in their career, communication skills become even more important. In spite of the increasing importance of communication skills, many individuals struggle to communicate their thoughts and ideas effectively in both verbal and written format. This inability makes it nearly impossible for them to compete effectively in the workplace and stands in the way of their progress.

## About the Book

The main objective of this book is to provide the reader with adequate exposure to the various forms and practices of business communication, primarily focusing on the communication needs of management students. At the same time, the book would also serve as a comprehensive guide for other students and business professionals who want to enhance their communication skills. The in-depth discussions on business conversations, instructions, team briefing, team presentation, business ethics, functional areas of communication, and core issues in corporate communication would not only help readers understand the nuances of business communication, but also enable them to enhance their communication skills at the workplace. Although a large number of books are available in the market to cater to the communication needs of students and professionals, this book is unique inasmuch as it discusses communication concepts and practices from the Indian business perspective. It includes caselets and excerpts pertaining to Indian businesses, such as Aditya Birla Group, Infosys, Wipro Industries, Merrill Lynch (India), and Reliance Industries. Each of the eighteen chapters contains either a case study or an excerpt relevant to the topic of discussion in that chapter, providing a practical approach to the ideas discussed. Moreover, numerous examples are given to illustrate the various forms of business communication and facilitate readers' understanding of the communication practices prevalent in contemporary business scenario.

## Pedagogical Features

Each chapter of the book begins with learning objectives and concludes with a case, caselet, or excerpt relevant to the development of a specific skill in communicating for business purposes discussed in that chapter. The assignments given at the end of each chapter help to assess not only the reader's understanding of the concepts but also their ability to apply those concepts in appropriate business situations. For example, in Chapter 4, the speech by Mr Aditya Vikram Birla is included in the critical thinking exercises to expose the readers to the fine techniques of public speaking discussed in the chapter. The case on Reliance Industries' image in the chapter on corporate communication is a direct indication of how the authors have tried to use recent corporate issues as a tool to drive home the concepts discussed in the book. Chapter 16 presents the WIPRO identity case to enunciate the advertising strategies discussed in the first part of the chapter. Similarly, the Pentagon case in the chapter on ethical communication brings out the emotional aspect of media reporting and other related issues.

Besides the three types of exercises—concept review questions, critical thinking questions, and projects—the book is also accompanied by an Instructor's Manual that provides guidance to instructors as to using it effectively in the classroom. The Instructors' Manual, which is available on demand, also outlines solutions to all the exercises given at the end of each chapter.

## Acknowledgements

Any project of this magnitude requires the goodwill, encouragement, guidance, and support of many people.

We are grateful to Prof. S. Venkateswaran, Vice Chancellor, BITS Pilani, for being a constant source of inspiration and encouragement in all our academic endeavours. We thank Prof. L.K. Maheshwari, Pro Vice Chancellor and Director, BITS, Pilani, for his unflinching support and guidance. Our heartfelt thanks are due to Prof. K.E. Raman, Deputy Director (Administration) and Prof. V.S. Rao, Deputy Director (Off Campus Programmes), BITS Pilani, for their valuable guidance. We are indebted to Prof. R.N. Saha, Dean, Faculty Division III & Educational Development Division, and Prof. A.K. Sarkar, Dean, Faculty Division I & Instruction Division, BITS Pilani, for extending their support and expert advice throughout the course of this project.

We acknowledge with gratitude the timely suggestions and consistent cooperation received from the faculty members of the Management Group and the Languages Group of BITS Pilani. Kavikrut, Sujeev Reddy, and C.S. Srivatsan, students of BITS Pilani, deserve our special thanks for assisting us in collecting data for writing certain chapters of this book.

Reviewers are an indispensable part of the making of a good textbook. Although we do not know them by name, we found ourselves in anonymous debate with several remarkable thinkers, especially about some of the important but not so common topics discussed in the book. Their keen eye and questioning attitude sharpened each chapter so as to benefit both the authors and the readers. In this regard, we appreciate the tremendous efforts of the editorial team of Oxford University Press, New Delhi, who were constantly communicating to us on all review matters.

We do not have enough words to express our gratitude for the unstinting cooperation and affectionate concern of our family members—Raman, Prabhu, and Priya of Meenakshi Raman's family, and Bindu and Paarth of Prakash Singh's family—during the course of this project.

We are indebted to the following persons and organizations for permitting us to include the information available on their websites as case studies or passages in various chapters of this book:

- Aditya Birla Group
- Wipro Technologies
- Infosys Technologies Ltd
- Reliance Industries Ltd
- Konica Minolta, Pentagon (USA)
- Merrill Lynch & Co., Inc.
- Dianne Schilling, www.womensmedia.com
- Bruce Wilson, Editor, www.businesslistening.com
- VNU Business Media, www.presentations.com
- Steve Tingas, www.marketingprofs.com
- Donna Shaw, Oregon State University, Oregon
- Dr Randall Hansen, Webmaster, Quintessential Careers
- Barbara Braham
- Carter McNamara, Authenticity Consulting, LLC
- www.proposalkit.com
- Michael A. Chwastiak, Publisher, Blue Boulder Internet Publishing, Ontario, Canada
- www.effectivemeetings.com
- Gail Miller, Human Resource Services, Washington State University, Washington
- Paul Treuer, University of Minnesota, Minnesota
- Rohit Sarda, www.wiprocorporate.com
- Conflict Research Consortium, University of Colorado, Colorado
- David A. McMurrey, University of Texas at Austin, Austin
- John D. Baker, Publisher & Editor, *The Negotiator Magazine*

**Meenakshi Raman**
**Prakash Singh**

# Brief Contents

*Preface to the Second Edition  iii*
*Acknowledgements  v*
*Preface to the First Edition  vi*
*Detailed Contents  x*
*Features of the Book  xviii*
*List of Case Studies  xx*

## PART I  UNDERSTANDING BUSINESS COMMUNICATION

1. Nature and Scope of Communication  3
2. Non-verbal Communication  46
3. Cross-cultural Communication  87
4. Technology-enabled Business Communication  104

## PART II  WRITING BUSINESS MESSAGES AND DOCUMENTS

5. Business Writing  133
6. Business Correspondence  154
7. Instructions  178
8. Business Reports and Proposals  195
9. Careers and Résumés  222

## PART III  DEVELOPING ORAL COMMUNICATION SKILLS FOR BUSINESS

10. Effective Listening  261
11. Business Presentations and Public Speaking  296
12. Conversations  336
13. Interviews  357
14. Meetings and Conferences  384
15. Group Discussions and Team Presentations  408
16. Team Briefing  432

## PART IV  UNDERSTANDING SPECIFIC COMMUNICATION NEEDS

17. Communication across Functional Areas  453
18. Corporate Communication  494
19. Persuasive Strategies in Business Communication  512
20. Ethics in Business Communication  546
21. Business Communication Aids  587

*Appendix A: Interview Questions  624*
*Appendix B: Impact Words  627*
*Appendix C: Transitions  629*
*Appendix D: British and American Vocabulary  631*
*Appendix E: Common Usage Errors  634*
*Appendix F: Commonly Misspelt Words  640*

*Index  648*
*About the Authors  651*

# Detailed Contents

*Preface to the Second Edition*   *iii*
*Acknowledgements*   *v*
*Preface to the First Edition*   *vi*
*Brief Contents*   *ix*
*Features of the Book*   *xviii*
*List of Case Studies*   *xx*

## PART I   UNDERSTANDING BUSINESS COMMUNICATION

1. **Nature and Scope of Communication**   3
    Introduction   3
    Definition   3
    The Mehrabian Model   4
    Business Communication   5
        Effective Business Communication   7
    Functions of Communication   9
        Information   9
        Control   9
        Motivation   9
        Emotional Expression   9
    Roles of a Manager   10
        Interpersonal Roles   10
        Informational Roles   11
        Decisional Roles   11
    Communication Basics   12
        Process   12
        Basic Facts about Communication   14
    Communication Networks   14
        Upward Communication   15
        Downward Communication   16
        Horizontal Communication   16
        Spiral or Diagonal Communication   17
    Informal Communication—Beyond
        the Organizational Hierarchy   18
        Informal Contacts with Outsiders   20
    Tips for Effective Internal
        Communications   20
        Downward Communication   20
        Upward Communication   21
        Supervisor and Employee
            Communications   21
    Interpersonal Communication   23
        Stages   23
        Styles   24
    Communication Barriers   25
        Organizational Structure   26
        Difference in Status   27
        Lack of Trust   27
        Closed Communication Climate   27
        Incorrect Choice of Medium   28
        Information Overload   28
        Message Complexity   29
        Message Competition   29
        Unethical Communication   30
        Physical Distractions   30
    Effective Managerial Communication   31
        Appropriate Communication Style   32
        Audience-centred Approach   32
        Understanding Intercultural
            Communication   33
        Commitment to Ethical
            Communication   34
        Proficiency in Communication
            Technology   35
        Control over the Flow of
            Communication   35
        Reducing the Number of Messages   36
    Strategies for Improving Organizational
        Communication   36
        Encourage Open Feedback   37
        Use Simple Language   37
        Avoid Overload   38
        Walk the Talk   39
        Be a Good Listener   39
    *Case Study 1: Goodwill Corporation Ltd*   *43*

*Case Study 2: Image and Rumours at Procter & Gamble* 44

## 2. Non-verbal Communication 46

Introduction 46
Definition 47
Significance of Non-verbal Communication in Organizations 48
Forms of Non-verbal Communication 52
   Conscious Non-verbal Communication 52
   Subconscious Non-verbal Communication 52
Types of Non-verbal Communication 53
   Kinesics 54
   Facial Expressions 55
   Posture 59
   Oculesics 66
   Haptics 68
   Proxemics 70
   Appearance and Artefacts 73
   Paralanguage/Vocalics 75
   Chronemics 80
Interpreting Non-verbal Messages 80
*Case Study: Charisma Corporation* 86

## 3. Cross-cultural Communication 87

Introduction 87
Concept of Cross-cultural Communication 88
Different Communication Styles 88
Ethnocentrism 89
Cultural Variables and Communication Sensitivity 90
   Variables of National Culture 92
   Technology 94
   Individual Cultural Variables 95
Cross-cultural Communication Strategies 98
   Potential Hot Spots in Cross-cultural Communication 99
Cross-cultural Communication skills—Basic Tips 101
*Case Study 1: Cultural Differences* 103
*Case Study 2: Conversation Styles* 103

## 4. Technology-enabled Business Communication 104

Introduction 104
Technology-based Communication Tools 105
   Telephone and Voicemail 105
   Facsimile Machines 107
   Computers 107
   Desktop 108
   The Internet 110
   Conferencing 114
   Instant Messaging 117
   Emails 119
   Groupware 121
   CD-ROM and DVD-ROM Databases 121
Positive Impact of Technology-enabled Communication 122
Negative Impact of Technology-enabled Communication 123
   Overcoming Negative Impact 124
Selection of Appropriate Technology 124
Effectiveness in Technology-based Communication 126

## PART II WRITING BUSINESS MESSAGES AND DOCUMENTS

## 5. Business Writing 133

Introduction 133
Importance of Written Business Communication 134
   Types of Business Messages 135
Direct and Indirect Approaches to Business Messages 137
   Direct Approach 137
   Indirect Approach 138
Five Main Stages of Writing Business Messages 139
*Case Study: Communication Complication in English* 152

## 6. Business Correspondence 154

Introduction 154
Business Letter Writing 154
Effective Business Correspondence—Basic Principles 155

Place the Reader First  155
Keep to the Point  155
Set the Right Tone  155
Write Effective Openings  156
Write Effective Conclusions  156
Common Components of Business
 Letters  156
Strategies for Writing the Body of a
 Letter  158
  State the Main Business, Purpose, or
   Subject Matter Right Away  158
  Keep the Paragraphs Short  159
  Provide Topic Indicators in the
   Beginning of Paragraphs  159
  Place Important Information
   Strategically  159
  Develop a 'You-attitude'  160
  Give an 'Action Ending' Whenever
   Appropriate  161
Kinds of Business Letters  161
  Routine Letters  161
  Covering Letters for Job Applications  163
  Recommendation Letter  163
  Thank-you/Follow-up Letters  166
  Acceptance and Rejection Letters  167
  Resignation Letter  167
  Inquiry Letters  169
  Persuasive Letters  170
Writing Effective Memos  171
  Memo Report Format  172
*Case Study: Missing Briefcase*  177

## 7. Instructions  178

Introduction  178
Written Instructions  179
  How to Write Instructions  180
  Groupings of Tasks  181
  Introduction  181
  General Warning, Caution, and Danger
   Notices  181
  Graphics in Instructions  182
  Format in Instructions  183
   Headings  183
   Lists  184
   Numbers, Abbreviations, and Symbols  184
Oral Instructions  185
Audience Analysis  186
  Types of Audience  186

Factors for Audience Analysis  186
Audience Adaptation  187
Product Instructions  188
  Characteristics of Good Product
   Instructions  189
  Function of Instructions  189
*Case Study: How to Operate the
 Minolta Freedom 3 Camera*  192

## 8. Business Reports and Proposals  195

Introduction  195
What is a Report?  196
  Kinds of Reports  197
  Who Writes and Reads Reports?  197
  Characteristics of Business Reports  197
  Elements of Effective Business Report
   Writing  198
  Purpose of Business Reports  199
Steps in Writing a Routine Business
 Report  199
  Determine the Scope of the Report  199
  Consider the Audience  200
  Gather Your Information  200
  Analyse Your Information  201
  Determine Solutions  201
  Organize Your Report  201
Parts of a Report  201
Corporate Reports  203
  Director's Reports (Board's Reports)  203
  Auditor's Reports  204
  Cost Audit Reports  205
Business Proposals  205
  Types of Business Proposals  205
  Components of a Proposal  207
  Format of Proposals  211
  Proposal Layout and Design  216
  A Simple Proposal Formula  216
  Five Key Elements of Winning Business
   Proposals  217
*Case Study 1: Handling Unsolicited
 Proposals for Private Infrastructure
 Projects*  220
*Case Study 2: The Keyboard Syndrome*  221

## 9. Careers and Résumés  222

Introduction  222
Career Building  223
  Today's Workplaces  223

Understanding Yourself  223
Setting a Career Goal  224
Job Search/Looking at Various
 Options  224
Preparing Your Résumé  225
Résumé Formats  230
Chronological  232
Functional  232
Combination  232
Targeted  232
Mini  232
Traditional, Electronic, and Video
Résumés  233
Types of Electronic Résumé  233
Guidelines for Preparing Electronic
 Résumés  234
Video Résumés  234
Sending Résumés  246
Follow-up Letters  248
Online Recruitment Process  251
Online Recruitment Techniques  251
Advantages of E-recruitment  251
*Case Study: Recruitment Drive
at SOBER*  256

## PART III  DEVELOPING ORAL COMMUNICATION SKILLS FOR BUSINESS

### 10. Effective Listening  261

Introduction  261
What does 'Listening' Mean?  262
Active and Passive Listening  263
Process of Listening  263
Advantages of Listening  264
Common Myths about Listening  265
Types of Listening  265
Informative Listening  265
Attentive Listening  266
Relationship Listening  266
Appreciative Listening  268
Critical Listening  268
Discriminative Listening  269
Effective and Ineffective Listening
 Skills  269
Barriers to Effective Listening  270
Content  270
Speaker  271
Medium  271
Distractions  271
Mindset  271
Language  272
Listening Speed  272
Feedback  272
Other Barriers to Effective Listening  273
Leadership and Role of Listening
 in Leadership Styles  274
Six Styles of Leadership  277
Listening at Three Managerial Levels  279
Level 1  279
Level 2  279
Level 3  280
Benefits of Listening for Leaders
 and Teams  280
Motivational Benefits of Listening
 in the Workplace  281
Why are Managers Inherently Poor
 Listeners?  282
Poor Listening Habits  284
Specific Poor Listening Habits in
 Customer Care Jobs/BPOs  287
Categories of Poor Listeners  287
Strategies for Effective Listening  288
Decide What Your Goals are for
 the Conversation  288
Be Aware of Your Options  289
Pay-offs of Effective Listening  291
*Case Study 1: Lyman Steil*  294
*Case Study 2: The Farewell Speech*  295

### 11. Business Presentations and Public Speaking  296

Introduction  296
Business Presentations and Speeches  297
Planning  299
Structuring  302
Delivery  304
Introduction to a Presentation  319
Function of an Introduction  319
Components of an Introduction  320
Main Body  323
Message-based Approach  323
Creativity in Presentations and

　　　　Speeches  324
　　　　Mind Mapping Your Presentations  324
　　Conclusion  325
　　　　Signalling the End  325
　　　　Reviewing  325
　　　　Emphatic Closing  325
　　Effective Sales Presentations  327
　　　　Sales Presentation—Sample  328
　　　　Integrating Levels of Content  330
　　Controlling Nervousness and Stage
　　　　Fright  331
　　　　Symptoms of Stage Fright  331
　　*Case Study*: *Business Leaders and*
　　　　*Public Speaking*  335

## 12. Conversations  336

　　Introduction  336
　　Importance of Business Conversations  337
　　Essentials of a Business Conversation  337
　　　　Conversations must be about the Issues
　　　　　　that Matter Most  337
　　　　Conversations must be Collective
　　　　　　and Public  338
　　　　Conversations must be Structured  338
　　　　Change-in-strategy Conversations  338
　　　　Conversations must Allow Employees
　　　　　　to be Honest without Risking
　　　　　　their Jobs  339
　　Conversation Management  340
　　　　Involve Everyone  340
　　　　Arouse and Sustain Interest  340
　　　　Engage in Active Listening  341
　　　　Make Effective Requests  341
　　　　Use Verbal Cues Appropriately  341
　　Non-verbal Cues in Conversations  346
　　　　How to Identify Cues and Clues  347
　　　　Signs and Signals  348
　　Stressful Conversations  348
　　　　Dealing with an Argumentative
　　　　　　Communicator  350
　　*Case Study*: *Creating a Conversation*
　　　　*with Potential Customers*  355

## 13. Interviews  357

　　Introduction  357
　　Fundamental Principles of
　　　　Interviewing  358
　　General Preparation for an Interview  358

　　Assess Yourself  359
　　Track and Leverage Your
　　　　Accomplishments  359
　　Updating Your Résumé  360
　　Re-assessing Your Résumé  360
　　Prepare Questions to Ask  361
　　Follow-up  361
Success in an Interview  361
　　Dressing for the Interview  361
　　Establishing Rapport  361
　　Using Body Language  362
　　Answering Questions  362
　　Asking Questions  362
Types of Interviewing Questions  362
　　Permission Questions  362
　　Factual Questions  362
　　'Tell Me about' Questions  363
　　'Feeling' Questions  363
　　'Checking' Questions  363
Important Non-verbal Aspects  363
Types of Interviews  365
　　Screening Interview  365
　　Selection Interview  365
　　Group Interview  365
　　Stress Interview  366
　　Walk-in Interview  366
　　Virtual Interview  366
　　Campus Interview  366
　　Panel Interview  367
　　Telephonic Interview  368
　　Behavioural Interview  368
　　Case Interview  369
Styles of Interviewing  370
　　Traditional Job Interview  370
　　Behavioural Job Interview  370
Case Interviews  376
　　Facing a Case Interview  376
　　Types of Case Questions  377
Mastering On-site Interviews—A
　　Guide to Company Visits  378
　　Preliminary Arrangements  378
　　Preparation  378
　　Corporate Culture and Fit  378
　　Salary  378
　　Testing  378
　　End of the Visit  379
　　Follow-up  379

*Case Study: A True Tale of a Case Interview Gone Bad* 381

## 14. Meetings and Conferences 384

Introduction 384
Purposes of a Meeting 385
Planning a Meeting 385
  Be Specific 386
  Create an Agenda 386
  Prepare in Advance 386
Meeting Process 386
  Who will Participate? 386
  What should be the Discussion-management Process? 387
  Plan, Discuss, and Assign Roles 387
  Pre- and Post-meeting Communication 387
Leading Effective Meetings 388
  Starting Time 388
  Opening Remarks 388
  Getting Down to Business 388
  Participation 388
  Agenda 389
  Closing 389
Strategic Issues Related to Effective Meetings 389
  To Meet or Not to Meet 389
  Non-verbal Communication in Meetings 389
  Reaching Rapid Consensus in Meetings 390
Evaluating Meetings 392
  Attendee Evaluations 392
  Internal Evaluations 392
Minutes 392
Planning a Conference 393
  Purpose of the Conference 393
  Conducting a Conference 394
  Promote the Conference 396
  Preparation 396
  After the Event 396
Teleconferencing 396
  Types of Teleconference 397
  Advantages of Teleconferences 398
  Disadvantages of Teleconferences 399
  Applications of Teleconferencing 399
Effective Meetings via Video Conferencing 401
Web Conferencing 403
*Case Study: A Special Meeting of the Executive Committee* 407

## 15. Group Discussions and Team Presentations 408

Introduction 408
Benefits of a GD 409
Workplace GD Guidelines 410
  Planning and Preparation 410
  Organizer's Role 410
  Procedure 410
Functional and Non-functional Roles in Group Discussions 411
  Functional Roles 411
  Non-functional Roles 413
Improving Group Performance 414
  Criteria for Effective Groups 414
  Problems Hindering Group Effectiveness 415
Assessment Group Discussions 415
  Content vs Process in GD 416
  How does One Ensure Excellence in Both Quantity and Quality of Content? 416
  What Role should You Specialize in? 416
  Holding Centre Stage in a GD 416
  Steps in a GD 417
  Opening the GD 417
  Approach to Topics and Case Studies 418
  Tips for Success in GDs 420
  Sample GD topics 421
Team Presentations 422
  Benefits of Team Presentations 422
  Purposes of Team Presentations 423
  Planning and Preparation 423
  Execution 426
  Towards Effective Team Presentations 428
*Case Study 1: Developing Presentation for a Training Programme* 430
*Case Study 2: Career Couselling* 431

## 16. Team Briefing 432

Introduction 432
Briefing 432
  Features 434
  Process 434
  Briefing down the Line 435

Benefits  435
Techniques  439
Team Briefing Formats  440
  Information Briefing  440
  Decision Briefing  441
  Follow-up Briefing  442
Effective Briefing  442
Sample Briefings  443
*Case Study 1: Team Briefing*  448
*Case Study 2: Briefing on 'Maximizing Your Business with Modern Telephone Techniques'*  449

## PART IV  UNDERSTANDING SPECIFIC COMMUNICATION NEEDS

### 17. Communication across Functional Areas  453

Introduction  453
Marketing Communication/Integrated Marketing Communication  454
  Cola Wars  454
  Definition of Marketing Communication  456
  Medium of Marketing Communication  456
  How Marketing Communications Works  459
Direct vs Indirect Selling  460
Project Management Communication  464
  Managing Project Communication  465
  Ideal Project Communication Mix  467
  Branding a Project/Marketing Communication in a Project  468
Human Resource Communication  469
  Human Resource Communication in Indian Industries  471
  Business Process Outsourcing in India—Victim of Poor HR Communication  473
Financial Communication  475
  Constituents of Financial Communication  477
Corporate Governance  482
Management Information Systems—A Communication Tool  482
  The E-business Enterprise  483
  Communication between Functional Areas  483
  Marketing and Production  485
  Finance and Other Functional Areas  486
  HR and Other Functional Areas  487
*Case Study 1: The Pentagon*  490
*Case Study 2: Merrill Lynch*  491

### 18. Corporate Communication  494

Introduction  494
What is Corporate Communication?  495
  Practice Areas  496
Corporate Citizenship and Social Responsibility  497
  Corporate Social Responsibility  497
  Corporate Reputation—A Benefit to Organizations  499
Corporate Communication Strategy  499
Crisis Management/Communication  500
  Crisis Preparedness  501
  Crisis Communication Planning—Organizing and Completing a Plan that Works  503
  Media Release in Crisis Situations  505
  Key Audience  507
*Case Study: How to Repair the Reliance Image*  509

### 19. Persuasive Strategies in Business Communication  512

Introduction  512
Advertising  514
  Definition  514
  Advertising as a Form of Communication  515
  Advertising Communication Elements  517
AIDA—Master Formula  519
  Attention  519
  Interest  520
  Desire  520
  Action  520
Planning Advertisements for Results  520
Effective Online Advertising  521
Conflict Management  523
  Organizational Conflicts  524

Strategies for Managing Conflict  525
Negotiation  531
   Communication and Effective Negotiation  532
   Basic Approaches to Negotiation  533
   Six Basic Steps of Negotiations  533
   Planning and Preparation  535
   Guidelines for Successful Negotiation  537
Intercultural Negotiation  539
   Five Intercultural Negotiation Skills  540
*Case Study: Launching the New Wipro Identity*  544

## 20. Ethics in Business Communication  546

Introduction  546
Ethical Communication  547
   Why Ethics in Organizational Communication?  549
   Ethical Code in Communication  550
Values, Ethics, and Communication  553
   Ethical Perspectives  555
   Ethical Issues Involved in Business Communications  558
What does a Professional Communicator Do?  559
Ethical Dilemmas Facing Managers  560
   Secrecy  560
   Whistle-blowing  561
   Leaks  562
   Rumours and Gossip  562
   Lying  563
   Ambiguity  565
Strategic Approaches to Corporate Ethics  565
   Corporate Culture  566
   Organizational Policy  566

Relevancy  569
Accuracy  570
Timing  570
Ethical Communication on the Internet  570
   The Internet  570
   Some Areas of Concern  571
   Ethical Implications of Privacy in Electronic Mail  573
   Need for Better Protocol  575
   Application of Computer Ethics to Problems Identified  576
Ethics in Advertising  577
   Benefits of Advertising  578
   Harms Done by Advertising  579
   Advertising and Social Responsibility  581
*Case Study: Electronic Mailing and Ethics*  586

## 21. Business Communication Aids  587

Introduction  587
Elements of Effective English  587
   Grammar and Syntax  588
Effective Paragraphs  597
   Topic Sentence  597
   Coherence  599
   Unity  601
   Adequate Development  602
Power of Reading  602
Punctuation and Capitalization  602
   Punctuation  604
Referencing Styles  612
   MLA Style  612
   APA Style  613
   Chicago Manual Style  614
Email Etiquette  615
Business Terms  617

*Appendix A*   Interview Questions  624
*Appendix B*   Impact Words  627
*Appendix C*   Transitions  629
*Appendix D*   British and American Vocabulary  631
*Appendix E*   Common Usage Errors  634
*Appendix F*   Commonly Misspelt Words  640
*Index*  648
*About the Authors*  651

# Features of the Book

**LEARNING OBJECTIVES**

After reading this chapter, you will be able to understand
- the terms communication, business communication, and effective business communication
- the importance of communication in business
- the basic processes and concepts of communication
- the roles of a manager in business communication
- the formal and informal communication networks
- the nuances of interpersonal communication
- ways to overcome barriers to communication
- the characteristics of, and develop strategies for, effective communication

**Learning Objectives**
Each chapter begins with learning objectives that focus on learning and the knowledge you should acquire by the end of each chapter.

**Business Communication Tool**
A new addition, this feature will help you understand the concepts and avoid mistakes related to business communication.

**COMMUNICATION TOOL**

**Tips for Effective Use of Non-verbal Communication**

Excellent communication skills are the key to success in your personal and professional life. Research shows that non-verbal communication is actually more important than verbal communication. Here are some tips for using non-verbal communication to improve your business and personal relationships:

**A. Observe and understand the non-verbal signals being sent your way on a moment-to-moment basis** Stop and ask the other person what his/her non-verbal behaviour means if you

tiveness and responsiveness, making it a more enjoyable experience for you and for them.
**G. Soak in the pats/hugs that others give you** Many people have difficulty being 'present' in the

**BUSINESS COMMUNICATION INSIGHT**

**Non-verbal Communication across the World**

Non-verbal communication differs all around the world. This section will give you an idea about the differences in non-verbal communication across various countries.

**Japan**
- Japanese rely on facial expression, tone of voice, and posture to tell them what someone feels.
- Frowning while someone is speaking is interpreted as a sign of disagreement.

Americans and depend on nuances of meaning in many cases.
- It is considered rude to speak to someone with your hands in your pocket and gum in your mouth

**The Middle East**
- Business and personal friendships are one and the same, and Arabs generally prefer to do business with people they know and like.
- The best way to communicate is always face-to-face. If this is not possible, make a phone call. The written word is considered less personal and less

**Business Communication Insight**
This new feature will aid you in understanding the various aspects of business communication at the workplace.

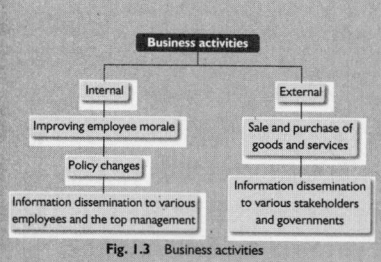

**Fig. 1.3** Business activities

**Table 1.2** Extent of message distortion

| Message | Amount of Message Passed (%) |
| --- | --- |
| Written by board of directors | 100 |
| Received by vice president | 63 |
| Received by general manager | 56 |
| Received by plant manager | 40 |
| Received by team leader | 30 |
| Received by worker | 20 |

**Figures and Tables**
All chapters contain figures and tables to illustrate the topics discussed in the chapter.

**Examples and Sidebars**
The text has been interspersed with examples and sidebars throughout the text, which will enable in understanding the concepts thoroughly and recapitulating the ideas.

2. *Sets off items in a date or address*

   The committee met on August 20, 2003, to discuss the plan.
   The study was conducted from January 15, 1975, to February 1, 1979.
   The committee met in August 2003 to discuss the plan.

- Unofficial communication channels in an organization are referred to as grapevines.
- Rumours are usually baseless and unverifiable information.

**SUMMARY**

Powerful communication skills are most needed in today's diverse workplace and, hence, the importance of these skills can never be overlooked. To achieve to become a successful communicator in the professional setting. Above all, it is necessary to understand and appropriately deal with the communication fail-

**KEY TERMS**

**Communication** It is the passing of information and understanding from one person to another at the same

Information, instructions, directions, feedback, etc. flow in this direction.

**Summary and Key Terms**
The summary at the end of each chapter draws together the main concepts discussed in the chapter. This will help you to reflect and evaluate important concepts. All technical terms have been explained at the end of each chapter as key terms.

**Exercises and Cases**
Each chapter contains a series of concept review and critical thinking questions, and project assignments that can be used for review and classroom discussions. It ends with a case study that is designed to consolidate your understanding of the concepts discussed in the chapter.

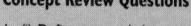

**Concept Review Questions**

1. (i) Define non-verbal communication in your own words, giving an appropriate example.

**Projects**

1. Using your favourite search engine, surf the Internet to find tips for effective presentations. Identify and

**Critical Thinking Questions**

1. How do you interpret the following non-verbal cues being sent by others? Do they always mean the

**CASE STUDY**

**Goodwill Corporation Ltd**

The president of Goodwill Corporation Ltd, Mr Abhishek Mukherji, wanted to facilitate upward communication. He believed an open-door policy was a good option. He announced that his own door was open to all employees and encouraged senior managers to do the same. He felt this would give him a way to get early warning signals that would not be filtered or redirected through the formal chain of command. Mr Mukherji found that many

# List of Case Studies

| | | |
|---|---|---|
| Chapter 1 | Case Study 1: Goodwill Corporation Ltd | 43 |
| | Case Study 2: Image and Rumours at Procter & Gamble | 44 |
| Chapter 2 | Case Study: Charisma Corporation | 86 |
| Chapter 3 | Case Study 1: Cultural Differences | 103 |
| | Case Study 2: Conversation Styles | 103 |
| Chapter 5 | Case Study: Communication Complication in English | 152 |
| Chapter 6 | Case Study: Missing Briefcase | 177 |
| Chapter 7 | Case Study: How to Operate the Minolta Freedom 3 Camera | 192 |
| Chapter 8 | Case Study 1: Handling Unsolicited Proposals for Private Infrastructure Projects | 220 |
| | Case Study 2: The Keyboard Syndrome | 221 |
| Chapter 9 | Case Study: Recruitment Drive at SOBER | 256 |
| Chapter 10 | Case Study 1: Lyman Steil | 294 |
| | Case Study 2: The Farewell Speech | 295 |
| Chapter 11 | Case Study: Business Leaders and Public Speaking | 335 |
| Chapter 12 | Case Study: Creating a Conversation with Potential Customers | 355 |
| Chapter 13 | Case Study: A True Tale of a Case Interview Gone Bad | 381 |
| Chapter 14 | Case Study: A Special Meeting of the Executive Committee | 407 |
| Chapter 15 | Case Study 1: Developing Presentation for a Training Programme | 430 |
| | Case Study 2: Career Couselling | 431 |
| Chapter 16 | Case Study 1: Team Briefing | 448 |
| | Case Study 2: Briefing on 'Maximizing Your Business with Modern Telephone Techniques' | 449 |
| Chapter 17 | Case Study 1: The Pentagon | 490 |
| | Case Study 2: Merrill Lynch | 491 |
| Chapter 18 | Case Study: How to Repair the Reliance Image | 509 |
| Chapter 19 | Case Study: Launching the New Wipro Identity | 544 |
| Chapter 20 | Case Study: Electronic Mailing and Ethics | 586 |

# PART I
# UNDERSTANDING BUSINESS COMMUNICATION

1. Nature and Scope of Communication
2. Non-verbal Communication
3. Cross-cultural Communication
4. Technology-enabled Business Communication

CHAPTER 1

# Nature and Scope of Communication

## LEARNING OBJECTIVES

After reading this chapter, you will be able to understand

- the terms communication, business communication, and effective business communication
- the importance of communication in business
- the basic processes and concepts of communication
- the roles of a manager in business communication
- the formal and informal communication networks
- the nuances of interpersonal communication
- ways to overcome barriers to communication
- the characteristics of, and develop strategies for, effective communication

## INTRODUCTION

Achieving success in the workplace is closely associated with the ability to communicate effectively, both in the workplace and with outsiders. Unlike in the past, today we face a highly volatile world where everything is in a state of flux. Most of the changes associated with this transformation revolve around the processing and communication of information. A number of communication challenges exist at workplaces. Identifying a problem, arriving at an appropriate solution, supervising work, coordinating various functions, coordinating people and their activities, developing products and services, and developing relationships—all these activities call for effectiveness and efficiency in communication. This chapter aims at providing an insight into the process, certain basic concepts, and the importance of communication in business.

## DEFINITION

> Communication is the process of exchanging information.

Communication is the process of exchanging information, usually through a common system of symbols. It takes a wide variety of forms—from two people having a face-to-face conversation to hand signals to messages sent over the global telecommunication networks. The process of communication facilitates interaction

**4** Business Communication

**Image 1.1** Communication is the process of exchanging information

among people; without it, we would be unable to share our knowledge or experiences with anybody else. Common forms of communication include speaking, writing, gesturing, and broadcasting (Image 1.1).

The term 'communication' comes from the Latin word *communicare* that entered the English language in the fourteenth and fifteenth centuries. It is, however, difficult to define communication. The Latin root word *communicare* has three possible meanings, which are as follows:

1. 'to make common', which is probably derived from meaning number 2 or 3 below
2. *cum + munus*, that is, having gifts to share in a mutual donation
3. *cum + munire*, that is, building together a defence, like the walls of a city

Therefore, in essence, communication entails the act of spreading information. When a person communicates, he/she establishes a common ground of understanding. In the organizational context, it brings about unity of purpose, interest, and effort. Communication can also be defined in the following ways:

- The process by which information and feelings shared by people through an exchange of verbal and non-verbal messages
- The successful transmission of information through a common system of symbols, signs, behaviour, speech, writing, or signals
- The creation of shared understanding through interaction among two or more agents

Communication depends on the interpretation of a message by the receiver. Shared understanding evolves through detection and correction of misunderstandings (as opposed to a one-way transmission of data). The understanding created through one communication cycle can never be absolute or complete. It is an interactive and ongoing process in which common ground, that is, assumed mutual beliefs and mutual knowledge, is accumulated and updated (Clark & Brennan 1991).

## THE MEHRABIAN MODEL

Albert Mehrabian, Professor Emeritus of Psychology, UCLA, is a pioneer in the field of understanding communications. Mehrabian established the following statistics (Fig. 1.1), which have now become a classic, for the effectiveness of spoken communication:

1. 7 per cent of meaning is in the words that are spoken.
2. 38 per cent of meaning is paralinguistic (the manner in which words are said).
3. 55 per cent of meaning is conveyed through facial expressions.

> The Mehrabian model stresses the importance of non-verbal factors in communication.

This model, though widely referenced in communications, should not be oversimplified or used indiscriminately to cover all manner of situations. While

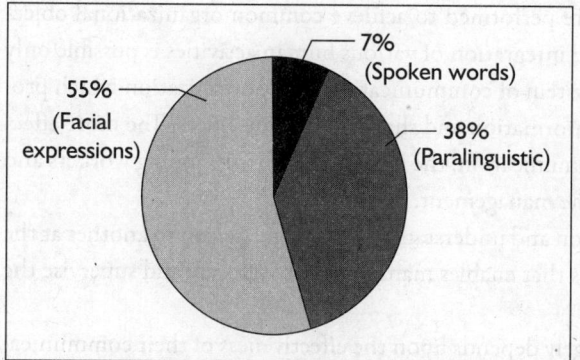

Fig. 1.1  The Mehrabian model

it serves to underline the importance of non-verbal factors in a communication situation, it is important to consider the context of the communication when applying this model. Mehrabian's research concluded that 93 per cent of the meaning inferred by the people in the experiment could indeed be accounted for by factors such as style of speaking, tone, facial expression, and body language. However, this is not a hard-and-fast rule that can be applied across board to any form of communication.

For example, the conclusions of this model would be unreliable in the case of written or telephonic communications, where without visual clues, the chances for miscommunication are greater. A fair way then, to apply this model to modern communications where visual inputs are absent (telephone, email, memos, etc.), is to infer that in the absence of visual signs, even greater care needs to be exercised while communicating.

Fig. 1.2  A 'No entry' sign

With the Mehrabian model as a reference point, one can understand why very short emails or memos can sometimes cause offence or result in a lack of understanding. However, this does not mean that all written communications, due to lack of visual inputs, are inevitably ineffective. For instance, legal documents, written contracts, and public notices when well written convey their meaning in no uncertain terms. Also, signs such as 'NO ENTRY' or 'VISITORS ONLY' convey their meaning perfectly well (Fig. 1.2).

In a telephonic communication, words and tone of voice are conveyed, but facial expressions are missing. Therefore, if a telephonic discussion is of a sensitive or emotional nature, according to Mehrabian's model, this communication is not an effective one, as without facial expressions only 45 per cent of the meaning can be conveyed successfully. However, this conclusion cannot be extended to all such communications. For example, if one is calling home to ask for the address of a friend, telephonic communication is perfectly adequate. It is also far more efficient and cost effective than to drive all the way back home just to ask the question directly and receive an answer face-to-face.

Thus, it is more than clear that the Mehrabian model gives us tremendous insight into the nature of human communications and helps explain the importance of careful and correct communication. The basic principles can be used as a guide and an example. However, it should not be blindly applied to every communication situation.

## BUSINESS COMMUNICATION

An organization is a group of persons constituted to achieve certain specific objectives. The achievement of these objectives largely depends upon proper coordination and integration of human effort in an organization. People working in an organization are interrelated; their activities are also inter-

> Communication is a process that enables management to allocate and supervise the work of employees.

related because these are performed to achieve common organizational objectives. Coordination and integration of various human activities is possible only if there is an effective system of communication in the organization which provides for exchange of information and sharing of various ideas. The more effective the systems of communication, the better relations are among workers and between workers and the management.

Communication is the flow of information and understanding from one person to another at the same level or at different levels. It is a process that enables management to allocate and supervise the work of employees.

The effectiveness of the management largely depends upon the effectiveness of their communication. Communication system is the medium through which an organization adapts to its environment. It not only integrates the various sub-units of an organization but also, in a systematic sense, serves as an elaborate set of interconnected channels designed to sift and analyse information imported from the environment. It also exports processed information to the environment.

As an organization grows in size, complexity, and sophistication, the role of communication also undergoes a change, and it becomes more critical to organizational functioning. It, therefore, becomes necessary to upgrade the system according to the needs of the organization from time to time.

Communication keeps the workers informed about the internal and external happenings, which helps them in accomplishing their respective tasks and are also of interest to the organization. It coordinates the efforts of members and facilitates them in achieving their organizational objectives. It also influences the actions of a person or a group. Communication is necessary to facilitate meaningful interaction among human beings in order to initiate, execute, accomplish, or prevent certain actions.

Though business communication is a specialized branch of general communication, there is no basic difference between the two. The process is the same and so are the principles that regulate them. The difference lies in their application to situations. Whereas general communication plays diverse roles, business communication is specifically concerned with well-defined business activities.

There are two types of business activities—internal and external. Internal activities include maintaining and improving the morale of employees, giving orders to workers, prescribing methods and procedures, announcing policies and organizational changes, and keeping the management informed. External activities relate to sale and purchase of goods and services, reporting to the government and the shareholders on the financial condition and business operations, and creating a favourable business climate (Fig. 1.3). Every activity, internal or external, leads to some result. Therefore, the main purpose of business communication is to obtain some results, that is, to secure an action by the receiver. The sender expects the receiver to do something on receiving the message—

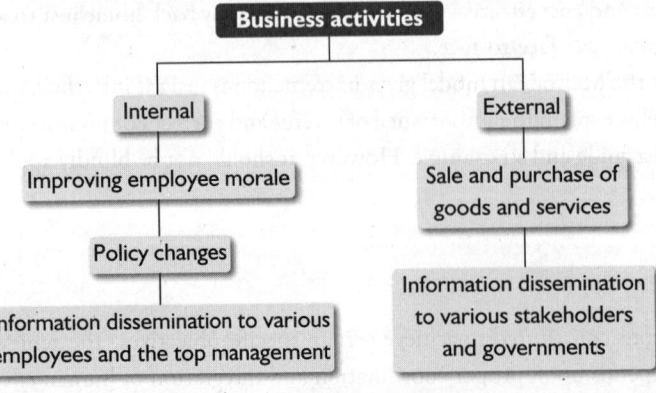

**Fig. 1.3** Business activities

write a cheque, place an order, approve an action, send some information, etc. The main features that lend business communication a distinct identity of its own are as follows (Fig. 1.4):

1. It deals with various commercial and industrial subjects.
2. It is characterized by certain formal elements, such as commercial and technical vocabulary, the use of graphic and audio-visual aids, and conventional formats.
3. It is impartial and objective as extreme care is taken to convey information accurately and concisely.
4. It entails formal writing techniques and procedures.
5. The language used should be direct, plain, and concise, and the style should be able to draw attention, arouse interest or create desire, develop conviction, and induce action.

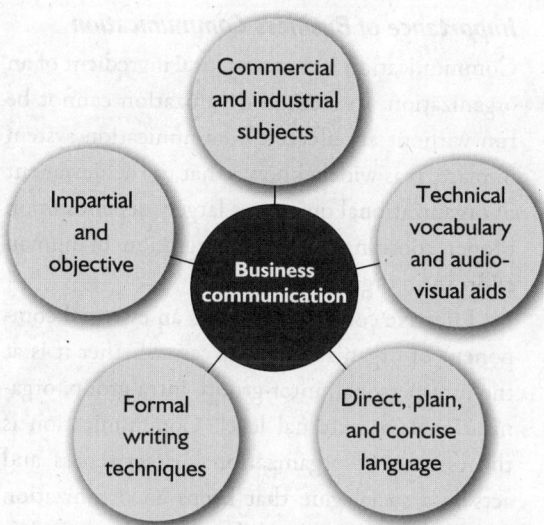

**Fig. 1.4** The features of business communication

## Effective Business Communication

Business communication becomes effective only when the language used is appropriate, the message conveyed is clear, and the predetermined purpose is achieved. Hence, effective business communication can be defined as *the use of effective language to convey a clear business message to achieve a predetermined objective.*

### Characteristics of Business Communication—A Two-way Traffic

Since communication is an exchange of views, opinions, directions, etc., it is a two-way traffic. It moves upwards and downwards. Messages, directives, opinions, etc. are communicated upwards, that is, from workers (lower level) to management (higher level), as well as downwards, from management to workers. George Terry has rightly remarked, 'Simply talking or writing, without regard to the recipients' response, is conducive to misunderstanding.' Thus, communication should be both ways. The characteristics of business communication are as follows:

**Continuous process** Communication is a continuous process. More often than not, it is repeated to achieve the desired results.

**Short-lived process** The process of communication is complete as soon as a message is received and understood by a receiver in the right perspective. Hence, it is a short-lived process.

**Needs proper understanding** The basic objective of conveying a message is to make the other party understand the message. For this purpose, it should be clearly and concisely worded.

**Leads to the achievement of the organizational objective** Effective communication does this by creating a sense of object orientation in the organization.

**Dispels misunderstanding** It leads to a clear understanding between people and thus builds camaraderie among people.

- Business communication moves upwards and downwards.
- Communication is the essence of organizational effectiveness.

## Importance of Business Communication

Communication is the most vital ingredient of an organization. In fact, an organization cannot be run without an effective communication system in place. It is widely known that the achievement of organizational objectives largely depends upon proper coordination and integration of human effort in an organization.

Effective communication is an essential component of organizational success whether it is at the interpersonal, inter-group, intra-group, organizational, or external level. Communication is the essence of organizational effectiveness and acts as a social glue that keeps an organization together. In short, the ability of the executives to communicate effectively increases not only their own productivity but also the productivity of their organization. Communication effectiveness

**Fig. 1.5** Benefits of effective communication

also fetches several other benefits to an organization (Fig. 1.5).

**Effective communication** A manager's job is varied and complex. A manager needs certain skills to perform the duties and activities associated with his/her job. The three essential skills or competencies a manager should possess are technical, human, and conceptual. Of course, the relative importance of these skills varies according to a manager's level within an organization. Human skill refers to the ability to work well with other people, individually as well as in a group. This skill is crucial, and is as important at the top levels of management as it is at the lower levels, since managers deal directly with people. Managers with good human skills—skills to communicate, motivate, lead, and inspire—can get the best out of their people.

Therefore, communication is intricately linked to managerial performance. Almost everything a manager does involves communication. He/she cannot make a decision without adequate information, and to obtain this information he/she needs to communicate. Once a decision is made, it needs to be communicated. The finest plan, the best idea, or the most creative suggestion cannot take shape without communication.

---

### Dhirubhai Ambani

Dhirubhai Ambani, the Founder Chairman of the Reliance Group, firmly believed that education empowered people. A great communicator, he inspired, educated, and motivated people. He actively used the telephone to surpass distance, to compress time, and to remain up-to-date of events. He was conscious of the power of information and communication. It was his vision to make the tools of infocomm available to people at affordable cost so that they would be able to overcome illiteracy and immobility.

# FUNCTIONS OF COMMUNICATION

Given the importance of communication in organizations, it is not surprising that managers spend as much as 80 per cent of their time communicating, such as giving press interviews, reading reports, listening to employees' grievances, preparing proposals, etc. It will not be wrong to say that the growth and success of any organization can be gauged by the quantity and quality of information that flows through its personnel.

Communication serves four major functions in an organization—information, control, motivation, and emotional expression.

## Information

*Information* refers to the role of communication in facilitating decision-making and problem solving. Managers, by means of adequate and effective communication, receive and transmit information that enables them to solve problems and make decisions. For instance, in case of a strike in an organization, it is the duty of the manager to call workers for interaction—listen to them, explain the organization's stand, etc. These communication activities enable managers to solve a problem in a better manner. Likewise, when managers have to take any decision, say, whether a particular location is suitable or not for setting up a branch of their company, they need to go through the field reports and related documents before arriving at a final decision.

## Control

In the organizational context, *control* refers to the power to influence people's behaviour. When the employees are required to comply with company policies and procedures, adhere to their job description, or first communicate their job-related grievances to their immediate boss, communication performs the control function. Similarly, when two managers do extraordinarily well in whatever project they take up and if some other manager teases them in an informal manner, and if it affects their behaviour in some way, the latter is not only communicating with the two managers but also controlling their behaviour.

## Motivation

- Communication serves four major functions in an organization: information, control, motivation, and emotional expression.
- An employee's communication skills acquire utmost importance in this changing business scenario.

*Motivation* refers to the fostering of motivational spirit among the employees. Effective communication is needed in setting and defining clear goals, giving feedback on the progress made in achieving these goals, and reinforcing the desired behaviour. Consider the function of the vice president of a company in motivating his/her junior executives to accomplish a project related to setting up of a training division in the company. The vice president should define the goal clearly at the first instance. Once some work is completed, along with giving feedback on the progress made, he/she should specify the steps for implementation. In all these tasks, communication plays an extremely significant role.

## Emotional Expression

Finally, *emotional expression* relates to the function of communication in expressing or letting out the feelings and emotions of employees under various circumstances. Today, organizations depend on teams rather than individuals for achieving the set goals. Besides its other advantages, teams have an in-built mechanism which provides the members an outlet to express their feelings of satisfaction, dissatisfaction, and frustration. This mechanism works entirely on the basis of communication. Consider the example of a team in a consultancy firm that has undertaken the project of preparing a code for export operations of another company. If some members of this team do not agree with a part of the code designed by some other member, they can express their dissatisfaction or disagreement to the team. In this context, communication provides a release for their emotional expression.

All the four functions of communication discussed so far are of equal importance in an organization. The members of a team need to

- interact for making decisions;
- be persuaded to perform effectively;
- exercise some form of control in order to check their behaviour; and
- be provided a means for emotional expression in order to be free from pent-up feelings.

Besides other factors, a person's communication skills are of phenomenal importance in today's dynamic and demanding workplace. How well one communicates with one's superiors, peers, and subordinates is one of the crucial factors for success in the workplace. Contemporary corporate sector or for that matter any other professional world is changing dramatically. The work environment, the kind of jobs assigned, the tools used, and the people in the organization are undergoing dramatic transformation. Various changes and upheavals in organizations revolve around conceiving, encoding, transmitting, decoding, and receiving information. As a result, a person's communication skills acquire utmost importance in the changing business scenario. By now you would have got a fairly good idea of the importance of communication in general as well as in an organizational set-up. However, before going into the nuances of communication basics, it would be better to understand the role of managers in the workplace and the kind of activities they perform for communicating effectively. An understanding of these roles will further asseverate the importance of managerial communication.

## ROLES OF A MANAGER

Managers engage themselves in a large number of varied, unpatterned, and short-term activities. Figure 1.6 depicts a categorization scheme, which helps in defining a manager's roles. These are primarily concerned with interpersonal relationships, transfer of information, and decision-making.

### Interpersonal Roles

Every manager is required to perform duties that are ceremonial and symbolic in nature. While performing such duties a manager plays an interpersonal role for his/her organization.

When Mr Kumaramangalam Birla, the Chairman of the Aditya Birla Group, presides over a convocation function of a university, he performs the role of a *figurehead*. When he is hiring, training, motivating, and disciplining employees, he acts as a *leader*. He plays the role of a *liaison person* when he is contacting external sources that provide him with information. These sources may be individuals or groups outside a particular unit of his organization and may be inside or outside his organization.

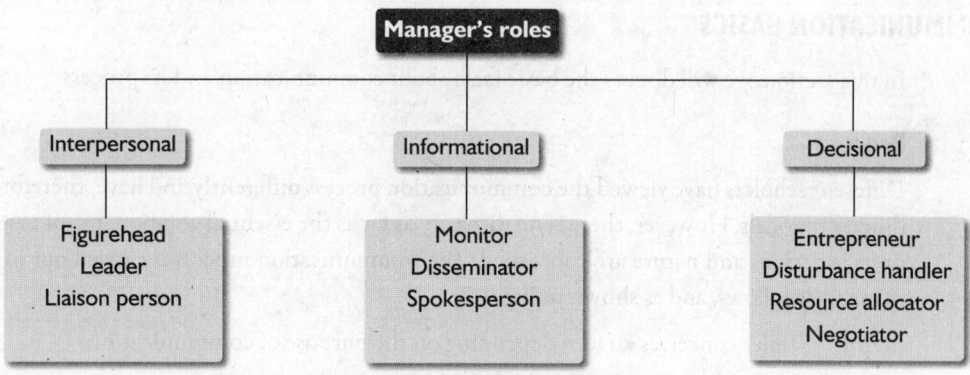

**Fig. 1.6** A manager's roles

For example, a production manager obtaining information from the marketing manager of his/her company plays an internal liaison role. When the production manager confers with other marketing executives through a trade association, he/she plays the role of an outside liaison person.

## Informational Roles

Collection of information by managers from organizations and institutions in their external environment indicates the informational role played by them. A manager becomes a *monitor* when he/she reads magazines, talks to others to learn the changes in the public's tastes, and what the competitors are planning, etc., with a view to collect information. The same manager becomes a *disseminator* when he/she acts as a conduit to transmit information to organizational members. However, when he/she represents his/her company to outsiders and transmits information on company's policies, plans, actions, results, etc., he/she becomes a *spokesperson*.

## Decisional Roles

The decisional roles played by a manager comprise four subcategories. As an *entrepreneur,* a manager initiates and supervises new projects that will potentially improve the organization's performance. As a *disturbance handler*, he/she is responsible for corrective action when his/her organization faces unexpected disturbances and crises. As a *resource allocator*, he/she allocates human, material, and financial resources. Finally, as a *negotiator,* he/she discusses and bargains with external groups to gain advantage over other organizations.

Irrespective of the type of organization they work in or the level at which they work, managers perform similar roles. However, the emphasis they give to the various roles changes with the change in their hierarchical levels and the size of their organization. For example, the role of a disseminator, figurehead, negotiator, liaison person, and spokesperson is practised at the higher levels of an organization than at the lower ones. On the other hand, the role of a leader is more important for lower-level managers than it is for either middle- or top-level managers. Similarly, a manager's role also differs according to the size of the organization. For example, the entrepreneurial role is least important to managers in large firms, whereas the spokesperson's role is extremely important to managers in small firms.

> A manager may play the roles of an entrepreneur, disturbance handler, resource allocator, and negotiator.

## COMMUNICATION BASICS

In this section, we will discuss the basic facts about communication and its process.

### Process

Different scholars have viewed the communication process differently and have, therefore, developed different models. However, there is no disparity as far as the essential components of communication or its functions and nature are concerned. The communication process is carried out in a systematic manner, as follows, and as shown in Fig. 1.7.

**Step 1** Sender conceives an idea depending on the purpose of communication.
**Step 2** Sender chooses appropriate symbols, encodes the idea, and formulates the message.
**Step 3** Sender sends the message through a suitable channel (oral or written).
**Step 4** Receiver receives the message.
**Step 5** Receiver decodes the symbols, and comprehends, and interprets the message.
**Step 6** Receiver sends response that is observed by the sender.

The entire communication process takes place within a communication environment, which is also called communication context or frame of reference. Table 1.1 gives us the components and functions of communication.

Both the sender and the receiver should be familiar with the context. If even one of them is not aware of the context, communication may suffer, and hence, lead to ineffectiveness. For example, when the managing director of a company gives a press interview on TV, he/she is the sender and the TV viewers are the receivers, though the implicit receiver is the person who interviews. At the time of telecasting, the interviewer must initially provide a brief background of the managing director and the company to prepare the viewers for the interview. If this context is not established, the viewers may find it difficult to comprehend what is being said in the interview.

When a sender (A) selects a channel and sends a message through it, it first enters the sensory world of the receiver (B) from where he/she picks it up through his/her senses. However, B's senses cannot gather all the information that exists in the world around him/her. How much he/she can gather depends on various factors such as the ability of his/her senses—sight, hearing, smell, taste, and touch—mental alertness, his/her cultural background, and his/her will. In other words, his/her unique mental make up is formed from his/her experiences, knowledge, prejudices, emotions, cultural background, etc.

The mental make up of a receiver influences the message and filters it. Besides the message, the receiver's sensory world may contain external noises, movements of objects, the non-verbal signals perceived, etc. In fact, the receiver's mental filter continually picks up such things from the world around him/her. Hence, there is a possibility that these things may affect the message

**Table 1.1** Components and functions of communication

| Components | Functions/Nature |
|---|---|
| Sender (encoder) | Selects, composes |
| Message | Verbal/non-verbal/combination |
| Channel | Oral/written |
| Receiver (decoder) | Identifies, comprehends, interprets |
| Response and feedback | Verbal/non-verbal/combination |

## Nature and Scope of Communication 13

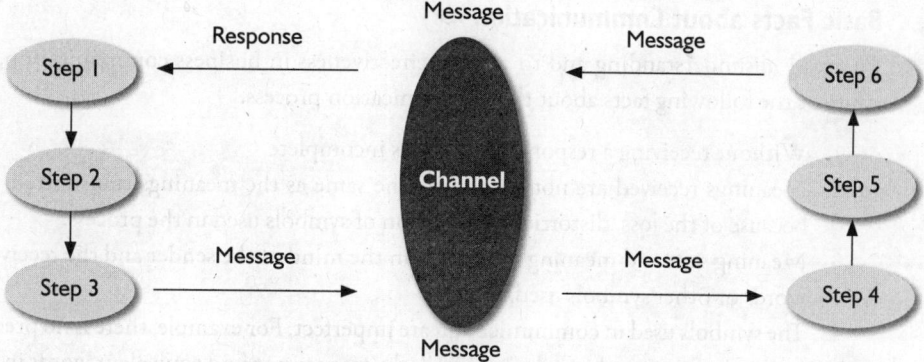

**Fig. 1.7** Steps in the communication process

he/she receives at a particular moment during a specific communication process in which he/she acts as a receiver.

This filtered message is sent to the receiver's brain where it is given some meaning. The receiver's experience, knowledge, biases, emotions, cultural background, etc. enable him/her to assign a meaning to the message. Depending upon what he/she is and what he/she has been, the message is interpreted.

No two people have identical filters because their mental make up is not the same. Hence, the meaning they give to two comparable messages may differ. For example, when your boss asks you to prepare a bi-monthly report, he/she might have meant a report prepared twice a month, whereas you may understand the same as a report prepared once in two months.

After assigning some meaning to the message, the receiver may respond in the form of words, gestures, or physical actions. When he/she decides to send a response, he/she takes into consideration the general meaning that the response will carry. This process of replying involves the most complex workings of his/her mind. His/her ability is directly proportional to his intelligence and also the extent to which he/she applies his/her mind in this step of communication process.

Once the receiver decides upon the response, he/she converts it into symbols and sends it. If he/she is engaged in oral communication, the response may be in the form of words or non-verbal means, such as gestures, facial expression, movement, touch, etc., or a combination of these. If the communication process happens in the reading or writing mode, the response may be in the form of words, diagrams, signs, or a combination of these.

When the response enters the sender's sensory world, his/her unique mental filter gives a meaning to the response and then another cycle of communication begins. The process may continue as long as two people wish to communicate.

Written communication also follows a similar process with some minor differences. These differences may be related to the creative effort, time gap between the two communication cycles, the number of cycles, etc. In fact, some written communication contexts may even end up with one cycle. For example, when the vice president, marketing, of a company seeks some clarification through a memorandum from the vice president, sales, and gets the required response, the communication cycle is completed and it need not be repeated.

> The mental make up of a receiver influences the message and filters it.

## Basic Facts about Communication

To avoid misunderstanding and to achieve effectiveness in business communication, we should be aware of the following facts about the communication process:

1. Without receiving a response the cycle is incomplete.
2. Meanings received are not necessarily the same as the meanings transmitted. This is mainly because of the loss, distortion, or creation of symbols used in the process.
3. Meaning sent and meaning received is in the mind of the sender and the receiver—not in the words or other symbols used.
4. The symbols used in communication are imperfect. For example, there is no precise translation for our jargons in other cultures. Similarly, we may not find equivalent words in our culture for certain words used in other cultures.

Although these facts bring to light the difficulties, complexities, and limitations of communication, on the whole, we as human beings cannot live without it.

## COMMUNICATION NETWORKS

Let us compare the following two communication situations: First, when the CEO of a business group announces new product plans to the stockholders of his/her company. Second, one day in the lunchroom, two office assistants gossip about their colleague whose services have been terminated recently. Though these two situations satisfy the essential steps of a communication process and relate to the same organization, they differ significantly.

The first describes a situation in which the CEO shares official information, which the stockholders need to know; the second one involves the sharing of an unofficial information about what is going on in the company. The former is known as formal communication while the latter is called informal communication. As both are very common forms of communication in organizational set-ups, it is beneficial if one understands the ins and outs of formal and informal communication networks existing in organizations.

Organizations are often described in the way they dictate who may or may not communicate with whom. The organizational structure of a workplace is the formally prescribed pattern of inter-relationships existing between its various units. This structure influences in many ways the various forms of communication in an organization. An organizational chart provides a graphic representation of an organization's structure and an outline of the planned, formal connections between its various units. Figure 1.8 depicts the structure of a small part of an organization and an overview of the types of communication expected to occur within it.

Each of the boxes shown in Fig. 1.8 represents a particular business function and the lines connecting the boxes represent the formal lines of communication between the individuals performing these functions. In other words, the lines indicate the flow of information in the organization or who is supposed to communicate to whom. People in organizations communicate formally with those immediately above and below them, as well as those at their own level. Formal communication between people several levels apart occurs rarely. However, in present times, such highly restricted hierarchical structures are giving way to more open forms of organizational structures.

> Information flows in an organization in three different directions—upwards, downwards, and sideways.

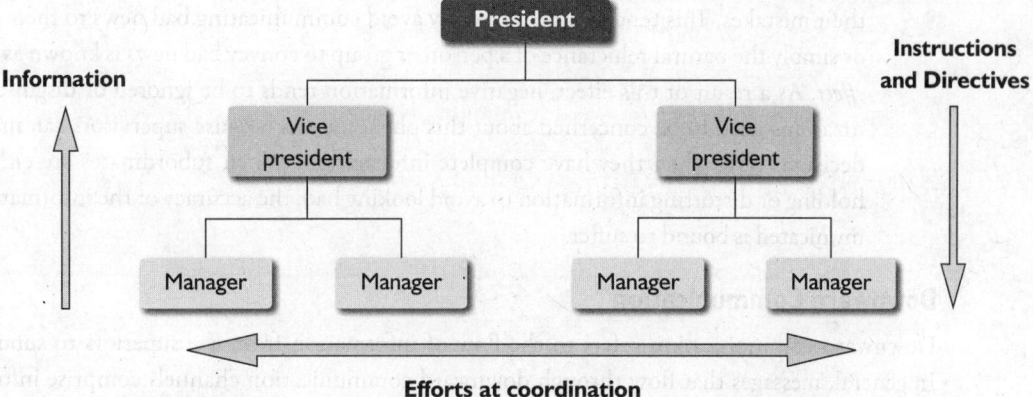

**Fig. 1.8** Organizational structure and types of messages

The nature of formal communication differs according to people's position in an organizational chart. Information about policies and procedures originates from executives and flows down through managers to supervisors and finally to lower-level employees. Many organizations have formulated official communication policies that encourage regular and open communication, suggest means for achieving it, and spell out responsibilities. Official information among the people of an organization typically flows through formal channels. Figure 1.8 clearly reveals that information flows in an organization in three different directions—upwards, downwards, and sideways.

## Upward Communication

Upward communication refers to the flow of information from lower levels to higher levels within an organization, such as messages containing information, requests, reports, proposals, and feedback (suggestions/recommendations). When a marketing manager submits the results of a recently conducted survey to the vice president, marketing, he/she is using the upward channel to communicate. Likewise, personnel officer of a company conveying the information regarding the continued absence of certain employees to his/her manager communicates vertically upwards. In the same way, when an employee in the production division of an industry expresses his/her grievances to his/her immediate superior, communication flows upwards.

Although we consider upward communication as the logical opposite of downward communication, there are some important differences between them. These differences arise because of the difference in status of the communicating parties. Some significant differences between upward and downward flow of communication are as follows:

1. Upward communication occurs far less frequently than downward communication. For example, communication between a shop-floor worker and his/her supervisor occurs less than once a month.
2. When people communicate upward, their conversations tend to be far shorter than the ones they have with others at their own level. This is mainly because of the difference in their status.
3. The information transmitted in the upward flow of communication is generally inaccurate because usually employees are interested in presenting their best when communicating with their bosses. Hence, they have a tendency to highlight their accomplishments and downplay

their mistakes. This tendency to purposely avoid communicating bad news to their superiors or simply the natural reluctance of a person or group to convey bad news is known as *the mum effect*. As a result of this effect, negative information tends to be ignored or disguised. Organizations need to be concerned about this phenomenon because supervisors can make good decisions only when they have complete information. When subordinates are either withholding or distorting information to avoid looking bad, the accuracy of the information communicated is bound to suffer.

## Downward Communication

Downward communication refers to the flow of information from the superiors to subordinates. In general, messages that flow through downward communication channels comprise information, instructions, directions, and orders, that is, messages instructing subordinates what they should be doing. You may also find feedback on past performance flowing in a downward direction. When a company introduces a new policy or procedure, it sends the information using the downward channel. A sales manager, after going through market surveys, may tell members of his/her sales force what products they should be promoting. A production manager may instruct his/her subordinates about the operational details of a new production process.

When formal information slowly trickles down from one level of an organization to the next lowest level through a downward communication channel, it becomes less accurate. This is more so when the information assumes a spoken form. In such cases, it is not unusual for at least part of the message to get distorted and/or omitted as it works its way down from one person to the next lowest-ranking person. When the message passes down several lines of hierarchy, there is a possibility of message distortion, as shown in Table 1.2.

There may be various reasons for this distortion, which will be discussed at length in the section on communication barriers.

## Horizontal Communication

In case of horizontal communication, messages flow not only up and down the organizational chart, but also sideways. When communication takes place among the members of the same work group, among members of work groups at the same level, among managers at the same level, or among any laterally equivalent personnel, we describe it as lateral or horizontal communication. Messages of this type are characterized by efforts at coordination or attempts to work together. For example, the marketing department of an organization has to coordinate its efforts with people in other departments while launching an advertising campaign for a new product. This necessitates the coordination of information with experts from manufacturing and production (to see when the product will be available) as well as those from research and development (to see what features people really want).

**Table 1.2** Extent of message distortion

| Message | Amount of Message Passed (%) |
|---|---|
| Written by board of directors | 100 |
| Received by vice president | 63 |
| Received by general manager | 56 |
| Received by plant manager | 40 |
| Received by team leader | 30 |
| Received by worker | 20 |

> Horizontal communication plays a significant role in organizations where functions are decentralized.

While vertical communication flows among the parties at different organizational levels, horizontal communication involves people at the same level. Therefore, it tends to be easier and friendlier. It also is more casual in tone and occurs more frequently as there are fewer barriers between the parties. This does not mean that horizontal communication is without its potential pitfalls. Indeed, people in different departments sometimes feel that they are competing against each other for valued organizational resources, leading them to show resentment towards one another. When an antagonistic, competitive orientation replaces a friendly, cooperative one, work is bound to suffer. Nevertheless, messages flowing through horizontal channels of organizational communication save time and facilitate cooperation. Lateral communication is more beneficial since strict adherence to the formal vertical structure for all communications can impede the efficient and accurate transfer of information. However, it can create dysfunctional conflicts when the formal channels are overlooked, when members go above or around their superiors to get things done, or when bosses find out that actions have been taken or decisions made without their knowledge. Horizontal communication plays a more significant role in organizations where the functions are decentralized, as there are increased possibilities of the gaps in communication among the various divisions.

## Spiral or Diagonal Communication

Apart from the vertical—upwards and downwards—and horizontal directions, communication also flows in a circular or diagonal direction (Fig. 1.9). If the management circulates the copy of a new bonus and incentive scheme among all employees, it is circular, diagonal, or spiral communication. Sometimes, however, communication flows between persons who belong to different levels of hierarchy

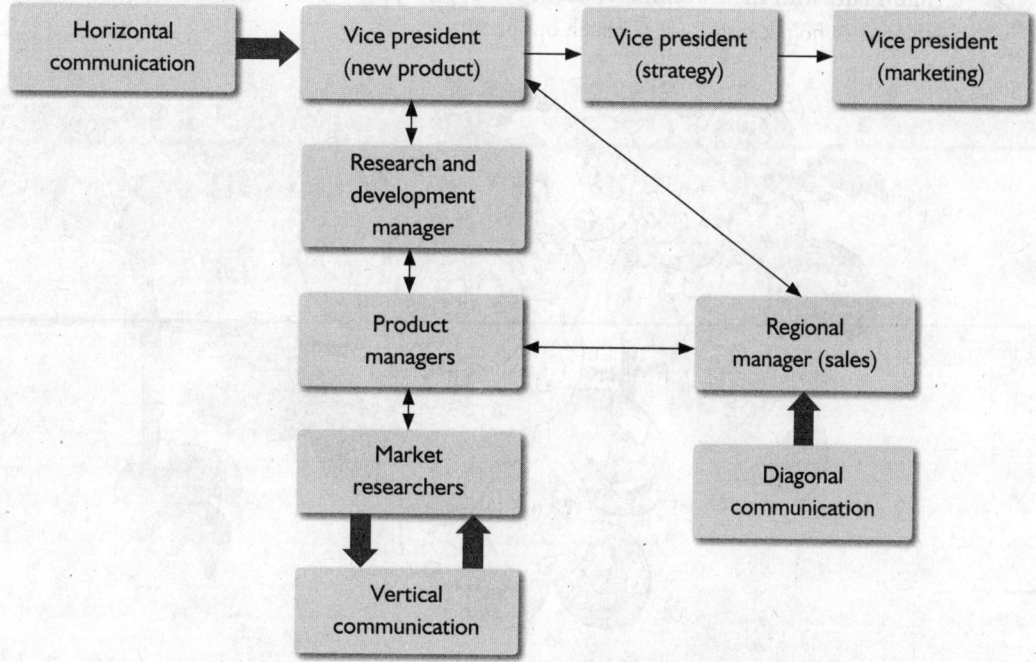

**Fig. 1.9** Vertical, horizontal, and diagonal communication

and who have no direct reporting relationship. This is used generally to quicken the information flow, improve understanding, and coordinate efforts for the achievement of organizational objectives. Such a movement of information flow is termed as *diagonal communication*.

## INFORMAL COMMUNICATION—BEYOND THE ORGANIZATIONAL HIERARCHY

Communication in organizations goes far beyond sending formal messages up, down, or across the organizational hierarchy. To get a complete picture of organizational communication one must also pay attention to informal communication—information shared without any formally imposed obligations or restrictions.

When people communicate informally, they are not bound by their organizational positions. Everyone is free to tell anybody anything. Although it would be inappropriate for an office assistant to share his/her thoughts with a senior manager about matters of corporate policy, both parties may be perfectly at ease exchanging funny stories. The difference lies in the fact that the funny stories are unofficial in nature and are communicated informally, that is, without following the formal constraints imposed by hierarchy.

It is easy to imagine how important the flow of informal information may be within organizations. People transmit information to those with whom they come into contact, thereby providing conduits through which all sorts of messages can travel. Research has shown that such informal connections may explain the important organizational phenomenon of turnover. For example, people who are planning to leave their jobs tend to be those who keep in touch with individuals who had left at an earlier date to take up new positions in other organizations. After all, people who communicate informally with their workmates about better job opportunities in other companies are likely to be the ones who take advantage of such opportunities.

'Hey! guys, listen up! Did you know that the boss is joining a rival firm?'

When anyone can tell anyone else anything informally, the result is a rapid flow of information along what is commonly called the *grapevine*. This refers to the pathways along which unofficial information travels. In contrast to formal organizational messages, which may take several days to reach their destination, information travelling along the organizational grapevine tends to flow rapidly. In fact, it is not unusual for some messages to reach everyone in a large organization in a matter of hours. This happens because informal communication crosses organizational boundaries and is open to everyone. There is another reason as well—informal information is generally communicated orally, and oral messages reach not only more people but also more quickly than written messages. However, oral messages run the risk of becoming inaccurate as they flow between people. Because of the possible confusion grapevines can cause, sometimes it is advisable to avoid them. However, grapevines are not necessarily bad. In fact, informal communication makes work groups more cohesive, and may also provide excellent opportunities to make social contacts that make life at work more enjoyable. Recall how some kings used to go around their kingdom to gather information through informal means. However, always remember to supplement information collected through the grapevine with information collected through formal channels, as certain inaccuracies may creep into informal messages.

> - Unofficial communication channels in an organization are referred to as grapevines.
> - Rumours are usually baseless and unverifiable information.

Regardless of whether it is helpful or harmful, grapevine is an inevitable fact of an organizational life. Although the information communicated along the grapevine may be accurate in some respects, it may be inaccurate in others. In extreme cases, the information transmitted through this channel may be baseless and unverifiable. Such messages are known as *rumours*. Typically, rumours are based on speculation, someone's overactive imagination, or wishful thinking, rather than on facts.

Rumours spread like wildfire through organizations because the information they contain is usually sensational and vague. This ambiguity leaves messages open to embellishment as they pass orally from one person to another. Before you know it, almost everyone in the organization has heard the rumour, and its inaccurate message comes to be regarded as fact.

If you have ever been the victim of a rumour, you would know just how troublesome it could be. Now, imagine how serious the consequences may be when organizations fall victim to it.

What can be done to counter the effects of rumours? You may be tempted to consider directly refuting a rumour. This approach works best whenever a rumour is highly implausible and is challenged immediately by an independent source. This was precisely what happened when the US Food and Drug Administration (FDA) carefully investigated cans of Pepsi after rumours about the presence of some syringes in the cans, and announced that there were not, nor could there have been, syringes in the Pepsi cans.

In the case of McDonald's, direct refutations (in the form of signs from the FDA stating that McDonald's used only wholesome ground beef in its burgers) had little effect because the rumour had spread so rapidly. In fact, directly challenging the rumour only led some customers to raise questions about why such official government statements were necessary in the first place, thereby fuelling the rumour. Not surprisingly, advertising campaigns (including public relations efforts by politicians rumoured to be involved in various scandals) devote more time in redirecting the public's attention away from negative thoughts and towards positive ones that they already have.

**Table 1.3** Grapevine communication—benefits, limitations, and guidelines

| Benefits | Limitations | Guidelines |
| --- | --- | --- |
| 1. Less expensive than formal channels | 1. Fast spreading nature can cause damage to the organization | 1. To be used as a supplementary channel only |
| 2. May give some information that you may find otherwise difficult to collect through formal channels | 2. If unverified, may cause troubles | 2. Information to be verified for facts and also the source |
| 3. An outlet for employees to share their anxieties, worries, and frustrations | 3. May lead to misunderstanding if incomplete | 3. Should not be ignored |
| 4. Used voluntarily by many employees | 4. May not be reliable as it is oral, and also nobody owns the responsibility for the information | 4. Employees using this channel should not be threatened or encouraged too much |
| 5. Fastest means of spreading information | | |

The benefits and limitations of grapevine communication along with the guidelines to use it more effectively are given in Table 1.3.

### Informal Contacts with Outsiders

As a member of an organization, you automatically become an informal conduit for communicating with the outside world. In the course of your daily activities, you unconsciously absorb bits and pieces of information that add to the collective knowledge pool of your company. During a trip to a shopping mall, you notice how a competitor's products are selling; as you read the paper, you pick up economic and business news that relates to your work; when you have a problem at the office, you ask your family or friends for advice. Every time you speak for or about your company, you send a message. In fact, if your job requires you to interact with the public, you do not even have to say anything. All you have to do is smile. Many outsiders may form their impression of your organization on the basis of the subtle, unconscious clues you transmit through the tone of your voice, facial expression, and general appearance—which is one reason to enforce a strict grooming code for all employees who interact with the public.

Top managers rely heavily on informal contacts with outsiders to exchange information that might be useful to their companies. Although much of the networking involves interaction with fellow executives, plenty of high-level managers recognize the value of keeping in touch with 'the real world'.

## TIPS FOR EFFECTIVE INTERNAL COMMUNICATIONS

Let us discuss the tips for effective communication in its different types.

> Top managers rely heavily on informal contacts with outsiders to exchange information that might be useful to their organizations.

### Downward Communication

The following are the tips for effective downward communication:

1. Ensure that every employee receives a copy of the strategic plan, which includes the organization's mission, vision, values statement, strategic goals, and strategies about how these goals will be reached.

2. Ensure that every employee receives an employee handbook that contains updated personnel policies.
3. Develop a basic set of procedures for how routine tasks are conducted, and include them in the standard operating manual.
4. Ensure that every employee has a copy of the job description and the organizational chart.
5. Regularly hold management meetings (at least every two weeks), even if there is nothing pressing to report. If you hold meetings only when you believe there is something to report, then communication will occur only when you have something to say—communication will be one-way and the organization will suffer. Have meetings anyway, if only to establish and affirm the communication process.
6. Hold full staff meetings every month to report how the organization is doing, major accomplishments, concerns, announcements about staff, etc.
7. Leaders and managers should have one-to-one meetings with employees at least once a week. Even if the organization has over 20 employees (large for a non-profit organization), the management should supervise the activities once in a while.
8. Regularly hold meetings to celebrate major accomplishments. This helps employees perceive what is important, gives them a sense of direction and fulfilment, and lets them know that leadership is all important.
9. Ensure that all employees receive yearly performance reviews, including their goals for the year, updated job descriptions, accomplishments, areas that need improvement, and plans to help them effect these improvements. If a non-profit organization has adequate resources (a realistic concern), it is better to develop a career plan with the employees.

## Upward Communication

Tips for upward communication are as follows:

1. Ensure that all employees give regular status reports to their supervisors. Include a section for what they did last week, will do next week, and any actions/issues to be addressed.
2. Ensure that all supervisors meet one-on-one at least once a month with their subordinates to discuss how it is going, hear any current concerns from them, etc. Even if the meeting is a chit-chat, it cultivates an important relationship between the supervisor and the employee.
3. Use management and staff meetings to solicit feedback. Practice the round-table approach so that each person is heard.
4. Act on feedback from others. Write it down. Get back to it—if only to say you cannot do anything about the reported problem or suggestion, etc.
5. Respect the grapevine. It is probably one of the most prevalent and, often, reliable forms of communication. Major 'movements' in any organization usually first appear when employees feel it safe to express their feelings or opinions to peers.

## Supervisor and Employee Communications

Supervision includes designing jobs, hiring people to fill those jobs, training them, delegating responsibilities to them, guiding them via performance reviews, helping them develop their careers, noting performance issues, and even firing them, if necessary. Obviously, small non-profit organizations may not be able to pay attention to all of these activities. However, there are several basic and regular activities, which provide a solid foundation for effective supervision. These basics ensure that everyone is working together towards a common goal.

Ironically, these basics are usually the first activities that stop when an organization is in a crisis. Consequently, an organization development specialist, when 'diagnosing' the workings of an organization, often looks to see if these basics are being practiced. A supervisor should conduct the following activities:

1. *Have all employees provide weekly written status reports to their supervisors*   Ask the employees to include the tasks undertaken in the past weeks, the tasks planned for the last week, any pending issues, etc., and date the report. Preparing these reports may seem a tedious task, but they are precious in that they ensure that the employees and their supervisor have mutual understanding of what is going on. These reports come in handy for the purpose of planning. They also make the otherwise harried staff and managers stand back and reflect on what they are doing.

2. *Hold monthly meetings with the staff*   Review the overall condition of the organization and review recent successes. Consider conducting 'in service' training where employees take turns describing their roles to the rest of the staff. For clarity, focus, and building morale, set an agenda and ensure follow-up. Consider bringing in clients to tell their story of how the organization helped them. These meetings go a long way toward's building a spirit of teamwork among the staff.

3. *Hold weekly or biweekly meetings with all staff together if the organization is small (e.g., under 10 people); otherwise, with all managers together*   Have these meetings even if there is not a specific problem to solve; just make them shorter. Holding meetings only when there are problems to solve cultivates a crisis-oriented environment where managers believe their only job is to solve problems. Use these meetings to give a brief overview to the employees of what they will do that week. Facilitate the meetings to support exchange of ideas and questions. Set an agenda, take minutes, and ensure follow-up. See that each person brings his/her calendar to ensure proper scheduling of future meetings.

4. *Have supervisors meet with their direct reports in one-on-one meetings every month*   This ultimately produces more efficient time management and supervision. Review overall status of work activities, enquire as to how things are going with both the supervisor and the employee, exchange feedback and questions about current programmes and services, and discuss career planning. Consider these meetings as interim meetings between the more formal, yearly performance review meetings.

5. *Develop a basic communication plan*   Planning your internal or external communications efforts helps a great deal to develop a communications plan, either informally or formally. While doing so consider the following questions:

    (a) What key messages do you want to convey?
    (b) To what key stakeholders do you want to convey the key messages (e.g., clients, funders, community leaders, service providers, etc.)?
    (c) What is the best approach to reach each key stakeholder, including who/how should the message be conveyed?
    (d) How will you know if you are reaching these stakeholders or not?

## INTERPERSONAL COMMUNICATION

Communication is as much a matter of human relationships as it is about transmitting messages. This fact is most appropriate to a business environment because an organization earns its reputation not because of its buildings or other material possessions but because of its people. Bonding among the various levels of employees needs to be strong and it is possible if the interpersonal communication in the organization is effective. Managers are far more than transmitters of information and instruction. They communicate with their subordinates and superiors on a day-to-day basis through interpersonal communication channels.

**Image 1.2**  Interpersonal communication

Interpersonal communication generally refers to spoken communication between two or more individuals on a personal, face-to-face level to send and receive information. It can also stand for written and non-verbal forms of communication that involves two or more people. It is called dyadic (dyad=two) communication if there are two participants (Image 1.2) and small group communication if there are a few more participants. Conversations, meetings, project discussions, sales visits, interviews, etc., are some forms which the interpersonal communication assumes in an organization. It differs from other forms of communication in that there are fewer participants involved, who are in close physical proximity to each other; many sensory channels are used; and feedback is immediate. We cannot deny the fact that managers and employees use various forms of electronic media, namely email, instant messaging, telephone, discussion forum, etc., for developing relationships through interpersonal communication. At times, using such media can enhance the quantity and quality of interpersonal communication if the senders and receivers are not effective oral communicators. Lack of immediacy in the online communication makes it easier to build close relationships.

### Stages

The act of developing relationships through interpersonal communication is carried out through various stages, which are as follows:

#### Stage 1: Initiating

This is the beginning of interpersonal communication through which senders initiate or start a conversation or chat with their audience. Conversation openers such as *How do you do?, How is everything?, Nice to meet you, Shall we begin?,* etc. can be used. Initiating relationships through conversations can be particularly difficult for people who have inhibitions. In such cases, making contact via the Internet can be helpful.

#### Stage 2: Experimenting

This stage is used to get acquainted with the receiver through small talk: *Where are you from? What is your role in the sales force? Do you know anybody else in the department? I guess Mr John also comes from the same town as yours.*

Though small talk does not add anything meaningful to a communication, it is necessary to open up the communication further and to develop familiarity among the participants. The relationship during this stage is generally pleasant and uncritical and the commitments are minimal.

### Stage 3: Strengthening

Here, the parties further develop their communication and try to understand each other's views. The sender needs to be an active listener and should try to understand others' perspectives on the topic of discussion or conversation. Similarly, the receiver should also try to comprehend the sender's message, the intentions behind conveying the message, and his/her objectives clearly. It is this stage during which the parties seek clarifications on various points in order to understand each other's views.

### Stage 4: Integrating

At this fourth stage of interpersonal communication, mutual decisions are made on the various issues related to the topic in discussion. This is the stage of intense friendships, close business partnerships, etc.

### Stage 5: Bonding

The final stage, bonding is meant for confirming the relationships formally through contracts, MoUs, agreements, and so on. Public announcements may also be made to stakeholders through a company's website and other means of internal and external communication.

All interpersonal communication need not necessarily end in bonding. If senders and receivers do not agree on the issues because of differences of opinion, then right from the initiating stage, the communication may turn out to be unpleasant as it may focus more on differences rather than on similarities. Hence there are minimum chances that the communication intensifies. Participants may not discuss much and the communication may reach a stagnation point where the participants express mutual disgust at each others' views. Such interpersonal communication fails ultimately if the parties do not go for damage control.

## Styles

Let us see the different kinds of style.

### Controlling Style

Here, senders keep the control with them and leave little or no room for receivers to provide feedback or reply. Managers who work in organizations with a closed communication climate may follow this style. Seniors in workplace hierarchy may also use it to communicate with their subordinates who generally do not like such one-way communication. Although this style might prove to be an efficient form of communication during crisis situations, it can intimidate receivers and can actually create a communication gap.

### Democratic Style

As against the controlling style, this style facilitates a healthy two-way communication wherein information is shared mutually. By encouraging participants to express their ideas freely, this style of interpersonal communication creates a cooperative and healthy atmosphere.

### Structured Style

Here, senders plan and structure their messages in such a way that they are well understood by their audience. For instance, a project manager who wants to communicate the specific goals of the project to his/her team members can follow this style. He/she can explain the objectives first and then gradually take his/her audience through his/her detailed plans. The structuring style of interpersonal communication is generally used to communicate specific goals and bring coordination in an organization. To avoid making this a one-way conversation it is always better for senders to modify this style and keep it more open to responses from receivers.

### Dynamic Style

This style allows senders to use motivation to influence the receivers. It is a high-energy approach involving the use of motivating words and phrases to encourage the audience to get inspired and achieve a certain goal. A sales manager can use motivating words and phrases such as *awesome, revitalize, spectacular, nice, solely, special, enjoyable, unmatched, amazing results, a fantastic new product, absolutely stunning, see for yourself, turn wishes to dollars, top notch, gear up, ground breaker,* etc. in his/her interpersonal communication with his/her team to motivate the team members. However, this style cannot be effective if the receiver does not have enough knowledge about the intended outcome.

### Quitting Style

When senders know that receivers are also equally interested in achieving the objectives through interpersonal communication, they can adopt this style. For instance, if a senior HR manager wants to hold a conversation with his/her junior managers on adopting a new incentive scheme and he/she knows that the juniors are also interested in this policy, he/she can leave the communicator's role to them. Also known as *relinquishing style*, this type of interpersonal communication is highly open to ideas to the extent that it can transfer the responsibility of the communication to the receiver.

## COMMUNICATION BARRIERS

At the height of the Cold War, an offhand comment made by the then Soviet Premier Nikita Khrushchev to a British diplomat was translated as 'We will bury you'. According to linguist Alan K. Melby, Khrushchev's remark, made in the context of a conversation about the competition between communism and capitalism, was essentially a restatement (in considerably more vivid language) of Marx's

---

 **COMMUNICATION TOOL**

**Tips for Effective Interpersonal Communication**

- Adapt your message to your receivers. In other words, consider their background before you present your message.
- Refer to your audience by name in order to make them feel that you are specifically addressing them to communicate your point.
- Avoid being dogmatic if you are the senior most among the participants. Remember that interpersonal communication is mainly aimed at developing and sustaining human relationships. Your audience will be receptive to even difficult tasks if they are communicated in a friendly manner.
- Remember to include all necessary details in your message so that there is no ambiguity and your audience can understand completely.
- As far as possible avoid using 'I' or 'me' frequently during interpersonal communication with your subordinates, peers, or superiors.
- Try to understand the feelings hidden behind your audience's words. Similarly, learn to express your feelings of sincerity, enthusiasm, etc. while communicating.

> - Communication fails when the message received is not the same as the message sent.
> - Communication barriers are not limited to only one or two people in an organization but may exist within the entire organization.
> - Communication barriers can be overcome by reducing hierarchical levels, increasing coordination, and encouraging two-way communication.

claim of communism's historic inevitability. Although 'we will bury you' is an acceptable literal rendering of Khrushchev's words, an equally accurate and contextually more appropriate translation would have been 'We will be present at your burial'. Such a rendering is consistent with Khrushchev's comment later in the same conversation that communism did not need to go to war to destroy capitalism, since the latter would eventually self-destruct. In the US, the common interpretation of 'we will bury you' was that *we* referred to the (erstwhile) USSR, *you* meant the US, and *bury* denoted annihilate. For many, especially those who maligned the doctrine of communism, the phrase became prima facie evidence of the (erstwhile) USSR's malevolent intentions toward the US.

The controversy over proper translation of Khrushchev's remark reveals a serious shortcoming of the encoder–decoder account of human communication. Although language is in some respects a code, in other respects it is not. The fact that 'we will bury you' could yield two equally 'correct' renderings that differed radically underscores the fact that humans do not use language simply as a set of signals mapped onto a set of meanings.

Although all communication is subject to misunderstandings, business communication is particularly difficult as the material is often complex. Moreover, both senders and receivers may face distractions that divert their attention. Further, the opportunities for feedback are often limited, making it difficult to correct the misunderstandings, thus ultimately leading to a breakdown in communication.

Communication barriers are not limited to only one or two people, they exist in entire organizations and communication fails when the message received is not the same as the message sent. There are many barriers that cause communication failure. These are as follows:

## Organizational Structure

All organizations, irrespective of their size, have their own communication techniques and each nurtures its own communication climate. In large organizations where flow of information is downward, feedback is not guaranteed. Organizations with a flat structure usually tend to have an intricately knitted communication network. Tall organizations generally have too many vertical communication links, as a result messages become distorted as they move through the various organizational levels.

Irrespective of the size, all organizations have communication policies that describe the protocol to be followed. It is the structure and complexity of this protocol that usually gives rise to communication barriers.

Organizations not only employ the formal methods of communication but also the informal ones, such as grapevine. Today, organizations have realized that a rigid hierarchical structure usually restricts the flow of communication. When the process of communication is hierarchical, information flows through a number of *transfer points*. There is a strong possibility that messages may get distorted, delayed, or lost at these points. To obviate this, the receiver should be contacted directly rather than through numerous transfer stations. Also, the message should be presented orally as this reduces the dependence on transfer stations. To further overcome structural barriers, opportunities should exist for communicating upward, downward, and horizontally (using techniques like employee surveys, open-door policies, newsletters, memos, and task groups). An attempt should be made to reduce hierarchical levels, increase coordination between departments, and encourage two-way communication.

### Difference in Status

When people belonging to different hierarchical positions communicate with each other, there is a possibility that communication may breakdown. Generally, employees at lower levels of the hierarchy are overly cautious while sending messages to managers and talk about subjects they think the managers are interested in. Similarly, people of higher status may distort messages by refusing to discuss anything that would tend to undermine their authority in the organization. In other words, they may want to retain the importance of their status. This tendency is beneficial neither for the employees nor for the organization. Limiting oneself to a particular department or being responsible for a particular task can narrow one's point of view so that it differs from the attitudes, values, and expectations of people who belong to other departments or who are responsible for other tasks.

Barriers arising due to differences in status can be overcome by keeping managers and lower-level employees well informed. Employees should be encouraged to keep their managers informed by being fair minded and respectful of their opinions. They should be brave and convey even such information that the boss might not like.

### Lack of Trust

Establishing credibility or building trust among subordinates or with colleagues is a difficult task. Subordinates may not know whether their manager will respond in a supportive or responsible way, and hence, it is necessary for the manager to ensure that they have faith in him/her. Without trust, free and open communication is effectively blocked, thereby threatening the organization's stability. You may be very clear in your communication, but that is not enough. People should trust you enough so as to willingly accept what you communicate or be able to freely discuss it with you.

Barriers to trust can be overcome by being visible and accessible. Hiding or insulating behind assistants or secretaries will not help; you need to share key information with colleagues and employees, communicate honestly, and include employees in decision-making. Creating an open communication environment in the organization, helping employees in times of distress, and assuring them of your suggestion or cooperation may help you to build trust in their minds.

- Barriers arising due to differences in status can be overcome by keeping the managers and the lower-level employees well informed.
- Managers should ensure that employees are willing to communicate both their problems and perspectives to them openly.

### Closed Communication Climate

An organization's communication climate is influenced by its management style. A directive, authoritarian style blocks free and open exchange of information that characterizes good communication. To overcome barriers related to organizational environment, one should spend more time listening than issuing orders. Managers should respond constructively to employees, and, of course, encourage employees and colleagues to offer suggestions, help set goals, participate in solving problems, and help make decisions. Managers should see to it that employees are willing to communicate both their problems and perspectives to them openly.

## Incorrect Choice of Medium

> Media richness relates to the importance of a medium in a given communication situation.

Choosing an inappropriate communication medium can distort the message and block the intended meaning. One should select a medium that suits the nature of the message and the intended recipient(s). *Media richness* relates to the value or importance of a medium in a given communication situation. It is determined by a medium's ability to convey a message using more than one informational cue (visual, verbal, or vocal) to facilitate feedback and establish personal focus. For example, a video conference is a richer communication medium than a phone call as it displays visual cues such as body language. Face-to-face communication is the richest medium because it is personal, provides immediate feedback, transmits information from both verbal and non-verbal cues, and conveys the emotion behind the message. Telephones and other interactive electronic media are not as effective. Although they allow immediate feedback, they do not provide visual non-verbal cues such as facial expressions, eye contact, and body movements. Written media can be personalized through memos, letters, and reports, but immediate feedback is missing along with the visual and vocal non-verbal cues that contribute to the meaning of the message. The leanest media are generally impersonal written messages such as bulletins, fliers, and standard reports. They lack the ability to transmit non-verbal cues and to give feedback. They also eliminate any personal focus. Table 1.4 summarizes the discussion on media richness.

The barriers that arise out of an inappropriate choice of media can be overcome by

- choosing the richest media for non-routine, complex messages,
- using rich media to extend and to humanize your presence to promote the employees commitment to organizational goals, and
- using leaner media to communicate simple, routine messages.

## Information Overload

At times, people load their messages with too much information. Remember that too much information is as bad as too little because it reduces the audience's ability to concentrate on the most important part of the message. The recipients facing information overload sometimes tend to ignore some of the messages, delay responses to messages they deem unimportant, answer only parts of some messages, or react only superficially to all messages. All these consequences of information overload failures lead to ineffective or poor communication.

**Table 1.4** Choice and quality of medium of communication

| Nature of Message | Type of Media | Cues | Nature of Feedback | Media Quality |
| --- | --- | --- | --- | --- |
| Personal (oral) | Face-to-face | Verbal and non-verbal | Immediate | Richest |
| Personal (oral) | Telephone, computers, etc. | Verbal and vocal | Close to immediate | Rich |
| Personal and impersonal (written)/addressed documents | Letters, memos, reports, etc. | Verbal and visual | Delayed/no | Leaner |
| Impersonal/unaddressed documents | Circulars, fliers, etc. | Verbal and visual | Almost nil | Leanest |

> Only relevant information should be part of a message.

To overcome information overload, as a sender, be focused, realize that some information is not necessary, include only the pertinent information, and give some meaning to the information rather than just passing it on. As a receiver, set priorities for dealing with information flow and do not get trapped in the sea of information.

## Message Complexity

There are two significant reasons for any message to become complex in a business setting—one, the dry and difficult nature of the message itself and the other, the difficulty in understanding it. For example, one may have to deal with subject matter that can be technical or difficult to express. Imagine trying to write an important insurance policy, a set of instructions on how to operate a sophisticated LCD projector, the guidelines for checking credit references, an explanation of why profits have dropped by 10 per cent in the last six months, or a description of some solid waste management programme. These topics are dry, and making them clear and interesting is a real challenge. When formulating business messages, you communicate both as an individual and as a representative of an organization. Thus, you must adjust your own ideas and style so that they are acceptable to your employer. In fact, at times you may be asked to write or say something that you disagree with personally. Suppose you work as a recruiter for your firm. You have interviewed a candidate who, you believe, would make an excellent employee, but others in the firm have rejected this applicant. Now, you have to write a rejection letter to the candidate. Regardless of your personal feelings, you must communicate your firm's message, a task communicators find difficult. It also happens many a time that you may not be clear about what needs to be communicated. Suppose your boss asks you to give a briefing to all the employees on the newly-introduced policy related to family pension, you may find it extremely complex unless you know the policy thoroughly.

Of course, it is not difficult to overcome the barriers to communicating complex messages. It can be done by keeping the messages clear and easy to understand, organizing them suitably, guiding readers by telling them what to expect, using concrete and specific language, and by being focused. Never forget to ask for feedback, which is essential for clarifying and improving a message.

## Message Competition

Invariably most of the business messages compete for the full and undivided attention of their receivers. This may happen at two levels—intra-personal and interpersonal. If you are talking on the phone while scanning a report, both these messages are apt to get short shrift. It may happen so that when you are the sender of a message, it may have to compete with a variety of interruptions—phone rings every five minutes, people intrude, meetings are called, and crises arise. In short, your messages rarely have the benefit of the receiver's undivided attention. Such barriers are true for both oral and written messages.

Avoid communicating to a receiver who does not have the time to pay attention to your message. Make written messages visually appealing and easy to understand, and try to deliver them when your receiver has time to read them. Oral messages are most effective when you take recourse to the face-to-face mode of communication rather than resorting to intermediaries or answering machines. Always set aside enough time for important messages that you receive, as you know that senders and receivers keep changing their roles in a communication process.

## Unethical Communication

> - Barriers arising out of unethical conduct may affect communication both within and outside an organization.
> - Communication barriers can also be due to bad connections, poor acoustics, or illegible copy.

Relationships within and outside organizations depend on trust and fairness. It does not mean that organizations should not be tactful. By all means it is possible for organizations to avoid illegal or unethical messages and still be credible or successful in the long run. Barriers arising out of unethical conduct may affect communication both within and outside organizations. Imagine a situation in which your colleague goes to your boss and takes credit for the success of a project, which in reality you have accomplished. Similarly, imagine a leading company that has created hype about the potential of its product, and in the process hoodwinked its prospective customers. These examples reveal that resorting to unethical means in communication may not drive you to success but to trouble.

Make sure that your messages include all the factual information that ought to be there. Ensure that your information is adequate and relevant to a situation. Above all, make sure that your message is completely truthful, not deceptive in any way, and does not mislead the audience.

## Physical Distractions

Recall the time when you delivered a talk to a large audience seated in a hall, which was poorly lit and inadequately seated. You might have observed that though you tried your best to attract the audience's attention through the various verbal and non-verbal means of communication, you found it difficult because of the shortcomings of the place. Communication barriers are often physical—bad electrical connections, poor acoustics, illegible copy, etc. Although barriers of this sort seem trivial, they can completely block an otherwise effective message. An uncomfortable chair, poor lighting, or some other irritating condition might also distract your receiver. In some cases, a barrier may be related to a receiver's health. Hearing or visual impairment or even a headache can interfere the reception of a message. These annoyances do not generally block communication entirely, but they do reduce receivers' concentration by distracting them.

To overcome physical barriers, exercise as much control as possible over the physical transmission link. If you are delivering an oral presentation, choose a setting that permits the audience to see and hear you without straining. When you are the audience, try to concentrate on the message rather than the distractions. On the other hand, if you are preparing a written document, make sure its appearance or layout suits the message contained in it.

Communication can easily make or break an organization's effectiveness. Just think about the times when you or others misunderstood or did not understand an oral or written communication. Most likely, you even passed on that message to others, believing it was correct and appropriate. Soon, too many people probably received the incorrect message. Feelings could have been hurt, products could have been ordered incorrectly, manufactured the wrong way, or even cancelled—all of it by mistake.

To decrease the possibility of communication problems arising out of various barriers, follow these four simple steps (Fig. 1.10):

1. Choose the recipients of your message carefully. Make sure that the key people who must receive the written or oral message are included. Omit the people who lack veto authority,

do not need to be informed, have no responsibility for the message or its results, will not act on the message, or should not have access to the information. One way to ensure you have involved the right people is to think about who should have a say in the context. Make your decisions accordingly.

2. Think about how to send the message, that is, should the mode be verbal or written. Verbal messages can be easily misinterpreted, especially when there are noises or distractions in the immediate surroundings; if the sender or receiver is anxious, uncertain, or fearful; if the words used are unclear; or if the message is complicated, detailed, unclear, and so on. Nonetheless, messages often do need to be verbal, such as those delivered on the phone, in a meeting, or while passing someone in a hallway. In such cases, as a leader, you must ensure that the receiver correctly hears what you want him/her to hear. How do you do that? Do not ask the person if he/she heard you or understood you. The answer to both questions is almost always 'yes'. Why? Because no one wants the boss to think he/she is ignorant or was not paying attention, or that he/she misinterpreted the message. Ask the receiver to repeat, in his/her own words, what he/she heard you saying, just to ensure that both of you have understood the same message. Otherwise, ask the receiver what will be the most difficult, easiest, or complicated steps in carrying out the task.

3. Follow up your verbal message with a written statement. In a meeting, if you make an important planned statement, distribute a copy of that message. If it was important, but not planned or not written down, ask someone to repeat the statement. After a phone call, a brief encounter with someone, or a scheduled meeting, follow up the statements with a written communication of understanding or confirmation.

4. Finally, decide who can communicate with whom. As a leader, your goal is to combine simplicity with effectiveness. You want messages to come in and go out; you want the right people to receive them in an efficient and effective manner. This means deciding who speaks and writes to whom. Do all communications have to go through your office for approval before being sent? Who speaks to the world outside your organization, that is, the public or the government? The managers or individual employees? Who communicates with or approves communication with other managers, departments, or sites? If all communications pass through your office, you will have direct and complete control over formal information. This is a very time-consuming, bureaucratic, and control-oriented approach with clear drawbacks. The disadvantage, however, of allowing everyone to speak with everyone is that the company messages probably would not be uniform. Therefore, consider the risks before deciding how to handle company information.

```
┌─────────────────────────┐
│ Consider the recipients │
│    of your message      │
└───────────┬─────────────┘
            ▼
┌─────────────────────────┐
│   Decide who can        │
│ communicate with whom   │
└───────────┬─────────────┘
            ▼
┌─────────────────────────┐
│ Follow up your verbal   │
│ message with a written  │
│       statement         │
└───────────┬─────────────┘
            ▼
┌─────────────────────────┐
│    Choose your          │
│  communication mode     │
└─────────────────────────┘
```

**Fig. 1.10** Steps in avoiding communication barriers

## EFFECTIVE MANAGERIAL COMMUNICATION

By being effective, managers can create and establish a healthy organizational environment. They can bring about vast changes not only in the management–employee relations but also in the external and internal communication networks of the organization. Effective communication enables managers in moving towards better functioning of departments and successfully dealing with the complexity of business activities. A manager with good communication skills would certainly have an edge over others in dealing with and solving problems arising out of turbulence in trade unions and other disturbances among abjurers. He/she will be competent in facing intercultural differences too. How to make managerial communication more effective? There are certain characteristics of managerial communication, an understanding of which would provide the managers with a proper perspective on effectiveness in communication.

The factors that render communication effective are as follows:

## Appropriate Communication Style

Every organization has its own culture, which is a reflection of its values, traditions, habits, and customs. Some companies tend to curb the upward flow of communication believing that it is time consuming and unproductive, whereas other companies foster candor and honesty, and employees feel free to confess their mistakes, to disagree with their boss, and to express their opinions.

There are several factors that influence an organization's communication climate, including the nature of the industry, the company's physical set-up, the history of the company, and passing events. However, one of the most important factors is the management style of the top management. Some managers regard workers as lazy and irresponsible, motivated by the fear of losing their jobs. Such managers adopt a directive style. On the other hand, some other managers adopt a more supportive style, assuming that people like to work and take responsibility when they believe in what they are doing. There is yet another set of managers who encourage employees to work together as a team. Such managers adopt a participative style. Although a company looks after its employees, it also gives them the opportunity to take responsibility and to participate in decision-making. The trend today is towards any style that encourages an open communication climate. In such a climate, managers spend more time listening than issuing orders, and workers not only offer suggestions but also help set goals and collaborate on solving problems. It expects special managers to create an open atmosphere and stay in touch with employees. Effective managers understand that free flow of information allows an organization to identify and attack problems quickly. Therefore, to promote the right atmosphere, these managers get out of their offices, walk around headquarters, meet often with small non-management groups, and travel the country and the globe to visit their 'troops'. To understand and to be understood by their workforce, they learn other languages when necessary, and even though they prefer face-to-face conversations, they use high-tech means like video conferencing.

As the participative style promotes and establishes an open communication climate, it is the best amongst the three styles of management.

## Audience-centred Approach

> Every organization has its own culture, which is a reflection of its values, traditions, habits, and customs.

Managers need to keep their audience in mind at all times during the process of communication. Their ability to empathize with, be sensitive to, and generally consider their audience's feelings is the best effective way of communication. Focusing on the audience is the impetus for everything else they do in the communication process. For example, communicating clearly and correctly is important because it ensures that the audience can respond to a message without having to sort out cluttered or incorrect language.

Further, managers need to take every possible step to get their message across in a way that is meaningful to their audience. They may actually create lively individual portraits of certain members of their audience so as to predict their reactions. They may simply try to put themselves in the audience's position and try to adhere strictly to guidelines about courtesy or gather information about the needs and wants of their audience. Whatever the tactic, the point is to write and speak from the audience's point of view.

More than an approach to business communication, the audience-centred approach is actually the modern approach to business in general (it is behind the concepts of total quality management and total customer satisfaction). The advantages of using this approach include successful communication by making it meaningful for an audience, enhanced credibility (because our audience perceives our sincerity), and staving off uncountable ethical questions (because when we concentrate on the benefits to our audience, our concern for others reduces the chance of an ethical lapse).

If managers are sincere towards their audience's needs and responses, they should work for an open communication climate inside and outside their organization. If they sincerely wish to satisfy the needs of their audience, they should approach communication situations with good intentions and high ethical standards. To understand their audience, managers need to do whatever it takes to understand intercultural differences and barriers. Finally, if managers value their audience's time, they should prepare and communicate oral and written messages as efficiently as possible. Hence, centring their attention on their audience helps managers accomplish the other five factors, which will be discussed in the following sections, that contribute to the effectiveness of managerial communication.

## Understanding Intercultural Communication

With the phenomenal advancement in the field of science and technology, more and more businesses are crossing national boundaries to compete on a global scale, and the make-up of the global and domestic workforce is changing rapidly. European, Asian, and US firms are establishing offices around the world and creating international ties through global partnerships, cooperatives, and affiliations. It is necessary for these companies to understand the laws, customs, and business practices of their host countries, and deal with business associates and employees who are native to these countries. Even within their nation, firms are working with a growing number of employees from diverse cultural backgrounds. So, whether managers work abroad or at home, they will encounter increasing cultural diversity in the workplace. To compete successfully in today's multicultural environment, they have to overcome the communication barriers arising out of various differences in language, culture, business practices, etc.

Understanding cultural differences in perception, greetings, and gestures is critical to all businesses. Success in business often depends on knowing the business practices, social customs, and etiquette of the host country. Ignorance in this regard and the mistakes committed may lead to miscommunication, which can cause businesses to lose their position in the market, keep firms from accomplishing their objectives, and ultimately lead to failure.

Today's managers must realize that it is not enough if they are able to speak a language; they must also be able to communicate effectively in various business situations.

Effective intercultural communication is a must in today's workplace.

## Commitment to Ethical Communication

The term 'business ethics' refers to the principles of conduct that govern a person or a group in any business enterprise. In general, ethical people are trustworthy, fair, and impartial. They respect the rights of others and are concerned about the impact of their actions on society. On the other hand, unethical people are essentially selfish and unscrupulous; they say or do whatever it takes to achieve an end. Under the influence of competition and job pressure, business people sometimes make unethical choices. Despite all the negative publicity, the level of ethical awareness has risen over the last few years. Firms like Hewlett-Packard are making sure that every employee is familiar with the company standards for business conduct. Citicorp trains its employees using an ethics broad game to solve hypothetical quandaries. General Electric employees have access to interactive software that answers their questions on ethics. Texas Instruments employees get a weekly column on ethics through an international electronic news service. Raytheon employees make some 100 calls a month to a hotline set-up to log complaints and ask about questionable behaviour.

Ethics play a crucial role in communication. Language itself is made up of words that carry values. So, by using certain expression or words effectively, managers influence others' perception of their message, and can, thus, shape expectations and behaviour. Likewise, when an organization expresses itself internally, it influences the values of its employees; when it communicates externally, it shapes the way outsiders perceive it. Ethical communication includes all relevant information, is true in every sense, and is not deceptive in any way.

Ethics affect every aspect of business communication. When sending an ethical message, managers are accurate and sincere. They avoid language that manipulates, discriminates, or exaggerates. They do not hide negative information

- In a multicultural environment, managers have to overcome the communication barriers arising out of various differences in language, culture, or business practices.
- Business ethics refers to the principles of conduct that govern a person or a group in any business enterprise.

behind an optimistic attitude, do not state opinions as facts, and portray graphic data fairly. They are honest with employers, co-workers, and clients, never seeking personal gains by making others look better or worse than they are. They do not allow personal preferences to influence their perception or the perception of others, and they act in good faith. On the surface, such ethical practices appear fairly easy to recognize. However, deciding what is ethical can be quite complex. Hence, managers should make sure that a certain code of conduct is prescribed and the employees strictly adhere to the same.

## Proficiency in Communication Technology

The ever-increasing quantum of information to be communicated and the speed of communication are two explicit results of the ever-changing technology that managers come across in their jobs. Hence, to be successful, they have to ensure that they not only develop their ability to understand, use, and adapt to these technologies but also motivate their subordinates to adapt themselves to the technological tools of communication.

Present-day technology is determining whom we communicate with, how frequently we communicate, and what sort of devices we use to communicate. Increasingly, employees are using desktop computers or laptops at their workplace, home, and during travel. Moreover, both employees and organizations are becoming increasingly accessible through fax, car phones, cellular phones, email, voicemail, satellite communication, and social media. In fact, today's businesses operate at such a fast pace, communicate across such great distances, and demand such professional-looking documents that the managers are left with no option but to master the technological tools and processes necessary to compete.

Irrespective of his/her designation, whether an entry-level employee, a manager, or a CEO, it is necessary for a professional to have access to the latest technological tools. For many such people, it means repeatedly adapting to new technologies and procedures. When a business purchases new computers or other new technologies, it expects to improve operations and increase productivity. However, because some employees are unable to adjust to new ways of performing work, some 30 per cent of such new technologies either fail or are never used to their fullest potential.

Technology has already blurred the lines between organizational responsibilities. For example, word processing is now an essential tool for executives and no longer an exclusive domain of secretaries. Technology is also helping companies communicate more easily and effectively; for example, Ford and FedEx Express are successfully using satellite television to communicate with their employees. There is no doubt that technology is becoming evermore useful. For example, fiber optics and electronic bulletin boards will put workers in touch not only with other workers but also with customers, clients, vendors, and regulators; satellites will improve shipment tracking so that businesses will know the location of every package and vehicle; and automated translations will help multicultural and international businesses overcome language barriers to improve intercultural communication.

Technology can be an invisible ally, helping managers perform the tasks necessary to succeed in business. As long as it is considered a boon and not a bane, technology can improve the effectiveness of business communication.

## Control over the Flow of Communication

It is necessary for managers to make sure that all communication messages flow efficiently across and outside their organizations. The sixth factor contributing to effective organizational communication is efficient flow of communication messages. If we consider the logistics of transmitting all the messages communicated, both within the organization and to and from the outside world, we will find that information does not flow efficiently because of several reasons, which are as follows:

- Information overload
- Lack of efficiency in preparing messages
- Lack of adequate training

All companies can keep the costs down and maximize the benefits of their communication activities by reducing the number of messages, by speeding up their preparation, and by training employees in communication skills.

### Reducing the Number of Messages

One useful way to reduce the number of messages is to think twice before sending one. Only about 13 per cent of the emails that executives receive are of immediate value, and not surprisingly, they tend to give it short shrift. They also tend to ignore many of the internal messages that are intended for them. In a study it was found that five CEOs received about 40 routine reports in five weeks and responded to only two of them.

Since organizations spend a lot of time and resources on producing letters and memos, they have to be concerned with how many messages they create. If an important message has to be sent, a letter or memo is a good idea. On the other hand, if it merely adds to the information overload, it is probably better left unsent or handled in some other way—say a quick telephone call or a face-to-face chat. However, with the alarming increase in the number of emails, SMSes, and fax messages, the managers have to devise an efficient method of not only reducing the number of such messages but also handling them appropriately.

In order to accelerate the pace of preparation, business people try to transmit messages as quickly as possible. One thing that helps in accelerating this process is to make sure that written messages are prepared correctly the first time around. Although eliminating errors entirely is an unrealistic goal, we can combat the ambiguity by making sure that everybody involved in preparing a message understands what is expected. If we are given an unclear writing assignment, we must ask for more guidance. If we are handling out assignments, we must explain what we want.

Another way to increase efficiency in the preparation of messages is through standardization. Most organizations use standard format letters for handling repetitive correspondence, and most employ a standard format for memos and reports that are prepared on 'Right-messages-at-the-right-time-add-value to-the-communication' motto. Although following a formula may inhibit creativity, it reduces the writing time. In case of memos and reports, standardization also saves readers' time because the familiar format enables people to absorb the information more quickly.

> Standard format letters can be used to increase efficiency in the preparation of messages.

## STRATEGIES FOR IMPROVING ORGANIZATIONAL COMMUNICATION

Given how important it is for people in organizations to communicate with each other in a clear, open, and accurate fashion, it is worthwhile to consider ways of improving organizational communication.

In the following paragraphs, several tried-and-tested techniques for improving organizational communication will be discussed.

## Encourage Open Feedback

In theory, encouraging open feedback is simple (Image 1.3). If accurate information is the key to effective communication, then organizations should encourage feedback. After all, feedback is a prime source of information. However, we say 'in theory' because it is natural for workers to be afraid of the repercussions they may face when being extremely open with their superiors. Likewise, high-ranking officials may be somewhat apprehensive about hearing what is really on their workers' minds. In other words, people in organizations may be reluctant to give and receive feedback—a situation that can wreak havoc on organizational communication.

**Image 1.3** Open feedback encourages communication

These problems would be unlikely to occur in an organizational climate in which top officials openly and honestly seek feedback and lower-level workers believe they can speak their mind with impunity. How can this be accomplished? Although this is not easy, several successful techniques for opening feedback channels have been used by organizations. The following are some of the techniques:

**360-degree feedback**   These are formal systems in which people at all levels give feedback to others at different levels and receive feedback from them as well as outsiders—including customers and suppliers. This technique is used in companies such as Hewlett-Packard, Motorola, and 3M.

**Suggestion systems**   These are programmes that invite employees to submit ideas about how something may be improved. Employees are generally rewarded when their ideas are implemented. For example, the idea of mounting film boxes onto cards that hang from display stands, which is common today, originally came from a Kodak employee.

**Corporate hotlines**   These are telephone lines staffed by corporate officials ready to answer questions and listen to comments. These are particularly useful during times of change when employees are likely to be full of questions. For example, AT&T used hotlines in the early 1980s during the period of its anti-trust divestiture.

- 360-degree feedback, suggestion systems, and corporate hotlines may be used as successful feedback channels.
- Avoid jargon—communicators should speak the language of their audience.

## Use Simple Language

No matter what field you are in, chances are that it has its own special language—its jargon. Although jargon may greatly help communication within specialized groups, it can severely interfere with communication among the uninitiated.

The trick to using jargon wisely is to know your audience. If the individuals with whom you are communicating understand the jargon, using it can help facilitate communication. However, when addressing an audience whose members are unfamiliar with the specialized language, simple, straightforward

> **BUSINESS COMMUNICATION INSIGHT**
>
> **Good Communication is Good Business**
>
> Why is communication important to business? Couldn't we just produce graduates good at numbers?
>
> Good communication matters because business organizations are made up of its employees. As Robert Kent, former dean of Harvard Business School has said, 'In business, communication is everything.'
>
> Research spanning several decades has consistently ranked communication skills as crucial for managers. Typically, managers spend 75 to 80 per cent of their time engaged in some form of written or oral communication. Although often termed a 'soft' skill, communication in a business organization provides the critical link between core functions.
>
> It has been observed that people unable to express themselves clearly in writing limit their opportunities for professional, salaried employment. Also, organizations are increasingly focusing on teams—both local and international—to get their competitive advantage. Therefore, communication had become more important than ever. How can you be effective?
>
> - Think before you communicate.
> - Be an active listener.
> - Be focused on your audience in your response.
> - Be brief.
>
> *Source:* Adapted from 'Why Good Communication Is Good Business' by Marty Blalock, http://www.bus.wisc.edu/update/winter05/business_communication.asp, accessed on 14 September 2011. Copyright © 2006 The Board of Regents of the University of Wisconsin System. Reproduced with permission.

language is bound to be most effective. In either case, the rationale is the same: communicators should speak the language of their audience. Although you may be tempted to try to impress your audience by using big words, you may have little impact on them if they do not understand you. The general advice is to follow the KISS principle, that is, keep it short and simple.

## Avoid Overload

Imagine this scene: You are up late one night at the end of the term. You are writing a paper and studying for finals, all at the same time. Your desk is piled high with books when your roommate comes in to explain what you should do to prepare for the semester-end party. If this sounds familiar to you, then you probably know that it is unlikely that you would be able to concentrate on the things you are doing. After all, when people are confronted with more information than they can process at any given time, their concentration level, and hence, their performance tends to suffer. This condition is known as *overload*.

Staying competitive in today's hectic world often requires doing many things at once—but without threatening the performance, which is often the result when communication channels are overloaded. Fortunately, several things can be done to avoid, or at least minimize, the problem of information overload. Some of these are given in this section:

*Rely on gatekeepers*   People whose jobs require them to control the flow of information to potentially overloaded individuals, groups, or organizations are known as gatekeepers. In making appointments for top executives, administrative assistants actually provide gatekeeping services to them.

*Practice queuing*   Queuing involves lining up incoming information so that it can be attended to in an orderly fashion. Air traffic controllers do this when they 'stack' incoming planes in a holding pattern so as to prevent them from tragically 'overloading' the runway.

## Walk the Talk

When it comes to effective communication, actions definitely speak louder than words. Too often, communication is hampered by the practice of saying one thing but meaning something else. Also, whenever implicit messages (e.g., 'we may be cutting jobs') contradict official messages (e.g., 'don't worry, the company is stable'), it is bound to result in confusion.

This is especially problematic when the inconsistency comes from the top. In fact, one of the most effective ways of fostering effective organizational communication is for CEOs to 'walk the talk', that is, to match their deeds to their words. After all, a boss would lose credibility if he/she told his/her employees 'my door is always open to you', but was never available for a consultation. Good communication demands consistency. For words to be heard as loud as actions, the two must match.

## Be a Good Listener

Effective communication involves more than just presenting messages clearly. It also involves doing a good job of comprehending messages sent by others. Although most of us take listening for granted, effective listening is an important skill. In fact, given that managers spend about 40 per cent of their time listening to others, but only 25 per cent on effective listening, the latter is a skill that could be developed in most of us. When we speak of effective listening, we are not referring to the passive act of just taking in information. Rather, effective listening involves the following three important elements:

- Being non-judgemental while taking in information from others
- Acknowledging speakers in ways that encourage them to continue speaking
- Attempting to advance the speaker's ideas to the next step

Individuals can be the root cause of a communication problem. In a business scenario, we do not attempt to change individual personality traits, nor, for that matter, is it possible; but we can surely understand the role of an individual when there is communication breakdown.

---

### Questionnaire

Research shows that in India many employers and employees lack good communication skills. This results in problems with productivity, workplace effectiveness, and job satisfaction.

To assess the level of your communication skills, take the following quiz.

**Questions**

**1. Listening**

(a) Do you listen to others' opinions? Yes O No O
(b) If you think someone is making a good point, do you acknowledge it? Yes O No O
(c) In a group, do you encourage people to listen to each other? Yes O No O

**2. Blaming and Praising**

(a) If someone makes a suggestion that is successfully implemented, do you ensure he or she receives thanks and praise? Yes O No O

(b) If someone makes a mistake, do you start the conversation by discussing the error? Yes O No O
(c) If you hear someone blaming another classmate/colleague, do you join in with your own negative comments? Yes O No O
(d) Do you criticize your classmates/colleagues in front of others? Yes O No O

### 3. Availability

(a) If you know an awkward colleague/classmate wants to talk to you, do you hide? Yes O No O
(b) If you're too busy to see someone, do you make a point of letting them know that you will get back to them? Yes O No O

### 4. Adapting

(a) Do you adapt your communication style for different people and circumstances? Yes O No O

### 5. General Communication Issues

(a) Do you prefer to give advice or instructions by discussing matters with colleagues or staff face-to-face? Yes O No O
(b) If a colleague or member of staff is struggling to understand something, do you go out of your way to help them? Yes O No O
(c) Do you try to write letters, documents, etc. in plain English? Yes O No O

### Answers

1. Listening: Award yourself a point for each of the following correct answers: (a) yes; (b) yes; (c) yes (maximum three points).
2. Blaming and Praising: Award yourself a point for each of the following correct answers: (a) yes; (b) yes; (c) no; (d) no (maximum four points).
3. Availability: Award yourself a point for each of the following correct answers: (a) no; (b) yes (maximum two points).
4. Adapting: Award yourself a point for the following correct answer: (a) yes.
5. General Communication Issues: Award yourself a point for each of the following correct answers: (a) yes; (b) yes; (c) yes (maximum three points).

### Your Score

13 points: You clearly know how to communicate well at work. Good communication isn't easy, though, and you need to maintain your success day in, day out.

11/12 points: Address the areas where you've failed to score points, and keep working at your communication skills. You should soon become a good workplace communicator.

Fewer than 11 points: You have some work to do. Try to improve your communication skills in the areas where you've lost points. If you're still struggling, you may be able to find a place on a relevant training course to assist you.

*Source:* Kevin Watson, http://www.workcommunication.co.uk/questionnaire-do-you-have-good-communication-skills.html. Reproduced courtesy of www.WorkCommunication.co.uk—how to communicate effectively in the workplace, accessed on 10 November 2011.

## SUMMARY

Powerful communication skills are most needed in today's diverse workplace and, hence, the importance of these skills can never be overlooked. To achieve effectiveness in communication, one needs to understand the basics of business communication. A clear comprehension of the communication process, its fundamentals, the various channels through which communication flows in an organization, etc. is essential to become a successful communicator in the professional setting. Above all, it is necessary to understand and appropriately deal with the communication failures arising out of certain significant factors. One can enhance communication effectiveness by adhering to the characteristics of effective communication and also by adopting certain strategies for improving communication skills.

## KEY TERMS

*Communication* It is the passing of information and understanding from one person to another at the same level or at different levels. It is the process through which management organizes work. The term can also be defined as the management of messages for the purpose of creating meaning.

*Communication barriers* It refers to certain factors that may pose problems in the communication process thereby causing failures in communication.

*Communication networks* It refers to the formal and informal network in an organization used for the purpose of communicating within and outside the organization. Vertical, horizontal, and diagonal flow of communication is possible in the formal networks. Grapevine flows through the informal network.

*Components of communication* It refers to the essential components of communication process, which are sender, channel, message, receiver, response, and feedback.

*Diagonal communication* It refers to communication that ignores the hierarchical structure and that flows between persons who belong to different levels of hierarchy and who have no direct reporting relationships.

*Downward communication* It refers to the flow of communication from the superiors to subordinates. Information, instructions, directions, feedback, etc. flow in this direction.

*Effective business communication* It is the use of effective language to convey a clear business message to achieve a predetermined purpose.

*Grapevine* It refers to the informal communication flowing in an organization. If used judiciously, this form of communication can benefit the organizations.

*Horizontal communication* It refers to communication among the various divisions of an organization in order to share and coordinate the multifarious activities.

*Managers' roles* It relates to the large number of varied, un-patterned, and short-term activities concerned with interpersonal relationships, the transfer of information, and decision-making.

*Organizational structure* It refers to the hierarchical structure of an organization. While some organizations have a tall and narrow structure having too many transfer stations, other have a short and wide structure having few transfer stations.

*Upward communication* It refers to communication flowing from subordinates to superiors. Information, analysis, feedback, etc. flow in this direction.

## Concept Review Questions

1. Discuss how communication plays a crucial role in the progress of an organization.
2. What are the activities that managers perform when they play the informational role in their organizations?

3. 'Your audience receives the message exactly as you intend it to be.' Do you agree or disagree with this statement? Justify your answer.
4. Discuss any three barriers that lead to communication breakdown in an organization.
5. Explain the role of horizontal communication in an organization by giving suitable examples.
6. What are the advantages and disadvantages of grapevine communication?
7. Discuss how you can put to use the grapevine form of communication for organizational effectiveness.
8. What are the characteristics of effective business communication?
9. Discuss the strategies for bringing about effectiveness in communication for business purposes.
10. Explain the process of communication through a diagram depicting the essential components of the process.
11. Elaborate the following statements in about 75 words each:
    (i) For an organization to prosper, both vertically upward and vertically downward flow of communication are essential.
    (ii) Grapevine communication can be used to the management's benefit.
12. Explain the following terms in about 75 words each with reference to managerial communication:
    (i) Decisional role
    (ii) Diagonal communication
    (iii) Open communication climate

## Critical Thinking Questions

1. Distinguish between each of the following pairs of roles performed by managers in an organization. Give one specific example of each to support your answer.
    (i) Liaison person and spokesperson
    (ii) Negotiator and disturbance handler
    (iii) Monitor and leader
2. For each of the communication situations given below, identify the direction/type of flow of communication. Choose the most appropriate form of communication for each situation and give reasons for your choice:
    (i) The president of Expert Engineering Corporation has just come back from his/her international tour and wishes to share some important information with everybody in the company.
    (ii) You, as the vice chairman of an MNC, wish to find out certain details about the new export policy of the central government from the vice president of another organization Novel Software.
    (iii) The supervisor of the production unit of a company needs some immediate clarifications from his/her manager on a proposal he/she has to submit.
    (iv) Your close friend and fellow officer Mr Mehra wants to share with you, in the company canteen, some unhappy incident that occurred this morning.
    (v) As a personnel manager, you want to announce details of this year's company picnic.
    (vi) As a director of internal communication, you want to convince the top management of the need for a company newsletter.
    (vii) As a production manager, you want to make sure that both the sales manager and the finance manager receive your scheduling estimates.
    (viii) As a marketing manager, you want to help employees understand the company's goals and its attitudes towards workers.
3. Give three ways in which you might encourage your employees to give you feedback on daily operations.
4. Identify and briefly discuss the communication barriers in the following situations:
    (i) 'My boss will fire me if I tell him/her about what had happened in my division this afternoon.'
    (ii) 'I'm sick of this. As soon as I'm just about finished with a project, I get six more to complete.'

(iii) 'This room is an awful choice for delivering a talk. There's a lot of discomfort and distraction.'

(iv) 'In this office nobody tells me anything and nobody listens to what I have to say.'

5. Explain the lines of formal and informal communication in your institute organization. Give suitable examples.

## Projects

1. List the various types of communications that exist in your institution/organization and discuss the strategies for making them more effective.
2. Form a group of seven and assign each member one of the following roles: president, vice president (marketing), vice president (operations), vice president (HR), manager (operations), manager (marketing), and manager (HR) of a large MNC in India. Devise dialogues for a discussion on introducing a new policy related to improving communication strategies. Try to incorporate both vertical and horizontal communication in your roles.
3. Observe for a week how people communicate with you. Note down the situations where you experience some difficulty in understanding the message. At the end of the week, discuss these barriers with the senders and jointly work out some strategies for overcoming the same.

## REFERENCES

Adair, John 2002, *The Effective Communicator*, Jaico Publishing House, Mumbai, pp. 6–7.

Adler, Ronald B. and George Rooman 2006, *Understanding Human Communication*, Ninth Edition, Oxford University Press, New York, pp. 197–201.

Adler, Ronald B. and Jeanne Marquardt Elmhorst 2002, *Communicating at Work*, Seventh Edition, McGraw Hill Higher Education, NY, pp. 410–11.

Clark, H.H. and S.E. Brennan, 'Grounding in Communication,' in L.B. Resnick, J.M. Levine, and S.D. Teasley (eds), *Perspectives on Socially Shared Cognition*, American Psychological Association, 1991, pp. 127–149.

Courtland, Bovee L. and John V. Thill 2003, *Business Communication Today*, Seventh Edition, Pearson Education (Singapore) Pvt Ltd, Delhi, pp. 28–33.

Guffey Mary Allen 2002, *Business Communication: Process and Product*, Thomson Asia Pvt Ltd, Singapore, pp. 297–306.

Lesikar, Raymond V., John D. Pettit, and Marie E. Flately 2002, *Lesikar's Basic Business Communication*, Eighth Edition, Tata McGraw-Hill, New Delhi, pp. 462–65.

Ludlow, Ron and Fergus Panton 1999, *The Essence of Effective Communication*, Prentice-Hall of India, New Delhi, pp. 2–3.

Penrose, John, Robert Rasberry, and Bob Myers 2001, *Advanced Business Communication*, Fourth Edition, Thomson Asia Pvt Ltd, Singapore, pp. 27–37.

Prasad, P. 1998, *Communication Skills*, S.K. Kataria and Sons, Delhi, pp. 63–72.

Robbins, Stephen P. and Mary Coulter 1996, *Management*, Fifth Edition, Prentice Hall of India, Delhi, pp. 610–17.

Roberts, K.H. 1984, *Communicating in Organizations*, Science Research Associates, Chicago, pp. 4.

Terry, George 1968, *Principles of Management*, Richard D. Irwin Inc., Homewood, Illinois.

### Goodwill Corporation Ltd

The president of Goodwill Corporation Ltd, Mr Abhishek Mukherji, wanted to facilitate upward communication. He believed an open-door policy was a good option. He announced that his own door was open to all employees and encouraged senior managers to do the same. He felt this would give him a way to get early warning signals that would not be filtered or redirected through the formal chain of command. Mr Mukherji found that many employees who used the open-door policy had been with the company for years and were comfortable talking to the president. Sometimes messages came through about inadequate policies and procedures. Mr Mukherji would raise these issues and explain any changes at the next senior managers' meeting. The most difficult complaints to handle were those from people who were not getting along with their bosses.

One employee, Anand, complained bitterly that his manager had over committed on behalf of the department and put everyone under tremendous pressure. Anand argued that long hours and low morale were major problems. However, he would not allow Mr Mukherji to either bring the manager into the discussion or seek out other employees to confirm the complaint. Although Mr Mukherji suspected that Anand might be right, he could not let the matter lie and said, 'Have you considered leaving the company?' This made Anand realize that a meeting with his immediate boss was unavoidable.

Before the three-party meeting, Mr Mukherji contacted Anand's manager and explained what was going on. He insisted that the manager come to the meeting willing to listen and without hostility towards Anand. During the meeting, Anand's manager listened attentively and displayed no ill will. He learned the problem from Anand's perspective and realized he was over his head in his new job. After the meeting, the manager said he was relieved. He had been promoted into the job from a technical position just a few months earlier and had no management or planning experience. He welcomed Mr Mukherji's offer to help him do a better job of planning.

**Questions**

1. What techniques increased Mr Mukherji's communication effectiveness?
2. Do you think that an open-door policy was the right way to improve upward communication? What other techniques would you suggest?
3. What problems do you think an open-door policy creates? Do you think many employees are reluctant to use it? Give reasons for your answer.

### Image and Rumours at Procter & Gamble

Since the late 1970s, Procter & Gamble has been plagued by rumours connecting the company with Satanism and devil worship. The rumours have come in two cycles: from late 1981 to the end of the summer of 1982, and from the autumn of 1984 into early 1985. Procter & Gamble primarily manufactures and distributes household products, including Crest toothpaste and Pampers disposable diapers. The company attributes its success to developing products based on consumers' needs and promoting these products with extensive advertising. It contacts consumers through an extensive network of toll-free telephone numbers and market research projects.

The first rumour that surfaced was that the company was owned by the Church of Satan. The 'proof' of this relationship was Procter & Gamble's hundred-year-old trademark, a quarter moon and 13 stars. Procter & Gamble was not overly concerned until late October 1981, when a second rumour began to circulate. It claimed that John Smale, President and Chief Executive, had appeared on the 'Phil Donahue Show', or a similar talk show, where he supposedly stated that he was a member of the Church of Satan, that the company contributed money to the church, and that 'there aren't enough Christians in the world to stop it'. He had never been on any such programme, of course, but the rumours also urged a boycott of all Procter & Gamble products.

Calls began flooding the toll-free telephone lines asking about the legitimacy of the rumours. Most of the calls were from retailers informing the company that some customers were returning Procter &

Gamble products or asking why the goods were not being taken off the shelves. Employees were being threatened, and some had had their tyres slashed.

The number of calls peaked at 15,000 in July 1982. Procter & Gamble counter-attacked by sending out a fact sheet to 48,000 churches in southern US. This group was targeted because the rumours were being spread by fundamentalist religious groups, mostly in the south. The company also enlisted the aid of certain members of the clergy, including Rev. Jerry Falwell, President of the Moral Majority, and Rev. Donald E. Wildmon, Chairman of the Coalition for Better Television. These clergymen issued statements discrediting the rumours and suggesting that people continue using Procter & Gamble's products. The company also obtained statements from television talk show producers confirming that no one from Procter & Gamble had appeared on their programmes. The public relations campaign dispelled the notions about the company's supposed link to the devil.

The rumours died down and the number of calls decreased to 30 or 40 a month. After the success of this counter-attack, Procter & Gamble was surprised when the number of calls suddenly jumped to 1,000 in September 1984, and then tripled to 3,000 in October.

This time the rumours concerned the company's trademark and its supposed symbolism in devil worship and Satanism. Unlike the first wave of calls, these calls seemed to come from across the country. Procter & Gamble began sending around media information kits, similar to those used previously, containing a brief history of the logo. They included letters from the producers of the television talk shows and letters from the clergymen. The company also sent a security team to track the rumour's source and to look for patterns in its transmission. They even threatened to sue anyone caught spreading the rumour.

However, by spring 1985, the problem had gotten out of control. The company was forced to change the logo, which was then 103 years old. Observers agreed that this was the right move, because hysterical rumours can outlast reasoned explanations and even lawsuits. By the time the logo had been changed, the company had spent several hundred thousand dollars on anti-rumour public relations and on extra telephone staff to handle calls on the matter.

The final result was that the company lost a historical symbol that had stood for trustworthy, reliable products to millions of consumers for over a 100 years.

### Questions

1. What category of communication is Procter & Gamble concerned with in this case?
2. What change, if any, would you have recommended for the company's initial strategy in 1982 to stop the rumours?
3. Were the toll-free telephone lines advantageous or disadvantageous to the company?
4. Do you agree with the decision of Procter & Gamble to change their established logo? Justify your view.

CHAPTER 2

# Non-verbal Communication

### LEARNING OBJECTIVES

After reading this chapter, you will be able to understand

- the term non-verbal communication
- the significance of non-verbal communication in organizations
- the two major forms of non-verbal communication
- the various types of non-verbal cues
- the interpretation of non-verbal messages
- the tips for effective use of non-verbal means

## INTRODUCTION

Demosthenes, the famous Greek orator, when asked what the first part of oratory was, answered, 'Action'; asked about the second, he replied, 'Action'; for the third he still answered, 'Action'. Generally speaking, people tend to believe in actions more than in words. Our actions are, in fact, a means of communication, subject to interpretation by others. Even the failure to act is a way of communicating.

Today, many researchers are concerned with the information sent through communication that is independent of and different from verbal information, namely the non-verbal communication. While verbal communication is organized by language; non-verbal communication is not. In business organizations, understanding the messages of team members as well as those of anyone else with whom you are communicating often involves more than merely listening to the spoken words. Non-verbal cues, in fact, can speak louder than words. Your personal appearance, facial expressions, postures, gestures, eye contact, voice, proximity, touch—all these non-verbal signals influence the way your message is interpreted or deciphered by your partners in a communication process. These silent messages communicate your feelings during any form of interpersonal communication you have with your seniors, subordinates, or colleagues. Non-verbal communication includes all unwritten and unspoken messages, both intentional and unintentional. Though they have a profound impact on your receivers, it is difficult to interpret them accurately. Nevertheless, they are not to be ignored, but to be recognized and understood as correctly as possible. To do this, you need to know about each of these resourceful means of

> Non-verbal signals play an important part in the communication process.

communication. This chapter will enable you to understand what we mean by 'non-verbal communication', its various types and forms, how to interpret them, and also some tips to enhance your non-verbal communication.

## DEFINITION

Communication is the transfer of information from one person to another. Most of us spend about 75 per cent of our waking hours communicating our knowledge, thoughts, and ideas to others. However, most of us fail to realize that a great deal of our communication is in a non-verbal form as opposed to oral and written forms. Non-verbal communication includes facial expressions, eye contact, tone of voice, body posture and motions, and positioning within groups. It may also include the way we wear our clothes or the silence we keep.

**Image 2.1** Non-verbal cues affect communication

In person-to-person communications, our messages are sent on two levels simultaneously. If the non-verbal cues and the spoken message are incongruous, the flow of communication is hindered. Right or wrong, the receiver of the communication tends to base the intentions of the sender on the *non-verbal cues* he/she receives (Image 2.1).

Imagine that you are comfortably seated inside a movie hall and waiting for the movie to begin. The hall is noisy with people talking to each other, chatting over cellular phones, enjoying the music being played, etc. All of a sudden the hall becomes dark and the music stops. Now you sense a totally different mood in the auditorium. You and the others become silent, as you know that the movie is about to start in a few seconds. The *darkness* and the *silence* in the hall communicate something to you.

Recall a conversation during which you *raised your eyebrows* to convey your disbelief at a statement made by your partner or a meeting in which you appreciated a member by *patting his/her back*.

Reminisce that *deafening roar of applause* you received at the end of an inaugural address, which was delivered by you to a large audience in a huge conference hall of an organization.

All the situations mentioned above convey a significant fact—we communicate not only through words but also through means other than words. Your smiling or frowning face, furrowed brows, immaculate clothing, animated movements, vibrant voice, firm or limpid handshake—all communicate something to your receivers. Likewise, your communication often involves more than merely listening to the spoken words. Words are not the only means we use for communicating with others. We also use silence, signs, symbols, space, objects, voice, touch, body movements, etc. along with our words to convey our messages. All these means are known as *non-verbal cues*. If 'non' means 'not' and 'verbal' means 'words', then it appears to be logical that non-verbal communication refers to communication that does not involve words.

> Silence, signs, symbols, body movements, etc. are known as non-verbal cues.

The term non-verbal communication was coined in the twentieth century and includes many features—communication through touch and smell, clothing, masks, and vocal features such as intonation, stress, speech rate, accent, and volume. It also refers to communication through body movements—facial expression, gaze, pupil size, posture, and interpersonal distance.

We can define non-verbal communication in several ways:

- *It is communication through any means other than words.*
- *It is the transmission of messages by some medium other than speech or writing.*
- *It refers to all external stimuli other than the spoken or written words and that includes body motion, characteristics of voice, appearance, and space distancing.*
- *It is the communication that uses non-linguistic means to convey the message.*
- *It refers to the transfer of meaning by body language, space, time, and paralanguage.*

Because the term *non-verbal* only excludes communication through words, the features it may include are virtually limitless. As this vital means of communication permeates all speech and much, if not all, of written communication, let us try to explore further by looking at the significance of non-verbal cues in organizational communication and also by understanding the nuances involved in this unique means of communication.

### Business Communication Insight

**Non-verbal Communication across the World**

Non-verbal communication is different all around the world. This section will give you an impression about the differences in non-verbal communication across various countries.

**Japan**

- Japanese rely on things like facial expressions, tone of voice, and posture to know how someone is feeling.
- If you frown when someone is speaking, it is read as a sign of disagreement.
- Looking or staring into another person's eyes is taken as a sign of disrespect, particularly a person who is senior to you because of age or position.
- Non-verbal communication is quite significant. In fact, there is a book for 'gaijins' (foreigners) on how to understand the signs.

**Hungary**

- Hungarians are never as direct as Americans in their communication and mostly rely on nuances of meaning in many cases.
- Talking to someone with your hands in your pocket and chewing gum in your mouth is considered impolite.

**The Middle East**

- Arabs don't treat business and personal relationships as different, and they generally prefer to conduct business with the people they know and like.
- Written communication is considered distant and less important. The best way to connect is always in person. If not possible, make a phone call.

## SIGNIFICANCE OF NON-VERBAL COMMUNICATION IN ORGANIZATIONS

Samuel Morse, the inventor of the first electric telegraph, also invented special alphabet of dots and dashes called the Morse code that is still used today. While the Morse code was used to communicate words quickly over distances, other codes have been developed to conceal the meaning of messages.

Such codes have played a significant role in a variety of military battles and are still used in contemporary times to secure important information that travels across the Internet.

Belief in the importance of non-verbal communication is nothing new. 'Don't watch a person's mouth but his fists' was the advice of Martin Luther, the sixteenth century religious reformer. We tend to place a great deal of emphasis on the written and spoken word, while overlooking the profound effects of non-verbal communication. As we all know, our communications early in life successfully take place without words. That is to say, as babies we communicate with everybody only through non-verbal means. However, after we learn to speak and start going to school, non-verbal language is often disregarded—at least superficially. However, it continues to have a profound subconscious effect on us. Once we become professionals, we find that we are ill-equipped to cope with the contradictions between the verbal and non-verbal messages we come across is our organizations. We should realize that to communicate effectively, using, understanding, and interpreting non-verbal cues appropriately is very important. The words we use generally convey objective information; non-verbal messages reveal our emotions and attitudes. When we do use words to talk about our emotions, we often talk about what we think we ought to feel, not what we really feel. Meanwhile, we express our true feelings non-verbally. When words and actions contradict each other, we tend to distrust the words and subconsciously rely on the non-verbal cues. Especially in oral communication, what we say is less important than how we say it.

Non-verbal communication is more suitable than words for some communication tasks. It is often quicker and easier to point to an object than to describe it. As body movement is visual, it is also a silent means of communication and may be used when it is difficult to use speech. For example, gestures may be used by people, who are not actually talking, to comment on what is being said without breaking the flow of the speaker. Body movement can be used without the mutual obligation or ritual conduct that seems to be required by conversation. It may sometimes be used as a substitute for speech where the words might be regarded as too explicit or indelicate.

One study showed how at parties people used hand gestures as initial salutations to capture another's attention before entering into conversation. Another study showed how patients used flamboyant gestures to attract the doctor's attention away from his medical notes. In this context, a gesture has the additional advantage of indirectness as well as visibility. A direct request for attention might be seen as a challenge to the doctor's authority.

Communication is more than verbal. Verbal exchanges account for only a fraction of the messages people send and receive. Research has shown that between 70 and 90 per cent of the entire communication spectrum is non-verbal. Consequently, you should be aware of the different forms of non-verbal communication that you are likely to encounter during negotiation conferences.

Although we continually send and receive non-verbal messages, most of us are not fully aware of the ways in which we communicate non-verbally. Still, if you watch carefully, you will see that most leading professionals (e.g., doctors, lawyers, and corporate chief executive officers) are excellent non-verbal communicators.

If you are aware of a sender's verbal message only, you are likely to miss the major portion of the overall communication. Being aware of both non-verbal and verbal messages give you an important edge. Skills in interpreting non-verbal

> - Understanding and interpreting non-verbal messages is an essential part of business communication.
> - Verbal exchanges account for only a fraction of the messages people send and receive.

communications help you glean useful information from others involved in the communication process. An awareness of non-verbal communication may also prevent you from harming your own position by inadvertently sending non-verbal signals that disclose confidential information or a weaknesses in your position.

When we display non-verbal signs, we may not intend to do so. Indeed, non-verbal communication may take place even against our own intentions. For example, as a member of an audience, you may try to look attentive, but be unable to suppress a yawn. The speaker may see that you are bored, despite your best intention not to show it. Sometimes non-verbal communication can take place even when no one present can describe the non-verbal cues that transmitted the message. We may believe that another person is angry without being able to say exactly how we got that impression.

Non-verbal communications can also be unique to one individual. Hand gestures, for example, may take their meaning from objects or actions they relate to or from the way they are used in conjunction with speech.

The fact that non-verbal communication can be unintentional, unconscious, and idiosyncratic makes it very difficult to study. Indeed the scientific study of non-verbal communication became possible only with the development of sophisticated recording—film or videotape—which allows repeated viewing, if necessary in slow motion. However, the major disadvantage of videotape is that the human observer still has to transcribe the behaviour into appropriate categories. To overcome this, researchers have tried attaching recording apparatus to the body, but this can make participants in experiments self-conscious; it also restricts their movements. Developments in computer image analysis hold the promise of fully-automated coding, which will increase speed and also improve reliability and precision.

Since non-verbal cues are important in emotional communication, they have also been regarded as central to interpersonal relationships. Non-verbal cues are not just important within a relationship but also to an outside observer, as they can also provide important signals about relatedness.

Knowledge of non-verbal communication is important for managers who serve as leaders of organizational 'teams' for at least two reasons:

First, to function effectively as a team leader a manager must interact with the other members successfully. Non-verbal cues, when interpreted correctly, provide the manager with one means to do so. The team members project attitudes and

- The study of non-verbal communication is difficult as most of the time it is unintentional and unconscious.
- In a team, various members project attitudes and feelings through non-verbal communication.

### Different Strokes for Different Folks

Non-verbal behaviours in different cultures can cause even greater problems than the ones related to language differences. There is the story of an Indian sales team of a company who were in a meeting in Japan. After winning a big business contract, they started laughing and talking in their own language in such a way that the Japanese customer became confused about the commotion around him and suspected that something may have gone amiss during the negotiations. The customer halted the negotiations and the business contract was lost. The client had not signalled a culturally appropriate response to the successful bid and the celebration was misinterpreted. Also, if the customer had understood the way of celebration as normal in another culture, he may not have thought it necessary to change his business decision.

feelings through non-verbal communication. Some personal needs, such as approval, growth, achievement, and recognition, may be met in effective teams. The extent to which these needs are met is closely related to how perceptive the team leader and the team members are of non-verbal communication among themselves and among others in the team. If the team members show a true awareness to non-verbal cues, the organization will have a better chance to succeed, for it will be an open, honest, and confronting unit.

Second, how something is expressed may carry more significance and weight than what is said, that is, the words themselves. Accompanied by a smile or a frown, said with a loud, scolding voice or a gentle, easy one, the contents of our communications are framed by our holistic perceptions of their contexts. Those sending messages should learn to understand themselves better as well as learn to exert some greater consciousness about their manner of speech. Those receiving messages may learn to understand their own intuitive responses better—sometimes in contrast to what seems to be 'reasonable'. Part of our culture involves an unspoken rule that people should ignore these non-verbal elements—as if the injunction were, 'Hear what I say, and do not notice the way I say it'. These elements are often ignored in school or overridden by parents, so the task of incorporating conscious sensitivity to non-verbal communications at a later stage is made more difficult.

Non-verbal communication occurs not only between people, but also internally. People grimace, stand in certain postures, and behave so as to reinforce to themselves certain positions, attitudes, and implicit beliefs. Unconsciously, they suggest to themselves the role they choose to play, submissive or dominant, trusting or wary, controlled or spontaneous, etc. People, especially people who work with or help other people—managers, teachers, etc.—would do well if they read about non-verbal communications. Although social scientists have long been interested in non-verbal language, it is only recently that the business world has started exploring the potential of this subtle yet powerful aspect of communication. Silent or non-verbal language has recently been shown to play an important role in two areas directly related to management—how managers motivate their employees, and how executives communicate their leadership and decision-making style. Studies have also shown the importance of non-verbal cues in the processes of job interviews and advertising.

> Non-verbal communication plays an important part in employee motivation, leadership, and decision-making.

### Walking the Talk

A good body posture is usually an indicator of confidence and uprightness. However, without internal, mental, and emotional 'posture', your words will sound hollow to your audience. For instance, a used-car salesman from a dubious franchise may have great body posture, greet you with a warm smile and a firm handshake. However, if in his heart he sees you as just another customer whom he can take for a ride, then sooner or later, his internal conflict between what he says and what he really thinks will cause him to 'trip up'. His movements and gestures will start giving away his real intentions. You will start feeling uncomfortable around him, even though you may be unable to pinpoint why. However, if the same used-car salesman is genuinely interested in helping you find the right car and puts your needs before his own, then his words and actions will remain in harmony with his underlying intentions, and you will instinctively trust him, even though you might not be able to identify the reason for such trust.

## FORMS OF NON-VERBAL COMMUNICATION

Non-verbal communications can involve conscious or subliminal, that is, subconscious, messages.

### Conscious Non-verbal Communication

Senders of conscious non-verbal communications are aware that they are sending a message and are also aware of the general meaning of that message. For example, the individuals extending a hug know that they are embracing someone and that the action is normally perceived as indicating affection. Receivers of conscious non-verbal communication are aware of receiving a message and its intended meaning. The receiver of a hug, for example, generally realizes that the message is a sign of friendship.

### Subconscious Non-verbal Communication

Subconscious messages are also called subliminal messages. These messages are communicated to the mind of the receiver unintentionally. Receivers of such messages are not consciously aware of the message. However, these messages are important. Some are listed as follows:

1. Gut reactions are frequently based upon your subconscious reading of subliminal non-verbal communications.
2. Police and military uniforms subliminally communicate the authority of those wearing them.
3. Well-dressed executives project success and credibility.
4. A poor sense of dressing up transmits a message of failure and lack of credibility.
5. Young, beautiful people are often seen in advertisements to communicate the subconscious message that the advertised product is associated with youth and beauty.

Although subliminal messages do not create awareness at a conscious level, they still influence receivers. In fact, subliminal messages are often more powerful than conscious messages. The advertising world is replete with examples that reinforce the value of subliminal non-verbal messages.

Companies pay large sums of money to have their products appear in movies. While these appearances are not typical product advertisements, the mere association of the product with the movie transmits subliminal messages that will influence viewers.

### *Voluntary or Involuntary Messages*

Conscious and subliminal messages can be both transmitted voluntarily or involuntarily.

**Involuntary non-verbal communication**   Most non-verbal messages are involuntary. In fact, many communicators are not aware that they communicate non-verbally.

> - Receivers of subconscious messages are not aware of the message.
> - Most non-verbal messages are involuntary.

1. Body language is one area where the involuntary nature of non-verbal communication is particularly evident. Everyday people unintentionally convey non-verbal signals by their facial expressions, gestures, and body postures. For example, people telling lies often involuntarily send a telltale non-verbal message to listeners by frequently blinking their eyes.
2. Since involuntary non-verbal communication represents unplanned physical responses, this communication form tends to be particularly revealing and more honest than verbal communication.

> ### Of Popcorn, Coke, and Nike
>
> James Vicary was the first to use a subliminal message in an advertisement in 1957. His goal was to make people want popcorn and Coke by flashing 'Eat popcorn' and 'Drink Coke' briefly on screens during movies. He claimed that popcorn sales rose by 57.5 per cent and Coke sales by 18.1 per cent. Subliminal slogans have come a long way since then. One of the best-known examples of subliminal advertising slogans is Nike's 'Just do it'. This slogan could mean different things to different people depending on their personal experience or cultural background. To a cricketer, it could mean just going out to the field and making a century. To a teenager, on the other hand, it could mean do what you feel like doing, even if it means breaking some rules. Closer home, Britannia (India) Ltd revamped its essential image of a biscuit company into a healthy eating, processed food company through its now famous 'Eat Healthy, Think Better' slogan. Similarly, Bharat Petroleum Co. Ltd, a major retail arm of the oil industry, projects its image under the banner 'Pure for Sure' at its various fuel pumps around the country.

> ### Arms and the Man
>
> An interesting example of an involuntary message is the position of the arms during a negotiation. In general, an open arm position suggests that someone is receptive to the negotiation process. Watch for changes in this position. If your counterpart's arms are lying open on the table where both of you are sitting as you start the negotiation, and he/she takes his/her arms off the table and crosses them over his/her chest when you mention that your company has a standard deposit of 50 per cent on all first time orders, it is a fairly reliable signal that he/she is not particularly pleased with this information. At this point, you may want to clarify your words, or even better, ask your counterpart if he/she would like to express his/her concern about the deposit.

**Voluntary non-verbal communication** Non-verbal communication can, however, be controlled by a person who has studied or knows about the various non-verbal cues and their significance. Let us look at the following examples:

1. A person who knows that people telling lies often blink their eyes can take special care not to blink when telling a lie.
2. A person who knows that a hug indicates friendship can consciously hug his/her worst enemy as a trick to put the person off guard or as part of an effort to improve their relationship.

## TYPES OF NON-VERBAL COMMUNICATION

The categories of non-verbal communication certainly provide a framework from which to conceptualize non-verbal communication, however, it is, in reality, a combination of cues and codes that work together to produce a certain meaning. Codes are distinct, organized means of expression that consist of both symbols and rules for their use. Although these codes are presented within classes, they occur together and are naturally integrated with verbal expression. It is inefficient to look at one cue or code for specific meaning.

> Cues and codes work together to provide a meaning to non-verbal communication.

A better way to grasp the integration of non-verbal codes is to consider their functions. In general, non-verbal communication helps people accomplish various goals.

> ### Legs can Talk too
>
> People often say they cross their legs for comfort, but this is only partially true. If you have ever crossed your legs for a long period of time, you know that this position can be extremely uncomfortable. Crossing your legs can be disastrous in business negotiations. Gerard I. Nierenberg and Henry H. Calero, in their book *How to Read a Person Like a Book*, describe a study in which they found, after videotaping 2,000 transactions, that no sales were made by people who had their legs crossed. If you want to give the impression of being cooperative and trustworthy, sit with with your legs uncrossed, feet flat on the floor, and body tilted slightly towards the other party. This posture sends a positive signal.

**Image 2.2** Emotions during non-verbal communication

**Create impressions**  First, non-verbal communication is used to create impressions. Physical appearance cues weigh heavily on this function, but kinesics, chronemics, and other cues can contribute to how others form perceptions of competence and character.

**Manage interactions**  Second, non-verbal communication is used to manage interaction. Facial expressions, vocalics, and even proxemics are used to signal turns in conversations.

**Express emotions**  Third, non-verbal communication is a primary means of expressing emotion. In fact, some experts have identified non-verbal expression to be a part and parcel of emotional experience. In addition, each cultural community has its own rules for display of emotions (Image 2.2).

**Send relational messages**  Fourth, non-verbal communication allows people to send relational messages. We convey affection, power, respect, and dominance through non-verbal cues.

**Convey deception**  Fifth, deception is conveyed and detected via non-verbal cues.

**Send messages of power and persuasion**  Finally, non-verbal communication is also used to send messages of power and persuasion. Leadership is conferred on the basis of non-verbal cues.

The functional approach to non-verbal communication illuminates how people use it. In this way, non-verbal cues can be considered in conjunction with each other in patterns. Several cues contribute to a single message or thread of messages, making treatment focused only on a single non-verbal behavior (e.g., gaze), a less effective means of achieving the functional goal of sending messages such as friendship, willingness, sadness, or anger. Hence, we would elucidate the various types of non-verbal codes in order to facilitate your understanding of their importance in various communication contexts (Table 2.1).

> Kinesics is the interpretation of body language, such as facial expressions and gestures.

## Kinesics

The best way to access executives' managerial potential is not just to listen to what the executives have to say, but also to observe their body language when they are saying it. Body language is the unspoken communication that goes

**Table 2.1** Types of non-verbal communication

| | |
|---|---|
| Kinesics | Facial expressions, posture, and gestures |
| Oculesics | Eye contact |
| Haptics | The communication of touch |
| Proxemics | The communication of space and proximity |
| Appearance and artefacts | The physical characteristics, the attire, and the accessories such as perfume, make-up, jewellery, etc. |
| Paralinguistics/vocalics | Variations in pitch, speed, volume, and pauses that convey meaning |
| Chronemics | The effects of time on communication |

on in every face-to-face encounter with another human being. It tells you their true feelings towards you and how well your words are being received. About 60–80 per cent of our message is communicated through our body language, and only 7–10 per cent is attributable to the actual words of a conversation.

Kinesics is articulation of the body, or movement resulting from muscular and skeletal shift. This includes all actions, physical or physiological, automatic reflexes, posture, facial expressions, gestures, and other body movements. Body language, body idiom, gesture language, organ language, and kinesic acts are just some terms used to depict kinesics. In ways that body language works in non-verbal acts, body language parallels paralanguage. Kinesic acts may substitute language, accompany it, or modify it. Kinesic acts may be lexical or informative and directive in nature, or they may be emotive or empathic movements. It is also the anthropological term for body language.

Our body says a lot about us in different ways as we communicate. Body movement can indicate attitudes and feelings while also acting as illustrators and regulators. Our body movement includes our head, eyes, shoulders, lips, eyebrows, neck, legs, arms, fingers, hands, and gestures. Together these pieces can convey if we are comfortable, unhappy, friendly, anxious, or nervous. With so many parts conveying messages, you can see how easily things can get confused and how difficult it is to manipulate non-verbal communication. Just think of the different messages that are communicated through facing a person, touching, standing at various distances, and in different stances. With careful thought, however, we may begin to use our bodies to further the clarity and meaning of what we say.

## Facial Expressions

Your boss's smile makes you feel happy while his frown leaves you discomfited; your subordinate's confused expression indicates the need to continue with an explanation; your customer's smile and nodding signal the time to close a sale.

However, most facial expressions are more subtle than extremes. You can use them in a variety of ways—to aid or inhibit other people's communication, to complement your own, and to replace spoken messages.

The face seems to be the most obvious component of body language, but it is certainly the most confusing and difficult to understand. Modern studies of facial expressions date back to the nineteenth century, starting with Charles Bell who, in 1806, published *Essays on the Anatomy and Philosophy of Expression: As Connected with the Fine Arts*. Charles Darwin's *The Expressions of Emotions in Man and Animals* (1872) was apparently influenced by Bell's earlier work. Facial expressions are like sentences in human language—infinite in variety. The relationship of facial expression to other components of body language and to language itself has been sparsely examined, and such observations as have been made are recent. It does not take a very extensive scientific study to observe that a smiling face makes

> **The Message Within**
>
> If you read the verbatim minutes of a meeting, you will not be able to grasp the nature of the proceedings in their entirety, in the same way as you would have if you had been present in the meeting or if you had seen it on video. This is because there is no record of non-verbal communication. The emphasis given to words or phrases is missing. To illustrate how *intonation* can change the meaning of a message, consider the example of a subordinate who asks his/her manager a question during a meeting. The manager replies, 'What do you mean by that?' The subordinate's reaction will be different depending on the tone of the manager's response. A low, smooth tone creates a different meaning from an intonation that is abrasive, with strong emphasis placed on the last word. The facial expression of the manager will also convey a message. A hostile or suspicious glare will convey something different from a smile.

a sentence sound different from a sentence articulated by a sorrowful, droopy physiognomy. There are five basic physical descriptions of facial expressions—neutral, relaxed, tense, uplifted, and droopy. These are described as follows:

1. The neutral expression could result in various expressions, such as pleasure, mask, respect, thoughtful, and quiet attention.
2. The relaxed expression could result in love, pleasure, and submission.
3. The tense expression could result in fear, surprise, determination, contempt, and extreme interest.
4. The uplifted expression could result in happiness, anxiety, rage, love, astonishment, and attention.
5. Finally, the droopy expression could result in distress, suffering, grief, dismay, and shock.

Facial expressions may portray the actual emotion felt and accurately accompany the speech. On the other hand, facial expressions, as with other body language and non-verbal components, may contradict the verbal expression, thus giving the real message. One's facial expression may be practised and may thus be made to lie convincingly, along with the speech act, about one's real feelings. Artists and clowns have effectively exploited facial expressions and gestures as social weapons and/or for entertainment.

The face can be used to communicate emotional meaning more accurately than any other medium in interpersonal communication (Image 2.3). Facial expressions tell the attitudes of the communicator. Researchers have discovered that certain facial areas reveal our emotional state better than others. For example, the eyes tend to reveal happiness or sadness, and even surprise. The lower face can reveal happiness or surprise; the smile, for example, can communicate friendliness and cooperation. The upper face, brows, and forehead can also reveal anger. Albert Mehrabian, Professor Emeritus of Psychology, UCLA, believes verbal cues provide 7 per cent of the meaning of the message; vocal cues, 38 per cent; and facial expressions, 55 per cent. This means that, as the receiver of a message, you can rely heavily on the facial expressions of the sender

**Image 2.3** The face expresses emotional meaning

> - The face can be used to communicate emotional meaning more accurately than any other medium in interpersonal communication.
> - Facial expressions are a crucial part of non-verbal communication.

because his/her expressions are a better indicator of the meaning behind the message than his/her words.

Facial expressions also provide information about a communicator's thought process. For example, one could judge the confidence of the communicator in the information being given, or the reliability of this information. Facial expressions also serve as a source of positive or negative feedback from the receiver. The face has the capability to produce messages of very high quality, in which the meanings are identical to the expressions. However, many believe that facial expressions are open to various interpretations of the receiver. Despite questions of this accuracy of facial expressions, they remain a non-verbal form of communication that is crucial within human interaction.

A facial expression is exceptionally communicative and can 'stand in' for verbal communication in some instances. Facial expressions that indicate an emotion that a person is communicating without actually feeling it are called *facial emblems*. These emblems serve as a kind of short hand that is widely understood. Facial expressions also serve as listener responses, indicating attention to the speaker. There are six categories of facial expressions that are generally agreed upon by researchers—happiness, sadness, surprise, fear, anger, and disgust.

Mouth movements can give away all sorts of clues. For example, we purse our lips and sometimes twist them to the side when we are thinking. Another occasion we might use this movement is when we want to hold back an angry comment. Nevertheless, it may probably be spotted by other people and although they may not know the comment, they may get a feeling that you are not too pleased. There are also different types of smiles and each gives off a corresponding feeling to its recipient.

Researchers estimate that the human face can display over 250,000 different expressions. Although a few people can control these emotions and maintain a 'poker face' when they want to hide their feelings, most of us display our emotions openly. Raising or lowering the eyebrows, squinting the eyes, swallowing nervously, clenching the jaw, yawning, sneering, smiling broadly—these voluntary and involuntary facial expressions supplement or entirely replace the verbal message. Yet, all facial expressions convey information. Facial expressions continually change during interaction and are monitored constantly by the recipient. Image 2.4 presents a set of six expressions.

The human face is the most complex and versatile of all species, serving many different functions. It serves as a window to display one's own motivational state. This makes one's behaviour more predictable and understandable to others and improves communication. The face can be used to supplement verbal communication. A quick facial display can reveal the speaker's attitude about the information being conveyed. Alternatively, the face can be used to complement verbal communication, such as lifting of the eyebrows to lend additional emphasis to a stressed word. Facial gestures can communicate information on their own, such as a facial shrug to express 'I don't know' to another's query. The face can serve a regulatory function to modulate the pace of verbal exchange by providing turn-taking cues.

The preceding discussion brings to light the fact that how we use our mouth, eyes, eyebrows, and other facial muscles reveals our emotional state. As in other aspects of non-verbal communication, facial expressions must be read in context. A smile might be a sign of happiness, amusement, or pleasure at seeing a friend. It might also indicate that the person is insecure and seeking approval.

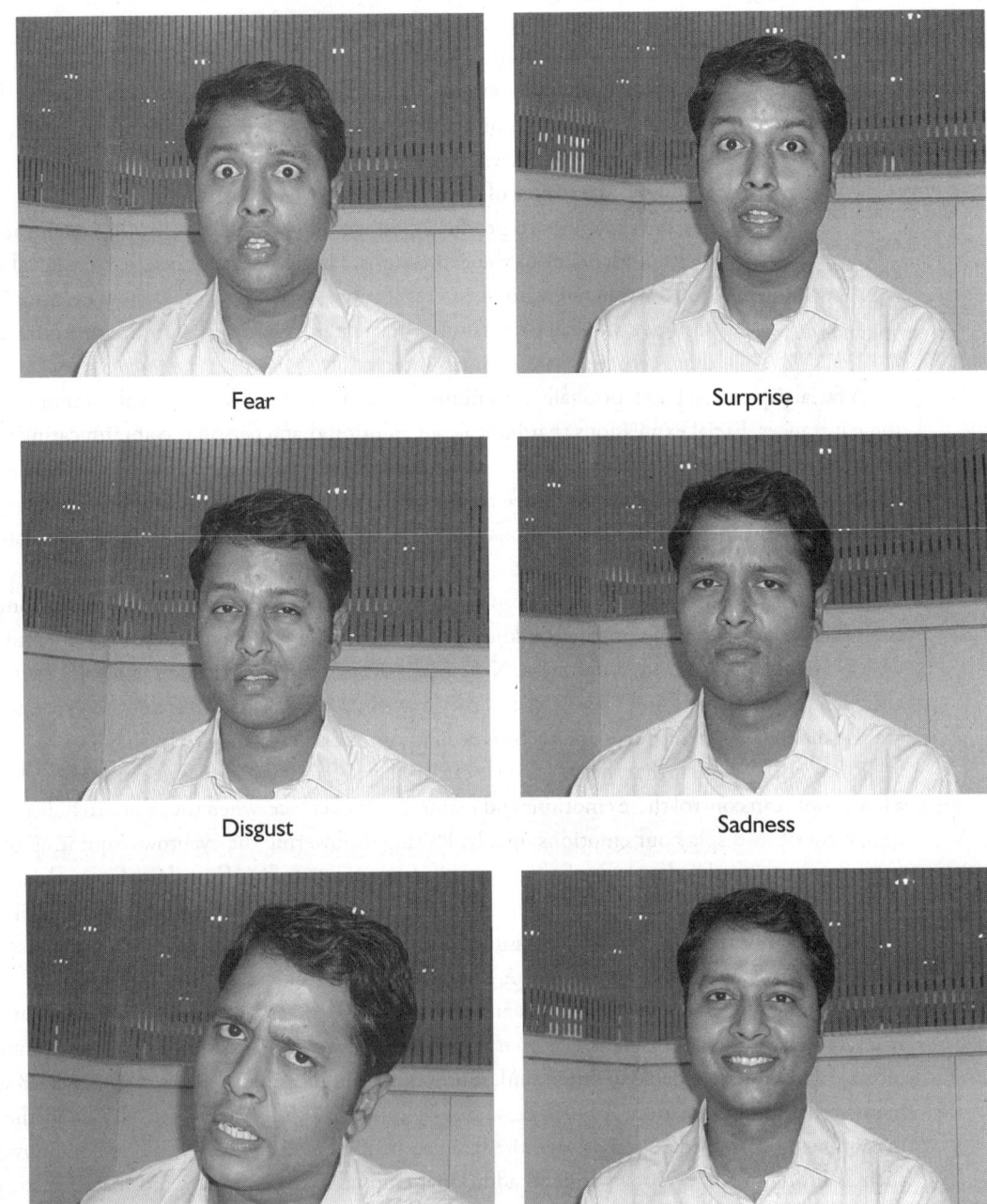

**Image 2.4** A set of six expressions

> The overall facial expression is important to a receiver's perception of credibility.

For example, when you see a beaming smile on the face of your interviewer, you feel that he/she is happy with your performance. At the same time when he/she gives an affected smile, it does not take too long for you to understand that your answer is not appropriate. Similarly, in another context, when you observe a frown on your boss's face, you decide to leave him/her alone as his/her face communicates that he/she is not in a good mood. You might also have observed that there are some people who exhibit a substitute expression on their face. For example, in the case of an employee being upbraided by his/her superior, though he/she would normally show his/her response on his/her face. He/she withholds that emotion and adopts some other expression at that time, as he/she knows very well that he/she cannot afford to exhibit anger or frustration on his/her face if he/she would like to retain his/her job.

The overall facial expression is important to a receiver's perception of credibility. An expression of dullness detracts from an image of dynamism. A speaker's face must show interest and attention. This helps considerably in rating credibility.

## Posture

Have you ever watched great presenters in action—men and women who are alone on stage yet make us laugh, cry, and be swept along by their words and enthusiasm? If you watch them carefully, you would note that they do not stand rigidly in one spot. They bounce and run and stroll and glide all around the stage because they know that human beings are drawn to movement. As part of our genetic heritage, we are programmed to pay attention to movement. We instantly notice it, whether we want to or not, assessing the movement for any hint of threat to us. Images 2.5 and 2.6 show the display of confidence through body posture and non-verbal expressions of different types of communication.

 See the PowerPoint presentation on body language in the Online Resource Centre.

**The right posture**  It can be stated that once you get your posture right, you will automatically start feeling better. The next time you notice that you are feeling a bit down, take a look at how you are standing or sitting. Chances are that you will be slouched over with your shoulders drooping down and inward. This collapses the chest and inhibits good breathing, which can help make you feel nervous or uncomfortable. Let us now look at certain body postures.

*Head position*  It is a great one to play around with, with yourself and others. When you want to feel confident and self-assured keep your head level both horizontally and vertically upright. You can also use this straight head position when you want to be taken as authoritative and serious. Conversely, when you want to be friendly and in the listening, receptive mode, tilt your head just a little to one side or the other. You can shift the tilt from left to right at different points during the conversation.

*Legs*  These are furthest from the brain, consequently, they are the hardest parts of our bodies to consciously control. They tend to move around a lot more than normal when we are nervous, stressed, or being deceptive. So the best strategy is to keep them as still as possible in most situations, especially during interviews or work meetings. Be careful too in the way you cross your legs. Do you cross at the knees or bring your leg up to rest on the knee of the other? This is more a question of comfort than anything else. Just be aware that the last position mentioned is known as the 'Figure Four' and is generally perceived as the most defensive leg cross, especially if it happens as someone tells you something that might be of a slightly dubious nature, or moments after.

> Good communicators are sensitive to small cues and modify their behaviour accordingly.

*The angle of the body in relation to others* It gives an indication of our attitudes and feelings towards people. We angle towards people we find attractive, friendly, and interesting, and angle ourselves away from those we do not. Angles include leaning in or away from people, as we often just tilt from the pelvis and lean sideways to someone to share a bit of conversation. For example, we are not in complete control of our angle at a cinema, because of the seating, nor at a concert when we stand shoulder to shoulder and are packed like sardines. In these situations, we tend to lean over the other person. Good communicators are sensitive to small cues like these and tailor their behaviour accordingly. They will notice a forward-leaning position as an indication that their remarks are being well received and will capitalize upon the point that led to this action. When a remark results in pulling back, a smart communicator will uncover the damage and try to rectify it. Awareness of such subtle messages can make the difference between success and failure in a variety of business settings: interviews, presentations, group meetings, and one-to-one interactions.

*Body relaxation and tension* It is a strong indicator of who has the power in one-to-one relationships. As a rule, a more relaxed person in a given situation has the higher status. This is most obvious in job interviews and high-stake situations in which subordinates meet with their superiors—such as requesting a raise or describing a problem. The person in control can afford to relax, while the supplicant must be watchful and on guard. While excessive tension does little good for either the sender or the receiver, total relaxation can be inappropriate for a subordinate. A job candidate who matches the interviewer's casual sprawl would probably create a poor impression. In superior-subordinate interactions, the best posture for the subordinate is probably one that is slightly more rigid than that of the powerholder.

*Height* It also affects perceptions of power: tallness usually equates with dominance. Standing up tall can help you appear more authoritative, whereas a slumped posture or slouched shoulders create an appearance of submissive or passive demeanour. Getting your body at the same level as others is a way of non-verbally diminishing status. To literally have to look up to someone may make the shorter person feel like a subordinate. Sitting down with someone could signal your desire for collegiality rather than status, while standing over or behind someone signals power or status. If you are taller than others or are standing when others are sitting, they may be seeing you as an authority figure or higher-status individual, even if you do not wish to appear as one.

**Perceived competence** Posture also can influence perceived competence. The difference between gesture and posture is that a gesture conveys a message by using one part of the body, whereas a postural shift involves the movement of the body as a whole. Closed postures, with features such as folded arms and crossed legs, indicate a closed personality and a lack of confidence. Open posture, with arms spread in a relaxed manner, is a much more confident pose than a closed stance. One should change posture periodically to show confidence because postural stiffness is usually

**Image 2.5** Body posture displaying confidence

Relaxed expression

Bored expression

Informal communication

**Image 2.6** Non-verbal expressions of relaxed, bored, and informal communication

perceived as nervousness. Like gestures, postural movements should flow with the conversation so that they look natural.

There are many different examples of non-verbal communication that can be included into this category. There are certain types of postures that convey inclusion or exclusion. One can place his/her body in a way that will include or exclude an individual from a conversation. Also, one can take on a certain posture that agrees with the person with whom one is communicating. Furthermore, postures may generally communicate involvement or withdrawal, superiority or inferiority, or feeling or unresponsiveness. Both gestures and postures tend to be more reliable indicators of the intensity rather than the kind of emotion being conveyed. Movement in one's face, gestures, and postures takes on very active roles in interpersonal communication.

In a nutshell, posture is indicative of attention, involvement, relative status between persons, and the degree to which another person is liked. Posture can also reveal the intensity of emotional states and is almost always studied in conjunction with other kinds of non-verbal communication behaviours.

A list of some postures and the messages they communicate is as follows:

- Slumped posture = low spirits
- Erect posture = high spirits, energy, and confidence
- Lean forward = open and interested
- Lean away = defensive or disinterested
- Crossed arms = defensive
- Uncrossed arms = willingness to listen

### Gestures

Gestures are observed actions. By moving parts of your body, you can express both specific and general messages, some voluntary and some spontaneous. Many gestures—for example, a wave of the hand—have a specific and intentional meaning, such as hello or goodye. Most of us, when talking with our friends, use our hands and face to help us describe an event or an object. We wave our arms about, turn our hands, roll our eyes, raise our eyebrows, and smile or frown. Yet, when included in a more formal setting, many of us tend to 'clam up'. Our audience of friends is no different from our business audience—they *all* rely on our face and hands (and sometimes legs, feet, and other parts of our body) to 'see' the bigger, fuller picture.

**Clear or vague gestures**   Gestures can be either clear or vague. Point at water and then point to your mouth. This is an example of an unambiguous gesture. Another person watching you is almost certain to understand that you want to drink water. There is hardly any chance of misinterpretation here. On the other hand, when you observe some listeners nodding their head to what you have just said, you are confused whether they agree or disagree with you.

Gestures make a large portion of a message. A speaker simply standing and talking with no movement whatsoever is dull. This does not mean that all gestures enhance communication; some can be detrimental. Ideally, a person's gestures should flow with the vocal channel so as to enhance the content. Gestures should also agree with the vocal message; if they do not, they will be detrimental. Use of good gestures at the proper time is beneficial to credibility. There is no 'correct' gesture for any given situation, but one of the keys to using good gestures is the appearance of spontaneity and naturalness. In other words, gestures should be performed without nervousness.

**Unnatural gestures**   Unnatural gestures, such as touching the body and playing with objects like clothing or pens, are detrimental to the message being sent and hurt credibility. Leg and foot movements also are known to represent discomfort and should be avoided. Finger-tapping, lip-licking, and smiling too often are tentative gestures that show lack of confidence. These gestures do not enhance the communicator's message and should not be used.

**Beneficial gestures**   Beneficial gestures are usually performed with the hands, arms, and head. These should be used to emphasize a point. Communicators should keep their hands and elbows away from their bodies to avoid the appearance of nervousness. In short, gestures that show participation and dynamism are beneficial to anyone who wishes to establish his/her credibility.

Arms give away the clues as to how open and receptive we are to everyone we meet and interact with. So keep your arms out to the side of your body or behind your back. This shows you are not scared to take on whatever comes your way and that you meet things head-on. In general terms, the more outgoing you are, the more you tend to use your arms with big movements. The quieter you are, the less you move your arms away from your body. So, try to strike a natural balance and keep your arm movements midway. When you want to come across in the best possible light, crossing the arms is something you should always avoid. Obviously, if someone says something that you disagree with, then by all means show your disapproval by crossing them.

**Hand gestures**   These are so numerous it is hard to give a brief guide. Palms slightly up and outward are seen as open and friendly. Palm down gestures are generally seen as dominant, emphasizing, and possibly aggressive, especially when there is no movement or bending between the wrist and the forearm. The palm up, palm down gesture is very important when it comes to shaking hands, and where appropriate we suggest you always offer a handshake upright and vertical, which should convey equality. One of the most frequently observed, but least understood cues, is a hand movement. Most people use hand movements regularly when talking. While some gestures (e.g., a clenched fist) have universal meanings, most of the others are individually learned and idiosyncratic. Hand

- Gestures and movements play very active roles in interpersonal communication.
- Beneficial gestures are used to emphasize a point.
- Gestures are of two types—conscious and spontaneous.

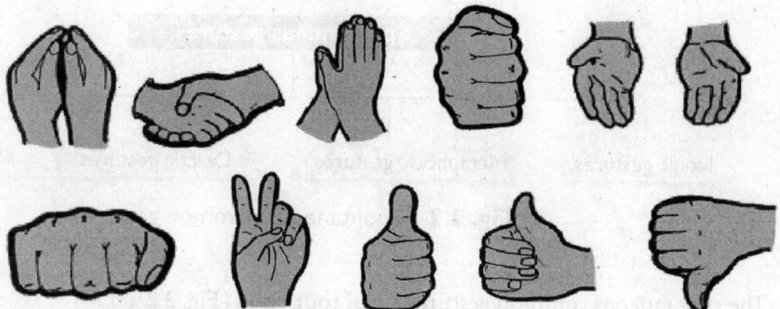

**Fig. 2.1** Hand gestures—universal and culture specific

gestures are ubiquitous in face-to-face communication, and appear to be integral to the production and comprehension of language in face-to-face contexts. In fact, listeners take into account the information conveyed by gestures, even when this information is not related to the information conveyed in speech. Figure 2.1 shows different hand gestures.

Gestures can be broadly classified into two categories: conscious and spontaneous.

### Conscious Gestures

When we reflect on what kinds of gestures we have seen in our environment, we often come up with a type of gesture known as *emblematic*. For example, when you enter an office and the receptionist is on the phone, he/she may flash an emblem such as a hand movement to signal you to sit down and wait. Some emblems communicate specific messages only within certain cultures or subcultures. The American 'V-for-victory' gesture can be made either with the palm or the back of the hand towards the receiver. In Britain, however, a 'V' gesture made with the back of the hand towards the receiver is considered impolite. Examples of emblems in American culture are the thumb-and-index-finger gesture that signals 'okay' or the 'thumbs up' gesture. Emblematic gestures are *consciously produced* and are, therefore, easier to remember.

Another conscious gesture that has been the subject of some study in the interface community is the so-called *propositional gesture*. An example is the use of hands to measure the size of a symbolic space while saying 'it was this big'. Another example is pointing at a chair and then pointing at another spot and saying 'move that over there'. These gestures are not unwitting and in that sense not spontaneous, and their interaction with speech is more like the interaction of one grammatical constituent with another than the interaction of one communicative channel with another; in fact, the demonstrative 'this' may be seen as a place holder for the syntactic role of the accompanying gesture. These gestures can be particularly important in certain types of task-oriented talk. Gestures such as these are found notably in communicative situations where the physical world in which the conversation is taking place is also the topic of conversation.

### Spontaneous Gestures

Spontaneous (unplanned, unselfconscious) gestures accompany speech in most communicative situations and cultures (despite the common belief to the contrary). People even gesture while they are speaking on the telephone. We know that receivers attend to such kinds of gestures, and that they use gestures in these situations to form a mental representation of the communicative intent of the speaker.

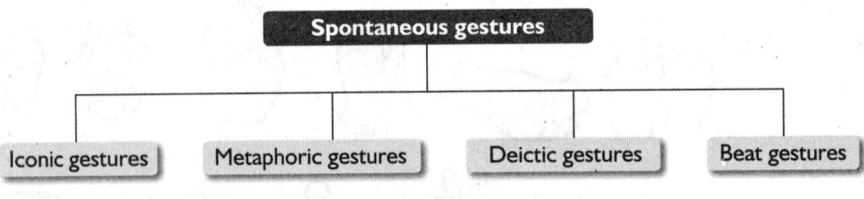

**Fig. 2.2** Spontaneous common gestures

The spontaneous common gestures are of four types (Fig. 2.2).

**Iconic gestures** Iconic gestures depict, by the form of the gesture, some feature of the action or event being described. Iconic gestures may specify the manner in which an action is to be carried out, even if this information is not given in the accompanying speech. For example, when a person illustrates a physical item by using the hands to show how big or small it is. Iconic gestures may also specify the viewpoint from which an action is narrated. That is, gestures can demonstrate who narrators imagine themselves to be, and where they imagine themselves to stand at various points in the narration, when this is rarely conveyed in speech, and listeners can infer this viewpoint from the gestures they see.

**Metaphoric gestures** Metaphoric gestures are representational, but the concept they represent has no physical form; instead the form of the gestures comes from a common metaphor. An example is 'the meeting went on and on' accompanied by a hand indicating rolling motion. There need not be a productive metaphor in the speech accompanying metaphoric gestures; sometimes the 'metaphors' that are represented in gesture have become entirely conventionalized in the language. There needs to be a recognizable vehicle that mediates between the form of the gesture and the meaning of the speech it accompanies.

Some common metaphoric gestures are the 'process metaphoric' just illustrated, and the 'conduit metaphoric', which objectifies the information being conveyed, representing it as a concrete object that can be held between the hands and given to the listener. Conduit metaphorics commonly accompany new segments in communicative acts; an example is the box gesture that accompanies 'In this [next part] of the talk I'm going to discuss new work on this topic'. Metaphoric gestures of this sort contextualize communication; for example, it is placing it in the larger context of social interaction. In this example, the speaker prepared to give the next segment of discourse to the conference attendees. Another typical metaphoric gesture in academic contexts is the metaphoric pointing gesture that commonly associates features with people.

**Deictic gestures** Deictics spatialize, or locate in the physical space in front of a narrator, aspects of his/her discourse; these can be discourse entities that have a physical existence, such as the tube of caulk that the narrator pointed to on the workbench, or non-physical discourse entities. An example of the latter might be pointing left and then right while saying, 'Well, Rekha was looking at Tina across the table....'

Deictic gestures populate the space between the speaker and listener with the discourse entities as they are introduced and continue to be referred to. Deictics do not have to be pointing index fingers. One can also use the whole hand to represent entities or ideas or events in space. An example from a conference comes from a speaker who referred to another researcher's technique

- Metaphoric gestures help to explain a concept.
- Deictic gestures are used to point at things or persons.
- Rhythmic beating of a finger, hand, or arm are examples of beat gestures.

of modelling faces and then said, 'We [don't] do that; we [bung] them all together'. During the word 'don't', this speaker used both hands to demarcate or wave away the space to his right, and during 'bung', he/she brought both hands together to demarcate a space directly in front of him/her. In this example, the speaker is positioning the techniques that he/she chose not to use to one side, and the techniques that he/she used directly in front of him/her.

**Beat gestures**  Beat gestures are small baton-like movements that do not change in form with the content of the accompanying speech. They serve a pragmatic function, occurring with comments on one's own linguistic contribution, speech repairs, and reported speech. An example is, 'She talked first, I mean second' accompanied by a hand flicking down and then up.

Beat gestures may signal that the information conveyed in the accompanying speech does not advance the 'plot' of the discourse, but is an evaluative or orienting comment. For example, the narrator of a home repair show described the content of the next part of the TV episode by saying, 'I'm going to tell you how to use a caulking gun to [prevent leakage] through [storm windows] and [wooden window ledges]...' and accompanied this speech with several beat gestures to indicate that the role of this part of the discourse was to indicate the relevance of what came next, as opposed to imparting new information in and of itself.

As far as the nature of gestures is concerned, emblems vary widely from language to language community. Interestingly, and perhaps not surprisingly, the *form* of metaphoric gestures appears to differ from one language community to another. Conduit metaphoric gestures are not found in narrations in all languages. The metaphoric use of space, however, appears in all narratives collected regardless of the language spoken. Thus, apart from emblematic gestures, the use of gestures appears to be more universal than particular.

Unlike language, gesture does not rely on a one-to-one mapping of form to meaning. That is, two fingers pointing towards the centre may convey dancing robots at one point, and at another point in the very same discourse, the same gesture may indicate rolling up a carpet in a room. The fact that gesture is not a code makes it a powerful index of human mental representation. Spoken languages are constrained by the nature of grammar, which is arbitrary and non-iconic (for the most part). Language is mediated by the ratified social code. Gesture, on the other hand, can play out in space what we imagine in our minds.

Though gestures are culture specific, there are certain gestures that are universally understood. Some of these are given in Table 2.2.

**Table 2.2**  Universal hand gestures

| Meaning | Hand Gesture |
| --- | --- |
| I am tired | Pressing the palms together and resting the head on the back of the hand while closing the eyes as if sleeping |
| I am hungry | Patting the stomach with the hands |
| After eating, I am full | Taking the hand and making a circular motion over the stomach |
| I am thirsty | Using the hand and making a circular motion over the throat |
| I am cold, or it is cozy, or a sign of eager anticipation | Rubbing the hands together |

> Oculesics is the study of the role of eyes in non-verbal communication.

Studying each one—facial expression, gesture, and posture—independently is justified for the purpose of analysis, but these should be recognized as a whole unit that functions as an expression.

## Oculesics

Oculesics is the way eyes are used during a communication exchange. This may include eye contact or the avoidance of eye contact. It may also include all other eye movements, such as looking at other body parts of the other person. Oculesic movements are also frequently associated with kinesic movements. For example, regulators often rely on both a kinesic component, such as raising of an eyebrow, and an oculesic component, such as looking into the eye of the other person, to get a message across.

Eye contact is a direct and powerful form of non-verbal communication. For example, the superiors in an organization generally maintain eye contact longer than the subordinate. The direct stare of the sender of a message conveys candour and openness. It elicits a feeling of trust. Downward glances are generally associated with modesty. Eyes rolled upward are associated with fatigue. Your eyes can tell your subordinate whether you are listening to his/her complaints about the company's management, where your attention is focused, and even how you feel about what he/she is saying. Your eyes can also assert your authority over others. In fact, only physical force can challenge another person more than a direct eye gaze or a stare. Thus, such a look from you might reform a lazy employee more quickly than would all the harsh words you can think of. Eyes can communicate a wide range of meanings, from a fleeting glance to a shifty gaze to a killer look. You might suspect the motives of your clients, employees, or customers who refuse to look at you directly. But again, the meaning might not be that simple because the facial expression may be combined with another non-verbal means of communication. For example, a firm handshake accompanied by an indirect gaze is harder to interpret than a simple glance.

A major feature of social communication is eye contact. It can convey emotion, signal when to talk or finish, or aversion. The frequency of contact may suggest either interest or boredom. Eye contact is also the most noticeable non-verbal behaviour that affects credibility. Like the old saying, 'Eyes are your windows to the world', eyes can be the window to credibility. Studies on eye contact and its effect on communication and credibility have found that maintaining your gaze while communicating is beneficial to credibility, and, conversely, averting eye contact is detrimental to credibility. Eye contact studies have produced information about the effect of eye contact on the three components of credibility—dynamism, competence, and trustworthiness. In tests where these three components were isolated, eye behaviour had little effect on dynamism. The competence and trustworthiness categories, however, produced a significant link. It can be used as a 'regulator' in conversations in an informal way, and it can be used as a more precise signal, for example, between the chairman of a meeting and a member who is asking for the floor. At the end of a social evening, people may signal 'Let's go!' only by eye contact.

The avoidance of eye contact also signals something meaningful. Looking away contributes to maintaining psychological distance. Other eye behaviours can indicate symptoms of abnormalities in human beings, such as excessive blinking, depressed look, dramatic gaze, guarded gaze, and absent gaze. The blink frequency can be a measure of tension, or even of sobriety as some researchers have concluded.

Eye contact and the length of eye contact may be confusing. For example, many of us feel embarrassed or uncomfortable when looked at for a prolonged period by others. Conversely, we may perceive others as diffident because of their relatively short eye contact with us.

Other strange eye behaviours, such as shifting eyes, looking down at notes for extended periods, and blinking excessively, have been shown to lower credibility. The most important eye behaviour in increasing credibility is to maintain eye contact while communicating. Eye behaviour can be controlled by a communicator, but credibility cannot be. Through the use of beneficial eye behaviour, a communicator can raise his/her credibility with the receiver.

As one of the most important aspects of dealing with others, eye contact helps us especially in interactions with people we have just met. Maintaining good eye contact shows respect and interest in what they have to say. By doing this you will not make the other person feel self-conscious. Instead, it will give them a feeling of comfort and genuine warmth in your company, however, any more eye contact than this and you can seem too intense, any less and you give off a signal that you lack interest in them or their conversation.

Eye behaviour (Fig. 2.3) is usually divided into two categories, *gaze* and *mutual gaze*. Gaze refers to an individual's looking behaviour. Mutual gazing is present when two individuals interact and look at each other, usually in the face. Gazing serves four functions—regulatory, monitoring, cognitive, and expressive. Some regulatory functions of gazing are to signal that communication may take place and to indicate turn taking. The monitoring function of gazing serves to show concern for the other person. Gazing indicates cognitive activity when the gaze is averted or shifted to one side or other. This occurs more when the listener is asked to reflect on some question. As a component of facial expression, the eyes' gaze is a powerful part of emotional expression. Communication through facial expression is marked heavily by the eyes.

Like other non-verbal means, eye behaviour also can differ greatly among cultures. People from some cultures may lower their gaze to convey respect, whereas this may be understood as insulting in other cultures. Direct eye contact may be seen as insulting in some cultures or conveying attention in others.

Good eye contact helps your audience develop trust in you, thereby helping you and your message appear credible. Poor eye contact does exactly the opposite.

People rely on visual clues to help them decide on whether to attend to a message or not. If they find that someone is not 'looking' at them when they are being spoken to, they feel uneasy.

Wise business communicators make a point of attempting to engage every member they are talking to by looking at him/her because they consider the eyes to be the most accurate predictor of a speaker's true feelings and attitudes. Effective business communicators can tell from people's eyes

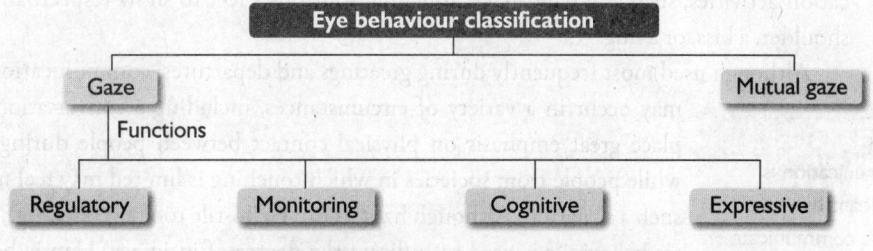

**Fig. 2.3** Eye behaviour—a classification

whether they are focused, receptive, or distant. They also note the frequency of eye blinks when judging a person's honesty.

In short, good eye contact enables the sender of a message to determine whether the receiver is paying attention, showing respect, responding favourably, or feeling distress. Likewise, from the receiver's perspective, good eye contact reveals the speaker's sincerity, confidence, and truthfulness. Since eye contact, like other non-verbal signals, stands for different interpretations, you must be respectful of people who do not maintain it. At the same time, you should remember that maintaining good eye contact with those you meet or with whom you interact would enhance the effectiveness of your communication.

The following can serve as effective guidelines on eye contact:

1. If you have trouble staring someone in the eye, look at something else on their face.
2. When speaking to a group look at everyone.
3. Look at people who are key decision makers or hold power.
4. Look at reactive listeners.
5. Do not look at the floor, scripts, or anything that causes you to tilt your head away from the receiver.
6. Do not look at bad listeners who may distract you.

## Haptics

Haptics or tactile communication or touch is an important form of communication for many primate species. Primates are social animals. They live in large groups. Touch helps the group form bonds and stay peaceful. Primates often groom each other. Female primates often hold and frequently cuddle and comfort their young. Mother tigers lick and nuzzle their babies, chimpanzees groom each other, and bear cubs wrestle with each other. Touch is used to comfort and establish dominance and bonds. Humans are no exception.

You feel elated when your boss pats you on your back after your presentation at a board meeting. You feel good because you think that he/she is pleased with your work. Your boss has communicated his/her satisfaction and appreciation just by his/her touch. You realize that a pat can convey much more than words. Most people feel the same way when such a touch comes from someone with whom they wish to communicate—a friend, a professor, or a colleague. The sense of touch is our first non-verbal experience in life. Through touch we learn to relate to people and objects. In fact, experiencing the sense of touch is critical to our sense of well being; we feel loved, cared for, respected, appreciated, and emotionally supported. This form of non-verbal communication also exists in other communication activities, such as a handshake, touching someone's feet to show respect, an arm around the shoulder, a kiss, or a hug.

Although used most frequently during greetings and departures, communication through touch may occur in a variety of circumstances, including a conversation. Some cultures place great emphasis on physical contact between people during a conversation, while people from societies in which touching is limited may feel uncomfortable in such a situation. Although haptics can be hostile too (e.g., kicking), more often haptic behaviour is used to indicate the degree of intimacy. Haptic behaviour may be divided into the following degrees of intimacy (Fig. 2.4):

> Haptic communication is the means by which people communicate through touch.

# Non-verbal Communication

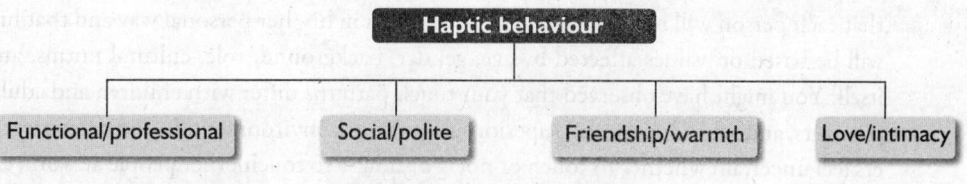

Fig. 2.4 Haptic behaviour

- Functional/professional
- Social/polite
- Friendship/warmth
- Love/intimacy

The boundaries between the different levels of intimacy are somewhat fuzzy, even in one culture. For example, touching the feet of elders is considered to be respectful in our country, whereas this behaviour does not exist in many other countries. As different cultures have different haptic standards communication through touch may frequently cause misinterpretation of what is intended with the touch. For example, in many Arab countries, men frequently touch each other in public or walk arm-in-arm. Such behaviour could easily imply an intimate sexual relationship between those two men in some other cultures.

If used properly, communication through touch can create a more direct message than dozens of words; if used improperly, it can build barriers and cause mistrust. You can easily invade someone's space through this type of communication. If it is used reciprocally, it indicates solidarity; if not used reciprocally, it may to indicate, among other things, differences in status. Touch facilitates not only the sending of the message but also the emotional impact of the message (Image 2.7).

Successful persuaders often touch those they are seeking to persuade. Touch can indicate the relationship between people. Touch is especially good at imparting a sense of empathy.

The sense of touch is an extremely strong sense and is often considered the strongest. Variation in the strength of the skin's electrical currents seems to be directly related to the emotional state of the person being touched. Also, the skin's use for communication is highly related to subliminal perception, or communication in which the meaning is less obvious. Touch can also deliver communication that is considered motherly or intimate. Touch can also be offensive if a relationship is misread and too much or not enough contact is made.

Touch can convey many factors such as intentions, feelings—both positive and negative—relationship, respect, and so on. In interpreting touch, you need to consider when, where, and how it is used. The extent of touch you need, tolerate, receive, and initiate depends upon the extent and kind of tactile communication you receive in your family. In business situations, touching suggests dominance. In other words, a person of higher status is more likely to touch a person of lower status. It is important to realize

Image 2.7 Touch as a message of non-verbal communication

that each person will respond to the sense of touch in his/her personal way and that his/her reaction will be based on values affected by age, gender, background, role, cultural norms, and the context itself. You might have observed that your touch patterns differ with children and adults, friends and strangers, and subordinates and superiors in your work environment. In Indian context, many managers feel uncertain whether to touch or not—or how—to touch other people at work, especially when the other person is of the opposite sex. But the fact that touch is an important way to convey warmth, comfort, and reassurance cannot be ignored.

## Proxemics

For most of us, someone standing very close to us makes us uncomfortable. We feel our 'space' has been invaded. People seek to extend their territory in many ways to attain power and intimacy. We tend to mark our territory either with permanent walls, or in a classroom with our coat, pen, paper, etc. We like to protect and control our territory.

Personal space is your 'bubble'—the space you place between yourself and others. This invisible boundary becomes apparent only when someone bumps or tries to enter your bubble. How you identify your personal space and use the environment in which you find yourself influences your ability to send or receive messages. How close do you stand with respect to the one with whom you are communicating? Where do you sit in the room? How do you position yourself with respect to others at a meeting? All of these things affect your level of comfort, and the level of comfort of those receiving your message.

A fascinating area in the non-verbal world of body language is that of spatial relationships, or proxemics—the study of man's appreciation and use of space. As a species, man is highly territorial, but we are rarely aware of it unless our space is somehow violated. Spatial relationships and territorial boundaries directly influence our daily encounters. Maintaining control over such space is a key factor in personal satisfaction; observing spatial interactions in everyday life is a key to personal awareness.

Decades of psychological and anthropological research have formulated the concept of proxemics. Proxemics is the study of the nature, degree, and effect of the spatial separation individuals naturally maintain. It defines regions around people and the acceptable social behaviours in those zones. As the distance between two people decreases, the degree of intimacy is increased, culminating in physical contact.

Space, distance, and territory are factors related to proxemic communication. Space is defined as the distance a person maintains between him/herself and his/her fellows and which he/she builds around him/her in his/her home and office. The ways in which a person uses space may be very significant to communication. There are many different types of space that include ways in which we keep our home and office, and how we maintain personal space, which is the area around our bodies which we do not want to be intruded. Distance, in contrast to space, is more relational and involves how far one individual is from the other. There are different types of distances, and each varies in degree. Distance can communicate messages that are sent and received as degrees of formality and intimacy. The concept of territory has many implications for communication. This involves the instinctive establishment of certain controlled areas. Humans establish territories as areas that communicate

> - Space, distance, and territory are factors related to proxemic communication.
> - Personal space directly relates to our interpretation of the meaning of the messages conveyed by the other person.

possession and defense. Studying proxemics helps one to understand many non-verbal cues that communicate intimacy, formality, and other factors for social interaction.

Personal space, or the distance from other persons, is a powerful concept. Research suggests that it directly relates to our interpretation of the meaning of the messages conveyed by the other person. For example, a person expressing anger is perceived as less threatening the further away that person is. However, if the person is close, the expression of anger becomes more threatening. In fact, physical closeness may itself be used to threaten others.

Distance from others is crucial if you want to send the right signals (Image 2.8). Stand too close and you will be marked as 'pushy' or 'in your face'. Stand or sit too far away and you will be 'keeping your distance' or 'stand-offish'. In a group situation, observe how close all the other people are to each other. Also notice a person's reaction when you move closer to him/her. If the person backs away, you have probably just intruded on his/her personal space or comfort zone. In other words, you may have overstepped the mark and should pull back a little.

The term 'proxemics' was coined by the researcher E.T. Hall in 1963 when he investigated use of personal space by humans in contrast with 'fixed' and 'semi-fixed' feature space. Fixed feature space is characterized by unmovable boundaries (divisions within an office building), while semi-fixed feature space is defined by fixed boundaries, such as furniture. Informal space is characterized by a personal zone or 'bubble' that varies for individuals and circumstances. While the use of each of these spatial relationships can impede or promote the act of communication, the area that humans control and use most often is their informal space. This zone constitutes an area that humans protect from the intrusion of outsiders. The study of spatial territory for the purpose of communication uses four categories of space:

- Intimate distance for embracing or whispering
- Personal distance for conversations among close friends

**Image 2.8** Physical distance communicates mental attitudes

- Social distance for conversations among acquaintances
- Public distance used for public speaking

It is very important for the effectiveness of a communicator that he/she observes the distance conventions called for by the situation. For example, being too close in what is considered to be a formal situation, such as an interview, can negatively affect the communicator's credibility in the eyes of the recipient. Observing the distance maintained in a given setting reveals the degree of formality and gives cues about what is and is not expected.

Behavioural study indicates that individuals perceive distances that are appropriate for different types of messages; they also establish a comfortable distance for personal interaction and non-verbally define this as their personal space. Research supports the hypothesis that the violation of this personal space can have a seriously adverse effect on communication. Thus, if individuals are to be mutually satisfied in a communication encounter, their personal space must be respected. Should an intruder invade this personal space while also trespassing within territorial boundaries, he/she places him/herself in double jeopardy and must compensate for the other's increased anxiety.

Another worthwhile example of such proxemic concepts is that of stepping behind the desk of an associate at work and intruding into his/her personal zone. If it is the boss, do you really have that much leeway? If it is your friend—you probably do. An office desk is a primary tool in establishing spatial communications, and a person's liberty to place that desk where and how he/she desires is a key element in personal considerations. The office cubicles do not allow the occupant to rearrange furniture to allow for personal preferences. They are not large enough to allow for a visitor's chair—another proxemic key. An extra chair to a pool employee can easily become a symbol of status—professional reasons for having visitors. The proxemic key resides in where the chair is placed, and in what relation to the desk. There are several basic arrangements for the desk:

- The occupant is enthroned and protected from intrusion on three sides (corner)
- The occupant's back faces the entry
- The occupant allows entry and space at the front and on one side of desk

Not only is a vocal message qualified and conditioned by the handling of distance, but the substance of a conversation can also often demand special handling of space. Spatial changes give a tone to a communication, accent it, and at times even counteract the spoken word. There are certain thoughts that are difficult to share unless one is within the proper conversational zone. Sharing a secret from a distance of 20 feet, for example, is not only difficult but also negates the confidentiality of the message itself. Another example might be of a person who enters an office and stands opposite a seated occupant. Even without the manipulation of invading personal space, such dominant body language influences potential conversation at a subconscious level. The further the stance, the less dominant the body language.

> In organizations, people use space and distance to communicate important information about themselves.

In organizations, most people use space and distance to communicate important information about themselves. The proximity or distance they keep in relation to others in the various situations in which they find themselves during the course of a business day results from their sense of territoriality. For example, two employees who are acquainted will be careful not to break each other's personal bubble at lunch hour. Neither will they thrust themselves on their boss—it is more

**Table 2.3** Interpersonal distances for various categories of interaction

| Distance | Relation | Volume |
|---|---|---|
| Close (8 in. to 12 in.) | Highly personal, seldom used in public | Audible whisper, very confidential |
| Near (12 in. to 36 in.) | Many dyadic social interactions occur | Indoors, soft voice |
| Neutral (4.5 ft to 5 ft) | Most social gatherings and business transactions | Outdoors, full voice |
| Public distance (5.5 ft to 8 ft) | Business and social discourse; more formal; desks in offices are placed to hold off visitors | Full voice with slight over loudness |
| Across the room (8 ft to 20 ft) | Used by teachers or speakers at public gatherings | Loud voice talking to a group |
| Far distance (20 ft and more) | Public speaking by public figures | Hailing distances, public-address systems |

likely that they will keep a greater distance from their boss than they will from the person who shares their office. You might have noticed how much closer you stand to a friendly colleague than to the one you do not know too well. By becoming aware of the non-verbal clues of distance, you can learn much about the people you come in contact with. The impact of the use of space on the communication process is related directly to the environment in which the space is maintained.

There are three basic principles that summarize the use of personal space in an organization. The higher your position (status) in the organization,

- the more and better space you will have,
- the better protected your territory will be, and
- the easier it will be to invade the territory of lower-status personnel.

Table 2.3 shows the interpersonal distances for various categories of interaction. It can assist you in determining how far away you should be from your audience, and in showing what volume you should use in speaking to the audience.

## Appearance and Artefacts

Potential employers, customers, and colleagues are usually impressed by people who are trim, muscular, and good in shape. One's physical appearance creates an image of the person in the same way that other non-verbal messages do. People who look attractive are considered to be likable and persuasive.

Personal appearance is a major factor used to judge a person simply because the first impression of a person is based on appearance. People can change their appearance by changing their clothing styles, hairstyles, and other accessories or artefacts. This channel of non-verbal communication confers a meaning that is transmitted by physical characteristics of the body, attire, and accessories. The physical characteristics of the body include facial shape, body shape, height, skin colour, body odour, hair, deformities, etc. Attire refers to clothing and accessories refer to other appendages or manipulable objects in the environment that may reflect messages from the designer or the user, such as fragrance, cosmetics, furniture, art, pets, or other possessions such as glasses, jewellery, handkerchief, flowers, helmet, and so on.

> Personal appearance is a major factor used to judge a person.

The meanings associated with physical characteristics have changed dramatically over time, especially with regard to what traits are associated with attractiveness. It is difficult to change your physical characteristics. However, you can enhance your physical appearance by using appropriate clothing and suitable accessories.

In today's society, the purpose of clothing has changed from merely fulfilling a need to expressing oneself. Clothing and other artefacts are especially powerful signifiers and convey a great deal of detailed information about someone's job, personality, values, and lifestyle. For example, uniforms of one sort or another are a feature in many, if not most, fields. Some uniforms are obvious—the army, the navy, or the air force, the police, schools, and some colleges, and even hospitals. Most of the other occupations and organizations have more subtle uniforms, which consist of a clearly defined range of regular clothing that are acceptable. In other words, there is an unspoken dress code in many organizations. The importance of clothing is a central aspect of impression management as prescribed by writers for the business market. Generally, people are treated on the basis of the social status their dress indicates, that is to say, poorly-dressed people are treated poorly and the well-dressed ones are regarded favourably and treated well. To establish credibility, you should wear styles that fit the environment and make you feel comfortable. The kind of clothing you wear can influence how people react to you. For example, if you are aware that discussions will hardly take place if you appear in a business suit and tie when you are among the shop floor employees, you should dress down. It is undeniable that garments form a large part of people's first impressions. In a large part of the world, a person dressed inappropriately will not be taken seriously, especially in a business situation. Whether to dress up or dress down depends on several factors, including the industry or the field of work. Geography also makes a difference in determining an appropriate working wardrobe. In addition, the culture of an individual organization also has an impact on the dresscode. Image 2.9 illustrates various attire for formal occasions.

Adornments are another form of appearance. Wearing expensive jewellery communicates one message while wearing ceremonial ornaments sends a completely different message. Appearance also takes into account personal grooming. Overall appearance is the non-verbal factor that people are most aware of and manipulate the most. Appearance communicates how we feel and how we want to be viewed. Your appearance says a lot about you, from the clothing you wear, to your hairstyle and jewellery, these artefacts often communicate information about you. The most influential artefacts you own are your

> Appearance is the non-verbal factor that people are most aware of.

**Image 2.9** Attire for formal occasions

clothes. Before you even speak, your artefacts will speak for you. Be aware that bad breath, body odour, and overpowering cologne or perfume will also speak for you.

Refer to the video exercise on body language.

Personal physical appearance usually provides the first available data about a stranger. Right or wrong, people make inferences based on this 'superficial' data daily. Inferences are made based on others' height, weight, skin colour, hair style, clothing, and any other physical attributes and artefacts.

In a nutshell, remember that the way you look—your clothing, grooming, and accessories—telegraphs an instant non-verbal message about you to your audience who make quick judgements about your status, personality, credibility, and capability. If you look the part, you are more likely to be successful in working with teams, other colleagues, and customers. You may be surprised to know that some aspiring professionals may even turn for help to image consultants because appearance is such a powerful force in business. You must always keep the following in mind:

1. Pay attention to good grooming, including a neat hairstyle, body hygiene, polished shoes, and clean nails.
2. Invest in professional-looking clothing and accessories.
3. Avoid flashy garments, clunky jewellery, garish make-up, and overpowering perfumes.
4. Ensure that you feel comfortable in your attire and that your accessories suit you before embarking on your business day.

## Paralanguage/Vocalics

You may have overheard two people arguing in the adjoining room, even though you could not make out their words, their emotions and the fact that they were arguing were explicit from the sound and tone of their voices. Likewise, you might have heard two of your colleagues talking to each other in a different language other than yours, though you could not understand the contents, you would have had some idea about their talk or at least their feelings—excitement, delight, frustration, exhaustion, boredom, or grief—from the tone of their voice and other non-verbal means.

The voice is an extraordinary human instrument. People from different walks of life recognize that the human voice communicates something beyond language. These effects are referred to by impressionistic descriptions, such as tone of voice, voice quality, manner of speaking, or 'the way they said it'. There are modifying features that can occur independently, such as crying, laughing, groaning, or whining. Every time we speak, our voice reveals our gender, age, geographic background, level of education, native birth, emotional state, and our relationship with the person being spoken to. All these cues (and many more) are contained in small fragments of speech, and other people can 'read' our voices with remarkable accuracy. When we speak, we 'encode' important information about ourselves; when we listen to others, we can 'decode' important information about them.

Paralanguage refers to all vocally-produced sound that is not a direct form of linguistic communication. Thus, paralanguage includes utterance that may have strong signifying traits but no semantic meaning. This 'non-lexical' vocal communication may be considered a type of non-verbal communication, in its broadest sense, as it can suggest many emotional nuances. This category includes a number of sub-categories:

> Paralanguage is communication that goes beyond specific spoken words.

- Tone (direct, commanding, loud, harsh, derisive, disguised, soft, gentle, comforting, pleasing, wheedling, volatile, scheming, sharp, boisterous, rage, nasal, etc.)

> Tone is the physical level at which the sound of human voice is transmitted.

- Inflection (spread–narrow)
- Pitch (high–low)
- Intensity (loud–soft)
- Articulation (precise–imprecise)
- Rhythm (smooth–jerky)
- Quality
- Dysfluencies/Pauses (silence–vocalized)
- Tempo/Pacing (rapid–slow)

## Tone

Tone, taken in its most literal meaning, is a feature of non-verbal communication. It is the physical level at which the sound of the human voice is transmitted.

To a linguist (or speech therapist), tone means the quality of sound produced by the voice in uttering words. In a general sense, tone is the attitude of the speaker as revealed in the choice of vocabulary or the intonation of speech. This attitude might be immediately apparent—for instance in the tone of a voice. It might, on the other hand, be a complex and subtle manner, which takes time to establish—for instance, in an extended piece of writing.

Tone is used to convey an attitude. This may be done consciously or unconsciously. It could be said that there is no such thing as a text or verbal utterance without a tone. In most cases, tone is either taken for granted, or perceived unconsciously.

Linguists and speech therapists chart intonation patterns by a system of marks on a page to suggest the rise and fall of a tone. Intonation is the term by which we refer to the patterns of sound that are evident in every utterance. We sometimes use the term 'monotone' to imply an absence of intonation. This usually suggests some negative state of mind on the part of the speaker. Every language has its standard set of intonation patterns. These have to be learnt by the non-native speaker as an essential constituent of the transmission of meaning. The intonation patterns of a language are the first things a child learns in its progress as a speaker.

Interestingly, intonation is a difficult hurdle while learning the second-language. The intonation of one's own native language becomes deeply internalized, and the ability to hear the intonation of a second language is not as sharp as it is in a young child. We can, perhaps, appreciate these difficulties if we take the single word 'hello' and consider the variations possible in expressing it to imply an attitude:

| | | | |
|---|---|---|---|
| 'Hello, hello, hello.' | A stereotypical policeman | 'Hello!' | 'Here we go again!' |
| 'Hello?' | 'Is anyone there?' | 'Hello!' | 'Fancy meeting you.' |
| 'Hello!' | 'At last I've found it!' | 'Hello!' | Greeting a friend |

Even a non-verbal utterance, such as a cough or a clearing of the throat, can be eloquent by means of its tone. An example of this is the cough that says, 'Be careful! People are listening in to what you are saying'. A slightly different cough acts as a warning not to go any further with an action or an utterance.

## Voice Inflection

Voice inflection is the way we change the tone of our voice to emphasize key words. You can vary your voice by stressing a word or phrase, stretching a word or phrase, or pausing before a word or phrase.

Stressing—I've got a BIG project.  Pausing—I've got ... a big project.
Stretching—I've got a b—i—g project.

> Pitch is a measure of how high or low a voice is.

### Pitch

Pitch is a measure of how high or low a voice is, and is mainly determined by the speed of vibration of the vocal folds; the higher the pitch, the faster the rate of vibration, and the lower the pitch, the slower the rate of vibration. When we are angry, many biological functions (e.g., our heart beat or respiratory rate) accelerate as our nervous system prepares our body for the response. The vibration rate of our vocal folds is affected in a similar manner, and the pitch of our voice therefore automatically rises. The pitch of a communicator's voice usually varies, depending on the subject. During a conversation, pitch almost always changes if the subject changes from, say, a sports event to macabre violence. Changes in pitch are expected by receivers and make a communicator more colourful and dynamic. A monotonous pitch throughout a conversation will be perceived as neither competent nor dynamic.

### Intensity or Volume

Intensity or volume refers to the loudness or softness of your voice. It represents more than a level of sound. A person with a weak voice is usually perceived as lacking confidence, which lowers credibility. A strong voice, on the other hand, shows great confidence. While pitch refers to the number of vibrations per second, volume refers to the amplitude of these vibrations. Volume can be controlled depending upon the situation, type and number of audience, size of the room, and the acoustic sharpness. For example, you may not like your subordinates speaking to you in a loud voice in your cabin because it is considered to be discourteous. At the same time they need to speak loudly in a meeting where there are a large number of people.

### Articulation

Articulation is the process by which sounds, syllables, and words are formed when your tongue, jaw, teeth, lips, and palate alter the air stream coming from the vocal folds. Poor articulation emerges when the sounds of words are omitted, substituted, distorted, or just plain slurred. The two most common problem areas are adjacent words that are blended together, as in 'shoulda' for 'should have', and sounds in words that are omitted, as in 'fishin'' for 'fishing'. Here is a list of some of the more common problem words:

gonna = going to  probly = probably
woulda = would have  gimmie = give me
coulda = could have  importn = important
ta = to  ya = you
finely = finally  dropping the 'g' from any word ending in 'ing'

Let us now consider an example that indicates the effect of poor articulation. Let us imagine that you are the human resources director for a large firm. You are reviewing applications and seeking candidates to fill a top-level position. After searching through hundreds of résumés, you come across a candidate that looks absolutely perfect on paper and you arrange an interview. Within the first 30 seconds of the interview, you realize you have made a mistake when the candidate says to you, 'Thanks for invitin' me here. It's freezin' outside—I prob'ly shoulda worn a heav'yer coat.' Although the candidate might look like a professional and have the credentials to back him/her up, you might not give him/her the job because you believe that his/her poor articulation will evoke negative perceptions in customers who speak with him/her.

Not everyone is gifted with the ability to clearly articulate words. However, the large majority of articulation problems are due to factors within our complete control. If you are one of those people fortunate enough to have the ability to clearly articulate words, you must not take it for granted. Poor articulation can certainly be due to physical or mental disorders beyond our immediate control. However, it is often a result of years of bad habit. The good news is, while it may seem challenging at first to clearly articulate all of your words, clear articulation can quickly replace poor articulation and become a new habit. You have already started to become aware of your articulation and you will now notice whenever you slur your words. Good articulation does not mean 'changing who you are' or 'speaking like a snob'; think of it as just being appropriate. Good articulation is not the same as being formal, it is just not being lazy. Nobody will think less of you for using good articulation. Articulation and the adequacy of our speech affect our social, emotional, educational, and vocational status, as well as the overall quality of our lives. When you make a conscious effort to no longer slur your words, you will find that others will perceive you to be well educated. You will find yourself to be well self-confident than ever before while having more opportunities that can lead you to success.

### Rhythm

Rhythm refers to the modulation of weak and strong (or stressed and unstressed) elements in the flow of speech. It ranges from smoothness to jerkiness during your speech. Commonly used for expressing emotions, rhythm is not much appreciated in business communication. In other words, you need to avoid rhythm while communicating on formal occasions such as presentations, interviews, group discussions, etc. On the other hand, you can use rhythm to make your communication livelier when you are appealing to the emotions of your employees.

If we consider the great speeches of Winston Churchill or Martin Luther King Jr, we can see that one of the things that raises simple public speaking to the level of oratory is the ability of the speaker to use rhythmic devices to reinforce meaning and to control the emotions of the audience. Their rhythms enabled them to express the emotions they were creating. When speakers learn to move in different rhythm patterns, they automatically develop different styles. The more flexible the speakers are with different rhythms, the more flexible they become with their styles of speaking.

### Quality

Imagine, a criminal is being tried in court. He/she denies saying something. The prosecution brings a recording, saying they have his/her confession on tape. As the accused vigorously denies the voice being his/her, an expert shows just why the voice could be no one else's. It is a reality that no two persons in the world have exactly the same voice.

The voice of most adult men is deeper than those of women. This is because a man's larynx is larger than that of a woman. It also has longer cords. The pitch of voice depends upon the length of the vocal cords. Each voice has a certain range of frequencies. It is this range that determines the kind of voice a person has. Voices can be divided into six groups: bass, baritone, and tenor for men, and alto, mezzo-soprano, and soprano for women.

> • Rhythm refers to the modulation of stressed and unstressed elements in the flow of speech.

> Breaks or irregularities result in dysfluent speech.

The quality of human voice also depends on many other things, such as resonating space, lungs, nasal cavities, etc. The nose, sinuses, pharynx, and oral cavity act as resonating chambers and modify the vocal tone produced by the vocal cords. The movement of the tongue against the palate, the shaping of the lips, and arrangement of the teeth also bring about changes in the voice. Since the structures and movements of all these organs are different in different people, the voices of no two persons in the world can be identical.

### Dysfluency

A 'dysfluency' is any break in fluent speech. You may find a subordinate who begins to stammer as he/she says, 'Everything is fine', sounding nervous or doubtful—as if everything is not fine and he/she were afraid that the truth would be discovered. There are many different kinds of dysfluencies. Dysfluencies heard in the speech of normal speakers include silences, fillers (um, ah), hesitations, whole word and phrase repetitions, and revisions. Dysfluencies that are more characteristic of stuttering include sound or syllable repetition, prolongations (unnatural stretching out of sounds), and blocks (sound gets stuck and cannot come out). Stuttering can be differentiated from normal dysfluencies by the type, frequency, and duration of the dysfluency. Following are certain utterances causing disfluency in your oral communication:

Phew, Uh-oh, Ahhah, Mmmmm, Tsk! Tsk, Oops, Shhh ..., Uh-huh, Humphf, Hah, Huh-uh, Whew, Hmmmm, etc.

Silence can be a positive or negative influence in a communication process. It can provide a link between messages or sever relationships. It can create tension and uneasiness or create a peaceful situation. Silence can also be judgemental by indicating favour or disfavour—agreement or disagreement. Let us suppose that a manager finds a couple of his/her staff members resting. If he/she believes these staff members are basically lazy, the idleness conveys to him/her that they are avoiding work or responsibility and should be given additional assignments.

During an oral interaction, you may use silence to enable the receiver to think about what you are emphasizing and to anticipate what you are going to say. Silence can also be used to convey one's opinion—agreement or disagreement. For example, if you are talking to your colleague and during your conversation you say, 'Well, I know you'd tell me if your operating expenses were too high' and he/she says nothing to this. After a long pause, the conversation resumes on a different topic. This silence probably means the operating expenses are too high. At times silence can communicate more than words.

### Tempo/Pacing

Tempo/pacing refers to the rate at which someone speaks. This factor is vital to understanding a message and to the credibility of the communicator. If a person speaks too slowly, the audience will likely lose interest, and the speaker's credibility will drop. Speaking too quickly may make a voice unintelligible, also leading to lower credibility. A speaker should, therefore, use a rate that is fast enough to keep the audience interested and show confident knowledge of the subject. However, the rate should be intelligible to the audience and slow enough not to reveal nervousness.

> Tempo/pacing refers to the rate at which someone speaks.

Vocal cues can serve as a way to communicate emotions within a message. These cues are sometimes not as strong as some other non-verbal cues because individuals vary in their ability to convey meaning in their voice, while receivers of messages have a limited decoding ability. However, voice is used to exchange meanings accu-

> Chronemics is the study of the use of time in non-verbal communication.

rately and efficiently. Many meanings can be exchanged by way of sound. The most accessible of instruments, the 'voice' is one of the easiest instruments through which the 'intention' can be directed and focused.

The famed poet Henry Wadsworth Longfellow once wrote, 'The human voice is the organ of the soul'. Your voice is an extremely valuable resource and is the most commonly used form of communication. Your voice is invaluable for both your social interaction as well as for your occupation. It is a major determiner of the receiver's first and final impression. Proper care and use of your voice improves the likelihood of having a healthy voice for your entire lifetime.

At times, paralanguage is actually more important than the words. In general, the communicator should avoid long pauses, repetition of words, and constant filler words. These vocal actions reduce credibility. A good combination of volume, varying rate and pitch, and fluency gives the impression of a competent and energetic communicator.

## Chronemics

Chronemics refers to the use of time as a message system, including punctuality, amount of time spent with another, and waiting time. The way we use time provides a number of silent messages. Coming on time, or a little earlier, to office not only reveals your interest, sincerity, and serious attitude towards work but also creates a good impression in the mind of your boss. Most of us may agree that being particularly scrupulous about our use of time during the first few months we are on the job is necessary to create a positive impact on our superiors and colleagues.

The amount of time we spend on a task or with a problem is also a good indication of how much importance we give it. When a business magnate gives a visitor a prolonged interview he/she signals his/her respect for, interest in, and approval of the visitor or the topic being discussed. By sharing his/her valuable time he/she sends a clear non-verbal message. A manager who never has time to talk over a problem with an employee or who postpones performance reviews because he/she 'doesn't have time' is conveying his/her lack of regard for subordinates, while a manager who takes time out to converse casually with employees every few weeks is sending a message that he/she cares. The person who cuts one meeting short to attend another is making a statement about the relative importance of the two meetings.

It is important, however, to remember that the rules and customs about time vary widely from one culture to another. Getting down to business quickly can be seen as a rude and insulting move on the part of a potential business associate from a nation other than yours. In many cultures, the relationship not only is much more important than the business at hand, but is also the foundation of the business venture and, therefore, determines whether there will be any business conducted. If the personal relationship is not established by taking time for dialogue and discussion, there will be no business relationship.

## INTERPRETING NON-VERBAL MESSAGES

Imagine yourself to be the president of a large firm. You have called a meeting of all your vice presidents and senior executives to discuss the presentation that you have prepared for a very important client. They all seem to be listening to you, but their non-verbal behaviour indicates boredom and restlessness. Somewhat puzzled and unsure of yourself, you seek their agreement and several of them concur verbally through verbal expressions such as 'Great!', 'Wow!', 'Perfect', 'You've done it again!', etc. Nevertheless their non-verbal language conveys the impression that they are far from confident about the presentation. What would you do in such a situation?

In situations where it is taboo to say what we really think, our words become empty rituals and our true feelings are conveyed almost entirely by non-verbal cues. Take, for example, a situation in which a marketing manager of a company discusses his/her presentation before the board members. No one in the board room would, obviously, tell him/her that he/she had bungled his/her presentation but if the presenter were intelligent enough, he/she would have read the non-verbal cues such as the facial expressions, gestures, tones of voice, etc., of the board members and understood clearly what they thought about his/her presentation. Managers should learn to recognize patterns of non-verbal language, beginning with their own. The goal should be to always be aware of how non-verbal language operates throughout any organization.

According to psychologists, people use non-verbal behaviour to express their emotional attitudes: the degree of like or dislike, dominance or submissiveness we feel towards them, and/or the degree of responsiveness—the amount of positive and/or negative feelings—the other person arouses in us. Non-verbal messages are expressed in a number of ways, as discussed in the earlier part of this chapter. For example, it is your boss who initiates a conversation when he/she meets you somewhere. It is generally up to a person with the perceived higher status to do so. We also need to interpret the cues of proxemics while communicating in formal occasions. People with a perceived higher status are granted a larger 'personal bubble' of space than those of lower status. However, people from different cultures have different concepts of appropriate proximity. Standing or sitting too close to somebody during formal interactions may make him/her uncomfortable.

When managers communicate instructions to their subordinates, they need to take care that they transmit appropriate non-verbal signals along with their spoken words. Inadvertently giving different non-verbal messages to different subordinates for the same verbal message would puzzle them. For example, you give instructions to three employees of yours—your secretary, assistant manager, and purchase manager—about the revised procedure for placing orders for some goods. Assume that you are using non-verbal means, such as eye contact, proximity, gesture, posture, and facial expression, differently for these three and you ignore the non-verbal responses that they send during this interaction. All of them will most likely miscommunicate the seriousness, interest, and attention your message is expected to receive. Hence, the importance of paying attention to the silent messages we send and

### English is by Nature a Rhythmic Language

There is rhythm in all spoken English, whether poetry, prose, or simple conversation. The rhythm patterns also develop vocal variety. The movement expresses emotion vocally and physically. By moving in different rhythm pattern styles, a speaker's voice becomes varied and interesting, losing its monotone. This is important for all communication and is especially important when relying only on voice, for example, when on the telephone or radio. We notice that very often speakers of all languages talk with an obvious rhythm to their speech.

receive. The fact is—silent language is a tremendously underestimated element in the way we communicate. The more accurately we learn to understand and use it, the more effectively we will be able to perform our job.

---

 **COMMUNICATION TOOL**

**Tips for Effective Use of Non-verbal Communication**

Excellent communication skills are the key to success in your personal and professional life. Research shows that non-verbal communication is actually more important than verbal communication. Here are some tips for using non-verbal communication to improve your business and personal relationships:

A. **Observe and understand the non-verbal signals being sent your way on a moment-to-moment basis** Stop and ask the other person what his/her non-verbal behaviour means if you are uncertain about it. It is more effective to be 'in the moment', tuning in to your audience, than to drone on with what you were trying to say.

B. **Use good eye contact** Many people stop using eye contact when they are speaking about their successes due to fear or embarrassment. Others stop using eye contact when they are talking about painful things.

C. **Stop what you were doing when your listeners look glassy-eyed or bored** Take ownership and responsibility for the situation by saying, 'I must be "off" tonight because I'm not getting that "you're interesting" look'. Change something drastically about what you were doing.

D. **Use the tone of your voice the way a musician uses an instrument** When you are expressing concern, you can speak in soft tones. When you are setting limits on a subordinate's behaviour, you can use a tone of authority and firmness.

E. **Adopt the most appropriate posture that suits the occasion** Your dynamic posture could instill enthusiasm and exuberance in your audience. Your concerned posture could evoke the much needed sympathy and seriousness during a counseling session.

F. **Express gratitude to your audience when they are being attentive and responsive** The encouragement could increase the level of attentiveness and responsiveness, making it a more enjoyable experience for you and for them.

G. **Soak in the pats/hugs that others give you** Many people have difficulty being 'present' in the moment to truly receive the affection that comes with a hug or a pat. You need to stop resisting and try to express your happiness over that non-verbal signal.

H. **When you are confronting someone who you are in a close relationship with, reach out to take his/her hand in both of yours** This kind of gesture will communicate that you want the difficult words that you are sharing to increase your level of comfort rather than to put a wedge in it. A caring gesture during a confrontation can assist the other person in hearing you instead of defending himself/herself.

I. **Understand the cultural nuances of the various forms of non-verbal communication** Are you aware what the non-verbal forms you use in your country mean in the country in which you would like to embark on a business venture?

J. **When there is a contradiction between the verbal and non-verbal messages of a person, try to assess the situation with the help of non-verbal cues** We form impressions of others mostly from non-verbal observations. Once we form these impressions, they influence our subsequent impressions and judgements. Even after first impressions have been made, the impact of non-verbal behaviour is powerful, and hence, observe speakers carefully along with listening to their message.

## SUMMARY

It may be possible to shut off the linguistic channels of communication by refusing to speak or write, but it is impossible to avoid communicating non-verbally, as your body keeps sending signals consciously or subconsciously. The field of non-verbal communications has grown rapidly over the last few decades, and it has applications in business, media, international relations, education, and indeed any field which significantly involves interpersonal and group dynamics. Non-verbal behaviour always has a communicative value and plays a significant role in all communication activities of an organization. Appearance and artefacts, facial expressions, postures, gestures, eye contact, proximity, touch, and voice—all communicate to your receivers your like or dislike, dominance or submission, positive or negative response, enthusiasm or indifference, respect or disrespect, agreement or disagreement, and so on. Non-verbal communication is powerful. It primarily expresses your attitude. Though it is ambiguous and subject to incorrect interpretation at times, it greatly enhances the possibility of understanding the true feelings of the speaker. Hence, it is given importance in interpersonal communication in organizations. Though your words may conceal what you really feel about a particular issue, your actions reveal that explicitly to the onlookers. When you notice a contradiction of verbal and non-verbal messages, the verbal part carries less weight than the non-verbal part. An awareness of the various non-verbal cues can certainly boost your understanding of others in both your professional and personal lives. As most of the non-verbal cues are culture specific, you need to understand their nuances when there is a need to communicate with people from other countries. Also, training in visible codes or non-verbal cues is as important as the training in verbal codes.

## KEY TERMS

*Chronemics* It refers to the use of time as a message system, including punctuality, amount of time spent with another, and waiting time.

*Facial expressions* The face can be used to communicate emotional meaning more accurately than any other medium in interpersonal communication. Facial expressions tell the attitudes of the communicator. They also provide information about a communicator's thought process.

*Gestures* These are actions. In other words, the term refers to the movement of the parts of body to express or elaborate some messages. Gestures can be broadly classified into two categories—conscious and spontaneous.

*Haptics* It refers to tactile communication or touch, and is an important form of communication. Touch helps groups form bonds and stay peaceful. Touch can convey many factors such as intentions, feelings—both positive and negative—relationships, respect, and so on.

*Kinesics* It can be defined as the non-verbal behaviour related to movement, either of any part of the body, or the body as a whole. It is also the anthropological term for body language. It includes facial expressions, postures, and gestures.

*Non-verbal communication* This form of communication includes all unwritten and unspoken messages, both intentional and unintentional. It includes facial expressions, eye contact, tone of voice, body posture and motions, and positioning within groups. It may also include the way we wear our clothes or the silence we keep.

*Oculesics* It is the way eyes are used during a communication exchange. This may include eye contact or the avoidance of eye contact. It may also include all other eye movements, such as looking at other body parts of the other person. Oculesic movements are also frequently associated with kinesic movements.

*Paralanguage/vocalics* It refers to all vocally-produced sound that is not a direct form of linguistic communication. Thus, paralanguage includes utterances that may have strong signifying traits but no semantic meaning. This 'non-lexical' vocal communication may be considered a type of non-verbal communication, in its broadest sense, as it can suggest many emotional nuances.

*Personal appearance* It is a major factor used to judge a person simply because the first impression of a person is based on his/her appearance. People can change their appearance by changing their clothing styles, hairstyles, and other accessories or artefacts. This channel of non-verbal communication confers meaning that is transmitted by physical characteristics of the body, attire, and accessories.

*Posture* It refers to the way we conduct ourselves in front of an audience—the way we sit, stand, or move.

In a nutshell, posture is indicative of attention, involvement, relative status between persons, and the degree to which another person is liked. Posture can also reveal the intensity of emotional states and is almost always studied in conjunction with other kinds of non-verbal communication behaviour.

*Proxemics* It is the study of the nature, degree, and effect of the spatial separation individuals naturally maintain. It defines regions around people and the acceptable social behaviour in those zones. As the distance between two people decreases, the degree of intimacy increase, culminating in physical contact. Space, distance, and territory are factors related to proxemic communication.

## Concept Review Questions

1. (i) Define non-verbal communication in your own words, giving an appropriate example.
   (ii) Discuss at least three ways in which non-verbal communication helps managers to interact with their subordinates effectively.
2. What are the two major forms of non-verbal communication? Explain each one.
3. List the various types of non-verbal cues, giving a one sentence description of each one.
   (i) Explain the terms kinesics, paralanguage, oculescis, haptics, chronemics, and proxemics in 100 words each.
4. What are the characteristics of the human voice? Discuss any three.
5. Explain the concept of 'personal bubble' in the context of non-verbal communication.
6. 'Gestures are observed actions.' Elucidate.
7. How do postures help you assess a person's confidence or diffidence?

8. Can you rely entirely on your colleagues' non-verbal cues during your interaction with them? Justify your answer with two examples.
9. What factors contribute to the appearance of a person? What can the person communicate through his/her appearance?
10. 'The eye is an extension of your brain and the window to your soul.' Do you agree or disagree? Why?
11. What does the statement 'Incongruity between peoples' verbal and non-verbal codes puzzles the observers' mean.
12. Do you feel that non-verbal behaviour is ambiguous? Explain your answer with a few examples.
13. Name and explain the six categories of facial expressions that we observe during our communication with others.

## Critical Thinking Questions

1. How do you interpret the following non-verbal cues being sent by others? Do they always mean the same to you? What role does the context play in your interpretation?

Yawning, keeping silent after a question or remark, drooping shoulders, leaning on a chair, raised eyebrows, standing off, and clearing the throat off and on.

2. You are narrating an interesting incident to your colleague and ask his/her opinion at some point. You are in utter dismay when you see him/her asleep. You cannot tolerate this and tell your colleague, 'I'm asking you for your opinion and you fall asleep?' Your colleague innocently says 'Isn't sleeping an opinion?' What will be your reaction?
3. Do you give importance to peoples' appearance? What impression do you develop when you meet two strangers at a dinner organized by the vice president of your company at his/her house—one dressed casually and the other is in formals?
4. Prepare a list of 10 idiomatic expressions containing the names of the parts of human body. Given below are two examples to help you out:
   - Seeing eye to eye
   - Tongue in cheek
5. Most non-verbal cues have a multitude of possible meanings and it is a serious mistake to assume that you can decide which is true in a given case. Did you ever have an opportunity to check the accuracy of this statement? Recall one such situation explaining the strategy you adopted to overcome your misinterpretation.

## Projects

1. Analyse the kind of non-verbal cues you send and receive when you interact with your professors/boss/colleagues. Discuss with your friends in a group how these silent messages enhance or blemish the communication effectiveness.
2. Conduct a survey to find out the impact of non-verbal cues in business communication. Prepare and circulate a questionnaire among 50 people, each from the age group 20–30 and 40–50. Analyse the responses and present your findings under the categories of non-verbal cues that you have learnt in this chapter.
3. It is interesting to observe how various birds and animals use non-verbal cues to communicate among themselves. Spare some time to observe nature and understand what signs and sounds birds and animals send to communicate.
4. Visit a primary school, a senior secondary school, a college, and a business house. Analyse the difference in the use of and the importance given to the use of non-verbal cues in their formal communication. Discuss with a few of your colleagues.
5. Collect pictures to show non-verbal cues, such as facial expressions, artefacts, postures, gestures, and haptics, as used in business settings and paste them on a chart paper. Label each, mentioning the message being sent through such cues.
6. Carefully observe the non-verbal behaviour of a person you work with. What messages do you get from your observation? Think about an alternative interpretation for each non-verbal cue you have received. Discuss which of your interpretations is more accurate. What are the factors you need to decode the non-verbal cues?

## REFERENCES

Adair, John 2002, *The Effective Communicator*, Jaico Publishing House, Mumbai, p. 92.

Adler, Ronald B and J.M. Elmhorst 2002, *Communicating at Work*, Seventh Edition, McGraw Hill Higher Education, New York, pp. 90–92.

Courtland, Bovee L. and John V. Thill 2003, *Business Communication Today*, Seventh Edition, Pearson Education (Singapore) Pvt Ltd, Delhi, pp. 45–48.

Guffey, Mary Ellen 2002, *Business Communication: Process and Product*, Third Edition, Thomson Asia Pvt Ltd, Singapore, pp. 51–52.

Hamlin, Sonya 1988, *How to Talk So People Listen*, Thorsons, London, pp. 58–59.

Lesikar, Raymond V. and M.E. Flately 2002, *Basic Business Communication*, Ninth Edition, Tata McGraw-Hill Publishing Company Limited, New Delhi, pp. 456–59.

Ludlow, Ron and Fergus Panton 1999, *The Essence of Effective Communication*, Prentice-Hall of India, New Delhi, pp. 63–64.

Pearce, Glenn C., Ross F. Figgins, and Steven P. Golen, 1988, *Business Communication: Principles and Applications*, Second Edition, John Wiley & Sons, Inc., USA, pp. 226–28.

Penrose, John M., Robert Rasberry, and Bob Myers 2001, *Advanced Business Communication*, Fourth Edition, Thomson Asia Pvt Ltd, Singapore, pp. 27–37.

Prasad, P. 1998, *Communication Skills*, S.K. Kataria and Sons, Delhi, pp. 65–66.

Robbins, Stephen P. and Mary Coulter 1996, *Management*, Fifth Edition, Prentice Hall of India Pvt Ltd, Delhi, pp. 614–15.

http://members.aol.com/doder1/bodylan1.htm, last accessed on 05 December 2004.

http://www.csupomona.edu/~tassigestures.htm# american, last accessed on 15 December 2004

http://www.thinkquest.org/librarysite_sum.html lib_id=4123&team_id=C005295, last accessed on 10 December 2004

### Charisma Corporation

Charisma Corporation (CC) has recently embarked on a new kind of training. The corporation is teaching many of its employees—especially those in marketing and sales—to make decisions on the basis of non-verbal communication cues. For Ms Malini Varma, vice president of CC, focusing on non-verbal communications has become an important part of her interpersonal dealings.

Several years ago, Ms Varma became interested in how body movements and mannerisms truly reflect what an individual is saying. Continually reading in this area of study, Ms Varma has been able to make decisions about potential employees and potential customers by 'reading' them. For example, Ms Varma believes that body language can give a person a competitive advantage. It can make the difference when closing a sale, or in CC's case, hiring new employees. For example, during interviews, Ms Varma pays constant attention to the job candidate's eye movements and mannerisms. She believes that she can correctly predict if the candidate will be an aggressive salesperson while simultaneously being personable and friendly. How does she do this? She does this by looking at candidates' eyes and the way they present themselves. In one case, a hiring decision came down to two people. The first candidate was animated and made constant eye contact. The second candidate never looked her in the eye, leaned back in his chair, and crossed both his legs and arms. The first candidate demonstrated the communication skills that Ms Varma found aligned with successful performance in her organization.

Ms Malini Varma is convinced that non-verbal communications can play a significant role in helping her organization achieve its annual sales goals. Personally, she has found that it has helped her 'quality' customers. For instance, even though a potential customer says, 'Yes', with his/her arms and legs crossed emphatically, it means, 'No!' Understanding this, Ms Varma is in a better position to probe further into the possible objections the customer has. She has found that, in many cases, she is able to steer the conversation in a direction that ultimately leads to successfully closing a sale. And that is a major competitive advantage.

### Questions

1. Describe the communications process that Malini Varma uses in her dealings with candidates and employees.
2. What problems might Varma encounter by her heavy reliance on non-verbal communications?
3. What communication guidance would you give to Varma and individuals like her who place an inordinately high value on body language? Explain your position.

# CHAPTER 3

# Cross-cultural Communication

## LEARNING OBJECTIVES

After reading this chapter, you will be able to understand
- what is meant by cross-cultural communication
- the concept of ethnocentrism
- communication styles and their significance
- cultural variables and their impact on communication
- cross-cultural communication strategies

## INTRODUCTION

Culture is communication and communication is culture.

–Edward T. Hall

Culture and communication go hand in hand. It is virtually impossible to say or convey anything which does not have any linkages to a cultural context, direct or indirect. This is true for written/spoken words as well as any action/gesture that are part of any message.

Our culture influences the way we approach problems and participate in groups and communities. When we participate in groups, we are often surprised at how differently people approach their work together. Culture is a complex concept, with many different definitions. Simply put, culture refers to a group or community with which we share common experiences that shape the way we understand the world. It includes groups that we are born into, such as gender, race, or nation. It also includes groups we join or become part of, for example, we can acquire a new culture by moving to a new region or by a change in our economic status. Such an all-inclusive manner of defining culture makes us realize that we all belong to many cultures at once.

Our histories are a critical piece of our cultures. Historical experiences—whether five years ago or 10 generations back—shape who we are. Knowledge of our history can help understand one another and ourselves better. Exploring the ways in which various groups within our society have related to each other is the key to opening channels for cross-cultural communication.

Not acknowledging cross-cultural similarities and intercultural variations may lead to stereotyping people from different backgrounds, exaggerating and caricaturing other cultures, and judging their specific ways of communication as fundamentally different and implicitly wrong. On the other

> Cross-cultural communication looks at how people, from differing cultural backgrounds interact and communicate.

hand, an understanding of cultural differences will pave way for effective communication at various workplaces. This will, in turn, lead to organizational effectiveness and subsequent progress.

## CONCEPT OF CROSS-CULTURAL COMMUNICATION

Communication is more than just speaking, writing, and editing; it also involves information gathering and teamwork. In the economy of the new century, this means communicating cross-culturally. There are three main components to any communication.

- Subject matter
- Medium of delivery
- Cultural considerations

Of the three aforementioned components, the third is generally ignored. While fashionable phrases are uttered—mostly, celebrating cultural diversity—what results are mostly exercises in politically-correct language or attempts at controlling personal irritation. Few people seem to feel the need to truly face the underlying issues that cloud even the simplest of delicate, and frequently confusing, cross-cultural interactions.

Cross-cultural communication looks at how people, from differing cultural backgrounds, endeavour to communicate. Cross-cultural communication tries to bring together such relatively unrelated areas as cultural anthropology and other established areas of communication. Its core is to establish and understand how people from different cultures communicate with each other. Its charge is to also produce some guidelines with which people from different cultures can better communicate with each other.

Communicating across cultures

In the context of cross-cultural communication, misunderstandings and misinterpretations are probably the most common problems people face; and 'culture' is often at the root of communication challenges.

## DIFFERENT COMMUNICATION STYLES

Communication style refers to the way people communicate and it varies widely between, and even within, cultures.

One aspect of communication style is language usage. Across cultures, some words and phrases are used in different ways. For example, even in countries that use the English language, the meaning of 'yes' varies from 'maybe, I will consider it' to 'definitely so', with many shades in between.

> Communication style refers to how people communicate between and within cultures.

Another major aspect of communication style is the degree of importance given to non-verbal communication. Non-verbal communication not only includes facial expressions and gestures but also involves seating arrangements, personal distance,

> Indirect and direct communication refers to the extent to which the words/gestures convey the main theme in the process of communication.

and sense of time. In addition, different norms regarding the appropriate degree of assertiveness in communicating can add to cultural misunderstandings.

### Direct/Indirect or High/Low Context

There are numerous ways in which communication styles in one culture may differ from the other. Interculturalists have identified two main distinctions—indirect/direct and high/low context. Context here implies the innate and shared understanding people are expected to bring into a particular communication setting, or shared nuances of a language, for example, shared meanings attached with a physical gesture, etiquette, etc. while interacting with another person of the same culture.

In high context cultures, people are homogeneous and collectivist (e.g., Thailand, Japan, Russia), whereas in low context cultures, people are heterogeneous and more individualistic in nature (e.g., the US). In high context cultures, for example, people have a reasonably good idea about how a particular interaction/discussion would progress and how the other person would probably react to a comment. However, in low context cultures, the communication style is more direct and people have lesser assumptions about other's reactions. Here the literal meaning of words is more important, blunt questions are not avoided, and people prefer discussing the main issue directly.

The differences between these two contexts can be experienced during business meetings and sales negotiations where people from different contexts meet. This happens particularly in the case of multinational organizations. For example, in Japan, the senior-most manager would enter a room first. If someone from a low context culture, who is not aware of this, enters the room first, he/she would, most likely, offend the Japanese manager. In Turkey and Greece, people may talk at length about things which may apparently have no direct relation with the meeting agenda. For them, people and trust building gets prominence. At times, the same word/gesture conveys different meaning to people belonging to different cultures. Sensitivity and knowledge of all this is integral to a successful cross-cultural business communication.

Table 3.1 gives us an idea about the kind of questions/comments people from high and low context cultures may prefer to use.

**Table 3.1** Communication across contexts

| Direct/Low Context | Indirect/High Context |
| --- | --- |
| Are you listening? | Hope you would have found the idea interesting. |
| You are doing that wrong. | Are you satisfied with the result? |
| Where are the sales figures? | Your presentation is good. I am sure you have all the sales data with you as well. |
| What would be the rent of this house? | The house is spacious and well maintained. I wonder if I would be able to afford it. |
| I do not agree with you. | Exploring other ideas may provide us with more insights. |

## ETHNOCENTRISM

People often perceive others' actions as being peculiar without understanding the reason for reacting differently than the other person would have. For example, an Indian employee working in the

UK may bow slightly to greet his manager who may pass a mocking comment, 'These Indians always behave like this,' to his fellow colleagues. We often say that British drivers drive 'on the wrong side' of the road. But we seldom say that the driver drives on the 'opposite side' or even 'left hand side'. An Arab is likely to perceive an American who wants to set a deadline for completion of some work as aggressive. But the same Arab is likely to prefer a handshake over a written contract, and is likely to be perceived as naive and perhaps untrustworthy by the American. These kinds of attitudinal differences develop due to *ethnocentrism*.

Ethnocentrism refers to perceiving other cultural groups from one's own cultural point of view. Thus, it implies making invalid assumptions about others' ways based on one's own narrow experience. Here, the key word is *assumptions*, since people are not even aware that they are being ethnocentric. The assumptions one makes about others' ways can involve negative judgements, which may in fact be invalid. Ethnocentrism often leads to misunderstanding others by misinterpreting what is meaningful and purposeful to other people through one's own points of view.

We often tend to judge their ways in terms of *our* life experience, not *their* context. We fail to understand that their ways have their respective meanings and functions in life, just as our ways have for us. These problems in perceiving may lead to adverse situations at the workplace. Nowadays, however, crossing the boundaries that individual cultures normally subscribe to, that in earlier times seldom took place, has become a rather regular affair. While technological advances in the field of communication have helped in taking care of various kinds of obstacles to communication, ethnic barriers to communications are still extant. Ethnocentric reactions may be taken care of by gaining knowledge of other cultures and developing an increased level of multicultural diversity. Recognizing cultural differences as well as becoming tolerant of other cultures by being empathetic, and avoiding unjustified assumptions and invalid notions may prove to be of great help in overcoming ethnocentrism. Furthermore, delving a little deeper than the surface stereotypes and labels may help to discover individual personalities as well as enable us to get rid of such ethnocentric behaviour.

## CULTURAL VARIABLES AND COMMUNICATION SENSITIVITY

The culturally diverse workplace of modern times differs significantly from that of the earlier generations in two ways. First, it is constituted of individuals from different national and cultural backgrounds. Apart from promoting diverse national and cultural backgrounds, workforce diversity represents different groups that have always been present there though the factor of diversity was never this prominent. Ethnic balance is changing. Diversity lends a much richer workplace environment, and a greater variety of viewpoints. Thus, an attempt at operating such a multinational firm without having taking into consideration the diversity in the human-related aspects may face personnel-related issues. So, managers who do not have the skills to manage workforce diversity may prove to be incompetent. Multicultural skills are not only of paramount importance to people who work within their respective regions but may prove to be important since global talent is likely to become a priority in the coming years.

Cultural factors considerably influence the typical ways in which individuals interact with others, present their ideas, or negotiate. The norms as well as values we assimilate in terms of our socio-cultural conditioning shape our views about the world apart from the way we interact with each other.

It is commonly held by most people that the word culture refers to people from a specific nationality. National cultures indeed exist and have an important role to play in shaping the way people interact. But culture has other dimensions as well. Within a country, regional differences may have a powerful influence on the way people interact. Attitudes, ethnicity, values customs, race, etc. can influence behaviour. Socio-economic backgrounds, physical disabilities, gender, sexual orientation, religion are also important determinants in this regard.

Figure 3.1 gives a clearer view of the cultural variables that may familiarize us with the various aspects of culture.

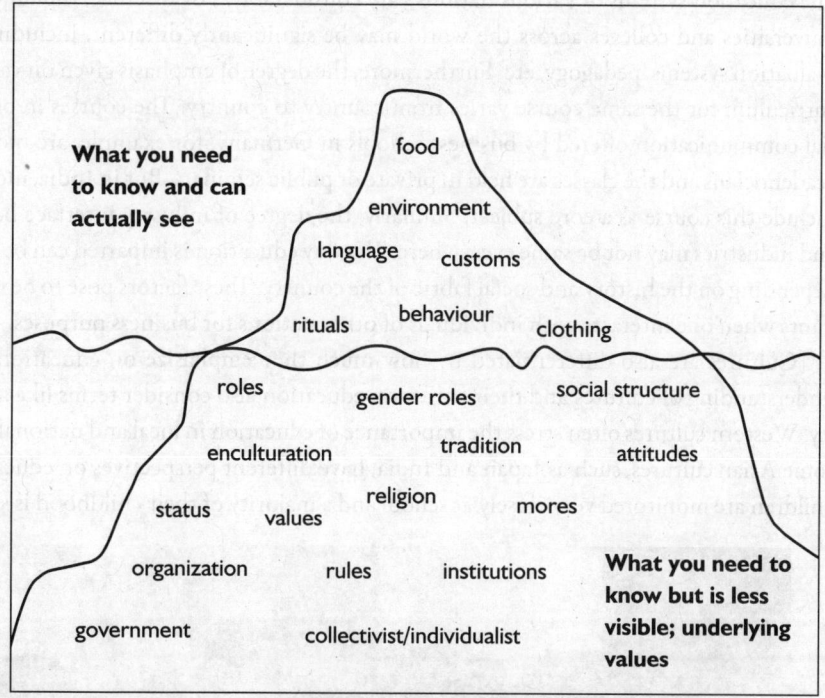

**Fig. 3.1** The iceberg of culture

The figure signifies culture as an iceberg and only the tip of an iceberg is visible while most part of it is hidden underneath. Now, if our perception on cultures is solely based on the external or visible attributes of culture, that is, food, clothing, rituals, language, etc., then we run the risk of slipping into stereotypical labelling, holding prejudices, and subsequently resorting to discriminatory action. Till the time we make a proper estimate of the underlying values, which are not overtly visible, one may misinterpret the visible attributes of the person.

A proper understanding of the differences between individualist (ego-centric) cultures and collectivist (socio-centric) cultures can hardly be ignored while learning about people from different cultures and promoting intercultural communication. Individualists stress on individual goals that promote self-realization, while collectivists need individuals to fit into the 'group'.

In matters concerning business, it is important to understand the values and traditions that shape people's behaviour. Even in our own environment, we regularly interact with people hailing from diverse cultural backgrounds.

## Variables of National Culture

Both the sender and the receiver of the message are influenced by external and internal stimuli. While interacting with people for business purposes in a foreign nation, one should realize that the overall national as well as individual cultural differences within cultures further influence those stimuli. There are various constraints and variables that communicators are faced with while working with foreign nationals. One should understand them and acknowledge of their existence.

### *Education*

The education systems of various nations vary considerably. For instance, the functioning of various universities and colleges across the world may be significantly different, including the curriculum, evaluation systems, pedagogy, etc. Furthermore, the degree of emphasis given on various aspects of the curriculum for the same course varies from country to country. The courses in business or managerial communication offered by business schools in Germany, for example, are mostly taken by non-academicians and the classes are held in private or public seminars. But in India, most business schools include this course as a core subject. Similarly, the degree of industry interface between universities and industries may not be same everywhere. The way education is imparted can be formal or informal depending on the history and social fabric of the country. These factors pose to be important determinants when one interacts with individuals of other nations for business purposes.

Cultures are also differentiated by how much they emphasize on education (Image 3.1). Our understanding of cultures and their thrust on education also consider terms like access and availability. Western cultures often stress the importance of education in local and national politics. However, some Asian cultures, such as Japan and India, have different perspectives on education. For example, children are monitored very closely at school and a majority of their childhood is spent in classrooms.

**Image 3.1** Students in a multicultural classroom
© Monkey Business Images / Shutterstock

This factor becomes important while doing business across cultures. Also, it indicates that the same educational/professional criteria cannot be applied uniformly to all cultures while recruiting people for an organization.

### Law and Regulations

Government regulations largely influence business communication as well as the sale of products. For instance, advertising targeted at children is closely monitored in America, Canada, and Scandinavian countries. European nations put restrictions on the advertising of cigarettes and even on the budget allocated on these advertisements. Many countries, such as Mexico, France, and the Province of Quebec, also have a limit on the usage of foreign language in advertisements. It had become difficult to forecast various tournaments in Iran given that the spectators shown on television exposed more than the permissible limits prescribed by Iranian law. Cosmetics and fashion magazines are prohibited in Iran among other things. Men are not even allowed to wear T-shirts in Iran. Women are required to wear either a *chador* (a head-to-toe veil) or a *manteau* (a loose smock worn over pants) along with a scarf on the head.

### Economics

Various important determinants such as per capita income, capital availability, and transportation infrastructure vary from country to country. The communication concerning a business depends on various parameters, such as the rate of inflation, regulatory laws like free enterprise system, or degree of ease to borrow capital. Under the US free-enterprise system, competitors usually set their own prices. In comparison, the Organization of Petroleum Exporting Countries (OPEC), as a cartel, sets oil prices. Some Japanese businesses take cues from the government before initiating major changes in the production and trading practices.

### Politics

The form of government and also the concept of democracy differ from country to country. Also major political changes within a country may influence the way businesses take place. The political stability or instability of the country in which one wants to enter or communicate for business needs to be assessed. All these events influence communication.

### Religion

Various nations around the world have a concept of single-religion or multi-religion. Also, there are many nations that are tolerant towards religious diversity. For instance, India and the US patronize religious diversity. Besides being tolerant towards several religions, these nations allow the practice of other personal beliefs as well. However, some nations like Iran, for example, do not accept multiple religions. Buddhism, Hinduism, and Islam are found in many parts across the world influencing the values (and lifestyle) of individuals professing these faiths. Religious holidays influence international communication, hamper work schedules, or postpone responses to queries. Religion can influence the position of women in society, and their buying patterns and lifestyle. To communicate well internationally, it is beneficial to comprehend the diversity in the religious practices in various countries.

### Social Norms

All the above-mentioned categories—politics, law and regulations, religion, education, economics—influence a country's social norms. Many nations have a patriarchal society and that largely affects business decisions. The family structure and how its members relate to one another—decisions, buying patterns, pooling of resources, special interests—influence behavior as well as business communication. Beyond the immediate family, a bond may exist between people, based on caste and creed, age, class, or even special interests. Perception regarding materialism, roles and status, culture and manners, punctuality, etc. may affect communication. Thus, it is necessary to be aware of the social norms of the country.

Most nations have several hundred different societal cultures. The most important factor to consider, then, is how affective that society is. An example could be of McDonald's which introduced different products in India instead of their regular beef containing products.

McDonald's failed to consider the Chinese culture when they released a commercial that featured a Chinese man kneeling and begging for a discount. Chinese were insulted because they view kneeling as a sign of respect or in this case disrespect.

## Technology

When communicating, we also need to consider a culture's advancement in technology. This is important because technology affects knowledge, language, society, and sometimes their work values as well.

### Language

An important determinant that encompasses all the preceding factors is language. Obviously, unless both the sender and the receiver understand a common language, the opportunities for successful business communication are largely limited. English is a language used throughout the world—and to a large extent the language of business. However, one may do a better job overseas if he/she knows some basic vocabulary of the host country, in case he/she may have to travel to places where English may not be used. Each language has its own grammatical patterns and lexicon. Thus, both verbal and written communication in a second language is more liable to errors. Language problems are often the cause of communication misunderstandings. To avoid these misunderstandings, one needs to understand the language as spoken in that particular cultural context in which one wishes to communicate.

---

**Linguistic Coding Examples**

*Homomorphs-antonyms* Same form but different meaning, for example, in America, when index and thumb fingers touch and the three other fingers are extended, it means everything is good. In Japan, it means the person has no worth.

*Homomorphs-synonyms* Same form and meaning, for example, having your palm facing the receiver with all five fingers extended is considered a hello or greeting in England, America, and Australia.

*Antomorphs-antonyms* Different form and meaning, for example, in India, shaking your head side to side indicates 'no', and in Greece, flipping your head slightly to one side indicates 'yes'.

*Antomorphs-synonyms* Different form and same meaning, for example, in Japan, pointing an index finger to the nose indicates 'I'. Americans point to the chest for 'I'.

*Source:* www.knightswrite.wikidot.com/chapter-3-navigate-cultural-differences-cross-cultural-commu, accessed on 3 May 2012.

An interesting case here is of the Chevy Nova car which was hugely successful in the US but failed in Mexico. In Spanish, *no va* roughly translates as 'does not go'. Mexicans did not want a car that 'did not go'. This linguistic variable affected the sales for a line of cars in a whole country. Hence, being aware of various languages is important in cross-cultural communication.

## Individual Cultural Variables

In this section, we shall discuss the individual variables—factors concerning the distinct lifestyle related to individual habits and ethnic diversity. So, within each culture, there are further differences in verbal and non-verbal communication expressed through varying non-verbal signals, food, individual speech, concepts of time, acceptable dress, decision-making patterns, manners at home and at work, and other non-verbal variations.

### Non-verbal Signals

Non-verbal cues, such as gestures, eye contact, facial expressions, and postures, vary considerably across the world. For example, traditional greetings, such as embracing and folding hands, may be common in some countries. Eskimos rub their noses to greet each other, whereas a kiss on the cheek or lips may mean the same in many cultures. The concepts of touching and facial expressions vary in meaning. One may comprehend wrongly when some Filipinos smile or laugh, since they may also be angry even while smiling or laughing. Also, the enigmatic facial expression of a Japanese may not signify disinterest, but rather stand for an unwillingness to express one's inner thoughts publicly. One should be aware and cautious and know the non-verbal variations that could cause failures in communication if he/she wishes to be understood correctly by the people of other cultures.

### Time (Chronemics)

The concept of time is looked at differently across the world. Latin Americans and people in the Middle East are more casual about timeliness than are Americans, who are quite prompt. Germans are very particular about time; rarely is one kept waiting beyond the stipulated time. In Latin American and Buddhist cultures, it is normal to wait for long before the host comes and meets the visitor since arriving late is a socially accepted custom. Hence, punctuality is one aspect of time that is treated differently across cultures.

Taking afternoon naps, closing shops, and postponing times for business meetings and dinner are common in some countries. German law specifies definite opening and closing hours for business and even dictates which evening(s) retail stores may be open. Even while referring to the different seasons of a year, people from different cultures differ in their expressions. Some only consider the rainy and dry seasons, whereas Americans and Europeans refer to spring, summer, fall, and winter. Again, in the US, people think of time as linear entity—days begin, days end; seasons start, seasons stop; and journeys begin, journeys end. Others think of time as a circular entity—all in good time—is appropriate enough for some cultures.

We should recognize which is the time-conscious culture and which is the one less concerned with precision in time. Knowing culture perceptions of time can help us understand why some responses are slow—by others' standards.

> Cultures differ in how people conceive of and handle time.

Managers spend 50 to 90 per cent of their time talking to internal and external customers. The nature of their communication gets affected by attitudes, social

### The Concept of Time—Monochromic and Polychromic Cultures

Cultures differ in how people conceive of and handle time. The concept of time affects interactions among people. Two extremes of this dimension would be monochromic and polychromic cultures. In monochromic cultures, time would be the focus and everything else would be arranged keeping in mind the constraints, deadlines, and schedules. On the other hand, in polychromic cultures people may never be too busy. Time here is a tool and never more important than the convenience of people. Doing multiple things at one time is another feature here.

Time, hence, is a cultural phenomenon. In Turkey or India, waiting for half an hour for a well-placed official is normal, whereas, in US, a delay of five minutes would be noticed. Time is probably a byproduct of industrial society.

### Exercise 3.1 Concept of time in different cultures

This exercise helps us understand the concept of 'time' in different cultures. The picture below represents a grocery store cashier in the shop. Quite a few customers (including you) have selected various groceries and wish to check out. Draw a diagram representing four–five customers who have gathered around the cash counter to pay.

Explain the basis of your suggested arrangement. Also, on the basis of your understanding of concepts discussed in the chapter till now, explain how the customers would have arranged themselves if the context were just opposite to your culture.

organizational patterns, thought patterns, roles, non-verbal communication, language, time, and context.

On a different level, cultural variables that can affect the communication process by influencing a person's perceptions are attitudes, social organization, thought patterns, roles, language, non-verbal communication (including kinesic behavior, proxemics, paralanguage, and object language), and time. The effects of these variables are interdependent and inseparable.

Managing cross-cultural communication involves the following essential steps:

1. *Cultural sensitivity* The person sending a message makes it a point to know the recipient and encodes the message in a form that will most likely be understood as it is intended. This inadvertently means that the manager must be aware of one's own and the other culture, and understands the expectations involved in the interaction.
2. *Careful encoding* The sender must consider the receiver's frame of reference to make the best choice regarding words, pictures, and gestures. Also, the sender has to understand that

the language translation is only a part of the process, and considers the non-verbal language as well.
3. *Selective transmission*   This involves choosing the channel medium after considering the nature of the message, level of importance, context and expectations of the receiver, timing, and personal interactions.
4. *Careful decoding*   This would involve the same points (at the receiver's end) as required by the sender while encoding the message. Further, it requires an understanding that your beliefs and perceptions are only valid for you and not everyone else.
5. *Follow-up actions*   This would include maintaining eye contact, an interactive posture, ability to respond in a descriptive, non-evaluative, and non-judgmental way. A careful follow-up would help avoid three types of miscommunications namely, receiver misinterpreting the message, receiver encoding response incorrectly, and sender misinterpreting the feedback.

Exercise 3.1 focuses on the concept of time in cross-cultural situations.

## Space (Proxemics)
The concept of space distancing is also culture-specific. While most Indians do not mind people standing close to them while speaking, Americans demand more room—called buffer space—between themselves and others when speaking. In some cultures, such as Arabs, Latin Americans, and Americans, not standing close may seem cold and uninterested. On the other hand, some cultures consider those who stand close to you as intrusive, rude, pushy, and overbearing.

As far as businesses are concerned, the concepts of office space differ. In some countries, several people occupy the same office, even the same desk. Furniture is arranged according to astrological beliefs. You cannot assume that one particular concept of space is accepted and understood throughout the world.

## Food
The preparation, serving, type of food, or even the time of the day when it is had vary widely throughout the world. Even the way one should behave when the food is served, the way it should be eaten, the sequence of courses of the meal, or table manners vary widely from country to country. Chinese are proficient with the use of chopsticks, whereas South Indians offer food on banana leaves. A large section of people in Asia eat with their hands, whereas Europeans prefer spoons, forks, and knives to eat. Comprehending and appreciating the different cuisines as well as food habits of various countries may pose to be crucial to the success of global business.

## Acceptable Dress
Generally the most accepted dress code for American males is a business suit and for females it is tailored suits. Moreover, these days business 'uniforms' have become common almost all over the world. Although some Britons still prefer to wear the bowler along with a dark suit and carry an umbrella; or for that matter some Indians still prefer a Nehru jacket; or in Singapore a long-sleeved shirt with a tie, the uniformity in business dresses can be seen throughout the world.

However, one may find exceptions to the same. For example, in the Middle East *thobes* are acceptable. One may also find the Mao dark-blue jacket and pants, the Iranian *chador*, the Japanese kimono, the Polynesian sarong, or the Hawaiian *muumuu* as part of the business attire in different parts of the world.

**Table 3.2** Attributes of high context and low context cultures

| Low Context Culture | High Context Culture |
|---|---|
| Relationships may not last longer | Aims at long-lasting relationships |
| Less dependent on context | Exploits context |
| Values only written agreements; relies more on verbal | Respects oral agreements also; relies less on verbal |
| Insiders and outsiders less clearly distinguished | Insiders and outsiders are clearly distinguished |
| Cultural patterns change faster | Cultural patterns are ingrained; change is slow |
| Individualistic in carrying out many tasks | Group orientation for almost all tasks |
| Shuns arguments and other similar tactics | Enjoys confrontation and debates |
| Tries to reach decisions quickly and efficiently | Spends more time on each little point |
| Less sensory involvement | More of sensory involvement |
| Negative messages are communicated directly/explicitly | Negative messages are indirect/implicit |
| Time is linear/monochromic; events happen one after another | Time is circular/polychromic; many events happen simultaneously |

### Decision-making

Decision-making is another area that varies with culture. Americans, for example, prefer individual decision-making as compared to the Japanese who prefer collective decision-making. Again, one cannot deny the time involved in reaching a consensus in a collective decision-making process. Thus, one should take into consideration the differences and nuances involved in decision-making styles across the countries.

Table 3.2 summarizes the features of high context and low context cultures discussed in this section.

## CROSS-CULTURAL COMMUNICATION STRATEGIES

Effective cross-cultural communication requires knowledge about the potential problems of cross-cultural communication coupled with a conscious effort to overcome these problems. There is always a significant possibility that cultural differences may cause communication problems. We need to be very observant and careful while dealing with such problems. Some precautions are as follows:

1. During cross-cultural exchanges, one should understand the interaction completely before reacting. Jumping to conclusions about what is being thought and said may lead to ineffective (and at times offensive) communication. Active listening can sometimes be used to check this—by repeating what one thinks he/she heard, one can confirm that one understands the communication accurately.
2. Sometimes words are used differently between languages or cultural groups and can lead to misunderstandings. Prior knowledge about such words is desirable.

> For cross-cultural communication to be effective, all the parties involved require knowledge about its potential problems.

3. Taking the aid of intermediaries who are familiar with both cultures can be helpful in cross-cultural communication situations.
4. In some cultures, people move quickly to the point; while in others, they talk about other things long enough to establish rapport or a relationship. Sensitivity to such cultural nuances help one to win the trust or establish a rapport smoothly.
5. Direct experience is the best way to begin to understand any culture. This may not always be practical, but access to sources that cater to members of the target group can be helpful ways to begin.
6. We tend to overlook similarities and notice just the differences when we first begin to interact with members of another culture. Here, one should understand that standards of interpretation that are used in one culture cannot be applied to interpret the behaviour of those belonging to another culture.
7. Avoid stereotyping. This can happen due to overgeneralization, especially among those who interact with other cultures rarely.
8. One should be sensitive to variation within groups as well as among them. There may be similar people, in terms of personality, attitudes, etc. in different groups and dissimilar people within a group. Group members may share the customs and rituals only. A metaphor can be given here of Apple and Microsoft which have developed different operating systems. Both those systems allow us to accomplish work with a word processing system. The output as we see is the same, but the language and the coding through which that output is accomplished are different.
9. Our own cultural identities become apparent to us when we begin to interact with people from different cultures.
10. Cultures witness changes with the passage of time. Updating one's knowledge of different cultures is very crucial, especially for a business manager whose job involves interacting with people from different cultures.

## Potential Hot Spots in Cross-cultural Communication

In cross-cultural communication, especially when working with other people or travelling abroad for work or pleasure, it may pay to ask some experts about the communication styles of the areas you plan to visit. A little research at the outset can stave off a host of misunderstandings.

### *Opening and Closing Conversations*
Different cultures may have different customs concerning who addresses whom, when, how, who has the right/duty to speak first, and what is the proper way to conclude a conversation. Think about it—no matter where you are, certain ways of commencing a conversation or concluding one will be considered rude, even disrespectful. These are artificial customs, to a certain degree, and there is probably no universally right or wrong way to go about these things, short of behaviour that all cultures would likely consider vulgar or abusive. Knowledge regarding modes of address, salutations, levels of deference to age or social position, gender differences, acceptable ways to conclude gracefully, etc., is certainly required.

### *Taking Turns during Conversations*
In some cultures, it is more appropriate to take turns in an interactive way; in others, it is more important to listen thoroughly and without comment/immediate response, lest it be taken as a challenge/

humiliation. This depends particularly on the context of the conversation, the audience, and the levels of personal knowledge/relationship between the people interacting. For example, a Western couple or pair of executives may feel perfectly comfortable interacting in a give and take way in a public market, but if that public market is in a part of the world where such a public display of give and take is considered to be in bad taste, then they may be giving offense without even realizing it.

### Interrupting

In some cultures, interruptions—vocal, physical, or emotional expression, etc.—are considered default conversational styles, particularly among those considered to be equals, or among men. Many people from Northern Europe or the US might mistake this kind of conversation for argument and hostility, but that might not be the case.

### Use of Silence

In some forms of communication, silence is expected before a response, as a sign of thoughtfulness and deference to the original speaker, yet at other times, silence may be perceived as a sign of hostility. In the West, 20 seconds of silence during a meeting is an extraordinarily long time, and people feel uncomfortable with that. Someone will invariably break in to end the uncomfortable silence. But the same reactions to silence are not universal.

### Appropriate Topics of Conversation

In some places, it is considered vulgar to speak openly about money, let alone about the kinds of intimate family issues that commonly form the basis of afternoon television talk shows in the West. Travellers or business people should learn the customs that surround the making of deals, the transaction of commerce, and the degree to which details are specified in advance and enumerated in writing across cultures (not all places are as prone to hiring lawyers and creating detailed contracts as the West).

### Use of Humour

In the West, people often try to build immediate rapport through humour, but this is not universally seen as appropriate. The use of humour can be seen as a sign of disrespect by some, and it is important to understand that this is another area where misunderstandings can often arise.

### Knowing How Much to Say

In some places, brevity is appreciated, whereas in other places, it is better to explain a rather small point using a longer preamble, followed by extended closing remarks. For Westerners, this can be maddening, as they tend to value speaking directly and to the point. Then again, there are clearly circumstances where Westerners say too much and lose their ability to communicate well, depending on the context. Of course, patterns around presumed areas of deference based on age and social standing can influence how long a speech is appropriate, depending on the culture.

### Sequencing Elements during Conversation

> Sequencing and timing of asking questions do matter in cross-cultural communication.

During a conversation, an extended conversation, or negotiation, the appropriate time to touch upon issues that are more sensitive, is a matter of concern for cross-cultural experts. Also, it is important to understand the influence that sequence has on effectiveness. It is important that the right question should be asked in the right way and also at the right time. The same question asked too soon or at an inappropriate time (as per the custom) may connote very different things to the listener and influence subsequent behaviour.

## CROSS-CULTURAL COMMUNICATION SKILLS—BASIC TIPS

Some simple tips to help you improve your cross-cultural communication skills are given as follows:

**Slow down** Even when English is the common language in a cross-cultural situation, this does not mean you should speak at normal speed. Slow down, speak clearly, and ensure your pronunciation is intelligible.

**Separate questions** Try not to ask double questions such as, 'Do you want to carry on or shall we stop here?' In a cross-cultural situation, only the first or second question may have been comprehended. Let your listener answer one question at a time.

**Avoid negative questions** Many cross-cultural communication misunderstandings are caused by the use of negative questions and answers. In English, we answer 'yes' if the answer is affirmative and 'no' if it is negative. In some cultures, a 'yes' or 'no' may only be indicating whether the questioner is right or wrong. For example, the response to 'Are you not coming?' may be 'Yes', meaning 'Yes, I am not coming'.

**Take turns** Cross-cultural communication is enhanced through taking turns to talk, making a point, and then listening to the response.

**Write it down** If you are unsure whether something has been understood, write it down and check.

**Be supportive** Effective cross-cultural communication is in essence about being comfortable. Giving encouragement to those with weak English gives them confidence, support, and trust in you.

**Check meanings** When communicating across cultures, never assume that the other party has understood. Be an active listener. Summarize what has been said in order to verify it. This is a very effective way of ensuring that accurate cross-cultural communication has taken place.

**Avoid slang** Even the most well-educated foreigner will not have complete knowledge of slang, idioms, and sayings. The danger is that the words will be understood but the meaning missed.

**Watch the humour** In many cultures business is taken very seriously. Professionalism and protocol are constantly observed. Many cultures do not appreciate the use of humour and jokes in a business context. When using humour, think whether it will be understood in the other culture.

**Maintain etiquette** Many cultures have certain etiquette when communicating. It is always a good idea to undertake some cross-cultural awareness training or at least do some research on the target culture.

Cross-cultural communication is about dealing with people from other cultures in a way that minimizes misunderstandings and maximizes your potential to create strong cross-cultural relationships. The list just discussed should be seen as a starting point to greater cross-cultural awareness.

## SUMMARY

Cross-cultural communication establishes and understands how people from different cultures communicate, and is charged with producing some guidelines with which people from different cultures can better communicate with each other. You can communicate effectively in different cultures by taking the time to understand their differences and similarities. You should always respect all cultures. Be patient with people when misunderstandings arise. Be flexible. Observe others and listen actively. Choose your words carefully when you communicate by avoiding slang, idioms, and cultural references. Be polite and professional, and you will avoid many potential cultural conflicts.

## KEY TERMS

*Communication style* It refers to the way people communicate between and within cultures.

*Cross-cultural communication* It looks at how people, from differing cultural backgrounds, endeavour to communicate. Its core is to establish and understand how people from different cultures communicate with each other. Its charge is to also produce some guidelines with which people from different cultures can better communicate with each other.

*Cultural variables* There are economic, educational, linguistic, political, religious, social, and technological variables. People grouped under the same cultural variable experience and share some common issues/beliefs.

*High/low context* These refer to different cultural contexts; cultures can be distinguished on the basis of homogeneity of people and shared nuances. Higher homogeneity would lead to high context cultures and low context cultures would see more heterogeneity of people.

## Concept Review Questions

1. Define cross-cultural communication.
2. Discuss about different communication styles highlighting low/high context cultures.
3. How do you see cultures differing in the way they perceive time?
4. How has increased market globalization and cultural diversity contributed to the increased relevance of cross-cultural communication?
5. Why do you think use of slangs and idioms should be avoided while talking to a multicultural audience?
6. What are some basic traits which a global manager must possess besides normal administrative and functional capabilities to manage a global organization?

## Projects

1. There are numerous examples of situations in the past where print advertising or television advertising by an MNC has caused serious unanticipated problems to the company because of the huge cultural differences between the countries that the company sells its products to.

   Collect some specific examples, analyse them, and suggest how they could have been avoided.

2. Choose a specific country such as Korea, Japan, Sweden, or Nigeria, whose culture you are not familiar with. Research in detail the culture and write a summary of what an Indian manager would need to know about rules of social behaviour in order to conduct business successfully in the country.

## REFERENCE

Alcoff, Linda, 'The Problem of Speaking for Others', *Cultural Critique*, 20 (Winter 1991), pp. 5–32.

### CASE STUDY 1

**Cultural Differences**

Wise Web Analytics is a California-based multinational company that has set up its offices in Hyderabad and Bengaluru. Santosh recently joined this company in its Hyderabad office. He is part of a team that has members from New York, Shanghai, and Malaysia for a major project in the area of risk analysis. His project manager Julie is based in San Jose. In the first week of his joining the company, Julie wanted to call for a project meeting of all the members through videoconferencing. She asked Santosh whether it would be convenient for him to join the meeting at 7 p.m. Santosh knew that he had another important assignment at 6 p.m. and he was not sure whether that would be over or not by 7 p.m. But he did not directly say 'No' to Julie. He said that if the team could wait for some time, it was fine or else they could go ahead with the meeting and he would join later. Put off by his reply, she firmly asked him whether he said 'Yes' or 'No'. And this confused Santosh.

**Questions**

1. Analyse the cultural differences involved in this case keeping in mind the discussion in this chapter.
2. What do you feel about Santosh's way of answering?
3. What would Julie think about Santosh?

### CASE STUDY 2

**Conversation Styles**

There are three conversations presented here which are of a misunderstanding due to differences in communication styles—indirect in one culture, direct in the other.

**The trip**

A: Hi! How did the visit to the plant go?
B: Quite well, I think they're interested in using my expertise.
A: That's great. Did they show you around?
B: Yes. I saw the whole plant.
A: The whole thing! That must have taken hours.
B: Actually, we were in and out in less than 30 minutes. They said another guy was coming at noon.
A: Oh!

**The meeting**

A: How did it go with the board members?
B: A lot easier than I was expecting.
A: Really? Did you ask about investing in the new building for storage?
B: Yes. I explained we had to have it and told them how much it would cost.
A: Ok. So what was their reaction?
B: There was no discussion. They said fine and asked me to move on to the next point.

**Getting back**

A: How was your meeting with the Director?
B: Very well, I think, for the first meeting.
A: When will you see the director again?
B: In the end, I didn't meet with the director. I met with his assistant.
A: Did she ask you a lot of questions about your proposal?
B: A few.
A: When are you going back?
B: Probably next week.
A: You're not sure?
B: I asked for another appointment and she said she would get back to me.

**Need help?**

A: Hi! What can I do for you?
B: Excuse me. I need some help with this new machine.
A: Of course. Let me explain it again.
B: I asked Kanti, but she couldn't help me.
A: No, she hasn't tried it yet.
B: It's a little bit complicated.
A: It's very complicated, but after I explained it to you and asked you if you understood, you said yes!
B: Yes. Please excuse me.

**Question**

Analyse the conversations and deduce the difference between what was said or done and how the receiver interpreted it.

# CHAPTER 4

# Technology-enabled Business Communication

## LEARNING OBJECTIVES

After reading this chapter, you will be able to understand
- the various modern technologies available for communication
- the positive and negative impact of technology-enabled communication
- how to select appropriate communication technology
- the effective use of technology-based communication tools

## INTRODUCTION

Technology has come to exercise an ever-increasing impact on communication in recent times. More and more enterprises, large and small, are trying to incorporate the latest technology into their operations. Educational institutions use technology for teaching, and many academic courses thus include technology-based practical components in their curricula.

Technology plays a pivotal role in the various functions of an organization. Among these functions, communication serves as the link among people both inside and outside the organization. Technology is completely revolutionizing the way organizations communicate. Nowadays, information is transmitted and exchanged by emails, faxes, voicemails, social and business networking sites, such as Orkut, Twitter, LinkedIn, and Facebook, and blogs, which are sites maintained by individuals.

We can use teleconferencing and video conferencing for conducting meetings with our associates around the world. Executives rarely make a presentation without using some presentation software. Above all, we now extensively use the Internet for collecting information and carrying out research.

Of all the new technologically advanced machines, computer is the one machine that all organizations are heavily dependent on. It is, in fact, an important component of almost all organizational communication functions, including preparation and distribution of memos, letters, proposals, and reports through internal and external networks. Today's organizations have more or less become paperless.

> Technology has completely transformed the way organizations communicate.

Gauging the importance of modern communication media, we have discussed in this chapter the various technology-based communication tools used for acquiring, transmitting, and processing information. The chapter also explains the positive and negative impact of such technologies on the organizational environment and on individuals. In addition, it explains the criteria that are needed to choose a technology for meeting a specific communication task. The chapter closes with providing certain guidelines for the effective use of technology in communication.

## TECHNOLOGY-BASED COMMUNICATION TOOLS

Specific tools that can be used for communication include telephones—mobile phones, facsimile machines, and computers—desktop computers, laptops, and personal digital assistants (PDAs). The distinguishing lines between modern devices are blurring steadily. For example, a mobile phone can now contain all the functions of a PDA and it can also allow access to emails and the Internet. For the discussion in this chapter, however, each of these devices is presented as a separate entity.

### Telephone and Voicemail

There are many types of telephones available, allowing us to choose the types or combinations that suit us best. Even the standard landline installed in an office has several options. As the most important feature apart from the basic functionality, a telephone also sometimes has the capability to record messages in case it is not answered personally.

A telephone can not only be used to contact those who may be difficult to reach in person, but can even be used to get through to busy people who are nearby. Office hermits who barricade themselves behind closed doors will often drop everything when the telephone rings. A telephone conversation does lack the visual feedback that often reveals how a message is getting across, although vocal cues—tone, pauses, interruptions, pitch, and rate—do, however, convey the person's reaction to the message considerably well.

Real-time communication is not the only type of telephone communication. Voicemail is a high-tech version of the answering machine. Many communicators are not very fond of voicemail, often with justification. Some voicemail menus and sub-menus can take too long, and 'clever' greetings can be annoying. However, voicemail does have its advantages. It allows one to leave a message at any time of the day or night, and the recipient actually receives the message without the omissions and distortions that come when an intermediary transcribes the message.

### Mobile/Cellular phones

A mobile phone has become a necessity today. Not only does it help us to follow calls anywhere, anytime, but it also possesses unlimited features, such as email, multimedia, the Internet, contacts, calendar, and interactive games; one can select a phone with features as per individual requirements.

There are many features that can also be added to a mobile phone, such as call waiting, call forwarding, conferencing capabilities, and voicemail after a phone connection is obtained by signing up with any service provider.

In fact, a service provider has many plans that one can also choose from. Intense competition in this market has created many options that bundle popular features, making them very cost effective. One should, however, ask relevant questions about the specific needs before selecting a service provider and plan. One of the important considerations for mobile phone connections is network coverage and acceptable reception in the places we are likely to use it the most, such as at home and the workplace.

> - Organizations use telephones, pagers, facsimile machines, and PDAs as tools for communication.
> - Vocal cues, such as tone, pauses, interruptions, pitch, and rate, help to convey a person's reaction to a message.

A mobile phone has become a part of everyday life for millions of people across the world. The ability to communicate by a cellular phone across the country (and the world) has become so common that it is no longer considered a luxury. It offers the following advantages:

**Accessibility** The biggest advantage of a mobile phone is that it makes it makes it much easier to contact a person at any time. For example, even if a person is not in his/her office, it is unlikely these days to not be able to telecommunicate with him/her, as a mobile phone always makes him/her accessible, unless the network is out of coverage area or the person does not wish to communicate. Especially, in the event of a critical problem, the problem can be communicated and a decision taken, without a person being present personally at any required place, thus saving crucial time.

**Connectivity** Mobile phones allow people to remain connected constantly. Especially if in a job a person is out of office for considerable amounts of time, people at the workplace can still constantly be connected with him/her through mobile phones. Also, a person can reach out to other people immediately in case of an emergency.

**Time** A mobile phone gives mobility and saves time as one can communicate even when one is on the move. An important conversation can take place anywhere (e.g., on a train), which puts fewer restrictions on time. For example, you travel for three hours every working day, then without a mobile phone, you would not be able to communicate in those three hours. A mobile phone, however, makes business communication during those hours possible.

**Information access** A mobile phone allows one immediate access to information. For example, if you were on your way to an important meeting, and suddenly, realized that you had forgotten a piece of vital information at office, then rather than getting stuck without it, a mobile phone would allow you to access it with just one call or text message to a colleague.

**Bookings and appointments** A mobile phone allows one to make bookings and appointments. It also helps one to confirm, clarify, or alter meeting details (e.g., location and time) instantaneously.

**Email messages** Using mobile phones it is now possible to be informed by a phone call or a text message of all (or specifically selected) new emails. Some newer phones also allow access to all emails via the WAP (wireless application protocol) and GPRS (general packet radio service) mobile Internet connections. Also, now, an advanced technology, 3G, the third generation of wireless technology, is mostly used with mobile phones and handsets as a means to connect the phone to the Internet in order to make voice and video calls, download and upload data, and surf the Net.

**Redirection and answer services** A mobile phone can act as a good extension of a landline. Calls to a landline can be forwarded almost instantly to a mobile number, if the person is not available at the time of the call. For an extra cost, mobile phones can also be used as part of an existing switchboard. This allows callers to be put straight through to a person from the office switchboard or reception without the inconvenience of dialling two numbers.

**International access** Nowadays, most phones are able to work in a number of countries, which means that one can be instantly accessible even when travelling outside the country. However, the only problem is the huge cost incurred, as incoming as well as outgoing calls get charged on roaming (i.e., being outside one's home network).

Despite its advantages, communication through mobile phones is not a perfect medium. Possibly the greatest disadvantage is the temporary nature of the spoken word. The spoken word is especially prone to being forgotten or misunderstood. Listeners quickly forget much of what they hear—half of a message almost immediately and the remaining half two days later. Even if they remember an oral message, listeners are likely to distort it. Some details are dropped out with each transfer of a message—facts and figures change. Receivers may even invent variations of the original fact, just to make the story more interesting or fit it to their own idea of what ought to have happened. The farther the message travels in space and time from its original sender, the greater the chance of distortion.

## Facsimile Machines

A facsimile (fax) machine scans a printed page, converts it into a signal, and transmits the signal over a telephone line to a receiving fax machine, which prints out the page. Although the fax facility has been available for many years, until recently it was slow and expensive. A fax can be used when a written document of some importance (such as a document containing a signature) needs to be urgently sent to another place that is at some distance.

Consider the budget and space constraints before deciding whether to get a simple fax machine or whether to get an all-in-one model that not only faxes but also prints and scans. Some vendors can even provide a fax number that allows one to receive a fax as an attachment to an email. This can be very handy for those who travel frequently and cannot always be near a fax machine.

## Computers

A computer is 'an electronic machine that can store, organize, and find information, do calculations, and control other machine. It has become a very affordable tool today.

The following discussion will focus on software and auxiliary products, followed by the three basic types of computers—desktop computers, laptops, and personal digital assistants (PDAs).

### *Software*

Software is a collection of computer programs and related data that are used to operate a computer. It is the interface between the computer hardware and user. The operating system, which acts as a host for all applications that are run on the computer, is the basic software that must be installed on any computer system. Many software packages (for various application programs) are often bundled with the system software at the time of purchase. At the bare minimum, one should know how to work on word processing, spreadsheet, and presentation software.

### *Auxiliary Products*

Auxiliary products are those products that can be used in conjunction with a computer to enhance its functionality. These products also require software that are specifically designed to facilitate their usage. The following are some examples of auxiliary products:

**Digital camera** A picture taken by this type of camera can be directly loaded onto a computer for a variety of uses.

**Scanner** It is a device that copies and then stores pictures and other documents on a computer. When a printed copy of a text needs to be included as part of a digital document, a digital image can be created by scanning the printed copy with the help of a scanner. The higher the resolution of the scanner, the better the image produced.

> A fax machine scans a printed page, converts it into a signal, and transmits the signal over a telephone line to a receiving fax machine.

**Wireless transmission** This feature allows one to communicate with other devices equipped with the same feature without using wires. Bluetooth is one technology that makes use of this feature. It is an appealing radio technology as it allows computers (and other electronic devices) to be wirelessly linked over short distances, however, it has its drawbacks, namely data rate and security. It offers only up to 24 Mbits per second data rate, and the greater range and radio frequency (RF) make it much more open to interception and attack.

The importance of making regular external backups of crucial data should not be avoided. Backups are commonly stored on DVDs, CDs, or zip discs, but there are also services provided on the Web to facilitate this process. Such backups help retain a copy of the data in case a computer is affected by viruses, which can lead to a loss of the data stored in the computer. Given below are few tips to protect the computer from a virus attack:

1. Install antivirus software such as McAfee, Avast! Antivirus, BitDefender, AVG, or Norton.
2. Keep the computer updated on all the software installed.
3. Install only trusted software.
4. Disable autoplay when plugging in USB devices or inserting CDs and DVDs, run antivirus software on the device drive, and then access it.
5. Run virus scans regularly.
6. Install a firewall that prevents hackers from getting access to the computer.
7. Delete unknown emails and never open attachments from an unknown sender; also never open attached files with .vbs or .js extensions.
8. Avoid clicking on (pop-up) advertisements on websites.

We will now discuss the desktop computer, the laptop, and the PDA.

## Desktop

A desktop computer or desktop is the most common type of computer, which is set up to operate in an office or an institute. It may also include a monitor/flat panel, central processing unit (CPU, including a modem/Ethernet card, a CD/DVD drive, and USB ports), a keyboard, a mouse, uninterrupted power supply (UPS), speakers, a web camera, and a printer. Printer prices have come down considerably. When purchasing a printer, assess the long-term cost. Laser printers cost more upfront, but are less expensive in the long run if one takes printing costs into account. Some type of backup storage should also be considered, such as a zip drive or a read/writable CD or DVD.

Nowadays, desktops can be purchased for a wide range of prices, depending mainly on the amount of memory and processing speed. Given the rapid advances in technology, enabling higher memory and speed capacities, any computer being bought today very soon becomes obsolete. Hopefully, this may not mean that a computer purchased today will not meet the requirements for a long period of time. Basic word processing, email, accounting, and spreadsheet work will not require a top-of-the-line computer.

> A desktop is the most common type of computer that is used in an office, institute, or at home.

### Laptop/Notebook

A laptop is a small computer that can work with a battery and is also portable. A single unit contains a combination of the capabilities mentioned for the desktop. It usually does not include a printer; hence, it is purchased as an additional item.

A laptop can also be used as a docking station that allows one to plug the laptop into a unit at office, enabling the laptop to be used as the basic processing unit while enjoying the use of a larger monitor and a full-sized keyboard.

Laptops tend to be a bit more expensive than desktops, but serve well if one travels considerably and needs computing capability. These days all laptops come with wireless capabilities. This allows Internet access when within range of a wireless network connected to the Internet.

Laptops are not typically as easy to upgrade as desktop computers due to the nature of their construction. Hence, one has to ensure that all the features required are obtained when the laptop is purchased. Getting a laptop with an extended battery life is a good idea. However, this may not be an issue if access to an electrical outlet is always available.

**iPads** Introduced by Apple Inc., in January 2010, iPad is a rectangular tablet or slate computer that weighs just 700 g and is 0.5 inches thick. It has a 9.7-inch-long touchscreen and is easy to carry anywhere. iPads can be used for web browsing, watching movies, playing games, reading e-books, viewing emails and photos, etc. While travelling, 3G or higher technology-based iPads enable us to get a fast connection for surfing the Internet, downloading emails, or using the global positioning system on the go, even where there is no Wi-Fi (Wireless Fidelity) network.

**Netbook** Netbooks are small, lightweight, inexpensive laptops, suitable for general computing and accessing web-based applications; most of them do not have an optical device such as a DVD or CD drive. They are mainly intended for accessing email, and other online documents. When they were introduced in 2007, they were called notebooks and over the years they have evolved as mini-notebooks with less computing power and features. However, netbooks have changed the way of teaching and learning in educational institutions. They are fully capable of accomplishing most school/college-related tasks such as word processing, power point presentations, Internet browsing, multimedia applications, and photo management. Students can have online conversations and complete online projects when they are working at different places or in different time zones.

### Personal Digital Assistant

A personal digital assistant (PDA) is a mobile device that manages personal information and can also be connected to the Internet. Although palmtop computers were used as PDAs earlier, newer mobile phones are now widely being used as PDAs by professionals. These phones combine the features of a palmtop computer and an ordinary mobile phone into a single device. They can access the Internet, intranets, or extranets via Wi-Fi, and wireless wide area networks (WWAN).

Many mobile phones or smartphones such as Blackberry, Sony Ericsson, Nokia N-series, Palm Treo, and I-mate are seen as an extension of their users' personal computers (PCs). Besides contacting people, they can be used for checking or sending emails, playing music, taking videos, browsing the Web, or in other words, for a variety of purposes, and also from anywhere. In today's busy and fast world where every minute counts, professionals find these technological marvels a boon to manage their information in a smart and efficient manner, and have become heavily dependent on them. Image 4.1 shows a smartphone.

> Netbooks have changed the way of teaching and learning in educational institutions.

> A web browser is a software application that enables a user to display and access information located on the website.

# 110 Business Communication

**Image 4.1** A smartphone

© Umberto Shtanzman / Shutterstock

## The Internet

The Internet is an international computer network connecting other networks, computers, and servers, and accessible to the public via modem links. It is a 'network of networks' that consists of millions of private and public, academic, business, and government networks linked by copper wires, fibre-optic cables, wireless connections, and other technologies.

The Internet has become an indispensible tool. It can be used at a basic level for email and for research, and it can be used at a more comprehensive level as a channel for selling business products and services.

A web browser is required to gain access to the Internet. It is a software application that enables a user to display and access information typically located on a web page. Microsoft Internet Explorer and Mozilla Firefox are the two leading web browsers. Once a browser is installed, access to the Internet can be obtained through an Internet service provider (ISP). The providers may differ in the features they provide, but all will allow one to send and receive emails. As with other forms of communication, there are many plans and prices from which to choose. Image 4.2 shows the Google home page, which is also a very famous search engine.

### Applications of the Internet

The following are some applications of the Internet.

**Email** Electronic mail (email) is a store-and-forward method of writing, sending, receiving, and saving messages over the Internet. Email has been discussed in detail a little further in the chapter.

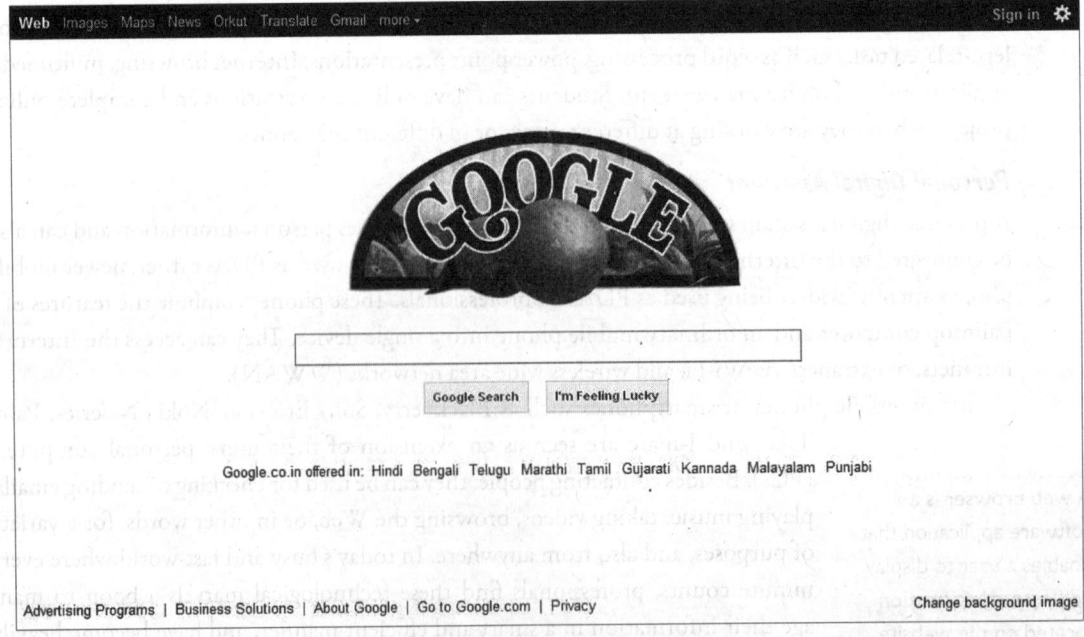

**Image 4.2** Google home page

> Social networking sites are very interactive and promote collaborations among the users.

**Remote access**  The Internet allows computer users to connect to other computers and store information easily, wherever they may be across the world. They may do this with or without the use of security, authentication, and encryption technologies, depending on the requirements. This is encouraging new ways of working from home, collaboration, and information sharing in many industries.

**File sharing**  The Internet has made it very convenient for people or organizations separated geographically to share information in a lot of different forms. A computer file, which contains a video, image, data, or an application, can be emailed to customers, colleagues, and friends as an attachment. It can be uploaded to a website for easy download by others. It can be put into a 'shared location' for instant use by colleagues on the same network. Internet collaboration technology enables business and project teams to share documents, scheduling tools, and other information. Such collaboration occurs in a wide variety of areas including scientific research, software development, conference planning, political activism, and creative writing.

**Social networking**  Social networking through the Internet is the way most people irrespective of their age communicate these days. People can gather and share information and experiences on various topics through social networking sites on the Web, such as Facebook, Twitter, Orkut, LinkedIn, and WAYN, as well as blogs, which are usually maintained by individuals with regular entries on descriptions, events, etc. These sites allow people to remain connected to the people they know through regular feeds and updates. As against static websites of organizations or individuals that appear on the Web, social networking sites are very interactive and promote collaborations among the users.

**Marketing**  The Internet has also made business-to-business (B2B) and business-to-consumer (B2C) marketing very easy for companies. Some of the well-known companies today, such as Amazon.com and eBay, have grown by taking advantage of the efficient nature of low-cost advertising and commerce through the Internet, also known as *e-commerce*. It is the fastest way to spread information to a vast target audience simultaneously. The Internet has also subsequently revolutionized shopping—for example, a person can order a book online and receive it in mail within a couple of days, or download it directly in some cases. Moreover, the Internet has significantly facilitated personalized cyber marketing, which allows a company to market a product to a specific person or a specific group of people more so than any other advertising medium. For instance, if the company has access to a person's browsing history and know that he/she looks mostly for flowers and books online, they can send him/her mailers only about these products, and can avoid sending irrelevant information about other products that are not demanded by the prospective consumer. Although the emergence of this technology is considered a revolution in marketing, its ethical implications are very sensitive. Debates are ensuing on the issue of accessing someone's browsing history without their knowledge and permission.

**Education**  The Internet has also revolutionized the concept of distance learning. Institutes offering such courses host websites that offer complete information and support to students about the courses, assignments, examinations, and schedules. Some institutes also offer online assignment submissions and examinations, thereby making distance education a very pleasant experience for the student. A large number of universities offer distance learning programmes to their off-campus students. Using Internet applications, online/web classes are conducted for the students who may even be professionals. The software used can make such classes as interactive and dynamic as those offered face-to-face. Further, online tutoring companies such as Tutorvista.com, Vienova, Kidspan, Planettutor,

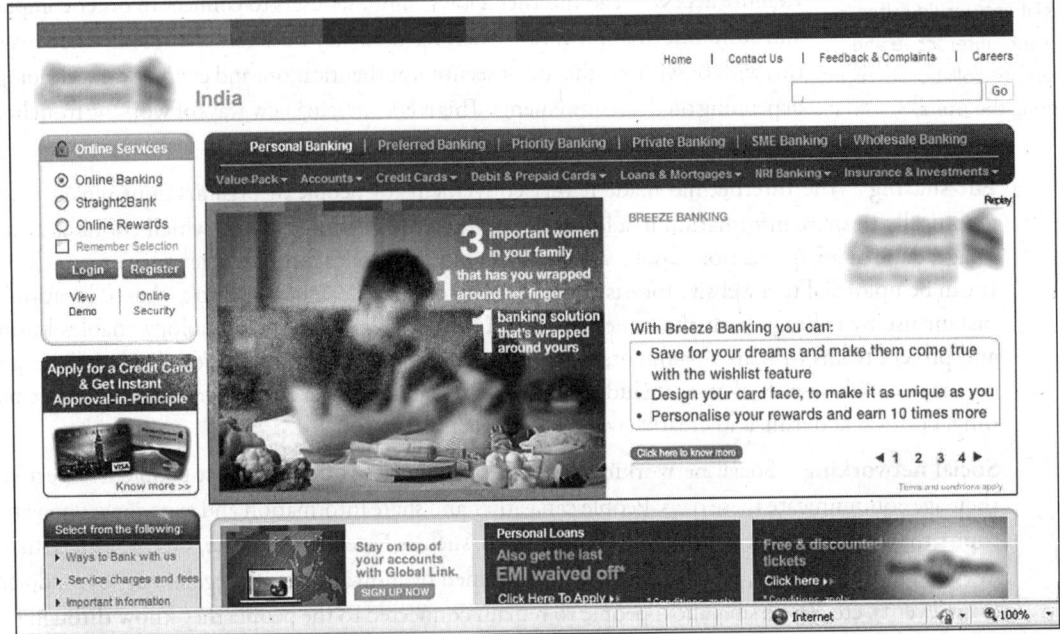

**Image 4.3** An online banking website

Tutorbene, etc. help students—both national and international—in various subjects. Online classes combine the best of traditional classroom experiences and the marvels of technology to provide students with the best possible educational instruction.

**Banking** It is now also possible to bank through the Internet. Banks host their own websites, which offer a vast range of services, such as checking account balances, determining status of issued or deposited cheques, and carrying out fund transfers between different bank accounts. Image 4.3 shows an online banking website. Most banks also tie up with various other service providers, such as mobile cellular service providers or the electricity department, and facilitate online payment of bills. On the flip side, the number of malicious applications targetting online transactions has increased drastically in recent years. These are of two types—local and remote. Local attacks occur on local computers, while remote attacks redirect the victim to a remote site. Attackers can steal money from a victim's online account via unauthorized transactions, which may be possible if the victim's computer is infected with virus. The criminals get access to the login details of the victims and then use the details for transferring money to other accounts and withdraw the money. To prevent such frauds, some banks use one-time passwords (OTP), which are messaged to the user's mobile phone, required to complete the transaction.

Credit card fraud is yet another swindle associated with online transactions. It can have devastating consequences for cardholders and business owners. *Payment gateways* are employed to avoid such fraud. A payment gateway is an e-commerce application service (offered by companies) for protecting credit card details by encrypting sensitive information to ensure that information is passed securely between the customer and the merchant and also between the merchant and the payment processor. Thus, payment gateway performs several tasks to process the transaction. VeriSign, Verified by Visa (VBV), etc. are reputed service providers for secure payment gateway.

**Reservations and submissions** One of the most useful applications of the Internet is the facility of making airline, railway, cinema, and other ticket reservations and, submitting various types of forms such as income tax returns and passport applications. However, in India, although ticket reservation systems work quite effectively, form submission systems have not yet been implemented completely. Therefore, some of these services are partial services, which can only be used to download and fill the forms, as of now.

## Netiquette

Netiquette includes certain social conventions for acceptable behaviour and usage of the Internet in a safe and non-invasive way. The following is a list of guidelines that must be followed when using any information service such as the Internet:

1. Know how file names work on your own system.
2. Although there are naming conventions for the file types used, do not depend on these file-naming conventions to be enforced. For example, a '.doc' file is not always an MS Word file.
3. Information services also use conventions, such as www.xyz.com. While it is useful to know these conventions, again, do not necessarily rely on them.
4. Be aware of conventions used for providing information during sessions. File transfer protocol (FTP) sites usually have files named README in a top-level directory, which have information about the files available. However, do not assume that these files are necessarily up to date and/or accurate.
5. Do not assume that any information one comes across is up to date and/or accurate. Remember that new technologies allow just about anyone to be a publisher, but not all people assume the responsibilities that accompany publishing.
6. Respect the copyright on material whenever reproducing the content. Almost every country has copyright laws.
7. If there is a problem with any form of information service, try to resolve the problem by checking locally first—check file configurations, software setup, network connections, etc. Do this before assuming the problem is at the provider's end, and/or is the provider's fault.
8. When there is trouble with a site and ask for help, be sure to provide as much information as possible about the problem in order to help debug the problem.
9. Remember that, unless you are sure that security and authentication technology is in use, any information submitted to a system is being transmitted over the Internet openly, with no protection from hackers.
10. Since the Internet spans the globe, remember that information services might reflect culture and lifestyle markedly different from one's own community. Materials that we find offensive may originate in a geography that finds them acceptable. Keep an open mind.
11. When information is required from a popular server, be sure to use a mirror server which is an exact copy of the data set and it is used to provide multiple copies of the same information.
12. Do not use someone else's FTP site to deposit materials you wish other people to pick up. This is called 'dumping' and is not generally acceptable behaviour.
13. When starting up your own information service, such as a home page, be sure to check with the local system administrator to find what local guidelines are in effect.

> Netiquette is the short for Internet etiquette or network etiquette.

> Audio conferencing uses conference calls to bring together clients or colleagues across the globe.

14. Consider spreading out the system load on popular sites by avoiding the 'rush hour' and logging in during off-peak times.

## Conferencing

Advances in computer technology, such as faster processors and better data compression algorithms, have enabled the integration of audio and video data into the computing environment. The growth of network technology, and the Internet in particular, has led to a greater awareness of the potential of conferencing systems for teaching, collaborative work, assessment, and student support. While synchronous conferencing systems require all the participants to be connected at the same time, asynchronous conferencing systems, such as bulletin boards, do not require this.

Let us now describe the various kinds of conferencing (Fig. 4.1).

### Audio Conferencing

Audio conferencing uses conference calls to bring together clients or colleagues at a moment's notice, or uses audio streaming to simultaneously reach hundreds of individuals across the globe. Regardless of where the participants are located geographically, an audio conference is just a local, national, or international call away with a telephone network. Telephone conferencing, however, does not permit one to see the facial expressions of the other participants, be it displeasure or a supportive smile or nod.

In voice conferencing, or telnet, five or six people in different locations can hold a conference call using conventional telephone equipment. Voice conferencing saves time. One disadvantage of basic voice networks such as this, however, is that calls must be re-established each time a meeting is held. This problem, however, can be avoided by using dedicated lines.

All telephone-conferencing networks have a time-lapse framework called *store-and-forward*. This feature is useful if a conference member is unable to attend the call. This allows messages to be recorded for replay in the same way as on a telephone answering machine. As a result, receivers can review the message and respond when it is convenient. The advantage of the store-and-forward feature lies in the freedom it offers receivers, allowing them to decide when to communicate.

### Video Conferencing

Video conferencing is an example of a synchronous conferencing system that takes place in real time between individuals or groups who are usually separated geographically. It allows the individuals participating in the conference to view each other. This allows one to gauge the reactions of all the other participants of the conference call.

Video conferencing can be achieved by adding software and relatively inexpensive hardware to standard desktop computers. Such systems also have the ability to easily incorporate data from other desktop computer applications into the conference. Video-conferencing systems can be broadly grouped into three categories:

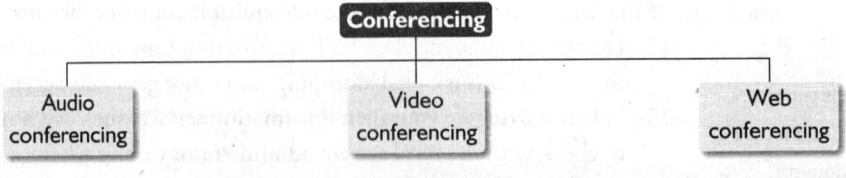

**Fig. 4.1** Types of conferencing

> Video conferencing allows the individuals participating in the conference to view each other.

- Room-based or 'studio' systems, designed for use by perhaps five participants up to a lecture theatre or even a large conference
- Roll about systems, designed to enable the system to be portable, typically used by small groups
- Desktop-based systems, designed for use by individuals or small groups

Video conferencing is useful whenever there is a clear communication need. The benefits of video conferencing are as follows:

- Reduced travel costs
- Face-to-face rather than telephone meetings
- Better quality teaching
- Easier collaborative working

Price reductions and technological improvements are helping disseminate video-conferencing technology. First, standards have been agreed to, which enable video-conferencing systems to 'talk to each other'. Add to that user-friendliness and segmentation of the systems. Most organizations benefit from a combination of desktop, group, and compact systems. Key people use desktop systems in their offices; conference rooms have group systems for shared use; and compact systems fill in wherever they are needed. Second, integrated services digital network (ISDN) has become more widely available. Third, video-conferencing technologies have managed to compress the amount of bandwidth required for video and enable acceptable quality bandwidth at lower bandwidths.

Video conferencing cuts costs and raises productivity. It also has other applications. At this point, it would be most appropriate to mention Cisco's Telepresence, a video conferencing system that enables collaboration through video meetings and conferences. With this system, launching a meeting is as simple as making a phone call and the participants can meet in many rooms at once—up to 48 locations in one meeting. It is easy to schedule a meeting without information technology (IT) support and it is also easy to integrate the existing video-conferencing systems to integrate with Telepresence. Set up initially by Cisco in 2006, this system mainly aims at linking two physically separated rooms in order to make them resemble one single conference room even though the two rooms may be on opposite sides of the world.

The basic hardware components required to establish a video conference include the following:

- Camera, usually attached to the top of the monitor
- Microphone
- Speakers—even where speakers are built into a workstation, external ones will provide better quality audio; alternatively, headphones may be useful, particularly in a shared office
- Video board, to capture the signal from the camera and convert it to digital form
- Network card, usually an Ethernet card for connection to the LAN or an ISDN card

Video conferencing has the following applications:

*Managing a global company* Video conferencing helps large multinationals operate in truly worldwide environments; it facilitates communications between individual sites, groups, and divisions.

*Facilitating new working practices* Video and data conferencing enable virtual teamwork. Geographically dispersed peer groups, such as engineers or product designers, can be brought together at short notice.

*Access to remote expertise*   Faults in manufacturing facilities can be quickly identified and fixed.

*Increased competitive advantage*   Video conferencing helps achieve faster time-to-market and 'steal a march' on competition.

*Supply chain management*   It fosters effective working relationships among partner companies, suppliers, and customers.

## Web Conferencing

Web conferencing is also called computer conferencing (CC). It usually refers to systems that allow numerous users to connect via a network, send email messages to the conference address, and receive messages posted by other users. Computer conferencing resembles an ongoing discussion in which people drift in and out as per their schedule and interests.

Interactive communication takes place between networked computers in which data are shared. Data may take the form of audio text (conference/bulletin board discussions), email, video conferencing, etc. This type of conferencing can happen in 'real time', which means the messages appear as they are being typed, or they can happen asynchronously with the messages being stored for later use.

Computer conferencing has become very popular in the last decade. This system of communication uses the filing and organizational capabilities of a computer to promote powerful interactions among groups of people. There are several varieties of CC, based on the needs of a group of people being served. These include groups organized by topics (e.g., within a discipline), for specific projects (e.g., research, editing a book), or for the purpose of meeting (e.g., information exchange, support group). These run on many platforms from PCs to mainframes and traverse networks that may be encompassed by the four walls of one room, or extend beyond national boundaries.

Computer conferencing is sometimes referred to as computer-mediated communication (CMC), although this term usually encompasses other technologies, such as text chat and video conferencing. Let us now introduce briefly the two types of computer conferencing that are used widely.

**Bulletin board/message board/online forum/web forum**   These are used to distribute information or to have an online discussion on topics (threads and blogs). Messages are arranged by the thread and remain available as long as desired. Users need to log on to see messages. Microsoft Outlook's public folder facility is an example.

**Email discussion list**   These are used for similar purposes as a bulletin board or web forum, but in this case messages are sent by email (discussed later) to all participants. There may be an archive of messages that can be viewed, sorted by date, author, or thread.

Web conferencing is most commonly used for sales presentations, product demonstrations, training, meetings between geographically dispersed team members, and brainstorming sessions. The following are the advantages offered by web conferencing:

> Web conferencing refers to a service that allows conferencing events to be shared across locations.

*Create virtual teams*   No matter what the geographical distance, Web conferencing can keep the team members linked together. Through a web conference, one can set up team meetings, brainstorming sessions, and new product demos.

*Expedite the decision-making process*   Like telephone conferencing, but with the added demonstration component, web conferencing is good for laying out an idea, building a quick consensus, and making a decision.

*Expedite the close*   Prospects can watch the live demo of a product and ask questions, all in one sitting, without ever leaving their desk. This convenience enables the sales team to immediately address concerns and move the sale along more quickly.

*Decrease costs*   Web conferencing is considerably less expensive than travelling for face-to-face meetings.

A real-time communication, web, or computer conferencing allows users to meet and collaborate while viewing and sharing documents electronically. As more attention is focused on ideas than on the communicators, this channel offers democracy. Considering the fact that people play a more important role than the messages being communicated in organizations, computer conferencing can be a threat to the corporate culture as it emphasizes the messages over the person who communicates them.

Web conferencing is the future of interactive technical communication. Online-enabled voice conferencing, audio conferencing, and web conferencing are making it easier for people in different cities, states, or even countries to communicate easily.

## Instant Messaging

Instant messaging (IM) has acquired a new dimension as a tool for enhancing productivity, fostering team-building efforts, and enabling cost-effective and speedy communication. Although the thought of striking important business deals over IM might be a little far-fetched, this channel is indeed being used to drive complex business deals, interact with project team members, discuss project details, take project approvals, and seek clarifications. Especially in the case of IT software and service companies, where projects need to be managed and delivered across multiple locations, IM tools are gaining popularity as an informal and, more recently, a formal communication channel.

### Growing Acceptance

Take the case of Newgen Software. The company uses a host of IM tools, the most prominent ones being MSN and Yahoo Messenger, for all its formal and informal communications, ranging from discussions and query redressal of employees and clients to fixing up the menu and venues for birthday parties and get-togethers. The communication can be within the company or with outsiders—clients, vendors, dealers, business associates, resellers, etc.

CSC India uses IBM's Lotus Sametime IM tool. Kale Consultants, which has a corporate Intranet with Microsoft NetMeeting embedded as the IM tool, encourages its employees to use it for intra-office communications. In addition to this, a large number of its support staff interacts over publicly available tools such as MSN and Yahoo Messenger.

Infosys uses Microsoft IM based on Microsoft Exchange 2000 Server as a communication tool within the organization to exchange short informal messages. The company, however, does not use it for official purposes. While none of these companies has plans to replace email as the primary channel for both formal and informal communication, the examples testify to the growing acceptability of IM within the corporate culture.

> Organizations with offices at multiple locations are now leveraging IM to keep disparate teams together.

### Building Collaboration

Organizations with offices at multiple locations are now leveraging IM to keep disparate teams together. In addition to this, with projects getting more complex and demanding, IM tools are being looked upon to provide the much needed collaboration to simplify process. The advantages are that it is almost a real-time communication, which is simple and user-friendly. It is also instantaneous, easy to use, cheap, and helps in multitasking and collaboration as many people can chat at the same time with one another.

Instant messaging helps in multitasking

Companies are trying to put the characteristic features of IM to best use to foster better employee relationships and accelerate team-building efforts. This includes posting birthday messages, anniversary wishes, or simply chatting with colleagues. An HR consultant points out that constant communication through IM helps in developing a better understanding at a personal level, thereby helping in building stronger teams. The informality leads to open discussion on matters that one might otherwise be reluctant to discuss in a formal environment.

Organizations have now consciously started using IM as a tool for more collaborative work among project teams and started integrating it with their work process targeted towards improving efficiency and driving down the communication costs. In this light, the use of IM is gaining even more significance. Apart from utilities such as discussing project details, taking project approvals, and client recommendations, IM tools are also becoming a part of other processes such as knowledge management (KM), where it is used for instant knowledge sharing and collaboration.

### IM Clients

At present, communication over IM is mostly informal in nature, as it is still in the early stages of evolution in the professional environment to take on the status of a truly formalized communication tool. Being a form of instant chat, IM is generally meant for informal communication.

Pidgin (formerly known as Gaim) is a multi-protocol IM client for Linux, BSD, Mac OS X, and Windows. It is compatible with AOL's AIM and ICQ (Oscar protocol) IM systems, MSN Messenger, Yahoo!, IRC, Jabber, Gadu-Gadu, and Zephyr networks. Pidgin supports many features of the various networks, such as file transfer, away messages, typing notification, and MSN window-closing notification. It also goes beyond that and provides many unique features. A few popular features are Buddy Pounces, which provide the ability to notify you, send a message, play a sound, or run a program when a specific buddy goes away, signs online, or returns from idle; and plug-in, consisting of text replacement, a buddy ticker, extended message notification, iconify on away, and more.

> Instant messaging allows improved communication and enhanced productivity at the workplace.

Pidgin runs on a number of platforms, including Windows, Linux, and Qtopia. Pidgin users can log in to multiple accounts on multiple IM networks simultaneously. This means that one can be chatting with friends on AOL Instant Messenger, talking to a friend on Yahoo! Messenger, and sitting in an IRC channel all at the same time.

## Advantages

Instant messaging allows improved communication and enhanced productivity in the following ways:

1. As it is instant and real time, the person does not have to wait for responses. It can give a response and receive an acknowledgement from the recipient instantaneously.
2. Being an n-way communication, involving many people makes collaboration possible. It also provides a solution to most queries at the same time by mutual discussion.
3. Files can be transferred online in real time without waiting for receiving emails.
4. As queries are resolved quickly, issues do not remain pending, saving precious time and improving overall productivity.
5. It is a great tool for multitasking. If we are on a phone call, addressing some user, and we get an IM, we can still respond to it.
6. People can see who is online, and so they do not waste time swapping emails or voicemail with people who are not available.

## Disadvantages

Experts feel that all IM tools are good as long as they are deployed within the perimeter of the institute's or company's firewall. As soon as IM is used to communicate with the outside world, there can be a number of challenges. These are as follows:

*Security* The widespread use of public IM tools, such as AIM (AOL Instant Messenger), may well be a security threat waiting to happen. Not only are services such as AIM, MSN Messenger, and Yahoo! Messenger entryways for viruses, but the conversations that take place on these IM applications are also transmitted unencrypted.

*Cross-platform compatibility* As with any consumer IM application, enterprise IM faces the challenge of cross-platform compatibility. Just as AIM cannot send instant messages to MSN Messenger, Lotus Sametime cannot automatically communicate with e/pop.

*Duplication* A high dependency on IM without a mechanism for the parties involved to show documentary evidence of a business transaction could result in duplicate communication, one using IM, backed up by a second one via email.

## Emails

One of the most common forms of exchanging digital messages over computer networks across the world, email has come a long way since its emergence three decades ago. Images 4.4 and 4.5 show the MS Outlook main page and Gmail web page, respectively. Besides being used extensively by almost all sections of the global society for communicating routine and important informal and formal messages, emails are also used for marketing.

Email marketing is a form of direct marketing on the Internet to communicate commercial and fund-raising messages to an audience. The software available for email marketing enables the users to create professional email newsletters, build and manage unlimited email lists, create and send online surveys, and enable them to track emails. Email marketing helps companies in cutting the cost on their marketing expenditure and enables them take their business worldwide.

 Refer to the Online Resource Centre for more on email.

**120** Business Communication

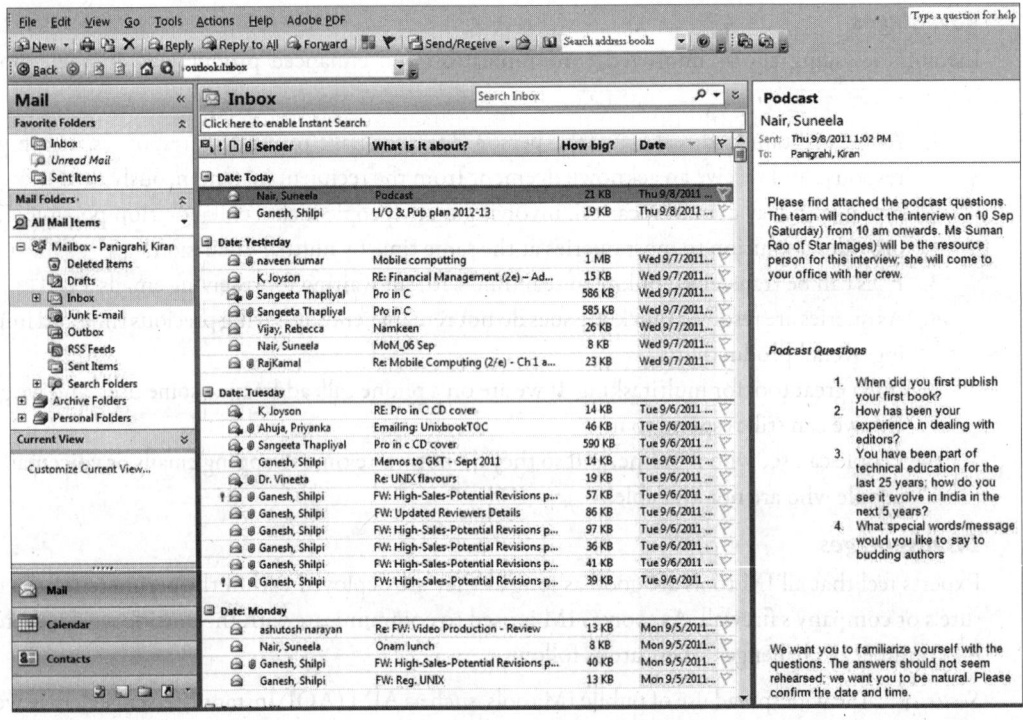

**Image 4.4** MS Outlook

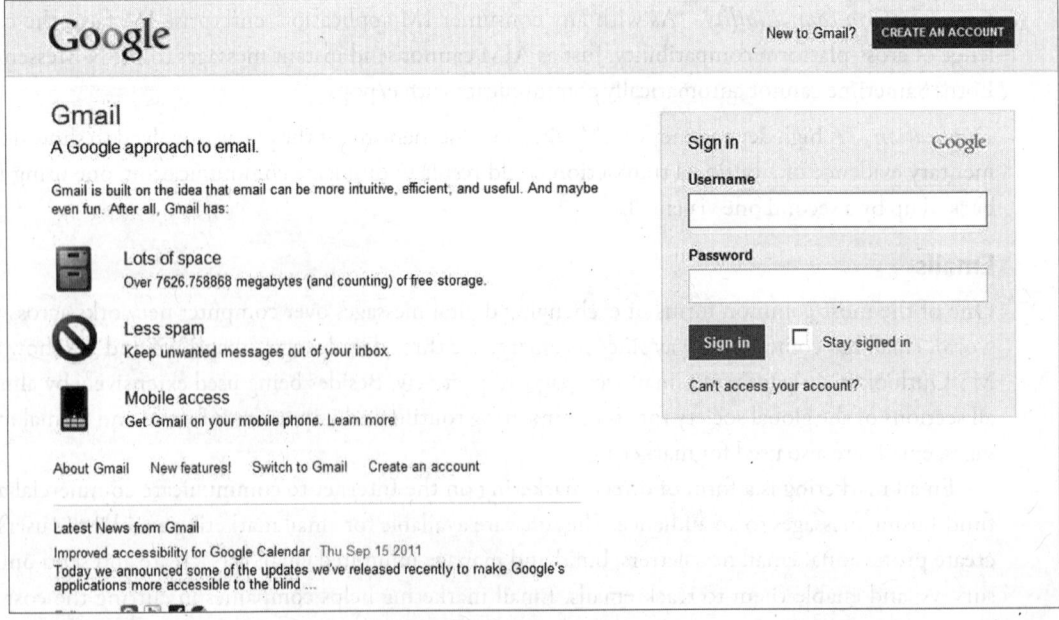

**Image 4.5** Gmail web page

## Groupware

Groupware allows several people to use the same software simultaneously to create documents, keep track of projects, route messages, and manage deadlines. It enables a supervisor to manage workflow via individual computers instead of physically moving people from place to place or having face-to-face meetings.

Groupware is central to the current theories of team-based organizations in which hierarchies are breaking down, allowing teams to work interactively from their individual locations. Groupware represents a basic shift in the communication culture and can be a threat to the traditional work culture that follows norms of privacy, hierarchy, face-to-face meetings, reports, and memos.

Lotus Notes released by IBM in 1989 is a groupware and can be used for many collaborative applications including emails, calendaring, personal information manager (PIM), instant messaging, and web browsing. The current version of Lotus Notes is 8.5, which provides added advancements in building custom software applications. Although it may take many companies a few more years to become comfortable with this new development, companies that want to remain viable and continue to grow will have to make the effort. Novell Groupwise is another Groupware that gives a range of collaborative tools to create a truly connected work environment.

## CD-ROM and DVD-ROM Databases

Compact disc-read only memory (CD-ROM) and digital video (or versatile) disc-read only memory (DVD-ROM) are pre-pressed discs that contain data accessible to but not writable by a computer. CD- and DVD-ROMs—with memory capacities of 194 MB (8 cm) or 650–900 MB (12 cm) and 4.7 GB (single-sided, single-layer), or 8.5–8.7 GB (single-sided, double-layer), or 9.4 GB (double-

---

**BUSINESS COMMUNICATION INSIGHT**

### Email Etiquette

The fact that working people are always short of time has affected modern business communication significantly. Communication these days, especially in the form of email, should be clear and succinct. Thus, it is vital to learn email etiquette.

Since non-verbal signals that are part of phone calls or face-to face meetings are missing in email communication, it is important to organize your views before writing an email.

Always take your time while composing emails and other business communication so as to make sure that they are clearly written. Do consider the following advice:

- Write clear messages; the receiver should not have to guess your meaning.
- Your emails should neither be too short nor too long. Write just enough to make your point.
- Always read your email before sending to make sure it is correct.

Emails drafted carelessly can lead to information overload. It becomes problematic for the receiver to understand poorly composed and grammatically incorrect emails.

Take care to avoid information overload which can happen when you use the 'copy all' option. Some people in the list may be uninterested in the information and find your message irritating.

> Groupware allows several people to use the same software, keep track of projects, route messages, and manage deadlines.

sided, single-layer), or 17.08 GB (double-sided, double-layer—rare), respectively—are used for storing huge amounts of information in a form that is easy to access. Some kinds of information typically found in these formats are encyclopaedias, dictionaries, telephone directories, and articles and abstracts on various subjects. They are popularly used to distribute computer software, including games and multimedia applications.

These discs can store a huge amount of text as well as high-resolution photos and other graphics. Multimedia applications, including video, audio, graphics, and text, are making CD-ROM and DVD-ROM storage of information essential. At the time of its introduction, the CD-ROM had more capacity than computer hard drives at the time. However, this is no longer the case, with the emergence of hard drives (main and external USB) far exceeding CDs, DVDs, and Blu-ray discs (BDs) with capacity up to 128 GB.

## POSITIVE IMPACT OF TECHNOLOGY-ENABLED COMMUNICATION

Today, we live in an increasingly interconnected world. We are more mobile than the previous generation—and that mobility is extending to our data. Process data are routed from the factory floor to the boardroom. A technician can access wireless sensors in remote locations to see what is happening, and an engineer in Bengaluru can troubleshoot an automation problem in Hyderabad while sitting at his/her PC.

Technology has tremendously changed the way companies, professionals, and institutes operate. Phenomenal advancements in computer technology have enabled small as well as huge organizations to communicate more closely and frequently within and outside. In today's technology-driven world, organizations that do not embrace technology may not be able to survive.

Of course, there are many organizations in our nation that still follow the traditional way of communicating, not because they do not realize the importance of technology but because they may not have adequate resources to establish technology-oriented communication networks. Given the resources, every organization would wish to own new technologies, as they have the following advantages:

1. Distance is no longer a major barrier. The importance of personal contact between people has been replaced with face-to-face communication. Communication across the country, or even around the world, has become as easy as communication with the office down the hall.
2. The organizational structure has become more streamlined as managers have increased direct contact with subordinates. Since this also means fewer intermediaries (people who pass messages on), the organization itself is more flattened.
3. More people in an organization have access to more information. This reduces the 'information float'—the rate of information flow—and tends to change the traditional role of managers as primary information sources.
4. The time required to make decisions has decreased because managers have access to increased information resources. The time taken to consider decisions, though, has also decreased because of increased pressure to act quickly.
5. The timelines and quality of information are increasingly important as more people have access to more sources of information. The difficulty is that more information does not necessarily mean better information.

6. The implementation of projects, particularly those depending on communication or involving strict time schedules, has been enhanced.
7. Teamwork in organizations has increased. More people, with a broader range of skills, can provide inputs on projects. In fact, many newer organizational charts are designed around computer links.
8. Finally, as technology increases in scope, managers are required to learn more about the communication process at all levels.

## NEGATIVE IMPACT OF TECHNOLOGY-ENABLED COMMUNICATION

Despite the advantages of an electronic office, technology at work and in communication also creates its own set of barriers—those specifically related to the interactions between people and machines. One such barrier that we can observe in formal communication is technophobia, or the fear of new technology itself. This can be resolved through familiarization and education. Besides technophobia, there are other, more subtle, barriers that can create a negative impact on the parties involved in organizational communication.

### Information Overload

The acceleration of change in society is accompanied by an increase in the volume of information needed to keep up with all these developments. This also leads to psychological, physical, and social problems. A worldwide survey found that two-thirds of managers suffer from increased tension and one-third from ill health because of information overload. Other effects of excessive information include anxiety, poor decision-making, difficulties in memorizing and remembering, and reduced attention span. These effects merely add to the stress caused by the need to constantly adapt to a changing situation.

### Less Time for Organizational Activities

Because of the time spent on checking emails and Internet browsing, the time required for decision-making or problem-solving is curtailed; this trend may lead to increased problems in future.

### Blurring Lines between Professional and Personal Lives

Technology-enabled communication has blurred the lines between the professional and personal lives of many people. For example, with the increased use of mobile phones, just as executives can be disturbed by their family members while they are at an important meeting, they can also be disturbed by their superiors or subordinates while they are on a vacation with their family.

### People Isolation

Technology's isolating effects are easy to observe. Prior to the widespread use of the printing press, people had to congregate and verbally interact with each other in person in order to communicate. With the advent of media technologies, such as record players, televisions, people no longer have to gather together in one place for entertainment. Innovations in telephone services such as voice-mail and caller ID make it possible for people to deliver messages without a personal interface at all.

However, several groups of people who do not have access to recent technologies feel isolated from the privileged lot. For example, there are many promising men and women in India who may not be able to apply for a job advertised on the Internet.

### Overcoming Negative Impact

As the advantages of technology-enabled communication override the limitations, it is appropriate to find some solutions to overcome its negative effects. One strategy to consider is instituting information 'filters'. To cope with volumes of data, email filters can be used to screen out less-than-critical messages and prevent an overwhelming amount of data from being thrown at a person. Deleting one's name from list servers may be another way to limit the influx of email. Likewise, properly managing the usage of mobile phones can reduce the blurring of lines between personal and professional lives.

Simply realizing the fact that computer technology is not the only means of communication would surely enable one to resort to other means of communication, thereby achieving one's predetermined purpose of communication.

## SELECTION OF APPROPRIATE TECHNOLOGY

As already discussed, new technologies have given people a wider range of choices for communication than ever before, and each channel has its uses. Hence, it is important not only to decide as to which communication channel to use, but also when to use each one most effectively.

Each channel has its own advantages as well as drawbacks. It is, therefore, important to identify some parameters to decide the technology that would be most efficient in accomplishing a specific communication goal. The following criteria may be considered for selecting an appropriate communication channel (Fig. 4.2).

**Purpose**  Generally, the purposes for which we communicate in an organization may fall into three major categories—to inform, persuade, and collaborate. For example, as the vice-president of a company, you may like to inform your managers about the company's new set of policies, motivate the managers for better sales, or have discussions with your counterparts in other branches to implement a new marketing strategy.

**Audience**  Adapting oneself or choosing a communication technology to suit the audience is vital for successful communication. Knowing the number, status (designation), composition, possible reactions, level of understanding, relationship, and needs of the audience before selecting a technology for communication purposes is essential. Imagine the impatience and anxiety that can be caused by the delayed response or no response for an email message sent to somebody who does not have easy access to emails.

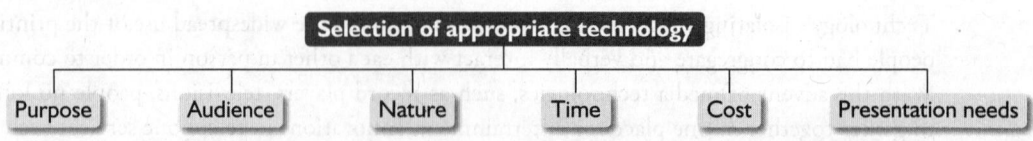

**Fig. 4.2**  Criteria for selecting an appropriate communication channel

**Nature**  Besides the purpose of a message and the type of recipients, there is yet another parameter to be considered for choosing the communication technology—the nature of the message. This can be ordinary, confidential, or even strictly confidential. For example, it would be inappropriate to convey a strictly confidential and sensitive message such as suspending the services of an employee through email.

**Time**  The urgency of a message is also an important factor in selecting a method of communication. For instance, there might be important decisions that have to be quickly communicated to an individual or group concerned. Employees would be happy to receive an email announcing a 10 per cent increase in their DA quickly rather than transmitting the message through the formal channels of communication, such as memos and circulars.

**Cost**  The cost factor has to be given due importance while deciding on a communication technology. For instance, using conventional phone lines is not only expensive but also does not provide several benefits offered by the Internet phone (voice calls made over the Internet). There are many web servers, such as MSN, Yahoo!, and Skype, which are efficient and have made communication very affordable. Hence, it is important to consider the cost of conveying messages.

**Presentation needs**  If a presentation—oral or written—contains complex data, graphs, maps, diagrams, or photographs, one has to carefully select an appropriate technology to present them effectively. For example, visual presentations can be made more effective through animation or colour contrasts, etc. by using any suitable presentation software.

We may not always have the luxury of choosing a technology. However, when we do, it would serve us well to consider all the factors and select the most appropriate means. Table 4.1 presents in a

**Table 4.1**  Factors affecting the choice of technology

| Technology | Nature of Message | Speed of Establishing Connection | Type of Information Conveyed | Time to Receive Feedback | Control over Composing and Delivering | Receivers' Attention | Permanency |
|---|---|---|---|---|---|---|---|
| Email | Formal/informal, routine, non-routine | Fast | Brief, non-complex; text only, no formatting | Delayed/ not always immediate | High | Low | Yes |
| Fax | More formal | Fast | Words, numbers, and images | Delayed | High | Low | Yes |
| Telephone | Formal/informal | Varied | Vocal, not visual | Immediate | Moderate | High | Usually none |
| Voicemail | Mostly personal | Fast | Vocal, not visual | Delayed | High | Low | Possible |
| Teleconferencing | Formal/informal | Slow | Vocal, not visual | Immediate | Moderate | High | Usually none |
| Video conferencing | Formal | Slow | Both verbal and non-verbal messages | Immediate | Moderate | High | Possible |
| Computer conferencing | Formal/informal | Moderate | Text and sometimes visual images | Immediate | Moderate | Low | Possible |

nutshell the various factors that have to be considered before selecting a suitable technology for communication.

## EFFECTIVENESS IN TECHNOLOGY-BASED COMMUNICATION

Like any other activity, technology-based business communication also requires planning before its implementation.

Before starting on a venture, plan for the technology that will be required. Get extra telephone lines if required, purchase and learn how to use a computer, decide how you will/will not use the Internet. Keep in mind that monitoring employees' use of the Internet while at work is not a violation of their right to privacy. Any policy should be in writing and signed by the employees. The appropriate use of technology can make work more efficient and easy from the very beginning.

 **COMMUNICATION TOOL**

**Top 10 Dos and Don'ts When Using Technology-based Communication**

| Dos | Don'ts |
| --- | --- |
| 1. Learn to work on word processing, spreadsheets, writing clear and concise presentations, and emails. | 1. Do not begin work without a basic knowledge about computer tools. |
| 2. Consider using an accounting software program suitable to the work. | 2. Do not overlook making regular external backups of computer files. |
| 3. Consider a laptop if work demands mobility. | 3. Do not overlook the Internet as an important communication tool. |
| 4. Learn the use of digital technology. | 4. Do not purchase more equipment than required for the next two years. |
| 5. Consider using a headset for cordless and cell phones. | 5. Do not spend on a top-of-the-line computer unless it is really required. |
| 6. Plan ongoing internal communications including awards, newsletters, and discussions. | 6. Do not sign up for extended time periods on any service including landlines and mobile phones. |
| 7. When leaving messages, clearly and slowly repeat your name and number. | 7. When tariff plans change, do not overlook to request information on communication plans that more closely meet the new requirements. |
| 8. Use a remote voicemail answering system rather than an answering machine. | 8. Do not fail to exercise rights on return policies within allowed time limits. |
| 9. Use a separate dedicated phone line for business and fax machines. | 9. Do not think that a toll-free telephone number is important unless orders are received by phone. |
| 10. Develop a logo to represent the business on stationery, signs, cards, and websites. | 10 Do not sign up for long-term plans with Internet service providers. |

## SUMMARY

Technology offers innovative ways of improving communication within and between organizations. Businesses that use emerging technologies to create communication solutions and strategies will maintain a competitive advantage. Email and other communication technologies are changing the landscape of business communication. As business communicators, we must be familiar with these technologies. This means understanding the equipment available to us—its advantages and disadvantages. In this context, consider once again the basic communication model. We are in a time marked by the use of new technologies designed to meet traditional communication goals—all intended to increase quality and productivity. These rapid advances in the technology of business communication require both employers and employees to reassess their communication goals as well as their methods of achieving them.

## KEY TERMS

*Audio conferencing* It uses conference calls to bring together clients or colleagues at a moment's notice, or uses audio streaming to simultaneously reach hundreds of individuals across the globe. Regardless of where you and your participants are, an audio conference is just a local or national call away with a telephone network.

*Bulletin board/message board/online forum/web forum* These are used to distribute information or to have an online discussion on topics (threads). Messages are arranged by the thread and remain available as long as desired. Users need to log on to see messages. Microsoft Outlook's public folder facility is an example.

*CD-ROM* It is short for compact disc-read only memory and is a powerful storage device for putting masses of information in a form that is easy to digest. Some kinds of information typically found on CD-ROMs are encyclopaedias, dictionaries, telephone directories, and articles and abstracts on various subjects.

*Desktop* It is the most common type of computer. This computer system should include a basic processing unit, monitor/flat-panel, a modem/Ethernet card, a CD/DVD drive, USB ports, and a printer.

*Email* It lets you send a message to a person without making direct contact or knowing where that person is located. Subscribers to email services are called users, and as a user, you can access messages on your system from your home, office, hotel, or anywhere you happen to be.

*Instant messaging* It is a type of communication service that enables you to create a kind of private chat room with another individual in order to communicate in real time over the Internet. It is analogous to a telephone conversation, but uses text-based, not voice-based, communication.

*Internet* It refers to an international computer network connecting several other networks and computers from companies, universities, etc. It has become a very important business tool, as it is used at a basic level for email and research and can be used at a more comprehensive level as a channel for selling products and services.

*Laptop/notebook* It is a portable computer. A single unit will contain a combination of the capabilities mentioned for the desktop.

*Personal digital assistants* These are units that allow users to synchronize their key organizational elements with their computer. In a very small package, users can have their entire contact list and calendar as well as a list of things to do.

*Technology-based communication tools* These are specific technological tools that can be used for communication. These include telephones, pagers, facsimile machines, computers, and personal digital assistants (PDAs).

*Video conferencing* It is a synchronous conferencing system that takes place in real time between individuals or groups who are usually separated geographically. It can be achieved by adding software and relatively inexpensive hardware to standard desktop computers. Such systems also have the ability to easily incorporate data from other desktop computer applications into the conference.

*Voicemail* It is a high-tech version of the answering machine. It allows users to leave a message at any time of the day or night.

*Web conferencing/computer conferencing* This system allows numerous users to connect via a network, send email messages to the conference address, and receive the postings of others.

## Concept Review Questions

1. Discuss the need for using technology in business communication.
2. Explain the following technology-oriented means of communication used for business purposes: voice-mail, video conferencing, and instant messaging.
3. Discuss in detail the pointers for email effectiveness.
4. What do you understand by computer conferencing?
5. Discuss the various ways in which telephones can be used as a means of communication in organizations.
6. Elaborate on the merits of using technology in business communication.
7. Discuss the negative effects that technology-oriented communication creates in business organizations.
8. Is planning necessary before selecting any particular technology for your business communication? Explain why.
9. Discuss in detail the various criteria necessary to choose an appropriate technology for business communication.
10. Elaborate how information can be transmitted and interchanged effectively by means of technology in organizations.

## Critical Thinking Questions

State whether the medium chosen for communicating each of the following messages is effective or ineffective. Give reasons for your answers. Also identify an alternative channel if you feel that the given channel is ineffective.

1. The managing director of Four Sigma Computers is disgusted by the behaviour of Mr K.N. Gupta, sales representative of the company. Mr K.N. Gupta has misbehaved with a female employee of the company who in turn has lodged a complaint against him. This is not the first time Mr K.N. Gupta has behaved in this fashion. Therefore, he receives a fax message, marked confidential, which gives him the last warning.
2. You have returned from BITS after attending a conference on technical communication. You are excited by your experience and want to share it with your boss. You want to tell him/her all about BITS, the conference, schedule, hospitality, and the utility of such conferences in detail. You send the message to your boss via an email.
3. WIPRO is concerned about the various rumours floating around on the deterioration of the quality of its goods. The Chairman feels that this will have a negative impact on the reputation of the company. Hence, he/she decides to clarify the matter to all the employees in order to remove the misunderstanding. He/she sends circulars to all the branches.
4. As the personnel manager you are apologizing to a customer for a mistake your company has made. You send him/her a fax.
5. The HR manager of a company wishes to complain to the vice chairman about a difficult colleague. He/she chooses to email.

## Projects

1. Read any current magazine on information technology or computers, or search the Internet to identify an article on business communication. Send this article electronically along with your comments to your friend. Ask him/her to send his/her feedback on your communication.
2. Discuss in groups the extent to which technology is being used in India for business communication.
3. Identify the various technologies used in your academic institution/business organization for the transmission of information. Prepare a three-page write up on the various technologies. Use print media or the Internet to get some appropriate illustrations to be included in your write-up.
4. Get prior appointment with a few executives of various small-, medium-sized, and large business

organizations. Find out through discussions what they feel about using technology for business communication. After gathering information from them, share and discuss with your friends.

## REFERENCES

Adler, Ronald B. and Elmhorst J.M. 2002, *Communicating at Work*, Seventh Edn, McGraw Hill Higher Education, NY, p. 371.

Bovee, Courtland L. and John V. Thill 2003, *Business Communication Today*, Seventh Edn, Pearson Education (Singapore) Pte Ltd, Delhi, pp. 364–70.

Guffey Mary Allen 2000, *Business Communication: Process and Product*. Thomson Asia Pte Ltd, Singapore, pp. 59–60.

Lesikar, Raymond V. and Marie E. Flately 2002, *Lesikar's Basic Business Communication*, Eighth Edn, Tata McGraw-Hill, New Delhi, pp. 489–90.

Penrose, Rasberry and Myers 2001, *Advanced Business Communication*, Fourth Edn, Thomson Asia, Singapore, pp. 38–41; 69–72.

http://computersathome.com/gsm/etiquette.html, last accessed on 10 October 2004.

www.letstalk.com/promo/unclecell/unclecell2.htm, last accessed on 05 October 2004.

www.10meters.com/manners.html, last accessed on 12 October 2004.

# PART II
# WRITING BUSINESS MESSAGES AND DOCUMENTS

5. Business Writing
6. Business Correspondence
7. Instructions
8. Business Reports and Proposals
9. Careers and Résumés

CHAPTER 5

# Business Writing

### LEARNING OBJECTIVES

After reading this chapter, you will be able to understand
- the importance of written communication in business
- the various types of business messages
- the direct and indirect approaches to business messages
- the five main stages to writing business messages

## INTRODUCTION

*You have undertaken to cheat me. I won't sue you, for the law is too slow. I'll ruin you.*
*Yours truly,*
*Cornelius Vanderbilt*

One of the most effective business letters ever written contained only 19 words. Composed by the business tycoon Cornelius Vanderbilt, the masterpiece shown above was sent to his business associates who tried to swindle him when he was vacationing in Europe.

In any business, to write and convey your thoughts clearly during a presentation are essential skills that are required for success. If you have positive ideas but are unable to express them, it is very hard to be successful. Writing is crucial to modern organizations as it serves as a major source of documentation. Reports, proposals, procedure manuals, guidelines, business plans, memorandums, letters, emails, circulars, notices, newsletters, websites—all these business documents provide information, persuade readers, establish, strengthen and sustain relationships, and also remain as repositories of information. Good communication skills are one of the most important skills employers look for in a potential employee. Today's technology-driven workplaces expect their managers to compose and edit their own emails, memos, letters, and other documents, though they may take help from their secretaries. No matter what the job, in order for you to be successful, you need to effectively communicate your business messages with your boss, your co-workers, auditors, bankers, and customers. You may have to write business documents to convey routine matters, goodwill messages,

> Writing is crucial to business organizations as it serves as a major source of documentation.

> Written communication is convenient as it can be composed and read when the schedules of the communicators permit and, if necessary, can be reviewed too.

negative messages, or persuasive messages while playing your professional roles. It is necessary that you use the right approach, words, and right style that most suit your message and readers. This chapter enables you to understand the various types of business messages, the most commonly followed approaches to writing these messages, and also the five main stages to accomplish the writing task.

## IMPORTANCE OF WRITTEN BUSINESS COMMUNICATION

Today's world of business is replete with various types of written communication, which is a convenient way for any business to reach across to people within the locality and the neighbourhood, as well as to customers and prospects in other cities. Business messages are so much a part of everyday business that one cannot think of a business without related business messages.

Organizations rely on written communication for many reasons. It provides a permanent record, a necessity in these times of increasing litigation and extensive government regulation. Also, writing out an idea instead of delivering it orally enables communicators to develop an organized, well-considered message. Written documents are also convenient. They can be composed and read when the schedules of the communicators permit, and can also be reviewed, if necessary. Written messages have

---

**BUSINESS COMMUNICATION INSIGHT**

**Reach Your Reader—How to Make Your Letters a Success**

Business letters and emails have the power to win over your reader like no other marketing material can. As soon as you start treating your business correspondence as routine letters, they may lose their personal touch and competitive edge. Keep the following points in mind to make your letters succeed:

**Know your reader**  The first thing you need to consider when writing letters is its reader. What do you want to tell that reader? How does a reader's perspective differ from yours? What impression do you want to leave? And what action do you want the reader to take? Let the answers to these questions determine your tone and how you present your information.

**Know your purpose**  Letters can be sent to confirm or request information, deal with misunderstandings and complaints, and sell new ideas and services to prospects and clients. And your letter's purpose will dictate the best way to organize the message. Before you even start to write, you should think about how the readers will react to the contents of the letter.

**Be concise and specific**  The length of your letters will vary depending on your purpose and the amount of information you need to convey. But regardless of what you need to include, you should always aim for conciseness. In general, experts suggest that all letters should be kept short so that the message is conveyed as effectively as possible. Be as specific as possible and tell the readers only what they need to know.

**Using letters successfully in your future**  Your letters have the potential to build new relationships, win over new business, and establish rapport with your clients—one reader at a time. Regardless of your letter's purpose, a great amount of care should be taken to ensure that the contents are the best they can be.

*Source*: Copp Melinda, 'Reach Your Reader: How to Make Your Letters a Success', http://www.evancarmichael.com/Business-Coach/2714/Reach-Your-Reader-How-to-Make-Your-Letters-a-Success.html, accessed on 23 September 2011. Reproduced with permission.

drawbacks too. They require careful preparation and sensitivity to audience and anticipated effects. Words spoken in a conversation may soon be forgotten, but words committed to hard or soft copy become a public record if conveyed to the media—like the emails that were communicated to the employees of RIL by the Ambani brothers.

'I am personally saddened like all of you at the developments of last two weeks. As already communicated, I will not comment on any issue at this stage and may do so at an appropriate time, if necessary', Anil wrote in an email to RIL employees (*The Hindu Business Line*, 30 November 2004).

Well-written business documents create your image as professional and strong. In other words, a sharp business writing skill is a key to rising to the top.

Choosing the right words and style wins the job interview, lands a new client, or gets a new product approved. Choosing the wrong approach or writing one improper phrase makes a poor impression and kills business. Poor writing can also make a bad impression on clients and funding bodies. Your writing may be the first thing your clients see; it is essential to get it right.

 Refer to the Online Resource Centre for a sample of a bad business letter.

## Types of Business Messages

Most of the written messages in businesses can be classified as positive, negative, neutral, and persuasive (Fig. 5.1).

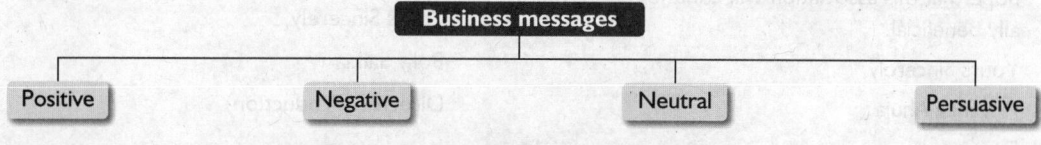

**Fig. 5.1** Types of business messages

**Positive messages or good news messages** These messages convey a positive information that mirrors your goodwill (offering adjustment, expressing appreciation, sending a note of thanks, expressing sympathy, etc.) in order to keep alive the business relationships. Some positive messages are as follows:

> A sales manager of a company offering to replace the desert coolers that the client company received in a bad shape
> 
> The CEO of an MNC sending an appreciation letter congratulating an employee for having been selected in the national football team
> 
> The president of a business writing a note of sympathy to commiserate with a deceased employee's family

**Negative messages or bad news messages** These deliver information that is undesirable or disappointing to readers. These messages may frustrate them. Messages revealing contract denials, job rejection, refusal of a request for an adjustment or credit, etc, come under this category. Some negative messages are as follows:

> A manager (personnel) of a consultancy firm sending a message to the candidate who was rejected for a job in the company

### Positive Message

Home World Interior Decorators
403, Anna Street
Chennai 600041

Purva Gupta
Chief Architect
SeaView Architects
7A, Vasant Vihar
Chennai 600024

14 December 2011

Dear Ms Gupta,

We would like to thank you for recommending your esteemed patrons to our store. You would be happy to note that we have opened two new stores at Spencers and City Centre. Please find enclosed the brochures of the two news stores with this letter.

I take this opportunity to inform you we have enlisted you as our preferred business partner. We hope that this association will continue to be mutually beneficial.

Yours Sincerely,

Priyanka Ahuja
Director

### Negative News

Springfield Textiles
Jafri House, Worli, Mumbai
www.springfieldtext.com

11 January 2012

Kiran Panigrahi
Star Garments
432, Block 7A,
Gurgaon 122001

Dear Mr Panigrahi,

It is with regret that I would like to inform you about the termination of our contract. Even after repeated reminders you have failed to deliver the material on time, and so, as per Clause 15 of our contract we are cancelling the orders that were placed in July this year.

We wish you luck on your company's future endeavours.

Yours Sincerely,

Polly Saikia
Director (Production)

---

A manager (HR) of a business corporation refusing an association's request for a donation

A manager of a bank refusing loan to a university student

**Neutral messages or routine messages** These carry information of equal or even higher importance than positive messages, but their emotional content and involvement is usually lower. Order acknowledgements, inquiries, requests for credit information, personal evaluation, and compliance with requests can be neutral messages. Most of the routine messages may be included under this category. Some neutral messages are as follows:

A government agency responding to a request for a brochure

A manager of a large corporation sending a memo notifying employees of a change in policy

A sales manager sending a weekly sales report to the head office

Although neutral and routine, such messages are of interest to their respective readers because the information the message contains is necessary, among other reasons, for day-to-day operations.

**Persuasive messages or influential messages** These try to motivate their readers to agree with the senders or to make them act in a desired way. As a businessperson you may need to influence your superior to adopt a particular proposal, your supplier to replace a defective product, or a prospective customer to buy your new product. Some persuasive messages are as follows:

## Routine Letter

Madura Ceramics
22, Grant Road
Bangalore 560095

04 April 2012

S. Srivatsan
Sree Ambica Agencies
Vinayaka Nagar
1st Main, Bangalore 560030

Dear Mr Srivatsan,

We are organizing a corporate social responsibility seminar for our vendor associates on 19 May 2012 at our corporate headquarters. As you are aware, this is an annual event that helps in creating awareness among our extended team.

Please send us the final list of participants by 20 April 2012.

Yours Sincerely

Kavita Phookan

CSR Manager

## Persuasive Message

The Association of Physiotherapists
270/40 Lake View, Kolkata 700045
Email: contact@physioasso.org

10 October 2011

Dr Shilpi Ganesh
HOD, Physiotherapy Dept
AIIMS Hospital, New Delhi 110022

Dear Dr Ganesh,

Your article in the August issue of *The Indian Medical Journal* on the need of developing soft skills in practicing physiotherapy struck a cord with the members of our association.

We are interested explore this area further to know more about soft skills, and your expert opinion would be a big help in persuading our members to include this aspect in their profession. We would like to invite you to be our guest presenter at our annual conference to be held at St Joseph's Auditorium at 6:00 p.m., Friday, 16 December.

We would reimburse you for transportation, hotel accommodation at the Orchid Hotel for the night of the 16th, and any other expenses associated with your presentation to our group.

As the programme for the annual conference must go to the printer on 7 November, we'd appreciate receiving your decision by the 1 November. Please send me an email to let me know.

The Association of Physiotherapists would be glad to hear your presentation on 16 December.

Yours Sincerely,

Asmita Mallik

Vice President

A publishing company sending a brochure of the latest edition of its book on business communication to all management institutions

An advertising firm sending a proposal in response to the demand from a bank for a nationwide advertisement campaign

A marketing manager writing a memo report containing her/his recommendations for introducing some changes in the existing marketing strategies

 Refer to the Online Resource Centre for more samples.

## DIRECT AND INDIRECT APPROACHES TO BUSINESS MESSAGES

There are two available approaches for writing a business message, namely direct and indirect approach.

### Direct Approach

Most business messages are written using the direct approach. Under this approach, a sender's primary objective agrees with that of his/her receiver's, that is, a sender transmits a message that the recipient

> - The direct approach to business messages is also known as the deductive approach.
> - Messages with negative information or persuasive content are often the most difficult to write.

is looking for or requires. For example, if you are writing to inform, use this approach. The direct approach immediately and clearly presents the most significant or most important thought. Additional thoughts follow by order of importance. When a reader is expected to be pleased, mildly interested, or neutral, start with the main point and then follow through with details. In other words, when the purpose of the message is to convey routine information and the analysis of the audience indicates that the reader will probably be interested in its contents, use a direct approach in preparing the message. The direct approach is also known as the deductive approach, in which the main idea such as a recommendation, conclusion, or request is stated first and then is followed by any needed explanation, which is followed by a friendly closing.

You can use this approach to convey positive information that pleases your readers, neutral messages that may not elicit either a positive or negative reaction but may have a strong information value, and negative messages that your readers will not want to read. The positive messages you deliver will greatly vary from extremely positive ('You are appointed.') to only slightly positive ('Here is our order for this month.'). The more positive your message is, the more positive your language should be, and vice versa.

## Indirect Approach

An indirect approach refers to a style of writing in which a message is conveyed to a reader not immediately, but only after an explanation. Under this approach, you do not reveal the main idea until after you have offered an explanation and some evidence. In other words, you explain your reasons for saying 'no' before you say 'no'. Most of the negative messages and persuasive messages use the indirect approach, which is also known as the inductive approach. Here, the evidence comes first, and the main idea comes later.

If positive messages with direct approach are among the easiest to write, then those with negative information or persuasive content are among the most difficult. The difficulty of writing a negative message stems from its twin objectives—to transmit the bad news clearly and to maintain the reader's goodwill. Persuasive messages too use the indirect approach because they try to overcome the reader's resistance. The indirect approach eases your audience into your message by explaining your reasons before delivering the bad news. Presenting the reasons first increases your chances of gaining audience acceptance by gradually preparing readers for the negative news to come.

A few sample messages (excerpts) written using both direct and indirect approaches are given in the box.

### Direct Approach vs Indirect Approach

**Direct approach**

- Congratulations! Your proposal for our nationwide advertising campaign is right on target. You have clearly foreseen the market value in terms of our customers in the northern region as per our expectations. We are adopting your proposal immediately.
- Thank you again for taking charge of the difficult task of meeting the two parties in my absence and doing an excellent job. Within just an hour's notice,

> you managed to pull the two relevant heads of the parties so that they could also present their views. I have noted your dedication and communication abilities and truly appreciate your efforts.
> - The Elegant Flyover Project report was due yesterday. We both know how important the completion of report is to the overall strategic plan. Submit the report to me no later than 5 p.m. today.
>
> **Indirect approach**
> - Applicants other than you, ones with equally solid educational background but extensive consulting background, have been selected to be interviewed.
> - Our department shares your goal of processing orders quickly and efficiently. But we may find it difficult to spare two employees today as we have been asked to complete the assignment related to Quality Enterprises by this evening itself.
> - We consider it as a golden opportunity to design this publicity campaign for a reputed organization like yours. You may find our proposal in order with all your requirements. We would feel ourselves fortunate if you accept this proposal.

## FIVE MAIN STAGES OF WRITING BUSINESS MESSAGES

Figure 5.2 identifies the five major stages involved in writing effective business messages.

### Prewriting

This is the planning stage in which you think through your writing assignment and develop a plan for accomplishing it. During the prewriting stage, you should

- determine your purpose,
- know your readers,
- search and collect data for your message, and
- organize and prepare an outline.

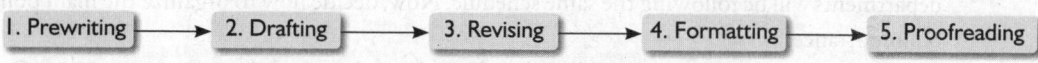

**Fig. 5.2** Five stages of writing business messages

**Determining your purpose** There are many different reasons for writing a business message. Reporting information, requesting payment, inviting some proposals, asking for an advice, assuring cooperation, recommending changes—any of these may serve as a valid purpose for writing a business message. For example, on any given day, a person at work probably writes a combination of emails, memos, and letters, such as informing employees about their health insurance coverage or answering a co-worker's question about a project via email, or writing a letter to a customer. Each one of these messages has a different purpose.

To help organize your thoughts, it is important to put together a purpose statement, 'The purpose of this memo is to ...' and then fill in the rest of the sentence. Using the examples listed earlier, you could surely put together the following two purpose statements:

> The purpose of this memo is to inform employees about the change in health insurance coverage.
>
> The purpose of this letter is to apologize to a customer.

> A persuasive message is more successful if it appeals directly to the wants and needs of its reader.

**Keeping your readers in mind** A message needs to convey information that is required by its target readers. Therefore, a message needs to be positioned from its readers' perspective. The target audience is important. For example, a persuasive message is more successful if it appeals directly to the wants and needs of its reader.

> It is necessary to collect and organize all the supporting points during the prewriting stage.

The tone in your writing reflects how a reader feels after reading a message. If the words in the message are demanding, authoritative, and harsh, the reader is going to react with anger or refusal to cooperate. Quite often one sees this type of writing coming from the top brass of an organization. The management is in charge, so it often tends to write from a position of power where the phrasing of the message is from its own viewpoint, not its reader's viewpoint, forcing the reader to develop an anti-authority stance.

**Appealing to your audience** Unless you make an effort to connect with your audience, chances are that your message is not going to be communicated correctly. The best way to connect is to create a positive tone in your writing by using the reader's point of view. Emphasize what the reader wants to know, not what you can do for the reader. Completely change your mindset from 'I' to 'you'. Instead of saying, 'I will allow you to take a vacation beginning June 1', say, 'Your vacation will start on June 1'. This is the difference between writing in the 'I-viewpoint' versus the 'you-viewpoint'. Notice how it also gets the reader involved in the message.

The key to keeping a reader's interest is getting the reader involved in the message. Do not just think about what you are going to say, think about how what you are saying is going to affect your listener.

**Organizing and preparing an outline** In order to get started on writing business messages, an outline of where one wants to head with it is needed. Start by making a list of the main points. Assume that you are writing a memo telling your employees that, during the summer season, the company will be working extended hours. This is your purpose. Some of the main points might be—working a 7–10 schedule will decrease the company's utility costs, childcare services will be available on-site, and all departments will be following the same schedule. Now, decide how to organize the main points based on importance.

The main points are organized based on how the audience might react to a message. During the prewriting stage, it is necessary to collect and organize all the supporting points also. For example, consider Fig. 5.3. Here, you need to collect all details related to each of the four main points of the

**Fig. 5.3** Mind map—employee behaviour subject to disciplinary action

**Table 5.1** Topical outline—employee behaviour subject to disciplinary action

| 1. Unsatisfactory Work Performance | 2. Violation of Safety Rules | 3. Insubordination | 4. Absence from Work |
|---|---|---|---|
| 1.1. Inability to meet deadlines | 2.1. Indifference | 3.1. Insolence | 4.1. No prior information |
| 1.2. Poor quality output | 2.2. Inadequate knowledge | 3.2. Hostility | 4.2. Backlog of work |
| 1.3. No initiative | | | |

> Good business writing should be concise and to the point.

business message, which is employee behaviour subject to disciplinary action. You can prepare a complete outline as shown in Fig. 5.3 or Table 5.1 before you proceed to draft your business message.

### Drafting

Drafting implies writing one or more rough versions of a message before it is finalized.

To make sure your message is well understood, you need to be clear and not ramble when writing a message. To prepare a good draft, you need to find the right balance of words and the right words for the balance.

**Right balance** Good business writing is concise and to the point. The shorter the sentences and paragraphs, the more likely the message would be understood. Studies have shown that as a sentence or paragraph becomes longer, comprehension starts dropping. Table 5.2 illustrates this point.

The first step towards a right balance of words is to separate your thoughts by writing short sentences. Do not try to string everything together using clauses like and, but, and however. For example, read the following sentence:

> It has come to my attention that the second Thursday of the month is the best opportunity for development to meet with management to review the latest technology advances being made by our competitor and the ways our company is prepared to deal with this direct attack on our company vision of always being the first to introduce products that improve the lives of consumers and make it easier for them to use everyday business products like their computers, PDAs, scanners, faxes, and photo copiers.

It is 85 words and totally off the scale of comprehension. Some words need to be eliminated.

**Right words** Now that we have our basic ideas in place, we need to formulate the above unclear sentence into a logical, concise paragraph using short sentences. Here is what to write instead:

'Starting from June 2012, the Product Management team will meet on the second Thursday of every month from 1 to 3 p.m. in room H-108. The topic of discussion for the June meeting will be the recent technological advances made by our competitor.'

Now, it is a 44 word paragraph consisting of two sentences. The first sentence is 26 words and the second sentence is 18 words. According to Table 5.2, the first sentence is a little long. However, every piece of information in that sentence is important for the understanding of the readers. So, let us break it up into two sentences as follows:

**Table 5.2** Relation between sentence length and comprehension

| Sentence Length (in Words) | Comprehension Rate (in %) |
|---|---|
| 8 | 100 |
| 15 | 90 |
| 19 | 80 |
| 28 | 50 |

The Product Management team will meet on the second Thursday of every month. The first meeting is on 9 June 2012, from 1–3 p.m. in room H-108. The topic of discussion will be the recent technological advances made by our competitor.

Now, it is a 42 word paragraph consisting of three sentences. The first sentence has 13 words. The second sentence has 15 words. The third sentence has 14 words. Notice how just these few changes made all the difference in reading comprehension.

It is important to get used to counting words when putting a message together. It may be the easiest trick to communicate effectively. Only essential words should be used to get the message across to the reader. Following are some strategies to help us find the right balance and words in drafting a business message.

*Redundancies* As good writing should be to the point, the fewer words you use, the more likely your message will be understood. Why 10 words should be used, when five words can get the message across? There seems to be a misconception that business writing needs to sound formal. People want to use fancy language to impress the reader. However, wordiness is not only irritating to a reader, it is also confusing and the message becomes unclear.

Sometimes, redundancies are easily spotted, and at other times, you really have to look hard to find them because redundancies are common in spoken English. Let us take a look at the following two sentences:

Kiran realized the possible potential that foreign imports had on her country's economy.
Mohan also included a ₹25,000 expenditure on the Humane Society Proposition.

Can you identify the redundancies? In the first sentence, eliminate 'possible' and 'foreign'. In the second sentence, eliminate 'expenditure'. Instead say, 'Mohan also included ₹25, 000 for the Humane Society Proposition.'

> Avoid using too many words to express simple, unimportant, or obvious ideas.

Let us now consider the following sentences:

It is absolutely necessary for all employees to refer back to our procurement manual when writing purchase orders.

If at all possible, our end-of-year annual report needs to be mailed out by 15 June 2012.

Past history has shown us that advance warning is necessary.

It was an unexpected surprise to find out that true facts were included in the article.

Mr Edwards did not hesitate to give his personal opinion to the reporter.

The redundancies are as follows:

absolutely, back          unexpected, true
at all, end-of-year       personal
past, advance

Avoid using too many words to express simple, unimportant, or obvious ideas. Table 5.3 illustrates a few more examples.

*Opening fillers* You can also reduce wordiness by carefully constructing the beginning of your sentences. Try not to use the phrases such as 'there is' or 'it is' to start a sentence. These words are commonly referred to as fillers because they do not add meaning to the sentence. Starting your sentence without a filler creates a more powerful and concise sentence. Look at the fillers in the following sentences:

There are four different proposals I want you to review before our next meeting.

It is company policy that prevents us from contributing to political campaigns.

The above sentences have been reworked and made concise as follows:

Please review these four proposals before our next meeting.

Company policy prevents us from contributing to political campaigns.

**Table 5.3** Sentences reworked to be concise

| Wordy | Concise |
|---|---|
| Sale of surplus tappers is one of our primary needs. (10) | Our surplus tappers must be sold. (6) |
| This manual of instructions was prepared to aid our dealers in being helpful to their customers. (16) | This instruction manual was prepared to help our dealers serve their customers. (12) |
| It is the responsibility of our Production Department to see that it meets the requirements of Sales Division's requirements. (19) | Our Production Department must meet the requirements of our Sales Division. (11) |
| The collision had the effect of a destructive force on the duplicator. (12) | The collision destroyed the duplicator. (5) |
| We have enclosed a pamphlet which shows further details of construction on page four. (14) | Page four of the enclosed pamphlet shows further construction details. (10) |
| Three days ago you asked us to investigate the problem of discomfort among your office workers... We have conducted our study. Too low humidity is apparently the main cause of your problem. Your building is steam-heated; therefore, your solution is to... (41) | Too low humidity is apparently the cause of your workers' discomfort. Since your building is steam-heated, your solution is to... (21) |

A business message becomes easier to read and understand if familiar but unnecessary phrases that just clog up a sentence are eliminated. Depending on the context, one can decide which phrases are not needed. Let us take a look at the following examples:

Because of the degree of classroom participation the school will win the contest.
Except for the instance of TCS, tech stocks lost 30 per cent or more in the last quarter.
The dealership's cars are noted for being excellent in quality.

Eliminating unnecessary words from the above sentences improves readability as follows:

Because of classroom participation, the school will win the contest.
Except for TCS, tech stocks lost 30 per cent or more in the last quarter.
The dealership's cars are noted for being excellent.

*Hedging and emphatic words*   Writing balanced statements is difficult. If you use too many qualifiers, your statement is ineffective; too many extremes, and your writing becomes dogmatic. Using too many words from either category will tell your reader that (a) there was no purpose to the communication, or (b) you did not do your research before writing. Check your writing for hedging and emphatic words (Table 5.4), and eliminate most of them.

*Removing nouns*   Your message can become confused and lengthy when you use a wordy noun phrase instead of a verb. For example, instead of using the phrase, 'give consideration to', use the verb 'consider'. By doing this, you will not only reduce the number of words in your sentence, but also convey a direct message that is easier to understand. Some common noun phrases and their verb replacements are as follows:

make a discovery of (discover); perform an analysis of (analyse); take action on (act); create a reduction in (reduce); engage in preparation (prepare); etc.

*Compound prepositions*   It is easy to replace compound prepositions with single words by simply asking yourself, 'Would I talk like this?' Most people do not use wordy phrases when speaking, so it is easy to identify them in one's writing.

**Table 5.4**   Hedging and emphatic words

| Hedging Words | | Emphatic Words | |
|---|---|---|---|
| often | in some respects | always | central |
| usually | might | undoubtedly | cardinal |
| perhaps | can | everyone knows/agrees | basic |
| almost | may | it is obvious that/certain | primary |
| that | could | the fact is | essential |
| possibly | attempt | indisputable | fundamental |
| virtually | seek | indeed | principal |
| apparently | hope | certainly | the rule is |
| seemingly | tend | clearly | common knowledge |
| in some ways | try | it is true that | absolute |
| to a certain extent | | | generally agreed |
| sort of | | | known conclusion |
| somewhat | | | |

Some compound prepositions and their shorter forms are as follows:

> despite the fact (although); for the amount of (for); the manner in which (how); until such time as (until); at a later date (later); etc.

*Trite business phrases*   Clichés and trite expressions are perhaps the most overused expressions in business writing. These tired expressions make you look like a very dull writer. Most people use them because everyone else does and it is easier than trying to think of an original way of expressing oneself. So, you write, 'Please do not hesitate to' instead of, 'Please' or 'Enclosed please find' instead of, 'Enclosed is'. Some more examples of trite phrases and the corrected version are as follows:

> every effort will be made (we will try); thank you in advance (thank you); under separate cover (separately); with reference to (about); pursuant to your request (at your request); etc.

*Use conversational style*   It is also more interesting to read a business message written in a conversational style that is warm and friendly, but not chatty. You want your business message to be professional, but not formal. In fact, you can test out your writing by asking yourself, 'Do I talk like this?' If the answer is no, you are probably trying too hard to make it sound formal. Instead, aim to make it professional and friendly.

> **Business writing should be conversational in tone and tailored to the audience and the subject.**

Business writing should be informal writing. It should be conversational in tone and tailored to the audience and the subject. But instead of writing conversationally, many business writers lapse into the stiff and stilted verbiage of the late nineteenth century and early twentieth century. That was when business letter writing, especially, reached a stylistic high. Many of the words and phrases used then (which today are considered clichés) still stubbornly show up in business communications, especially letters. Following are some of the clichés; try and see how many of these you have used:

> this is to inform you ..., I am in receipt of your recent ..., enclosed please find ..., please be advised ..., enclosed herewith ..., trusting to hear from ..., thanking you in advance, I remain ..., I appreciate your timely response ..., you may deem it advisable ..., may I take the liberty of ...

*Tailoring language for the reader*   In selecting the exact tone and words to use, rely on the relationship with the reader. Approach business writing as you would approach a face-to-face conversation. Think of your writing as talking on paper, and select the language level that fits the reader, subject, and requirements of the communication. Ask yourself the following:

> Have I expressed my ideas so that the reader will feel that I am helpful, courteous, and human?
> Have I tailored my message to my reader's desires, problems, circumstances, and probable reactions?
> Have I emphasized 'you', the reader, instead of 'I' or 'we'?
> Have I expressed my ideas so they reflect good public relations for the company (letters) or good human relations with my colleagues (reports)?
> Have I stressed the positive and avoided emphasizing ideas my reader may view unfavourably?

Refer to Tables 5.5–5.10 to see how effective business messages can be created through well-written sentences.

**Table 5.5** Sentences reworked to be accessible and direct

| Excessive, Overwritten | Accessible, Direct |
|---|---|
| The defendant is renowned as a person of intemperate habits. He is known to partake heavily intoxicating beverages. Further, he cultivates the company of others of the distaff side, and wholly, regularly, and consistently refuses and abstains from earnest endeavours to gain remuneration. | The defendant drinks, chases other women, and refuses to work. |
| The choice of exogenous variables in relation to multi-collinearity is contingent upon the derivations of certain multiple correlation coefficients. | Supply determines demand. |

**Table 5.6** Sentences reworked to be polite

| Tactless | Tactful |
|---|---|
| You neglected to take care of the requirements of form 123. | To enjoy the full benefits, of your new ABC, simply follow the procedures outlined on form 123. |
| We want our cheque. | To keep your account in the preferred customer class, send our cheque for ₹ ... today. |

**Table 5.7** Sentences adapted to reader requirements

| Flat Detail | Detail Adapted to Reader Need |
|---|---|
| This cookware is guaranteed to withstand temperature changes. | Because XYZ Cookware can withstand extreme changes in heat and cold, you can safely move any piece from your freezer to your microwave. |

**Table 5.8** Sentences reworked to focus on readers

| 'We' Attitude | 'You' Attitude |
|---|---|
| We are happy to have your order. We shipped it this morning. | You will receive your solid walnut desk by Tuesday, 23 October. |
| We regret that you have had so much trouble with our product, and we apologize for not solving your problem sooner. | You were right to ask me about the troubles you have been having with your new car. Thank you for this opportunity to answer your questions. |

**Table 5.9** Sentences reworked to show positive attitude

| Poor Attitude | Good Attitude |
|---|---|
| You must remember that we have more responsibility here at CEC than worrying about someone's fingers getting caught in some machine. | I have asked Mr Jeevan Singh, a safety consultant from Health Enterprises, to investigate and suggest possible procedure and machine modifications. |
| It is hardly possible that our trigger could have misfired without some contributing cause; nevertheless to help out those who lack technical know-how, a company as responsible as Creative Guns can gladly replace the trigger you have. | To prevent your gun from misfiring again, we will gladly replace the trigger you have. |

**Table 5.10** Sentences reworked to be positive

| Negative | Positive |
|---|---|
| I regret to inform you that your admission to candidate status has been delayed until you complete the following requirements. | Before you are admitted to candidate status, you will need to complete the following requirements. |
| On 3 March 2012, we sent you the accidental injury forms and requested that you return them to the Health Center. It is now 27 March 2012, and we have not yet received your reply. | To receive your cheque from Employee Insurance, please file the accidental injury form we sent you on 3 March 2012. |

## Revising

In most cases, your first draft may well be your final draft because you may not often have time to do any additional work on the document. Many businesspersons give a final shape to their business documents just on the day on which they are expected to send the document—be it a report, proposal, or letter. However, it is advisable to review your business messages carefully after completing your first draft.

Revising is the process of modifying a document to increase its effectiveness. Once you have the raw material—your first draft—in front of you, you can refine it into an effective document, considering its importance and the time constraints under which you are working. Look at each word. Is it the right one? Would another one be more precise? Are there better, more concise ways of structuring the sentence? Did you say what you mean? Could someone read other meanings into the words? Is the chosen organization the best for your situation? Be your own critic. Challenge what you have done. Look for alternatives. Then, after conducting a thorough and critical review, make any changes that you think will improve the draft. Input from others can also help you refine your writing. It is often difficult to find errors or weaknesses in your own work; yet others seem to find them easily. Receive criticism with an open mind; objectively evaluate it so that your draft benefits from it. In short, revise your document for content, clarity, conciseness, vigour, and readability by using the right words in the right context and with the right tone.

Table 5.11 helps you check whether your business message has been structured appropriately.

**Table 5.11** Appropriate structures for business messages

| Message Type | Opening | Body | Close |
|---|---|---|---|
| Direct requests | Request or main idea | Provide necessary details | Close cordially and state specific action desired |
| Routine, good news, and goodwill messages | Main idea or good news | Provide necessary details | Cordial comment, a reference to the good news, or a look towards the future |
| Bad news messages | Buffer/neutral statement that acts as a transition to the reasons of the bad news | Give reasons to justify a negative answer; state or imply the bad news, and make a positive suggestion | Close cordially |
| Persuasive messages | Statement or question that captures attention | Arouse the audience's interest in the subject. Build the audience's desire to comply | Request action |

## *Formatting*

In business, no one format for any type of business document is universally accepted as standard; a fair amount of variation is common. However, the success of a communication surely depends on the packaging of its ideas. The first thing the readers notice about a message is generally its appearance. An interesting message definitely gets noticed more. The messages in Amul butter advertisements are a case in point. You can see the most commonly adopted formats for different types of business documents in Chapters 6 and 8 that discuss them at length.

To some extent, technology is changing the formatting standards. For example, although formatting is traditionally the next-to-last step in the writing process, you may in fact, make some formatting decisions at the planning or drafting stages. You may, set your word processing program with default side margins of 1 or 1.25 inches, which are appropriate for most documents.

Use a variety of design elements, such as white space, margins, line justification, typefaces, and type styles to make your message look professional, interesting, and up-to-date. However, be careful not to overdo.

Email messages all look like memoranda—whether they are sent to someone inside or outside the organization. They typically contain elements such as to, from, subject, date, etc., just as memorandums do, and they do not contain any inside address as is typical of letters. The important point is to use the format that is appropriate for each specific message.

Regardless of who actually types your documents, you are the one who signs and submits them, so you must accept the responsibility for not only the content, but also the mechanics, format, and appearance of your documents. Moreover, the increasing use of word processing means that executives now create/type many of their own documents—without the help of an assistant.

## *Proofreading*

Proof reading in a kind of reading for detecting typographical errors in a printed text. Some tips for proofreading your business messages are as follows:

1. Do not try to proofread a document by reading it on your computer screen. Read from a printed copy.
2. Proofread your message only after you have composed its first draft.
3. Leave double space between lines in the text so that it is easier to read, because the added space helps your eyes rest between all the text.
4. Take time to proofread. When you are rushed, you cannot do a good job of proofreading.
5. Reading your message aloud is a great technique for finding errors in construction.
6. The final look should be for capitalization, spelling mistakes, and numbers used in sentences. Double-check all the proper names because it is so easy to misspell a person's name.

It does take added time to proofread a business message, but it is well worth your time. Remember every single piece of written correspondence you send out is a representation of your business. The errors you missed will be quite obvious to the reader; so, proofread for the finishing touch. Some common proof reading symbols are displayed in Table 5.12.

Now even a single aberrant comma shall not escape my eye.

Table 5.12 Communication tool—proofreading symbols

| Symbol | Meaning | Example |
|---|---|---|
| ⌐ | Delete | Cancel this wr8ong order |
| ⌒ | Close up | He is w⌒orthy |
| ¶ | Begin a new paragraph | ¶ Roshan began his career in … |
| (cap) or ≡ | Set in CAPITALS | Set wto as Wto |
| (rom) or ⊬ | Set in roman | Set *writing* as writing |
| (ital) or __ | Set in *italics* | Set business communication as *business communication* |
| ∧ | Comma | However∧ this is |
| :̂ | Colon | The various factors are:̂ |
| ∨ | Apostrophe | This is Ragini∨s laptop |
| ⌒= | Hypen | Multi⌒=talented personality |

## SUMMARY

Most businesses communicate through technology, however, traditional skills needed for effective writing still reign supreme in today's business organizations. Writing different types of business messages demands different approaches. While a direct approach is used for conveying business messages that are positive or neutral in nature, an indirect approach is used to express negative or persuasive messages. Of course, business messages that take care of their readers are seen to be more effective. There are five major stages in preparing business messages—prewriting, drafting, revising, formatting, and proofreading. Each of these stages is important in its own respect. By adopting strategies appropriate to each stage, it can be ensured that business documents appear concise, clear, correct, complete, and courteous. Business documents should reflect the values and standards of an organization whose products and services they market. Prospects may not read beyond the first few lines if a business document lacks clarity, succinctness, and impact. A polished presentation can make the difference between a business that flourishes and one that falters or even fails.

## KEY TERMS

***Business messages*** These are messages written in the form of letters, memos, reports, proposals, newsletters, etc. to achieve several business goals.

***Direct approach*** It refers to a style of business writing in which information is conveyed to a reader directly, using no extended prelude.

***Drafting*** It is the second stage in preparing business messages. After collecting necessary information, it is appropriately organized and the first draft of a business message is written, keeping in mind the principles of effective writing.

***Formatting*** It refers to the way you package your ideas before sending it to your reader.

***Indirect approach*** It refers to a style of business writing in which information is conveyed to a reader not immediately, but after an explanation.

**Negative messages** These are messages that deliver information that is undesirable or disappointing to the readers.

**Neutral messages** These are messages that carry information of equal or even higher importance than positive messages, but their emotional content and involvement is usually lower.

**Persuasive messages** These are messages that try to motivate their readers to agree with the senders or to make them act in a desired way.

**Positive messages** These are messages that convey a positive information that mirrors your goodwill in order to keep alive the business relationships.

**Prewriting** It is the planning stage in which you think through a writing assignment and develop a plan for accomplishing it.

**Proofreading** It is an essential part of rewriting and a careful review of the final draft of your business message.

**Revising** It refers to the third stage in business writing. It is the process of modifying a document to increase its effectiveness.

## Concept Review Questions

1. Why do business organizations give importance to written communication?
2. Discuss the two approaches to writing business messages with suitable examples for each.
3. If you wish to convey a negative message to your business customer, which approach you would choose and why?
4. Discuss briefly the four factors you need to consider at the planning stage of business writing.
5. Why is 'revising' considered as an essential step to preparing business messages?

## Critical Thinking Questions

1. Write a clear and effective business message of about 100 words for each of the following situations:
    (i) The CEO of a company has recently moved his/her residence to a nearby locality. On his/her behalf you, as the personnel manager, draft a message to be sent to your counterparts in other divisions.
    (ii) The vice president of a business firm is impressed by the report submitted by her sales manager. Hence, she sends an email appreciating the efforts of the manager.
    (iii) You are the senior manager, HR, of your company. You are away from Mumbai for an important conference in Delhi. Just the day before you plan to return, you receive an important assignment at Dehradun. Now draft a message to be sent to the chairman of your company.
2. Critically analyse the following websites:
    (i) http://www.infosys.com
    (ii) http://www.bits-pilani.ac.in
    Give your comments on the following:
    Home page, headings, navigation to hyperlinks, use of colour, highlighting techniques, and reader friendliness.
    What changes, if any, would you recommend?
3. Revise the following business messages so as to make them simpler, more concise, and effective:
    (i) The expectations of the chairman for a stock dividend were accentuated by the preponderance of evidence that the company was in good financial condition.
    (ii) After a trial period of three weeks, during which time she worked for a total of 15 full working days, we found her work was sufficiently satisfactory so that we offered her full-time work.
    (iii) It seems as if this letter of resignation means you might be leaving us.
    (iv) It would be greatly appreciated if every employee would make a generous contribution to the bereaved family of Mr Mayank Sharma.

(v) It is imperative that the pay increments be terminated before an inordinate deficit is accumulated.
(vi) Following the government task force report recommendations, we are revising our job applicant evaluation procedures.
(vii) The production department quality assurance program components include employee training, supplier cooperation, and computerized detection equipment.
(viii) It is our suggestion that you do not attempt to move forward until you seek and obtain approval of the plan from the team leader prior to beginning this project.

## Projects

1. Review and reinforce your grammar and language skills by visiting the following websites and taking the tests and quizzes offered at these sites. Then focus on those areas of the English language where you are weak with a view to improve your business writing skills.
   (i) www.4tests.com
   (ii) www.ManyThings.org
   (iii) http://a4esl.org/
   (iv) http://www.usingenglish.com/quizzes/index.php
   (v) http://www.englishforum.com/00/interactive/
2. Choose two websites launched by any two business organizations of your choice. Along with two of your friends, identify any messages sent by the head of these organizations on any special occasions to their employees. Evaluate these messages on the basis of the writing strategies you have learnt in this chapter.

## REFERENCES

Adair, John 2002, *The Effective Communicator*, Jaico Publishing House, Mumbai, pp. 102–03.

Adler, Ronald B. and Jeanne Marquardt Elmhorst 2002, *Communicating at Work*, Seventh Edition, McGraw Hill Higher Education, New York, pp. 76–83.

Anderson, Paul V. 2003, *Technical Communication*, 5th Edition, Thomson Asia Pvt Ltd, Singapore, pp. 239–43.

Bovee, Courtland L. and John V. Thill 2003, *Business Communication Today*, Pearson Education Asia, Delhi, pp. 79–82, 107–09, 144–47.

Guffey, Mary Allen 2000, *Business Communication: Process and Product*, Thomson Asia Pvt Ltd, Singapore, pp. 152–65.

Lesikar, Raymond V. and Marie E. Flately 2005, *Basic Business Communication*, Tenth Edition, Tata McGraw-Hill Publishing Co. Ltd, New Delhi, pp. 63–64, 88–93.

Madhukar, R.K. 2001, *Business Communication and Customer Relations*, Vikas Publishing House Pvt Ltd, New Delhi, pp. 57–58.

Ober, Scot 2004, *Contemporary Business Communication*, Fifth Edition, Biztantra, New Delhi, pp. 187–94.

Penrose John M., Robert Rasberry, and Bob Myers, *Advanced Business Communication*, Fourth Edition, Thomson Asia Pvt Ltd, Singapore, pp. 115–44.

Poe, Roy W. and Rosemary T., Fruehling 2000, *Business Communication: A Case Method Approach*, 5th Edition, A.I.T.B.S. Publishers & Distributors (Regd), Delhi, pp. 7–12.

## CASE STUDY 1

**Communication Complication in English**

Woodrow Wilson once said, 'If I am to speak for 10 minutes, I need a week for preparation; if 15 minutes, three days; if half an hour, two days; if an hour, I am ready now.'

With Indian businesses growing globally, one of the most important factors in sustaining success is effective communication with both international and domestic clients. From a fresher (young graduate) needing to ace an interview, to a corporate executive wanting to forge a strong relationship with a client, to an MD giving an impactful presentation in hope of acquiring a big business deal, effective communication has become vital in our professional world. Sushmita Pant, Communication Training Head at Spectramind, Pune, explains, 'Globalization in India today has made it impossible for us to ignore communication. You can be very thorough technically but if you are not able to communicate your skills, you are most likely to end up stuck doing one type of thing with limited growth.' To be able to work for any multinational today, soft skills are necessary. Prem Kanth, HR Head, Unibrics, states, 'It is assumed that in order to get a job with a company such as Unibrics, you need to know how to communicate effectively in both oral and written contexts.'

Unfortunately, majority of our youth today lacks in fluency in English language and are also painfully poor in grammar. Although many students have studied in English medium schools, they are still unable to construct grammatically accurate sentences. Others struggle with pace, tone, and pronunciation. It's not just about conquering a British or American accent to work in a call centre, but about articulating one's thoughts coherently and using the language correctly. Reema Singh, communication specialist and trainer, states, 'Youth, nowadays, has either a poor command over the English language or very weak delivery. Communication is futile if not chosen for the right audience—this is missing too.' HR and training managers are made sorely conscious of this fact.

Suneela Nair, Training Head at OOP Technologies, explains, '90 per cent of the applicants for voice-based job positions are rejected due to poor communication skills.' Pant adds, 'Apart from poor grammar, the youth have serious problems in understanding, assimilating, and replying.' It's not just call centres that are facing these difficulties, as explained by an HR manager, 'We want our employees to be able to express themselves clearly. Since we do not provide soft skills training, how can we expect our employees to have good communication skills to begin with?' Ironically, individuals most dissatisfied by this obvious lack of adequate communication training are the graduates themselves. Neema Khaire, a 23-year old commerce graduate, had to work right after after she graduated. 'I went to around 20 call centres, and was told by the last one that I shouldn't apply to a job that requires spoken English. I was so mortified,' she confesses. Dev Mehta, another commerce graduate, was forced to work for a small pay of ₹2,500 per month as no other positions were available. 'I went for about 25 interviews but because I could not speak fluent English, I was rejected.'

Today, people from all walks of life understand that communication is a vital skill for any profession. As Avijit Bannerjee, an IT specialist, shares, 'Having just the technical knowledge and no communication skills is like having only one leg to walk.' A group of engineering students opine, 'We need English in everything as 99 per cent working professionals communicate in English.'

It seems that organizations and young graduates both understand the need for communication. Then, why is there a big gap between actual and desired skills? Why is today's youth struggling in the art of self-articulation?

Two main ways through which individuals can develop communication skills are exposure and education. Even though global exposure is available to urban youth, they lack formal training in communication.

Universities and postgraduate educational institutions admit that there is no space in their curriculum for soft skills courses and that these skills should be learned at the undergraduate level. Suresh Patil, Founder Trustee and Vice Chairman of Maharashtra College Trust, further clarifies, 'A large number of our postgraduate management students come from the undergraduate level without having any work experience. Efforts should be made for personality development and improving soft skills at the undergraduate level, as at the postgraduate level, there is hardly any time to work on these skills.

And after our graduates get into the industry, there is no room to fix their faults.'

Students also agree with these views 'Our curriculum is not practical. Students must learn how to ace an interview, how to communicate—whether a management graduate or not, one has to know these skills,' states Dev Mehta, a student. 'Classes in communication should be mandated by all universities,' says Piyush Khare, another student. Neela Asrani, an educator from Jai Hind College, MMK College, Mithibhai College, and NM College, states, 'It is difficult to imagine how our students would write formal correspondence and communicate effectively in the corporate world. There is grammar comprehension, but limited skills when it comes to practical application.'

College principals are divided in their views on the importance of establishing formal courses in communication at the undergraduate level. Some feel that soft skills of their students are 'good enough'. A principal stated, 'If a person is looking for a career in communication or PR, then it is essential that these skills are taught. Otherwise, it is valuable but not of the utmost concern.'

The good news is that certain universities recognize the need for better communication and are designing widespread courses so that their students graduate with enough skills to face the corporate world. Dr Indira Shah, Principal of HVM College, comments, 'Over the last couple of years, we realized that while our students were good in theory, they were lacking in analytical and communication skills. To change this, we have taken some steps.'

Vernacular and English medium students who underwent intense, industry-driven, and interaction-based soft skills training at the corporate level, stated that their grammar, diction, intonation, conversation skills, and speaking confidence improved in 10 days.

An effective solution would be for the corporates to come and work with educational institutions to help establish such courses. Dr Medha Patkar, principal of DC College, points out, 'We are striving to improve the communication skills of our students, but it would be great if the corporate sector could help us shoulder this responsibility. We could use their help in drafting courses and students would do better if we understood the requirements of various corporates.'

In order to be proficient in today's globally competitive economy, focus should be on enhancing communication skills at the undergraduate level. There would be considerable improvement if university management accepts this as a need and begins training students in the first year. It is our responsibility to create an atmosphere where our youth can develop the expertise they need to achieve success.

## Questions

1. Comment on the views of Sushmita Pant, Communication Training Head at Spectramind, Pune and Prem Kanth, HR Head, Unibrics on organizational communication.
2. Reema Singh, communication specialist and trainer states, 'Youth, nowadays, has either a poor command over the English language or very weak delivery. Communication is futile if not chosen for the right audience—this is missing too.' Discuss Ms Singh's views with reference to the significance of audience analysis in written communication.
3. Explain the role of colleges and universities in shaping the communication skills of their students.
4. Exposure and education are the two key ways in which individuals develop communication skills. Explain with suitable examples.
5. Neela Asrani, an educator, says, 'There is grammar comprehension, but limited skills when it comes to practical application.' Would you agree? Share your views in 150 words.

CHAPTER 6

# Business Correspondence

## LEARNING OBJECTIVES

After reading this chapter, you will be able to understand

- the seven characteristics of business letter writing
- the basic principles of effective business correspondence
- the various common components of business letters
- strategies required for writing business letters
- the various kinds of business letters
- how to write effective memorandum reports

## INTRODUCTION

When *Fortune* magazine once questioned many successful executives about what business schools should teach, the answer was, 'Teach them to write better.' The message that these top executives were reiterating was that managers should be made to learn the functional importance of effective business writing. Persuasive letters are important. And so are the routine ones, such as writing an application for leave, or explaining a situation, which has gone wrong, through a letter or a memo. In business deals, precision of writing and clarity of meaning are extremely important. Time is a valuable factor and those who can save time through precise communication will be able to use it as an asset for the organization. An organization that values time and communication is bound to gain out of their sagacious use of communication skills.

When you write a letter you create an image of your company and yourself in the reader's mind. A good letter should be effortless reading that makes the reader want to read more. It should be clear and concise, with short sentences and simple words. It should keep to the facts, and be easy to read and understand.

In this chapter, we will focus more on business letters, although the principles involved in effective written communication also apply entirely to business letters.

> A good letter should be clear and concise, with short sentences and simple words.

## BUSINESS LETTER WRITING

Business letter writing is effectual when one knows why one is writing a letter, understands the reader's needs, and then clearly writes what is needed. Every business letter should be clear, human, helpful, and as friendly as the topic allows. The best letters have a conversational tone and read as if the reader was being spoken to. In brief, the seven Cs of business letter writing include being:

- clear,
- concise,
- correct,
- courteous,
- conversational,
- convincing, and
- complete.

In a business letter, sometimes, a reader has to be convinced to act or react in a constructive way towards the business. The reader will respond quickly and constructively only if the letter is clear and concise, and has a friendly and helpful tone. The company business should not be represented in any business letter as one that cannot make a mistake and is always in the right.

## EFFECTIVE BUSINESS CORRESPONDENCE—BASIC PRINCIPLES

Let us now consider certain basic principles for communicating effectively in business situations.

### Place the Reader First

For all writers, the most important people are their readers. It is also true for business letter writing. If you keep the readers in mind when you write, it will help you use the right tone, appropriate language, and include the right amount of detail. What do readers want from business letters? They want relevant information, presented in a clear and easy-to-understand style. They do not want muddled thinking, background information they already know, business-speak, and jargon. Above all, they want to get the gist of your message in one reading—they do not want to dig for the meaning through long sentences and a boring style. The better picture you have of the readers, the better you can communicate.

### Keep to the Point

In business letter, try not to waste a reader's time. The first step in any writing task is to set down the aim. Ask yourself, why am I writing and what do I want to achieve? The clearer you are in your own mind about what you want to achieve, the better your letter. It will help you focus on the information that supports your central aim, and to remove information that is irrelevant. You may also draw an outline to plan your letter, by adhering to the following steps:

1. Make a list of the topics you want to cover but do not worry about the order.
2. Under each topic list keywords, examples, arguments, and facts.
3. Review each topic in the outline for relevance to your aim and audience.
4. Cut out anything that is not relevant to your aim or audience.
5. Sort the information into the best order for the readers.

> Always try to present information in a clear and easy-to-understand style.

### Set the Right Tone

In a business letter, it is important to use a tone that is friendly, yet efficient. Readers want to know that there is someone at the other end who notices and takes an interest in their concerns. Therefore, you need to observe a helpful and friendly tone, by maintaining a conversational approach throughout the letter.

> - Try to be direct and use your words positively so that the reader has a good impression from the beginning of your letter.
> - A closing paragraph should end the letter on a polite and business-like note.

## Write Effective Openings

Your first job when writing a letter is to gain your reader's attention. It is an important principle of effective writing to put the most important information first. The opening paragraph is both the headline and the lead for the message that follows in the rest of the letter. Some examples of openings in business letters are as follows:

> Thank you for your letter dated 8 March 2011, which has been brought to my attention.
>
> I refer to the previous correspondence in respect of the above, please note that to date we have not received your cheque for those outstanding arrears.
>
> With reference to our telephone conversation yesterday regarding ...

Make your first paragraph stand out—get straight to the message and do not waste the reader's time. As the opening paragraph sets the tone for your letter, avoid using tired phrases that are wordy, give little information, and create a formal and impersonal tone. Be direct and use your words positively so that the reader has a good impression from the beginning of your letter. Include the most important information in the first paragraph. Do not be afraid to start your letter strongly.

## Write Effective Conclusions

A closing paragraph should end the letter on a polite and business-like note. Typical final paragraphs in business letters invite the reader to write again or use overused and meaningless phrases that detract from the impact of the letter. Consider the following examples of good closing sentences for business letters:

> I again apologize for the delay in replying and trust that this letter has clarified the points you have raised. However, if you wish to discuss any points I have not clarified, or need any further information, you may certainly contact me again.
>
> I look forward to hearing from you and in the meantime, should you have any queries, please do not hesitate to contact me.
>
> I regret that I cannot be of more assistance in this matter, and should you have any further queries, please do not hesitate to contact me.

In a longer letter, the last paragraph can summarize the key points or repeat the key message. If some action is needed, explain what you want the reader to do or what you will do. Use positive words such as 'when' not 'if'. The letter should end positively and politely. Use the final paragraph to explain or repeat what you want your reader to do.

## COMMON COMPONENTS OF BUSINESS LETTERS

This section discusses the common components of business letters (Fig. 6.1).

**Heading** The heading of a business letter contains the writer's address and date of the letter. The writer's name is not included and only a date is needed in headings with letterhead stationery.

**Inside address** The inside address shows the name and address of the recipient of the business letter. This information helps prevent confusion. Also, if the recipient has moved, the inside addresses

| Letter | Annotation |
|---|---|
| 6 June 2012<br>11/17 Campian Street<br>Egmore, Chennai 78703 | Heading—the date and the sender's address. |
| Mr Raji Patricks<br>30/05 Aruna Asaf Ali Road<br>New Delhi 110067. | Inside address—name and address of the recipient of the letter. |
| Dear Mr Patricks, | Salutation |
| I received your 6 June 2012 letter requesting consultation, and am providing my recommendation in the following. First, let me review my understanding of your inquiry. The question you raise revolves around whether the heating registers should be located in a low sidewall, or in the ceiling, and if ceiling registers are used, which type—step down or stamped-faced—will deliver the best results. Additionally, the problem concerns whether there is any benefit to having heating registers near the floor, whether moving heated air down in ducts negatively affects blower performance, and whether adequate injection that can be achieved on the low speed of a two-state furnace.<br><br>My recommendations are as follows:<br><br>• I can find nothing in either Carrier, Trane, or ASHRAE design manuals that indicates drop as being a factor in duct design any different from normal static losses. If you have different information on this, I would like to have references to it.<br>• I cannot see any advantage to low sidewall application. The problem is injection and pattern. I do see an advantage to low sidewall return; Carrier Design Manual-Air Distribution is a good reference on both items.<br>• I recommend step-down diffusers with OBD because they have pattern and volume control that is superior to stamped-faced diffusers.<br>• I am opposed to low sidewall diffusers or floor diffusers in the application you describe. The increased static losses that result from trying to get the ducts down through the walls will only increase installation cost and reduce efficiency. | Body text of the letter: single spaced text with double spacing between paragraphs; no paragraph indentation.<br><br>Use of special formatting within the letter—use bulleted or numbered lists, even headings and graphics. |
| If there is anyone in your organization who is uncomfortable with these recommendations, let me know. I would be very interested in reviewing any actual documented test results. Let me know if you have any further questions or if I can be of any further assistance.<br>Sincerely, | Complimentary close |
| *[signature]*<br>Sheeba Mathew<br>HVAC Consultants | Signature block |
| Encl: Invoice for consulting services | End notations |

**Fig. 6.1** Parts of a business letter

helps to determine what to do with the letter. In the inside address, include the appropriate title of the recipient, and copy the name of the company exactly as that company writes it.

**Salutation** In a business letter, the salutation—the 'Dear Sir' of the letter—is usually followed by a comma, except sometimes when a colon is also used. If you do not know whether the recipient is a man or woman, traditionally you simply write 'Dear Sir' or 'Dear Sirs'. More recently, however, salutations such as 'Dear Sir or Madam', 'Dear Ladies and Gentlemen', 'Dear Friends', or 'Dear People' have been recommended.

**Subject or reference line** The subject line replaces the salutation or is included with it. It announces the main business of the letter.

**Body of the letter** The actual message is contained in the body of the letter, the paragraphs between the salutation and complimentary close. Strategies for writing the body of the letter are discussed later in the chapter.

**Complimentary close** The 'Sincerely yours' element of a business letter is called the complimentary close. Other common ones are 'Thanking you', 'Cordially', 'Respectfully', or 'Respectfully yours'. Notice that only the first letter is capitalized, and it is always followed by a comma.

**Enclosures** To make sure that the recipient knows that items accompany the letter in the same envelope, use such indications as 'Enclosure', 'Encl.', or 'Enclosures' (when two or more attachments accompany the letter). For example, if you send a résumé and writing sample with your application letter, you would write this: 'Encl.: Résumé and Writing Sample'. If the enclosure is lost, the recipient will know.

**Copies** If you send copies of a letter to others, indicate this fact among the end notations also. If, for example, you were upset by a local merchant's handling of your repair problems and were sending a copy of your letter to the Better Business Bureau, you would write: 'Cc: Better Business Bureau'. If you plan to send a copy to your lawyer, you can write, 'Cc: Mr Saurav Mishra, Lawyer'.

## STRATEGIES FOR WRITING THE BODY OF A LETTER

In this section, various strategies that help in writing effective business letters have been discussed.

### State the Main Business, Purpose, or Subject Matter Right Away

The very first sentence of a business letter should talk about its main objective. When business people open a letter, their first concern is to know what the letter is about, what its purpose is, and why they need to spend their time reading it. Therefore, roundabout beginnings need to be avoided. If you are responding to a letter, identify that letter by its subject and date in the first paragraph or sentence. To illustrate, let us look at the following examples:

> Dear Mr Anupam
>
> I am writing in response to your 1 September 2011 letter in which you described the problems that you have had with one of our chainsaws. I regret that you have suffered this inconvenience and expense and ...

> Business letters should include short paragraphs, between three and eight lines long.

Dear Ms Rehman:

I have just received your 4 August 2011 letter in which you list names and other sources from which I can get additional information on the manufacture and use of plastic bottles in the soft-drink industry ...

## Keep the Paragraphs Short

The paragraphs of business letters tend to be short, some only a sentence long. To enable the recipient to read your letters more rapidly and to comprehend and remember the important facts or ideas, create relatively short paragraphs that are anywhere between three and eight lines long.

## Provide Topic Indicators in the Beginning of Paragraphs

Analyse some of the letters you see in this chapter in terms of the contents or purpose of their individual paragraphs. In the first sentence of any paragraph of a business letter, try to locate a word or phrase that indicates the topic of that paragraph. If a paragraph discusses your problems with a personal computer, include the word 'problems' or phrase 'problems with my personal computer' into the first sentence. Doing this gives recipients a clear sense of the content and purpose of each paragraph. Let us now examine how an excerpt is modified after the topic indicator, 'work experience', is incorporated into it.

*Original excerpt*   I have worked as an electrician at the Bhilai Steel Plant for about six years. Since 2005 I have been licensed by the city of Bhilai as an electrical contractor qualified to undertake commercial and industrial work as well as residential work.

*Revised excerpt*   As for my work experience, I have worked as an electrician in Bhilai for about six years. Since 2005 I have been licensed by the city of Bhilai as an electrical contractor qualified to undertake commercial and industrial work as well as residential work.

## Place Important Information Strategically

Information in the first and last lines of paragraphs tends to be read and remembered better. Therefore, important information should be placed in these high-visibility points. For example, in job application letters that must convince potential employers that you are right for a job, appealing qualities should be mentioned at the beginning or end of paragraphs for greater emphasis. Less positive or detrimental information should be placed in less visible points in your business letters. If you have some difficult things to say, a good (and honest) strategy is to de-emphasize by placing them in areas of less emphasis. For example, if a job requires three years of experience and you only have one, bury this fact in the middle or lower half of a body paragraph of the application letter. The resulting letter will be honest and complete; it just will not emphasize weak points unnecessarily. The following are some examples of these ideas:

> Place important information in high-visibility points.

1. *Original draft*   In July, I will graduate from the University of Bengaluru with a Bachelor of Science in Nutrition and Dietetics. Over the past three years in which I have pursued this degree, I have worked as a lab assistant for Dr Sunetra Roday and have been active in two related organizations, the Student Dietetic Association and the Indian Home Economics Association.

In my nutritional biochemistry and food science labs, I have written many technical reports and scientific papers. I have also been serving as a diet aide at Apollo Hospital in Bengaluru the past year and a half.

As the job calls for a technical writer, in the revised version, emphasize that first, then mention the rest.

*Revised draft*   During my three years at the University of Bengaluru, I have had substantial experience writing technical reports and scientific papers. Most of these reports and papers have been in the field of nutrition and dietetics in which I will be receiving my Bachelor of Science degree this July. During these years, I have also handled plenty of paperwork as a lab assistant for Dr Sunetra Roday, as a member of two related organizations, the Student Dietetic Association and the Indian Home Economics Association, and as a diet aide as Apollo Hospital in Bengaluru in the past year and a half.

2. *Original draft*   To date, I have done no independent building inspection on my own. I have been working the past two years under the supervision of Mr Sridhar Saha who has often given me primary responsibility for walk-throughs and property inspections. It was Mr Saha who encouraged me to apply for this position. I have also done some refurbishing of older houses on a contract basis and have some experience in industrial construction as a welder and as a clerk in a nuclear construction site.

Do not lie about the lack of experience, but do not highlight it either, as follows in the revised draft:

*Revised draft*   As for my work experience, I have done numerous building walk-throughs and property inspections under the supervision of Mr Saha over the past two years. Mr Saha, who encouraged me to apply for this position, has often given me primary responsibility for many inspection jobs. I have also done some refurbishing of older houses on a contract basis and have some experience in industrial construction as a welder and clerk in a nuclear construction as a site as well.

## Develop a 'You-attitude'

In a business letter, the primary focus should be on the concerns of the recipient rather than the writer's. Even if you must talk about yourself in a business letter a great deal, do so in a way that relates your concerns to those of the recipient. This recipient-oriented style is often called the 'you-attitude', where the 'you' refers to the recipient. Let us look at a few examples.

1. *Original draft*   I am writing to you about a change in our pricing policy that will save our company time and money. In an operation like ours, it costs us a great amount of labour time (and thus expense) to scrape and rinse our used tableware when it comes back from large parties. Also, we have incurred great expense on replacement of linens that have been ruined by stains that could have been soaked promptly after the party and been saved.

*Revised draft*   I am writing to inform you of our new policy that will be effective from 1 September 2012. It will enable us to serve your large party needs more efficiently. In an operation like ours in which we supply for parties that have guests up to 500, turn-

> An 'action ending' makes clear what the writer of the letter expects the recipient to do and when.

around time is critical; unscraped and unrinsed tableware causes us delays in clean-up time and, more importantly, less frequent and less prompt service to you, the customer. Also, linens ruined by stains, which could have been avoided if they had been immediately soaked after the party, cause you to have to pay more in rental fees.

2. *Original draft*   For these reasons, our new policy, effective 1 September 2012, will be to charge an additional 15 per cent on unrinsed tableware and 75 per cent of the wholesale value of stained linens that have not been soaked.

   *Revised draft*   Therefore, in order to enable us to supply your large party needs effectively, we will begin charging 15 per cent on all unrinsed tableware and 75 per cent of the wholesale value of stained linens that have not been soaked.

## Give an 'Action Ending' Whenever Appropriate

An 'action ending' makes clear what the writer of the letter expects the recipient to do and when. Ineffective conclusions to business letters often end with rather limp, non-committal statements, such as 'Hope to hear from you soon' or 'Let me know if I can be of any further assistance'. Instead, or in addition, specify the action the recipient should take and the schedule for that action. If, for example, you are writing a query letter, ask the editor politely to let you know of his/her decision if at all possible in a month. If you are writing an application letter, subtly try to set up a date and time for an interview. Some examples are as follows:

> As soon as you approve this plan, I will begin contacting sales representatives at once to arrange for the purchase and delivery of the microcomputers. May I expect to hear from you within the week?
>
> I am free after 2:00 p.m. on most days. Can we set up an appointment to discuss my background and this position further? I shall look forward to hearing from you.

# KINDS OF BUSINESS LETTERS

In this section, some common kinds of business letters such as routine letters, covering letters for job applications, follow-up letters, acceptance letters, rejection letters, resignation letters, inquiry letters, complaint letters, adjustment letters, and persuasive letters are discussed.

 You can refer to the Online Resource Centre for several samples of business letters.

## Routine Letters

Any routine correspondence can be planned in three steps—opening, middle, and closing paragraph. These are discussed as follows:

### Opening Paragraph

Most routine business letters begin by referring to a previous correspondence. While it is not an exciting way to open a letter, it is efficient and saves the reader the time spent on searching for what is being referred to. Rather than forcing the recipients of letters to match replies with copies of related letters or documents, it is better if the correspondence begins with references to specific communications. Some examples are as follows:

> **BUSINESS COMMUNICATION INSIGHT**
>
> **Tips and Tricks for Better Letters**
>
> The first step in drafting an effective business letter is following the right formatting style. A poorly formatted letter is not likely to be read—as per a study of HR personnel, more than 80 per cent said they wouldn't consider a résumé even if it had only one or two mistakes in the cover letter. However, a well-formed letter might not be considered unless the text is potent and engaging.
>
> The age-old copywriting formula that can be very useful in letter writing is AIDA—attention, interest, desire, and action.
>
> First, you gain the reader's attention, then you make them interested, then you arouse their desire, and then you convey to them what action they should take. Consider the following openings for a business letter:
>
> - Please find attached a résumé for your consideration for …
> - I am writing to let you know that …
> - This letter is regarding your recent …
>
> None of the above openings can grab the reader's attention. Some attention-grabbing approaches and examples are as follows:
>
> - *Flattery*: I am a huge fan of your work …; I have always dreamed to work for your company …
> - *A question*: Are you aware that …; Have you also had this problem …
> - *Surprise*: 20 million people will die in road accidents this year; in the last two years, I've pursued and brought down to justice 6 of the CBI's 10 most wanted criminals.
>
> As soon as the reader's *attention* is caught, create *interest* in whatever you are presenting. For example, you may promise to overcome their shortcomings—with a great service, with innovative solutions, with a partnership, or with whatever it is that you are writing about.

    Here is the information you asked for in your letter dated 12 November 2011.
    In your letter dated 9 June 2012, you asked for …
    In reply to your letter dated 8 August …

If your letter is in response to a telephone call or an in-person conversation, you might use the following beginnings:

    Following our conversation this morning …
    Your telephone call this morning reminded me that …

### Middle Paragraph

In the middle paragraph, complete information needs to be given to the reader. Providing complete information means giving all the necessary details. This involves trying to answer any possible questions that the reader may want to ask. A bulletin or brochure, whenever possible, is a useful way to minimize detail in letters.

### Closing Paragraph

Letters should be closed with a note of goodwill to avoid sounding abrupt. When we walk away from someone, we tend to say something like 'Look after yourself', 'It was good to see you again', or 'See you soon'. In the same way, in a letter, it is good to end the communication in a way that will enable the reader to think well of the company.

## Covering Letters for Job Applications

> A covering letter is the first step in the selection process.

A covering letter is the first step in the selection process, whereby the prospective applicant puts forward his/her candidature to the employer so that he/she can be considered for the necessary assignment/work. It has to be meticulously written since it creates the first impression, and many a times, it is here where half the battle is won or lost. It is normally accompanied by a detailed résumé. The format of a typical covering letter is given in Fig. 6.2 and sample of a covering letter is given in Fig. 6.3.

## Recommendation Letter

A recommendation letter is a written reference that offers information about your character, work history, and or/academic history. Recommendation letters can help you find a job or get into college. Figure 6.4 provides two sample recommendation letters.

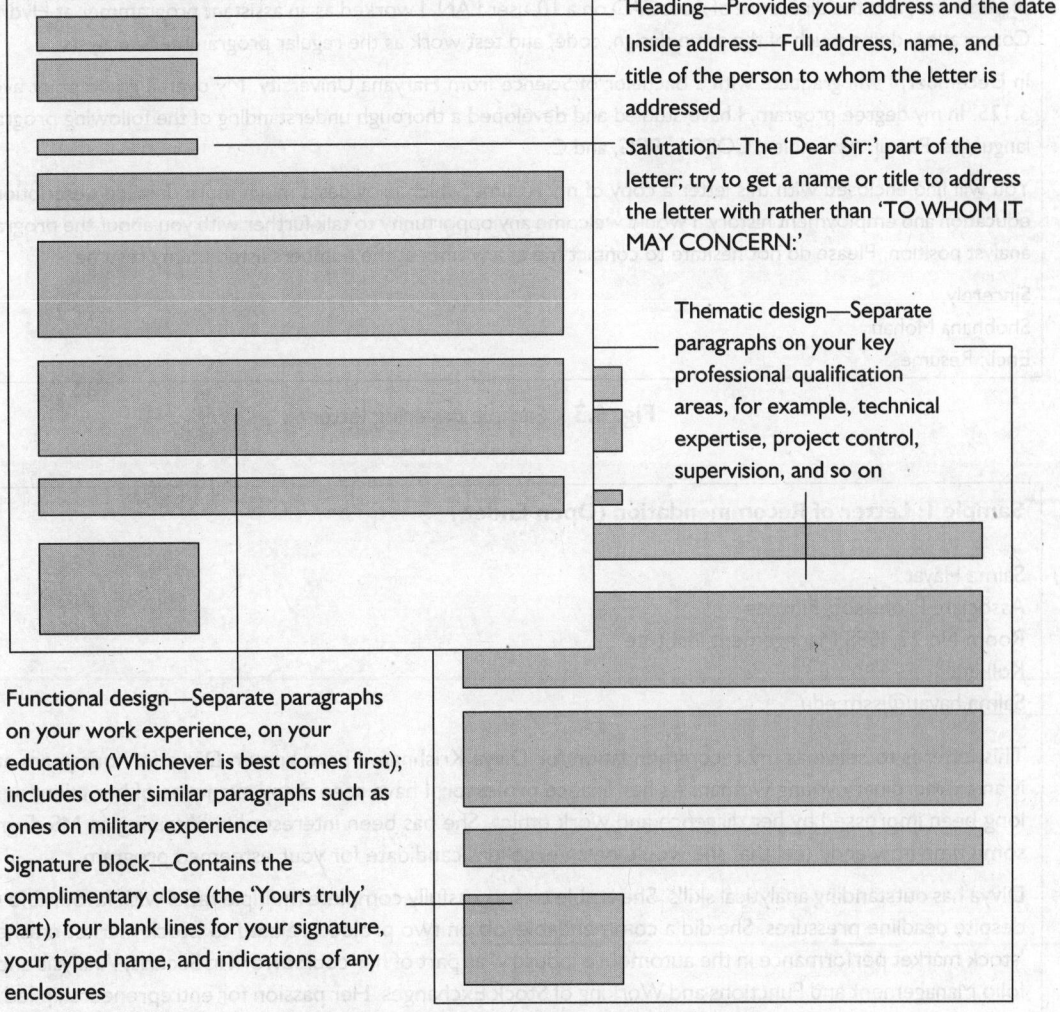

**Fig. 6.2** Format of a typical covering letter

83 DLF Carlton
Gurgaon 78719

4 August 2012
Personnel Department
Techmax Ltd
P.O. Box 178
Gurgaon 78733

Hi,

I am writing with regard to your newspaper advertisement in *The Hindu* dated 2 August 2012 concerning your need for a programmer. I believe that I have the qualifications, experience, and enthusiasm that you are looking for.

As for my work experience, I have been employed with two organizations over the past three years that have drawn on my computer-programming skills. My work at Logani Corporation involved the setting up of new software, training of personnel, and the direct use of AutoCAD on a 10-user LAN. I worked as an assistant programmer at HydroLogics Corporation, doing much of the same design, code, and test work as the regular programmers/analysts.

In December, I will graduate with a Bachelor of Science from Haryana University. My overall grade point average is 3.125. In my degree program, I have studied and developed a thorough understanding of the following programming languages: Pascal, Assembler, COBOL, RPG, and C.

You will find enclosed with this letter a copy of my résumé which provides a much more detailed description of my education and employment history. I would welcome any opportunity to talk further with you about the programmer/analyst position. Please do not hesitate to contact me at any time at the numbers listed on my résumé.

Sincerely,
Shobhana Mohan
Encl.: Résumé

**Fig. 6.3** Sample covering letter

**Sample 1: Letter of Recommendation (Open Ended)**

Salma Hayat
Associate Professor, Finance
Room No 22, ISSS Management Institute
Kolkata
Salma.hayat@issm.edu

This letter is to serve as my recommendation for Divya Krishnan. I have known Divya for four years and she is an extraordinary young woman. As her finance professor, I have seen many examples of her talent and have long been impressed by her diligence and work ethics. She has been interested in obtaining an MS degree for some time now and I feel that she would be an excellent candidate for your esteemed program.

Divya has outstanding analytical skills. She is able to successfully complete multiple tasks with favourable results despite deadline pressures. She did a commendable job on two projects related to 'stock market crashes' and 'stock market performance in the automobile industry' as part of her coursework in Security Analysis and Portfolio Management and Functions and Working of Stock Exchanges. Her passion for entrepreneurship led her to spearhead the Centre for Entrepreneurial Leadership which is one of the centres for excellence at BITS, Pilani.

This is a student-led think-tank organization functioning in collaboration with the National Entrepreneurship Network (NEN). As the vice-president of the sales and marketing team, she has organized Conquest—the nationwide business challenge.

I must also make note of Divya's exceptional academic performance. Out of a class of 75 students in the management group, Divya stands in the top 5 per cent. Her above-average performance is a direct result of her hard work and strong focus.

She has also been an active member of the BITS Management Association. Her leadership skills were reflected during her tenure as the student coordinator for INTERFACE 2005, the Annual Management Convention. She was also the chief editor of the management magazine *Phoenix*.

Divya is a good team player. She also has excellent communication and negotiation skills. She has always taken the initiative to motivate her team and been at the forefront in guiding her peers and colleagues. She has successfully demonstrated leadership ability in group discussions, class projects etc. and is quite comfortable in the role.

If your graduate program is seeking superior candidates with a record of achievement, Divya is an excellent choice. She has consistently demonstrated an ability to rise to any challenge that she must face.

To conclude, I would like to restate my strong recommendation for Divya Krishnan. If you have any further questions regarding Divya's ability or this recommendation, please feel free to contact me at the details given on the letterhead.

---

**Sample 2: Letter of Recommendation (Close Ended)**

*Recommendation letter*
Sun Technologies Ltd
32, Race Course Road
Coimbatore, Tamil Nadu

Please answer the following questions regarding the applicant, making sure to save your work regularly.

**How long have you known the applicant and in what connection?**
I have known Sindhura for the last three years. She was my student at the Birla Institute of Technology & Science (BITS), Pilani, where I was teaching finance and management. She completed three courses—Fundamentals of Finance & Accounting, Security Analysis & Portfolio Management, and Management Accounting, and also worked on a project—'Role of Indian stock market regulator in curbing insider trading practices'—under my guidance. It was during this period, that I interacted with Sindhura and closely monitored her performance as well as assessed her capabilities. Over these years, I became an informal career counselor and mentor to Sindhura, and we have discussed her career aspirations at some length.

**What do you consider to be the applicant's major talents and strengths?**
While there are several positive attributes of Sindhura, a few things that I wish to highlight are—team work, leadership, and creativity. Sindhura thrives in a team environment—a critical skill for success at the BITS program as the evaluation process includes several group assignments.

As a member, she is very hard-working and works closely with rest of the team members to achieve the team goal. She is an excellent leader as well. She seeks to get a clear sense of what is expected and collaboratively arrives at common goals, role-delegation, and timelines. She works towards creating a trusting, participative environment and motivates her team to deliver more than what they set out to achieve.

For instance, as the student coordinator of the Economics and Finance Association at BITS, she effectively interfaced with the student body and the faculty to initiate and organize university events throughout the year such as technical conferences, guest lectures, inter-university competitions/festivals.

**What do you consider to be the applicant's major weaknesses or areas for improvement?**
Sindhura is an exceptional student with several talents. One area of relative weakness that I have observed is oral communication skills. She needs to work on her voice-modulation and diction.

**In what developmental areas has the applicant changed most over time?**
In her initial years at BITS, she had difficulty in conceptualizing the larger picture to understand real-life business scenarios and needed regular guidance. By the junior year, her continued analysis and research gave her thorough understanding of business environment. This learning is reflected in a paper on 'Mergers and Acquisitions' that she authored. The paper was selected at the prestigious All India Input Output Conference (2005).

**What will this individual be doing in 10 years? Why?**
While in her junior year, the annual academic festival—APOGEE—was facing a revenue crunch. As the head of photography club, Sindhura pioneered the idea of generating revenues through selling photographs taken during the event to the audience. This was a successful idea that continues to be a revenue source even today. She is a problem-solver who is not afraid of taking the road less traveled.

She was a topper of her class and also led various extra-curricular initiatives. She does not shy away from taking responsibility for her mistakes, nor does she blame others for the consequences of her decisions.

These qualities of Sindhura make me believe that she will be a very successful entrepreneur. I am sure she will be a great role-model that BITS would be proud of.

I strongly recommend Sindhura for admission to the London Business School. If you require any elaboration, please feel free to contact me.

**Fig. 6.4** Sample recommendation letters

## Thank-you/Follow-up Letters

Thank-you letters are critical to your job search success, and interviews are not the only occasions to send thank-you and follow-up letters. If you have ever helped or done something for someone, and not received a thank you, you understand how employers view this lack of courtesy on the part of job seekers.

A thank-you letter should be written after an interview; when a contact is helpful to you in a telephonic conversation or email; provides information; helps you at a career fair; or any other reason for which you want to express thanks and develop a good relationship. Figure 6.5 provides a sample thank-you letter after an interview. It can be observed how the letter creates a positive impression, and shows that Shubendu has exceptional follow-up skills and consideration for the interviewer's time. This letter creates yet another opportunity for Shubendu to offer her skills.

> **SHUBENDU GHOSH**
> 78 Siddhi Apartments,
> Goa 403516
> Residence: (0832) 2734134, Mobile: 9890035172, Email: shubendu@internetserver.com
>
> 10 April 2012
>
> Purva Gupta–Director of Education
> The IFSC School
> Road 58/97 School Road
> Ahmedabad
>
> Dear Ms Gupta,
>
> I appreciate the time you recently took to discuss the position you currently have available at The IFSC School with me. It was a pleasure speaking with you and meeting your very competent staff—the conversation was extremely informative. The tour of the school was very impressive—it is truly a 'state of the art' design. As I mentioned during our interview, I am confident that, given the chance, I could contribute a great deal to your overall learning institutes' objectives and goals.
>
> In addition to my experience, skills, and qualifications, I am an experienced team player who brings enthusiasm and unique concepts into a group environment that secures 'win-win' results. I have been known to encourage a free exchange of ideas among students, and generate measurable progress in classroom participation and knowledge retention—which is so important to the learning process. I know that I can meet and exceed your expectations.
>
> As you recommended in our interview, I have enclosed a list of references that you may contact regarding my prior work accomplishments and skills. If you feel my talents and endless energy are in line with your thoughts, please call so we can further discuss The IFSC School requirements.
>
> Sincerely,
> Shubendu Ghosh,
>
> Enclosure: Reference List

**Fig. 6.5** Sample thank-you letter

## Acceptance and Rejection Letters

An acceptance letter is required to formally notify the employer of your decision to accept his/her offer of a job. In the acceptance letter, specify the job you are accepting and the name of your supervisor. Also, review your starting salary, basic job responsibilities, and the date on which you will start work. In the rejection letter, tactfully state your reasons for not taking the job. It is beneficial to convey your appreciation for the interview and the employer's time because you may want to work for him/her in the future. Figures 6.6 and 6.7 provide sample letters of acceptance and rejection.

## Resignation Letter

Many job seekers do not understand the importance of a carefully-worded resignation letter. When people resign, it is imperative that they do not 'burn any bridges'. As you will see, the sample resignation letter (Fig. 6.8) is very carefully worded. Even if the person concerned (Roshan) may have disliked his supervisor's attitude, the letter does not convey his actual opinion.

Hamilton College 198
College Hill Road, Pune
30 April 2012

Mr Peter Selvaraj
Director, Human Resources
Biotech, Inc., Ferry Brand Building
34th Floor, Noida City Centre, Noida

Dear Mr Selvaraj,

I am delighted to accept your offer to join Biotech as a sales representative. Your phone call this morning made my day! To review our conversation, I will be starting at Biotech on 17 July 2012 at an annual base salary of ₹325,000, a 5 per cent commission, and a review after six months. My primary duties will be selling pharmaceutical products to hospitals and drug stores and researching organizations in the Delhi NCR region under the supervision of Mr Gautam Gupta.
I am very excited about joining the Biotech team.

Sincerely,
Harish Madan

**Fig. 6.6** Sample acceptance letter

---

Hamilton College 198
College Hill Road, Jangpura, New Delhi
13 October 2012

Mr Kiran Rao
Principal
Windsor School
Green Park, New Delhi

Dear Mr Rao,

Thank you for offering me the position of a French teacher at Windsor School. The offer is very appealing and I appreciate your giving me extra time to make a decision.

After much consideration, I have decided to decline your offer. The decision was very difficult, but I have accepted a position as a teacher at Darpan School. The opportunity to work with a mentor teacher with a reduced teaching load seems to be the most appropriate course of action for me as I begin my career in independent school teaching. Perhaps our paths will cross again in the future.

Thank you again for your interest. Your consideration has been greatly appreciated.

Sincerely,
Elsa Mathew

**Fig. 6.7** Sample rejection letter

---

Roshan William
Recruiter
Power Recruiters Ltd
Chennai

30 April 2012
Ms Mini Mohan
Manager, Power Recruiters Ltd
8595, Sunset Road, Chennai

Dear Ms Mohan,

Please accept this letter as resignation of my position as Recruiter, effective 30 April 2012. I am offering two weeks' notice, which will give you an opportunity to find a suitable replacement. If you would like, I am more than willing to provide training and orientation to the newcomer.

My decision to resign was finalized after a long and careful consideration of all factors. I regret leaving friends here; however, I feel the change will be beneficial to my long-term career goals and objectives. I assure you that I will complete any outstanding projects and business affairs before my departure—the transition will be handled professionally to ensure no internal or external problems.

Again, it has been a pleasurable learning experience working as part of your team and I wish nothing but success for Power Recruiters Ltd.

Sincerely,
Roshan

---

**Fig. 6.8** Sample resignation letter

## Inquiry Letters

An inquiry letter is useful when you need information, advice, names, or directions. Be careful, however, not to ask for too much information or for information that you could easily obtain in some other way, for example, by a quick trip to the library.

### Solicited and Unsolicited Inquiry Letters

A solicited letter of inquiry is written when a business or agency advertises its products or services. For example, if a software manufacturer advertises some new package it has developed and you cannot inspect it locally, write a solicited letter to that manufacturer asking specific questions. If you cannot find any information on a technical subject, an inquiry letter to a company involved in that subject may put you on the right track. In fact, that company may supply much more help than you had expected (provided of course that you write a good inquiry letter).

A letter of inquiry is unsolicited if the recipient has done nothing to prompt your inquiry. For example, if you read an article by an expert, you may have further questions or want more information. You seek help from these people in a slightly different form of an inquiry letter. As the steps and guidelines for both types of an inquiry letters show, you must construct the unsolicited type more carefully, because recipients of unsolicited letters of inquiry are not ordinarily prepared to handle such inquiries.

> An inquiry letter is useful when you need information, advice, names, or directions.

## Persuasive Letters

> Persuasive letters are an attempt to convince your reader to do something.

Persuasive letters are an attempt to convince someone to do something. These are requests to a reader. Persuasive letters may have two consequences: either a request will be granted or declined. When writing letters of request that the reader is very likely to grant, simply bottom-line the request, then give all the necessary details. A perfect example of this type of letter is the request for a letter of recommendation. If you find yourself writing such a letter, make sure that you tell your reader the name of the person or organization to whom the letter of recommendation is to be addressed. Also, include all information you have concerning what the letter of recommendation should include—in particular a job description or an account of what the organization is looking for.

The purposes of persuasive letters are threefold. First, the letter wants the reader to act. Therefore, you must provide enough information so that readers know exactly what to do, and you must anticipate and overcome any possible objections. Second, the letter should build a good image of the writer and his/her organization. Finally, the letter should create or cement a good relationship between the reader and the writer—just in case you wish to contact this reader again. In order to meet these purposes and write a good persuasive letter, you must know four things—the details of what you are requesting, facts about your reader, specific action desired from the reader, and any possible objections the reader might have. Refer to Fig. 6.9 for a sample persuasive business letter.

---

The Society of Insurance Agents
R.S. Puram, Basavanagudi
Bengaluru 560 056
10 November 2012

Dr Rahila Khan, Ph.D.
Hyderabad University
Prof. C.R. Rao Road, Gachibowli
Hyderabad 500046
Phone: (040) 3632145

Dear Dr Khan,
Your recent article, 'Are Insurance Agents taking Themselves too Seriously?', which appeared in the July 2012 issue of *Insurance Monthly*, rang a familiar note with our group. We, at the Society of Insurance Agents, agree with the important messages of your article and heartily concur that 'insurance must closely monitor our colleagues and must protect against an attitude of righteous self-importance'. In addition, your views and vision have drawn favourable comments from our sister group, Women in Insurance.
Both groups have often felt the need for more information in the area of self-monitoring, especially from the point of view of an expert such as yourself. Shortly after the first of the year, about 200 members will be attending our annual meeting, whose theme this year is 'Self Appraisal'. We would be gratified if you could meet with us and make the keynote address.
By accepting our invitation to be our featured speaker, you will be able to assist the appraisal profession and make your message heard on a personal level. The annual meeting will be held on 18 and 19 January 2013 in Bengaluru at the City Tower Convention Centre. We would love to have you and your spouse as our guests for the entire weekend. We can promise lovely weather and an attentive as well as receptive audience.

> We would appreciate receiving your acceptance so we can schedule your flights and accommodations as soon as possible.
>
> Sincerely,
> Asmita Malik, President
> Enc: Annual Meeting Schedule

**Fig. 6.9** Sample persuasive business letter

The organization of a persuasive letter is like an inverted pyramid. You should begin broadly by capturing the reader's interest and stating the common ground—get the reader to buy into your problem or situation. Then you should specifically detail the shared problem and its solution. Should you suspect that your reader might sense negative elements (and this is the norm), outline the benefits. Then you should narrow the focus by telling the reader exactly what he/she should do. A very special type of persuasive letter is direct mail. More commonly known as 'junk mail', direct mail is common to sales and fund raising and usually asks readers to part with their money. We get scores of this type of mail every year—and usually toss them out. Yet, organizations continue to send them—for one good reason. They work. Direct mails usually contain an emotional and convincing appeal. The mailing lists are carefully compiled and monitored. The writing is thoughtfully crafted. Next time you receive direct mail, read it closely and try to identify what the writers have done.

## WRITING EFFECTIVE MEMOS

The key to writing an effective memo is to keep the goal of all business communications in mind: to get our readers do what we want them to do and to promote goodwill. Understanding how memo reports are written is a very important aspect of business correspondence. Memos, once organized, can help us accomplish organizational goals effectively. Memos and memorandum reports are not the same thing. A memo can be a handwritten note to your co-worker about meeting for lunch. On the other hand, a memo report is a report. It is always typed, and usually has an introduction, a well-developed body with headings, and a conclusion. In this chapter, we will use the term memo to mean memorandum reports. Since the purpose of writing a memo is to convey news and information, any word that is meant to give order or advice should be avoided.

The following command words—called imperative verbs—with 'you' as their subject, which should be avoided, are as follows:

> Come here.
> Do not overuse bullets.
> Please pick up your messages.

In all of these examples, the subject is not stated because it is understood to be 'you'. These sentences tell the reader what to do giving instructions, advice, and by requesting. It is inappropriate to use a memo report to give instructions and advice. Memo reports must not tell the readers what they should do.

 Refer to the Online Resource Centre for memo templates and style.

Imperative verbs (and the 'you' pronoun) are condescending; they 'talk down' to readers. For example, if our boss tells us to 'be courteous', s/he is implying that we are rude. Insulting our readers is

---

An In-house Memo of The Blue Motors Company, New Delhi

Date: 14 December 2012
To: T.R. Rao (VP-Sales-India)
From: Shantanu Mitra (Director Marketing)
Re: Marketing Plan Review

As you requested, the Marketing Plan Review process has been established and is ready to be put in motion. Initial meetings with all divisions, territories, and marketing and sales staff have been scheduled to begin early next month and will continue until March 2013. Here is the schedule for the meetings:

| North | Leela Hotel, New Delhi | 15–19 Jan. |
| West | Tulip Hotel, Mumbai | 1–4 Feb. |
| South | Chennai Grand, Chennai | 20–24 Feb. |
| East | Century Hotel, Guwahati | 5–9 Mar. |

Attendees will discuss the new marketing plan and give their opinions. In particular, we are anxious to have the following questions answered:

- Will the plan work in all areas?
- Are any regional adjustments needed?
- How does each region react to our new image?
- What is each region's gut-level reaction to the plan?

I have prepared a 16-page questionnaire to be distributed at the meetings. Hopefully, we will receive input from everyone. I have attached a copy of the questionnaire.
Please let me know if you have any questions.

Attachment: Questionnaire
CC: All the members of the Strategic Marketing Team (India)

---

**Fig. 6.10** Sample memo report

not the way to get them to do what we want them to do. Instead of giving instructions that tell what the readers must do, a memo report should focus on giving information.

### Memo Report Format

All business documents, and therefore, a memorandum report too, requires a specific format and organization. A memo report is carefully designed so that the reader acts upon it correctly the first time it is read, thereby avoiding the need for follow-up messages. It also has an introduction, main body, and conclusion that are discussed in detail here. Refer to Fig. 6.10 for a sample memo report.

#### *Introduction*

An introduction to a memo report (a) builds goodwill and (b) answers the two questions a busy executive asks every time he/she receives a piece of correspondence—'what is this' and 'why me'? It has the following characteristics:

1. The topic tells a busy executive what the memo is about. It answers 'What is this?'

> The body is the main and largest part of a memo report.

2. The reason for sending tells why that reader is getting the memo, answering 'Why me?'
3. The language is conversational and plain and avoids the outdated and unfriendly 'Per your request' or 'Pursuant to your request'.
4. The tone is friendly, courteous, and positive to make a good first impression. An effective introduction establishes a rapport with the reader. Memos and letters should not begin with 'I' or 'we' since the focus must be on the reader and not on the writer.
5. The length is short and the writing concise so the reader can understand the message in a quick reading without being scared off by a long paragraph.

## Body/Discussion

The body is the main and largest part of a memo report. Its function is to report complete, correct, and current information. It includes the following points.

1. The headings (first, second, and third levels) help the reader follow all the ideas within the text. A memo has level headings to help your eye make sense of the content before you actually read it. Main headings are usually centred, while sub-headings are at the left margin. This hierarchy is easy for every reader to see.
2. Conversational and plain language reaches the reader, who might not have the education, vocabulary, or experience that you have. Short sentences and paragraphs are much easier to understand.
3. Concise and precise language gets to the point and ensures that the messages are clear. Concise messages save time and money by being clear the first time, thus eliminating the need for follow-up letters and explanations.
4. The eight C principles—completeness, clarity, concreteness, correctness, conciseness, consideration, courtesy, and candidness—are the guidelines for effective messages.
5. Good document design—bullets, spacing, and headers—make memos look professional and help the reader to understand them the first time he/she reads it.
6. Visual aids are used if they help the reader understand the message better.

## Conclusion

The conclusion of a memo summarizes it and ties up any loose ends. It includes the following points:

1. It restates the topic of a memo in one–two sentences.
2. A polite closure offers the best way to contact the writer to ask questions, look at samples, or talk story. It is friendly, uses conversational, plain language, and avoids wordy and vague sentences such as 'feel free', 'do not hesitate to', and 'contact'. An effective polite closure provides extension numbers or email addresses with sentences such as 'If you have any questions, please call me at Ext. 1234.'
3. Its tone is friendly, courteous, and positive to make a good last impression. An effective conclusion also builds goodwill. It avoids implying that the reader needs the information. For example, 'Following the guidelines will make you a good writer' implies that the writer is not good now. A better sentence is, 'Following the guidelines makes us better writers' or 'Following the guidelines results in better messages'.

## SUMMARY

Business letters are written to inform readers of specific information. However, a business letter can also be written to persuade others to take action or propose new ideas. At times, business letters even function as advertisements. For example, the letters long distance phone companies send to those not signed up for their services or even the cover letter to your résumé, both serve to promote or advertise.

Business letters can be challenging to write, because you have to consider how to retain the readers' attention. This is particularly the case if your readers receive large amounts of mail and have little time to read. Writing business letters is like writing any other document—first, you must analyse your audience and determine your purpose. Then you gather information, create an outline, write a draft, and revise it. The key to writing business letters is to get to the point as quickly as possible and to present your information clearly.

In this chapter, the importance of communicating information in a simple, clear, concise, and precise form for a successful manager and for his/her organization's smooth functioning has been discussed. The chapter also emphasizes the necessity of planning for achieving clarity of thought and expression, knowing your audience, purpose, language, and tone, etc.

## KEY TERMS

*Acceptance and rejection letters* In an acceptance letter, you should specify the job you are accepting and the name of your supervisor. Also, review your starting salary, basic job responsibilities, and the date on which you will start work. In a rejection letter, tactfully state your reasons for not taking the job, keeping in mind that you may wish to work for the organization at a later date.

*Covering letter* It is the first step in the whole selection process whereby the prospective applicant puts forward his/her candidature to the employer so that he/she can be considered for the necessary assignment/work.

*Effective business correspondence* It is the hallmark of organizational effectiveness in dealing with both internal and external agencies, and therefore has to be strategically analysed and meticulously planned.

*Formats* These are structured, standard, and universally accepted ways in which business letters related to jobs, routine inquiries, adjustment, sales orders, etc. are written.

*Memos and memorandum reports* These are an important aspect of business correspondence. Memos, once organized, can help us to accomplish organizational goals effectively. Memos and memorandum reports are not the same thing. A memo can be a handwritten note. On the other hand, a memorandum report is always typed, and usually has an introduction, a well-developed body with headings, and a conclusion.

*Persuasive letters* In these letters an extra effort is made to get a request granted through writing and drafting the letters in a particular format so as to emphasize the need more emphatically and effectively.

*Solicited and unsolicited inquiry letters* These letters of inquiry are written when a business or an agency advertises its products or services and any information on these cannot be found locally or if the recipient has done nothing to prompt an inquiry as such.

*Thank-you/follow-up letters* These letters should be written after an interview; when a contact is helpful; provides information; helps you at a career fair; when you visit a contact at their work site; and any other reason for which you want to express thanks, or have a desire to maintain friendly relations.

## Concept Review Questions

1. Is there any strategic approach to handling an unpleasant business situation? How does one say 'No'?
2. 'Organizations need to remember that an emotionally sensitive letter needs to have tact, as there is a human mind at the other end. The reader has feelings too.' Discuss.
3. Rewrite the following negative ideas in positive terms:
   (i) Our office is closed on Monday.
   (ii) I have no experience other than writing accounts in my father's garments store.
   (iii) We are sorry to inform you that the goods cannot be delivered until Tuesday.
   (iv) We cannot ship the electric clocks till you inform us what colours you want.
4. Improve the following statements so that they become more sincere and friendly:
   (i) We are surprised that we have not received your order since a long time.
   (ii) The inconvenience is regretted.
   (iii) While we understand your position, you must also realize that we cannot wait indefinitely for receiving our dues.
   (iv) We note with regret that you are not satisfied with the goods.
5. Improve the tone of the following sentences by using passive voice:
   (i) You damaged the camera by dropping it.
   (ii) An inexperienced clerk in our dispatch department committed the error.
   (iii) Everyone believes that Messrs A and bros have a high credit reputation.
   (v) You have returned the form without signing it.
6. What are the basic ingredients of an effective office memo? How can it be used as a very strong tool to send the right messages and get the necessary action?
7. Persuasive business letters use a tone which runs through the whole message and most of the times, the effect is very positive. How do you think this style is different from simple business writing? Critically examine the efficacy of persuasive writing.

## Critical Thinking Questions

1. You are a chief engineer (constructions) at Sulabh Mills. Your company recently constructed a new administrative building on a five-acre plot. You have landscaped the unused four acres with walkways, fountains, and ponds for employees to enjoy during their lunch hours and before and after work. Your lovely campus-like site is one of the few such locations within the city limits. The mayor of the city is running for re-election. He/ she has written to you seeking permission to hold a public rally-cum-fund raiser on your grounds.

    Her/his election committee will take care of all catering, security, and clean-up. You do not want to give your place for a political activity for various reasons. Write to the mayor and decline his/her request. Structure your reply on the following major heads:
    (i) Your primary and secondary audience
    (ii) Brainstorm—list as many reasons as you can think of, stating why you are refusing her/his request. Determine the best and the most effective reasons.
    (iii) Write a buffer opening—relevant, supportive, interesting, neutral, and short.
    (iv) Write the actual refusal itself—positive, subordinated, and unselfish.
    (v) Write the closing for your letter—original, friendly, off the topic, suggestive, best wishes, etc.

2. Choose an advertisement from a newspaper/magazine of a product/service in which you have some interest. The advertisement probably does not have enough space to provide all the information you need to make an intelligent purchase decision. Write to the company, asking at least three questions about the product. Be sure to mention where you learned about the product. Try to encourage a prompt response. Attach a copy of the advertisement to your letter and submit both to your instructor. Then you can mail the letter along with the advertisement to the company so that the class can later compare the types of responses received from different companies.

3. You are applying for admission to a management college. You are required to write a composition of about 300 words stating your objective in seeking the admission. Draft the statement of your objective.

## Projects

1. Bring in a one-page composition you have written in the past—an essay, business letter, etc. Make sure your name is not on the paper. Exchange papers among several colleagues (so that you are not revising the paper of the person who is revising yours) and complete the following:
   (i) Read the paper once, revising for content. Make sure that all needed information is included, no unneeded information is included, and the information is presented in a logical sequence.
   (ii) Read the paper a second time, revising for style. Make sure that the words, sentences, paragraphs, and overall tone are appropriate.
   (iii) Read the paper a third time, revising the corrections. Make sure that the grammar, punctuation, and word-choice are error free.

   Return the paper to the writer. Then, using the revisions of your paper as a guide only (after all, you are the author), prepare a final version of the paper. Submit both the marked-up and the final version of the page to the instructor.

2. Work in a group of three–four people for this assignment. Assume that a large shopping centre is next to your campus and many students park their cars and bikes for free while attending classes. The shopping centre management is considering closing this space for students' use, citing the need for additional space for customer parking. The members of your team represent different student organizations in the campus—students' union, campus welfare group, NSS volunteers, etc. who have decided to write a joint letter to the manager of the shopping centre, trying to convince him to maintain the status quo. Brainstorm to generate ideas for the contents of the letter; have each member call out possible points to include, while one person writes all the ideas. Do not evaluate now. After 10 to 15 minutes, discuss each point and then decide which to include and in what order. Revise the letter and prepare the final draft.

3. Working in a team of three–four people, assume the role of the grievance committee in your company union. Your company has just reported its first known case of an employee with AIDS. The employee wants to continue working as long as he/she is physically capable of doing so. The company has also allowed him/her to keep working. However, you have received letters from at least five members of the union working in his/her department who have strongly objected to his/her continuing work, worried about the risks of contracting the disease. Although they have compassion for him/her, they want him/her to be allocated some work that will not require frequent interaction. Your committee has done some research on the topic, and based on your findings, you decide not to intervene. Write a memo to the chairman, giving her/him your decision.

# REFERENCES

Brusaw, Charles T., Gerald J. Alred, and Walter E. Oliu 1999, *The Business Writer's Companion*, Second Edition, St. Martin's Press, New York.

'Career Development and Job-search Advice for New College Graduates', 2004 National Association of Colleges and Employers, Bethlehem, PA, JobWeb.com.

Eva Lai 2005, *Writing a Job Application Letter: Major Points to Consider*, Job Search Communication Package, The Independent Learning Centre, The Chinese University of Hong Kong, Hong Kong.

Garratt Lesley 2005, *Revising the Style of the Job Application Letter*, Job Search Communication Package, The Independent Learning Centre, The Chinese University of Hong Kong, Hong Kong.

Hurley, Pat Kamalani 2005, *Good News and Neutral Messages*, University of Hawaii, Hawaii.

McMurrey, David A. 2004, *Online Textbook for Austin Community College's Online Technical Writing Course*, Capital Community College, Hartford, CT.

Perelman, Lesli C., James Paradis, and Edward Barett 2002, *The Mayfield Handbook of Technical Scientific Writing*, Massachusetts Institute of Technology, Cambridge, MA.

Tebbe, Lesley 2005, *Business Correspondence*, Needham, MA, www.salary.com.

## Missing Briefcase

It was Saturday afternoon and Rajesh was determined to take care of all pending correspondence before leaving for the weekend. A few days back, he had received a memo from Sunit John, a sales representative, which went as follows:

'Last week I made a sales presentation to TechIndia Electronics and carried two briefcases with me—my regular one plus a second one filled with brochures and pamphlets. At the conclusion of my presentation, I distributed the brochures, picked up my regular briefcase and left—completely forgetting about my other suitcase. When I discovered the following morning what had happened, I immediately called TechIndia Electronics, but so far they have been unable to locate the suitcase. This leather suitcase was around a month old and cost ₹3,500. Since the company policy manual states that employees will be reimbursed for all reasonable costs of carrying their assigned duties, may I please be reimbursed for the loss of the briefcase? The cash memo is attached.'

Rajesh has been thinking about this situation all week long, he had even discussed it with Deepak Barua, Marketing Chief, who has told him to make whatever decision he thought was reasonable. Sunit is a good sales representative and the policy manual does contain the exact sentence he has quoted. On the other hand, Rajesh feels that assuming responsibilities for such mistakes would not only be expensive but also might encourage padded expense accounts. Finally, Rajesh decides to do two things. First, he would write a memo to all the sales staff, interpreting more fully the company policy. He wants the sales staff to know that in future he intends to interpret this policy to mean that any personal property that is stolen will be reimbursed at present value only if reasonable care has been taken to secure such property, if the incident is reported within two working days, and if the value can be determined. Any sales representative can, however, appeal Rajesh's decisions to Deepak. Second, because the present policy may not have been sufficiently clear, Rajesh would write a memo to Sunit and agree to his reimbursement request.

### Questions

1. How reasonable was John's claim? Was the intent of the policy clear? Should Rajesh have reimbursed him? Why or why not?
2. How reasonable is John's interpretation of the company policy?
3. Compose the two documents that Rajesh intends to write the memos to the sales staff and—Sunit. Format them in appropriate styles.

# CHAPTER 7

# Instructions

## LEARNING OBJECTIVES

After reading this chapter, you will be able to understand

- the term 'instructions'
- why instructions are so important in organizational communication
- how written instructions are framed
- the various steps involved in written instructions
- the importance of headings, tables, charts, and graphs in written instructions
- the importance of oral instructions
- audience analysis and issues like audience adaptation in instructions
- product instructions and its significance for customers

## INTRODUCTION

One of the most common and most important uses of technical writing is *instructions*—the step-by-step explanation of how to do things. However, for something seemingly so easy and intuitive, instructions are some of the worst-written documents one can find.

As an instructor, you should aim at having listeners or readers follow your explanations, learn from your instructions, and then apply this knowledge within the organization.

Instructions generally contain the following elements:

- An announcement of the subject or topic
- A declaration of what can be achieved by following the instructions
- A description of the intended readers
- Information about the scope of the instructions
- Details about the organization of the instructions and how to use the instructions effectively

> Instructions are simple steps that explain how to do a particular task.

Instructions, in general, are simply steps explaining how to do a particular task. They shape a reader's attitude towards a process, a product, or the writer of the instructions.

# WRITTEN INSTRUCTIONS

> Instructions should be so clear that readers will not have to ask for additional help.

Written instructions are the most common kind of instructions. These are generally used in organizations by managers to dictate the process to be followed by the subordinates and companies to specify exactly how a product is to be used. The goal in writing instructions is to make the point so obvious and the steps so self-explanatory that readers will not have to ask for additional help.

Good instructions are not necessarily easy to write. The following steps should be followed while writing instructions:

1. They must be clear enough to be followed.
2. They must be correct.
3. They must contain the appropriate amount of information.
4. It should be obvious where the reader is to begin and what the next step might be, and the connections between the steps should be easy to grasp.
5. The steps should be numbered within the instructions clearly and illustrations should be placed next to the related text.

The key with instructions is to take nothing for granted. Assuming that readers know nothing about the process you are describing is better than risking confusion and possible damage or harm by overlooking some basic information. A few rules for writing instructions are as follows:

1. Include four elements as needed—an introduction, a list of equipment and materials, a description of the steps involved in the process, and a conclusion.
2. Explain in the beginning why the process is important and how it is related to a larger purpose.
3. Divide the process into short, simple steps, presented in order of occurrence.
4. Present the steps in a numbered list, or present them in paragraph format, making plentiful use of words indicating time or sequence, such as 'first' and 'then'.
5. If the process involves more than 10 steps, divide them into groups or stages identified with headings.
6. Indicate, when appropriate how readers may tell whether a step has been performed correctly and how one step may influence another. Supply warnings that performing a step incorrectly could result in damage or injury, but limit the number of warnings so that readers do not underestimate their importance.
7. Include diagrams of complicated devices, and refer to them in the appropriate steps.
8. Summarize the importance of the process and expected results in the conclusion.
9. Present the steps of your directions in a numbered or bulleted list.

'This door is stuck with glue!'

> **BUSINESS COMMUNICATION INSIGHT**
>
> **Effective Product Instructions**
>
> Product instructions should be easily understood and usable by your target audience. The following tips will help you in writing better instructions:
>
> 1. Make sure your instructions are written for your audience, not your organization—people who buy products need to know how to assemble/install/use the product as easily as possible. And because many people may not be tech savvy, instructions need to be understood by the lowest common denominator.
> 2. Instructions should never be written by experts, as they are very prone to making the mistake of assuming that the reader knows a little bit about the subject matter already.
> 3. Instruction writing must match your target audience—for any form of instructions to be followed by non-technical users, the writer should assume zero prior knowledge. Approach with logic and common sense.
> 4. Keep an open mind: No matter how thoroughly you know your product, a fresh outsider's view will often pick up on ways of improving the instructions.
> 5. Test the instructions on people who are genuinely typical of the target audience.
>
> Source: Maur, Suzan St, 'How To Write Product Instructions', http://www.articleslash.net/Business/Marketing.1076_How-To-Write-Product-Instructions.html accessed on 14 September 2011. Reproduced with permission.

10. Number or label the steps and sub-steps clearly. Often, a major step is numbered 1, and the sub-steps are numbered 1.1 and 1.2. The sub-sub-steps are numbered 1.1.1 and 1.1.2, etc. For example:

   1. First major step
      1.1 First sub-step
      1.2 Second sub-step
         1.2.1 First sub-sub-step
         1.2.2 Second sub-sub-step

   2. Second major step
      2.1 First sub-step
      2.2 Second sub-step
         2.2.1 First sub-sub-step
         2.2.2 Second sub-sub-step

11. Restrict each step, sub-step, or sub-sub-step to an individual piece of information.
12. Make liberal use of headings and sub-headings.
13. Tell your readers what to do in case of a mistake or an unexpected result.
14. List alternative steps that readers may take. Place the alternative steps where readers can find them easily.
15. Include a troubleshooting guide at the end of your instructions. The guide will list potential problems and their solutions. Troubleshooting guides often use a table format with the problem in the left column and the solutions to the right.

## How to Write Instructions

At the beginning of a project, before writing instructions, it is important to determine the structure or characteristics of the particular procedure you are going to write about. The following are three ways to ensure that effective instructions have been framed (Fig. 7.1).

**Audience and situation** Early in the process of writing instructions, define the nature of your readers and situations. Remember that defining the readers means defining their level of familiarity with the topic as well as other such details.

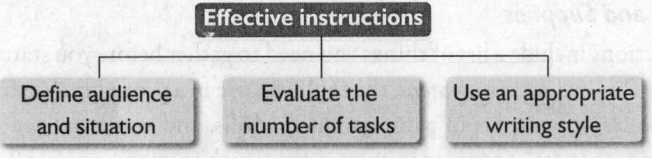

**Fig. 7.1** Effective instructions

**Number of tasks** A task is a semi-independent action within a procedure, for example, setting the clock on a microwave oven is one task in the big overall procedure of operating a microwave oven. A simple procedure like changing oil in a car contains only one task; there are no semi-independent groupings of activities. Some instructions have only a single task, but have many steps within that single task. A good approach is to group similar and related steps into phases, and start renumbering the steps at each new phase. (A *phase* is a group of similar steps within a single-task procedure.)

**Writing style** Notice how 'real-world' instructions are written—they use a lot of imperative (command or direct-address) kind of writing; they use a lot of 'you'. This style is entirely appropriate for writing instructions, to get your reader's full attention. For example, 'Now, press the Pause button on the front panel to stop the display temporarily' or 'You should be careful not to ...'. Also, articles (a, an, and the), punctuation, etc. should be carefully and appropriately used.

## Groupings of Tasks

Listing tasks may not be all that you need to do. There may be so many tasks that you must group them so that readers can find individual ones more easily. For example, the following are common task groupings in instructions: unpacking and set-up tasks; installing and customizing tasks; basic operating tasks; routine maintenance tasks; troubleshooting tasks; and so on.

## Introduction

The introduction to instructions need to be planned carefully. It may indicate

- the specific tasks or procedure to be explained as well as the scope of coverage,
- what the audience needs in terms of knowledge and background to understand the instructions,
- a general idea of the procedure and what it accomplishes,
- the conditions wherein these instructions should (or should not) be used, and/or
- an overview of the contents of the instructions.

The introduction ought to be brisk and to the point. It should not trudge labouriously through each of the above mentioned elements.

## General Warning, Caution, and Danger Notices

Instructions must alert readers to the possibility of ruining their equipment, bunging the procedure, and hurting themselves, and also emphasize key points or exceptions, by using special warning, caution, and danger notices.

### Technical Background or Theory

> Instructions must emphasize key points or exceptions.

At the beginning of certain kinds of instructions, you may need a discussion of the background related to the procedure. For certain instructions, this background is critical—otherwise, the steps in the procedure would make no sense. For example, for certain instructions for using cameras, some theory might be needed as well.

> - Most instructions include a list of things required to start a procedure.
> - Graphics, such as diagrams, tables, and flow charts, are crucial to instructions.

### Equipment and Supplies

Most instructions include a list of things you need to gather before you start a procedure. This includes *equipment*, the tools you use in a procedure (such as, mixing bowls, spoons, bread pans, hammers, drills, and saws) and *supplies*, the things that are consumed in a procedure (such as, wood, paint, oil, flour, and nails). In instructions, these are typically listed either in a simple vertical or a two-column list. Use a two-column list if you need to add some specifications to some or all the items—for example, brand names, sizes, amounts, types, or model numbers.

## Graphics in Instructions

A lot of professional, business, and technical writing contains graphics—drawings, diagrams, photographs, illustrations tables, pie charts, bar charts, line graphs, and flow charts. Once you know how to put graphics into your writing, you should use them wherever appropriate. Graphics are crucial to instructions. Sometimes, words simply cannot explain a step. Illustrations are often critical to readers' ability to visualize what they are supposed to do.

### Graphics—Types and Functions

Figure 7.2 shows a type of graphic used in presentations. Let us consider the types of graphics and their functions. You can use graphics to represent the following elements in your writing:

**Objects** Photographs, drawings, diagrams, and schematics are the types of graphics that show objects. For example, if you are explaining how to graft a fruit tree, you may use cartoon illustrations showing how that task is done.

**Numbers** Numerical data can be represented using tables, bar charts, and pie charts. If you are discussing the rising cost of housing in a city, you could use a table with the columns being for five-year periods since, say, 1970; the rows could be for different types of housing. Tables, bar charts, pie charts, and line graphs are some of the principal ways to represent numerical data.

*Tables* Tables are made up of rows and columns of numbers and words, though they contain mostly numbers. They permit rapid access to and relatively easy comparison of information. If the data is

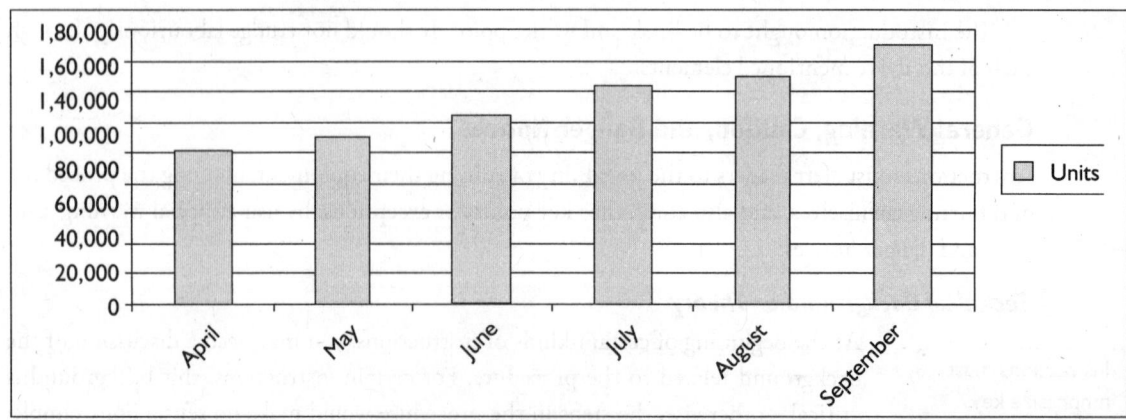

**Fig. 7.2** Graphics in presentations

arranged chronologically, tables are not necessarily the most vivid or dramatic means of showing such trends or relationships between data—that is why we use charts and graphs.

*Charts and graphs* Charts and graphs are actually just another way of presenting the same data that is presented in tables—although a more dramatic and interesting one. At the same time, a chart or diagram has less detail or precision than a table. For example, observe a table of sales figures for a 10-year period and a line graph for that same data. You get a better sense of the overall trend in the graph, but not the precise sales figures.

### Formatting Requirements

When you create charts and diagrams, keep the following requirements in mind (Fig. 7.3):

*Axis labels* In bar charts and line graphs, do not forget to indicate what the *X*- and *Y*-axes represent. One axis might indicate millions of dollars; the other, five-year segments from, say, 1960 to the present.

*Keys* Bar charts, line graphs, and pie charts often use special colour, shading, or line style (solid or dashed). Indicate what these mean; translate them in a key (a box) in some unused place in the chart or graph.

*Figure titles* For most charts and graphs, include a title, and in many cases, a numbered title. Readers need some way of knowing what they are looking at. Cite the source of any information you borrowed in order to create the graphic.

*Cross-references* Whenever you use a chart or graph, do not forget to put a cross-reference to it from the related text. With that cross-reference, provide some explanation of what is going on in the graphic, how to interpret it, and what its basic trends are.

*Documentation* When you borrow information to create a graphic, be sure to use the standard format to indicate the source. It does not matter whether you photocopy the graphic and tape it into your report, re-type the graphic (e.g., a table), trace or draw the graphic freehand, or take some subset of the data (e.g., using data from a table to create a bar chart)—it is all borrowed information, which someone also worked hard to develop and who deserves credit for that effort.

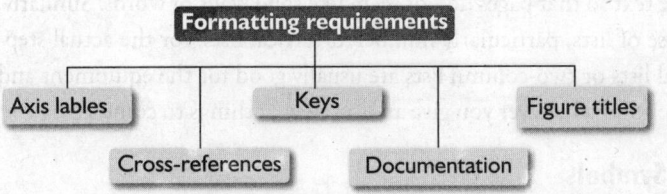

**Fig. 7.3** Important considerations in formatting

## FORMAT IN INSTRUCTIONS

In this section, we shall discuss different instruction formats.

### Headings

Headings are the titles and sub-titles you see within the actual text of professional, scientific, technical, and business writing. They alert readers to upcoming topics and sub-topics, help them find their way around long reports and skip what they are not interested in, and break up long stretches of straight text. Headings are also useful for writers. They keep you organized and focused on the topic. When you begin using headings, your impulse may be to insert the headings *after* you have written the rough draft. Instead, visualize the headings *before* you start the rough draft, and plug them in as you write.

### Communication Tool

**Tips for Headings**

- Use headings to mark off the boundaries of the major sections and subsections of a report.
- Try for two to three headings per regular page of text.
- For short documents, begin with the second-level heading and skip the first level.
- Make the phrasing of headings parallel.
- Make the phrasing of headings self-explanatory: instead of 'Background' or 'Technical Information', make it more specific, such as 'Physics of Fiber Optics'.
- Make headings indicate the range of topic coverage in the section. For example, if the section covers the *design* and *operation* of a pressurized water reactor, the heading 'Pressurized Water Reactor Design' would be incomplete and misleading.
- Avoid 'lone' headings—any heading by itself within a section without another of the same kind. For example, avoid having a second-level heading followed by only one third-level heading (the third-level heading would be the lone heading).
- Avoid pronoun reference to headings. For example, if you have a third-level heading 'Torque', do not begin the sentence following it with something like this: 'This is a physics principle …'.
- When possible, omit articles from the beginning of headings. For example, 'The Pressurized Water Reactor' can easily be changed to 'Pressurized Water Reactor' or 'Pressurized Water Reactors'.
- Do not use headings as lead-ins to lists or as figure titles.

### Lists

Lists are useful because they emphasize certain information in a regular text. When you see a list of three or four items strung out vertically on a page, rather than in a normal paragraph format, you naturally notice it more. Certain types of lists also make for easier reading. For example, in instructions, it is a big help for each step to be numbered and separate from the preceding or following steps. Lists also create more white space and spread out the text so that pages do not seem like solid walls of words. Similarly, instructions typically make heavy use of lists, particularly numbered vertical lists, for the actual step-by-step explanations. Simple vertical lists or two-column lists are usually good for the equipment and supplies section. In-sentence lists are good whenever you give an overview of things to come.

### Numbers, Abbreviations, and Symbols

Instructions also use plenty of numbers, abbreviations, and symbols.

#### *Numbers and Words*

Following are some of the rules which are useful regarding some issues with respect to numbers and words:

1. Do not start sentences with numerals—write the number out or, better yet, rephrase the sentence so that the numeral does not begin the sentence.
2. For decimal values less than 1, add 0 before the decimal point: for example, .08 should be 0.08.
3. Make a firm decision on how to handle 0 and 1 when they refer to key, exact values.
4. Use numerals for important, exact values, even when those values are below 10.

> Lists are useful because they emphasize on relevant information within the text.

5. Use words for numerical values less than 10 that are unimportant, such as in the sentence, 'There are six data types in the C programming language'.
6. When using fractions, avoid the symbols that may be available in the character set used by your software or typewriter. Construct the fraction like this: 5-1/4. Be sure to put the hyphen between the whole number and the fraction.
7. Stay consistent with either decimals or fractions in these situations.
8. Do not make numerical values look more exact than they are. For example, do not add '.00' to a rupee amount if the amount is rounded or estimated.
9. For large amounts, you can write, for example, 36 lakh or 45 crore, but not 23 thousand.

### *Abbreviations and Symbols*

In technical-writing contexts, you may often have to decide whether to use " or ' for inches or feet or to use 'inches', or 'in'. First of all, remember that symbols and abbreviations are distracting to readers; they are different from the normal flow of words. However, there are plenty of cases where the written-out version is more distracting than the symbol or abbreviation. Also, the context also decides whether to use symbols and abbreviations. For example, if a document has only one or two references to numerical measurements in inches, there is no reason to use symbols or abbreviations. But in a document with numerous feet and inch references, using symbols or abbreviations is more efficient.

Which standard symbols and abbreviations are to be used? Follow the standards in the field in which you are writing, or those found in a standard reference book, such as a dictionary. Do not make them up yourself (e.g., 'mtr' for metre). Very few abbreviations take an 's' to indicate plurality, for example, 5 in. means 5 inches. For the few that you think might take the 's', check a dictionary. What about obscure abbreviations and symbols? If you are concerned that readers might not recognize the abbreviation or symbol, write its full name in regular text and then put the abbreviation and symbol in parenthesis just after the the first occurrence of that word.

## ORAL INSTRUCTIONS

Oral instruction is a form of dyadic communication. Speaking in such situations as reporting, briefings, etc. gives you less freedom than when instructing. Here you have more room for individual creativity. You have to choose the best and most effective way of making the listener understand your instructions completely. Since instructing involves preparing employees to do a better job of managing and then preparing them to instruct others, it cannot be taken lightly.

Most often you will be required to give instructions to your subordinates. The following guidelines have been written with the aim to help an instructor:

1. Keep in mind the background knowledge of the subordinates, their psychological make-up, capacity to grasp, and ability to act upon your instructions.
2. Make sure that you restrict yourself to the one task which you want to be performed.
3. Separate each instruction by a time-gap or a clear signal in case you want to give more than one instruction.
4. Use plain, direct, and polite language.
5. Keep the sentences short.

**Image 7.1** Make sure your instructions are understood clearly

6. Find out whether your instruction was successful by observing whether the action implied in the instruction had been performed according to your visualization (Image 7.1).

## AUDIENCE ANALYSIS

You 'adapt' your writing to meet the needs, interests, and backgrounds of the intended readers. Lack of audience analysis and adaptation is one of the root causes of most of the problems found in professional documents. Therefore, let us now discuss the various types of audience and factors required for audience analysis.

### Types of Audience

One of the first things to do when you analyse an audience is to identify its type (Fig. 7.4). The common division of audience into categories is as follows:

**Experts** These are people who know the theory and its products. They design and test products, and know everything about them. Often, they have advanced degrees and operate in academic settings or in research and development areas of government and business worlds. More often, one of the challenges faced by an expert is communicating to technicians and executives.

**Technicians** These are people who build, operate, maintain, and repair products that the experts design and theorize about. Theirs is a highly technical realm as well.

**Executives** These are people who make business, economic, administrative, legal, governmental, and political decisions on the products that the experts and technicians work on. Executives are likely to have as little technical knowledge about the subject as non-specialists.

**Non-specialists** These people have the least technical knowledge. Their interest may be as practical as technicians', but in a different way. They want to use new products to accomplish their tasks or, they may just be curious about a specific technical matter and want to learn about it.

### Factors for Audience Analysis

It is important to determine the category of each target audience with respect to the four just discussed. However, audiences, regardless of these categories, must also be analysed in terms of the following factors:

**Background—knowledge, experience, training** One of the most important concerns while instructing is just how much knowledge, experience, or training you can expect from your readers. If

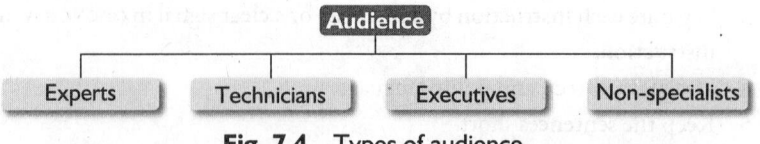

**Fig. 7.4** Types of audience

you expect some of your readers to lack certain background information, do you automatically supply it in your document? Consider an example: assume that you are writing a guide to using a software product that runs under Microsoft Windows. How much can you expect your readers to know about Windows? If some are likely to know a little about Windows, should you provide that information? Obviously, there is no easy answer to this question—part of the answer may depend on the size of the segment of the audience that needs that background information.

**Needs and interests**   To plan your document, you need to know what your audience is going to expect from that document. Imagine how readers will want to use your document; what will they demand from it. For example, imagine that you are writing a manual on how to use a new microwave oven—what are your readers going to expect to find in it and, equally important, what do they not want to read about?

**Other demographic characteristics**   There are many other characteristics about your readers that might have an influence on how you should design and frame your instruction—for example, age groups, type of residence, area of residence, sex, and political preferences.

**More than one audience**   You are likely to find that your report is for more than one audience. For example, it may be seen by technical people (experts and technicians) and administrative people (executives). You can either write all the sections so that all the audience of your document can understand it, or you can write each section strictly for the audience that would be interested in it, then use headings and section introductions to alert your audience about where to go and what to avoid in your report.

**Wide variability in an audience**   You may realize that, although you have an audience that fits into only one category, there is a wide variability in its background. If you do not cater to that lowest level, you lose that segment of your readers. Most writers put the supplemental information in appendixes or insert cross-references to beginners' books.

## Audience Adaptation

Once you have understood your audience, pay attention to how you write. The business of writing to your audience may have a lot to do with in-born talent and intuition. However, there are some controls you can use to have a better chance to connect with your readers (Image 7.2). The following controls have mostly to do with making information more understandable for non-specialist audience:

**Add key information**   Check to see whether certain key information is missing.

**Omit unnecessary information**   Unnecessary information can confuse and frustrate readers—after all, it is there so they feel obligated to read it. For example, you can probably remove theoretical discussion from basic instructions.

**Change the level of the information**   You may have the right information, but it may be 'pitched' too high or too low. It may be directed at the wrong kind of audience—for example, at an expert audience.

> A report should be adapted keeping in mind the kind of audience it will cater to.

**Add examples**   Examples are one of the most powerful ways to connect with audience, particularly in instructions. Analogies are particularly helpful.

**Change the organization of your information**   Sometimes, you can have all the right information, but arrange it in the wrong way. For example, there can

**Image 7.2** Connect with your readers

be too much (or too little) background information up front such that certain readers get lost. Sometimes, background information needs to be woven into the main information.

**Strengthen transitions**  It may be difficult for readers, particularly non-specialists, to see the connections between the main sections of your report, between individual paragraphs, and sometimes even between individual sentences. You can make these connections much clearer by adding *transition words* and by echoing *keywords* more accurately. Words like 'therefore', 'for example', and 'however' are transition words—they indicate the logic connecting the previous thought to the upcoming thought. You can also strengthen transitions by carefully echoing the same keywords.

**Write stronger introductions**  People seem to read with more confidence and understanding when they have the 'big picture'—a view of what is coming, and how it relates to what they have just read. Therefore, make sure that you have a strong introduction—one that makes clear the topic, purpose, audience, and contents of your document. For each major section within your document, use mini-introductions that indicate at least the topic of the section and give an overview of the sub-topics to be covered in that section.

**Work on sentence clarity and economy**  Often, writing style can be so wordy that it is difficult or frustrating to read. When you revise your rough draft, go through it line by line trying to reduce the overall word, page, or line count by 20 per cent. Try it as an experiment and see how you do. You will find a lot of fussy, unnecessary detail and inflated phrasing you can chop out.

**Use more or different graphics**  For non-specialist audience, you may want to use more graphics—and simpler ones at that. Writing for specialists and experts tends to be less illustrated, less graphically attractive—even boring to the eye.

**Use readable type styles**  For non-specialist readers, you can do things like making the lines shorter (bringing in the margins), using larger font sizes, and other such tactics. Certain type styles are friendlier and more readable than others.

## PRODUCT INSTRUCTIONS

With the growth of high technology products and more complex features in existing products, proper product instruction has become an integral part of a company's marketing strategy, and corporations are going all out to make it as effective as possible. Good product instructions are accurate, can be easily understood and used, and are suited to the environments in which they are used. Instructions are needed whenever the design of a product alone is not sufficient to guide people to use the product properly. Product instructions should give people the information they need, when and where they need it.

> Product instruction has become an integral part of a company's marketing strategy.

## Characteristics of Good Product Instructions

Effective product instructions have the following characteristics:

- Logical sequences of actions, discriminations, and judgements leading to successful outcomes
- Concise, understandable, and direct, and therefore, appropriate for users
- Identification and emphasis on hazards
- Formatted for the way people use them
- Physically attractive to encourage use

### Good Product Instructions Rely upon Good Analysis

A thorough understanding of the people, tasks, and conditions is essential to insure that both products and their instructions work well with the people using them. A systematic analysis of these factors creates the needed foundation for the design of instructions. Some examples are as follows:

- Users are identified and characterized
- Task logic is developed and tested
- Needed behavioural skills and abilities are delineated
- Working conditions are investigated and described
- Hazards are identified and strategies are developed

### Product Instructions can Take Any Form

The primary purpose for product instructions is to convey essential information to users when it is not available or cannot be communicated through the design of the product itself. There are many different ways to accomplish this.

### Instruction Sheets, Control Labels, Stickers, Tags, etc.

The familiar instruction sheet packaged with many products is only one of many ways to provide information to users. Control labels and symbols, dial markings, name plates, and other signs and marks on products also serve as instructions.

### Warnings, Cautions, Notices

Hazard labels and other cautionary notices affixed to devices or mounted in their vicinity instruct users to be careful while handling those devices. However, instructions alone cannot make dangerous products safe, they can only help people avoid accidents and injury.

### Embedded Helps

On-demand information is widely used in software applications. Similar techniques are available for non-computer uses also.

### Non-visual Stimuli

Auditory tones or brief spoken messages can be instructional. Even tactile stimuli have been used to successfully communicate information.

### Function of Instructions

The function of instructions can vary widely. *Procedural guides* help people assemble, install, and operate products. *Decision aids* help people choose among alternative applications and actions. *Troubleshooting guides* help users isolate problems and find the resources they need to make repairs.

## SUMMARY

Instructions are a very important form of communication tools, quite useful when it comes to explaining a technical product or a process to an audience that is not from the same field as required for an easy product/process understanding.

Instructions generally contain the announcement of the subject or topic, a declaration of what can be achieved by following the instructions, descriptions of the intended readers (those for whom the instructions are intended), and information about the scope of the instructions—what they cover, details about the organization of the instructions, and how to use the instructions effectively.

Written instructions, generally have to follow a definite format for proper understanding and effective transfer of the message to a receiver.

Instructions must be clear, correct, and contain appropriate amount of information. Visual design and page layout are also very important. Instructions must be easy to read, and the connections between steps should be easy to grasp.

## KEY TERMS

**Audience analysis**  It is the detailed study of a target audience (intended or potential readers) of a piece of writing.

**Oral instruction**  It is a form of dyadic communication that helps you choose the best and most effective way of making the listener understand your instructions completely.

**Product instruction**  It has become a very integral part of a company's marketing strategy with the growth of high technology products and more complex features in the existing products. Corporations are going all out to make this as effective as possible as they have realized that this is a very important aspect of product communication to a customer.

**Troubleshooting**  It helps users isolate problems and find the resources they need to make repairs.

**Written instruction**  These are the most common kind of instructions generally used in organizations by managers to dictate a process that needs to be followed by the subordinates so that they know exactly how a product is to be used.

## Concept Review Questions

1. Why are instructions so important and determine how instruction strategies allow a manager to give simple and effective instructions to his/her sub-ordinates?
2. A clear and straight instruction not only reflects the clear thought process of the manager but also reflects the overall corporate vision of an organization. Discuss.
3. Product instructions have become a very important area of focus for companies manufacturing technical products. Illustrate with an example.
4. What is audience analysis? Why it is so critical and how can it be effectively undertaken and used by a company while issuing instructions.
5. What are the key points which differentiate oral communication from written? Discuss in detail.

## Critical Thinking Questions

1. In the following list, select the statements that you think are important while writing instructions. Justify your selection.
   - Adding some jokes to your instructions.
   - Writing your instructions in the right order.
   - Giving a detailed description of what the video player looks like.
   - Making your writing clear and easy to understand.
   - Displaying your knowledge of the technical side of the video.
   - Giving direct and simple commands/directions.

2. Read the two sets of instructions below. Decide which one you think is more successful and why.
   
   (i) Set A
   
   Mother: 'Let us see if we can get it right this time. I do not want to be watching Des O'Connor like last time! You need to put the video in the machine and then press the record button. That is the small red one which is a little to the left of the play button, which looks like a Smartie with an arrow on it—you cannot miss it. The stop button is just below the play button, I think. Oh, by the way, do not forget to rewind the tape first, and you will need to change the channel too probably.'
   
   (ii) Set B
   - Put the tape in the machine.
   - Press rewind and wait until the rewinding has finished.
   - Change the channel to 5.
   - The record button is the red one in the top left corner. Press it.
   - Check whether the recording light is on.
   - Press stop when the programme has finished.

3. Your mother left some instructions for you on how to clean the car. However, they are a bit of a jumble and could be a lot clearer. Put them into the right order by numbering them 1 to 6.
   - Using the chamois leather, polish the car until it sparkles.
   - Wash the car thoroughly.
   - First clean the inside of the car with the vacuum cleaner.
   - Fill with soapy water.
   - Then fetch a bucket from the garage.
   - Rinse the car with clean water.

## Projects

1. Write instructions for a new student on how to get from one part of your university to another, for example, from your classroom to the library.
2. Write down the recipe of one of your favourite dishes.
3. Choose a useful computer program and write instructions on how to use it. You may use up to 10 different instructions.

## REFERENCES

Clampitt, Philip G. 2005, *Communication for Managerial Effectiveness*, Sage Publication, California, pp. 17–29.

Mathew, Subin, 'Instructions for a Good Life', Subins software, http/members.tripod.com, last accessed on 21 November 2004.

McMurrey, David A. 2001, *Power Tools for Technical Communication*, Thomson Learning/Heinle Publishers, Boston, pp. 45–52.

Rai, Urmila and S.M. Rai 2002, *Business Communication*, Himalaya Publishing, Mumbai, pp. 74–86.

Sen, Lalita 1998, *Communication Skills*, Prentice Hall India Ltd, New Delhi, pp. 35–47.

Tribe, Jennifer, 'Seven Tips for Writing Effective How-To Instructions', www.netwrite-publish.com, last accessed on 27 November 2004.

'Writing Skills for Effective Instructions', www.englishonline.com, last accessed on 22 November 2004.

Ysseldyke, Jim and Peggy Wiltse, University of Minnesota, 'Strategies and Tactics for Effective Instruction', American Society of Technical Communication website, www.mayorsonacademy.org., last accessed on 21 November 2004.

e-instruction, www.icicibank.com, last accessed on 21 November 2004.

www.webwritingthatworks.com, last accessed on 25 November 2004.

## CASE STUDY 1

**How to Operate the Minolta Freedom 3 Camera**

The Minolta Freedom 3 is a very versatile camera that is very easy to operate, making it the perfect camera for the beginner photographer. Most 35mm cameras require you to adjust the amount of light to be allowed onto the film and to focus the camera. The Minolta Freedom 3 does this for you, as well as advancing each picture to the next frame. You will be able to take professional quality pictures after mastering these following easy steps: 1. loading the film, 2. taking the picture, and 3. unloading the film.

**Equipment and supplies**  To get started using your camera, you will need the following items:

- Minolta Freedom 3 camera
- Roll of 35mm film

**Warning:** *Different films are for different occasions. Just remember that lower ISO numbers (this will be on the film box as 25, 100, 200, 400, or 1000) need more light and less movement. Higher numbers are for taking pictures inside or where there is a lot of activity.*

**Loading the film**  Before you can begin taking pictures with your camera, you need to put an unexposed roll of film into your camera. This can be done by following these easy steps: 1. opening the back of the camera, 2. putting the film in the camera, and 3. advancing the film.

**Opening the back of the camera**  This camera will help you load the film. All you need to do is perform the following steps:

1. Turn the camera face down so you are looking at its back with the viewfinder pointing away from you. You will notice the film door covers the entire back of the camera beneath the viewfinder.
2. Find the film door opener on the left-hand side of the door. Push this switch up and the door will swing open.

**Putting the film in the camera**  You are now ready to put an unexposed roll of film into the camera. This is done in the following ways:

1. Take the film out of its box.

**Warning:** *Film producers recommend that the film should be loaded in low light levels. This is to protect the film from being exposed before it is put in your camera. Do not pull the film out of the cassette except as indicated below.*

2. Hold the film cassette so the little inner hub is pointing toward you. Place the film into the left-hand side of the camera. The film will only go in one way so do not force the cassette into place.

**Advancing the film**  The camera will now do the hard work of advancing the film. All you need to do is perform the following steps:

1. Hold the cassette in place with your left hand as you pull enough film from the cassette to reach the right side of the camera. Slide this end piece of film around the rubber hub and press the notched holes of the film onto the matching notched teeth of the hub.
2. Locate the clear, plastic door on the right-hand side of the film door. Close this door onto the film and hub. The camera will now advance the film. If it does not, repeat the previous step.
3. Close the main film door. As you do this, the motor will advance the film to exposure 1. On top of the camera in the centre, the display window will now say 1 in the lower right-hand corner.

**Taking the picture**  Now that the film has been loaded into the camera, you are ready to start taking pictures. The majority of the work is done by the camera, but a few easy steps must be followed to maintain a consistent quality in your pictures. These are 1. holding the camera, 2. framing the picture, and 3. taking the picture.

**Holding the camera**  Holding the camera is a very important part of picture taking; an improperly held camera can result in blurred pictures caused by camera movement. To ensure a good picture, you must perform the following steps:

1. Grasp the camera with its front pointing away from you in your right hand so that your index finger is wrapped around the top, right-hand corner of the camera. Your remaining fingers should be in the notch of the lens cover and your thumb should be on the film compartment door.
2. Place the camera into your left palm so it has a flat, sturdy platform to rest on.

**Warning:** *Make sure your shoulder strap is held out of the way of the lens. This can cause pictures to be partially blacked out.*

**Framing the picture**  Framing the picture means getting everything into the picture that you want. To frame a picture, you need to perform the following steps:

1. Hold the camera up to your face with the front facing away from you. Position the viewfinder to the eye that you will be looking through. Close the other eye.
2. Aim the camera at the subject that you will be photographing and look through the viewfinder. You will see a representation of the picture.
3. Centre the main item of your picture into the middle of the viewfinder. The white box around the outside edge of the viewfinder is a representation of the outer edge of your picture. If something you want in the picture falls outside this edge, back up to squeeze this in.
4. Make sure the small inner box in the very centre of the viewfinder is on the subject you want photographed. This is the spot where the camera will focus.

**Warning:** *Failure to centre the focusing box on your subject can result in blurred pictures.*

**Taking the picture**  The final step in picture taking is actually taking the picture. All you need to do is:

1. Make sure that there is nothing, fingers or shoulder strap, directly in front of the camera.
2. Find the shutter release. This square silver button, located under your right index finger on the top right-hand side of the camera, is what triggers the camera to actually take the picture.
3. Depress the shutter release. Your picture is taken and the film is automatically advanced to the next frame. (The Minolta Freedom 3 automatically adjusts for different lighting situations and turns the flash on automatically when needed.)

**Warning:** *When taking a picture, if a red light appears in the viewfinder, this means the flash needs a moment to charge itself. Wait a few seconds until a green light comes on, then take your picture. Failure to wait will result in dark pictures due to lack of light.*

**Unloading the film**  After you have finished taking your pictures, you need to get the exposed roll of film out of your camera so that you can get it processed into pictures. This is done by 1. rewinding the film and 2. removing the cassette.

**Warning:** *Never open the back of the camera before the film is rewound back into its cassette. Doing so will expose the entire roll to light which will ruin all of your pictures.*

**Questions**

1. Critically analyse the above set of instructions from the point of view of completeness, conciseness, headings, and use of format for instructions.
2. Whom do you think the instructions are meant for? Do you think the product uses the right audience analysis?
3. Do you think the above instruction pattern is required for all kinds of products or it is required for only technical products like a camera. Justify your view.
4. Use the above sets/patterns of instructions and rewrite it for a recipe for lemon tea.

# CHAPTER 8

# Business Reports and Proposals

## LEARNING OBJECTIVES

After reading this chapter, you will be able to understand

- what are business reports and proposals
- types of reports and proposals
- the steps in report writing
- the various components of reports and proposals
- format and layout of reports and proposals

## INTRODUCTION

Imagine that you have a terrific idea for installing a new technology where you work and you write a document explaining how it works, point out the benefits, and end by urging the management to go for it. Is that a proposal? No, it is more like a feasibility report, which studies the merits of a project and then recommends for or against it. Now, all it would take to make this document a proposal would be to add elements that ask management for approval for you to go ahead with the project.

Some proposals must sell the projects they offer to do, but in all cases proposals must sell the writer (or the writer's organization) as the one to do the project. In today's competitive business environment, it is hard to get new orders, customers, or business partners. Therefore, most businesses have to prepare proposals to get new orders to increase their profits. This may be a bid on contract, a business proposal to a government authority, or to another company/organization. Likewise, when these businesses accomplish their projects or assignments, they need to prepare reports to record the details.

> - A report is a logical presentation of facts and information.
> - A proposal is a special analytical type of report prepared to get products, plans, or projects accepted by others.

In business, virtually, every aspect of any job involves report writing—annual reports, monthly sales reports, or production and project reports—all of which require extensive analysis of data and figures. Almost everyone in a management job has to do some report writing. The higher the job, the more reports it usually entails. Besides, every organization has a system of routine periodical reporting on the progress and status of different activities. The management may assign certain special studies, time to time, for taking some special decisions. The information normally presented in the report is needed for reviewing and evaluating progress,

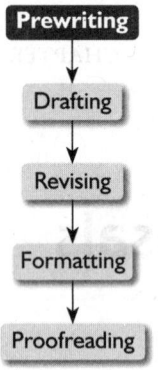

**Fig. 8.1** The five-step report writing process

for planning a future course of action and taking critical and strategic decisions. They act as a perfect feedback mechanism on various aspects of the organization. However, only a well-prepared proposal and the ensuing well-documented report on completion of the proposed project will be successful. Most managers rely on reports to provide information and analysis so that they can make decisions and solve problems. As a businessperson, you may need to write and read all kinds of reports that objectively communicate information about some aspect of the business.

A proposal, on the other hand, is a special analytical type of report prepared to get products, plans, or projects accepted by others. Proposals are an important part of job-related writing because their acceptance can lead to significant operational improvements, new business, additional jobs, and safer working conditions. Proposals can be one or two pages long, or they can be hundreds of pages if they involve large and complex plans.

As with other business messages, when writing reports and proposals, you benefit from the following five step writing process: prewriting, drafting, revising, formatting, and proofreading (Fig. 8.1). However, when preparing these longer messages, you may need to add some tasks to the familiar categories or you may need to pay special attention to tasks you are already familiar with. For example, besides analysing your purpose and audience, you might want to study the situation carefully to determine whether a report is called for and which type of report would be most appropriate. This chapter focuses on the definition, types, structure, contents, and organization of business proposals and business reports.

## WHAT IS A REPORT?

A report is a logical presentation of facts and information. A good business report must be an orderly arrangement of some factual information that is objective in nature and serves some business purpose.

It is designed to give a complete picture of what has taken place at a distance from the reader who does not know about it and gathers knowledge about it from what the writer presents in the report. According to the American Marketing Society, the purpose of a report is 'to convey (to) the interested persons the whole results of the study in sufficient details and so arranged as to enable each reader to comprehend the data and so determine for himself the validity of conclusions'. The British Association for Commercial and Industrial Education has defined a report as 'a document in which a given problem is examined for the purpose of conveying information and findings, putting forward ideas first, and sometimes making recommendations'.

> Reports are broadly categorized into information reports and research reports.

## Kinds of Reports

A report is a compilation of information that has been sought, collected, organized, and written to convey a specific message. The objective is either to present information or analyse a particular situation. Consequently, reports are broadly categorized into information and research reports (Fig. 8.2).

An *information report* may present a record of previous events, or it may periodically cover past and new information that will allow readers to stay current on a topic, see progress on a project, or gain insight on product development. The purpose of the information report is to convey ideas and data as clearly, concisely, and correctly as possible.

A *research report* is concerned with analysing information. A writer looks at a problem that needs to be solved, gathers data and analyses the data that are available, arrives at a decision, and then makes recommendations. Research reports may solve merchandizing or production problems, offer remedies for better ways of financing, or give insights into anticipated acts by competitors. The objective is that the reader of a research report will desire to take some action as a result of the new information presented in the report.

**Fig. 8.2** Kinds of reports

## Who Writes and Reads Reports?

Consider the following routine informational needs of a large complex, multinational organization:

A marketing manager at company headquarters uses some information provided by the field sales representative to ascertain sales for the next three months.

A manager prepares proposals for the company to submit bids for a government project.

The vice president—administration informs all subordinates about a new company policy on hiring temporary personnel.

An HR manager relies on the legal cell of the company to interpret government regulations for completing a compliance report.

A production head asks subordinates to gather and analyse information needed to make an operational decision.

These common situations, just mentioned, show why a wide variety of reports have become such a basic part of the typical management information systems. As a result of constraints imposed by geographical separation, time pressures, and lack of technical expertise, managers have to rely on others to provide the information, analysis, and recommendations they need for making decisions and solving problems. Moreover, because they travel upward, downward, and laterally within the organization, reading and writing reports is a typical part of nearly every manager's duties.

## Characteristics of Business Reports

Business reports should be an orderly and objective presentation of information that may help in decision-making and problem solving. The report must be orderly so that the reader can locate the

> Business reports should be accurate and objective.

needed information quickly. It must be objective because the reader will use the report to make decisions that affect the health and wealth of the organization. It must present information and facts. Where subjective judgements are required such as in making recommendations, reports must be presented ethically and be based squarely on the information presented in the report. Finally, the report must be useful—there should be a 'need-to-know' dimension in business reports that is sometimes missing. They must provide the specific information that management needs to make a critical decision. This objective should be of top priority in a report writer's mind during all phases of the writing process.

## Elements of Effective Business Report Writing

In presenting information, an effective business report should be accurate and objective.

### *Accuracy*

Accuracy in a business report includes accuracy of information and writing. Since information in a business report is used to make decisions, inaccurate information can lead to inaccurate decisions. Therefore, make sure your report deals with factual information only. The accuracy of any report depends upon the correctness of the data that was gathered to prepare it. Use reliable sources and be accurate in reporting all information. The accuracy of writing depends on accuracy in writing mechanics (spelling, punctuation, and grammar) and writing style. To avoid writing style errors, use precise words and terms that are not likely to be misinterpreted by readers. Some examples are given in Table 8.1.

### *Objectivity*

In writing, objectivity means presenting material free from personal feelings or prejudices, which is sometimes difficult to accomplish. Some tips to achieve objectivity in writing are listed as follows:

**Make a distinction between facts and opinions**   Minimize unsupported judgements and inferences.

**Example:** You are gathering information on the quality of service offered by your bank's tellers. In an interview, a customer tells you, 'The tellers are always well-mannered and pleasant, even when they serve customers who rush them or complain because they had to wait in line.'

While this information is valuable for your report, it should be included as an opinion rather than a fact.

**Report all pertinent information** Present both positive and negative aspects.

**Example:** You are reporting on the effects of your company's experimental flexi-time system for work hours. Look for both benefits and problems resulting from the system.

**Table 8.1**   Examples of precise terms and references

| Unspecific Terms | Specific Terms |
|---|---|
| • Profits have increased | • Increase of $100,000 annually |
| • Improved efficiency | • 20 per cent increase in efficiency |
| • Staff reduction | • One less operator |

| Unspecific Reference | Specific Reference |
|---|---|
| • Procedures have changed. | • Procedures have been changed. |
| • This is the reason for the delay. | • These changes account for the delay. |

> The purpose of a business report is to aid in decision-making.

If you enjoy the new system and want to see it become a permanent arrangement, it may be difficult for you to present a fair-minded view of the negative aspects. However, your credibility as a writer and the value of your report depends upon your objectivity.

## Purpose of Business Reports

A business report conveys information to assist in decision-making. Some reports might present the actual solution to solve a business problem; other reports might record historical information that will be useful in making future decisions. Either way, the information being reported will be useful in making decisions. In order for a writer to have a clear understanding of why a report is written, a written statement or question purpose is essential. Let us look at the following examples:

Statements of purpose

- To determine ways to improve employee morale.
- To design a new procedure for the company's annual inventory.

Questions of purpose

- Should new computers be purchased to replace the older models?
- Should the office arrangement be open or modular?

Now that you know why you write business reports, let us go through the steps of how to write one.

 Refer to the Online Resource Centre for samples of business reports.

## STEPS IN WRITING A ROUTINE BUSINESS REPORT

Your assignment will be to write a memo report to help solve a business-related problem. Think of a job you currently have (or have had in the past). Is there something you would change? Have you noticed a procedure or an on-going situation that could be improved? Perhaps new equipment is needed or the physical layout is inefficient. Perhaps the work-flow needs to be revised or company policy needs to be re-evaluated. There is sure to be something you would like to see improved. Once you have a topic, you are then ready to start thinking in terms of a report. Do not decide on a solution right now. Go through some steps to arrive at the right solution. In creating your report, follow these steps:

1. Determine the scope of the report.
2. Consider the audience.
3. Gather information.
4. Analyse the information.
5. Determine the solution.
6. Organize the report.

> A common fault of many reports is making the scope of the report too general or too vague.

### Determine the Scope of the Report

A common fault of many reports is making the scope of a report too general or too vague. When you choose a subject for a report, one of the first steps is to narrow the scope to a report length. The scope of the report is defined by determining the factors that you will study. You need to limit the amount of information you will gather to the most needed and most important factors. For example, factors to be studied to determine ways to improve employee morale might include the following:

- Salaries
- Fringe benefits
- Work assignments
- Work hours
- Evaluation procedures

## Consider the Audience

Unlike letters and memos, reports usually have a far wider distribution. Many people may be involved in a decision-making process and may need to read the information in the report. Your job is to make it easy for the reader. Usually, there are multiple audience (Table 8.2) and each audience has unique needs.

Some audience considerations include the following factors:

- Need
- Education level
- Position in the organization
- Knowledge of the topic or area
- Responsibility to act
- Age
- Biases
- Preferences
- Attitudes

**Table 8.2** Kinds of audience

| | |
|---|---|
| **Primary** | People who have to act or make decisions on the basis of a report |
| **Secondary** | People who are affected by the actions taken by the primary audiences in response to the report |
| **Immediate** | People who are responsible for evaluating the report and getting it to the right people |

## Gather Your Information

Now that you have a clear understanding of the purpose and scope of your report and the audience, you are ready to gather your information. This information you gather can be of two types: secondary and primary. *Secondary information* is gathered and recorded by others. *Primary information* is the information you gather and record yourself. However, each type has its drawbacks (Table 8.3), and you must be alert while employing these.

At this point, research is what is required. Think about where you are going to find your information. For example, if the purpose of your report requires purchase information, you might want to check with vendors and distributors for features and pricing information.

**Table 8.3** Types and sources of information with their drawbacks

| Type | Sources | Drawbacks |
|---|---|---|
| **Secondary** | Books, Internet, reports, newspapers, magazines, pamphlets, and journals | Information may be inaccurate, out of date, or biased |
| **Primary** | Questionnaires, surveys, observations, experiments, historical information, and raw data | Information must be gathered carefully to ensure it is accurate and bias free |

## Analyse Your Information

> Report writing involves two types of information—secondary and primary.

After information has been gathered it needs to be analysed. The purpose of the analysis is to make sense, objectively, of the information you have gathered. Separate facts and figures need to be interpreted by explaining what they mean—what significance they have. For example, if you were wondering which computer to buy for your office, you would collect information on the type of work you are currently doing in your office and the kind of work you want to do. Then you would gather information on computers. This information might include cost, compatibility, speed of operation, machine capacity, machine dependability, maintenance availability, potential for upgrading, and other factors. Then you would compare and contrast (analyse) the different computers to determine how well they can do what you want done, what their potential is, how dependable they are, and so on. Once all the information is gathered, you are ready to determine solutions.

## Determine Solutions

Based on your analysis, you will then be ready to offer solution(s) to the problem you have been studying. For example, the solution to the question, 'What office arrangement would be the best for effective work-flow?' should be based solely on the gathered information. A tendency in business report writing is to 'slant' information in the report to lead the reader to the decision the writer wants. Make sure you report all pertinent information—good and bad.

## Organize Your Report

You have the topic, the information, and the decision. Now you are ready to determine how to present your information. Before actually writing, organize your information into an outline form. You can formulate an outline for your report by choosing the major and supporting ideas, developing the details, and eliminating the unnecessary ideas you have gathered. This outline becomes the basic structure of your report. A report could be presented as a memo report, a standardized form report, or a formal report. A memo report will involve the following five steps:

1. Provide identifying information (usually in the To, From, Date, and Subject fields).
2. Define the project or problem (purpose of the report).
3. Give the background.
4. Give the supporting data.
5. State your conclusions and recommendations.

## PARTS OF A REPORT

A few general guidelines are applicable to many types of business reports. If your report is extensive (more than two pages), you should include descriptive headings for the major sections, to help readers navigate the report easily (Table 8.4).

> A report could be presented as a memo report, a standardized form report, or a formal report.

**Introduction**   Begin the report with a brief overview of its contents.

**Summary**   Summarize the situation on which you are reporting, or describe the problem or opportunity that your report is exploring.

**Table 8.4** Various types of headings

| Descriptive | Parallel | Unnecessary to Transition |
|---|---|---|
| Headings should talk about the content. Poor: Supporting Data Better: Comparison of Three Computer Models | All headings of the same level should start with the same grammatical structure. | Headings should not be relied upon to give meaning to that section of the report. Headings do serve as guides, but the report should be understood even if no headings are used. Poor: *Changes Must Be Communicated to Employees:* This problem has been a persistent one throughout the industry. Better: *Changes Must Be Communicated to Employees:* The problem of communicating changed procedures to employees has been a persistent one throughout the industry. |

> **BUSINESS COMMUNICATION INSIGHT**
>
> **How to Write Reports that Get Read**
>
> In a report, you are supposed to provide the facts and not embellish or influence. This does not, however, mean that reports need to be dull and boring. The following key points will help you in preparing an objective and interesting report:
>
> **Do not use jargon**  Try to minimize the use of business jargon and phrasing no matter how much you or other people may feel it's more appropriate. Use language and tone of voice that your key readers will feel comfortable with. If your report is to be read by a wide variety of different audiences, focus your language on the most important groups. Include a short glossary of terms as an appendix within the report.
>
> **Create a logical structure**  Start by writing a list of headings for your entire text. If a lot of background information also has to be included, in addition to the main information, section it off clearly with headings that say that it's background so those who know it all already can skip straight to the important stuff. Make sure your headings are clear enough to communicate the basic message.
>
> **The executive summary**  Depending on the nature of your report, you may be expected to include an executive summary, or at least an introduction that captures the key points of your information. Write the summary after you have written the body of the report, not before. Use the list of headings as a guide.
>
> **Keep your views separate**  If part of your remit is to comment on the report and/or its conclusions, keep this separate from the main body of information.
>
> **Graphs and charts**  Try, also, to keep graphs and charts physically adjacent to the text that talks about the same thing. As before, there is nothing more irritating for the reader if they have to keep flipping from front to back of a document, whether online or paper-based.
>
> **Keep it simple**  Try to avoid including too many diverse elements in your report, no matter how long and involved it is. If you do need to include appendices and various bits of background material, research statistics, etc., make sure they are neatly labelled and contained at the back of your document.
>
> **Looks matter**  How your document looks goes a long way to creating the right impression of your work, and of you. Organizations usually have a format for internal reports. If a report is meant for clients or customers, make sure that it is polished and clearly branded with the organization's corporate identity.
>
> Source: Maur, Suzan St, 'How to Write Reports that Get Read', http://howtowritebetter.net/how-to-write-reports-that-get-read-part-2/, accessed on 29 November 2011. Reproduced with permission.

**Discussion**  Provide some explanatory detail, including the results of whatever research you may have conducted. List the available options. Explain your methods, if appropriate. If you are writing an analytical report or recommendation, give the criteria by which you are making judgments. If you are

> Corporate reports are usually statutory reports.

reporting on more than one task or situation, consult for suggestions about organizing your material.

**Conclusion** If you are writing an analytical report or recommendation, explain the implications of each of the available options. If you are writing an analytical report, offer your evaluation here. If you are writing a recommendation or feasibility study, explain which option you think is best, and why.

## CORPORATE REPORTS

Corporate reports are special kinds of reports brought up by public or listed companies periodically as part of their corporate communication exercise to the shareholders, creditors, government, etc. (Fig. 8.3). Sometimes, corporations have to publish such reports as part of compliance, while, sometimes, it is done to bring in more transparency and an element of corporate governance where the companies try to share relevant information with interested parties. Corporate reports are usually statutory reports. Reports that are statutorily required are called statutory reports. Section 165 of the Companies Act, 1956 includes auditor's report, director's report, etc., under statutory reports. The board of directors has to send such reports to all members of their corporation. The Act specifically lays down the particulars that must be set out in the statutory report to enable the shareholder to get

**Fig 8.3** A sample corporate report

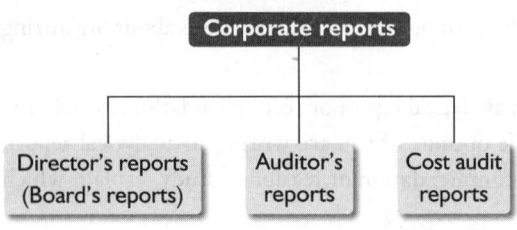

**Fig. 8.4** Corporate reports

all the necessary information. The various types of corporate reports are as follows (Fig. 8.4).

### Director's Reports (Board's Reports)

An annual report of directors, attached to every balance sheet, is called the director's report. Some of the issues the report normally contains are related to

- the state of affairs of the company,
- the amount, which it recommends for payment of dividends to the shareholders,
- future prospects of the company, changes in directors and auditors, etc., if any, and
- any other factual information which the company wishes to share with the shareholders.

### Auditor's Reports

Companies appoint auditors to scrutinize and check their accounts and submit their reports. The Companies Act, 1956 stipulates that companies must have auditors to audit the books and examine the affairs of the company on behalf of the shareholders and report to them. The auditor's report is usually attached to the balance sheet.

The report should state whether in the auditor's opinion, he/she obtained all the information to the best of his/her knowledge and also, whether proper books of account, as required by law, have been kept by the company. In addition, it ensures that the company's balance sheet and profit and loss accounts are in agreement with books of accounts and returns, etc. (Fig. 8.5).

---

We have examined the accounts of MALAYSIAN AIRLINE SYSTEM BERHAD (the Company) and the consolidated accounts of MALAYSIAN AIRLINE SYSTEM BERHAD AND ITS SUBSIDIARIES (the Group) as on 31 March 2012. Our examination was made in accordance with approved auditing standards and accordingly, included such tests of the accounting records and such other auditing procedures as we considered necessary in the circumstances. In our opinion,

a. the accounts are properly drawn up in accordance with the provisions of the (Malaysian) Companies Act, 1965 and give a true and fair view of the state of affairs of the Company and of the Group as at 31 March 2012 and of the results of the Company and of the Group and cash flow of the Group for the year then ended, and

b. the accounting and other records and the registers required by the Act to be kept by the Company and its subsidiaries of which we have acted as auditors have been properly kept in accordance with the provisions of the Act.

We have considered the accounts and the auditors' report of the subsidiary of which we have not acted as auditors, being accounts that have been included in the consolidated accounts.

We are satisfied that the accounts of the subsidiaries that have been consolidated with the Company's accounts are in form and content appropriate and proper for the purposes of the preparation of the consolidated accounts and we have received satisfactory information and explanations required by us for these purposes.

The audit reports on the accounts of the subsidiaries were not subject to any qualification or any adverse comment made under subsection (3) of Section 174 of the Act.

ABC & Co.
*Public Accounts*

**Place**: Kuala Lumpur
**Dated**: 26 June 2012

---

**Fig. 8.5** A sample auditor's report

### Cost Audit Reports

The cost audit reports involve the scrutiny of cost records of a company. The government has made cost audit rules, which apply to every company with respect to the auditing of the cost accounting records. It normally contains the following information: cost accounting system, capital employed, net worth, profit after depreciation, and production details (installed capacity, licensed capacity, actual utilization, raw material consumed in terms of quantity and value, power and fuel in quantity, rate per unit and total cost, wages and salaries of employees, depreciation, overhead, royalties, spare parts, abnormal expenses, etc.).

 Please refer to the Online Resource Centre for several samples of business reports.

## BUSINESS PROPOSALS

A proposal is a written document that seeks to persuade readers to accept a suggested plan of action. The objective of a proposal's argument can be almost anything, but it is usually to convince readers that the proposal is in their best interests. Some reasons for business proposals are to

- buy a service or product from the readers,
- convince readers of the existence of a situation, or to take a course of action,
- convince the concerned department of the need for a new technology, and
- provide funds (for example, a loan or grant, or to become a partner or shareholder).

By definition, a proposal is a persuasive presentation for consideration of something. In practice, some proposals fit this definition well—for example, a company's proposal to merge with another company, an advertising agency's proposal to promote a product, or a city's proposal to induce a business to locate within its boundaries.

Proposals are usually written, but they can also be oral presentations or a combination of both. They may be made by and for a variety of individuals or organizations such as government agencies, foundations, and businesses. They can even be made internally—by one department of a business to another or to management. For example, the IT department might outline its needs for new equipment in a proposal to the management.

A proposal is an offer to be sold to clients and should contain information that would enable them to decide whether to approve the project, to approve or hire you to do the work, or both. To write a successful proposal, put yourself in the place of the target audience—the recipient of the proposal—and think about the sort of information that would be needed for you to win over the audience and sell the proposal.

### Types of Business Proposals

> A proposal is a written document that seeks to persuade readers to accept a suggested plan of action.

Consider the situations that necessitate proposals. A company may send out a public announcement requesting proposals for a specific project. This public announcement—called a request for proposals (RFP)—could be issued through newspapers, trade journals, Chamber of Commerce channels, or individual letters. Firms or individuals interested in the project would then write proposals in

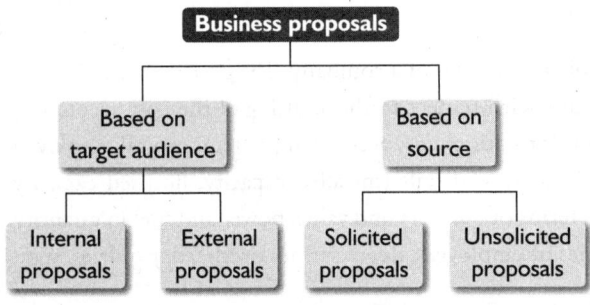

**Fig. 8.6** Types of business proposals

which they summarize their qualifications, project schedules and costs, and discuss approach to the project. The recipient of all these proposals would then evaluate them, select the best candidate, and finally work up a contract.

However, proposals can come about much less formally. Imagine that you are interested in doing a project at work (e.g., investigating the merits of bringing in some new technology to increase productivity). You visit your supervisor and he/she responds by saying, 'Write a proposal and I will present it to the upper management.' Business proposals can be divided into two categories (Fig. 8.6):

- Internal and external—according to the target audience
- Solicited and unsolicited—according to the source

In both cases, proposals are usually read by people in positions of authority.

### Internal Proposals

A proposal written to someone within an organization (e.g., a business, a government agency, etc.) is an internal proposal. Some business contexts in which internal proposals may arise are as follows:

> The chairman of a company asks a personnel manager to develop a training programme for new recruits.
> The vice president (production) of a company, asks a senior manager to suggest a new design for increased productivity in the plant.
> The CEO of a business organization asks a project manager to suggest a project management plan to deal with huge assignments to be carried out for companies abroad.

In internal proposals, you may not have to include certain sections (such as qualifications) or bulky information. These proposals can be submitted in the form of a manuscript or a memorandum. The proposal can be built within the memo or be attached to it.

### External Proposals

An external proposal is written from one separate, independent organization or individual to another such entity. The following situations are examples of external proposals:

> An independent consultant proposes to do a project for another firm.
> An advertising agency proposes to design a scheme for a nationwide advertising campaign for a bank.
> A company in India proposes to set up a waste water treatment plant in another country.

As opposed to an internal proposal, an external proposal is sent in the form of a letter as it goes outside the organization. As in the case of internal proposals, an external proposal can also be sent in the form of a manuscript along with a separate covering letter.

## Solicited Proposals

> - A solicited proposal arises out of a specific demand or when the customer asks for a proposal.
> - Brochures and unsolicited proposals tend to suffer from a lack of information about the reader.

A solicited proposal arises out of a specific demand or when a customer asks for a proposal. In other words, a proposal is solicited, if the recipient of a proposal in some way requested it. In proposals of this kind, a corporation or government body seeks a business to complete a project or task and thereby allows companies to bid for the project. An open bid is placed on the market with other companies competing for an interview spot. The winning candidate is offered the project. A solicited proposal provides you with a description of what the customer wants. Many also provide you with formatting instructions for your proposal and the evaluation criteria that will be used to make a selection. Sometimes you will make a suggestion to a potential customer and he/she will ask you to submit a proposal so that he/she can consider your suggestion. This counts as a solicited proposal because the customer is expecting it and you have a chance to talk to him/her and gain an understanding of his/her needs.

## Unsolicited Proposals

You can initiate a proposal yourself. When you initiate a proposal it is an unsolicited proposal, and can be either an internal or an external proposal, depending on whether the proposal is for your employer or some outside agency. In other words, a proposal is categorized as unsolicited when it is sent without the recipients asking for it. For example, you might perceive that some changes in the hiring policies of your company could improve the morale and performance of the company's employees. If you submit such a proposal, it is, technically, an unsolicited internal proposal. On the other hand, suppose a governmental agency is attempting to improve working conditions in your industry and advertises the availability of funds for rectifying common problems. The agency invites any qualified person to submit a grant proposal using the agency's guidelines. If you were to submit such a proposal, you would be preparing an externally solicited document.

An unsolicited proposal is a document about your products and services. They are usually produced individually, and given to someone specific (although it may be to someone you do not know very well). Unsolicited proposals are often in letter form, unless they are large documents, in which case they are bound. If you are writing an unsolicited proposal, try focusing as much effort on graphics design as you put into a brochure. Every piece of copy, every aspect of the layout, and every graphic should contribute to persuading the reader. Both brochures and unsolicited proposals tend to suffer from a lack of information about the reader.

## Components of a Proposal

A brief description of the sections you will commonly find in proposals is provided in this section (Table 8.5).

### Executive Summary

> The executive summary is a sales document designed to convince the reader that the project should be considered for support.

This first component of a proposal is the most important section of the entire document. Here, a reader is provided with a snapshot of what is to follow. Specifically, it summarizes all the key information and is a sales document designed to convince readers that this project should be considered for support. Be certain to include the following points:

**Table 8.5** Components of a proposal

| Component | Content | Approximate Length |
|---|---|---|
| Title page | Title, proposal writer, receiver, organization, and date | 1 page |
| Executive summary | Umbrella statement of your case and summary of the entire proposal | 1 page |
| Introduction | Overview of the entire proposal | 2 pages |
| Statement of need | Problem statement (Why is this project necessary?) | 1 page |
| Project description | Details of how the project will be implemented and evaluated (benefits and feasibility, description, method, procedure, and theory) | 3 pages |
| Project management | Schedules (work, implementation, and reporting) | 3 pages |
| Budget | Financial description of the project plus explanatory notes | 1 page |
| Organization information (qualifications) | History and governing structure of the non-profit; its primary activities, audiences, and services | 1 page |
| Conclusion | Summary of the proposal's main points | 2 paragraphs |
| Appendix | Additional material | 4–5 pages |
| Special section | Any other section specific to the project in question | 2 pages |

- *Problem*   A brief statement of the problem or need your agency has recognized and is prepared to address (one or two paragraphs)
- *Solution*   A short description of the project, including what will take place and how many people will benefit from the programme, how and where it will operate, for how long, and who will staff it (one or two paragraphs)
- *Funding requirements*   An explanation of the amount of grant money required for the project and what your plans are for funding it in the future (one paragraph)
- *Organization and its expertise*   A brief statement of the name, history, purpose, and activities of your agency, emphasizing its capacity to carry out this proposal (one paragraph)

### Introduction

Plan the introduction to your proposal carefully. Make sure it does all of the following things (but not necessarily in this order) that apply to your particular proposal:

- Indicate that the document to follow is a proposal
- Refer to some previous contact with the recipient of the proposal or to your source of information about the project
- Find one brief motivating statement that will encourage the recipient to read on and consider doing the project
- Give an overview of the contents of the proposal

### Statement of Need

Often appearing just after the introduction, this background section discusses the need for the proposal—the problem, opportunities available for improving things, and the basic situation. For example, the management of a chain of hospitals may need to ensure that all employees develop health awareness. The owner of a pine timberland in Shimla may want the land to produce saleable timber without destroying the ecology. It might be that the audience of the proposal already knows the problem very well. However, writing the background section might be useful in demonstrating your particular view of the problem.

If the audience reads beyond the executive summary, you have successfully piqued its interest. Your next task is to build on this initial interest in your project by enabling the audience to understand the problem that the project will remedy. The statement of need will enable readers to learn more about the issues. It presents the facts and evidence that support the need for the project and establishes that your organization understands the problems and can reasonably address them.

### Project Description

This section of your proposal should have five subsections—objectives, methods, staffing/administration, evaluation, and sustainability. They then become the focus of the evaluation to assess the results of the project. The project's sustainability flows directly from its success, hence its ability to attract other support.

### Objectives

Objectives are the measurable outcomes of a programme. They define the methods. The objectives must be tangible, specific, concrete, measurable, and achievable in a specified time period.

In any given proposal, you will find yourself setting forth one or more of these types of objectives, depending upon the nature of your project. Present the objectives very clearly. You might, for example, use numbers, bullets, or indentations to denote the objectives in the text. Above all, be realistic in setting objectives. Do not promise what you cannot deliver. The recipient will want to be told in the final report that the project actually accomplished these objectives.

### Methods

In proposals, it is important to explain the methodology that would be used in completing the proposed work, if approved to do it. This acts as an additional persuasive element; it shows the audience you have a sound and well thought out approach to the project. Here, the technical background relating to the procedures or technology that you plan to use in the proposed work can also be discussed. Once again, this gives the proposal writer a chance to show that he/she knows what he/she is talking about, and builds confidence in the audience that he/she is a good choice to do the project. By means of the objectives, you have explained to the recipient what will be achieved by the project. Therefore, in essence, this section describes the specific activities that would take place to achieve the objectives. It enables readers to visualize the implementation of the project and should be able to establish credibility with the readers.

### Staffing/Administration/Qualifications

Most proposals contain a summary of the proposing individual's or organization's qualifications. This section demonstrates the qualifications, knowledge, and experience of the proposal writer (or sender) and relates these to the required work to confirm that the individual or organization has the ability to deliver the proposed work. Usually, this section also includes examples of similar work the supplier has done for comparable requirements. Actually, this section is like a mini-résumé contained within the proposal. The proposal audience uses it to decide whether you are suited for the project.

> Objectives must be tangible, specific, concrete, measurable, and achievable in a specified time period.

> An evaluation plan helps an organization refine and improve its programme.

Therefore, it lists work experience, similar projects, references, training, and education that show familiarity with the project.

In describing the methods, staffing for the project, including the number of members of staff, their qualifications, and specific assignments alloted to each one of them, also has to be mentioned. Details about individual members of staff involved in the project can be included either as part of this section or proposal senders in the appendix, depending on the length and importance of this information. Proposal senders also provide thumbnail sketches of the people who will fulfil the project or requirement, and clearly demonstrate how their experience and qualifications enable them to carry out the proposed work effectively and efficiently. More detailed résumés or curricula vitae (CVs) for all team members are usually provided in an appendix or as supporting documents.

In addition, the proposal sender also needs to describe for the audience all the proposed plans for administering the project. This is especially important in a large operation, if more than one agency is collaborating on the project, or if you are using a fiscal agent. It needs to be clear who is responsible for financial management, project outcomes, and reporting.

### *Evaluation*

An evaluation plan should not be considered only after a project is over; it should be built into the project. Including an evaluation plan in your proposal indicates that you take your objectives seriously and want to know how well you have achieved them. Evaluation is also a sound management tool. Like strategic planning, it helps an organization refine and improve its programme. An evaluation can often be the best means for others to learn from your experience in conducting the project.

### *Sustainability*

Evidence of fiscal sustainability is a highly sought-after characterstic of a successful grant proposal.

### *Budget*

Most proposals also contain a section detailing the costs of the project, whether internal or external. For external projects, you may need to list your hourly rates, projected hours, costs of equipment and supplies, and so forth, and then calculate the total proposed cost of the project. For internal projects, there probably will not be a fee, but you should still list the project costs, for example, the hours you will need to complete the project, equipment and supplies you will be using, assistance from other people in the organization, and so on. The budget for a proposal may be as simple as a one-page statement of projected expenses. Sometimes, a proposal may require a more complex presentation of the budget, perhaps including a page on projected support and revenue, and notes explaining various items of expense or of revenue.

### *Organizational Information*

Normally, the résumé of an organization should come at the end of a proposal. The natural inclination may be to put this information up front in the document. However, it is better to sell the need for your project and then your agency's ability to carry it out. It is not necessary to overwhelm the reader with facts about your organization. This information can be conveyed easily by attaching a brochure or a prepared statement. In two pages or less, tell the reader when your organization came into existence,

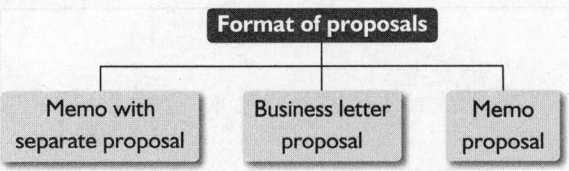

**Fig. 8.7** Proposal formats

state its mission, being certain to demonstrate how the subject of the proposal fits within or extends that mission, and describe the organization's structure, programmes, activities, and special expertise.

### Conclusion

The final paragraph or section of a proposal should bring readers back to focus on the positive aspects of the project. In the final section, as the proposal sender, you can end by urging them to get in touch with you to work out the details of the project, to remind them of the benefits of doing the project, and maybe to put in one last plug for you or your organization as the right choice for the project.

### Appendices

Ancillary material, which might be of interest to some readers, goes in appendices. Résumés of the principal investigators, testimonial letters, listings or examples of previous projects undertaken by the proposal sender, audit procedures, technical details, graphics, professional papers cited in the body of the proposal, and similar other material can be grouped and included in the appendices numbered in letters A, B, C, etc.

## Format of Proposals

You have the following options for the format and packaging of your proposal. It does not matter which you use as long as you use the memorandum format for internal proposals and the business letter format for external proposals (Fig. 8.7).

### Cover Letter/Memo with Separate Proposal

In this format, you need to write a brief cover letter/memo and attach the proposal after it. The cover letter/memo briefly announces that a proposal follows and outlines the contents therein. In fact, the contents of the cover letter/memo are pretty much the same as the introduction (discussed in the previous section). Notice, however, that the proposal that follows the cover letter/memo repeats much of what you see in the cover letter. This is because the letter/memo may get detached from the proposal or the recipient may not even bother to look at the letter/memo and just dive right into the proposal itself (Fig. 8.8).

### Business Letter Proposal

In this format, you need to put the entire proposal within a standard business letter. You should include headings and other special formatting elements as if it were a report (Fig. 8.9).

### Memo Proposal

In this format, you need to put the entire proposal within a standard office memorandum. Like in a business letter proposal, in a memo proposal too you should include headings and other special formatting elements as if it were a report (Fig. 8.10). It may take as much thought and data gathering to write a good memo or letter proposal as it does to prepare a full proposal (and sometimes even more). Do not assume that because it is only a letter, it is not a time-consuming and challenging task.

20 August 2017
Priyanka Ahuja
General Manager
ABC Ltd
116th Way
Bengaluru

Ms Ahuja,

Thank you for taking the time to talk with me last week. I know that your business office accounting has been a high priority problem for you. I am pleased to propose a cost effective solution that will minimize your in-house burden. As you know, we are specialists in accounting and payroll services with over 40 years of experience. We pride ourselves in providing our clients with a professional service, guaranteed accuracy, and the highest level of confidentiality. The attached cost summary is based upon your current needs and can be adjusted as we customize your services. I look forward to discussing your project with you in more detail shortly. Please contact me directly anytime you have additional questions or requests.

Sincerely,

Sheeba Mathew
President

**Fig. 8.8** A sample cover letter

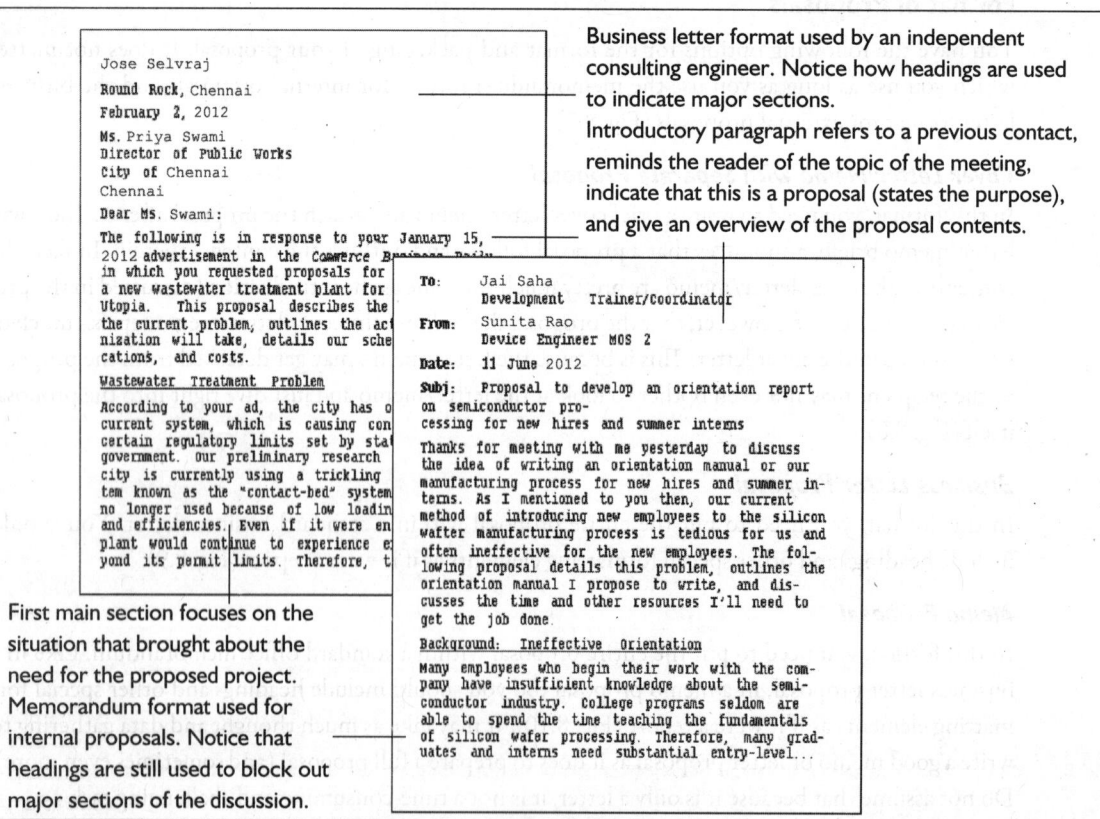

**Fig. 8.9** A sample business proposal

Aim Accounting Services,
D1/101, Sesame Street
Vasant kunj, New Delhi – 110022
(PH) 011-26164031
(FX) 011-26164032
www.AACServices.com
20 August 2017

**Prepared for: Priyanka Ahuja, General Manager**

**Prepared by: Sheeba Mathew, President**

VA Fitness requires **accounting** and payroll **services** to take over from (and report to) an overburdened owner. Being short-staffed, the **accounting** and payroll functions have been distressed. Outsourcing these office domains will allow the management team to give attention to other important areas of the business.

Proposal Request Number: 534-2002

**Table of contents**

**VA Fitness**

Executive Summary............................... 1
Client Operations.................................. 2

**The Project**

Cost Summary........................................ 3
Contract and Terms.............................. 4
Benefits..................................................... 5
Project Management............................. 6

Executive Summary

The Objective

VA Fitness requires **accounting** and payroll **services** to take over from (and report to) an overburdened owner. Being short-staffed, the **accounting** and payroll functions have been distressed. Outsourcing these office domains will allow the management team to give attention to other important areas of the business.

The Goals

VA Fitness is a small private organization that needs professional **accounting** and payroll services within their budget. The goals of **Aim Accounting Services** are as follows:

- Deliver professional **accounting** and payroll **services**
- Deliver **services** at a cost lower as compared to the cost of an in-house staff member
- Assure on-time payroll and other account payables

The Solution

**Aim Accounting Services (AAS)** specializes in complete **accounting** and payroll **services** for medium-sized companies. All accountants in our staff are chartered accountants with supplementary taxation **services** provided through our corporate office located in Bangalore.

We provide **accounting services** including the following:

- Periodical—daily, quarterly, and yearly **accounting** reconciliation

**Fig. 8.10** A sample memo proposal (contd)

- Year-end tax statements and synopses
- Quarterly tax payment reports
- Ledger maintenance
- Inventory account balancing

Payroll **services** including the following:

- Standard wage period check determination and initiation
- Withholding allotments
- Benefit synopses

Accounts payable **services** to include (upon request) the following:

- Payment of all bills owing
- Budget plan discussions
- Negotiation for terms

Client operations

VA Fitness is a private fitness club at three locations. Started in 2009 with six staff members, the club now employs 12 people per location and has a clientele of approximately 2000. Office **accounting** and payroll team currently consists of the owners who took over the charge when the FT accountant did not return from long medical leave. The lack of a FT **accounting** and payroll manager has led to a backlog of data entry, limited inventory control, delayed payroll, and late tax filings. Once **AAS** is in charge for all **accounting** and payroll, the owners will be relieved to return to the FT management of their sections.

AAS will be responsible for timely **accounting**, payroll, accounts payable, and tax filing.

Cost summary

The following is an estimation and summary of the costs associated with **AAS** offering for **accounting** and payroll **services**. These numbers are only initial estimates.

| Initial Account Set-up | Price |
|---|---|
| Conversion from Valley Fitness to AA **Services** | ₹ 10,000 |
| Time period to cover 1 January, 2009–Present | |
| Production of Q1, Q2 Reports | ₹ 2,000 |
| Production of Current Standing Report | ₹ 5,000 |
| **Total Set-up Costs:** | ₹ 25,000 |
| **Ongoing Monthly Costs** | |
| Daily Account Reconciliation | ₹ 6,000 p/mo |
| Bi-weekly Payroll | ₹ 3,000 p/mo |
| **Total Ongoing Monthly Costs:** | ₹ 9,000 |
| Ongoing Quarterly/yearly Costs | |
| Quarterly Tax Documents | ₹ 6,000 p/qtr |
| Quarterly Filings | ₹ 2,000 p/qtr |
| Quarterly Reports | ₹ 7,000 p/qtr |
| Year-end Summaries | ₹ 3,000 p/yr |
| Year-end Tax Filing Summaries | ₹ 5,000 p/yr |
| Maintenance of Employee Benefit Reports | ₹ 2,000 p/yr |

| | |
|---|---|
| **Total Ongoing Quarterly/yearly Costs:** | ₹ 19,000 |
| **TOTAL SET-UP AMOUNT** | ₹ 30,000 |
| **TOTAL MONTHLY AMOUNT** | ₹ 9,000 |
| **TOTAL QUARTERLY/YEARLY AMOUNT** | ₹ 20,000 |

**Standard Disclaimer:** The numbers represented above are to be used as an estimate only. The above cost summary does in no way constitute a warranty of final pricing. Estimates are subject to change if the project specification of terms of contract are changed in any way.

Contract and terms

Initial Set-up:

- 50 per cent at contract signing
- 50 per cent at conversion completion
- Any other balances owing

Monthly Fees:

- Due upon receipt of monthly invoice
- Net 15

Quarterly/yearly Fees:

- Will be billed on monthly invoice
- Net 15

Special/additional Reports:

- Will be billed on monthly invoice
- Net 15

Minimum Term of this contract

12 calendar months commencing on the first of the month following conclusion of conversion. After the preliminary term of this agreement, services will be delivered on a monthly basis at the current rate schedule. Current rates are revealed no less than 31 days prior to the end of the preliminary term of this agreement. If a new agreement for a period of 14 or more months is engaged, the rates will be locked in at the current rate at the time of signing. In the event of termination for any reason, 3 months' notice is required by either party. There are no pre-payment fines. Revocation of the agreement prior to the end of the preliminary term will require payment for all contracted services due to the end of the contract period or for 3 months, whichever is longer. Late payment levies will be calculated on any account past due by 30 days. Concluding terms and conditions will be delivered in the agreement for services.

Benefits

By employing AAS as your accounting and payroll resource, you will realize the following benefits:

- Proficient preparation of all tax, payroll, and benefit synopses
- Assigned account manager who is completely committed to your company's needs
- CPA level staff
- Lesser overall cost for accounting requirements
- Owner/manager are not tied to office for prolonged periods of time

- No need to employ or train to fill jobs
- Deadlines are of utmost priority
- No need to employ a separate tax attorney since we provide the staff in-house
- Initial set-up comprises of everything essential to get your business back on track
- Full discretion

Project management

AAS offers to provide our entire staff at your service. We will allocate an account manager to your organization with whom you can converse and add additional reports as required.

### Proposal Layout and Design

If there is no written request for proposals (RFP), or if the written RFP does not specify the outline or format, then there are no rules for the layout and design of a proposal. The only standard to apply to the proposal's appearance is whether it meets with the proposal evaluator's approval. If the evaluator has not made any specific references with respect to design, then all that is needed is make the proposal legible. A proposal layout should be highly readable and should make it easy to locate information. Extensive use of graphics can be made, because they enhance the readability of a document and convey information well. In the absence of instructions to the contrary, headings, typefaces, margins, headers/footers, and other formatting attributes can be anything that help achieve the goal of your proposal. The following tips should be kept in mind while preparing a proposal layout and design:

1. Use serif typeface, such as Times Roman (10–12 point type)
2. Use column width of 50–60 characters (either double column or 'scholar's margins') and margins of at least 0.5"
3. Use colour whenever possible
4. Use graphics extensively
5. Make full use of front matter (Table of Contents, List of Figures, etc.)
6. Use navigational aids such as a cross-reference matrix
7. Provide appendices for data that do not fit within the proposal
8. If the page count is large enough, use three ring binders or other binding
9. Use tabs that break the content down into sections and make finding material easier

### A Simple Proposal Formula

Here is a simple approach to help you cover all the bases in your proposal. For each section/requirement that you must address, make sure you answer: who, what, where, how, when, and why.

1. Who: who will do the work, who will manage the work, who does the customer call if there is a problem, who is responsible for what?
2. What: what needs to be done/delivered, what will be required to get it done, what can the customer expect, what it will cost?
3. Where: where will the work be done, where will it be delivered?

4. How: how will the work be done, how will it be deployed, how will it be managed, how will you achieve quality assurance and customer satisfaction, how will risks be mitigated, how long will it take, how will the work benefit the customer?
5. When: when will you start, when will key milestones be scheduled, when will the project be complete, when is payment due?
6. Why: why have the chosen approaches and alternatives been selected, why should the customer select the proposal writer?

These simple questions can help you ensure that your proposal contains everything needed to 'answer the mail'. For each of the customer's requirements, go through the list and you will probably have everything covered. You can use it for inspiration when writing, and you can use it like a checklist for reviewing a draft proposal.

## Five Key Elements of Winning Business Proposals

The five key elements required to win a business proposal are described as follows:

*Solutions*  Explain how your business is the best amongst other bidders to provide solutions. Also ensure that these solutions can be implemented successfully.

*Benefits*  State how your business can maintain confidentiality and meet prescribed deadlines. Outline the benefits to be gained by the funding company by doing business with you.

*Credibility*  Establish credibility by highlighting your previous projects—successful projects in the same area, you can also present some testimonials that speak for your potential.

*Samples*  Include in the appendix a small sample of your work in a similar area. This will serve as an evidence of your ability to accomplish the project if offered.

*Targeted*  A winning business proposal is all about communication. Speak in the language spoken by your intended audience. Depending on the background of the proposal evaluators, use the appropriate jargon.

Ultimately, if your company is well-positioned and unique in the marketplace, then you are most likely going to be the only party able to meet the needs of the company requesting the bids. For example, if a retail craft chain is looking for a web design firm and your company specializes in web creation for the crafts industry, your company, in all likelihood, should win the proposal process.

In the end, you may not win all bids, but will win business that best matches your company to the prospective business.

## SUMMARY

Both proposals and reports are major forms of business communication. While proposals offer to solve problems, provide services, or sell equipment, reports present information to decision-makers in business, industry, government, and education. These significant forms of business communication include several components depending upon the need and the existing practice in the respective organizations. They can be inbuilt in the body of a memo or a letter or can be attached to a memo or letter. As proposals and reports project the image of an organization, they need to be prepared with utmost care.

## KEY TERMS

**Business report** It is an orderly arrangement of factual information that is objective in nature and serves some business purpose. In other words, it is a document in which a given problem is examined for the purpose of conveying information and findings, putting forward ideas first and sometimes making recommendations.

**Corporate reports** These are special kind of reports brought up by public or listed companies periodically as a part of their corporate communication exercise to the shareholders, creditors, government, etc.

**Elements of effectiveness** These are accuracy and objectivity.

**Information report** It conveys ideas and data as clearly, concisely, and correctly as possible.

**Research report** It enables its readers to take some action as a result of the new information presented in it.

## Concept Review Questions

1. Why do we refer to a business proposal as a sales offer?
2. Mention any three situations in which proposals may be prepared in businesses.
3. Distinguish between the following:
   - Internal and external proposals
   - Solicited and unsolicited proposals
   - Letter and memo proposals
4. What are the contents of the following components of a business proposal:
   - Executive summary
   - Problem statement
   - Cost summary
5. Discuss with appropriate examples the essentials of winning proposals in business.
6. Before a manager begins the task of accumulating data or of writing a report, some important questions need to be asked. What are these questions?
7. Why, do you think, corporate reports are more important as compared to other kinds of reports? Base your answer by taking into consideration the annual report of the company.
8. Audience analysis is a very integral part of any effective report writing. Discuss?
9. With numerous reports reaching on the table of the top management, suggest some methods in report writing itself to immediately catch the attention of a busy manager?

## Critical Thinking Questions

1. Your company is considering a proposal to make an in-house canteen for office employees. Your office has around 100 employees. Make a report to give an estimate of the area, manpower, and money required to set-up and run the canteen.
2. As the marketing chief of Sahil Garments, you visited Europe to explore the possibility of entering the European market. You found that the company's garments were criticized for dull colours, and limited range of sizes. Write the executive report to the company's directors recommending the changes to be made in the product design to enable the entry into European markets.
3. It has been proposed that the working hour of your bank branch be changed to morning and evening hours, for the convenience of the customers. As a convener of the committee, formed to look into the feasibility of implementing the proposal, prepare your report with recommendations.
4. Assume that you are writing a solicited business proposal to establish a day-care centre for the benefit of the employees of a reputed group of companies.

Would you include as references the names and addresses of other clients for whom you had recently built similar centres? Would you include these references in an unsolicited proposal? Where in either proposal would you include these references and why?
5. An NGO sends a proposal to a private company requesting funding for running a health awareness programme in the nearby villages. Would this proposal include all the elements of a proposal discussed in this chapter? Discuss your answer in about 250 words.
6. Assume the role of the manager—HR of a corporation. You feel the need for introducing a refresher program for the secretaries of all managers in the areas of business communication, computer application skills, and management concepts and techniques. You see this program as a way of revising and updating their skills in all these three areas. You need funds for running this program. Now answer the following questions: What is the background of the problem? What will be the outcome of your proposal, if accepted?
7. The best institute of technology and science in Goa decides to conduct an online examination for about 50,000 graduates in India for their selection to postgraduate degree programmes and invites proposals from various consultancy firms. As the CEO of Excellent Consultants Ltd, Bengaluru, you respond to this request through a business proposal.
8. What are the elements you would include in this proposal? Which element is the most important one according to you and why? What are the factors you need to consider before preparing this proposal?

## Projects

1. Assume that you are the director of the placement office of your college. You believe it will help students who are also job applicants to know the preference of personnel managers with respect to the form and job content of written job applications. Do the following:
   - Draw up a questionnaire that will best serve your purpose
   - Write a letter designed to accompany the questionnaire
2. Obtain from your library or any government office a copy of a short government report in a field that interests you. Then:
   (i) Write a factual analysis of the report, using the following pointers:
       - Kind of report (informative or interpretive)
       - Origin and destination
       - Purpose and scope
       - Sources of information
       - Organization of material
   (ii) Construct a formal outline of the report.
   (iii) Does the outline reveal any deficiencies in the organization? If so, explain and illustrate.
3. Businesses today are doing more outsourcing than ever before. For any organization you know, select two problems from the list given below:
   Internet misuse, inefficient payroll practices, poor handling of customer orders, poor use of sales staff, or poor telephone techniques.
   Assume that the boss has asked you, as a consultant, to either solve the problem or study it and tell the organization what to do. Prepare a proposal describing your plan to solve the problem or perform a service. Describe how much you will charge and what staff you will need. Send your letter proposal to your boss.
4. Form a group with three of your friends/colleagues. Choose from newspapers at least four advertisements inviting tenders. Take one at a time. While two of you can play the role of the managers of the company that has invited tenders, the other two can play the role of proposal writers. Discuss thoroughly and prepare all the four proposals in letter format. You can interchange the roles.

## REFERENCES

Anderson, Paul V. 2003, *Technical Communication*, 5th Edition, Thomson Asia Pvt. Ltd, Singapore, pp. 503–14; 536–40.

Bovee, Courtland L., and John V. Thill 2003, *Business Communication Today*, Pearson Education Asia, Delhi, pp. 29–30.

Fulscher, Richard J., 'A No-Fail Recipe:/ Winning Business Proposals', *Journal of Property Management*, 1996, Vol. 61; No.1; pp. 62–65.

Guffey, Mary Allen 2000, *Business Communication: Process and Product*, Thomson Asia Pvt. Ltd, Singapore, pp. 360–375.

Lesikar, Raymond V. and Marie E. Flatley 2005, *Basic Business Communication,* 10th Edition, Tata McGraw-Hill Publishing Co. Ltd, New Delhi, pp. 444–45.

Scot, Ober 2004, *Contemporary Business Communication*, 5th Edition, Biztantra, New Delhi, pp. 330–45.

## CASE STUDY 1

### Handling Unsolicited Proposals for Private Infrastructure Projects

In developing countries, infrastructure projects with private participation increased dramatically in the past decade, attracting more than US$ 750 billion in committed new investment from 1990–2001.

Quite often, private companies initiated the projects on their own by suggesting concepts to governments, including detailed construction, operation, maintenance, and financing plans. For example, it is estimated that unsolicited projects have accounted for approximately 20 per cent and 50 per cent of total private infrastructure projects in the Philippines and South Korea, respectively. In theory, unsolicited proposals are a useful means for the private sector to propose beneficial ideas for project development. In practice, many of the world's most controversial and troubled private infrastructure projects were suggested to governments by private companies. A review of these and other troubled unsolicited projects reveals that many of the problems do not stem from the project concept being developed in the private sector, but from governments awarding the projects to the original private proponent without adequate competition and transparency. Private proponents often claim that the unique characteristics of their unsolicited proposals—intellectual property rights, small scale, remote locations, or cost efficiencies—dictate the need to sole-source and negotiate project details. Governments should not accept this argument. However, most governments still have no formal process for handling unsolicited proposals. This needs to change. There are three basic options. First option is to simply adopt a law prohibiting unsolicited projects—and some countries have done this. A second option is for governments to buy the concept and then award the project through a competitive bidding process in which no bidder has a predefined advantage. A third option—which has been adopted in such countries as Chile, South Korea, and the Philippines—is to offer the original proponent a pre-defined advantage in a competitive bidding process.

Under the third option, more and more countries are beginning to use one or a combination of two main approaches—a bonus system and the Swiss challenge. Under the bonus system, the government gives the original project proponent an advantage in the bidding process that takes the form of a bonus, usually about 10 per cent, credited to the proponent's bid. Under the Swiss challenge system, the government gives challengers an opportunity to make better offers than the original proponent, then allows the original proponent to countermarch.

### Questions

1. Ultimately, for a government awarding private infrastructure projects that originate as unsolicited proposals, a final objective should be to maximize competition and transparency. Do you agree?
2. Which of the three options would work best, depending on country conditions?
3. Under the bonus or Swiss channels systems, what are the major process issues? What is fair and not fair?

## CASE STUDY 2

### The Keyboard Syndrome

A manufacturing facility in Mumbai employs three data entry operators who work full time entering the records related to production, personnel, and inventory data into the computer. This data is then sent over the Internet to Brijlax Systems mainframe computer, where it becomes part of the corporate database for financial, production, and personnel management. As required by the labour agreement, in addition to a one-hour break as part of the lunch period, these three operators receive two 15 minutes break daily; they may take them at any convenient time, once in the morning and the other in the afternoon. Otherwise, they generally work at their keyboards all day.

Last year, Rajiv Sen, one of the operators, was absent from work for two weeks for a condition diagnosed as carpal tunnel syndrome, a neuromuscular disorder of the tendons and tissues in the wrists caused by repeated hand motions. His symptoms included a severe ache in the wrist and ever growing pain in the neck and shoulder. His doctor treated him with anti-inflammatory medicine and a few injections, and he had no problems thereafter. However, after a week, a second data entry operator experienced similar symptoms; his doctor diagnosed his ailment as 'RSI or repetitive stress injury' and referred to it informally as the VDT (video display terminal) disease. Because the company anticipates further automation in the future, with more data entry operators to be hired, Ramesh Chauhan asked his assistant, Sandeep Kaul, to gather additional information on this condition. In fact, Ramesh wants Sandeep to survey all workers in Mumbai to determine the type and degree of their use and to identify any related health problems. Once the extent of the problem is known, he wants Sandeep to make any appropriate recommendations regarding the work environment—posture, furniture, work habits, rest breaks, and the like—that will alleviate this problem. Sandeep develops a questionnaire as a first step and asks at least 50 clerical staff of the company to fill it. He then analyses the data carefully and uses it to prepare his final report.

### Questions

1. What are the ethical implications of this case?
2. Develop an employee questionnaire that elicits the information Ramesh had asked for. Include a short introductory paragraph at the top of the questionnaire explaining the purpose of the study and giving any needed directions.
3. Considering the findings from your questionnaire and the secondary sources, what does all this information mean in terms of your problem statement?
4. Prepare a recommendation report. Include an executive summary, use formal language for the body of the report, organize the body by criteria, and place the recommendations and conclusions at the end.
5. Assume the role of Sandeep Kaul, define the problem of the report and then identify the components of the problem.

CHAPTER 9

# Careers and Résumés

### LEARNING OBJECTIVES

After reading this chapter, you will be able to understand
- the process of building a career
- various résumé formats
- traditional, electronic, and video résumés
- the channels used to submit résumés
- the follow-up process
- the online recruitment process

## INTRODUCTION

*Choose a job you love and you will never have to work a day in your life.*
—Confucius

Time and effort has to be invested while searching for a job, irrespective of the kind of employment you seek. It would be difficult for you to find a job of your choice without knowing your career goals, the job market and also the recruitment process. A career is more than a job. It involves everything that you learn and practice during your lifetime. Building a career entails planning to reach your goals. Hence, it is important not only to decide what you would like to become in your life but also to pursue your goals with perseverance. Your goal may be to excel in the area of your interest by developing products; start your own business venture; pursue research; become rich; attain fame in your workplace by being innovative; or get a job as early as possible. But, irrespective of the nature of your goal, you need to put in your best efforts to achieve it. Getting the right job takes more than sending your résumé to a few companies. In fact, before entering the world of work, you need to know your potential and also the options available for you in the job market. Career building does not end with getting a job but continues till you are satisfied with your job and achievements. In fact, it takes time for fresh graduates to build their careers by building their individual brands. As career building and résumé writing are two important aspects pertaining to job search and interviews, various factors involved in these processes have been discussed in this chapter.

> Career building and résumé writing are two important aspects related to job search and interviews.

# CAREER BUILDING

Career building is an important aspect of a person's professional life. This section discusses various components that help in the process of career building.

## Today's Workplaces

We are living in a world that has been witnessing a great social and technological transformation and obviously today's workplaces have changed their practices in order to cope with such a revolution. Consequently, organizations demand from their employees those skills that would enable them to carry out various activities. For instance, a business analyst needs excellent analytical skills, while a project manager should possess brilliant leadership skills. In short, the core competencies of employees should be in tune with the needs of their respective industries. If we look at today's organizations, we realize that the type and nature of jobs also have undergone a sea change. Job titles such as knowledge analyst, event manager, video jockey, animator, ERP consultant, and software architect are quite novel and interesting as compared to their conventional counterparts. Many organizations expect their managers to possess multitasking skills. Hence, it is important to know the nature and type of the organization and the kind of job you wish to take up before applying for that job.

## Understanding Yourself

Before looking for a job and building your career, you need to know yourself—your education, skills, experience, personality and interest. In other words, you need to go for self-assessment. But in reality, how many of us take time out to self-assess our skills or our attitude? Although a majority of us generally believe we are right, we need to assess ourselves from time to time. Answering the following questions may enable you to understand your goals, aspirations, and potential:

1. What do I want to become?
2. Do I have enough subject knowledge to take up the career?
3. What is my academic area of interest?
4. Am I equipped with necessary skills to apply my knowledge?
5. What are my most enjoyable and greatest skills?
6. Am I a person with a positive attitude?
7. What are my likes and dislikes?
8. What activities do I like the most?
9. What are my strengths and weaknesses?
10. Have I ever tried to overcome my weaknesses?
11. Do I communicate effectively?
12. Do I possess adequate social skills?
13. How good am I in small talks?
14. What are my hobbies/extracurricular activities?
15. How am I different from others?
16. Am I creative?
17. What are the major achievements and failures in my life?
18. Am I confident in presenting myself to others?
19. Can I work in a team?

> Many organizations expect their managers to possess multitasking skills.

> Assess yourself continuously to gain knowledge about your skills, personality, and attitude.

Answering these questions will help you realize your strong and weak points regarding your knowledge, skills, attitude, interests, etc. This will also help you in motivating yourself.

When one is unemployed or fears lay-off, the time is right for reassessing one's current skills, talents, abilities, strengths, weaknesses, interests, and work values. In addition, it is the time to re-examine accomplishments and achievements, particularly those that may be relevant to a prospective employer. It is necessary to keep an on-going accomplishments file in which you maintain such items as articles, congratulatory letters, certificates from the boss or clients/customers, 360-degree evaluations, and descriptions of successful activities as they occur.

### Setting a Career Goal

Before setting a career goal, let us try to understand what the term 'career' means. To some of us, a career may identify our progression in professional life. Some others may feel that it refers to the various jobs or positions that earn us money. In other words, it refers to the job in which you have been trained in and will be continuing for some years. In fact, a career defines a person's professional life.

Setting a career goal implies thinking about your future. It enables you to stay focused and motivated. It may sometimes be difficult to have a very specific goal at this point. In that case, give a wider scope to your goal or be flexible. For instance, if you are interested in a marketing job, you should be ready to enter into any related areas, such as market research, advertising, transportation, processing, packaging, and selling. Setting a career goal is not a once-for-all process. Changes in your personality and environment may change your career goals. Hence, it is necessary to relook into your career goals every two years and make necessary changes. Remember to build a strong base for your career in the initial years so that it can take care of your future career aspirations and accomplishments. By doing so you are making your career strong and stable. In addition, ensure that your career journey is just as rewarding as reaching the goals. Enjoy every step of the way even when you start at the bottom. Your career will always have a learning curve. Make the most of it and keep as long as it satisfies you. Once you find that you are no longer satisfied, it is time to re-evaluate your position and career goals.

### Job Search/Looking at Various Options

After setting your career goal, you may need to answer the following questions, as honestly as possible, in order to proceed towards that goal:

1. What does career satisfaction mean to me?
2. Do I want to start a business on my own or wish to work for somebody?
3. If I don't have the skills necessary to achieve my career goal, do I have any means to acquire the same?
4. What specific compensation do I expect?
5. Which is more important for me—to work in my dream company or have my dream job in any company?
6. What type of working environment do I look for?
7. Do I want to work for a small or a large company?
8. What can I offer to my employer that others can't?

> Changes in your personality and in working environment may tend to change your career goals.

Now, with more clarity in your mind about your career goals, you can explore the various options available to you. One such option is to visit a company's website and gather information, such as its size, branches, products, achievements, ongoing projects, and working environment. You can also go for conventional job-search options, such as checking classified ads in newspapers, contacting companies in which you are interested, using personal contacts to get information, and attending job fairs. Like millions across the globe, you can also utilize online job search tools. For instance, you can have a look at the following websites:

- www.careerbuilder.com
- www.placementindia.com
- www.naukri.com
- www.monster.com
- www.timesjobs.com
- www.bestjobsinindia.in

Once you have identified a career and a promising industry of your choice, compile a list of specific organizations in that field. Then go to their websites and find out all the details. You can also email the organizations and ask for brochures or newsletters if they are not available on their websites. These days, companies have a separate web page for careers/job opportunities that contains information regarding the application process, mode of interview, etc. Some companies even present a few sample case studies that are similar to the ones given in interviews. So, by carefully reading the websites, you may be able to get an idea not only about the job openings but also about how to prepare for your interview.

Networking with your classmates, friends, business people, and professors can help you find more job openings. The broader the network, the better your chances are of making more employment contacts. Such professors often give consultancy to industries and businesses, stay in touch with them. During your academic tenure, demonstrate your work ethics and ability to make your professors realize your potential. Try to contact some business persons through family or friends and keep in touch with them. Your internships at some industries may also serve as a good source of career contacts for you. Also there are chances that your internships themselves may turn into jobs if you perform well. Your membership in various professional associations and organizations may also get you some job leads.

## Preparing Your Résumé

A *résumé* is a primary and potential marketing tool that is aimed not at getting a job but fetching an opportunity for an interview. It is a marketing document that presents your past and present credentials and achievements, so that your prospective employer can judge your future potential. Your résumé packages your qualifications, experience, and accomplishments into a convincing advertisement that can persuade employers. It is not necessary that a résumé should be prepared only at the time you are looking for a job. It can be prepared during the course of your study—say, second or third year, because you may need it for applying for internships or for some competition. Moreover, preparing your résumé early will enable you

> Résumé is a document that presents your past and present credentials and achievements so that your prospective employer can judge your future potential.

> A résumé should capture the attention of the recruiter on the first page.

to identify your weak areas and give you time to convert them into your strengths. But remember to invest your time, talent, and resources in preparing your résumé just as successful companies do in marketing their products.

Let us now understand how long a résumé should be and what its various parts entail.

## Length

There are no specific guidelines that tell us about the length of a résumé. But generally, recruiters prefer crisp, if not short, résumés. They expect the document to reflect not only the credentials of the candidates but also their attitude. Some universities prescribe a one-page or two-page format for résumés to be submitted to the recruiters who visit the campus for job interviews. Many fresh graduates may not have work experience, and hence may be able to stick to a one-page format. At the same time, other fresh graduates may have many projects, internships, extracurricular activities, achievements, leadership skills, etc. to be presented in their résumé. Hence, the résumés of fresh graduates or entry level job seekers may often, but not always, be one-page long. When it comes to the résumés of candidates seeking jobs above entry level, but below executive level, the length can be more than one page. Along the same lines, résumés competing for a senior-level position can be more than two or three pages long. In short, we can say that the résumé length is decided by each individual job seeker unless it is clearly specified by recruiters. But irrespective of its length, a résumé should capture the attention of the recruiter on the first page.

## Parts

Generally, résumés have the following standard parts that the recruiters expect and need to make valid appraisal of the candidates:

- Contact information—name, address, telephone number, email address
- Career objective or summary of qualifications
- Education
- Professional experience
- Special skills and aptitude
- Awards/honours/achievements
- Activities and interests
- References

**Contact information** The main heading of your résumé should start with your name, address, mobile and landline phone numbers, and email address/es—do not include 'Résumé' or 'Curriculum vitae' on the top as the heading. If you have a personal web page that highlights your accomplishments in a positive and professional way, you can include that as well. Among these details, your name should look prominent. After completing all the details, include a rule or line so that the reader's attention is drawn towards the visual centre (natural focal point lying within the first third of the page) of the page. Depending on the space available, you can arrange the details in many ways, as shown in Fig. 9.1.

|  |  |
|---|---|
| <div align="center">**Kanchan Kumar Agrawal**<br>S/o Ratan Kumar Agrawal<br>Opp. Ugmit Polytechnic College, Rayagada 765001, Orissa<br>91 9538285467/06856222401<br>kanchan@yahoo.co.in</div> ||
| <div align="center">**KANCHAN KUMAR AGRAWAL**</div> ||
| S/o Ratan Kumar Agrawal, Opp. Ugmit<br>Polytechnic College, Rayagada 765001, Orissa | 91 9538285467/06856222401<br>kanchan@yahoo.co.in |
| <div align="center">**KANCHAN KUMAR AGRAWAL**</div> ||
| S/o Ratan Kumar Agrawal<br>Opp. Ugmit Polytechnic College<br>Rayagada 765001, Orissa | Ph: 91 9538285467/06856222401<br>Email: kanchan@yahoo.co.in<br>Web page: careerfolios.com |
|  | S/o Ratan Kumar Agrawal, Opp Ugmit<br>Polytechnic College, Rayagada 765001, Orissa<br>91 9538285467/06856222401<br>kanchan@yahoo.co.in |
| **Kanchan Kumar Agrawal** ||

**Fig. 9.1** Résumé arrangements

**Career objective** Career objective is the statement that tells the reader the role you want to play, the skills that qualify you, and the benefits or value you can add to the company. It should be in line with the job that you have applied for. A clearly stated objective enables the recruiter to understand the candidate's commitment to his/her career. However, many candidates may have expertise in different areas and may not like to focus on only one area of expertise. Hence, they change the objective statement according to the job requirement. Experts disagree about the need for including your career objective on the résumé because they feel that it may limit your opportunity to only one field. If you wish to be considered for various openings, it is better to include a summary of qualifications in place of the career objective. A summary of qualifications is used to highlight your strongest points, especially if you have had varied experience. It is suitable for candidates with work experience, whereas a career objective is suitable for fresh graduates. The following are four choices for including/omitting career objective on your résumé:

1. Include this part only when applying for a specific, targeted position. (e.g., 'As a market analyst I can use my strengths in demographic research and analysis to target, develop, and maintain a dominant market share for your company.').
2. Include a general statement such as *Job Objective: Office Manager* or *Goal: Position in Public Relations, Marketing, or Communications* or *Objective: Field sales position with a large manufacturer.*

> A summary of qualifications is used to highlight one's strongest points.

3. Omit this part if you are preparing an all-purpose résumé or be ready to change this so as to suit the job profile.

Let us look at a few examples of career objective/job objective:

- To seek an opportunity in which my sales-support, customer-service, problem-solving, and human-relations skills will grow and retain your customer base.
- To obtain a position as a financial analyst with an opportunity for growth and career advancement
- To enhance my professional skills in a dynamic and stable organization
- To seek a responsible job with an opportunity for professional challenges
- To enter as a system analyst where my mathematical and analytical skills can be applied effectively, thereby contributing to the progress of the organization

Let us look at a few examples where a summary of qualifications has been given:

- Competent administrator with 15 years of experience in managing multi-site business office operations
- Experienced engineer with significant background in design and construction of large public work projects
- IBM-trained customer service engineer with an impressive 16 years experience in technical and customer support.

**Education** Unless your work experience has been extensive and directly related to your job profile, your education is probably a stronger qualification than your work experience and should, therefore, come as the next part of your résumé. Generally, all fresh graduates include this part after the career objective. In this part, include the name and location of your college and schools, graduating year, examinations passed, major subject, and your percentage or grade point average. One way to show your percentage in a better light is to mention the percentage in major subjects (e.g., 85% or GPA 8.5 in major). You can include your latest degree first and then mention the board examinations that you have passed for securing the $12^{th}$ and $10^{th}$ grades. Some recruiters who visit for campus recruitment want the students to mention only certain details, such as the programme of study, the college/board, and the percentage as mentioned in the following example:

Educational Qualifications:

- **Graduation:** B.E. (Hons) Mechanical, BITS-Pilani, Goa Campus, CGPA: 8.58
- **Intermediate:** I.S.C., Percentage: 93.8
- **High School:** I.C.S.E., Percentage: 86.5

**Professional/Work experience** Work experience of any type adds value to your résumé. It tells the employers that you have had experience in carrying out the task or project the organization had assigned you. It informs that you have followed directions, accomplished goals through team efforts, and have been rewarded for your endeavours. Fresh graduates can include their paid or non-paid internships at any organization during their academic career, experience of working as a volunteer for a social cause with an NGO, a project carried out by them as a part of their academic process, etc., under this category. Candidates who have already

> Work experience of any type adds value to your résumé.

worked in other organizations can include this part even before the section on education because work experience counts more than educational qualifications.

This part can also be called the 'Career Record', 'Record of Experience', or 'Work record', or 'Career Experience'. While writing this part, focus on the skills you have developed and your progression from assignments of lesser to greater responsibility. List your projects/internships/assignments in reverse chronological order with the current or the last one appearing first. Include details such as type of assignment (internship/project); dates/duration; project title; objectives; applied skills; results/accomplishments. Working professionals can give the details of their jobs—employer's name and address; details of employment; most important job title; and significant duties, accomplishments and promotions.

In giving details of work experience, be specific with statements such as *part of the project team for the Bizfest 2012, analysed data collected through a market survey among 1000 residents of Chandigarh city to find out the demand for the handmade toys prepared by underprivileged women and suggested necessary modifications.* Avoid using general statements such as *worked with my team for a market survey; successfully resolved problems related to ineffective functioning of the college canteen, etc.* Make your statements forceful and persuasive by using descriptive and action verbs. The following is a list of such verbs:

> Administered, analysed, addressed, applied, appraised, allocated, assessed, accomplished, assisted, budgeted, balanced, built, changed, controlled, counseled, customized, collected, coordinated, consolidated, computed, catalogued, directed, designed, devised, demonstrated, developed, drafted, delegated, evaluated, expanded, examined, expedited, edited, established, engineered, formulated, fabricated, facilitated, founded, handled, hired, implemented, interpreted, identified, instituted, introduced, generated, guided, identified, inspected, improved, instructed, led, managed, maintained, marketed, modified, motivated, monitored, operated, organized, oversaw, pioneered, processed, produced, persuaded, planned, publicized, promoted, programmed, performed, repaired, researched, represented, resolved, restored, recommended, spearheaded, scheduled, surveyed, specialized, streamlined, systematized, set goals, suggested, transformed, translated, tabulated, trained, updated, wrote.

**Special skills and aptitude** Variedly known as *Capabilities and Skills, Core Competencies, Talents, Abilities,* etc., this section of your résumé enables your recruiters to know what distinctively you can do for their organization. So list your specific skills here. For instance, if you are good in designing web pages, preparing financial reports, developing training programmes, etc., mention them using expressions such as *competent in, proficient with, skilled in, experienced in, ability to,* and *capable of.* This section can also include two categories—occupational and personal skills. While professional or technical skills, such as marketing, fundraising, and programming are included under the former, personal skills such as good communication skills, an analytical aptitude, working well under stress, quick learning, etc. can be included under the latter category. Foreign languages that you are proficient in can also be included in this section. Focus on top three or five skill areas and provide brief examples from your experience to support the same. In addition, remember to focus more on those skills that are relevant to the job you are applying for.

> Focus on top three or five skill areas and provide brief examples from your experience to support the same.

> A reference is a person who has agreed to provide information about the candidate to his prospective employer.

**Awards/Honours/Achievements** Any awards, honours, recognition, fellowships, certificates, and commendations you have received in the recent past (say, in the last five years) can be included, under this section in your résumé. Identify them clearly, for instance, instead of saying *Recipient of Google award,* give more details: *Selected by Google Inc. as Head for the Goa State Google Technology User Group.* If you have many achievements to list, present them in different categories, such as academic, non-academic, and professional. Also present them in reverse chronological order, selecting more of your achievements from the recent past. For example, a fresh graduate should include more achievements from his/her college years though he/she can also include a significant few from his/her high-school years.

**Activities and interests** Today's recruiters are interested in selecting well-rounded persons for their companies. Hence, in this section, you can include your extracurricular, community, or other professional activities to demonstrate your leadership, management, team, and interpersonal skills. Use action statements such as *Led the sponsorship and marketing team for the annual cultural festival Waves 2012 of the campus and collected a sponsorship of ₹10 lakh,* rather than saying *Chairperson of the Sponsorship and Marketing Team.* Membership of professional bodies can also be included here, but religious or political affiliations should be avoided.

This section can also include your hobbies and other interests, such as painting/dance/music/reading/photography/skating/teaching kids/compèring. It is better to avoid mentioning time-consuming/addictive pastimes such as computer games and car racing. If you don't have any hobby or interest worth mentioning, you can omit this part.

**References** A reference is a person who has agreed to provide information about a candidate to his/her prospective employer regarding the candidate's suitability for the job. Generally the names of references are not to be included in the résumé unless specified by the recruiting company. However, you should have the names of your references before you begin your job search. Talk to some professors or previous employers who know you very well and get their consent to use them as your references. Give them your résumé, so that they can go through the details. Keep a list of their full names and complete contact addresses ready with you, so that you can take it along with you while going for an interview.

## RÉSUMÉ FORMATS

After discussing the parts and contents of a résumé, it is appropriate to throw some light on the various formats in which a résumé can be presented. Résumé writers can use any of the following five formats depending on their requirements (Fig. 9.2):

- Chronological
- Functional
- Combination
- Targeted
- Mini

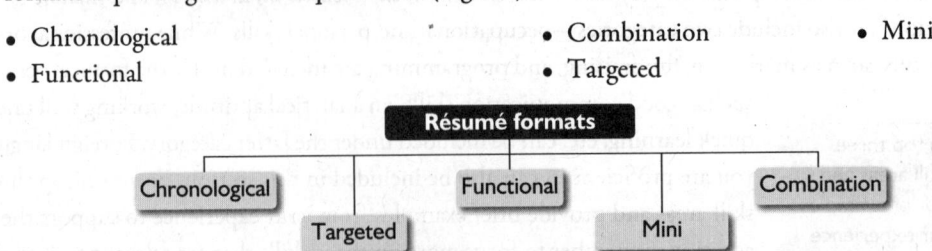

**Fig. 9.2** Résumé formats

### Business Communication Insight

**Avoid These 10 Résumé Mistakes**

Don't make the following résumé mistakes:

1. **Résumé lacks focus** A sharp focus is an extremely important résumé element. A 'general' résumé that is not focused on a specific job's requirements may be seen as non-competitive. You can use your profile/summary section to position yourself for each job you target by tweaking the wording to fit each type of position.

2. **Résumé is duties-driven instead of accomplishments-driven** Résumés should consist primarily of high-impact accomplishments statements that sell the job-seeker's qualifications as the best candidate. Focus on accomplishments that set you apart from other job candidates.

3. **Résumé items are listed in an order that doesn't consider the reader's interest.** Consider whether your education or your experience is your best selling point and list that first. Generally, brand-new graduates list education first, while job-seekers with a few years of experience list experience first.

4. **Résumé exposes the job-seeker to age discrimination by going too far back into the job-seeker's job history.** The rule of thumb for someone at the senior level is to list about 15 years worth of jobs. Similarly, don't provide the date of your college graduation if it was more than about 10 years ago.

5. **Résumé buries important skills, especially computer skills, at the bottom.** There are few jobs today for which computer skills are not important. If computer skills are relevant to your field, list them in your summary or profile section. If you are in the technology field, list your technical skills in a separate section called, say, 'Systems Proficiencies', but be sure it's on the first page of your résumé.

6. **Résumé is not bulleted.** Use a bulleted style to make your résumé more reader-friendly. In a study by Career Masters Institute, use of bullets was the second-highest ranked preference by employers, and density of type (paragraphs rather than bullet points) was ranked highly as a factor that would inspire employers to discard a résumé.

7. **Résumé uses a cookie-cutter design based on an overused résumé template.** Standard templates are somewhat inflexible and contain problematic formatting. The employer immediately senses a certain lack of imagination in the job-seeker.

8. **Résumé lacks keywords.** Inundated by résumés from job-seekers, employers have increasingly relied on digitizing job-seeker résumés, placing those résumés in keyword-searchable databases, and using software to search those databases for specific keywords that relate to job vacancies. In addition, many employers search the databases of third-party job-posting and résumé-posting boards on the Internet.

9. **References are listed directly on your résumé.** Never list specific references directly on your résumé. List them on a separate sheet, and even then, submit them only when specifically requested by an employer.

10. **Résumé's appearance is not available in other electronic formats.** Beyond a résumé that can be sent as an email attachment, it is crucial these days to have at least one type of electronic version of your résumé for sending via email and posting to the Internet job boards.

*Source:* Hansen, Katharine, 'Avoid These 10 Résumé Mistakes', http://www.quintcareers.com/resume_mistakes.html, accessed on 29 November 2011. Reproduced with permission.

### Chronological

This format presents information related to various activities in the reverse order of the sequence in which they were carried out. For instance, while preparing the education section, your recent education will appear first, followed by the earlier ones. Similarly, for all the other sections, namely work experience, projects, etc. the reverse chronological order is used. This format is primarily used when you are staying in the same profession, particularly in very conservative fields such as academia and law. Though it makes it easier for recruiters to get information on what you did under each job, it is difficult for you to highlight your best activities and credentials.

> - The chronological format presents the information related to various activities in the reverse order of the sequence in which they had been carried out.
> - Combination résumés start with a short skills and achievements section followed by a shorter chronology of job description.

### Functional

As against the chronological format, the functional format highlights your major skills and accomplishments from the very beginning. It helps the reader see clearly what you can do for them, rather than having to cull it from the job description. It enables you to choose the highlights from all your activities and target the résumé towards a new direction or field so as to match it with your job profile. In other words, it allows you to present the skills you acquired in an organization rather than describing the job names and titles. The functional résumé is a must for career changers, but is very appropriate for fresh graduates who have a wide range of skills and those who want to make slight shifts in their career direction. This is a very effective format, and hence, highly recommended.

### Combination

Combination résumés start with a short skills and achievements section, followed by a shorter chronology of job description. This format combines the elements of both the chronological and functional formats. It maximizes the advantages of both kinds of résumés, avoiding potential negative effects of either type. However, it tends to be a longer résumé and also may be repetitious—skills and accomplishments may have to be repeated in both the 'functional' and 'chronological' job descriptions. In short, with this type of résumé you can highlight the skills you have that are relevant to the job you are applying for, and also provide the chronological work history that employers prefer.

### Targeted

Candidates who wish to apply for jobs that match their skills and experiences can choose this format. It is customized so that it specifically highlights the experience and skills relevant to the job they are applying for. Candidates who wish to use one-size-fits-all type of résumé for any job should not resort to targeted résumé format, as it definitely takes more work to write a targeted résumé.

### Mini

A mini résumé contains a brief summary of your career highlights and qualifications. It can be used for networking purposes, or shared upon request from a prospective employer, or reference writer who may want an overview of your accomplishments, rather than a full length résumé.

> A mini résumé contains a brief summary of a candidate's career highlights and qualifications.

# TRADITIONAL, ELECTRONIC, AND VIDEO RÉSUMÉS

A *traditional* or *conventional résumé* is the résumé you prepare and send by post along with a cover letter or as an attachment to an email that acts as the cover letter. Students who appear for on-campus interviews prepare this kind of résumé and submit it to recruiters through the placement office of their colleges. Such résumés are generally short, only about one or two pages long.

Although traditional résumés are still used, *electronic résumés* are gaining popularity these days. An electronic résumé is essentially a résumé that is electronically formatted so that optical scanning systems can search or read (scan) it easily. Whatever you have gathered from the preceding discussion on traditional résumés holds good for electronic résumés as well; but as against the traditional résumés which are intended to be read by humans, electronic résumés are scanned by the computers, and so, are also called scannable résumés.

Electronic résumés are an increasingly widespread alternative to the traditional print variety. Since many employers look for, and sometimes even require, applicants to submit information electronically, it is important to know this type of résumé in some detail.

## Types of Electronic Résumé

There are two types of electronic résumés (Fig. 9.3). These will be discussed here.

### ASCII Résumé

ASCII stands for American Standard Code for Information Interchange. ASCII is the standard way printable characters are represented in the US. In other countries, computer systems, however, have additional ASCII codes, called extended ASCII. If the writer's computer has extended ASCII and the reader's does not, there is a problem.

ASCII résumés are widely used because (a) all computers read standard ASCII (b) many companies no longer hire people to read résumés. Instead they use OCR (Optical Character recognition) software for applying a modern technique called electronic applicant tracking.

### HTML Résumé

HTML stands for HyperText Mark-up Language. If you choose this form of electronic résumé, you need to create an HTML coded document that can be uploaded to the Internet via a web page.

HTML or web-based résumés have the following advantages:

1. Thousands of employers worldwide can access your résumé information as quickly as you post it.
2. You can update and change your résumé readily.

> Electronic résumés are an increasingly widespread alternative to the traditional print résumés.

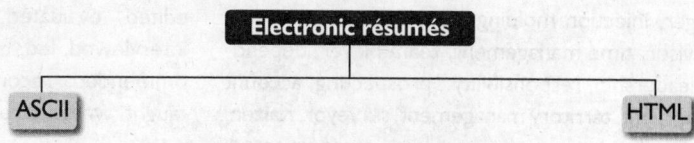

**Fig. 9.3** Types of electronic résumé

3. You can demonstrate your experience and showcase your expertise on the Internet by including portfolios with accessible graphics and sound.

Nevertheless, HTML résumés have one major drawback in that privacy is not assured; you have no control over who sees your résumé or where it is transferred, once you have uploaded it on the Web.

### Guidelines for Preparing Electronic Résumés

1. Electronic résumés should convey the same information as traditional résumés.
2. Format and style must be computer-friendly.
3. List as many facts, skills, and attributes as possible.
4. Use descriptive nouns, noun phrases, action words, and sentence fragments to describe your experience. Quantify your experience wherever possible.
5. Rely heavily on technical language, the current industry buzzwords, and technical acronyms associated with your field of study.
6. Be clear with the job description of the post you are applying for.
7. Place your full name as the first item on the résumé.
8. Put contact information on different lines and if you list more than one phone number, put each on a separate line.
9. Left justify the entire document, avoid columns, and use at least one-inch margins.
10. Avoid punctuation as much as possible.
11. Avoid vertical and/or horizontal lines or boxes.
12. Use a standard font (Arial, Courier or Times New Roman) and font size 10 or 12.
13. Use white space to demarcate various headings.
14. If you email your résumé, save the file in ASCII or plain text format.
15. Include a key word summary at the end of your résumé (see box below).
16. If you send a print copy, do not fold or staple.

### Video Résumés

A *video résumé* is a presentation that is recorded using various digital means (e.g., digital camera) and used for job applications. They enable job seekers to showcase their abilities beyond the level of traditional or electronic résumés, and allow prospective employers to actually see and hear the applicants'

| Sample Key Words | |
|---|---|
| manufacturing supervisor, design assistant, production manager, injection molding inspector, assembly line supervisor, time management, team player, dependable, leadership, responsibility., prospecting, account development, territory management, surveyor, Kaizen, Time Studies, programmer, advised, communicated, | conducted, designed, developed, directed, doubled, edited, evaluated, improved, increased, installed, interviewed, led, managed, persuaded, planned, recommended, reconciled, reduced, sold supervised, taught, wrote, hired |

> Video résumés enable job seekers to showcase their abilities beyond the level of traditional or electronic résumés.

strengths as presented by them. With the increasing power of technology, it is possible to transmit streaming videos via the Internet. Hence, video résumés are gaining popularity these days. They are now being accepted by companies across the world for various professions. Of course, the need for objectivity in these videos is a serious matter for concern as the receiver may get carried away by the appearance and presentation skills of the applicants even before an interview. At times, even business schools ask for a one-minute video, where you can present your skills, strengths, and objectives. A video résumé is a quick tool to gauge professional abilities and can speed up the screening process. However, it may not be practically possible for companies to invite video résumés if the number of applicants is very large. However, it may be appropriate to demand a video résumé for jobs involving performing arts, such as music, dance, and theatre, or those demanding excellent verbal and non-verbal communication skills.

The following are samples of cover letters (Fig. 9.4) and résumés (Fig. 9.5):

---

**Sample 1**

Pranav Kulkarni
932 Hailey Road 33/46
New Delhi 110541

25 May 2012

Mr Rohit Kumar
HR Manager
WCTG Group
780 Wolseley Avenue
Mumbai 220145

Dear Mr Kumar,

I am writing to apply for the position of Finance Trainee, as advertised on your home page on 10 May, 2012. Your recent move into the field of audit and tax is of particular interest to me as I plan to pursue a career in this area.

Recently, I graduated from Anna University with a Masters of Business Administration, majoring in Finance. This programme allowed me the opportunity to learn and practise the various financial analysis procedures necessary for this type of job. Of particular relevance is the research project I completed in my final year on 'The Evolving Role of Compliance and the Challenges in the Next Decade'. As many of my assignments involved working in groups, I have also developed strong teamwork skills, and enjoy working in such an environment. You will be able to get a clearer idea about my suitability for the position advertised from the attached résumé.

I will contact you in a fortnight from now to ensure that you have received this résumé and to answer any questions that you may have. Thank you for your consideration.

Sincerely,

Pranav Kulkarni

Encl: Résumé

**Sample 2**

Niharika Jain
Flat No.145
Royal Estate,
Bengaluru 432096
25 May 2011

Mr Vikas Gupta
Personnel Manager
Hindustan Unilever Limited
41 South High Street
Bengaluru 520124

Dear Mr Gupta,

When I saw the advertisement in the May 12$^{th}$ edition of *The Times of India* for the position of Brand Manager in Hindustan Unilever Limited, I felt that my qualifications matched with the job profile, and hence, I am writing to express my interest in the same. I am a graduate from NMIMS University with a Masters in Marketing Management.

You indicated a need for someone with both marketing experience and leadership skills. During my junior and senior years at Mumbai, I have worked as an assistant brand manager for various clients. Please see my enclosed résumé for a more complete view of my background.

I am eager to learn more about this opportunity with Hindustan Unilever Limited, and look forward to interviewing with you. I can be reached by phone at 9800050063 or by email at niharika.jain@yahoo.com. Thank you for your time and consideration.

Sincerely,

Niharika Jain

**Fig. 9.4** Sample cover letters

---

**Sample 1**

**PRANAV KULKARNI**

- 932 Hailey Road, New Delhi–110520
- Email: pranav.kulk@gmail.com

| | |
|---|---|
| **OBJECTIVE** | To apply my proven problem-solving, analytical, and interpersonal skills |
| **EDUCATION** | Anna University |
| | Master of Business Administration, expected May 2012 |
| | Specilization: Finance and Information Systems & E-business |
| | GPA: 3.8/4.0 |
| | |
| | St Xavier College, Kolkata |
| | Bachelor of Science in Business Administration, April 2009 |
| | Specialization: Finance |
| | GPA: 3.3/4.0 |
| **EXPERIENCE** | PRAXAIR Co., Kolkata |
| | • Corporate audit intern, 6/5/10 – 5/8/10 |

- Conducted year-end compliance audits of production facilities throughout West Bengal
- Created an audit profile for the company's Medigas division
- Recognized relatively high telephone expenses for an expatriate officer and developed a solution to minimize this expense with the help of the telecommunications department
- Recognized areas for improvement and discussed alternative solutions with local management after participating in a month-long accounting and operational audit of plant facilities in China

M&T BANK, Kolkata
Finance Intern, Summer 2008
- Analysed float operations of the newly acquired bank for Assistant Vice-president of Technology
- Recommended how to minimize cost of combined float operations

**COMPUTER SKILLS**
Proficient in Microsoft Office (Word, PowerPoint, Excel, and Access), Microsoft FrontPage, Basic HTML, Dynamic HTML, PageMaker, Visual Basic, Visual C++, JavaScript, Java

**KEY SKILLS**
- Have a mathematical mind with good analytical skills
- Able to co-ordinate and manage all aspects of payroll and VAT administration
- Able to prioritize individual workloads according to deadlines
- Confident attitude with a proactive approach to work
- Good knowledge of IRIS accounts production software
- Ability to manage multiple tasks simultaneously
- Experience in offering tax, accountancy, and business development advice to clients
- Up-to-date with all current accounting and taxation legislation
- Possessing commercial acumen
- Able to work as part of a team or alone

**ACTIVITIES/ AFFILIATION**
Vice-president of the Graduate Management Association (GMA)
Webmaster for the National MBA Consortium and GMA web sites
Volunteer Practice Interviewer for the School of Management Career Resource Centre Member of winning team in the IBM Career Advantage Competition

**REFERENCES**
Prof. Shanti Krishna
Professor, Anna University, Chennai
044-2624840
Email: skrishna@anna.ac.in

Prof. Shashi Dewan, Dean
Anna University, Chennai
044-2627892
Email: sdewan@anna.ac.in

**PERSONAL DETAILS**
Father's Name: Pradeep Kulkarni
Date of Birth: 30-05-1986
Gender: Male
Languages known: English, Hindi, French and Marathi
Contact number: 9542456395

## Sample 2
## Prem Kumar

Address: B 33/29, Raj Nagar  
Varanasi (UP) 221005

Mobile: 09000003877  
Email: prem.kumar@gmail.com

### CAREER OBJECTIVE

Looking for a challenging career which demands the best of my professional ability in terms of technical and analytical skills, and helps me in broadening and enhancing my current skill set and knowledge.

### SYNOPSIS

A fresher with B.Tech Degree in Electronics and Communication Engineering from Bharath University, Bhopal. Possess knowledge of practical-electronic circuit design and C/C++ programming.

### PROFILE

- Well versed in Electronic circuit design. Good knowledge of C, C++
- Analytical, good at problem-solving and excellent in maintaining interpersonal relationships
- Good verbal and written skills.

### EDUCATIONAL QUALIFICATION

- B. Tech (Electronics and Communication Engineering) with aggregate 7.8 CGPA (scale of 10.0) in 2006–2010 from Bharath University, Bhopal.
- 12th with aggregate 74% from Chakdwipa high school (W.B.C.H.S.E) in 2006.
- 10th with aggregate 80% from Chakdwipa high school (W.B.B.S.E) in 2004.

### SOFTWARE SKILLS

- **Languages & Skills**     C, C++
- **Operating Systems**      Windows 9x/2000/XP
- **Softwares**              Microsoft Word, PowerPoint, and Excel

### PROJECTS UNDERTAKEN

**IR Remote Control Jammer—Mini Project**  
An electronic circuit that jams IR signals. No infrared remote would work in the proximity of this circuit.  
**Role:** Electronic design and soldering

**Heart Beat Monitor—Mini Project**  
This project monitors the heart beat of a patient. An electronic circuit that is tied around the wrist of a patient, results of the heart beat are shown using a Matlab program in a PC.  
**Role:** Electronic design, soldering, and Matlab programming.

**Automatic Dark/Light Detector—Mini Project**  
This electronic circuit automatically switches on when there is darkness and switches off when light falls on the sensor.  
**Role:** Electronic design

## FIELDS OF INTEREST

- Hobby electronic circuits
- Mobile communications
- Digital signal processing
- Digital electronics
- Embedded systems

## EXTRA-CURRICULAR ACTIVITIES

- Won first prize in school drama
- Organized various cultural programmes in a club
- Won prizes in quiz competitions

## STRENGTHS

- Determined to learn with a practical approach
- Good communication skills
- Enthusiastic and can produce results under deadline constraints

## PERSONAL DETAILS

| | |
|---|---|
| Father's Name | Arun Kumar |
| Date of Birth | 27-02-1988 |
| Gender | Male |
| Languages known | English, Hindi, Bengali, Oriya, and Tamil |
| Permanent Address | B 33/29, Raj Nagar, Varanasi (UP) 221005 |
| Hobbies | Listening to music, drawing, playing cricket |

**Prem Kumar**

### Sample 3
### Rahul Kharbanda

- 1111 Varsha Tower, Saakar Heights, Bengaluru 44000
- 08023274968 (o) 08023254612 (h) 09962546541(m), Email: Rrk@gmail.com

## QUALIFICATIONS SUMMARY

Accomplished senior marketing professional with broad retail marketing experience, encompassing *strategic planning, qualitative and quantitative research, interactive marketing, creative development, media planning and buying, database/direct-marketing, public relations, sales promotion and visual merchandising,* with the ability and skill set to provide creative, innovative, enthusiastic and forward-thinking leadership in a team environment. Focused on achieving continuous, improved business performance.

**11/2011—Present Green and Fresh, Bengaluru, Karnataka**
A ₹800-crore national general retailer with nearly 1000 locations.

***Marketing Director—12345 Division*** *(5/00–present)*
Appointed to lead the entire marketing function through a turnaround. Assumed majority of responsibilities and accountabilities previously held by the vice-president and the director of field marketing.

- Led the development and implementation of annual marketing plans that resulted in consistent sales increases, in a flat growth industry. During this time, marketing played a key role in achieving sales growth that consistently out-performed key competitors and the industry as a whole. This growth resulted in 12345 becoming profitable in 2002, for the first time in over 10 years
- Led the development and implementation of annual marketing plans that resulted in consistent sales increases, in a flat growth industry. During this time, marketing played a key role in achieving sales growth that consistently out-performed key competitors and the industry as a whole. This growth resulted in 12345 becoming profitable in 2002, for the first time in over ten year.
- Directed development of business-to-consumer, business-to-business, and associate-to-family local store marketing programmes that drove incremental annual sales of ₹400 million
- Spearheaded the testing and rollout of a private label, retail-financing programme that has resulted in incremental sales of over ₹100 million, in the first three months and projected to drive annual incremental system-wide sales of over ₹30 billion
- Developed and implemented consumer research to improve results of our sales promotions. Increased annual vendor co-op fund by over 100%, in less than two years, resulting in an increase in consumer-facing media

***Director, Brand Management—P&G Inc.*** *(10/1999–10/2011)*
$900+ million division of Mith Company with 800+ corporate-owned and franchised stores in the US, Puerto Rico, and Canada. Promoted to lead the development and implementation of national-level, brand positioning, and general marketing initiatives.

- Directed development of interactive, direct marketing, media, creative, sales promotion, and PR strategies
- Built entirely new staff of nine marketing professionals, following company's acquisition and relocation
- Controlled ₹45 million national budget
- Conducted reviews for and hired four outside agency resources (general market, direct marketing, interactive, print media)
- Launched two, successful brand-building advertising campaigns
- Championed the development and launch of 'www.67890.com'—the most visited website in this retail category with nearly 2 million hits per month in less than one year
- Blueprinted public relations & publicity strategies resulting in 90+ million free, annual media impressions
- Initiated a comprehensive, relational database-marketing program, which increased customer retention by over 10%, in the first month, and achieved 8:1 ROI in less than 6 months
- Responsible for design, development, and implementation of consumer
- Designed two category and company first national sales events, resulting in record sales and the company's highest comp sales performance for the year
- Pioneered implementation of a toll-free, consumer 800# locator featuring direct-connect technology, which resulted in a 22% increase in store call volume
- Implemented a downloadable 'On-hold' messaging system reducing store labour hours and related costs
- Directed the development and implementation of new frame merchandising strategy resulting in consistent product presentation across all stores and increased ease of customer shopping process by 15%
- Controlled five outside agency partners including general market advertising, direct marketing
- Interactive marketing, print placement and Yellow Pages advertising agencies
- Created a charitable event programme, which married the efforts of independent optometrists, store operations staff, and two separate charities resulting in valuable community-service exposure

*Marketing Manager—Specialty Businesses (9/95–9/1999)*
Managed marketing disciplines for Specialty Business Group and served as lead member of a cross-functional business team accountable for all business decisions and P&L.

- Championed marketing programmes and general business solutions resulting in increased customer traffic and sales, in a declining Host sales
- Implemented company's most successful sales promotion resulting in record customer traffic increase of 13% comp sales increases of over 15%
- Pioneered implementation of a toll free, consumer 800# locator featuring direct-connect technology, which resulted in a 22% increase in store call volume
- Implemented a downloadable 'On-hold' messaging system reducing store labor hours and related costs
- Improved Host relations, resulting in increased business support, 30% decrease in host advertising media costs and increased exposure to Host customers
- Spearheaded successful employee sales contests
- Interactive marketing, print placement and Yellow Pages advertising agencies
- Pioneered a breakthrough media strategy improving ROI by nearly 100%
- Employed merchandising and promotional strategies for BJ that continue to drive record sales volumes

*Associate Director, Client Services (93–95)*
Recruited to direct account services group in development, implementation, and manage targeted, 'neighbourhood' marketing programmes. Clients included: Goodyear Tire & Rubber Company, Host Marriott, Taco Bell, Wendy's International, Coca Cola, Ruby Tuesday, Cracker Barrel Red Robin International, California Pizza Kitchen, Chevys Fresh Mex, Longhorn Steakhouse, and others

- Key member of strategic management team developing and implementing growth strategies, which resulted in year-on-year revenue increases of more than 200%
- Developed and implemented Goodyear's national Neighborhood Network, which achieved an ROI of 69% in four months
- Spearheaded targeted neighbourhood marketing programme for Red Robin resulting in a 16%+ net sales gain
- Developed a New Store Opening program for Red Robin International in a market with no brand awareness, resulting in record traffic and sales and a sustained weekly sales increase of more than 16%
- Developed and directed various programs achieving redemption rates of 15–25%
- Signed over $400,000 in new business, in 6 months, representing $2 million in expansion potential. Spearheaded successful employee sales contests
- Utilized sales prospecting and contact management database system, improving productivity by over 20%
- Built solid working relationships with all levels of client management

*Associate Director, Marketing Services (5/1992–8/1993)*
Promoted from Senior Manager, Sales Promotion. Appointed member of co-op marketing committee, new product development and concept re-imaging teams.

- Directed design, development, testing and subsequent national rollout of new menu presentation system resulting in average transaction increase of more than 5%
- Reduced annual department operating expenses by over 10%
- Led staff of eight and effectively managed annual budget of $7+ million
- Participated in strategic development and implementation of concept re-imaging, which resulted in double-digit comparable store sales increases

*Senior Manager, Sales Promotion (12/1989–5/1992)*
Promoted to this position responsible for planning and directing the development and implementation of print, merchandising, sales promotion and direct marketing programs, including national co-op marketing events, sales promotions, new product testing and introductions, and menu presentation

- Directed design, development, testing, and subsequent national rollout of new menu presentation system resulting in average transaction increase of more than 5%
- Blueprinted the chain's first, national direct mail promotion, which resulted in sales gain of over $1 million
- Expanded vendor resources resulting in improved finished quality of print and merchandising materials and shortened production schedules
- Renegotiated vendor contracts reducing budgeted expenses by $300,000–$1 million annually. Improved average FSI coupon redemption from 0.5% to over 2%.
- Implemented promotional tracking system resulting in accurate and timely results reporting
- Created promotional trade-up and add-on programmes resulting in average transaction increases of 5–15%.

*Manager, Sales Promotion* (9/1987–12/1989)
- Directed design, development, testing and subsequent national rollout of new menu presentation system resulting in average transaction increase of more than 5%
- Renegotiated print media contracts resulting in savings of more than $250,000
- Created kids' premium promotion resulting in sales increase of 11%
- Established in-house print media agency resulting in annual savings of over $750,000
- Spearheaded development and implementation of print and merchandising network improving franchisee participation in company-sponsored programs from 10–40%.
- Developed and implemented multi-tiered gift certificate sales promotion resulting in 25% sales

**SOFTWARE**    Microsoft Office (Excel, Access, Word, Outlook, PowerPoint)

**VOLUNTEER**   Director, Astha Foundation, Mysore (April 1999–Present)
Vice-president and Trustee, Saakar Football Club, Saaker Hts, Bengaluru (1994–Present)

## Sample 4
### RAKESH KUMAR
Mobile: +91 8962882001(M)
Email: Rakeeshkumar@yahoo .co.in, rakeshp.hr83@gmail.com

Seeking challenges in HRD/General Administration in an organization of high repute.

### SYNOPSIS

- ☐ HR Professional with over 5 years of experience in HR, general administration, recruitment operations, salary administration, and payroll and team management.
- ☐ *Presently associated with SEPCO Electric Power Construction Corporation (CHINA GOVT UNDERTAKING COMPANY) as Manager (HR & Admin).*
- ☐ Successfully implemented measures for welfare and administration in different capacities.
- ☐ Adept at analysing the financial viability of new ventures/new projects; demonstrated skills in strategic planning and securing mandatory loan/other approvals from regulatory/statutory authorities.
- ☐ Aware and up-to-date about the competitors in the industry and able to appropriately select the various resources for hiring best candidates based on 'Cost Effectiveness' and 'Urgency'.
- ☐ Comprehensive experience of handling complete general administrative functions. Expertise in formulating and benchmarking functional best practices in the organization.
- ☐ Effective in handling employee grievances, salary, and appraisals. Self-motivated, pro-active and reliable individual with ability to perform best in challenging situations.

## CORE COMPETENCIES

**HRM/HRD**
- Coordinating for smoother implementation of HR policies, manpower planning, induction, recruitment, job rotation, transfers, deputation, lien scheme, orientation, and development of new employees.
- Assisting in development and administration of performance management programmes in the organization, including periodic performance reviews and appraisals for all members of staff.
- Assisting in the compensation survey of management and non-management levels in related industries.
- Looking over the activities pertaining to attendance, shift schedules, overtime, leaves, employee loans, insurance claims, etc.
- Conducting screening interviews and making arrangements with employing departments to interview and select the qualified candidates and giving out reference check letters.

**CONTRACT LABOUR MANAGEMENT**
- Ensuring contract labourers are covered under ESIC & PF, timely distribution of wage, rotation of contract labourers, getting principal employer registration, ensuring contractor gets the Lice under Contract Labour(R&A) Act, etc.

**STATUTORY COMPLIANCE**
- Ensuring compliances under various labour legislations such as Factories Act, Payment of Wages Act, Industrial Dispute Act, PF Act, ESIC Act, Minimum Wages Act, WC Act, etc.

**PERFORMANCE MANAGEMENT**
- Ensuring timely and proper execution of the performance appraisal process.
- Evaluating the performance of employees as per identified KRA's (quarterly) by developing monitoring mechanism for measuring performance.
- Maintaining files of compensation of executives. Processing compensation related actions and benefits and preparing reports for management review and approval.
- Maintaining appraisal records, tabulating appraisal data, and analysing feedback received.

**GRIEVANCE HANDLING/EMPLOYEE RELATION MANAGEMENT**
- Handling employee's grievances.
- Conducting one-on-one discussions at 30/60/90 days interval with new hires.
- Conducting quarterly one-on-one meetings with existing employees.

**PAYROLL ADMINISTRATION**
- Ensuring timely feeding of attendance, leave etc.
- Salary calculation of 350 + employees.
- Formulating and implementing increment, incentive, and other remuneration policies.
- Performing surveys of salaries, allowances and benefits to ensure that the company maintains its competitive employment position in the market.

**TRAINING & DEVELOPMENT**
- Identify training requirement and prepare annual training calendar as per the need to enhance skills.
- Co-ordination of training.

**EMPLOYEE WELFARE**
- Rolling out various welfare scheme, namely medical facility, transportation facility, etc.

### GENERAL ADMINISTRATION

- Managing the entire gamut of tasks related to administration.
- Overseeing the implementation of values and regulations in the organization.
- Formulating long-term developmental and implementation strategies for achievement of goals.
- Heading the overall functions in line with organizational objectives, designing and implementing systems, policies and procedures to facilitate internal control.

### LAND ACQUISITION

- Framing, supervising land acquisition proposals as per various acts and regulations of the government.
- Carrying valuation, negotiation of property, and authentication/verification check of revenue records.
- Coordinating with the offices of the Government for various clearances, Negotiations with land owners to fix land rates on various parameters.
- Managing matters related to land registration, mutation, lease administration and payment of stamp duty, adjudication process, conflict resolution, and dealing with various court cases.

### PROFESSIONAL EXPERIENCE

**Since 5 Jan 2010 associated with SEPCO Electric Power Construction Corporation as Dy Manager (HR&ADMIN)**

**Role:**

- Assisting Head HR in organization-wide manpower budgeting and planning.
- End-to-end responsibility of recruitment for lateral and campus recruitment.
- Assisting head HR in organization-wide compensation management.
- Planning and execution of campus recruitment programme.
- Complete responsibility of induction of new employees.
- Complete responsibility for training and development of employees.
- Handling the performance appraisal management, promotion or increments of employee based on performance and seniority
- Handling staff duties, pay and allowances, payroll and timekeeping.
- Administering the site, establishing offices, mobilization of personnel and material,
- Liaising with various government agencies, contactors, and internal/external departments for coordinating operations. Managing the legal exercise related to project, accidents, and claims.
- Dealing with statutory authorities such as the Pollution Department, District Administration for Labour License, HSD License, quarry permission/NOC.

As a HR generalist for shared services, I am responsible for the following:

- End-to-end talent growth and talent management
- End-to-end performance appraisal and performance management
- Reward management
- Exit interviews, analysis, and follow-up on that
- Employee engagement activities

### ACHIEVEMENTS:

Individually handled the campus recruitment programme in BITS College, Bhilai and Guru Ghasi Das University, Bilaspur.
Individually executed training and development programme for trainees.

**Project:**
**SEPCO Electric Power Construction Corporation, Super Mega Thermal Power Project (6x600 MW)**
**Duration: 05/01/2010 to Present**

| PROFESSIONAL EXPERIENCE |
|---|

14 Oct 2008 to 2 Jan 2010 associated with **TOTEM INFRASTRUCTURE LTD as Assistant Manager (HR&ADMIN)**
**Role:**
- Expertise in handling staff duties, pay and allowances, attendance, timekeeping, safety, and liaising with the Government as well as local bodies.
- Extensive exposure in acquisition of land, preparation of compensation.
- Expertise in handling site, establishment of offices, mobilization of personnel and material.
- Hands-on experience in monitoring, co-ordination, and liaison activities with various government agencies, contactors, inter/intra departmental activities.
- Adept at handling legal exercise related to project, accidents, claims etc.
- All statuary compliance like P.F. contract labour, B.O.C.W. registration, 7-A enquire, all type of Fatal or non-fatal accidents.
- An enterprising leader, possess excellent communication, interpersonal, negotiation and people management skills to positively contribute to organizational growth and success and Excellent practice in dealing with Labour License, HSD License, Quarry permission, NOC from Pollution Dept and local bodies as well as District Administration.
- Statutory compliance (ESIS, PF, PT, Factory Act, leaves, etc.)
- Maintaining Files/Records., House-keeping, Admin;

**Project:**
**Mauda Super Thermal Power Project (2x500 MW) Duration: 14/10/2008 to 2/01/2010.**

May 2006 to Oct 2008 with **SCAW Industries Pvt. Limited, Dhenkanal as Sr Executive (HR & Admin)**
**Role:**
- Look after bachelor and family accommodation and allotment
- Performance appraisal management, promotion or increment of employee based on performance and seniority
- Look after staff and worker welfare
- Maintaining all records of leave and joining of staff as well as daily wages.
- Maintaining all records of all PRWs.
- Preparing monthly manpower report and recruitment
- Handling all camp related works
- Handling Land Liasoning with contractors for manpower mobilization
- Handling Purchasing of all camp related items
- Maintaining all records of camp administration.

**Project:**
**Scaw Industries Project**
**Duration: 01/05/2006 to 08/10/2008**

| ACADEMIC QUALIFICATIONS |
|---|

- M.B.A. having specialization in HR and Marketing from BPUT, Orissa in 2006
- Bachelor of Commerce (Accounting Hons) From Utkal University (Orissa) in 2004
- I.com (XII) from Talcher College, Talcher (Orissa) 2001
- Matriculation from Kendriya Vidyalaya MCL Talcher (Orissa) in 1999

| IT SKILLS |
|---|

- Well-versed in MS Office and Internet applications

| PERSONAL PARTICULARS | | |
|---|---|---|
| Name | : | Rakesh Kumar |
| Father's Name | : | Lt Lalan Pandey |
| Date of Birth | : | 13 March 1983 |
| Permenent Address | : | Q. No –1c/2, At/PO-South Balanda, Distt – Angul (Orissa) – 759116 |
| Last Salary Drawn | : | ₹4.5 Lakh pa |
| Exp-Negotiable | | |

DATE  
PLACE                                                                                          (RAKESH KUMAR)

**Fig. 9.5**   Sample resumés

## SENDING RESUMÉS

After carefully preparing the first draft of your resumé, go through it at least thrice for checking the accuracy of details, sequence of various parts, spelling and grammar errors, types of fonts used, margins, page layout, etc. Check whether your resumé reflects your skills and accomplishments properly and adequately. Delete any information that does not reflect these aspects. Change the order of various sections of your resumé or delete one section if you feel that such order or deletion would project you in better light to your recruiters. For instance, if you feel that your 'interests' may not impress your employers, you may omit the section. Once you revise the contents, you can seek the help of some of your friends, who have a good eye for spelling and grammar, to proofread the resumé. Request them to see if your resumé looks professional with the chosen font types, space, bullets, etc. It is a fact that even professional writers have a hard time proofreading their own writing. Remember that proofreading is an important step and cannot be ignored since a silly typo may turn out to be an easy excuse for a hiring manager to eliminate one from the thousands of resumés he/she receives for a job. For instance, a resumé containing the statement *recipient of a plague for …* instead of *recipient of a plaque for…*, or *unclear physics* in place of *nuclear physics*, or *2110* instead of *2011* will certainly create a poor impression in the reader's mind.

There are several ways to submit resumés to employers. Channels such as email, website traditional mail, fax, or in-person can be used. But it is always necessary to follow the directions and procedures, if any, specified by the employer. Though the content of a resumé remains the same, there are certain guidelines that need to be kept in mind while using each channel:

**Email**

1. Use the advertised job title as your 'subject' line in the email. Cite relevant job numbers or descriptors as noted in the ad or as specified by the recruiters.
2. If you are sending an unsolicited resumé (without knowing of an opening), put a few words stating your objective in the 'subject' line.
3. Read the instructions carefully and completely before sending. Some employers who advertise online may only accept responses by conventional mail or may want you to respond to a different email address. It is important to respond exactly as instructed in the directions.

> Always proofread the cover letter and resumé before sending them to a recruiter.

4. If you send your résumé and cover letter as an attachment, include them in the body of the message as well. Attach them as a .pdf document, not in word processed format.
5. Attach your cover letter and résumé as one document.
6. When sending your résumé and cover letter as an attachment, the name of the attached file should be your name, not simply 'résumé'. Attachments can be sent if your recruiter is using a compatible email program.
7. Either include the cover letter and résumé in the body of email or prepare an ASCII version (text only) if attachments are not accepted. Pronounced a *AS kee,* ASCII format offers text only and is immediately readable by all computer programmes. It eliminates italics, bold, underlining and usual keyboard characters.
8. Unless an employer specifically says not to, submit a hard copy résumé and cover letter in addition to the emailed format.
9. Before emailing your résumé to your recruiter, email it to your friends and check whether they have received it in the proper format.

**Website**
1. Provide recruiters with your URL if you wish to post your résumé online.
2. Do not use photos.
3. Avoid providing information related to your age, gender, marital status, religion, and references.
4. Include an ASCII version of your résumé on your web page so that your recruiters can download it into their company database.

**Traditional mail**
1. Use good quality paper for your résumé and cover letter, and ensure that the print is clean and dark.
2. Use a large envelope without folding, stapling, or pinning the documents.
3. Use mailing labels and computer print your return address and the name and address of the person to whom you are sending your résumé and letter.
4. Place the letter on top of the résumé with other supporting materials under the résumé.
5. The name and address on the label should match exactly the name and address on the letter you are enclosing.

**Fax**
1. Fax your letter and résumé only when an employer requests it, or to meet a deadline.
2. Select a font with adequate space between characters. Thinner fonts such as Times, Palatino, Century Schoolbook, Courier and Bookman are clearer than thicker ones.
3. Use a 12 point or larger font.
4. Avoid underlines.
5. Use plain white paper and black ink to ensure the best quality copy in transmission.
6. Call the employer to verify that your résumé and letter have been received.
7. Always follow-up with a mailed original.

**In-person**
1. Ensure that your personal appearance is making an impression. Dress as if you were going for an interview and act professionally; be courteous to everyone.

2. Present the cover letter and résumé in a neat envelope, with the addresses of both the receiver and sender.

## FOLLOW-UP LETTERS

> If your application fails to bring a response from its receiver within a month or so, you may send a short follow-up letter.

Follow-up letters are written in the following contexts:

- When you do not receive any response from the company within a month of sending your application
  - After you are interviewed for a job
  - After you are rejected by a recruiter

Let us now examine application, interview, and rejection follow-up letters.

### Application Follow-up Letter

An application follow-up letter is sent if your application fails to bring a response from its receiver within a month or so. It is sent to (i) remind the receiver, (ii) show your earnest desire in getting an interview, (iii) once again emphasize your qualifications or add any recent job-related information. It should be a simple and short letter. Figure 9.6 shows a sample application follow-up letter.

---

203, Prestige Street
Vasant Vihar
Gurgaon

20 August 2012

Mr Albert Pinto
Personnel Manager
Hotel Alila Diva
Goa

Dear Mr Pinto,

45 days ago, I had applied for the post of Associate Manager, Customer Care at Hotel Alila Diva and I would like to inform you that I am still very much interested in the job and am looking forward to an opportunity to be interviewed.

During the past month, I completed a short term course in Customer Care by Delhi School of Management and I feel that this course has further enriched my knowledge in customer care and enhanced my skills in dealing with public.

Please keep my application in your active file and kindly let me know when you need a skilled manager for your customer-care wing. I would consider myself fortunate to meet you.

Sincerely,

Shubhash Saboo

---

**Fig. 9.6** Sample application follow-up letter

### Interview Follow-up Letter

> It is a good gesture to thank your recruiters after you are interviewed or selected.

It is a good gesture to thank your recruiters after you are interviewed or selected. Acknowledging the interviewer's time and courtesy through a note of thanks sets you apart from other applicants. It may also enable your interviewers to recall their conversation with you and understand your good manners and genuine interest in the job. However, timeliness is very important in such follow-up letters. They will be effective if sent immediately after the interview. Include details such as the date of interview, job title for which you were interviewed, and specific topics discussed. Convey your enthusiasm and confidence, and avoid the overuse of 'I' especially in the beginning of sentences. Think about an innovative beginning and an emphatic ending for the letter. Figure 9.7 illustrates a sample follow-up letter.

---

Room No. 245, A-Hostel
Bright Institute of Management
New Delhi 110002

20 August 2012

Ms Smitha Kulkarni
Human Resources Manager
Young India Corporation
1200, Beach Road
Chennai 600002

Dear Ms Kulkarni,

It was very enjoyable to speak with you about the Assistant Sales Executive position at the interview on 18 August 2012, during your recruitment visit to Bright Institute of Management, New Delhi. The job, as you presented it, seems to be a very good match for my skills and interests. The creative approach to sales that you described confirmed my desire to work with you.

As mentioned during the interview, I will be graduating in June 2013 with an MBA in Marketing. Through my education and experience, I've gained many skills, as well as an understanding of marketing concepts and dealing with the general public. I have worked on two projects in the area of advertisement and sales promotion during my internship at Fashion Enterprises, Kolkata. I think my education and work experience would complement the responsibilities of the position that you have interviewed me for.

I have enclosed a copy of my college transcript and a list of references that you requested.

Thank you again for the opportunity to be considered by Young India Corporation. The interview served to reinforce my strong interest in becoming a part of your sales team. I can be reached at (011) 24524524 or by email at manish818@bim.ac.in, should you need additional information.

Sincerely,

Manish Tiwari

---

**Fig. 9.7** Sample interview follow-up letter

Nowadays, before an interview ends, most companies inform the candidates about the organization's follow-up procedures—from whom (same person who interviewed them, someone else), by what means (phone, email, etc.), and when they would hear again from the organization. If the interviewer did not tell you, and you did not ask, use your follow-up/thank-you letter to ask. If more than a week has passed from the date when you were told you would hear something from the employer, call or email to politely inquire about the status of the organization's decision-making process. Someone (or something) or an unexpected circumstance may be holding up the process. A polite inquiry shows that you are still interested in the organization and may prompt the employer to get on schedule with a response. In your inquiry, mention the name of the person who interviewed you, time and place of the interview, the position for which you are applying, and ask the status of your application.

### Rejection Follow-up Letter

Rejections also need to be accepted with humility and an open mind. The attitude should be to never give up, even when you feel angry, humiliated, isolated, or think that it's unfair. You may feel that you have the requisite qualities for the job but still you were not selected. The reason for rejection may not always necessarily lie with your inadequacies; it may be because of some organizational constraints. But, whatever be the cause, you are not going to lose anything by responding to a rejection letter (Fig. 9.8) if you are still interested in the type of job and think that you may best fit in. Your

---

789, Golden Gate Road
Sancole
Goa 403726

26 May 2012

John P. Mathew
Director of Human Resources
Bright Banking Corporation
123 Museum Road
Bengaluru-560001

Dear Mr Mathew,

I just received your letter today, indicating that you have selected another candidate for the post of Financial Analyst in Bright Banking Corporation. Although I am disappointed, I appreciate your gesture of informing me your decision in such a timely manner.

Thank you once again for giving me an opportunity to attend the interview. I enjoyed meeting you and your colleagues and learning about your company. My meetings confirmed that BBC would be an exciting place to work and build a career.

I want to reiterate my strong interest in working for you. Please keep me in mind should another position become available in the near future.

Thank you again for your consideration.

Sincerely,
Ravindran

**Exhibit 9.8** Sample rejection follow-up letter

response letter may bring about good fortune for you. In a rejection follow-up letter, it is natural that you would want to express your disappointment and it is okay to do so. However, use this letter to convey your continued interest in the job and inform the company that you will contact them again after sometime in case another job opens up. After a couple of months, send one more letter but do not overdo it as companies may like people with perseverance but they do not like those who pester them for a job.

## ONLINE RECRUITMENT PROCESS

The latest buzzword in recruitment is 'e-recruitment'. Also known as 'online recruitment', it is the use of technology or web-based tools to assist the recruitment process. The tool can be either a job website like naukri.com, or an organization's corporate website or intranet. Many big and small organizations are using the Internet as a source of recruitment. They advertise job vacancies through the Web. The job seekers submit their applications and résumés on the Web, which can be drawn by prospective employees depending on their requirements.

The two kinds of e-recruitment that an organization can use are as follows:

*Job portals* This includes posting a position with the respective job description and specification on a job portal and also searching for suitable résumés posted on the site corresponding to an opening in an organization.

*Complete online recruitment/application section on a company's website* A company can add an application system to its website, where 'passive' job seekers can submit their résumés into the database of the organization for consideration as and when roles become available.

### Online Recruitment Techniques

The first stage of online recruitment is giving detailed job descriptions and specifications in job postings to attract candidates with the right skill sets and qualifications. Some e-recruitment techniques are as follows:

1. E-recruitment should be incorporated into the overall recruitment strategy of the organization.
2. A well-defined and structured applicant tracking system should be integrated and the system should have proper backend support.
3. Along with the back-office support a comprehensive website to receive and process job applications (through direct or online advertising) should be developed.

### Advantages of E-recruitment

The following are some advantages of e-recruitment:

- Lower costs to the organization—posting jobs online is cheaper than advertising in the newspapers
- No intermediaries
- Reduction in the time for recruitment (over 65% of the hiring time)
- Facilitates the recruitment of the right type of people with the required skills
- Improved efficiency of recruitment process

> E-recruitment is the use of technology or web-based tools to assist the recruitment process.

- Gives 24×7 access to an online collection of résumés
- Helps organizations to weed out unqualified candidates automatically

Fig. 9.9 facilitates your understanding of the online recruitment system.

---

GlaxoSmithKline, one of the world's leading research-based pharmaceutical and healthcare companies, commonly known as GSK, adopts online recruitment system to recruit candidates. The system involves the following steps:

### STEP 1: JOB SEARCH

Before you apply for a job at GSK,

- you need to start by searching for a job opening that interests you and matches your skills, knowledge, and experience. You can search by job type, location, or areas of interest. When you find a job that matches your skills, knowledge, and experience, you need to apply online by clicking on 'Apply for this job' at the end of the job description.
- you need to create your personal account on the job search page. This will enable you to add or edit your details, view your application status, create and view saved job searches, receive email alerts, CV, and supporting documents.

### STEP 2: APPLYING

When you apply online at GSK, you need to enter the following:

1. **Personal details:** First name, last name, date of birth, marital status, nationality, gender, email address, etc.
2. **Source details:** Here you may have to answer/fill up.
    (i) Where did you hear about us?
      - Employee referral
      - Corporate website
      - Friends and family
    (ii) Referrer name:
    (iii) Is the referrer an employee in this organization?
    (iv) Employee code/number:
    (v) Email:
    (vi) If an employee refered you to this job, please indicate his/her employee code & work email address.
3. **Current address:** Address, postal code, country, province, phone number
4. **Education details:** Degree level, major fields of study, marks or cgpa, university, year of passing, study mode
5. **Work experience**
6. **Top skills:** IT-related skills such as C++, HTML, Oracle8

| | | | | |
|---|---|---|---|---|
| 7. **Language proficiency:** | **English:** | Speak | Read | Write |
| | **Hindi:** | Speak | Read | Write |
| | **Other Languages:** | Speak | Read | Write |

8. **Other particulars:** Work expectation (willingness to travel, salary expected etc.)
   Availability status (possible time as to when you can join the job)

9. **Additional details:** Career goals, achievement, awards and recognition

10. **References:** Minimum two references stating name, position, company, and email

11. **Document upload:** Upload the résumé or CV

12. **Declaration:** I hereby declare that all the particulars given by me on this application form are to the best of my knowledge and belief, true and correct. I understand that if or at any time after my employment the information given on this application form are found to be false, incorrect or incomplete, the Company reserves the right to terminate my services without notice or compensation. I further understand that my employment is contingent upon my satisfactory passing a medical examination at the Company's expense by the appointed Company's doctors.

Once all these columns are filled up, you need to click on the submit button. When you submit your application online, an on-screen message that the details have safely arrived will be displayed. In addition, you will receive a further acknowledgement email when your application arrives in the recruiter's inbox.

**STEP 3: PHONE INTERVIEW**
The recruiter will review your application and contact you to arrange a phone interview for around 30 minutes.

**STEP 4: ON-SITE INTERVIEW**
During this stage you will be asked competency-based questions which focus on how you have used your skills, knowledge, and experience in specific tasks in your past roles.

**STEP 5: FINAL STAGE**
Following the interviews, interviewers meet to evaluate all candidates against the job requirements and the hiring manager selects the most suitable candidate. This is followed by a written offer letter.

**Fig. 9.9** Sample e-recruitment process

## SUMMARY

Today's globalized workplaces offer innumerable employment opportunities for the job seekers. However, it is important for job seekers to know precisely the kind of job they would like to take up to formulate their career goals. Once they set their goals, they need to work towards accomplishing them. The prospects at the workplaces are so competitive that the job seekers invariably need to know the various strategies related to projecting their skills and personality to their prospective employers. Résumés not only play a crucial role in showcasing job seekers' competence and skills but can also be slightly modified to suit different purposes. In short, building a career and writing job-winning résumés are two very important steps in the process of job search.

## KEY TERMS

***Career building*** It is an important aspect related to a person's job search and interview.

***Career goals*** It entails the job-related objectives that a person wants to achieve in one's career.

***Job search*** It is an important component in the process of career building, which involves identifying a career and evaluating the various options available to the job seeker.

***Résumés*** It is a document that gives a summary of the job seeker's past and present achievements and credentials based on which the prospective employer can judge his/her potential.

***Résumés writing*** In involves the process of presenting the job seeker's qualifications, experience, and accomplishments convincingly in a document so as to persuade the employer to call him/her for an interview.

## Concept Review Questions

1. Define a résumé. What role does it play in getting you an interview for a job?
2. What is a career goal and how is it important for you?
3. *Before going for a job search, you need to understand yourself*—discuss this statement in about 150 words.
4. Discuss any three ways in which you can look for job opportunities.
5. Bring out two advantages and disadvantages each for traditional, electronic, and video résumés.
6. Which format (chronological/functional/combination) of résumé is suitable for a fresh graduate and why?
7. What is the role of the part *career objective* in a résumé?
8. What can recently graduated students include in their résumé under 'professional/work experience'?
9. List any five 'dos' for sending your résumé through email.
10. Discuss the various steps involved in applying online for a job.

## Critical Thinking Questions

1. Critically analyse the following parts of a résumé written by a student who has just graduated from a management school. Write down the shortcomings and then rewrite the résumé parts. Invent any necessary details.
   (i) Awards/honours
   - March 2008: Awarded NSF scholarship by the Government of Andhra Pradesh
   - June 2009: Course topper at the university
   - September 2010: Received the Chief Minister's award
   (ii) Work experience
   - Completed a project on 'cultural influences on customer preferences'
   - Was responsible for credit-processing functions
   - I have experience of preparing accounting reports
   (iii) Education
   2010—present: pursuing MBA from Indian Business School
   2006-08—Passed CBSE with 80%
   2007-2010—Received BBA from Indian Business School
   (iv) Activities and Interests
   Playing football, cricket and chess
   Leader of NSS of my college
   Interested in computer games and listening to music

2. Following are few sentences taken from the cover letters of some job applications, rewrite them so that they are free from grammar and punctuation errors and also sound more specific and effective:

(i) Mr Mukul Gupta of your company has told me about a position in your sales division I would like to apply for the same.
(ii) I express my desire in working for a company like you!
(iii) Kindly consider this my application for any position that you may find suitable for me.
(iv) I wanted to know you that my skills match the requirements of the job for which you have placed an advertisement in *The Hindu*.
(v) Please call me. As soon as possible and arrange an interview for me.
(vi) Please have a look at my résumé, I don't want to repeat anything and bore you.
(vii) This is to apply for a position in your company.
(viii) Your company is one of the finest in Marketing and I bet no other company can match yours. Hence no wonder, I wish to enter your company!
(ix) Because I must make my career soon, write me soon.
(x) I have completed all courses in marketing offered by my college.

3. Shift the calendar to your graduation date so that now you are ready to sell your working skills in the job market. You have come across the following advertisements through an online service. Prepare the cover letter and résumé for each of the following:

(i) A French investment firm is seeking an analyst who can assist the assessment of potential private equity investments and marketing of an existing and new leveraged buy-out fund. Applicants should have a bachelor's degree from a reputed college and some experience in banking. Strong analytical capabilities and excellent computer skills will give an edge over other applicants. Please email résumé and cover letter to ebif@mark.in.

(ii) Included in the Fortune 500 Companies, this multinational company is seeking management trainees in order to cope with the company's expansion plans. The challenging management training programme requires applicants with good communication skills, enthusiasm, and high energy levels to be successful. They must be graduates, computer literate, and should possess good interpersonal skills. Fax résumé to Mahesh Kalra at 022-22334455.

## Projects

1. Using your knowledge of career building, job search and résumé writing, visit the websites of the following organizations and understand their recruitment process. Then prepare brief notes on the steps involved in the process.
   - Ernest & Young Private Limited
   - HSBC
   - Ogilvy & Mather
2. Working in a group of five classmates complete the following tasks:
   - Select an occupation
   - Identify the jobs related to the selected occupation (e.g., if it is marketing it can include areas such as research, advertising, communication, etc.)
   - List any five people you know who might provide information about this career or possible job leads. Discuss why each person was chosen.
   - Search the Internet and find out what help you can get from the websites of companies that provide information regarding job openings.

## REFERENCES

http://owl.english.purdue.edu/handouts/pw/index.html, accessed on 10 January 2012.

http://www.adm.uwaterloo.ca/infocecs/CRC/manual/resumes.html, accessed on 12 December 2011.

http://www.resumania.com/arcindex.html, accessed on 2 March 2012.

## CASE STUDY 1

**Recruitment Drive at SOBER**

SOBER is the biggest private sector employer in India. The company has more than 200,000 employees worldwide. In India, SOBER stores range from small local SOBER MINI stores to SOBER MEGA supermarkets. Around 80 per cent of all sales are from India. The company also operates in eight countries outside India, including Singapore, China, and Thailand. The organization has recently opened new stores in India and also in the UK. This international expansion is part of SOBER's strategy to diversify and grow the business. As market leader in the Indian supermarket sector, it caters to local, national, and international needs.

SOBER seeks people across a wide range of both store-based and non-store jobs.

- In stores, it needs checkout staff, stock handlers, supervisors, as well as many specialists such as pharmacists and bakers.
- Its distribution depots require people skilled in stock management and logistics.
- Its head office provides the infrastructure to run SOBER efficiently. Roles here include human resources, legal services, property management, marketing, finance, and information technology.

SOBER aims to ensure all roles work together to drive its business objectives. It needs to ensure it has the right number of people in the right jobs at the right time. To do this, it has a structured process for recruitment and selection to attract applicants for both managerial and operational roles.

As the company is on its expansion mode, it is vital to plan ahead. It needs to recruit on a regular basis for both the food and non-food parts of the business.

Both managerial and non-managerial positions become available at SOBER because

- jobs are created as the company opens new stores in India and expands internationally,
- vacancies arise as employees leave the company—when they retire or resign—or get promoted to other positions within SOBER, and
- new types of jobs are created as the company changes its processes and technology.

The high level of motivation at SOBER helps the company achieve its business objectives and helps employees to achieve their personal and career objectives. An important element in hiring is to have clear job descriptions and person specifications. A job description sets out

- the title of the job,
- to whom the job holder should report,
- what are the areas of business the job holder is responsible for, and
- a simple description of roles and responsibilities.

A person specification sets out the skills, characteristics, and attributes that a person needs to do a particular job. Together, job descriptions and person specifications provide the basis for job advertisements. They help job applicants to know what is expected of them. As they are sent to anyone applying for jobs, they should

- contain enough information to attract suitable people,
- act as a checking device to make sure that applicants with the right skills are chosen for interview, and
- set the targets and standards for job performance.

Job descriptions and person specifications show how a person fits into the SOBER business. They help the organization to recruit the right people. They also provide a benchmark for each job in terms of responsibilities and skills. These help managers to assess if employees are carrying out jobs to the appropriate standards.

With its purpose to serve its customers, SOBER has the customer at the top in organizational structure. Hence it needs people with the right skills at each level of this structure. In fact, there are six work levels within SOBER. This gives a clear structure for managing and controlling the organization. Each level requires particular skills and behaviours.

Level 1: It includes frontline jobs, working directly with customers, doing various in-store tasks, such as filling shelves with stock, and requires the ability to work accurately and with enthusiasm and to interact well with others.

Level 2: It includes leading a team of employees who deal directly with customers—requires the ability to manage resources, set targets, manage, and motivate others.

Level 3: It includes running an operating unit—requires management skills, including planning, target setting, and reporting.

Level 4: It includes supporting operating units and recommending strategic change—requires good knowledge of the business, the skills to analyse information and to make decisions, and the ability to lead others.

Level 5: It includes jobs responsible for the performance of SOBER as a whole—requires the ability to lead and direct others, and to make major decisions.

Level 6: It includes jobs that create purpose, values, and goals for SOBER, holding responsibility for its performance—requires a good overview of retailing, and the ability to build a vision for the future and lead the whole organization.

For its various positions, SOBER advertises in different ways. The process varies depending on the job available. The company first looks at its internal pool of employees to fill a vacancy and if there are no suitable people SOBER advertises the post internally on its intranet for two weeks. For external recruitment, SOBER advertises vacancies via its website or through newspapers and other job search sites. Applications are made online for managerial positions. The chosen applicants have an interview followed by attendance at an assessment centre for the final stage of the selection process. People interested in store-based jobs with SOBER will approach stores with their résumé or register though Monster.com. The store prepares a waiting list of people applying in this way and calls them in as jobs become available. For more specialist jobs, such as bakers and pharmacists, SOBER advertises externally

- through its website and offline media,
- through television and radio, and
- by placing advertisements on Google or in magazines.

SOBER makes it easy for applicants to find out about available jobs and has a simple application process. By accessing the company website, an applicant can find out about local jobs, management posts, and head-office positions. The website has an online application form for people to submit directly.

At SOBER, the process of selecting external management candidates involves the following stages:

- Screening of applications and résumés to find the best fit with SOBER
- Inviting shortlisted candidates for interview
- Successful candidates attend assessment centre for team-working activities and problem-solving exercises
- Selected candidates attend a second interview
- Successful candidates receive job offer letters

Planning for aggressive recruitment drive and implementing the same efficiently is vital if a business is to meet its future demands for employees. It allows a business time to train existing staff to take on new responsibilities and to recruit new staff to fill vacancies or meet skill shortages. As a major multinational company with many job opportunities, SOBER needs to have people with the right skills and behaviours to support its growth and development. With its clear organizational structures, detailed job descriptions and person specifications, it provides user-friendly ways of applying for jobs and a consistent approach to recruitment and selection. This augurs well for its expansion and growth plans.

### Questions

1. What are the different channels, according to you, that companies like SOBER should use to advertise their job vacancies?
2. Describe how job descriptions and person specifications are helpful in the selection process? What other purposes might a job description be used for?
3. Critically analyse SOBER's methods of attracting and recruiting candidates. Outline what you consider to be the main strengths and weaknesses of one of these methods.
4. Evaluate the benefits of using both interviews and assessment centres in the selection process.
5. Discuss briefly the planning stages that are involved in SOBER's recruitment drive.

# PART III
# DEVELOPING ORAL COMMUNICATION SKILLS FOR BUSINESS

10. Effective Listening
11. Business Presentations and Public Speaking
12. Conversations
13. Interviews
14. Meetings and Conferences
15. Group Discussions and Team Presentations
16. Team Briefing

CHAPTER 10

# Effective Listening

## LEARNING OBJECTIVES

After reading this chapter, you will be able to understand

- the term listening
- active and passive listening
- the advantages of listening
- the various types of listening
- listening barriers
- leadership and the role of listening in leadership styles
- listening at three managerial levels
- why managers are inherently poor listeners
- poor listening habits
- strategies for effective listening

## INTRODUCTION

According to a recent survey conducted in a top blue-chip company in India on how members spent their time communicating, 63 per cent of their time was spent in listening to one another, while reading took 4 per cent, writing 11 per cent, and speaking 22 per cent of their time. Listening is an important aid to communication (Image 10.1). Undoubtedly, if people are bad listeners, they will also make bad communicators. Listening is not the end result of the communication process. As Charles Gragg, Professor at Harvard Business School, states, 'It can be said flatly that the mere act of listening to wise statements and sound advice does little for anyone.' In the process of learning, the learner's dynamic cooperation is required. Often when a misunderstanding occurs, it is attributed to a lack of communication, which most of the time implies that whoever was delivering the message did not do an effective job. However, what about the other side, the listener? Listening is the communication skill used most often in human interaction but it is not a skill that most people perform well. Communication involves a source

**Image 10.1** Listening skills will help you communicate effectively

# 262 Business Communication

> Listening is the art of hearing and understanding what someone is saying.

and a receiver. Listening consists of the roles receivers play in the communication process. It is a process that includes attending, perceiving, interpreting, assessing, and responding. This chapter discusses not only its advantages but also addresses key issues regarding poor listening, types of listening, strategies for effective listening, etc.

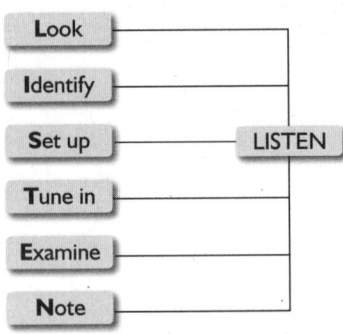

**Fig. 10.1** The word 'LISTEN'

## WHAT DOES 'LISTENING' MEAN?

Listening might be defined as the art of hearing and understanding what someone is saying. Each letter of the word 'LISTEN' will guide you towards becoming a better listener (Fig. 10.1).

**Look** Your understanding from listening will improve if you can see the order and consistency in the speech/talk and anticipate the next topics or words. Speakers should generally be consistent in their order of presentation as well as in what they present.

**Identify** Identify why, what the instructor is saying is important to you. You need a reason for wanting to listen or you will be unmotivated during the lecture. Do you want to learn the content? What part of it? To be interested in the talk and to understand its content are your responsibilities. It is up to you to get what you want.

**Set up** Set up your position to maximize the possibility of listening and staying in touch with the lecture. Your eyes, ears, and brain are parts of your listening apparatus; ensure that they are all in functioning order. Take adequate amount of rest. If you get sleepy, drink some orange juice or coffee. Maintain eye contact to facilitate listening. Block out the noise and distractions by sitting where you will be least bothered—the front row. If you cannot hear what is being said, by all means, move away from the problem—human or mechanical.

---

### The Power of Listening

If speaking is silver, then listening is gold—Turkish proverb.

- Listening is a magnetic and creative force.
- When we are listened to, it creates us, makes us unfold and expand.
- When we are listened to, ideas begin to grow within us and come to life.
- People are more happy and free when they are listened to.
- Creative listeners want others to be themselves, even at their very worst. True listeners know that if you are bad tempered, it does not mean that you are always so.
- As we listen, there is an alternating current that recharges us, so we are constantly being recreated as well.
- Unless you listen, you cannot know anyone. You will know facts and have impressions, but not really know people.
- The most serious result of not listening is boredom (for it is really the death of caring and love).
- Not listening seals people off from each other more than anything else does.
- Listening provides the fertile soil from which positive decisions and changes can develop.
- Listening is one of the best gifts of all we can offer to people experiencing homelessness.

*Source:* Adapted from Ireland, Brenda 1992, *Strength to Your Sword Arm: Selected Writings*, Holy Cow Press, Duluth, Minnesota.

> Listening has a number of direct and indirect benefits.

**Tune in** Learn to increase your attention span by timing just how long you can concentrate before you think of something else. Remember the brain works approximately four times faster then you can talk, so there is time for the mind to roam if you do not have a plan. Knowing how the speaker stresses important content will help to keep you tuned in.

**Examine** Examine the context to determine the main points. Action verbs and content nouns will help you to focus. Not all the content given during a talk is essential. Check the agenda or ask the speaker about the topics that are going to be covered each day. By skimming the topics in advance, you can get a general idea about the facts and ideas to be covered each day. This will keep your ears tuned to hear the important rather than the trivial topics. Use phrases or questions such as, 'Let me see if I understand you' or 'Is this what you mean?' to make sure that you are on the right track.

**Note** Taking notes while you listen will improve your concentration. The very act of taking notes may help you stay alert. Even if the material sounds familiar, write down a word or two to remind you that the topic was covered and to keep you listening. Once you start listening, think about how to write down the content you want.

## Active and Passive Listening

There are two types of listening—passive and active (Fig. 10.2). Active listening involves verbal feedback. One type of feedback involves questioning. You ask for additional information to clarify the speaker's message. For instance, you might ask, 'What do you mean?' By asking this type of question, you want the speaker to elaborate on the information already given. Another type of feedback is paraphrasing (e.g., 'Let me make sure I am with you so far', or 'What I hear you saying is ...'). Then you rephrase the speaker's ideas in your own words. With this type of feedback, you demonstrate that you have understood her/his concerns.

Passive listening occurs when a listener does not verbally respond to the speaker. The listener may deliberately or unintentionally send non-verbal messages through eye contact, smiles, yawns, or nods. Sometimes passive listening is appropriate. If the speaker wants to air a gripe, vent frustration, or express an opinion, you may want to listen passively. The speaker may not want or need a verbal response; rather he or she may want a sounding board. Passive listening is also appropriate when you want to ease back mentally and be entertained. It would be a mistake to interrupt the speaker as he/she narrates a good joke or story. For example, when we 'listen' to the stereo while we are cleaning the house. Also, watching TV or otherwise listening without responding is passive listening, because the communication is one-way, with no exchange or feedback.

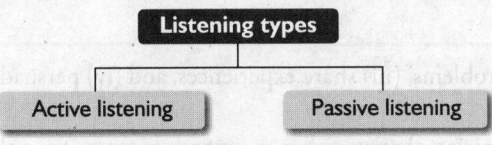

**Fig. 10.2** Types of listening

## Process of Listening

In order to be a good listener, it is necessary to understand the various stages of listening (Fig. 10.3). These are as follows:

**Sensing/Selecting stage** The listener selects, from among a multiple of stimuli, the only one that seems important at that point in time and converts it into a message.

**Interpreting stage** The listener is engaged in the act of decoding the message. It is at this stage that the listener is faced with multiple barriers that could be semantic, linguistic, psychological, emotional, or environmental.

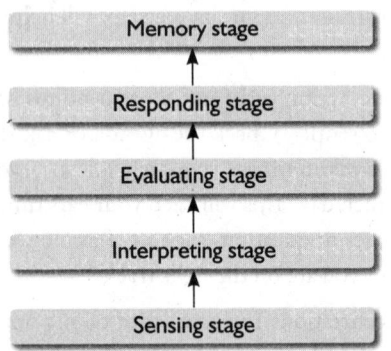

**Fig. 10.3** Various stages of listening

**Evaluating stage** A great deal of critical listening takes place at this stage. The listener assigns a meaning to the message, draws inferences, takes an overview of the messages, and seeks accuracy of information and evidence. Often, the listener is disturbed by prior experiences, beliefs, and emotions, which often come in the way of the evaluation process.

**Responding stage** This is the stage when the listener is ready to respond. In addition, this feedback stage is important for a speaker. The listener's non-verbal signals tell the speaker whether he or she has been understood or not. The speaker also has to be able to understand whether the listener is faking attention.

**Memory stage** This is the final stage of listening. Effective listening helps listeners retain chunks of what they have heard. 'Memorability' (the quality or state of being memorable) is an important index for listeners to test how much matter has been stored in their memory banks. Unfortunately, no matter how brilliant a speaker is, most listeners can retain only 10–25 per cent of a talk or a presentation the day after. That is why good speakers must always make it a point to organize their matter sequentially, supported by good visuals, so that listeners have a higher recall rate at the end.

## Advantages of Listening

Listening is the highest compliment one human being can pay to another. Effective listening will benefit you as well as those around you. Some of the ways that it helps us in our daily lives are as follows:

1. It breaks up barriers between people.
2. We can understand each other more.
3. It minimizes the losses of potential revenues, which may result from sending a customer the wrong product.
4. It prevents miscommunication of objectives and priorities among people.
5. It also prevents time lost because of having to communicate a second or third time to get things straightened out.

We listen to (i) obtain information, (ii) solve problems, (iii) share experiences, and (iv) persuade or dissuade.

However, it is hard to listen because of certain barriers that we either encounter or erect. If people are poor listeners: (i) only inaccurate and incomplete information is exchanged, (ii) problems are not clearly understood and remain unsolved, (iii) people are unable to share experiences, and (iv) being unable to understand each other through inattentiveness, they are unable to persuade or dissuade others.

> Effective listening helps listeners retain chunks of what they have heard.

@ Please refer to the Online Resource Centre for more on listening skills.

## Common Myths about Listening

You may think of listening as a 'soft' skill, but it is one of the most important business skills you can develop. To better understand what it takes to be a good listener, you will have to discard the following four common myths:

*Myth 1* 'I do not have to concentrate: listening comes naturally.'

*Truth* Being a good listener requires a conscious effort. You must keep your mind constantly engaged and in gear.

*Myth 2* 'I'm a good listener because I always get the facts and figures straight.'

*Truth* You may be a selective listener. You listen to the facts and figures, but do not hear or comprehend the rest of the information, such as questions raised, emotions of the speaker, context, opinions, and ideas discussed.

*Myth 3* 'You should not interrupt when someone is speaking.'

*Truth* A good listener does not hesitate to interrupt if the speaker's information is unclear. You must be an inquisitive listener to be an effective listener.

*Myth 4* 'A good listener paraphrases everything a speaker says.'

*Truth* If you constantly parrot people's statements back to them, they might think you are slow or—even worse—condescending. It is better to repeat key information and ask the speaker to verify it, but do not rephrase all of his/her comments.

## TYPES OF LISTENING

Certain skills are basic and necessary for all types of listening (e.g., receiving, attending, and understanding), however, each type requires some special skills. This section discusses those special skills and presents guidelines to improve listening behaviour in all situations. Before we can fully appreciate the skills and apply the guidelines, we must understand the different types of listening (Fig. 10.4).

### Informative Listening

Informative listening refers to a situation where a listener's primary concern is to understand the message. Listeners are successful in so far as the meaning they assign to a message is as close as possible to the meaning that the sender intended. Informative listening, or listening to understand, is found in all areas of our lives. Much of our learning comes from informative listening. For example, we listen to lectures or instructions from teachers—and what we learn depends on how well we listen. In the workplace, we listen to understand new practices or procedures—and again how well we perform depends on how well we listen.

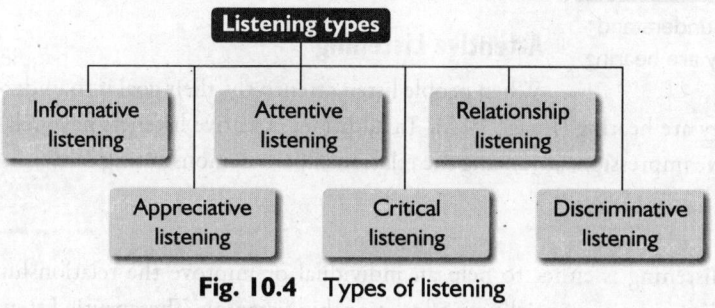

**Fig. 10.4** Types of listening

> - Informative listening refers to a situation where a listener's primary concern is to understand the message.
> - Memory is a crucial variable of informative listening.

We listen to instructions, briefings, reports, and speeches; if we listen poorly, we are not equipped with the information we need. At times, careful informative listening is crucial. Whatever the case, effective informative listening demands that you concentrate on the message—and know its source.

The three key variables related to informative listening are as follows:

**Vocabulary** The precise relationship between vocabulary and listening has never been determined, but it is clear that increasing your vocabulary will increase your potential for better understanding. Having a genuine interest in words and languages, making a conscious effort to learn new words, breaking down unfamiliar words into their component parts—all these things will help you improve your vocabulary.

**Concentration** You can probably remember times when another person was not concentrating on what you were saying and you can probably remember times when you were not concentrating on something that someone was saying to you. There are many reasons why people do not concentrate when listening. Sometimes listeners try to divide their attention between two competing stimuli. At other times, listeners are preoccupied with something other than the speaker of the moment. Sometimes listeners are too concerned with their own needs to concentrate on the message being delivered. Concentration requires discipline, motivation, and acceptance of responsibility.

**Memory** Memory is an especially crucial variable for informative listening; you cannot process information without bringing memory into play. More specifically, memory helps your informative listening in the following three ways:

**Image 10.2** Attentive listeners try to understand and remember what they are hearing

1. It allows you to recall experiences and information necessary to function in the world around you. In other words, without memory you would have no knowledge bank.
2. It establishes expectations concerning what you will encounter. You would be unable to drive in heavy traffic, react to new situations, or make common decisions in life without the memory of your past experiences.
3. It allows you to understand what others say. Without memory of concepts and ideas, you could not understand the meaning of messages.

## Attentive Listening

When people listen attentively, their goal is to understand and remember what they are hearing (Image 10.2). In addition, attentive listeners have relational goals like giving a positive impression, advancing the relationship, or demonstrating care.

## Relationship Listening

The purpose of relationship listening is either to help an individual or improve the relationship between people. Therapeutic listening is a special type of relationship listening. Therapeutic listening brings to mind situations where counsellors, medical personnel, or other professionals allow a

> **Power Listening**
>
> Listening to others gives managers the information needed. Listening to themselves gives them the information to act in their own best interests. As managers achieve self-awareness, they are more able to choose their responses rather than react automatically. They then respond to what is real, rather than to emotions or misconceptions. Information is power. Effective listeners are able to concentrate and find the most valid information in whatever they listen to. Effective listeners are people who have a positive influence on others.

*The purpose of relationship listening is either to help an individual or improve the relationship between people.*

troubled person to talk through a problem. It can also be used when you listen to a friend or an acquaintance and allow him/her to 'get things off the chest'. Although relationship listening requires you to listen for information, the emphasis is on understanding the other person. Three attitudes are key to effective relationship listening—attending, supporting, and empathizing.

**Attending** In relationship listening, attending behaviour indicates that the listener is focusing on the speaker. Non-verbal cues are crucial in relationship listening; that is, your non-verbal behaviour indicates that either you are attending to the speaker or you are not. Eye contact is one of the most important attending behaviour. Looking appropriately and comfortably at the speaker sends a message that is different from that sent by a frequent shift of gaze, staring, or looking around the room. Body positioning communicates acceptance or lack of it. Leaning forward, toward the speaker, demonstrates interest; leaning away communicates lack of interest. Head nods, smiles, frowns, and vocalized cues such as 'uh huh', 'I see', or 'yes' are all part of positive attending behaviour. A pleasant tone of voice, gentle touching, and concern for the other person's comfort are other attending techniques.

**Supporting** Many responses have a negative or non-supportive effect, for example, interrupting speaker, changing subject, turning a conversation towards oneself, and demonstrating a lack of concern for the other person. Wise relationship listeners know when to talk and when to just listen—and they generally listen more than they talk.

Three characteristics describe supportive listeners: (i) discretion—being careful about what they say and do; (ii) belief—expressing confidence in the ability of the other person; and (iii) patience—being willing to give others the time they need to express themselves adequately.

**Empathizing** Empathy is feeling and thinking with another person. The caring, empathic listener is able to go into the world of another—to see as the other sees, hear as the other hears, and feel as the other feels.

There is some risk involved in being an empathic relationship listener. You cannot be an effective empathic listener without becoming involved, which sometimes means learning more than you really want to know. However, commanders cannot command effectively, bosses cannot supervise skilfully, and individuals cannot relate interpersonally without empathy. Empathic behaviour can be learned. First, you must learn as much as you can about the other person. Second, you must accept the other person—even if you cannot accept some aspects of that person's behaviour. Third, you must have the desire to be an empathic listener. Empathy is crucial to effective relationship listening.

*Empathy is crucial to effective relationship listening.*

## Appreciative Listening

Appreciative listening includes listening to music for enjoyment, to speakers because you like their style, to your choices in theater, television, radio, or film.

The quality of appreciative listening depends upon three factors—presentation, perception, and previous experience (Fig. 10.5).

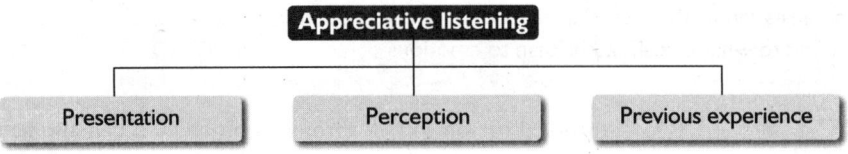

**Fig. 10.5** Appreciative listening

**Presentation** Presentation encompasses many factors—the medium, setting, style, and personality of the presenter, to name just a few. Sometimes it is our perception of the presentation, rather than the actual presentation, that most influences our listening pleasure or displeasure.

**Perception** Expectations play a large role in perception. Perceptions—and the expectations that drive them—have their basis in attitudes. Our attitudes determine how we react to, and interact with, the world around us. Perceptions influence all areas of our lives. Certainly, they are crucial determinants as to whether or not we enjoy or appreciate the things we hear. Obviously, perceptions also determine what we listen to in the first place. As we said earlier, listening is selective.

**Previous experience** Previous experience influences whether we enjoy listening to something. In some cases, we enjoy listening to things because we are experts in the area. Previous experience plays a large role in appreciative listening. For example, many people enjoy the sounds of large-city traffic; perhaps growing up in a large city was a happy experience for them.

## Critical Listening

Politicians, the media, salesmen, advocates of policies and procedures, and our own financial, emotional, intellectual, physical, and spiritual needs require us to place a premium on critical listening and the thinking that accompanies it. However, there are three things to keep in mind. These three things were outlined by Aristotle, the classical Greek rhetorician, more than 2,000 years ago in his treatise, *The Rhetoric*. They are as follows—*ethos*, or speaker credibility; *logos*, or logical argument; and *pathos*, or psychological appeals.

**Ethos** The credibility of the speaker is important. The two critical factors of speaker credibility are expertness and trustworthiness. When listening to a message that requires a critical judgement or response, ask yourself, 'Is the speaker a credible source, one who is both an expert on the subject and who can be trusted to be honest, unbiased, and straightforward?'

> Effective critical listeners carefully determine the focus of the speaker's message.

**Logos** Even speakers with high ethos often make errors in logic, not by intention, but by accident, carelessness, inattention to detail, or lack of analysis. Critical listeners have a right to expect well-supported arguments from speakers, arguments that contain both true propositions and valid inferences or conclusions. Both ethos and logos are crucial elements of critical listening. Reliance on just these two elements without consideration of pathos would be akin to attempting to sit on a three-legged stool with one leg missing.

**Pathos** The psychological or emotional element of communication is often misunderstood and misused. Simply said, speakers often use psychological appeals to gain an emotional response from listeners. Effective critical listeners carefully determine the focus of the speaker's message. Speakers may appeal to any one or several needs, desires, or values that are important, such as: adventure, thrift, curiosity, fear, creativity, companionship, guilt, independence, loyalty, power, pride, sympathy, altruism, etc.

Effective critical listening depends on the listener keeping all the three above mentioned elements of the message in the analysis and in perspective.

## Discriminative Listening

Discriminative listening may be the most important type of listening, for it is basic to the other five. By being sensitive to the changes in the speaker's rate, volume, force, pitch, and emphasis, the informative listener can detect even the slightest shift in nuances. Although discriminative listen-ing cuts across the other five types of listening, there are three things to consider about this type of listening.

**Hearing ability** People who lack the ability to hear well have a greater difficulty in discriminating among sounds. Often this problem is more acute for some frequencies, or pitches, than others.

**Awareness of sound structure** Native speakers become quite proficient at recognizing vowel and consonant sounds that do or do not appear at the beginning, middle, or end of words. For example, a listener might hear 'this sandal' instead of 'this handle'; but since English words do not begin with 'sb,' one would not mistake 'this bean' for 'this sbean'. Attention to the sound structure of the language will lead to more proficient discriminatory listening.

**Integration of non-verbal cues** As stated earlier, action, non-action, and vocal factors are important for understanding messages. Nowhere is attention to these factors more important than in effective discriminative listening. Words do not always communicate true feelings. The way they are said, or the way the speaker acts, may be the key to understanding the true or intended meaning.

## EFFECTIVE AND INEFFECTIVE LISTENING SKILLS

All of us can hear, but not all of us can listen. Hearing and listening are not the same thing. Hearing is involuntary whereas listening involves the reception and interpretation of what is heard. It decodes the sound heard into meaning.

Good listening requires a knowledge of technique and practice very similar to good writing or speaking. Many people believe that good listening skills are easy to learn or automatically part of every person's personality. Neither is correct. The difference is that poor listening skills are often not obvious to other people. If we cannot speak effectively, it is immediately obvious, but it may take a little time for other people to become aware that a person is a poor listener.

An active listener

- does not finish others' sentences
- does not answer questions with questions
- is aware of and guards against biases
- never daydreams or becomes preoccupied with his/her own thoughts when others talk
- does not dominate the conversation
- plans responses after the other person has finished speaking, not while he/she is speaking
- provides feedback, but does not interrupt incessantly
- analyses by looking at all the relevant factors and asking open-ended questions
- keeps the conversation on what the speaker says, not on what interests him/her
- takes brief notes, as this forces one to concentrate on what is being said

## BARRIERS TO EFFECTIVE LISTENING

Listening is never easy. There are a number of common barriers that you, if you are aware of them, can try to counteract (Fig. 10.6).

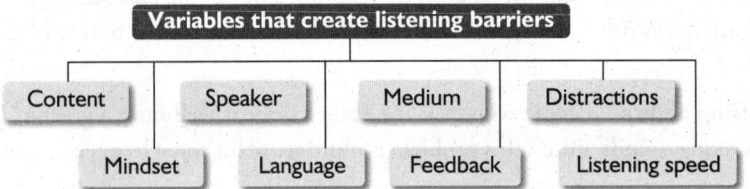

**Fig. 10.6** Variables that create barriers to effective listening

- An average person spends 70 per cent of waking hours communicating, 45 per cent of that involves listening
- In a 10-minute presentation, there is only 50 per cent retention
- To improve listening comprehension, one must overcome barriers created by variables like content, speaker, medium, distractions, mindset, language, listening speed, and feedback (Fig. 10.5).

The following are some reasons/variables that create barriers to listening:

### Content

- Listeners knowing too much
  - feel that their knowledge is so extensive that there is little left to learn
- Listeners knowing too little
  - tune out when faced with difficult intellectual or emotional content
  - only listen to information within their beliefs
- Remedy:
  - do not sit back passively and allow sound to enter ears
  - develop a positive attitude towards message
  - anticipate the importance of the message content
  - seek areas of interest in the message
  - remind yourself that something of value can be learned

## Speaker

- Delivery:
  - speaker's enunciation, organization, clarity, speed, volume, tone, inflections, emotions, and appearance affect interpretation of message
- Attitudes towards speaker:
  - listeners are influenced more by their attitude towards the speaker than the information presented
  - if a listener likes a speaker, he/she is more likely to empathize, and therefore, comprehend the message
- Remedy:
  - concentrate on the 'what' of the message, not the 'who' or 'how'

## Medium

- Distance and circumstances:
  - least effort is needed when the speaker is not visible
  - more effort is needed when the speaker is visible, but not present
  - most effort is needed in face-to-face interactions
- Reasons:
  - the amount and variety of both verbal and non-verbal stimuli increases
  - these stimuli can either help or hinder communication
- Remedy:
  - realize the potential for better understanding, and increase listening effort

## Distractions

- Extraneous stimuli:
  - sounds, lights, odours, mannerisms, voice inflections, and moving objects can easily distract listeners
  - psychological studies indicate that a listener's attention span is sometimes no more than two or three seconds
  - distractions can be categorized as environmental or physical, but most often they are psychological in nature
- Remedy:
  - identify and eradicate distractions
  - if distractions cannot be eliminated, increase concentration
  - free yourself from preconceptions, prejudices, and negative emotions

## Mindset

- Attitudes:
  - structured by a listener's unique physical, mental, and emotional characteristics
  - an individual's mindset can either magnify or diminish stimuli, distorting the message
- Remedy:
  - strive to not let personal biases interfere with comprehension

- respect other's freedom of values and beliefs
- accept that attempting to understand another's viewpoint is not necessarily agreeing with it
- realize that there may be more than one acceptable point of view

## Language

- Ambiguity:
  - listeners rarely hear every word spoken and may attach different meanings to words than the speaker
- Misinterpretation:
  - can occur when words are imprecise, emotional, technical, or overly intellectual
  - occurs most often when listeners interpret words based on personal definitions established by background, education, and experience
- Remedy:
  - realize that different words may have different meanings for different people
  - evaluate the context in which the word is used
  - see that the meaning is in the mind, not in the word

## Listening Speed

- Rate:
  - the average speaking rate is 125–150 words per minute
  - the average listening rate is 500 words a minute, leaving a lot of excess thinking time
- Think time:
  - poor listeners use the excess time to daydream, often missing part of the message
- Remedy:
  - use excess time to outline messages
  - identify the purpose and how it is supported
  - evaluate the soundness of logic
  - verify and integrate with existing knowledge
  - maintain eye contact to observe and interpret non-verbal signals
  - formulate questions to enhance and verify understanding and provide feedback

## Feedback

- Inappropriate:
  - premature comments or evaluations before a full understanding of the speaker's viewpoint
  - comments which are coloured with emotions of resentment, defensiveness, or suspicion
  - can hinder speaker by confusing or diverting into tangents
- Remedy:
  - supportive feedback can demonstrate interest through appropriate eye contact, smiling and animation, nodding, leaning forward, verbal reinforcements such as 'I see' or 'yes', and phrasing interpretations of the comments for verification
  - these must be timed to assist rather than hinder a speaker

## Self-inventory of Listening Habits

The purpose of this inventory is to help you gain a better understanding of your listening habits. After you complete the inventory, you should be able to describe some of your listening habits. This is, of course, a subjective inventory and not an objective test.

### Directions

First, read this list and put an X at the end of each habit that you now use sometimes. Second, reread the habits you have noted and put another X next to the habits you perform almost all of the time you spend listening.

1. I follow the speaker by reviewing what he or she has said, concentrating on what the speaker is saying and anticipating what he or she is going to say.
2. I analyse what I am hearing and try to interpret it to get the real meaning before I let the speaker know what I heard and understood.
3. I look at the speaker's face, eyes, body posture, and movement and listen to his other voice cues.
4. I think about other topics and concerns while listening.
5. I listen for what is not being said as well as for what is being said.
6. I fake attention to the speaker, especially if I am busy or think I know what the speaker is going to say.
7. I show in a physical way that I am listening and try to help set the speaker at ease.
8. I listen largely for the facts and details more than ideas and reasons.
9. I know the facial, body, and vocal cues that I am using while listening.
10. I evaluate and judge the wisdom or accuracy of what I have heard before checking out my interpretation with the speaker.
11. I avoid sympathizing with the speaker and making comments like 'I know just what you mean, it's happened to me' and then telling my story before letting the speaker know what I heard and understood.
12. I find myself assuming that I know what the speaker is going to say before he or she has finished speaking.
13. I accept the emotional sentiment of the speaker.
14. I think up arguments to refute the speaker so that I can answer as soon as he or she finishes.
15. I paraphrase or summarize what I have heard before giving my point of view.
16. I am easily distracted by noise or the speaker's manner of delivery.

Now you have an inventory of your **effective listening habits** (odd-numbered habits you noted), your **ineffective listening habits** (even-numbered habits you noted), your **most effective listening habits** (odd-numbered habits you marked twice), and your **most ineffective listening habits** (even-numbered habits you marked twice).

*Source*: Sprecher, Kim, http://www.englishrocks1.net/Listening/self.doc, accessed on 12 November 2011. Reproduced with permission.

## Other Barriers to Effective Listening

The communication process is so complex that many variables exert themselves whenever we try to listen. These can generally be categorized as follows:

> Distracting noises, poor acoustics, uncomfortable seating arrangements, etc. are examples of barriers.

**Physical conditions** Distracting noises, poor acoustics, uncomfortable seating arrangements, physical discomfort caused by uncomfortable temperature, etc. form barriers to listening. The most effective device for surmounting these difficulties is concentration if you cannot manipulate the distractions.

**Casual attitude**  Assuming that since you are hearing, you must also listening, the lack of effort and concentration forms one of the major barriers to listening.

**Speaking–thinking rate**  We usually speak at a rate of 125–150 words per minute but the mind is able to cope with approximately 400 words per minute. This means that there is a considerable amount of 'idle' time in which the mind can wander away from the task of critical and careful listening. It is during this 'free time' that many listeners surrender to external distractions.

**Premature evaluation**  It is the trait of jumping to conclusions. As psychologist Carl Rogers has noted, 'The problem is the very human tendency to evaluate what is said from one's point of view only, the inability to postpone an evaluation for the sake of communication in the particular situation. This immediate evaluation sets up a chain reaction that colors one's response to a speaker.'

**Status and role**  Your impression of a person's status will determine, to a large degree, what you learn from him/her and what influence he/she will have over your attitudes. Status relationships between the speaker and listener, as well as the various roles they both play, frequently determine the success or failure of the communication act.

**Communication context**  Still another ingredient that influences the process of communication is what we will refer to as the communication context. The place of the encounter (the 'where'), has an impact on the final outcome. We all behave differently at our homes, for example, than at school, on the job, or at a party. The 'arena' of our acts helps govern both our messages and responses.

## LEADERSHIP AND ROLE OF LISTENING IN LEADERSHIP STYLES

Communication does not just involve speaking and writing, it also includes listening. Studies have shown that a large percentage of people listen less effectively than they believe, and many are poor listeners. Many organizations, in an effort to improve interpersonal communications, have encouraged skill development in reading, writing, and speaking. Little, if anything, is ever suggested to improve listening habits. The misconception held by many is that listening is related to hearing. People may have perfect hearing, but because their listening skills are inadequate, what they understand is not necessarily what is being said.

Of all the communication skills, listening is the earliest learned and the most frequently used, yet it seems to be the least mastered. Listening is a skill that underlies all leadership skills. It is the key to developing and maintaining relationships, decision-making, and problem solving. As leaders, we spend as much as half of our communication time listening, and much of it is wasted since we do it so poorly. It is such a part of our everyday life, both in our careers and at home, that we sometimes take it for granted. In executive leadership, the creative managers are good listeners. They listen to their personnel and build on their suggestions. In particular, they seem to have the ability to draw out the best in their subordinates and then add to it. Why is it then that while the skill of listening is identified by many researchers as one of the most important qualities a leader can possess, poor listening is identified repeatedly as the most common deficiency in leaders? Unfortunately, listening skills are very often ignored or just taken for granted. As a result many communication problems develop.

Leadership is one of the most widely discussed topics in business today, yet it continues to be confusing and elusive to many of us. Understanding leadership and the act of leading is not merely

> ### The President and the Ensign
>
> Bill Marriott, Chairman and CEO of Marriott International, the world's largest hotel chain, has this inspirational tale to tell, which he described as 'the biggest lesson I have learned through the years'.
>
> 'It is to listen to your people. I find that if you have senior managers who really gather their people around them, get their ideas and listen to their input, you make a lot better decisions'. Mariott said he learned this during a visit by President Dwight Eisenhower when Marriott was a young ensign in the navy. He had been in the Navy for six months and the President was a visitor at Marriott's home during Christmas time. It was an extremely cold day, but Marriott's father had put up targets outside for shooting. He asked the President if he wanted to go out and shoot or stay home by the fire. Without hesitation, the President turned to the young ensign and asked, 'What do you think, ensign?' Marriott told the President that it was too cold to go outside for shooting and that they should stay home by the fire. Marriott says that the lesson he learned that day (asking another's opinion) has always remained with him and has proved a big asset in his business.

limited to a select few. It exists at all levels of an organization. Leadership and management are terms that are often used interchangeably. Since many of the human resource skills are valuable in both disciplines, this is often acceptable. They do, however, have a substantially different focus. Management is a bottom line focus, or in other words, is about how to accomplish things. Leadership is a top line focus, or in other words, is about what does the leader want to accomplish. 'Management is doing things right; leadership is doing the right things.' Leadership is not limited only to those elected or appointed. Many people have the potential to become effective leaders. In fact, people at all levels can and must exercise leadership if the group is to achieve its goals. People do differ in potential, but everyone can become more effective through increased knowledge of leadership concepts and increased self-understanding.

There are two basic types of leadership—transactional and transformational. Transactional leaders influence followers by means of a transaction. That is, they give followers money, praise, or some other reward (or punishment) in exchange for the followers' effort and performance. Competent transformational leaders help followers develop the confidence they need to achieve their goals. Transformational leadership, however, involves a strong personal identification with the leader. Followers join in a shared vision of the future, going beyond self-interest and the pursuit of personal rewards. They influence followers to perform beyond expectations. Even though there is a natural tendency to associate leaders and leadership with people at the top of organizations, true leadership will be needed across and throughout all types and levels of organizations. The character and qualities that are found in true leaders are essential at all levels of responsibility.

According to a survey, by *Time Magazine*, of more that 200 managers and leaders on what effective leaders do to make them effective, more than 70 per cent mentioned the same first five items. These five times in order of their frequency are: communicate well, listen effectively, demonstrate approachability, delegate effectively, and lead by example. The remaining items that were listed by at least 40 per cent of the responders are: read situations and people well, use a variety of power bases to lead, teach well, care about the people they lead and show it, and treat people fairly, honestly, and consistently. The vast majority of managers and leaders all agree that most, if not all, of their job

### Linda Dillman

Linda Dillman, the ex-CIO of Walmart is known as much for her business accomplishments as for her avoidance of media attention. Asked what makes her a unique leader, several employees point to her ability to not just listen to ideas but to turn them into reality. Says Dillman: 'It is all about pushing as much down to the people who are closest to the work so they can take on more responsibility.'

activities involve communication in some way, that is, message sending and message receiving, spoken and written. Leadership is more of a communication activity, certainly more than any other activity. Naturally, effective leaders communicate clearly, in a timely fashion, keep people they lead informed, and have the ability to listen empathically.

Leaders walk in others' shoes by listening and caring. These two critical and respected leadership characteristics are often missing for various reasons. One point is certain, when leaders take the time to listen with empathy, they build trust and commitment that creates an environment for success. Listening is an essential and undervalued skill. Since effective managers tend to be aggressive, they are sometimes better talkers than listeners. Most managers are promoted because they are noticed, and people do not usually get noticed by being silent. However, managers who are bad listeners tend to be bad managers. A tendency toward one-way communication stems from the misconception that management involves ordering people around. Listening requires us to understand that our staff is important. Leaders may wish they had more time to listen. These constraints are unavoidable, but they are not an excuse. They may not be able to listen as well as they would like, but to be an effective leader, they must avoid making listening the lowest priority. At times, action oriented, fire service leaders make the mistake of believing that speaking and doing are more important than listening. As effective leaders, nothing could be further from the truth. The need for effective leadership is undisputed. What is relatively unknown is the role of listening in leadership. Listening has been identified as the primary communication skill, in two senses of the word. It is primary because it is (i) the first communication skill acquired and (ii) in comparison with speaking, reading, or writing, used more often each day.

Goleman, Boyatzis, and McKee, authors of *Primal Leadership* with the goal of helping people become more effective leaders, identified six styles of leaderships and five steps towards learning leadership skills. Listening skills are essential for effectiveness at virtually every stage. They draw extensively from research into emotional intelligence or EI (which has no relationship to the better known theoretical construct known as the intelligence quotient or IQ) and use EI as the unifying principle and yardstick with which to evaluate leadership ability. Emotional intelligence is an innate ability which gives us our emotional sensitivity and our potential for learning healthy emotional management skills, which can help us to understand people and how they work, what motivates them, and how to work with them.

Like mental intelligence or IQ, emotional intelligence (EQ) is a function of the brain. IQ is made up of abilities, such as mathematical calculation, memory, vocabulary, and word use. It involves primarily the *neo cortex* or top portion of the brain. EQ is made up of emotional drives, and behavioural tendencies that are motivated by feelings. It involves the lower and central emotional section of the brain—called the limbic system. The central finding of EI research is that emotions are essentially contagious, and thus a leader's attitude and energy can 'infect' a workplace either for better or for worse. With this in mind, the authors stress the importance of 'resonance', which is the ability of leaders to perceive and influence the flow of emotions (including motivational states) between themselves and the others they work with. The fundamental importance of resonance rests in part upon a leader's ability to put into practice the skill of empathic listening. Due to the implications of improving resonance, the authors emphasize throughout *Primal Leadership* the importance to leaders of self-awareness, which includes the ability to perceive and moderate the effect one is having on others.

## Six Styles of Leadership

The authors of *Primal Leadership*, Goleman, Boyatzis, and McKoe, have distilled all leadership roles into six distinct styles based in part on research data from 3,871 executives—that effective leaders switch between depending upon circumstances—then explain the role of EI resonance within each style (Fig. 10.7). Skilful listening, the linchpin of resonance, is the crux of the first four styles.

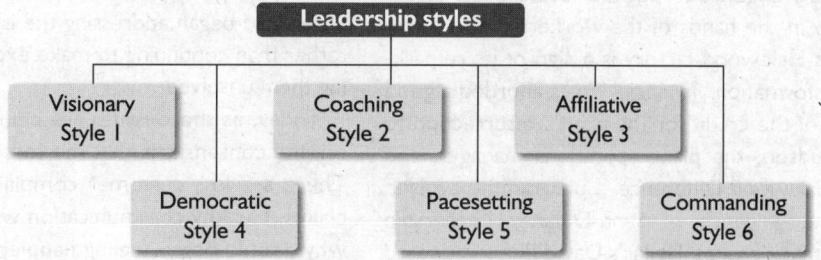

**Fig. 10.7** Leadership styles

**Style 1:** *Visionary* It describes leadership that inspires people by focusing on long-term goals. An effective visionary leader listens to the values held by the individuals within the group, and thus can explain his or her overall goals for an organization in a way that wins their support.

**Style 2:** *Coaching* It is in essence management by delegation, and describes leadership that helps people assume responsibility for a stretch of the road that leads to the organization's success. An effective coaching leader listens one-on-one to employees, establishes personal rapport and trust, and helps employees work out for themselves how their performance matters and where they can find additional information and resources. Delegation of decision-making authority to the employee within his or her area of responsibility—including the power to make and learn from mistakes—is crucial to the effectiveness of this leadership style. Coaching leadership not only frees leaders from doing work for others, but fires-up and accelerates innovation and learning at all levels of an organization.

> Coaching leadership accelerates innovation and learning at all levels of an organization.

**Style 3:** *Affiliative* It describes leadership that creates a warm, people-focused working atmosphere. An affiliative leader listens to discover employees' emotional needs, and strives to honour and accommodate those needs in the workplace. The danger of affiliative leadership, the authors' caution, is that it focuses on the emotional climate

## Jaguar

When a Jaguar automobile drives by, its uncommon elegance, sweep of design, and sheer beauty always catches the eye. This turnabout accomplished between 1998–2001 by the Jaguar plant at Halewood, UK, caused almost as great a stir as the magnificent cars themselves. What made this 180-degree turnabout so remarkable was that Halewood was not a new auto plant at all. This subsidiary of US carmaker Ford had been producing Fords for over 30 years, with questionable efficiency, deplorable working conditions, and commensurately poor quality.

However, by 2001, Halewood had turned a new corner. An article in the *London Financial Times* confirmed this remarkable accomplishment, noting that 'Ford's decision to put the future of its Jaguar subsidiary in the hands of the workers at the once-notorious Halewood factory is a sign of its remarkable transformation.' *Financial Times* afforded a good measure of the credit for the plant's resurrection to David Hudson, the plant operations manager, and to The Halewood Difference, a programme evolved under the guidance of Senn-Delaney Leadership (a consultancy group). Jaguar's David Perry is quoted in the article, saying that the hard evidence of the effect of this programme has been a '20 per cent productivity improvement since December 1998', less than 18 months after The Halewood Difference was launched. The challenge lay in overcoming over 30 years of deep-rooted fear, animosity, and mistrust in Halewood. As Steve Coultate, manager of the Trim and Final Department explained, 'First of all, we have to set an example of how we are going to behave and how we expect the team to behave, laying down some ground rules as to how we are going to operate. I think the other issues are respect on the floor, listening to people, and actually treating them as we would want to be spoken to. This isn't going to happen unless senior managers set up the environment to allow it to happen, and then encourage it positively.'

So, how did it happen? Hudson came to Halewood with a reputation for making things happen. But unlike his predecessors, he chose a very different approach. As Senn-Delaney Leadership's Clayton describes him, 'He is honest, forthright, and persistently encouraging people to change. He speaks a constant message and doesn't duck the issues.' As evidence of this, Hudson encouraged people at Halewood to write to him with their problems. He would then invite these people to come and talk to him. He spoke to them honestly and encouraged them to be a part of the change. The word quickly spread that he was very different from everybody else who had occupied that office. Halewood had been building Ford Escorts for years with varying degrees of quality problems. Now Halewood began addressing the issues that surfaced rather than continuing to make excuses for and leaving them unsolved.

Today, as those issues are being dealt with head on, the consensus is that the cars even look better. There are less customer complaints and warranty claims. Healthy communication was a prime reason why people began feeling happier and doing better work at Halewood. One example of this were the daily meetings that began to take place with the various line group leaders and the engineering and management staff. In a sheltered area just off the shop floor, the group leader would come forward with a large chart listing everything that needed attention in his group area. Speaking over a microphone to cut through the shop noise, he would go through his list one item at a time, notifying the engineering and maintenance managers of his area's issues and where they needed help. The microphone would then be immediately passed to one of the engineers or maintenance people who would respond, taking accountability for the issue and telling the group leader what could be done and/or when it would be done.

while ignoring the work itself, and thus should be used in combination with other leadership styles such as the visionary style.

**Style 4:** *Democratic* It describes leadership that obtains input and commitments from everyone in the group. When faced with uncertainty about how to proceed, a leader elicits fresh ideas and renewed participation by faithfully listening to everyone's opinions and information. The listening may be challenging, particularly in a diverse group and when sensitive issues are raised. Dangers include 'dithering', as when meetings drag on for weeks without making progress.

The authors describe styles 1–4 as 'resonance builders' and contrast these to styles 5 and 6, which they call 'dissonant' styles because these do not emphasize listening. They caution that while styles 5 and 6 are essential under some circumstances, effective leaders use them sparingly because of their potential side effects.

**Style 5:** *Pacesetting* It describes leadership that sets ambitious goals and continually monitors progress toward those goals. (This style is sometimes referred to as 'management by objective'.) Although this is a superior motivator for certain types of employees and under certain situations, the unrelenting pressure it creates over long periods of use can result in burn-out and loss of both creativity and productivity.

**Style 6:** *Commanding* It describes leadership that issues instructions without asking for input about what is to be done or how: 'do it because I say so'. The authors caution that while this style is invaluable during a true crisis, over the long haul it erodes motivation and commitment, leading to massive turnover and a downward spiral of morale and productivity. No listening is required for this style.

## LISTENING AT THREE MANAGERIAL LEVELS

Listening, as a model, has three levels. As managers move from Level 3 to Level 1, their potential for understanding, retaining what is being said, awareness, responsiveness, creativity, and effective communication increases. All managers listen at different levels of efficiency throughout the day, as their listening habits, attitude toward listening, mental alertness, and physical health change.

### Level 1

At this level there is conscious attention, understanding, awareness of the moment, respect, and a spirit of cooperation. This means managers will see things from the other person's point of view, be empathetic to the person's feelings, and thus avoid internal distractions that interfere with effective listening. They pay attention to the talker's total communication by listening to the content and the intent of what is being said, such as tone of voice, inflections, and volume. A critical ingredient of this level is the manager's attitude of mutual respect, which helps suspend negative personal labels and is non-intimidating.

### Level 2

This level of listening is characterized by a state of partial awareness, being in and out of consciousness, or listening to words but not fully understanding the meaning of the message. Managers at this level do not realize that information is being missed. This results in making little effort to understand the talker's intent or to clarify for understanding. When managers listen at Level 2, they mainly focus on the words. Much of what is communicated non-verbally is missed.

> Defensive listening is a major barrier to effective communication and problem solving.

### Level 3

This level has dangerous consequences. It is an automatic 'tuned-out' mode. Internal distractions include daydreaming, thinking about something else, self-dialogue, finding fault, and negative feelings. Not much of what is said will be remembered. Managers experience concentration problems resulting in difficulty while making decisions. A major factor that contributes to Level 3 is a blaming attitude that perpetuates negative feelings of frustration, anger, worry, impatience, and loss of humour. These factors cause stress, which then reduces alertness and creativity. Fatigue is often part of this level—a feeling of not being up to par, loss of initiative, or increased indifference.

The following example illustrates all the aforementioned three levels.

> A manager named Subodh Gupta met with one of his key employees. 'Anjali,' he said, 'I have the feeling there is something that disturbs you about our professional relationship.' Anjali took this encouragement as an opportunity to explain that she felt that he had made some very degrading comments to her a week ago. Instead of reacting defensively, Subodh listened to Anjali's whole explanation and acknowledged her feelings. 'I appreciate you telling me,' he said. 'I can see how you thought my comments were a putdown'.
> 
> 'Yes', Anjali remarked, 'I was upset about it.' Subodh listened to that too, and expressed concern that Anjali was upset, adding, 'I did not intend it as a putdown.'

This listening encounter proved a success because Subodh stayed at the Level 1 of listening throughout the conversation. By doing so, he influenced Anjali in a positive way that encouraged Anjali to feel comfortable talking about her negative feelings. Subodh's Level 1 behaviour impacted Anjali in such a way that she could respond to him at Level 1. A few days later, Anjali was heard mentioning her rapport with Subodh as an example of a good working relationship. Imagine what might have happened if Subodh had reacted defensively at Level 3 after inviting Anjali to discuss what was bothering her! Often, when managers offer someone the opportunity to express his or her feelings about their behaviour, they feel attacked and find it difficult to handle the feedback as Subodh did. Usually managers take what is being said personally, become defensive or even verbally attack the person. If Subodh had responded at Level 3 in a defensive manner to Anjali's expressed negative feelings, the conversation more than likely would have ended with no resolution and increased alienation. Defensive listening is a major barrier to effective communication and problem solving because it perpetuates resistance, hostility, and an argumentative atmosphere. Information is power. Effective listeners are able to concentrate and find the most valid information in whatever they listen to. Effective listeners are powerful people who have a positive influence on others.

## BENEFITS OF LISTENING FOR LEADERS AND TEAMS

Besides the deep implications of listening for leadership, explored leadership models, listening has a number of direct and practical benefits for executives, managers, and team members.

The following are the immediate tangible benefits of effective listening in the workplace:

**It helps in knowing an organization**   Listening, especially carefully listening to the grapevine, will tell you what the members of the staff think about the company's policies and activities. Hence, it will

> Better listening leads to a better recollection of important facts and issues.

help you understand your organization better. The 'listening manager', because he/she listens well, has his/her mental stethoscope on the heartbeat of the organization and can usually predict what changes are needed.

**It helps in making better policies**  If a manager listens to his/her subordinates carefully, he/she will know which policies are suitable for the organization. He/she will chalk out the policies that are acceptable to other members and will win their willing support.

**It mollifies complaining employees**  Very often employees have certain grievances. It is quite possible to come across an employee who has been boiling inside for a long time. All that he/she needs is a listener. If you listen to him/her patiently and sympathetically, his/her anger will be drained out and he/she will leave mollified. Harvey Mackay, a Minneapolis businessman, author, and columnist, says, 'You can win more friends with your ears than with your mouth.'

**It is important for the success of the open-door policy**  Many managers take pride in the open-door policy, that is, they always keep their doors open for the employees to walk into their room and talk to them. No doubt, their doors are always open, but they are themselves bad listeners. So, their employees are inhibited from talking freely. The result is a total failure of upward communication. However, if a manager listens sympathetically, employees will be encouraged to talk and there will be free upward communication.

**It helps to spot sensitive areas before they become explosive**  In an engineering firm, the management decided to meet the workers' union regularly whether or not there was any problem to sort out. The result was that they began to listen to each other properly for the first time. They were able to spot sensitive areas, find the solutions before they became explosive, and problems that could have led to serious disputes did not arise.

**It forms a bond of respect**  Genuine listening generates respect, rapport, and trust between the speaker and the listener. In particular, employees like and respond to, supervisors who they think are listening to them.

**It increases productivity**  Productivity will be higher and problems will be solved more quickly if people working on solving problems are encouraged to explain problems and start working towards solutions finding before 'advice-giving' begins.

**It can calm people down**  Focusing on listening helps both the speaker and the listener stay calm—and helps them cool down—when dealing with a crisis or discussing an emotionally-charged topic.

**It increases confidence**  A supervisor, who listens well, tend to have better self-esteem and self-image because he/she will get along better with others.

**It increases accuracy**  Better listening leads to a better recollection of important facts and issues, resulting in fewer miscommunications and mistakes. Thus, good listening techniques are even more important when complex issues are involved.

## MOTIVATIONAL BENEFITS OF LISTENING IN THE WORKPLACE

Following are certain motivational benefits of listening:

**Innovative solutions to problems and new production methods evolve through listening** By not listening to the people who have to get the job done, a leader not only chills innovation but also demotivates by reducing feelings of responsibility, control, and importance. Six sigma, the latest system for total quality management, explicitly recognizes not only the value of the employee viewpoint but also the value to the employee of being listened to. Listening makes employees feel better about themselves and the problems they work on seem more within their control.

**Cultivating the work environment** A company's leaders should seek out the creative voice of team members and encourage them to listen to one another in order to build an office environment that promotes cooperative teamwork and inspired problem solving.

A company should use empathic listening to discover ways to make the work environment comfortable and attractive in order to recruit and retain top people. Brainstorm, prototype, and take feedback from team members to zero in on what works. This approach to the work environment encourages a flow of creativity and problem solving.

**Encourage prototyping** Like brainstorming, prototyping is a way to solicit input from team members and develop empathy with customers. Prototyping is the process of creating multiple early versions of your products, perhaps with alternative features, before the final version is ready for sale. For example, when facing a one-month deadline, try to come up with outlines or prototypes after the first week and get feedback from team members about the prototypes to see what directions look most promising. Then prepare a final version. Prototyping early often breaks logjams, builds momentum, and allows one to change course before running into obstacles.

## WHY ARE MANAGERS INHERENTLY POOR LISTENERS?

Following are some reasons for the poor listening skills of managers:

**Listening training is unavailable** Listening is the skill we use most frequently; it is also the skill in which we have had little training. We had formal training in other major communication skills, such

---

### QinetiQ

When British Energy wanted to replace its Nuclear Emergency Management System to meet the Y2K requirements, it approached QinetiQ, an IT solutions firm that had designed NARIMS, a storage and management hub for important nuclear incident information for the Ministry of Defence. British Energy wanted QinetiQ to examine how the NARIMS core technology be adapted to suit its requirements. QinetiQ first conducted a feasibility study and an in-depth analysis of British Energy's specific needs. Prototyping and rapid application development were used during the project management phase to deliver a business-critical system. The advantages of their approach were as follows:

- It cost them no more than producing a book.
- The risks were lowered.
- The system was tested on the client's own network to demonstrate its effectiveness.
- The IT company worked closely with the client as it refined the prototype.

As a result of this, QinetiQ delivered an emergency management system, The Incident Information Management System, which provides core support to all information management requirements in case of any problem arising at any of the UK's nuclear power stations.

## Listening Well

*Listening well is as powerful a means of communication and influence as to talk well.*

—John Marshall

First, a good companion should be a good listener. It is important to listen carefully, to give the other person your complete attention, even through pauses and silence. Sometimes, people need time to remember the right word, to name a feeling, especially if their mind is troubled or their life situation is fraught with struggle. It's a good idea to turn off your cell phone when listening to other people to avoid interruptions. For someone in need, it's important to listen as carefully and as long as is necessary.

Second, listen not so much for details as for feelings and for the theme of the exchange. How can you acknowledge the emotions, the desolation or turmoil that the other person is going through? There are some common human themes—the need for shelter, food, survival, the desire for safety and security, concerns in relationships, struggles with decision-making, right and wrong, the desire for consideration and acceptance, queries of meaning and purpose, aspiration for useful and productive work, health.

Third, when you are listening, keep in mind that no single thing ever outlines or determines another person. With time and consideration, one can begin to fully know and comprehend who an individual may be.

Fourth, take great care with reactions. Ask for clarification. 'Help me understand', 'I'm don't know what that means. Could you explain more?', 'How it that so?', 'What are you undergoing?', 'Is this something that has occurred to you before?'

Fifth, as a listener, listen also to yourself. What are you feeling? What thoughts and memories are emerging? Not that you need to share this, but it'll help you to empathize. Listening to yourself is a reminder that in sharing this journey with another, you are opening yourself to a new experience. In engaging, you will also be affected.

Sixth, when you listen to another person, listen especially for the possibilities—the future that is available in this journey. What strengths, resources and capabilities does this person carry? Listen for the hope, dreams and the values that are important to the other person. What appeals the person? What gives the person a sense of drive and control?

Seventh, as you listen, ask how you can best promote the journey towards health and well-being. It's good to test your insights and ideas with the other person. 'What do you think?', 'Is this ok?', 'How do you feel about this?', 'Does this seem useful?' These ways of listening honour the other person. More than anything, these are the ways that help establish a feeling of camaraderie between two people.

---

as writing, reading, and speaking. Very few people undergo any training in listening. Workshops and conferences provide opportunities to improve our writing and speaking skills. It is difficult to find training to sharpen listening skills.

**Thinking speed is more than speaking speed** Another reason for poor listening skills is that people can think faster than they can speak. Most of us speak at the rate of about 125 words per minute. However, we have the mental capacity to understand someone speaking at 400 words per minute (if that were possible). This difference between the rates at which we speak and think means that when we listen to the average speaker, we are using only 25 per cent of our mental capacity. We still have 75 per cent left to utilize. So, our mind is sure to wander. This means that we need to make a real effort to listen carefully and concentrate more of our mental capacity on the listening act.

**We are inefficient listeners** Numerous tests confirm that we are inefficient listeners. Studies conducted by Gail Miller at Washington State University have shown that immediately after listening to a 10-minute oral presentation, the average listener has heard, understood, and retained

50 per cent of what was said. Within 48 hours, that drops off another 50 per cent to a final level of 25 per cent efficiency. In other words, we often comprehend and retain only one fourth of what we hear. We all want to be more than 25 per cent efficient. It is not difficult to see the problems inefficient listeners can create for themselves and others. Poor listening causes us many personal and professional problems.

## POOR LISTENING HABITS

Following is a list of some poor listening habits:

**Listening but not hearing**  Sometimes a person listens only to facts or details or to the way the speaker presented, and misses the real meaning.

**Rehearsing**  Some people listen until they want to say something; then they quit listening, start rehearsing what they want to say, and wait for the opportunity to jump in and talk.

**Interrupting**  The listener does not wait for the complete meaning to be determined, but interrupts so forcefully that the speaker stops in mid-sentence.

**Hearing what is expected**  People frequently think they heard the speaker say what they expected them to say; alternatively, they refuse to hear what they do not want to hear.

**Feeling defensive**  The listeners assume that they know the speaker's intention, or why something was said, or for various reasons, they expect to be attacked and react defensively.

**Listening for a point of disagreement**  Some listeners seem to wait for the chance to attack someone. They listen intently for points on which they can disagree and then attack or confront.

**Call the subject matter uninteresting**  A poor listener when faced with a topic he/she knows, might say to himself/herself, 'Gee, how dull can it get anyhow? You would think they could get a decent speaker on a decent subject.' He/she convinced that the topic is uninteresting and turn to the many other thoughts and concerns stored up in his/her mind for just such an occasion—to start using that unoccupied 75 per cent of the mental capacity. A good listener, on the other hand, might start at the

### Are You Listening—or Just Hearing?

When we think about listening, we tend to assume that it is basically the same as hearing; this is a misconception because it leads us to believe that effective listening is instinctive. As a result, we make little effort to learn, or develop listening skills, and unknowingly neglect a vital communication function. Consequently, we create unnecessary problems for others and ourselves: misunderstandings, hurt feelings, confused instructions, loss of important information, embarrassment, frustration, and lost opportunities. Listening involves a more sophisticated mental process than hearing. It demands energy and discipline. Listening is most often a learned skill. The first step is to realize that effective listening is an active, not a passive, process. A skilled listener does not just sit there and allow listening to happen haphazardly. The belief that the power of the talker plays a major role in communication is why many managers are poor listeners. In our society talking is viewed as more important, with listening categorized as only a supportive function.

> ### How Much are You Paid for Listening?
>
> A manager asked her secretary to keep track of the time she spent listening on the telephone. She was shocked to discover that her company was paying her 35 per cent of her salary, or $18,000, for this function. Amazingly, on the average, people are only about 25 per cent efficient as listeners. With this efficiency rate, she was being paid about $13,500 for the time she spent listening inefficiently!

same point, but would arrive at a different conclusion. The good listener says, 'Gee, that sounds like a dull subject and I do not see how it could help me in my work. But I am here, so I guess I will pay attention and see what the speaker has to say. Maybe there will be something I can use.'

**Criticize the delivery or appearance of the speaker**  Many of us do this regularly. We tend to mentally criticize the speaker for not speaking distinctly, talking too softly, reading from a script, not

> ### The Positive Influence of Listening
>
> Positive influence happens in a variety of forms between managers and those they supervise. It surprises many managers to learn that one of the most significant ways to influence others in a positive way is by effectively listening to them. 'I was astonished! All I had to do was listen, and this employee of mine worked through his own problem without me giving a bit of advice.' Newly aware of his own listening patterns, this manager stopped himself from jumping in with solutions when an employee began sharing a problem. Instead, he listened quietly and occasionally summarized what was being told. The employee came to his own conclusions right in front of him. The manager realized how much he had been interfering with his staff's ability to build confidence by being too quick to give advice. He was amazed that most people just want him to listen to them. Listening to the individual is the most important attribute of an effective manager. Managers who listen, earn their employees' respect and loyalty. They discover important things about how the business is going. One company hired an expensive management consultant to find out why workers had low morale. The consultant began searching for the cause of dissatisfaction using a method the company's managers could have used themselves. He directly asked the workers why they were unhappy—and listened to their answers.

> ### How to Solve Problems by Listening
>
> Employees frequently have excellent ideas about improving the productivity of the work environment. Managers who listen to these ideas solve more problems than those who do not. These managers create a sense of concern for their staff while receiving better-quality information. Ranjan Das, the foreman of a large manufacturing plant, called in Krishnan, a supervisor of a production line, into his office to explain the plans for a new way to assemble machinery. Ranjan described how he thought the procedure should be changed. Krishnan's only response was silence and a frown. The foreman, reading Krishnan's non-verbal communication accurately, realized that something was wrong and sensed that Krishnan might have something to say. So he said, 'Krishnan, you have been in the department longer than me. What is your reaction to my suggestion? I am listening.' Krishnan paused and then began to speak. He realized his manager had opened the door to communication and felt comfortable offering suggestions from his years of experience. As the two employees exchanged ideas, a mutual respect and trust developed, along with a solution to the technical problems. While listening, the manager remained in complete control of the situation. He was an active, not a passive, listener.

> Ensure that your concern for facts does not prevent you from hearing the speaker's primary points.

looking the audience in the eye, etc. We often do the same thing with the speaker's appearance. If speakers are not dressed as we think they should be, we probably tend to not listen closely or we may immediately classify the speaker as a liberal, conservative, hippie, etc. However, if we concentrate on what the speaker is saying, we may begin to get the message and may even get interested. The message is more important than the form in which it is delivered.

**Become too stimulated** We may hear a speaker say something with which we disagree. Then following our train of thought, we spend more time developing counter arguments and no longer listen to the speaker's additional comments. We are busy formulating questions in our mind to ask the speaker, or we may be thinking of arguments that can be used to rebut the speaker. In cases like this, our listening efficiency drops to nearly zero because of over-stimulation. So, hear the speaker out before you judge him or her.

**Listen only for facts** Too many of us listen for facts and, while we may recall some isolated facts, we miss the primary idea the speaker is trying to convey. Be sure that your concern for facts does not

---

### Six Habits of Highly Ineffective Listeners

1. *On–off listening* This occurs because most of us think about four times as fast as an average person can speak. Thus, the listener has ¾ of a minute of 'spare thinking time' in each listening minute to think about such things as personal affairs, concerns, and troubles.

   *(One can overcome this by paying attention to more than the words, watching non-verbal signs like gestures, eye contact, hesitation, or voice tone to pick up the feeling level.)*

2. *Red flag listening* Sometimes, when we hear certain words, ideas, or opinions expressed, we become upset and stop listening. These expressions, often cultural, political, or religious in nature, become 'like a red flag to a bull'. We find ourselves reacting and thus, tuning out the speaker.

   *(The first step to overcome this barrier is to discover our personal red flags. Also, try listening attentively to someone more sympathetic to the issue.)*

3. *Open ears–closed mind listening* Sometimes we decide rather quickly that either the subject or the speaker is boring, and what is being said makes no sense. We decide we can predict what the person knows or will say; thus, we conclude there is no reason to listen because we will hear nothing new.

   *(Better to listen and find out for sure if our predictions are accurate, rather than assume so.)*

4. *Glassy-eyed listening* Sometimes we look at a person intently and seem to be listening. However, our minds are far away, absorbed in our own thoughts. We get glassy-eyed with a dreamy expression on our faces. We can tell when other people look this way, and they can see the same in us.

   *(Postpone daydreaming till another time. If others appear glassy-eyed, suggest a change of pace or break.)*

5. *Too-complicated-for-me listening* When we are listening to ideas that are too detailed, wandering, or complex, we often stop paying attention and 'give up' trying to understand. Our thoughts then go elsewhere.

   *(It is important to keep trying to understand by asking clarifying questions.)*

6. *Do not rock the boat listening* We do not like to have our favourite ideas, prejudices, and points of view challenged or overturned. So, when someone says something that clashes with what we believe, we may unconsciously stop listening or even become defensive and plan a counterattack.

   *(It is best to keep listening carefully and non-defensively, so we can do a better job of responding constructively.)*

prevent you from hearing the speaker's primary points.

**Try to outline everything that is being said**   Many speakers are so unorganized that their comments really cannot be outlined in any logical manner. It is better to listen, in such a case, for the main point. A good listener has many systems of taking notes and selects the best one to fit a speaker.

**Fake attention**   This is probably one of the more common bad listening habits. When a speaker speaking to a group suddenly notices that most of the audience is sitting with chin in hand staring at him/her, it is a good signal that attention is being faked. Their eyes are on the speaker but their minds are miles away.

**Tolerate or create distractions**   People who whisper in an audience fall into this category. Some distractions can be corrected (e.g., closing a door, turning a radio off) to improve the listening atmosphere.

**Evade the difficult**   We tend to listen to things that are easy to comprehend and avoid things that are difficult. The principle of least effort will operate in listening if we allow it to do so.

## Specific Poor Listening Habits in Customer Care Jobs/BPOs

The most common traps we all fall into when we fail to really work at listening are given as follows:

1. *Mental verbal criticism*   We stop paying attention to what the customer is saying and start to judge him/her by what we hear. Do not pay any attention to the person's accent, dialect, lisp, or incorrect grammar. Pay attention to what he/she is trying to say to you, not the way he/she says it. Do confirm what you hear to be sure you understand what he/she meant.
2. *Faking attention*   Customers often keep talking to us when we start doing something else. You probably think you know what is wrong and are beginning to check billing records, etc. But you should stay focused on what the caller is saying.
3. *Tolerating or creating distractions*   Do not chew gum, tap a pencil, or shuffle papers. Be sure that the 'clicking' of your keyboard is not distracting the customer.
4. *Interrupting or finishing their sentences*   Some people speak slowly. They may even irritate you with their totally predictable storyline. However, even if you know exactly what they are going to say, wait for them to confirm that by saying it. Your attempt to promptly identify what to do can backfire if you interrupt.

## Categories of Poor Listeners

One reason behind ineffective listening at work is that we have developed bad habits and poor listening styles, prevent us from really hearing others. Some of the categories of poor listeners as follows:

**The faker**   Fakers only pretend to be listening. They may smile while you talk to them. They may appear to be intent, but they are either thinking about something else, or are so intent on appearing attentive that they do not hear what you are saying. Often their minds wander as they tune in and out of the conversation.

**The dependent listener**   Some people primarily want to please the speaker. Dependent listeners may agree excessively with what the speaker says (nodding head all the time), not because they really agree, but because they want to maintain the goodwill of the speaker. By trying to please, dependent

> Intellectual listeners may be in the danger of listening only to the words of the speaker and ignoring their non-verbal cues.

listeners are often frustrating.

**The interrupter**   Interrupters never allow the other person to finish talking. They may be afraid that they will forget something important they want to say, they may feel that it is necessary to respond to a point as soon as it is made, or they may simply be more concerned with their own thoughts and feelings than with those of others.

**The self-conscious listener**   Trying to impress the other person, they do not listen with understanding; therefore, they may be constantly framing their replies in order to be helpful.

**The intellectual listener**   Intellectual listeners attend only to the words of the other. They make a rational appraisal of what has been said verbally, but they ignore the non-verbal cues (including the feelings that are communicated non-verbally).

**The judge and jury listener**   These listeners often become so involved in judging the ideas or behaviour of others that they do not hear the full story. They may interrupt with a comment about being 'wrong' or 'incorrect' or may attack the other person without attempting to understand their position. When this happens, they shut their ears and do not try to listen.

## STRATEGIES FOR EFFECTIVE LISTENING

The human brain is built for conversation, but we achieve better results when we think strategically about listening and make a few simple, deliberate choices that support our conversational goals. Your skill as a listener can make or break your success in leadership, teams, customer relationships, and negotiations.

The following steps can make you a more effective conversationalist:

### Decide What Your Goals are for the Conversation

Skilled listeners think about their purposes for having a conversation and make their choices based upon those purposes. Valid business purposes for a conversation include the following:

**Exchanging information**   In many conversations, you will talk about what someone needs or is offering. You may also be trying to figure out whether someone else has complementary offerings or needs, for example, to figure out if one of you is a potential buyer and one a potential seller. Finally, part of the exchange of information is often about whether someone accurately understood what he/she heard.

**Building working relationships**   People who know and respect one another and have had a good experience working together, often work together more effectively. Personal style can make an enormous difference. Developing and maintaining positive personal relationships can be one of the most important components of customer-supplier, employer-employee and networking conversations, etc.

> Your skill as a listener can make or break your success in leadership, teams, customer relationships, and negotiations.

**Feeling good**   Having an enjoyable and/or productive conversation can make you feel valued, respected, and even liked. As such, conversations can be a key component of having a good day or even a good job, and of being motivated and productive.

**Making someone else feel good**   Good conversations can have the same effect on others as they have on you. Whether or not you have a vested interest in someone's state of mind—such as a customer, co-worker, or supplier—you may find merit in giving someone this experience.

## Be Aware of Your Options

With your conversational goal in mind, deliberately choose whether to talk, listen, focus, or clarify what you want to say. In conversations, people generally take turns talking and listening. Effective listeners are fully conscious of making a decision each time they decide to talk or to let someone else talk. If you have not already, you can develop this self-awareness and reap its benefits.

### When to Speak and When to Listen

There are a few rules of thumb when deciding whether to talk or listen.

**Never assume you should talk more**   In leadership, customer relationship building, negotiating, and virtually every other vital business function, skilful listening is often more valuable than talking. Simply because you are the boss, or more experienced, it does not necessarily follow that your conversational goals will be best served if you talk more. So, consider making listening your default choice in most situations. Even in employment interviews, applicants often need to be good listeners in order to form relationships with their interviewers and to discover how best to structure what they are going to say during the limited amount of time they have to showcase their abilities. A job applicant who demonstrates all of the necessary qualifications and manages to make the interview more interesting for the interviewer is more likely to get the job.

**You can ask**   If you are not sure whether to talk or listen, you can always ask them which they would prefer, whether they would like to talk or listen to something you are ready to say.

**Make an effort to share the floor**   If you think you have been talking too much, you can make an effort to give them a turn by asking them a non-leading question, then listening attentively to their answer.

**When the conversation lags, refocus**   If they are not talking, and you do not know what to say next, but your goals for the conversation have not been reached yet, there are two safe ways to continue. First, you can simply ask the other persons what else they want to say about the topic being discussed. Second, you can propose to talk more about a relevant topic, and ask them if they want to talk with you about it.

### Planning What to Say When You Speak—Focusing and Clarifying

When you speak, do you plan what to say—by focusing or clarifying—to best serve the business purposes of the conversation? Before you speak you may choose to focus what you are going to say, by using an appropriate structure and level of detail.

You may also decide to clarify what topics and background are important to your listeners before going ahead. It is worth remembering that people use the word 'rambling' to describe someone who talks about things that are not important, and the word 'pedant' to describe someone who lectures them about something they already know. Also, keep in mind that many people feel threatened or embarrassed if you assume that they know something that they do not.

> Speakers can try to clarify the topics and background that are important to their listeners.

## Types of Listening Skills

Communication scholars have identified three listening skill clusters and the accompanying behaviour that are used by attentive listeners.

### Attention Skills

Attention skills include the following factors:

**A posture of involvement**  It refers to inclining one's body towards the speaker, facing the speaker squarely, maintaining an open body position, and positioning the body at an appropriate distance from the speaker.

**Appropriate body motion**  It refers to occasionally nodding your head, using facial expressions to reflect emotions back to the speaker, adjusting the body position in non-distracting ways, etc.

**Eye contact**  It refers to sustained, direct, and reflective contact with the speaker.

**Non-distractive environment**  It refers to doing what it takes to eliminate distracting noises, movement, etc.

### Following Skills

Following skills include the factors that we shall discuss now:

**Door openers**  Non-coercive invitations to talk tend to take one of four forms as follows:

- Description of another person's body language (e.g., 'You're beaming, what's up?')
- An invitation to talk or to continue talking (e.g., 'Please go on.')
- Keeping silent, giving another person time to decide whether to talk
- Attending to show interest (e.g., displaying attention skills as described above)

**Minimal encouragers**  These refer to brief indicators to the other person that you are with them, for example, 'Hmm', 'Oh?', 'I see', 'Right', 'I understand', 'Really?', 'Go on', 'Sure', etc.

**Infrequent questions**  These are open ended and asked one at a time; beware of the key listening error of asking too many questions.

**Attentive silence**  Most listeners talk too much; learn the value of using non-verbal attentive listening behaviour with verbal silence.

### Reflecting Skills

Reflective skills include the following characteristics:

**Paraphrasing**  It refers to re-stating what you believe to be the essence of a speaker's comments, for example, 'So you are suggesting that we change the proposal?'

**Reflecting feelings**  It refers to understanding and expressing vocally the emotion you think the speaker is trying to convey, for example, 'It sounds like you are angry with your group members.'

**Reflecting meanings**  It refers to tying feelings to content, for example, 'So you were angry with your group members for pushing the proposal topic through without your input?'

**Summative reflection**  It refers to summarizing what has been said, For example, 'If I understand correctly, you want the proposal topic to be changed and you want some kind of guarantee that proposal topics must be passed by all group members, right?'

**Tip for people who worry about rambling**  Practise getting whatever you want to say said in 60 seconds or less. Practise this using a clock, a watch, or even an oven timer. Yes, some things might merit two and half minutes, or even an hour, but in general if someone is interested in what you say during your first 60 seconds, they will ask a follow up question, and then you can continue for another 60 seconds.

## Attentive Listening

> Attentive listening involves thinking and acting in ways that connect listeners with speakers.

Attentive listening means thinking and acting in ways that connect you with the speaker. There are several simple steps you can take to improve your listening. The quality of information exchanged, your own experience as a listener, the experience of the person you are listening to, and your relationship with the listener will all benefit. The steps are follows:

**Get over yourself** If you assert your own position at every opening in a conversation, you might eliminate many of the potential benefits of listening. In particular, people you are talking with might not feel respected by you, their thinking and brainstorming will be inhibited, and they may even withhold important information out of caution—or out of anger. Wait until they finish making their points before you speak. Do not interrupt, even to agree with them, and do not jump in with your own suggestions before they explain what they have already done, plan to do, or have thought about doing.

Listening carefully for a while first gives the talker and the listener both a chance to develop an understanding about what exactly the issue is.

**Stop multitasking** Do not multitask if you are supposed to be listening. You wind up listening to only part of what someone says, or pretending to listen while you do something else. You also sacrifice important non-verbal cues and information about their intent, confidence level, and commitment level. Even if you think that you can get enough of what people say while multitasking to serve your immediate purposes, you should assume as a general rule that people notice when you do not listen to them attentively. If you find your attention wandering, use this trick—decide why you do not want to listen, think about what you might get out of listening, then choose whether to listen or not.

**Recap regularly** Very skilled listeners practise and become good at recapping both the facts and level of importance (the emotional drift of the speaker) in a few brief words.

**Use body language** Use positive body language, such as making frequent eye contact and facing the speaker squarely. Avoid negative body language, such as frowning and looking away. A great deal of research has been done on body language. Books have been written about it. Some people claim to be experts at interpreting it. However, for the rest of us, it is enough to be aware that body language exists, and to use it constructively when we can.

## PAY-OFFS OF EFFECTIVE LISTENING

The first real evidence of effective communication is when each person really *understands* what the other person has said—the meanings, attitudes, and feelings behind the words. That takes time and concentration. Here are some *positive results* that can be gained from effective listening.

**Gaining knowledge** Each person can learn new information about topics, ideas, and people. Listen for the meaning beyond the words and the context of the communication. Listen to the person—get in touch with emotions, language, habits, and temperament.

**Receiving better work and cooperation from others** Showing a sincere interest in other peoples' problems, ideas, thoughts, and opinions can bring you more respect and cooperation.

**Winning friends** Not only does it help you to make new friends, but it will also enrich ongoing friendships.

**Solving problems and conflicts** Only after understanding the other person can you agree or disagree, and then work cooperatively to clarify thinking, seek solutions, and resolve conflict.

**Reducing tension** It gives the other person a chance to 'get it off the chest', to 'clear the air', or 'let off a little steam'.

**Preventing trouble** If people can learn to listen before speaking, before sticking their neck out, before taking untenable and unreasonable positions, or making commitments that cannot be kept, they will likely avoid many unfortunate experiences.

**Doing a better job** Try asking your partner or fellow workers for ideas about improving your listening performance. Then try some of their suggestions.

## SUMMARY

The chapter makes it evident that effective listening is an active process and not a passive one. It takes effort to concentrate on messages for a complete understanding to take place. Since it is an arduous task, it challenges the listener's mental faculties. Therefore, it is often remarked that listening is not like hearing and that a listener not only hears through the ears but also through the eyes. Good listening skills are a prerequisite for success in one's professional career. It is a critical area of effective communication skills, and when we listen carefully, we succeed in developing a rapport with people. We can become good listeners by actively and imaginatively entering the frame of reference of other person. However, this is not an easy task and, like any tough skill, requires lot of hard work, dedication, and training.

## KEY TERMS

*Brainstorming* It is an interactive session where employees or the parties involved discuss a specific issue with open minds and try to reach and arrive at as many alternative courses of action as possible.

*Effective listening* It can be defined as the art of hearing and understanding what someone is saying.

*Faking attention* It is the act of pretending to be listening.

*Informative listening* It is the name we give to the situation where the listener's primary concern is to understand the message. Listeners are successful insofar as the meaning they assign to message is as close as possible to that which the sender intended.

*Interpreting* It refers to the stage when a listener is engaged in the act of decoding a message. It is at this stage that the listener is faced with multiple barriers.

*Listening barriers* These are various variables in the communication process that exert themselves whenever we try to listen.

*Prototyping* This is a way of soliciting input from team members and developing empathy with customers. It is the process of creating and experiencing multiple early versions of your service products, perhaps with alternative features, before your 'final' version is ready for sale.

*Sensing* It allows the listener to select, from among multiple of stimuli, only the one that seems important at that point in time and convert it into a message.

## Concept Review Questions

1. Briefly, discuss the importance of listening in communication.
2. How can listening improve employee-employer relationships?
3. Narrate a specific incident in which listening proved helpful to you and another in which poor listening actually harmed you to some extent.
4. Listening is an art and like any other art, it has to be cultivated consciously. Discuss.
5. Mention some ways in which a person can learn the art of listening.
6. Explain how each type of non-verbal communication relates to listening.
7. How is listening an inherent skill required for effective leadership and team building?
8. What is passive listening and how can it be advantageous/disadvantageous in some situations?
9. List some of the common external and personal barriers to listening. How are they similar/dissimilar to the general barriers to communication?

## Projects

1. The class is divided into teams of some 4–5 members each; the teacher reads some factual information, which could be a newspaper article, a story, or any other text to only one member of each team. Each of these team members then tells what he/she has heard to the second member of the team, who in turn tells to the third member and so on until the last member of each team has heard that information. Now the last person receiving the information reports to the teacher what he/she has heard, who then verifies it with the original message. The team able to report the information with the greatest accuracy wins.
2. Identify two companies that you think have listened to their customers and redesigned their products or services accordingly. Mention specific situations and bring out their revised strategies.
3. Advertisements are generally considered the ultimate message styles and act as a direct communication between the company and the customer. Identify two specific advertisements and look at how companies have depicted in them their willingness to 'listen' to their customers.

## REFERENCES

Aristotle 2000, *Art of Rhetoric*, tr. J.H. Freese, Harvard University Press.

Goieman, Daniel, Richard Boijatzis, and Annie McKee 2002, *Primal Leadership*, Harvard Business Review Press, 1st edition.

Hill, Linda 1996, *Building Effective One-on-One Work Relationships*, Harvard Business School Technical Notes, 9-497-028, pp. 7–11.

Hulbert, Jack E. 1998, *Barriers to Effective Listening*, Sage Publications.

Ireland, Brenda 1992, 'Six Habits of Highly Ineffective Listeners', Adapted from *Strength to Your Sword Arm: Selected Writings*, Holy Cow Press, pp. 27–31.

Ireland, Brenda 1992, 'The Power of Listening', Adapted from *Strength to Your Sword Arm: Selected Writings*, Holy Cow Press, pp. 23–25.

Mackay, Harvey 2000, *Pushing the Envelope All The Way To The Top*, Ballantine Books, New York, pp. 50.

Nichols, Ralph G. and Leonard A. Stevens 1957, *Are You Listening?*, McGraw-Hill Book Company, New York, p. 18.

Pearson, Judy C., Paul E. Nelson, Scott Titsworth, and Lynn Harter 2003, *Human Communication*, McGraw-Hill, pp. 31–46.

Quick, Thomas L. 1989, *Unconventional Wisdom: Irreverent Solutions for Tough Problems at Work*, Jossey Bass, San Francisco, pp. 103–07.

Rennebohm, Craig, 'Approach and Companionship in the Engagement Process', in B. Compton and B. Galaway 1999, *Social Work Processes*, Brooks/Cole Publishing Company, Pacific Grove, pp. 30–43.

*The Times of India*, October 2004.

Verma, Vijay K. 2000, *Guide to the Project Management Body of Knowledge*, Chapters 2 and 10.

## CASE STUDY 1

**Lyman Steil**

Dr Lyman Steil is the CEO and president of Communication Development, Inc.; founding partner of The Masters Alliance; director of The Amara Institute; former director of debate, Macalester College, and former chairman of the Speech Communication Division, Department of Rhetoric, University of Minnesota. Steil is the founder of the International Listening Association (ILA) and author of several books on the subject. In 1979, Steil was working as a speech communication professor at Macalester College in St Paul, when he and his colleagues were hired by Sperry Corp., one of the original main-frame manufacturers that later became Unisys. Sperry was trying to incorporate the theme of listening into its advertising campaign, and was hoping that Steil and his peers could provide some insight on the subject. Instead, Steil suggested that, if listening was a corporate quality they wanted to convey to the public, the company's staffers should first learn about listening themselves. Over the next five years, Steil helped train thousands of managers at the company, who then trained their employees. In the end, 44,000 Sperry workers learned the tenets of listening, which eventually became one of the reasons that they became such a business success.

**Honing up on listening**  When Steil works with clients, typically in a group setting over one or two days, he starts with a personal assessment tool to help participants understand their strengths and weaknesses as listeners. Next, Steil teaches the fundamentals of listening concepts and discusses attitudes that get in the way of listening. Much of the workshop involves learning skills in the following four areas:

- Sensing—do you hear the words?
- Interpretation—do you understand the words?
- Evaluation/judging—do you accept or reject the words?
- Responding—do you take a final action that results from the conversation?

He also asks each participant to put together a chart of the 25 most significant people in their life, and categorize that list into a top-five list. Often, when examining this list, participants find that the most significant people in their lives are not the ones they listen to well. Making these connections is the first step on the road to becoming a good listener, he explained.

**How to be an active listener**  Anyone can learn how to be an effective listener if he or she is willing to commit the time and energy. In the first place, listening breaks down due to lack of attention—most people do not realize that there is a process to listening, and that process revolves around a purpose, says Steil. It is the listener's responsibility to make sure that he or she understands the other party's purpose and that their mutual purposes are aligned. In other words, you may have to listen to someone else's small talk or venting—no matter how much you want to walk away—before you can get the information you want or need. IT managers often do not feel like they have the time for small talk, which can be a big mistake. There is also the problem of selective listening—some people listen well on subjects close to their heart, but on other topics, they do not hear a thing. 'In the tech world, a lot of people have attitudes that work against them', Steil said. It is crucial that IT managers pay attention to emotions and distractions. According to Steil, emotional triggers include people, topics, and language. If a politician you loathe is on CNN discussing the war in Iraq, your feelings for the politician may override his or her message, which could be a valuable one. Conversely, you may respect a politician or have neutral feelings for him or her, but the topic of war is a negative one for you. As a result, your first reaction is to tune out. Listeners must be able to filter those emotions and understand how they impact their ability to listen. Distractions include noise in the room, people walking in and out of the office, emails popping up on the screen, or a person's own physical or emotional discomfort unrelated to the conversation. 'Good listeners identify and deal with [distractions] as best they can,' Steil said. If anything might be unclear, he added, good listeners will take the time to ask or clarify.

**Questions**

1. Do you believe that a skill like listening can be developed by hiring a professional who through training and other activities will help people become a better

listeners? Give your suggestions.
2. Steil suggested that, if listening was a corporate quality they wanted to convey to the public, the company's staffers should first learn about listening themselves. Justify the above point in the light of actual business situations.
3. In the above case, Steil says that we listen most carelessly to the people who are most important in our priorities list. Do you really buy this argument? Give illustrations from your daily life to substantiate your point.
4. 'Good listeners identify and deal with [distractions] as best they can,' Steil says. How would you interpret the above statement, in the light of the fact that distractions are bound to be present in any kind of communication.
5. How can organizations at large try to be better listeners? List some examples/situations where corporations have gained by being good listeners and some examples where companies that have failed to be good listeners have suffered enormously.

### The Farewell Speech

The vice-president of a company was being given a farewell by the employees with whom he had worked for more than 25 years. Camaraderie, reflections, sharing of thoughts and memories, lots of wine, and plenty of food could sum up the mood of the party. The CEO walked in to join the party and he was soon requested to deliver a short speech looking at the mood and the spirit of the occasion. The CEO, an eloquent speaker, stood up and delivered a great speech, marked with touches of gentle humour, about life after retirement, what the vice president meant to the company and to him personally, how he had reached such heights and yet never compromised his values, and that his exit would be a difficult space to fill in. As the CEO spoke, all eyes were fixed on him. Most employees were serious, watchful, and paying full attention. Some were clearly indifferent. A few proactive listeners, however, enjoyed every bit of what the CEO said which was quite evident from their body language. Their smiling faces, twinkling eyes, and occasional head nods, in agreement with what the speaker said, were indicative of their level of involvement and enjoyment. In other words, they had tuned themselves to whatever the CEO was saying. However, midway through his speech, the CEO sensed that his speech was becoming a little too stretched, he cut short his speech and wished the vice-president all the good health and peace.

### Questions

1. What happened in the case mentioned above? Explain.
2. Did everybody receive the message the same way? Why?
3. How should a CEO approach his speech preparation for such an occasion?
4. How do listening skills differ according to place, person, and time? Explain in the context of the above situation.

CHAPTER 11

# Business Presentations and Public Speaking

## LEARNING OBJECTIVES

After reading this chapter, you will be able to understand

- business presentations and speeches
- the importance of business presentations
- the basics of effective presentations
- the contents of an introduction, well-developed main text, and emphatic conclusion
- the importance of verbal, vocal, and visual elements in business presentations
- various media used for presenting the visual contents
- effective sales presentations
- strategies for overcoming stage fright

## INTRODUCTION

For businesspersons who have spent a considerable number of years in their profession, it is something of an occupational hazard to have to sit through regular presentations whether as a member of the audience or as a speaker trying to spice up a pitch.

No matter what your area of responsibility or the type of organization for which you work, you will, sooner or later, be expected to give a presentation or speech. You may be asked to talk to colleagues, clients, suppliers, or the general public. Each group requires different information about your business, which should be presented in a format appropriate to the situation. You may be asked to speak for 10 minutes or two hours. Regardless of whom you are talking to, the subject matter or the duration of your presentation and your ability to effectively communicate with your audience and engage them directly reflects on your company and you. As your career progresses, your presentation skills become even more important because, at the entry level, executives may require mostly technical skills but as they rise in management, they are required to rely less on technical training and more on their ability to sell their ideas and plans to their next level of management. Failure to professionally present your work, ideas, or organization in these situations may significantly affect your company's reputation. In addition, it will most certainly affect your own ability to achieve your career goals.

> Speaking effectively and powerfully is a skill that will help in your professional growth.

Speaking effectively and powerfully is a skill that is really worth learning. Fortunately, public speaking is something you can learn. Public speaking is a skill that can be studied, polished, and even perfected to some degree. All it takes is hard work. With tenacity and persistence, you can master it, which makes a significant difference to your career. This chapter facilitates your understanding of business presentations and public speaking and guides you through each stage of giving a presentation and a public speech, from the initial preparation to the conclusion and questions and answers.

## BUSINESS PRESENTATIONS AND SPEECHES

The ability to speak effectively in public is important. Members of groups, companies, or organizations often have to make speeches to large or small groups of people. We give speeches to explain our ideas or plans, to report on the results of research or investigations, to convince people of the advantages of a course of action, or to entertain at a lunch. Whether we can make a good speech or not, makes a big difference to what other people think about us. Being able to express information and ideas clearly and in a well-organized way in front of a group of people is a useful skill. Along with computer literacy, professional presentation skills are becoming a new survival skill in the workplace. People enjoy presenters who are inviting, engaging, and informative. Whether you present to internal or external audiences, your presentation basics remain the same.

Sales managers and financial managers deliver presentations to potential customers. Brand managers propose new ideas to the management and present the new product line to the sales force. Division heads and shop floor supervisors brief senior managers on recent developments in their respective divisions. They also explain new policies and procedural changes to their subordinates. Besides these situations in which presentations are delivered, there are presentations from the engineers and scientists involved in the research and development activities of their companies.

Let us see whether a business presentation differs from a public speech. A presentation is a formal talk addressed to one or more people and 'presents' ideas or information in a clear, structured way (Image 11.1). Public speaking is speaking formally to a group of listeners. Though, in most respects, both these types of oral communication remain the same, they differ subtly in terms of the purpose of the speaker, background and expectations of the audience, the amount of information that is to be delivered, and the level of interaction to be allowed. These subtle points of difference are tabulated in Table 11:1.

**Image 11.1** Business presentation

> A presentation is a formal talk addressed to one or more people and 'presents' ideas or information in a clear, structured way.

Some typical reasons why it may be in the interests of an organization to have an executive deliver a speech/talk are as follows:

- To influence important decisions
- To attract media and public attention

**Table 11.1** Differences between business presentation and public speaking

| Points of Difference | Business Presentation | Public Speaking |
|---|---|---|
| Aim of speakers | To give the audience what they know they need | To give the audience what they believe they want |
| Type of audience | Generally homogenous in terms of their knowledge, area of academic or professional interest, etc. | Mostly heterogeneous |
| Expectations of audience | Complete details about the topic | Do not expect a lot of details |
| Amount of information | More | Less |
| Level of interaction | More; as the audience wishes to understand the topic thoroughly | Less; as a general understanding is desired by the audience |

- To establish an image
- To explain the importance of organizational change
- To dispel rumours
- To present findings before a committee

As you examine these situations, you may observe that, though each one appears to belong to the category of business presentations, two of them, the second and the fifth, can be grouped under the category of public speaking, because of the differences discussed earlier.

---

### BUSINESS COMMUNICATION INSIGHT

**Effective Presentations**

Managers groan the most was when they receive a draft PowerPoint exceeding 50 pages. Ideally, the presentation should take 10 minutes and the discussion should last for hours.

Do your team's reports and presentations spark action by your clients? Do they utilize storytelling techniques to engage the audience and make an emotional connection that is remembered and passed along? Do they contain insights that connect with business action and impact? Do they get to the 'Now what?' (what your client should do) or do they stop at the 'What?' (what you did or found).

The five points listed here—in combination—will get you started on the road towards effective presentations.

- Set a limit of 15 slides (maximum), the rest goes in the report
- Use just one slide for business context and methodology
- Make sure you know the business context and decision to be made, and that you get to the 'Now What?' (what the client should do)
- Know who the audience is for the presentation, and how it will be delivered (in person, by webcast, phone, or just sent?)
- Make sure you have a true insight—that connects with business action of value—not just 'findings' that are labelled 'insights'

*Source:* Lewis, Ian, 'Do Your Reports and Presentations Create Action and Business Impact—or Groans?', http://www.consultcambiar.com/2011/07/do-your-reports-and-presentations-create-action-and-business-impact-%E2%80%93-or-groans/. Reproduced with permission.

> - Through effective preparation, you will be able to answer all the questions and doubts about your speech before they arise.
> - The factors that contribute to the occasion are the *facilities* available for your presentation, and *time* and *context* of your presentation.

## Planning

Preparing and delivering your first business presentation or public speech can be daunting. You may find it difficult to decide what you want to say and how to say it, or perhaps the thought of speaking before an audience scares you. It is true that some people are naturally talented at public speaking, but with some helpful guidance, anyone can prepare and deliver a successful speech that will be remembered for all the right reasons.

Your first instinct may be to sit down with a pen and paper and charge ahead into writing the first line of your speech. However, you will save yourself a lot of time and effort, not to mention much frustrating rewriting, if you begin instead by devoting some time to careful planning of your speech. Through effective preparation, you will be able to answer all the questions and doubts about your speech before they arise. The contents of your speech, and how you deliver it, are based on five important factors—occasion, audience, purpose, thesis, and material (Fig. 11.1).

### Occasion

The circumstances or the occasion will obviously have a great bearing on your speech. The factors that contribute to the occasion are the *facilities* available for your presentation, *time*, and the *context* of your presentation.

*Facilities* include the venue, keeping in mind the seating, light, projection facilities, ventilation, acoustic provisions, etc. Most experienced speakers check out the room in advance and come prepared for any lacunae.

*Time* refers to both the time of the day you are going to present and the duration of your talk. Straightforward and factual presentations may work well during the morning hours; but if you need to give an after-dinner speech, you need to adapt your remarks to the occasion. As far as the duration of the presentation is concerned, most business presentations are brief. Hence, you need to present the important points in the first few minutes.

*Context* refers to the events surrounding your presentation. When you are presenting in a team, for example, you need to consider the team members. They might have left a positive or negative impression in the minds of the audience and hence, you would need to adapt yourself to the existing situation just before presenting your part. Besides these events, the recent happenings in your company can also affect the presentation. For example, if you are about to present a new proposal on budget just after your company has suffered a financial loss, you should emphasize on those features of your budget that focus on reducing the costs.

The occasion will dictate not only the content of your speech, but also the duration, tone, and expectations of your audience. For example, humour may be inappropriate during a business

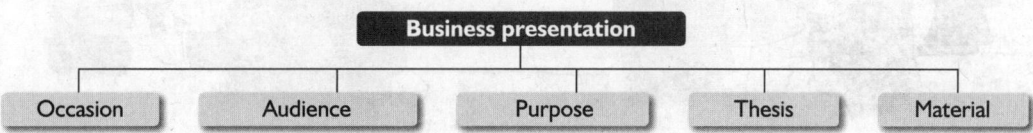

**Fig. 11.1** Success factors in a business presentation

> - The occasion will dictate not only the content of your speech, but also the duration, tone, and expectations of your audience.
> - Knowing your audience's preferences can make the difference between an effective and an ineffective presentation.

presentation or a eulogy, while it may be welcome during a wedding speech or sports event. You should also be aware of your role and any observations that you might make during your speech. For example, if you are presenting the final report of your project to a group of superiors, you need to take care of the short duration, firm but polite tone, and also the expectations of your superiors. Be mindful of the occasion and your role in it.

### Audience

Whatever the occasion, your speech must always be targeted to your audience, who know what they want to listen to just as speakers know what they need to convey. Hence, as a presenter, knowing the positions, personal preferences, significant demographic characteristics, size of the group, aim, knowledge, and attitudes of your audiences would greatly help you tailor your speech better. Your audiences may be internal or external to the organization, or a combination of both.

Begin your preparation by considering the positions/ranks/designations of the members of your audience. If they are specialists in their fields, you may find them to be more interested in the technical aspects of your talk. If they are non-experts, they would probably be bored if you give technical details. Most managers fall under the second category. Even executives, who come up through the ranks as engineers, take a different perspective upon becoming responsible for an entire job.

Your audience may have its idiosyncrasies. Some may insist on a formal presentation, while others on a casual one; some may appreciate humour, while others may be strait-laced; some may find your delivery fast, while some may wish you would speed up; some may prefer electronic presentations, while others the human touch; etc. Though it is difficult, knowing your audience's preferences can make the difference between an effective and an ineffective presentation. Consider the preferences of your most important clients before starting your preparation.

Keep in mind the demographic features, such as the age, sex, cultural background, and economic status, of your audience while preparing for the presentation. For example, you need to know the distribution ratio of men and women among the audience for your presentation on the new scheme for travel or medical reimbursement, as there may be special considerations for the men or women. Likewise, when you present a topic like a new insurance scheme, it is beneficial to consider the age groups and cultural backgrounds of your audience. For example, as an executive of a large organization, you

Adapt your speech to your audience

may have people from diverse cultural backgrounds or regions. The points you make, examples you give, or jokes that you insert in your presentation have to be shaped according to the audience's sensibilities. The economic factor is important, especially in sales presentations, where the purchasing power of the potential customers need to be considered for a product or service which your company may offer. It is difficult to consider all the variables in demographics. However, it is necessary to recognize the dimensions of your audience that are important for preparing your presentation.

The next factor in audience analysis is the number or size of the group. Ask yourself the following questions:

How many copies of the handout or questionnaire need to be prepared?
How large should the visual aid be, so that it is clearly visible to everyone?
How much time should be devoted to answering questions?

Certain factors have to be kept in mind, for example, it would not be wise to be seated while addressing a large audience, or standing behind a podium to make a presentation to four or five people. Also, you need to consider the audience's attitude towards you, as the presenter, and the topic. Keep in mind whether the audience is friendly or hostile towards you, and how they feel about the topic. You must know the audience for your message to have the best effect.

## Purpose

Before you start preparing a presentation, you should ask yourself, 'Why am I making this presentation?' Do you need to inform, persuade, entertain, train, or sell? Your objective should be clear to you if it is to be clear to your audience. A statement of purpose not only describes what you want to accomplish but also helps you know, at the end of your presentation, whether you have achieved the same. You can classify your purpose into two broad categories: general and specific.

Your general purpose can be further divided into three subcategories—*informing*, *persuading*, or *entertaining*. An informative presentation at the new employee orientation programme or another enlightening presentation for explaining your project status are typical presentations that have an informative purpose. Sales presentations, presentations by the marketing executives to convince sales representatives to be more enthusiastic about a product that has gone down in sales, etc. come under the second subcategory—persuading.

A specific purpose statement needs to specify *whom* you want to influence, what you want them to think or do, and *when* and where you want them to do it. For example, if you want your boss to accept the internal proposal you presented during the discussion at the end of your presentation, you have to formulate your specific purpose statement with the four 'wh'—*who, what, when*, and *where*. Your purpose statement should clearly specify the desired outcome of your presentation. For example in a training programme, when you are given the task of explaining the features of Microsoft Excel to a group of new employees, your purpose statement could be 'I want everyone in this group to show me that he or she can use all the features of Microsoft Excel with efficiency after my presentation'.

> A statement of purpose not only describes what you want to accomplish but also helps you know whether you have achieved the same.

## Thesis

The central or core idea of your presentation is referred to as the thesis statement, a single statement that summarizes your message. Just as the concentric circles revolve round the same centre, all your ideas should contribute something to your

> The central or core idea of your presentation is referred to as the thesis statement.

central idea. Your thesis statement reveals what the exact purpose of your presentation is. If it is not clear and leaves your audience confused about what you are trying to present, much of your presentation will be left unheard. It is necessary to understand the difference between your purpose statement and your thesis statement. For example, if your purpose statement is 'I want my project team members to change over to the new technique', your thesis statement could be 'Recent advances have changed the course of our project'. In other words, instead of explicitly revealing your purpose to the audience, you are informing them of the purpose lying beneath the thesis statement.

### Material

Once you have formulated your thesis, you need to develop the information that elaborates it. Collecting material requires some research. For example, when you are giving a product presentation, besides the complete information about the product, you may have to collect the information pertaining to the competing products, and their features. When you are explaining a process or procedure, the information is obvious.

The main text of your presentation will include the series of steps involved. For most of the business presentations, you may have to consult company records, statistics, and publications. Sometimes, you may have to collect information through surveys or interviews. You may have to contact external organizations to procure information for some of your presentations. Once you have collected material and ideas for your presentation, assemble them at one place. You may list all the ideas on a piece of paper and then organize them.

### Structuring

Structuring or organizing your material clearly is vital for an effective presentation. A well-organized presentation can make your messages more comprehensible, keep your audience happy, and boost your image as a speaker. On the other hand, rambling or taking too long to get to the point, including irrelevant material in your speech, omitting necessary information, or messing up the ideas can lead to a chaotic structure. Even experienced speakers may get into trouble if their material is not organized appropriately and they end up presenting their ideas disjointedly.

> Structuring or organizing your material clearly is vital for an effective presentation.

The key to all these problems is to organize your ideas into a well-known pattern. In other words, your presentation should have the following format (Fig. 11.2):

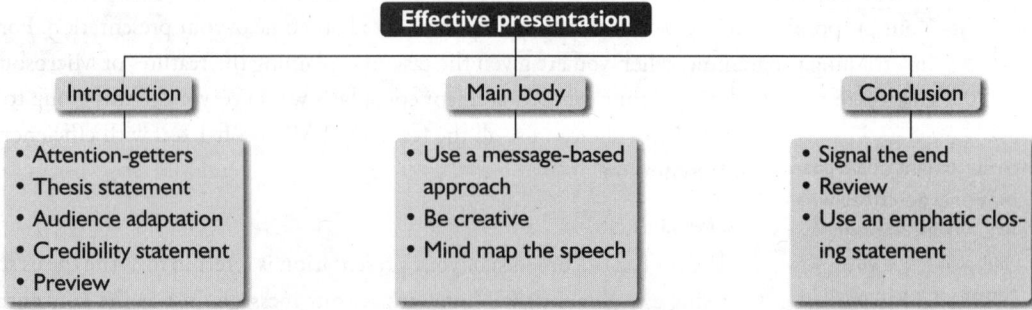

**Fig. 11.2** Components of an effective presentation

> Identify the key points that support your thesis and then decide which plan best develops these points.

**Introduction** Should grab attention, introduce topic, contain a strategy for establishing credibility, preview your speech, establish rules for questions, and have a smooth transition to the main text.

**Main body** Contains all topics/the entire matter organized into a logical sequence

**Conclusion** Contains signal, highlights/summary, closing statement/re-emphasis, a vote of thanks, and invites questions

These components of an effective presentation will be discussed in detail later in this chapter.

### Organizing/Outlining

Although you need to give an introduction first, it is appropriate to organize the main text of the speech. Even though it does not come first in your presentation, the main body requires organizing. Identify the key points that support your thesis and then decide which organizational plan best develops these points.

### Patterns

The body of a presentation can be organized in six basic patterns. You need to choose the best pattern that suits and develops your topic. The six patterns are as follows:

- Chronological
- Spatial/directional
- Topical/categorical
- Cause and effect
- Problem and solution
- Climactic

**Chronological pattern** A chronological pattern is one in which the points are arranged in the way in which they occurred or were observed. You can use this pattern for an informative presentation. You may present a business process or procedure such as developing a new product or giving a set of instructions to your subordinate. It can also be used to present the history and growth of your company over the years to a group of visitors.

**Spatial pattern** A spatial pattern organizes material according to how it is put together or where it is located physically. Some topics which may be organized using this pattern include the safety requirement on the shop floor including placement of equipment, and technical details on the support required ; description of your company building with the locations of its various divisions, etc.

**Topical pattern** The most commonly followed pattern is the topical pattern. Here, you divide the topic into some logical themes or categories. For example, when you want to present a proposal on a new timely inventory system, you can divide the major benefits of this system into three or four categories and present them one by one.

**Cause and effect pattern** You may like to discuss the causes of conflict escalation in the organizational teams and the resultant effects in your presentation. The first part of your speech may explain how and why conflicts are on the rise. The second part could discuss the effects of conflicts on the progress and the environment of the organization. Having organized the topic in the cause and effect pattern, you can now follow two approaches—either presenting the causes first and then the effects, or vice versa.

> A chronological pattern is one in which the points are arranged in the way in which they occurred or were observed.

**Problem and solution pattern**   Akin to the cause and effect pattern is the problem and solution pattern, which also divides information into two main sections, one that describes a problem, and the other a solution. This pattern is typically used in persuasive speaking where your general purpose is to convince the listener to support a certain course of action. The pattern is designed to compel the listener to make some kind of a change in opinion or behaviour by establishing that a problem exists, then providing a solution. In the problem section, you present different aspects of the problems being discussed and offer evidence of these problems. In the solution section, you discuss a potential solution and support its effectiveness over others.

**Climactic pattern**   In a climactic pattern or order of importance, items are arranged from the least important to the most important. For example, while presenting the details of an accomplished project, you may start from the basics, and slowly take the audience through the various stages of the project. This is a flexible pattern, and may guide the organization of all or part of an example, comparison or contrast, cause and effect, or description.

You have understood that speeches must have an organizational structure. An organizational structure or pattern makes the speech easier to understand. Though there exist several patterns in which you can organize your presentation, the type of pattern you choose will depend upon the topic and purpose of your speech.

## Delivery

Successful and inspiring speakers are remembered not only because they are eloquent, humourous, or have a good style, but primarily and principally because their message and ideas cause a change in their audience's actions, attitudes, lives, or make the purpose clear to them.

The statement mentioned above is true for all types of presentations—business presentations, business speeches, classroom lectures, and so on, especially in an age of instantaneous communication via telephone, computer, and fax. Face-to-face business presentations are enormous time consumers—from scheduling a date when everyone can attend to making every arrangement necessary for the presentation, it takes much more time and effort than it would have taken to send the same message as an attachment to an email, in the form of a memorandum, circular, or notice. Nevertheless, presentations still play an important role in business for obvious and good reasons. Face-to-face presentations have many advantages. If delivered effectively and efficiently, they can capture the audience's attention without the risk of being shuffled aside. You can reveal your enthusiasm to the audience better than any other means of presentation and can also address their questions or objections directly. Hence, it is important to know certain ideas related to delivering your presentations. The discussion that follows provides you not only with these ideas but also with some suggestions so as to enable you to deliver business presentations with greater effectiveness.

### *Types of Delivery*

Selecting one particular mode of delivery, or a combination of modes, is an important task for the preparatory stage, as this selection has bearings on the way in which you need to prepare the presentation. Business presentations can be delivered in any of the following four modes:

- Speaking from notes
- Speaking impromptu
- Reciting from memory
- Reading from a manuscript

**Speaking from notes** This mode of delivery, alternatively known as extemporaneous delivery, is planned and rehearsed, though not word for word. You can deliver your presentations with the help of outlines, note cards, or visual aids. You have a good chance of delivering an extemporaneous speech that appears spontaneous and effortless to the audience, if you plan and prepare carefully and rehearse your presentation several times in front of a mirror, your friends, or colleagues. Practically every business presentation—a project report to be presented to the management committee, a sales presentation, or a key note address to be delivered at a conference—should be delivered extemporaneously if you want them to have an impact on your audience.

The advantages of extemporaneous presentations are as follows:

*Conversational quality* With their own control over language, speakers sound spontaneous.

*Adaptability* It is often used for a wide range of situations because of its effectiveness.

*Control* Speakers have a more precise control over ideas and language.

*Effective non-verbal cues* Speakers will be able to freely use the non-verbal cues appropriate to the situation, as they are not restricted by the language in a written manuscript.

**Speaking impromptu** Unexpected, off-the-cuff talks are categorized as impromptu presentations. For example, you may discover all of a sudden at a weekly meeting that your subordinates are unaware of a process, the knowledge of which is necessary to understand the new project that your division is going to take up. To meet such unforeseen demands, you may have to deliver an impromptu talk. Similarly, you may be asked at a gathering to 'say a few words' or your superior may suddenly ask you to give a background to some problem.

In most business situations, you may be asked to talk about something that you know, or on a subject within your expertise—a problem that you have solved, project that you have undertaken, technical aspect of your area of expertise, etc.

It is possible to give impromptu presentations by applying the following guidelines:

*Anticipate that you may be asked to speak* Experienced businesspeople always know the questions they may be asked during a particular discussion. For instance, a senior marketing executive would know the explanations he may have to give on the market survey that he was be involved in. Even if you are new in your company, you may be able to think about the possible points which your boss may ask you to explain if he calls you for a discussion. In any case, if you prepare yourself, just in case you are asked to speak, your remarks will be more effective.

*Decide immediately upon the points to be spoken* As soon as you are invited to speak, take a minute or half to think of two or three points—one main and a few supporting—that you would like to make. If you are asked to speak at a large gathering, you may think about the points while proceeding towards the dais or podium.

*Present your viewpoint* Let the audience know your definite viewpoint at the outset. If you are asked to convey your opinion on a purchase and you give importance to the cost, state your view on the cost first. If you are not sure of your opinion, you can say, 'I'm not very sure about the cost-effectiveness of this purchase. I think we need to compare it with the purchase we made last week.' Then, provide some evidence to support your specific view. You can say, 'As I recall, last week's purchase was less expensive by about 10 per cent, though the quality was better.'

*Be as brief as possible* Impromptu messages should be kept as short as possible to avoid any exposure of your ignorance about a particular issue. Some people continue to talk even after explaining their specific viewpoint. Brevity is an important characteristic of all impromptu speeches, whether it deals with your remarks on a project or your best wishes at a farewell dinner to a retiring employee.

> Brevity is an important characteristic of all impromptu speeches.

**Speaking from memory** This is, by far, the most difficult of all the four modes of delivery. Unless you are a trained performer, avoid memorizing your speech as you are likely to forget your lines and the speech will end up sounding stilted. You might have noticed some novice speakers who fail to make purposeful eye contact with their audience when they try to recall sentences. They often focus on the ceiling or a particular location in the hall every time they search their memory, losing rapport with their audience. However, memorizing a quotation, a story, an incident, or an opening/concluding remark always strengthens your delivery.

**Reading from a manuscript** Some business presentations require verbatim reading from the manuscript. You may be aware that presidents and prime ministers read from a text when they deliver some important messages to the nation because the omission or addition of some word/s may be interpreted differently by their audience. Similarly, while delivering a highly technical or complex presentation for business purposes, you may want to use this mode. Some important decisions of the courts of law, policy statements by government, etc. are to be read out, rather than paraphrased.

### Guidelines for Delivery

The success of a business presentation depends on the various elements—verbal, non-verbal, vocal, and visual—used during your presentation (Fig. 11.3).

**Verbal elements** These elements are categorized as follows:

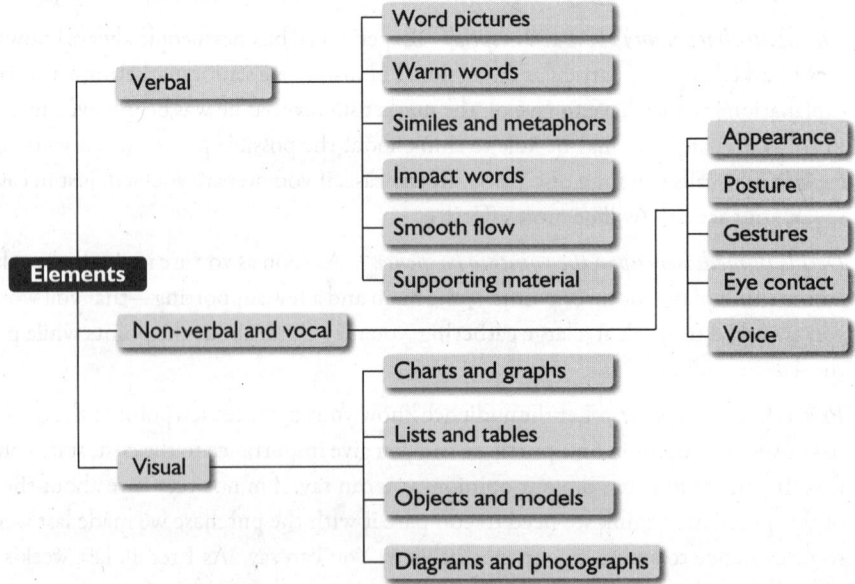

**Fig. 11.3** Guidelines for delivery

*Word pictures* Give your speech a graphic quality, by painting word pictures that allow an audience's own imagination to take over. Specific details allow an audience to see the scenes you are describing. Your major job as a speaker is to tell somebody something. Present your point clearly and just enough so that the listener clearly understands the message you intended. The task is not merely to get words out of your mouth, but to transfer ideas into the listeners' minds.

*Warm words* Cold words leave us uneasy and unsure while warm words make us feel secure and comfortable. Words are powerful. They conjure images, evoke emotions, and trigger responses deep within us and we react, often without knowing why.

In the early days of instant coffee, advertisers got off to a bad start by stressing words like 'quick', 'time-saving', and 'efficient'. These are all words without warmth and feeling. Makers of fresh coffee fought back with warm, happy, and appetizing words like 'aroma', 'fresh', and 'tasty'. The instant coffee industry learnt the lesson and its product became 'delicious', 'rich', and 'satisfying'. Sales soon boomed.

Words also suggest that something is good or bad. Use words that strengthen your arguments and weaken those of your opponents. For example, look at the following words:

| **Good** | **Bad** |
|---|---|
| Independent | Unaccountable |
| Well-regulated | Red tape |
| Free-thinking | Wishy-washy |
| Appropriately rewarded | Fat cat |

*Similes and metaphors* Although technical presentations do not require the use of similes and metaphors, we cannot deny the fact that they not only add flavour to a business speech but also make abstract ideas imaginable. Reach for vivid comparisons your listeners can understand and remember. Try the following metaphors in your business speeches:

> As inflexible as an epitaph
> As cold as outer space

> You can also make your speech flow smoothly and gracefully from beginning to end by using some transitional devices.

Building a business is like building an empire
As profitable as a gold mine
Delay is the deadliest form of denial

*Impact words*   'We' and 'you' are the most important words of all. You cannot stir the audience up if you do not address them directly and relate them to you and your topic. Remember the five-to-one rule—every time you use the singular 'I', try to follow it with five plurals. Given below are some words that you may use in your business presentations or speeches to get desired results:

discovery, guarantee, love, proven, safely, easy, health, vigour, money, results, save, protect, interest, challenge, opportunity, excitement, enthusiasm, flourish, progress, favorable, adaptation, circumstances

*Smooth flow*   You can also make your speech flow smoothly and gracefully from beginning to end by using some transitional devices. They promote clarity, emphasize important ideas, and sustain your listeners' interest. Some transitional devices are discussed as follows:

1. A *bridge* is a word that alerts your audience that you are changing direction or moving to a new thought. Some examples are as follows:

   We completed the project in January. *Meanwhile* other developments were taking place.
   That was bad enough. *However,* there was even worse to come.

2. A *number item* keeps your listeners informed about where you are in a presentation that covers several points. Two examples are as follows:

   The *first* advantage of the new plan is. ...
   A *second* benefit of the plan is. ...

3. A *trigger* is a repetition of the same word or phrase to link one topic with another. An example is as follows:

   That was what the debtor situation was *like* in March. Now I will tell you what it is *like* today.

4. An *interjection* is a word or phrase used into a commentary to highlight the importance or placement of an idea. Some examples are as follows:

   So what we have learned—*and this is important*—is that, it is impossible to control personal use of office telephones.
   Now here is another feature—*perhaps the best of all*—that makes this such a terrific plan.

5. *Internal summary* helps your audience stay oriented by providing a one-sentence summary during the course of delivering the main text of your presentation. An example is as follows:

   Now, you can see that the problem grew from several causes—a shortage of parts, inexperienced maintenance people, and the overload of opening a new warehouse.

> A rhetorical question can subtly change the direction of the discussion.

6. An *internal preview*, like an internal summary, orients an audience by alerting listeners to the upcoming points. An example is as follows:

   > You are probably wondering how all these changes will affect you. Well, some of them will make life much easier, and others will present some challenges. Let us look at three advantages first, and then we will look at a couple of those challenges I mentioned.

7. A *rhetorical question* can subtly change the direction of the discussion. An example is as follows:

   > That is what a change of image can do to a company. *So how can we improve our image?*

8. A *flashback* is a sudden shift/reference to the past, and breaks what seems to be a predictable narrative. An example is as follows:

   > Today, we are the market leader. However, *three years ago*, this was not the case.

9. A *list* is a very simple way of combining apparently unrelated elements. An example is as follows:

   > We made *four* attempts to solve the problem.

10. A *pause* is a non-verbal method of showing your audience that you have finished a section of your speech and you are about to move on to another.

11. *Physical movements* towards a visual aid such as a black/white board, flip chart, or screen suggest that you are moving on to something new.

12. A *quotation*, *anecdote*, or *joke* can serve as an excellent link. A joke may be a good link to an idea that one may wish to take up next. Consider the following joke:

    > The Chairman told me a story of a job applicant who said, 'I like the job, sounds fine, but the last place I worked at, paid more, gave more overtime, more bonuses, subsidies, travel allowances, holidays with pay, and generous pension schemes.' The Chairman said, 'Why did you leave?' The applicant answered, 'The firm went broke.'

*Supporting material*  Solid ideas will not always impress your audience. You need to back up your well-organized points in a way that makes the audience notice, understand, and accept your message. In other words, you need to use plenty of supporting material or develop your core points adequately.

Supporting material not only clarifies the main ideas, but also makes them more vivid and meaningful to your audience. In addition, they prove your main statement (Table 11.2).

Several kinds of supporting material are given in the following list (Table 11.3):

1. When you deliver your presentation on a topic that you feel that your audience is not too familiar with, you can use a *definition* to develop your idea. Let us look at the following short paragraph to illustrate how to use definition as a supporting material:

   > Harvesting, most often, *refers to selling a business or product line*, as when a company sells a product line or division or a family sells a business. Harvesting is *also*

**Table 11.2** Examples of supporting material

| Main Statement | Supporting Statement |
|---|---|
| Replacing the lens in the laser projector is not as complicated as it seems. | Let me show a diagram that demonstrates how to do it. |
| We could increase sales by extending the time until late in the evening. | An article in *Business Today* cites statistics showing that shops that extended their working hours to 10 p.m., boost profits by more than 20 per cent of the direct overheads involved with longer business day. |
| Our HR unit could develop the academic skills of our junior executives. | For example, Wipro supports its newly-inducted executives to further their education through the off-campus programs offered by BITS, Pilani. |

occasionally used to refer to sales of a product or product line towards the end of a product life-cycle.

2. Vivid and concrete *examples* have more impact on listeners' beliefs and actions than any other kind of supporting material. Without examples, the ideas you present may often seem vague, impersonal, and lifeless. When you give examples, the same ideas become specific, personal, and lively. Almost all effective speakers use examples in their presentations. The following

**Table 11.3** Kinds of supporting material

| Type | Definition | Function | Speech Occasions | Tips |
|---|---|---|---|---|
| Definition | Explaining difficult term(s) with the help of simple terms | To clarify | Used in informative/technical presentations | Use easy and known terms |
| Example | A brief reference that illustrates a point | To clarify and add interest | Used in all types of presentations | Use situations with which your audience may be familiar |
| Statistics | Quantification of the main point | To clarify, prove, and add interest | Used widely in presentations where sales figures, survey results, etc. are to be explained | Round off the numbers, support with visuals, and explain adequately |
| Analogy | Process that shows how one idea resembles another | To clarify, add interest, and prove | Used in business presentations involving products, processes, and procedures | Make the comparisons vivid; select familiar analogies |
| Testimony | Opinion of experts, peers, or celebrities | To clarify, add interest, and prove | Used in sales presentations | Memorize/paraphrase/read verbatim, cite source, use sources credible to your audience, and follow-up with re-statement or explanation |

excerpt from the talk delivered by Azim Premji, Chairman, Wipro Corporation, reveals how effectively an example can be used in presentations to drive home your point:

> The difference between great achievement and mediocrity is not extraordinary talent or intelligence, but perseverance. In fact, dreams and perseverance make a winning combination.
>
> In 1972, a chartered plane, carrying a Rugby team, crashed in the Andes. After a week-long futile search, the rescue team gave up, thinking that all of them must be dead. The passengers, after waiting for many days to be rescued, decided to help themselves, since apparently nobody else was going to do it. Two of them volunteered to cross the mountains by foot to reach the green valleys of Chile and bring back help. It was a walk of more than 50 miles. But they did it and came back to rescue their fellow passengers who managed to survive in the mountain 70 days after the crash.
>
> The core of heroism lies in the ability to walk that extra mile. As long as you can do that, you will never be defeated.
>
> *Source:* Address by Shri Azim Premji, Chairman, Wipro Corporation, at the annual convocation of the Indian Institute of Management, Kolkata at 2:15 p.m. on 3 April 2004 on 'Continuous Transformation'.

3. *Statistics* refer to the use of numbers to represent an idea or data explaining something in terms of size or frequency. They are probably the most common form of supporting material used in business presentations. They are used in presentations related to sales trends, sweeping change in profits, size of market segments, and many other aspects of business. Most statistics are collections of examples reduced to numerical form for clarity and easy comprehension of a complex idea. When handled well, statistics are especially helpful, because they are firmly based on facts and show that the speaker is well-informed. Consider the excerpt from the speech of Aditya Vikram Birla, 'Let the Competition be Afraid of Us', delivered at a conference organized by *Euromoney* on 22 March 1994 in New Delhi.

> We also have a vast bank of talent, with over 3.5 million scientific and technical personnel, trained in the English language, of a quality and at a cost unmatched. India has a well-developed capital market. We have 21 stock exchanges with over 2,000 actively traded scripts, compared to 220 in Indonesia, 354 in Thailand, 423 in Malaysia, 235 in Singapore, and 181 in the Philippines. China—one doesn't know.

Using statistics as evidence has, of course, its over share of problems. Statistics are powerful; however, they can be easily manipulated. When evaluating statistics, always consider the source. Compare your statistics to others—seek multiple sources—to ensure they are accurate. When presenting statistics, quote the statistics completely, and use only current information.

4. An *analogy* can make a point by showing how one idea resembles another. Analogies compare items from an unfamiliar area with items from a familiar

> The strength of your analogy lies in your choice of the points of comparison and the effectiveness with which you deliver it to your audience.

area. For example, when you are taking a shower and someone turns on another faucet at the washbasin. The flow of water drops for everybody. A similar thing happens with the flow of data over a cable modem connection—when more people are using the system, the speed at which the data flows is slower.

Whenever you propose adopting a policy or using an idea because it works well somewhere else, you can use comparisons. Business presenters mostly use literal comparisons that link similar items from two categories. Look at how N.R. Narayanmurthy, Chairman and CEO, Infosys Technologies Ltd, uses comparison as a device to explain his idea pertaining to professionalism in India and the western countries in the following excerpt:

> Yet another lesson to be learnt from the West is about their professionalism in dealings. The common good being more important than personal equations, people do not let personal relations interfere with their professional dealings. *For instance, they don't hesitate to chastise a colleague, even if he is a personal friend, for incompetent work. In India, I have seen that we tend to view even work interactions from a personal perspective.* Further, we are the most 'thin-skinned' society in the world—we see insults where none are meant. This may be because we were not free for most of the last thousand years.
>
> Source: Excerpt from a lecture delivered at the Lal Bahadur Shastri Institute of Management, New Delhi, on 1 October 2002.

Whether the purpose of using an analogy is to add clarity, interest, or proof, you should ensure that the familiar part of comparisons are well known to your audience and make sure that your comparisons are valid. The strength of your analogy lies in your choice of the points of comparison and the effectiveness with which you deliver it to your audience.

5. *Testimonies* are remarks made by others who are authoritative or articulate and could make a point more effectively than you could, on your own. For instance, when Piyush Pandey, Executive Chairman and Creative Director of Ogilvy & Mather's India and South Asia operations, says something about advertising, people will accept it without question because he is an authority in the field of advertising. For example, if you had to add punch to your talk on a comparative study of Asian and western advertising you could quote him as follows:

   > Asian advertising has stopped aping the West and is evolving a style of its own based on different cultures in the region. There is more self-confidence, and therefore more fresh ideas.
   >
   > Source: *Asia Times*, 27 September 2003.

   Other testimonies include: remarks made by a celebrity who may be a non-expert in the field, an article written by a relatively unknown person in a journal or newspaper, some good arguments put forth by your colleagues/relatives/professors, etc. They also help build a persuasive case.

   Whenever you use a testimony in your presentation, cite the source and quote verbatim if it is short. If it is lengthy or confusing, you should try to paraphrase.

   **Non-verbal elements** Your appearance, facial expressions, eye contact, postures, and gestures—all communicate your interest, enthusiasm, dynamism, intention, and

> Non-verbal elements communicate your interest, enthusiasm, dynamism, intention, and confidence to your audience.

confidence to your audience. Whatever the occasion, the following tips will help you to use non-verbal cues effectively during your presentation:

*Appearance* Though appearance is important in any setting, how you dress is even more important when you stand in front of an audience for delivering a message. However, dressing effectively does not always mean dressing up. If the occasion calls for casual attire, an overly formal appearance can be inappropriate.

*Posture* The best stance for delivering a presentation is relaxed, but firm. Your feet should be planted firmly on the ground, and spaced at shoulder-width. Your body should face your audience with your head upright, turning naturally to look at them.

Moving about can add life to your presentation and help you release nervous energy. You can move towards the visual aids, walk away from them, return to your original position, and then approach your audience.

You may have observed that many business presentations are delivered in small groups of 5–6 employees or potential customers. On such occasions, you may have to remain seated during the presentation. Sit straight and lean forward, as lounging back in your chair indicates indifference. Sit naturally in a posture that reveals your dynamism and interest, much as you sit while conversing with your friends.

*Gestures* People are more likely to pay attention to what we are showing them from the stage, rather than what we are telling them. So, our words and our body language must be in sync. Gestures should enhance—not distract from—the message. Remember the following hints during your next presentation:

- Gesture in your personal power zone: It is the length of your arm span, out in front of you and above your head. The gestures may feel 'big' at first, but they will look natural to your audience.
- Refrain from pointing at your audience.
- Resist the temptation to stick your hands in your pockets or behind your back. Your audience may think you are hiding something from them.

*Eye contact* Whether you are proposing an innovative, new product line, reassuring your employees about the effects of recent budget cuts, or trying to explain to your customers that your company is not involved in a scandal, your impression on the audience can determine your ultimate success. The impression that brings in success is possible to cultivate only when you talk directly to your audience, sharing your involvement and sincerity.

Make real, rather than desultory, eye contact with individuals in your audience, as if you are talking one-on-one with each person for three to five seconds. Divide the room into quadrants and alternate your focus to avoid favouring one side of the room (a common tendency among amateur presenters). If the audience is too large for you to make eye contact with each one, select a few people in different parts of the hall, making eye contact with each one for a few seconds.

**Vocal elements** Your voice can serve as an important tool to support your verbal message. How you sound is as important as how you look or what you say (Image 11.2). Your vocal elements, namely the tone, pitch, rate, and volume reflect your attitude about yourself, your message, and your audience. Try the following tips to help you use your vocal elements to enhance the impact of your presentation:

**314** Business Communication

**Image 11.2** How you sound is as important as how you look

- Speak with enthusiasm and sincerity
- Adjust the volume of your voice
- Avoid disfluencies or vocalized pauses
- Use your optimal pitch
- Avoid fast delivery
- Use silence and pauses effectively
- Articulate each word clearly

**Visual elements**   Your audience will remember facts easily if the ideas are connected to right brain stimulation. The way to simulate the right brain is to show pictures. Visual stimuli are more effective than verbal stimuli. For example, you often recall the colour of the cover of a book rather than its title and subtitle.

*Advantages*   People find your message more interesting, grasp it more easily, and retain it longer when you use visual support along with your words. Besides increasing the clarity of the message, visuals make presentations more interesting. For example, investment brokers often use an array of well-prepared charts, tables, models, and so on to add variety to information that would be dull without them.

Graphics can also boost your image in ways that extend beyond the presentation. They add a professional flavour to your presentation. Finally, your audience remembers a visual message longer than a verbal message.

*Types*   Charts, maps, diagrams, photographs, and other visual aids are part of most business presentations. As a speaker, you can choose from a wide array of visual aids to make your presentations more effective. Some of these aids are as follows:

- Lists and tables
- Charts and graphs
- Objects and models
- Diagrams and photographs

1. *Lists and tables* provide a way to organize related information so that users can easily make comparisons of the data and highlight key facts and figures These are especially effective when you list steps, highlight features, or compare related facts.

A list is a set of choices from which a user can select one or more items. Items in a list can be text, graphics, or both. You can use a list to present users with a set of exclusive or non-exclusive choices.

A table is a two-dimensional arrangement of data in rows and columns, which is particularly useful for displaying precise numerical data. The purpose of a table is to present complex data, to demonstrate patterns and relationships, and to present exact data. For example, a sales manager might use a table to compare this year's sales performance with last year's in several regions. However, a personnel officer explaining the advantages and disadvantages of two different health insurance plans available to employees might use a list or table to help individual employees decide which plan might work best for them.

As you design lists and tables for presentation, consider the following tips in mind:

> - Visual stimuli are more effective than verbal stimuli.
> - Graphics add a professional flavour to your presentation.

> Pie charts have the advantage of allowing the audience to quickly visualize proportional relationships.

- Keep the visuals simple; list only highlights; and use only key words or phrases, never full sentences.
- Use numbered and/or bulleted lists to emphasize key points—numbered lists suggest ranking of steps in a process, while bulleted lists work best for items that are equally important.
- Use text sparingly. If you need more than eight lines of text, create two or more tables. Lines of text should never exceed 25 characters across, including spaces.
- Use large fonts. Make sure that the words and numbers are large enough to be read by everyone in the audience.
- Enhance the list's or table's readability. Careful layout and generous use of white space will make it easy to read.

2. *Charts and graphs* are useful for comparing data, after you have organized the information for a presentation. The comparison you make ultimately determines the type of graphic to use. For example, a bar chart is an obvious choice for comparing data across a number of years, and a pie chart efficiently shows the relationship of parts of a whole. Figure 11.4 shows different types of charts and graphs. Essentially, there are five choices:

- Correlation to the whole as percentage (pie chart)
- Comparing items at one point in time (horizontal bar chart)
- Change over time (vertical bar or line graph)
- Intervals between events (vertical column or histogram frequency distribution charts)
- Correlation between two variables (scatter graph)

Pie charts compare the parts to the whole and visually display percentages and proportions. The circular pie chart represents the whole and the size of each wedge of the pie shows the components share. Pie charts have the advantage of allowing the audience to quickly visualize proportional relationships.

Bar graphs consist of simple horizontal or vertical bars, each representing one type of data. They use various lengths (but equal widths) to show different value, so that they can be compared.

Line graphs show continuous change over time. The ordinate ($Y$-axis) typically depicts quantity and the abscissa ($X$-axis) depicts time. By plotting several lines on the same graph, it is possible to compare the trends of several variables.

Scatter graphs consist of dots on a graph that can be used as analytical tools. The dots usually represent the intersection of two bits of data showing the relationship of one variable to another.

For many oral presentations, the audience does not have the benefit of accompanying text. To simplify information for listeners, keep the following points in mind:

> - Scatter graphs consist of dots on a graph that can be used as analytical tools.
> - Diagrams and photographs are graphics used to present a visual picture of the topic under discussion.

- Do not overload your presentation with charts and graphs.
- Keep your charts and graphs simple.
- Use upper and lower case letters, rather than all capitals. They make the type easier to read.
- Keep the focus on the audience, not on the visual.

3. *Objects and models* are often used to convey an idea of the object under discussion or to give an accurate idea about a real model. This is especially

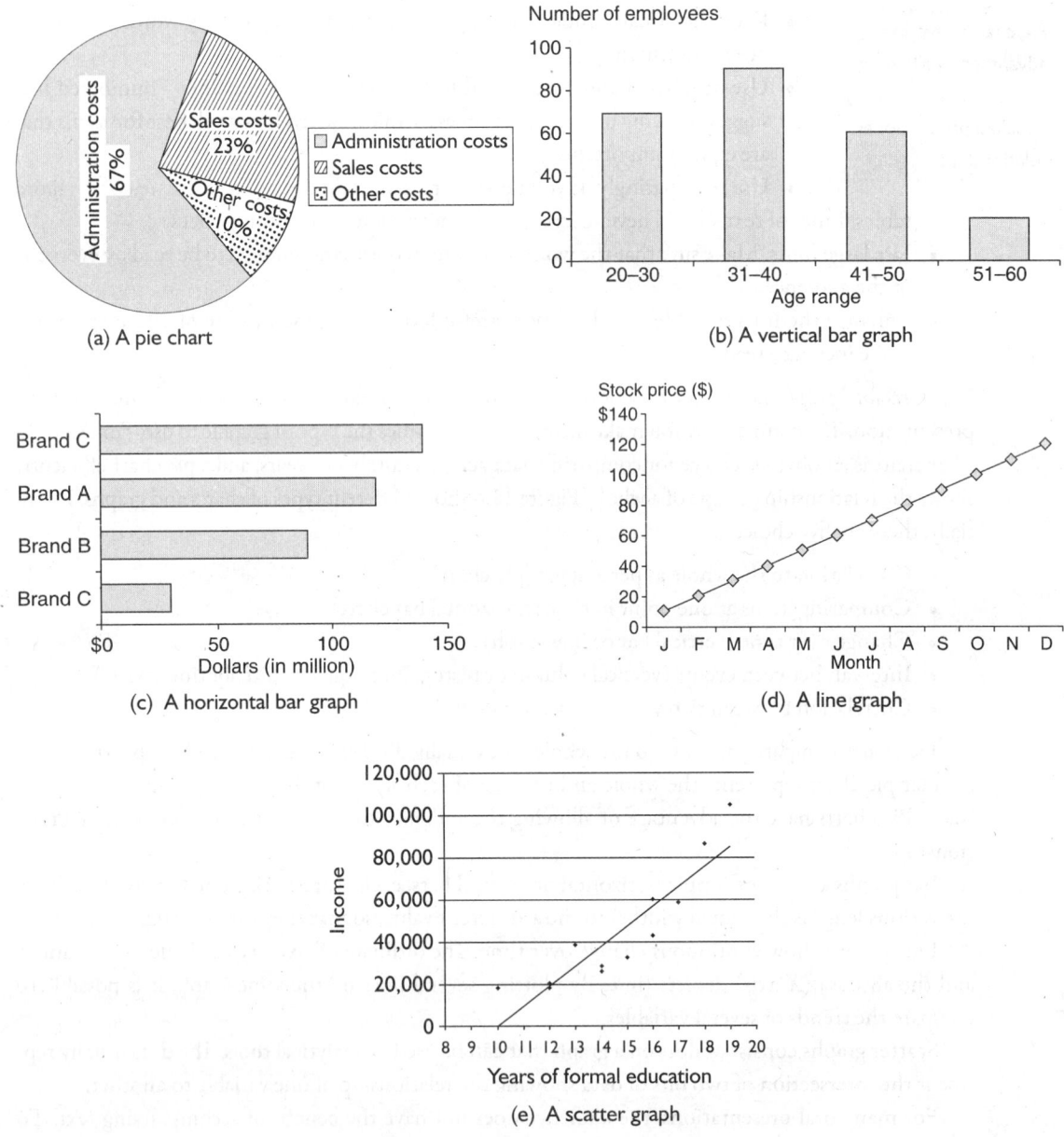

**Fig. 11.4** Different types of graphs and charts

true in training sessions and in some types of selling, where hands-on experience is essential. It is difficult to imagine learning how to operate a piece of equipment without actually trying it, and few customers would buy an expensive, unfamiliar piece of merchandise without seeing it demonstrated.

4. *Diagrams and photographs* are graphics used to present a visual picture of the topic(s) under discussion. They add colour and, if used properly, greatly enhance the quality of the presentation.

## Business Presentations and Public Speaking

> Time lines provide historical perspectives or assist with future planning.

Diagrams are graphic attempts to simplify and explain the relationships of component parts or stages of a process or structure. They can

- emphasize the flow of processes over time or depict a hierarchical order of relationships
- make labels compact to conserve space (within the diagram)

Organizational diagrams show relative positions, roles, and responsibilities within an organization. Time lines provide historical perspectives or assist with future planning. Exploded diagrams show parts and details that are usually hidden. Maps and floor plans that include data as symbols or shading are some other examples of useful diagrams. Figure 11.5 shows a flow chart showing an organizational hierarchy. In general, diagrams can be used to show

- ideas, facts, priorities, and processes
- where things are located or how they work
- relationships, when quantitative information is not the primary focus

*Media for presenting visual aids*  Choosing the most advantageous way to present your visual aids is just as important as picking the right typeface. The best photograph, chart, or diagram will flop if it is not displayed effectively. The following means could come in handy:

1. *Flip charts* consist of a large pad of paper attached to an easel. You reveal visuals on a flip chart one at a time by turning the pages. You can also produce visuals on rigid *poster boards*, which you can display on the same sort of easel.

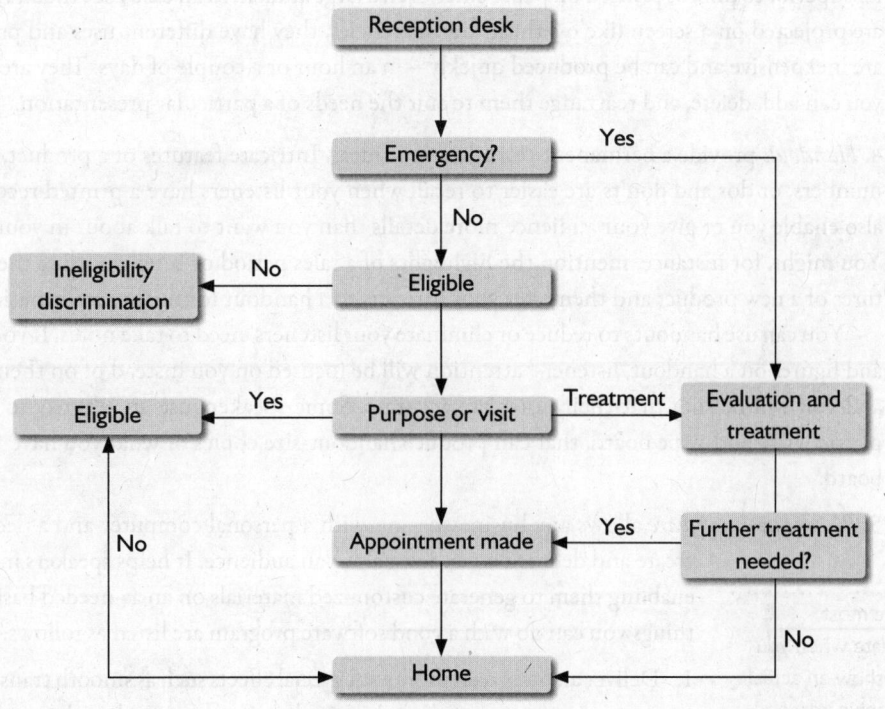

**Fig. 11.5**  A flow chart

> A major advantage of flip charts and poster displays is that they are relatively simple to prepare and easy to use.

A major advantage of flip charts and poster displays is that they are relatively simple to prepare and easy to use. You can create them with familiar materials—pens, rulers, and so on. They are relatively portable (most easels collapse into a carrying case) and easy to set up. They do not require electrical equipment, which can break down or be useless if the electricity goes.

2. *Transparencies* are clear sheets that are used with an overhead projector to cast an image on a screen. They are frequently the chosen visual aids when the audience is too large for flip charts or poster displays.

You can create original images with special pens or reproduce visuals from other sources by using a standard copying machine equipped with special acetate sheets. You can use a slide projector as well as an overhead machine.

Transparencies have several advantages, which are as follows:

1. They can be produced quickly.
2. They can be projected to a large size for all members of a large audience to see.
3. They are visible in a lighted room.
4. Using special pens, you can draw on them as you speak, underlining key words, circling important numbers, completing graphs, and so on. After the presentation, you can erase your additions and reuse the same sheets.
5. They are easy to store and do not wear out like flip charts and poster boards.

3. *Slides* are most appropriate when you want to show an actual photographic image. They are often far superior to photos printed on paper since even a large audience can easily see them. Although slides are projected on a screen like overhead transparencies, they have different uses and properties. They are inexpensive and can be produced quickly—in an hour or a couple of days. They are easy to edit—you can add, delete, and rearrange them to suit the needs of a particular presentation.

4. *Handouts* provide a permanent record of your ideas. Intricate features of a product, names, phone numbers, or dos and don'ts are easier to recall when your listeners have a printed record. Handouts also enable you to give your audience more details than you want to talk about in your presentation. You might, for instance, mention the highlights of a sales period or briefly outline the technical features of a new product and then refer your listeners to a handout for further information.

You can use handouts to reduce or eliminate your listeners' need to take notes. If you put key ideas and figures on a handout, listeners' attention will be focused on you instead of on their notebooks—and you will be sure that their notes are accurate. Some speakers use an 'electronic blackboard', a plastic write-and-wipe board, that can produce handout-size copies of what you have written on the board.

5. *Presentation software* allows any businessperson with a personal computer and a decent printer to create and deliver text and visuals to an audience. It helps speakers in many ways by enabling them to generate customized materials on an as-needed basis. Some of the things you can do with a good software program are listed as follows:

> Slides are most appropriate when you want to show an actual photographic image.

1. Deliver an on-screen show with special effects such as smooth transitions between screens, animation, and synchronized timing that reveals each point as you raise it.

# Business Presentations and Public Speaking

2. Create visuals in many formats, including slides, overhead transparencies, and screen output.
3. Prepare a variety of handouts for your audience, based on your speaking notes or displays.
4. Create charts, graphs, and tables.

*Guidelines for using visual aids*   Whether you are using handouts, poster boards, flip charts, transparencies, slides, chalkboard, or computerized display, be sure to follow the basic rules discussed as follows:

1. *Selection*   As with any part of your presentation, visual exhibits must be chosen with care.

2. *Appropriateness*   Visuals, used for their own sake, will distract your audience from the point that you are trying to make.

3. *Simplicity*   Show only one idea per exhibit and avoid unnecessary details. If an exhibit needs further explanation, supply it verbally.

4. *Condense*   Most exhibits are visual images, so you should avoid excessive text. Captions should contain only key words or phrases, not sentences. Omit subtitles. Follow the 'Rule of Seven': each slide should contain no more than seven lines, and each line should have no more than seven words. Use simple typefaces. If a visual needs more explanation, supply it orally.

5. *Label*   Make sure each exhibit has a descriptive title. Label each axis of a chart, each part of a diagram, and so on.

6. *Using colour*   Colour is one of the biggest reasons why visual presentations have such enormous impact. When used correctly, colours can help audience sort out the various elements of a slide, add interest to a presentation, highlight important points, and add to the 'professional quality' of visuals. However, remember that a slide is a supplement to your presentation, and it should not distract from it. Therefore, keep the text the same colour from line to line and slide to slide. Similarly, the titles and subtitles should be the same colour from slide to slide. It is permissible to alter the colour of an occasional word for emphasis (e.g., a red word in a string of black text).

## INTRODUCTION TO A PRESENTATION

The introduction to a presentation is as important as the foundation of a house. It gathers ideas together to separate them from the rest of the information in the world, and it unites those chosen ideas into a thesis. A separate unit from the body of the essay, the introduction should grab the reader's or audience's attention and introduce the main idea through the thesis statement.

To understand the introduction you need to understand its function in the presentation, and the various components that constitute an effective introduction.

### Function of an Introduction

An effective introduction serves the main purpose of preparing the audience for what is coming up, and of establishing the purpose of your talk. In other words, your introduction should arouse the audience's interest in your topic and lead towards what you are going to talk about.

## Components of an Introduction

An introduction sets the tone of the entire speech. The main components of an effective introduction are as follows:

- Attention-getters
- Thesis statement
- Audience adaptation
- Credibility statement
- Preview

### *Attention-getters*

No matter how effective a presenter you are, or how important your topic is, you can quickly lose an audience if you do not use your introduction to grab their attention and arouse interest. It is, therefore, essential for you to begin your presentation by grabbing their attention. You have to sound interesting and establish the right tone. You have to ensure that the opening remarks are related to the topic. For example, when you are giving an internal presentation to your colleagues with whom you are familiar, you can begin your speech on the steps involved in cutting the costs, like the following:

> You would be pleased to know that we have made fairly good progress on formulating our cost-cutting expenses as instructed by our VP. We have found that it is possible to reduce our operating expenses by almost ten per cent without compromising on efficiency. Let me introduce you to the five steps involved in this process.

On the other hand, when you are presenting to an unfamiliar group with diverse backgrounds, you would like to start by grabbing their attention before you present your topic preview. The attention-getter is designed to intrigue the audience and motivate them to listen attentively for the next several minutes. Most importantly, an attention-getter should create curiosity in the minds of the listeners, and convince them that the speech that follows will be interesting and useful.

Following is an array of attention-getting devices from which you can choose the one that suits your topic:

- A story
- A question
- A quotation
- A startling statement
- Humour
- Reference to audience
- Reference to occasion

**Story or personal experience**  Most people enjoy a good story. So, beginning your presentation with a story or personal experience may prove to be effective. Imagine that your company has decided to move its office to some new location, you are in charge of this move, and you are standing in front of a gathering of the divisional managers of your company to present the topic, 'Office Move'. You have come up with all the details regarding the location, size, and cost along with a comparative study with the existing office for this presentation.

**Question**  Rhetorical questions are designed to arouse curiosity without requiring an answer. Many speakers use this device to begin their presentations. Let us take the same example of the topic 'Office Move'. If you want to begin your presentation with a question, you may start as follows:

> How many of you have moved house in recent years? How many of you know when our company moved last?

When you want to present a talk on, 'Setting Up a Training Division', you can begin by asking a series of questions, as follows:

> Does training matter? Is it not essential to have a highly-skilled workforce? Should we not spend a few minutes thinking about this?

Here, when you ask the first question, if you notice some hands rising among the audience, acknowledge the same and then move to your second question.

**Quotation** A quotation from a famous person or from an expert on your topic can make a catchy introduction. The quotation immediately launches you into the speech and draws audience focus to your topic. For example, if as the personnel manager of your company, you would like to automate all the procedures in various divisions. However, you know that your company has some managers who do not believe in depending on technology. Your presentation on 'Office Automation' can then start with the following quote by Bill Gates:

> The first rule of any technology used in business is that automation applied to an efficient operation will magnify the efficiency. The second is that automation applied to an inefficient operation will magnify the inefficiency.

**Startling statement** You may choose to secure audience attention by shocking the audience. People tend to focus on that which is amazing or unique. Startling statements or events, shocking facts or statistics, are effective for engaging audience attention. For instance, producing a good product is no longer enough. Today, people expect, or indeed deserve, excellent customer care. When someone says to you that pleasing a customer is hard, you could ask them:

> Compared to what? To having to find new ones? Believe me, it is far harder to get new customers than to take good care of the existing ones. Yet, even so, we have lost six out of every ten customers who were on our books five years ago.

**Humour** Yet another effective way of catching your audience's attention, making a point, and increasing your audience's liking for you is beginning with the right joke. Humour is an effective attention-getter, and it can be used to motivate people and influence an organization's culture. It also helps people relax, which facilitates learning.

Humour helps lighten the atmosphere, and allows you to make your next point after becoming more comfortable with your audience. Jokes are not the only humourous openers. You can sometimes use cartoons, amusing remarks, or humourous definitions that will set the tone perfectly for your message.

**Reference to audience** Opening your presentation by mentioning your audience's needs, concerns, or interests clarifies the relevance of your topic immediately and shows that you understand them. A senior executive, who addresses the employees with a purpose of dispelling the rumours floating about the company, may start the speech as follows:

> I know that all of you are disturbed by the rumours about laying off employees. I called you today specifically to explain just what it means to our company, and why you should ignore such baseless talk.

> Humour is an effective attention-getter, and it can be used to motivate people and influence an organization's culture.

**Reference to an occasion** If the reason for your speech is tied to some event, occasion, or institution, the audience members will expect to hear you tie the subject of the speech to that event or institution. Here, the event or institution itself will provide a good starting point. Consider the occasion nothing more than a starting point.

> *Thesis statement and preview are crucial to communicate your topic and purpose to your audience.*

### Thesis Statement and Preview

Thesis statement and preview reveal and present your topic. It should be blended with your attention-grabbing remarks. The thesis statement and preview are crucial to communicate your topic and purpose to the audience. Be sure to clearly state the topic of your presentation to capture the attention of the audience, without keeping them in suspense for long. Make sure that the statement and preview are clear, concise, and easy for the audience to remember. See how the following opening emphatically blends the attention-grabbing remark, topic, and three aspects of the topic:

> The best way to predict the future is to create it. In today's competitive marketplace, it is not enough to build a better mousetrap; the world will not beat a path to your door. You must build them a highway. The need for an overall marketing plan is acute.
>
> And that plan has to have three parts: research your market, position yourself against your competitors, then develop a promotional plan to highlight your uniqueness. During the next 30 minutes, you will learn how to create your future.

### Audience Adaptation

It is but natural that, as a speaker, you would like to achieve your desired outcome, but not at the cost of ignoring your audience. You need to think how you could best act as a catalyst to achieve the desired outcome. The best way is to be outcome-centred in your focus on results, and audience-centred in your delivery.

In a business speech, facts should be secondary to messages. While you may well have drawn your message from facts, when you make a speech, begin with that message and then support it with relevant facts, not vice versa.

The best way to grab and hold the attention of your audience is to convince them that your message is important or interesting to them. Relate your message to them and how they will benefit from it.

### Credibility Statement

If your audience perceives you as a qualified speaker, there is more possibility that you will be listened to attentively. Credibility is mostly a matter of being qualified to speak on the specified topic.

Explanatory remarks can convey your interest in the subject. A sentence establishing your credibility, would come in handy. Consider the following examples:

> *The best way to hold the attention of your audience is to convince them that your message is important or interesting to them.*

> I have developed a deep interest in emotional intelligence since the day I had a discussion with Prof. Breckenridge, an expert in this field.
>
> The information I am going to share with you on motivation comes essentially from the book by Shiv Khera, and an article I came across recently in Harvard Business Review.

Credibility statements establish your qualifications as a speaker. They can refer to your extensive research on a topic, life-long interest in an issue, personal experience, or desire to better the lives of your listeners by sifting through the topic and providing crucial information.

### *Preview*

Previewing your material is of the utmost importance because that will prepare your audience for whatever you are going to say during the rest of your speech. In other words, in the preview during the introduction, you are telling the audience what they should listen for in your presentation ahead.

The preview has to be delivered quickly and emphatically in a sentence or two. For example, if you are giving a product presentation on a photocopier, you can tell the audience about its benefits and special features as follows:

> Owning Crystal Photocopier would prove to be not only practical in cost and size, but also beneficial with its executive relevance and sophisticated international appearance.

This preview informs your audience that you will be talking about the cost, size, relevance, and appearance.

Preview statements serve another purpose as well. As they usually come at the end of the introduction, they provide a smooth transition to the body of the speech.

Let us consolidate all the essential components of an introduction, both internal and external, and try to formulate certain guidelines for an effective introduction. The following tips may help you in preparing a smart introduction:

- Choose any of the attention-getters that suit your topic.
- While revealing your topic, also use visual and non-verbal cues
- Relate the topic to your audience by using words such as *we, us, ours* in your internal presentations and *you, yours* in your external presentations.
- Project your personality and competence to establish credibility.
- To preview your presentation, show the presentation outline with sub-topics under each main topic.
- Look for material (anecdotes, questions, quotations, statistics, etc.) in some books or on the Internet while preparing for your presentation.
- Rehearse your introduction several times until it is smooth.
- Remember that the introduction provides you the first opportunity to impress your audience and establish your credibility.

## MAIN BODY

The message that you impart has to be yours. Yet, the way you convey it, the way you structure a speech can be analysed and perfected. Organization is the key to clarity. Remember the following when creating the body a speech:

- Use a message-based approach
- Be creative
- Mind map the speech

> A message-based approach orients itself to delivering the facts related to the point in question.

### Message-based Approach

A message-based approach makes facts secondary. Listeners need to be given only those facts that support the message and are necessary to understand the message. In other words, the facts that you present should prove that your message is sound. A message-based approach orients itself to delivering the facts related to the point in question. Consider the situation where you deliver a product presentation. Here, you may divide your message into sub-topics, such as the product description, comparative study, and advantages. When you deliver the first part, that is, product description, you may have a lot of facts regarding the difficulties you had faced in designing, and the struggles you had to overcome in improving the appearance. Focus on your message and only on those facts that are vital for supporting that message.

## Creativity in Presentations and Speeches

The essence of creativity is to be able to look at familiar objects and situations, enriched by experience, but not constrained by it. Knowing the following four steps in a creative process may help you understand and implement it better:

### *Preparation*

Know precisely what you want to achieve. Obtain detailed knowledge about your subject. Converting content skills into process skills may help you prepare well. For instance, when you want to talk about how to prepare for organizational change with your subordinates. Instead of only talking about the details of the change and its expected outcome, you can be creative by talking about people who resist change and then add on the other messages.

### *Incubation*

At this stage, you allow your subconscious mind to take over and let your critical faculty relax. Think over the topic. Make a note of all your thoughts. The relevance of some of them may not be apparent for hours, days, or weeks. Ideas come into being when thoughts collide, it is necessary to give some time for this to happen.

### *Illumination*

Creative ideas are breakthroughs. Nevertheless, remember to ensure that such an idea is well connected to your message.

### *Verification*

Here, you need to allow your conscious brain to take over and evaluate the suggestions it has been given by its subconscious counterpart. In other words, you are testing your assumptions to check their validity.

## Mind Mapping Your Presentations

A mind map is made of one central idea or concept, and 5–10 related concepts. You can define the type of relationships between the centre and the branches. Mind maps become very good techniques for starting to think in purely associated ways. However, depending on what you are using it for, you can visualize any complex knowledge. You can draw relationships among the branches and describe their type with a textual note.

> Mind mapping allows rapid expansion and exploration of an idea

Mind maps are recognized as the most effective and versatile thinking tool available. Mind mapping allows rapid expansion and exploration of an idea resulting in a clear and concise picture or 'map' of all the relevant interlinked points for inclusion. The use of shapes, colours, and dimensions as visual stimulants further adds to this simple and powerful tool.

## CONCLUSION

The conclusion of a presentation is as important as its introduction, but shorter. It includes the following main points:

- Signal the end
- Review
- Use an emphatic closing statement

### Signalling the End

In order to indicate to the audience that you are going to end your speech, you need to use a verbal or non-verbal cue.

**Verbal cues**   Consider the following examples:

In the end, I would like to say ...
Now I would like to summarize by emphasizing ...
Let me share with you one last thought ...
Let me conclude by saying ...
To recapitulate what I have been talking so far ...
Finally, I would like to wind up by saying ...

**Non-verbal cues**   A change in the tone of your voice, facial expression, etc. are examples of non-verbal cues that can be used to signal the end.

### Reviewing

Your review should contain a restatement of your thesis and summary of your main points. You can draw the attention of your audience to the reference made by you in your introduction as follows:

To recapitulate what I have been sharing with you so far this evening, our merchandising approach needs changing to become more profitable.

I hope, by now, you all would agree that with some basic merchandising changes we can improve our balance sheet. When we are able to convince people that we have a broad range of quality products, we will have more customers who will augment our profit by buying our products.

### Emphatic Closing

An emphatic closing statement will help your listeners remember you and your talk favourably. A weak ending can nullify many of your previous gains. Besides creating a favourable impression, a strong closing statement will give your remarks a sense of completion.

> An emphatic closing statement will help your listeners remember you.

Following is a sample outline of a speech on computer mediated communication (CMC). This is an extended speaking outline in which the key words and phrases are longer than they should be on the real speaking outline.

### Sample Outline of a Business Presentation

1. Introduction
1.1. Attention-getter: How many of you can actually remember the days when you had to communicate via the phone or through letters, when you had to actually write cheques and present them to people to get cash, or had to go to the library to do literally all of your research?
1.2. Link to audience: Most of us cannot imagine life without email, ATM machines, or the Internet, because we rely on these things every day to make our lives easier.
1.3. Speaker credibility: Besides being an avid user of each of these technologies, I have done research on the pros and cons of commuter mediated communication (CMC).
1.4. Thesis sentence: Today, I am here to convince you that CMC is just as useful as face-to-face communication, and in some ways, even better.
1.5. Preview of speech: First, I want to talk about the ways that CMC can help build strong interpersonal relationships. Next, I will show how CMC can positively affect the work place, and finally, I will discuss how CMC can make inter-group relationships in a large-scale organization better.

*Transition*: Let us begin by talking about the way in which the most common forms of CMC can help build strong interpersonal relationships.

2. Main Point 1
2.1. Strong interpersonal relationships: Some people argue that email is not a good form of interpersonal communication, because we do not see people's non-verbal cues, because the feedback is not instant, or because we may be less of an individual when typing.
2.1.1. We are beginning to find ways to add expressiveness:
   (a) Punctuation
   (b) Writing non-verbal expressions
2.1.2. We have unlimited interaction over the computer as opposed to limited interaction when using the phone or in face-to-face communication:
   (a) We are driven as humans to communicate
   (b) It may take longer with computers, but we will still learn as much about others
2.1.3. With the Internet, it is much easier to find many friends with the same interests:
   (a) Websites
   (b) Chat rooms

*Transition*: Besides a great way to meet and visit with people interpersonally, CMC will bring positive changes in the workplace.

Main Point 2
2.2.1. Workplace:
   (a) We will be more flexible
2.2.2. We will need less hierarchy:
   (a) One person can communicate with many

(b) Communication flow will follow work flow

2.2.3. More contact among ranks

2.2.4. More efficient use of expertise

*Transition*: CMC will not only positively affect the way we do business, it will help us to communicate interpersonally with our co-workers.

Main Point 3

2.3. Interpersonal relationships in the workplace:

2.3.1. Informality will increase

2.3.2. More people will be involved in decision-making

*Transition*: Let us go back over what we have learned today.

3. Conclusion

3.1. Restate thesis: Today, I have explained to you why CMC will positively affect our lives.

3.2. Restate main points: First, we talked about how CMC will help us build strong relationships, then we talked about how CMC will make the work better, and finally, we discussed how CMC can make the workplace a better place.

3.3. Call-to-action: I encourage you to learn all that you can about CMC not only because it is the wave of the future, but also because CMC will soon be an inevitable part of our lives.

3.4. Clincher: It is time to get on the information highway, before you get run over.

# EFFECTIVE SALES PRESENTATIONS

A sales presentation should focus on a central proposition, which should be the perceived benefit that the prospect gains from the product/service. During the questioning phase, the sales person would have refined the understanding (and ideally gained agreement) as to what this is. The presentation must now focus on 'matching' the benefits of the product with the needs of the prospect so that the prospect is entirely satisfied about the proposition. The sales person therefore needs an excellent understanding of the many different organizational benefits that accrue to customers, and why, from the product/service. These perceived benefits would vary according to the type of customer organization (size, structure, market sector, strategy, general economic health, culture, etc.).

A sales presentation must demonstrate that the product/service meets the prospective customer's needs, priorities, constraints, and motives or the prospective customer will not even consider buying or moving to the next stage; this is why establishing the situation and priorities during the questioning phase is so vital. The above point is especially important when the sales person has to make a presentation on more than one occasion to different people or groups, who will each have different personal and organizational needs, and will therefore respond to different benefits (even though the central proposition and main perceived benefit remains constant).

> The sales presentation must demonstrate that the product/service meets the prospective customer's requirements.

All sales presentations, whether impromptu or the result of significant preparation, must be well structured, clear, concise, professionally delivered, and have lots of integrity. The quality and integrity of the presentation is always regarded as a direct indication as to the quality and integrity of the product/service. It follows, then, that the sales person must avoid simply talking about technical features from the seller's point of view, without linking the features clearly to organizational context and benefit for the prospective client. Also, avoid using any jargon which the prospect may not understand.

Sales presentations must always meet the expectations of the listeners in terms of the level of information and relevance to the prospect's own situation, which is another reason for a proper preparation. A vague or poorly prepared sales presentation would stick out like a sore thumb and would be disowned immediately. When presenting to influencers, which is necessary on occasions, it is important to recognize that the sales person is effectively asking the influencers to personally endorse the proposition and the credibility of the selling organization and the sales person, so the influencers' needs in these areas are actually part of the organizational needs of the prospect company. The presentation must include relevant evidence of success, references from similar sectors and applications, and data all backing up the central proposition.

Business decision-makers buy only when they are totally satisfied with the decision. They need to be certain that the new product/service will be sustainable and reliable. Therefore, the presentation must be convincing in these areas. Individual buyers ultimately buy for similar reasons, but for more personal ones as well, like, image, security, ego, etc., which may need to feature in these types of presentations if they form part of the main perceived benefit.

## Sales Presentation—Sample

The following sample provides you with some useful ideas on a sales presentation:

As you begin to consider the main points of your presentation, imagine that you are creating two presentations that are entwined with one another. One presentation explains the features of your product, service, course, message, etc. The other explains the benefits and relevance of each point within those features.

 You can refer to the Online Resource Centre for more samples of presentations.

### Presentation Mapping

Mapping out a presentation and displaying specific points and their relevance is very important—you immediately begin to see what your presentation material lacks. Now, the trick is to consider these parallel tracks of thought throughout your presentation. Before you start you need to think further about these multiple messages and how they apply to your presentation.

### Connect Message to Audience

The main message of your presentation should be presented in a clear manner to the audience. This can be done in a sentence or two, as it should be succinct, but it must also immediately show why the material presented is relevant to the audience. This extra effort to communicate the larger picture will help the audience to focus on your presentation. It introduces the main message and its context to the audience and is a crucial step in the organizational process.

If you are training employees, they would want to know why each item they have to learn is important to them and to the company. If you are summarizing a project or quarterly results, people will want to know what it all means and where it is going. Any presentation will be improved by an explanation of how the content is relevant to the audience. The consultant can then break down the usability issues into three categories and explain them thoroughly. The outline slide in Example 1 (Fig. 11.6), begins detailing points the consultant will make to back up the overview material shown in the slide in Example 2 (Fig. 11.7).

Let us use the example of a consultant making a presentation to a client company, concerning the usability of that company's website. The consultant used test subjects to look at the website and recorded their answers to questions, how they completed given tasks, and their overall impressions. The test results provide detailed information about the usability of the company's website, the main facts, and the content of the consultant's presentation.

Beyond the content, the consultant wants the company to understand two important points throughout the presentation. First, how a combination of visual impressions, poor navigation, and unclear text works against the purpose of a website and leads to confusion, dissatisfaction, and (more importantly) fewer purchases from customers. Second, on a big-picture scale, the consultant wants to emphasize the importance of the website in the company's overall business strategy. Therefore, the consultant now has three levels to work with—the specifics of the usability testing, the placing of each of these specifics into one of three contextual categories, and a broader message about the importance of the website itself. At the designing stage of the slide show, keep in mind that the overview slide is a great place to explain why the message is important—to introduce the context of your presentation. In Fig. 11.6 (Example 1), the consultant's slide outlines why the website usability testing is important to the audience and their company. Based on the slide's text, the consultant can further explain the importance of the website to the company and how its poor usability affects the company's bottom-line. This allows the consultant to further emphasize the big picture of his/her message.

### Text and Design

There are some unique ways to lead the audience back to your overview points using the slide's text and design. The three-bullet overview in Fig. 11.7 is short enough for the audience to comprehend the importance of the talk ahead. It also gives the presenter the opportunity to establish the relevance of the points under discussion. The consultant can simply organize the presentation according to problems of visual impression, navigation, and lack of clear text, as listed in Fig. 11.7. The outline slide in Fig. 11.7 is a quick list of content categories that give the audience a road map of the data that backs up the presenter's message. By clearly introducing each section with its own title slide or by marking each slide with the section name, the audience will automatically connect each problem with one of the three categories.

### Colour Coding

> The three-bullet overview gives the presenter the opportunity to establish the relevance of the points under discussion.

A second design method is to use colour coding or icons for each category. At the beginning of the presentation and during the explanation of the three types of problems, the presentation can introduce a colour or icon next to each item. By referring to this mechanism, the consultant can make this connection clear to the audience. From that point on, when the presentation displays the appropriate colour or icon next to the point being discussed, the audience will understand. Icons added to the outline slide add visual appeal, provide a balanced look, and give the presenter a

**Importance of Usability Testing**

- The website takes the place of speaking to a person
- The website needs to be clear and self-explanatory
- Your website represents your entire business

Fig. 11.6  Example 1

**Three Categories of Results**

- Visual impression
- Navigation
- Clarity of text

Fig. 11.7  Example 2

graphical element that helps bring the audience back to the main points throughout the presentation in Fig. 11.8. Figure 11.8 (Example 3) shows the same outline information as Fig. 11.7 (Example 2), but with category icons that can be used throughout the presentation to visually make the appropriate connections.

 Refer to the Online Resource Centre for more on presentation strategies.

### Integrating Levels of Content

The final design method, of integrating levels of content, is more complex graphically but more open to your creativity. You can visually represent the levels using shadows or 3-D images for a layered effect. In Fig. 11.9 (Example 4), clip-art of a man, who appears confused, annoyed or even angry, depending on the usability problem being discussed, has been used. The image includes a shadow to make the man appear as though he is in front of the text and reading it. By inserting a clip art of a confused or annoyed website user in front of the text, you immediately relate the slide's content to visitors. This layer adds a relevance cue to illustrate to the audience how a customer may feel when facing confusing navigation on a website. As you design slides, look for ways to add such extra layers. Another example is a sales presentation in which you use an illustration of a happy customer to make the connection between your product's features and your prospect's need to serve better its customers, or a smiling accountant or piggy bank to show the ways audience members can save money for their company.

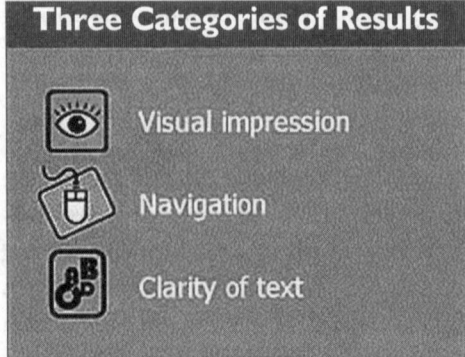

**Three Categories of Results**

- Visual impression
- Navigation
- Clarity of text

Fig. 11.8  Example 3

**Importance of Navigation**

- If users get lost, they don't find the information they want
- Confusing navigation gives the impression that you're confused
- Frustrated users give up quickly and don't purchase or contact you

Fig. 11.9  Example 4

## Summarize

> At the end of a presentation, bring together all the levels that have been discussed, fusing the content with its context.

At the end of a presentation, bring together all the levels that have been discussed, fusing the content with its context. Repeat the points of the overview and then reiterate the relationship between the details and the three main categories. Do not forget to leave a sentence or two for the big picture. This kind of organizing takes practice, but the end result is a more balanced presentation, and one that the audience will find useful and memorable.

A presentation must always focus on the main perceived benefit, nevertheless, it is important to show that all the other incidental requirements and constraints are met. However, do not overemphasize or attempt to pile high loads of incidental benefits as this simply detracts from the central proposition. Presentations should use the language and style of the audience. Technical people need technical evidence; sales and marketing people like to see flair and competitive advantage accruing for their own sales organization; managing and finance directors want clear and concise benefits relating to costs, profits, and operating efficiency; and generally the more senior the contact, the less time you will have to make your point—no nonsense, no frills, but plenty of relevant hard facts and evidence. If the sales person is required to present to a large group and in great depth, then it is extremely advisable to enlist the help of one or two suitably experienced colleagues, from the appropriate sections like technical, customer service, distribution, etc., in which case the sales person must ensure that these people are properly briefed and prepared, and the prospect notified of their attendance.

## CONTROLLING NERVOUSNESS AND STAGE FRIGHT

Before you learn how to deliver a speech, it is important to be ready to deliver your lines. Stage fright is a phenomenon that you must learn to control. Stage fright is not the most accurate term for the nervousness that occurs when considering a speaking engagement. In fact, most of the fear occurs before you step onstage. Once you are up there, the fear usually goes away.

People may never overcome stage fright, but they can learn to control it, and use it to their advantage.

### Symptoms of Stage Fright

You are suffering from stage fright if you have a dry mouth, tight throat, sweaty hands, cold hands, tremulous hands, nausea, fast pulse, wobbly knees, or trembling lips.

### Strategies for Reducing Stage Fright

Not everyone reacts the same and there is no universal remedy for stage fright. Following are a few categories of strategies or techniques to overcome stage fright, however, do not try to use all these strategies at once. Pick out the strategies from the various categories and try them out until you find the right combination.

> The sales presentation must demonstrate that the product/service meets the prospective customer's requirements.

### Visualization Strategies that can be Used Anytime
- Concentrate on how good you are.
- Pretend you are just chatting with a group of friends.
- Close your eyes and imagine the audience listening, laughing, and applauding.
- Remember happy moments from your past.
- Think about your love for and desire to help the audience.

### Strategies in Advance of the Presentation

- Even if you do not like the topic, develop an interest in it.
- Be extremely well-prepared.
- Anticipate hard and easy questions.
- Memorize your opening statement.
- Organize.
- Practise.

### Strategies Just before the Presentation

Remember, stage fright usually goes away after you start. The tricky time is before you start.

- Be in the room at least an hour early, if possible, to triple check everything. You can also mingle with the participants arriving early.
- Take quick drinks of tepid water.
- Concentrate on the ideas.
- Concentrate on your audience.
- Say something to someone to make sure your voice is ready to go.
- Use eye contact.
- Breathe deeply, evenly, and slowly for several minutes.

### Strategies when the Presentation Begins

Before each presentation, make a short list of the items you think will make you feel better. Use these steps to control stage fright so that it does not control you.

- If your legs are trembling lean on a lectern/table or shift your legs or move about.
- Use eye contact. It will make you feel less isolated.
- Look at the friendliest faces in the audience.
- Do not comment on your nervousness.

### On-camera Techniques

- If your presentation is being videotaped before a live audience, ignore the camera. Likewise, if

**COMMUNICATION TOOL**

**Tips for Effective Presentation**

- Keep control of the presentation, but do so in a relaxed way. If you do not know the answer to a question, do not waffle. Admit that you do not know and promise to get back with an answer later, and make sure you do.
- Never knock the competition. It undermines your credibility and integrity. Do not even imply anything derogatory about the competition.
- If appropriate, issue notes or a copy of your presentation.
- Use props, samples, and demonstrations, if relevant and helpful, and make sure it all works properly.
- During the presentation, seek feedback, confirmation, and agreement as to the relevance of what you are saying, but do not be put off if people stay quiet.
- Invite questions at the end, and if you are comfortable and in control of things, invite questions at any time, even at the outset.
- Whether presenting one-to-one or to a stern group, relax and be friendly. Let your personality and natural enthusiasm shine through. People buy from people who love and have faith in their products and companies.

- you are being interviewed before a camera, the viewer expects to see you communicating with your 'live' audience or interviewer.
- If you are interviewed by a television reporter, keep your comments short and to the point.
- If you *must* face a hostile interview on-camera, *avoid the appearance of surprise*. The only preparation is to expect an opening question that is hostile, direct, unfair, and unexpected. Do not let them lead you into unwarranted confessions, admissions, or explanations.

## SUMMARY

Presentations and speeches play a very significant role in business environment. Hence, when planning for presentations or speeches, you must take extra care to define their purpose and relate them to the audience's interests. You must also take care of the locale of the presentation in order to familiarize yourself with it. Business presentations are effective only when they are delivered with a catchy introduction, adequately developed main points, an emphatic conclusion, and also intelligent and focused answers to your audience's queries at the end. You also need to work out suitable strategies for sustaining the interest of your audience throughout your presentation. It is always helpful to select an appropriate mode of delivery—prepare a clear outline for your presentation chalking out all the main topics and sub-topics and meticulously follow the same. Using various devices such as internal previews and internal summaries enables you to maintain a smooth flow during the presentation. The language—words, phrases, clauses, quotations, and sentences you use, visuals you display, vocal cues—all contribute significantly to the success. You should be careful not only in selecting your visual aids but also in using them during your presentation. There is no harm in learning the strategies that help you to control nervousness. These strategies, if adopted suitably, would enable you to look forward to your presentations rather than shying away from them. To be an effective speaker, you should also be adept at handling the questions posed to you after your presentations. You need to focus carefully, respond precisely, and control arguments cleverly during the question-answer sessions. Also, conclude your presentations on time.

## KEY TERMS

*Audience*  It refers to a group or groups of listeners who attend a presentation. Audience know what they want to listen to and speakers know what they need to convey.

*Business presentation*  It is a formal talk delivered in a business context and environment to one or more people, which presents ideas or information in a clear and structured way.

*Conclusion*  It refers to the end remarks or summary of a presentation comprising a signal to the audience and a re-emphasis of the highlights.

*Introduction*  It refers to the opening remarks of a presentation comprising of an attention-getter, purpose, preview, and audience adaptation techniques.

*Non-verbal elements*  These refer to aspects of body language used during a presentation to reinforce the verbal statements.

*Occasion*  It refers to the circumstances that led to the presentation.

*Patterns*  These refer to the order in which a presentation can be organized. There are several patterns such as chronological, spatial, categorical, cause-effect, problem-solution, climactic, and psychological.

*Public speaking*  It is speaking formally to a group of listeners mostly heterogeneous.

*Purpose*  It is the objective of a presentation. It can be classified into two broad categories—general and specific.

**Stage fright** It is a phenomenon that one must learn to control. Stage fright may arise, disappear, or diminish, but it usually does not vanish permanently. You must concentrate on getting the feeling out in the open, into perspective, and under control.

**Thesis** It refers to the central or core idea of a presentation, a single statement that summarizes the message.

**Types of delivery** These refer to the four modes in which presentations can be delivered—speaking from notes, speaking impromptu, reciting from memory, and reading from manuscript.

**Verbal elements** These are words, or the linguistic devices, used in a presentation to make the meanings clear by providing a graphic quality.

**Visual elements** These refer to visual stimuli used during presentations to provide a professional flavour and to present complex details with clarity and accuracy. These can be graphs, maps, drawings, tables, charts, photographs, etc..

## Concept Review Questions

1. Mention any four occasions on which the CEO of a company delivers business presentations.
2. How does effectiveness in speaking help managers in their professions?
3. What are the five important aspects to be considered while planning for your business presentation?
4. Discuss the contents of an introduction to a speech.
5. What are the various patterns in which you can organize the contents of your presentation?
6. What are the ways in which you can develop your presentation contents?
7. How can you overcome stage fright during a presentation?
8. Do you agree that language plays an important role in ineffective presentations? Justify your answer.
9. Appropriate vocal cues enhance the impact of your business presentation. Discuss this statement with suitable examples.

## Projects

1. Using your favourite search engine, surf the Internet to find tips for effective presentations. Identify and write down 10 tips that have not been included in this chapter. Discuss them in a group and decide which is the most powerful.
2. Visit your nearest library or bookshop to identify a book containing some classic speeches. Read at least two of them and discuss the success factors that have contributed to the greatness of such speeches. Then present one of them in your own style and ask your friends to critically evaluate the same.

## REFERENCES

Adair, John 2002, *The Effective Communicator*, Jaico Publishing House, Mumbai, p. 90–91.

Adler, Ronald B. and J. M. Elmhorst 2002, *Communicating at Work*, Seventh Edition, McGraw Hill Higher Education, New York, pp. 310–17.

Bovee, Courtland L. and John V. Thill 2003, *Business Communication Today*, Seventh Edition, Pearson Education, (Singapore) Pvt Ltd, pp. 507–10.

Guffey, Mary Allen 2000, *Business Communication: Process and Product*, Thomson Asia Pvt. Ltd, Singapore, pp. 463–64.

Hamlin, Sonya 1988, *How to Talk so People Listen*, Thorsons, London, pp. 113–14.

Lesikar Raymond V. and John Pettit 2002, *Lesikar's Basic Business Communication*, Eighth Edition, Tata McGraw-Hill Publishing Co. Ltd, New Delhi, pp. 451–53.

Ludlow, Ron and Fergus Panton 1999, *The Essence of Effective Communication*, Prentice-Hall of India, New Delhi, pp. 60–61.

Penrose, John M. and Robert W Rasberry, and Robert J. Myers 2001, *Advanced Business Communication*, Fourth Edition, Thomson Asia Pvt. Ltd, Singapore, pp. 41–74; 240–56.

Prasad, P. 1998, *Communication Skills*, S.K. Kataria and Sons, Delhi, pp. 63–69.

Robbins, Stephen P. and Mary Coulter 1996, *Management*, Fifth Edition, Prentice Hall of India Pvt. Ltd, Delhi, pp. 9–14.

## CASE STUDY 1

### Business Leaders and Public Speaking

Here is a first-hand account of a very good public speaker who trains professionals in public speaking.

I train business professionals in public speaking and also in preparing their project proposals and presentations. One day, my friend Mohan called and asked if I could help his boss, Mr Andrew's, who had to speak at the convocation ceremony of a business school in Hyderabad. I asked if his boss knew what he wanted to say, and Mohan said yes, but the talk was not developed yet and his boss wouldn't have time to devote to it until the weekend.

I learnt from Mohan that Mr Andrews was really smart but not experienced in speaking to large groups.

We set up two meetings with Mr Andrews—the first to discuss what the message would be; the second to practise it. I asked for a general summary of what would be said. Mohan replied, 'He's going to talk about contemporary business scenario.' 'Is he going to say something unusual about today's business or is he going to talk about its future as well?' I asked. Mohan replied that he didn't know, but he assured me that I would be briefed on the day of the first meeting.

When I walked for the meeting, the receptionist escorted me into a meeting room off the lobby. Mohan too arrived, handed me his business card, and briefed me on the status of the script and slides (a work in progress). Shortly, Mr Andrews arrived with a handful of wrinkled papers in his hand. They were his notes. He did not know how to connect his computer to the projector, or how to use PowerPoint well enough to re-sequence the slides. However, his knowledge of contemporary business was encyclopedic and the rate at which he spoke was supersonic. When I asked questions about his topic so that he could clarify what he wanted to say, and in what order, he was wonderfully patient with my modest understanding of his discipline, and used analogies and metaphors to explain his point—a sign, I think, of a good communicator.

In addition to speaking very fast, he did not look me in the eye, and also did not relate what he said to the bar charts on the screen. But he spoke with visceral passion and emphatic verve about the way multinational companies are working these days —and that made up for his other flaws as a speaker. He could lift up his whole body and jump into a keyword with both feet—giving it real meaning and significance.

The challenge, however, was to develop his topic so that the audience would think they were hearing a standard pitch about the contemporary business scenario and then gradually realized that they were listening to something entirely new and exciting.

After two meetings, we cut the slides down to 20 and the timing down to less than 30 minutes. He had no time to rehearse. He promised he would work on it in his hotel room when he arrived in Hyderabad. I continued to email him suggestions over the weekend.

I learned from Andrews that he did not rehearse until he was on the plane, and then he stayed up most of the night in a panic working on it. Two days after the event, he called to say it went well, and that my emails had helped. I called Mohan to get his assessment, who said it was a little short—much shorter than the presentations made by other speakers. I pointed out that short presentations are not necessarily a bad thing—'For a speech to be immortal, it need not be interminable.'

The points Andrews needed to remember were as follows:

1. Get attention of his audience
2. Sustain the attention
3. Make a clear point in a memorable way
4. Be unique in his own way
5. Persuade people to come to talk to him

His job was to generate trust and curiosity among his audience and sustain their interest in his convocation address.

### Questions

1. 'Mr Andrews had not adequately planned and prepared his speech.' Do you agree or disagree with this statement? Discuss.
2. What are the factors that Mr Andrews need to keep in mind regarding the use of body language and voice so that his speech would be impressive.
3. Prepare and introduction to Mr Andrew's speech keeping the discussion in this chapter.

CHAPTER 12

# Conversations

## LEARNING OBJECTIVES

After reading this chapter, you will be able to understand

- the importance of business conversations
- the essentials of business conversation management
- the various aspects of conversations
- the role of non-verbal cues in conversations
- how to devise strategies for dealing with stressful conversations

## INTRODUCTION

> You are awake 16 hours a day—5840 hours a year. You spend more time contacting other people than in any other single activity. How well you converse with these people is the magic key to whether your days will be pay-off days filled with personal and social popularity.
>
> –James A. Morris

I wish I had said...
Why did he not promote me into the new job?
Why was I not invited to the party?
I could have made a better impression if...

These thoughts cross everyone's mind now and then. That is but natural. We all wish to do better and we all feel we would do better if only we had a few hints to help us master the art of conversing in such an engaging manner that people felt drawn towards us.

In organizations where informal conversation is seen as a waste of time, the rule has been to 'stop talking and get to work'. This rule may have been appropriate for the assembly lines of the industrial age, but it is not helpful in the workplace of the information age. The life-blood of the knowledge economy is conversation. Through all kinds of talk in the cafeteria and hallway, around the water-cooler, over the phone, or shop-talk over coffee, knowledge workers are not just chatting away, but often sharing critical business knowledge.

This chapter focuses on workplace or business conversations that are vital for any business to progress. Beginning with a brief discussion of the various types of conversations, the chapter attempts

> ## Types of Conversations
>
> **Chat** A friendly informal conversation, in fact the least formal of all conversations
>
> **Tête-à-tête** French for 'head to head', meaning a confidential conversation
>
> **Dialogue** A two-way conversation that may involve opposing points of view
>
> **Parley** A formal discussion between enemies regarding the terms of a truce
>
> **Colloquy** The most formal of all conversations (e.g., a colloquy on nuclear disarmament); can also be used to jocularly describe a guarded exchange (e.g., a brief colloquy with the arresting officer)
>
> **Communion** A form of conversation that may take place on such a profound level that no words are necessary (e.g., communion with nature)

to enunciate the characteristics of effective conversations and also the strategies that may be adopted to make conversations successful.

## IMPORTANCE OF BUSINESS CONVERSATIONS

A conversation is important, interesting, and indispensable in its own way. Whatever the type of conversation you may be involved in, it is in your hands to make it interesting, inspiring, and influential. Business conversations are interactions with a purpose. The degree of success that you achieve in business will ultimately come down to the degree of depth of your conversations.

The primary block in having necessary conversations at work is technology. While technology is a wonderful tool, however, as many instances seem to suggest, its unbridled use can have an adverse impact on our social as well as business relationships. For example, rather than walking down the hall to have a face-to-face conversation with a member of our team, we send an email. Rather than taking the time out to have lunch with a valued customer to further deepen our relationship, we leave a voicemail to save ourselves time. This kind of total reliance on technology severs human connections, which are the primary drivers of business growth. People love doing business with people who care about them, are trustworthy, and with whom they feel an emotional bond. Without regular and sustained conversations, no such bond can exist. So, as a leader, you need to have meaningful and healthy conversations with people you work with and your customers.

Improving the quality of relationships and the quality of conversations is the key to making your organization work. This way people who are geographically separated and who do not know each other very well work more effectively together. Also, the quality of relationships and conversations is at the core of learning to work effectively in teams.

- Each type of conversation is important, interesting, and indispensable in its own way.
- Meaningful conversations lead to healthy business relationships.

## ESSENTIALS OF A BUSINESS CONVERSATION

Business conversations should adhere to certain requirements to be effective. These necessities form the characteristics of effective and successful conversations.

### Conversations must be about the Issues that Matter Most

A conversation must be focused on the most important issues facing the organization—the company's strengths and the obstacles to performance. For instance,

'Hey, you look very familiar! Have we met before?'

a conversation between an HR Manager and his junior manager may focus on the grievances the latter might have received from a few employees. Certain serious grievances need immediate attention, which can be gained through such conversations. It is all too easy for senior managers to become swamped in the operational details of managing a business. What gets crowded out are tough and honest conversations about the fundamental issues that will determine long-term success. Formal conversations will be rewarding if focused on the issues that matter most to the business.

## Conversations must be Collective and Public

Successfully realigning an organization with a new strategic direction almost always requires simultaneously changing the worldview and the behaviour of a whole set of interdependent players—the CEO, senior leadership team, and managers down the line. This will not happen without a collective, public conversation (Image 12.1). The term 'collective' connotes that several levels of management

**Image 12.1** Collective conversations are effective conversations

across important functions and value-chain activities have to be engaged. 'Public' tells us that senior managers need to keep everyone three to four levels below them informed about what has been learned, as well as what changes are planned. For instance, a sales manager's conversation with the leaders of his/her project teams will enable the former to share new policies related to the sales strategies that may be introduced in the near future.

## Conversations must be Structured

Structured conversations, which are guided by protocols for listening and speaking, are an essential part of any business communication. A typical structured conversation allows productive conversations to occur in which all participants have a chance to speak and to actively listen. Practitioners meet in a group with a facilitator who leads them through a set of prescribed steps. These steps may include presentation of a focusing question, close. To achieve honesty and full engagement in these conversations, you need to structure them carefully.

> A conversation must be focused on the most important issues facing an organization.

### Change-in-strategy Conversations

When the top management advocates a new direction and begins to develop programmes for change without finding out what influential people in other parts of the organization think of the new focus, it usually results in failures. Similarly, taking the other extreme, when some top managers do not advocate at all and instead in the name of participation and involvement, depend entirely on inquiry—assembling a large group of managers and asking them to define a direction—the result is often widespread frustration. Managers and employees look to leaders to articulate a point of view about where the business is going, a point of view to which they can respond. Leaders need to advocate, then inquire, and repeat as needed. Hence, organization-wide conversations held in connection with effectuating any change have to take care of both promotion of change and inquiry. For example, a few years back, Infosys wanted to take to the market the new concept of process-driven business process management (BPM) to get into the global consulting business in a big way and also build value into customer deals. To bring out this new concept, several conversations involving advocacy and inquiry would have been held in this organization of global repute.

> - Structured conversations, which are guided by protocols for listening and speaking, are an essential part of peer observation practice.
> - Leaders need to advocate, then inquire, and repeat as needed.

### Conversations must Allow Employees to be Honest without Risking their Jobs

In many companies, managers talk about strategic problems with one or two people they trust but pull their punches in more public settings. For example, some companies might be aware of the tensions that exist between their regional entities and the functional departments. They also might be aware that the senior team has not been managing effectively, and many managers may also doubt their president's ability to lead the organization out of the mess. None of these issues may be discussed publicly, for two reasons. First, managers may fear that being honest would hurt their careers or even endanger their jobs. Second, they may be

> - Conversations should be held in such a manner that the participants are honest without risking their jobs.
> - By involving everyone, a conversation becomes more interesting, informative, and resourceful.

afraid that their president and his/her senior team would feel so hurt and defensive that the conversation would not lead to change and might even set back the organization. Hence, they may like to play safe in their conversations. Conversations should be held in such a manner that the participants are honest without risking their jobs.

## CONVERSATION MANAGEMENT

How many times do you walk away from a conversation wondering whether you got your point across, were understood, actually resolved the issue, or reached an agreement that would result in the outcomes you want, and through the conversation enriched the relationship rather than constricted it?

The precondition for learning how to converse of effectively requires a willingness to be (i) known, (ii) seen, and (iii) changed. Learning does not take place otherwise. Given these preconditions, how do you manage your conversations? Following are some strategies and tools that facilitate a profound shift in the course of a conversation or relationship, when you practise them consciously (Fig. 12.1).

### Involve Everyone

A good conversationalist is not one who holds his/her listeners spell-bound by his/her speech; but one who involves everybody in the conversation. You must remember that there are others in the group as well who may have something to contribute. You must give all those who wish to speak a chance to do so. Whether others add much or little is unimportant, for at the end of a conversation it is not remembered who said what; all that remains is a feeling of participation and the satisfaction of knowing that each one has contributed his/her bit. By involving everyone, a conversation becomes more interesting, informative, and resourceful.

### Arouse and Sustain Interest

A conversation is successful only when all the participants take an active interest in it, that is, have respect for and an interest in each other's points of view. It is a joint venture, and once a person joins, he/she needs to fully participate in it. For a conversation to be interesting, it should be peppered with questions, answers, views, expressions, statements, and information. This can also be achieved by having a fairly good idea of the various personalities present in the conversation. There may be participants who can be easily drawn into a discussion, are reticent and outgoing, use magniloquent words with a view to impress upon others, are aggressive or touchy, idealists or realists, and so on. Hence, it is

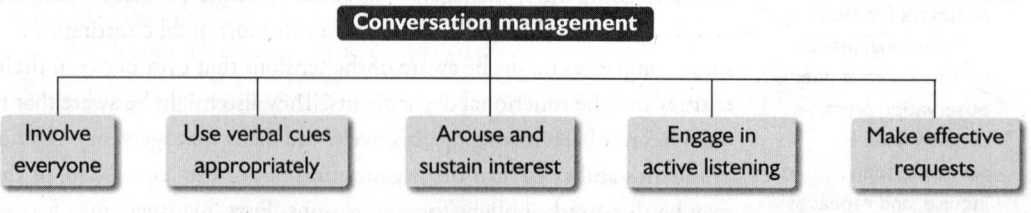

**Fig. 12.1** Various aspects of conversation management

necessary to take notice of the various attitudes so as to strike a balance, and arouse and sustain the interest of everybody.

## Engage in Active Listening

Active listening is as important in conversation as effective speaking. Active listening refers to taking personal responsibility to find out and be sure that what we consciously communicated was received and what we received was what was intended to be sent, and any distortions were clarified before proceeding with the conversation. Try to interpret, understand, and paraphrase the sender's message so as to fully comprehend it. This type of listening would be more rewarding and productive during a conversation (Image 12.2).

**Image 12.2** Active listening leads to a meaningful conversation

Listening to others helps them listen to you, thereby transforming the conversation. The three core listening skills to practise are as follows:

*Inquiry* Ask open questions that provide information and meaning such as 'What did you notice?', or 'What did you think?', or 'What conclusions did you draw?'

*Paraphrasing* Ask questions that check your understanding against what the other person meant such as 'When you said this, did you mean ...'.

*Acknowledgment* This may be the most underutilized but powerful tool for defusing negative emotions. Acknowledgement of another's frustration, irritation, or anger goes a long way in defusing the emotional charge that blocks communication. Phrases such as 'I can see how angry you feel' or 'If I were in your shoes, I would probably feel just as frustrated' honour the other person's reality even if you do not agree with their perspective.

## Make Effective Requests

Requests and promises are the lifeblood of business communication. An effective request has the following four elements:

1. Say exactly what you want.
2. Say exactly who you want it from.
3. Say exactly when you want it.
4. Make sure you have the same assumptions about what is needed to ensure the desired outcome.

Notice in the above elements that the operative word in the first three is 'exactly'. Too often, we sabotage the results we desire by not making requests at all, making unclear requests, not communicating expectations, and promising results when unclear about the request.

## Use Verbal Cues Appropriately

> Active listening is as important in conversation as effective speaking.

This is the most difficult aspect of a conversation. We use language in conversations to convey our ideas and feelings, paraphrase the presented thoughts, appreciate others, reflect upon implications and underlying feelings, and invite

> Requests and promises are the lifeblood of a business communication.

further contributions. How to do this? The following are some practical hints to accomplish these purposes:

- Encourage
- Acknowledge ideas
- Question
- Inform
- Direct
- Criticize

### *Encourage*

Encouragement is a key factor for a successful communication. It

- gives the other person permission to go on with what he or she is saying,
- promotes the other person's further exploration of an idea, and
- can make the other person start talking.

Typically, encourage when

- you want more information about ideas, facts, or feelings and
- the other person appears hesitant.

**How to encourage**   Make use of the following tips:

- Say things like 'Go on', 'Tell me more', and 'uh-huh'.
- Use non-verbal cues like head nodding and hand gestures, and
- Maintain good eye-contact, use appropriate body language, and remain quiet.

*Examples*   Let us imagine two conversations between you and a counterpart to illustrate the use of some verbal cues for encouragement.

1. Counterpart: 'I've been having a problem motivating my team.'
   You: 'Tell me more.'
   Counterpart: 'They just don't seem to work together well enough.'
   You: 'Could you tell me a bit more about that?'
2. Counterpart: 'I think additional security guards will reduce theft.'
   You: 'That's an excellent idea.'

A few more examples:

> Had it happened to me I'd have been rather upset.
> That must have been rather satisfying.
> I guess that must make you rather anxious.

### *Acknowledge Ideas*

> - Encouragement is a key factor for successful communication.
> - In acknowledging ideas, you let the other person know that you are paying attention to the content.

In acknowledging ideas, you let the other person know that you are paying attention to the content. Acknowledging ideas you focus on the other person's content—the ideas—rather than the emotion.

1. Demonstrates that you have listened actively,
2. Summarizes your understanding of the information presented to you,
3. Provides a basis for clarifying what you may have misunderstood, and
4. Establishes rapport.

Typically, acknowledge ideas when you

- think ideas should dominate,
- want more information about what has been said,
- are confused or unclear,
- have been given a lot of information, and
- want to make sure that you heard and understood correctly.

**How to acknowledge** First, listen to understand—not to judge—the ideas expressed by the other person. Then, repeat almost verbatim, or paraphrase using the other person's words as much as you can. Your restatement can interrupt, clarify, or summarize the other person's presentation. When you acknowledge ideas, refrain from adding some of your own comments and avoid evaluating what you are hearing.

*Examples*  Let us consider two examples that illustrate how to acknowledge ideas.

1. Counterpart: 'This policy manual is outdated. It cites procedures no longer in effect. We need annual revisions.'
   You: 'You think we should start revising the policy manual annually.'
   Counterpart: 'We must abandon all projects other than those which have a direct bearing on production.'
   You: 'Earlier, I understood that you wanted annual revision of the policy manual. Now, I think you're saying that we should engage only in projects having direct bearing on production.'
2. Counterpart: 'Flexitime could really solve a lot of problems around here, as there are only a few typewriters and word processors. The only problem might be for the company carpool. I guess they'd have to coordinate time schedules.'
   You: 'Let me see if I understood this correctly. You believe that if we institute flexitime, we can increase the use of office equipment, and alleviate some traffic problems, but there will some implications for carpooling.'

## Question

Questioning is the single most used category in conversations. Questions can clarify meaning and avoid problems. Insufficient or incorrect information can lead to an improper response or action. The intent of questioning is to

- seek information,
- clarify information, and
- gather additional information,
- help lead the other person to gain an insight.

There are two types of questions, open and closed. An open question allows the respondent wide latitude and opens up the conversation. It is phrased so that it requires a descriptive response. A closed question allows less latitude because it requires a 'yes' or 'no' response or a specific fact. It causes the respondent to focus on his or her thoughts.

Typically, question when you

> Questions can clarify meaning and avoid problems.

- know what information you need,
- want to guide the conversation.
- are unclear about something, and

> An open question allows the respondent wide latitude and opens up the conversation.

**How to ask an open question**   Phrase your question so your counterpart can choose from a variety of responses and can be descriptive.

**How to ask a closed question**   Phrase your question so that it limits the range of your counterpart's response.

*Examples*   Let us consider a few open and closed questions.

1. Open: 'What factors could interfere with your meeting the deadline for the report?'
2. Closed: 'Will we get the report on time?'
3. Open: 'We need to address the dependent care needs of our employees. What are some of the things we can do?'
4. Closed: 'What companies have programs for employees' dependents?'
5. Open: 'How have these insurance claims been handled in the past?'
6. Closed: 'Have past insurance claims been answered using this approach?'
7. Open: 'How could that help with the problem of absenteeism?'

## Inform

Informing conveys a message to your counterpart. The ability to share information is critical in the business world. Most discussions revolve around giving information and centre on an exchange of messages. The sender states facts, thoughts, feelings, and concerns about a subject. The receiver processes the message and gives back his/her own information. Informing may

- make your counterpart aware of something,
- answer your counterpart's question,
- move the discussion in a particular direction,
- change the subject under discussion,
- build on another's idea(s),
- contribute to problem solving or decision making, and
- stimulate discussion, as in a brainstorming session.

Typically, inform when

- more information is needed by your counterpart to go further in the interaction,
- explaining,
- your counterpart is ready to listen, and
- time is critical.

**How to inform**   In order to inform

- know your audience,
- state your message clearly, in appropriate language,
  - keep to the point,
  - offer only the quantity of information you believe your counterpart can assimilate at a time,
  - identify your opinion as such, and
  - then question to check for understanding before informing further.

> Most discussions revolve around giving information and centre on an exchange of messages.

*Examples*   Some examples of sentences that inform are as follows:

You have an opportunity to participate in a training programme, 'Conversations that Work.' It will help you to achieve your communication goals. The program will help you effectively use skills you already know but, perhaps, haven't thought to organize in this particular way.

I think there are two key audiences our newsletter must address—our clients and board of directors.

I was very pleased when I read your report.

Fantastic! How do you keep coming with such good ideas?

What a memory! Wish mine were as good ...

You learn fast! I wish I too ...

Praise, implied in the last few examples above, often has some of the elements of encouragement. However, as praise often reflects the judgement of the speaker and its intent is to share opinion, it is frequently classified as information.

### Direct

Directing involves one person giving instructions to another. In the most common business use, directing is the act of delegating. Directing helps you to

- guide someone and
- clarify expectations.

Typically, direct when you

- expect compliance from the other person,
- are delegating responsibility,
- are teaching,
- do not have time to do anything else, and
- believe that the other person has the knowledge and skill to carry out the direction.

**How to direct** In order to direct

- state the directions clearly,
- state the directions in sequence,
- use imperative sentences,
- be constructive, and
- question to check understanding.

*Examples*

Please review the year-end totals for last year and compare those with the year-end totals from the previous year.

I'd like you to retype the proposal, substituting the new regional manager's name for John's name.

I need your help in the beginning phase of this project. Please complete the following by 1 March—identity five experts, interview them, summarize the information in a report, send the summary to me and mail copies to each interviewee. Do you have any questions?

> In the most common business use, directing is the act of delegating.

In giving directions, one of the most important things is to be clear. Therefore, be concise and check for understanding.

### Criticize

> Since criticism increases defensiveness in a receiver, criticizing should be done carefully and with tact.

Criticizing intends to redirect negative behaviour to positive. It is necessary in business interactions because everyone makes mistakes. Since criticism increases defensiveness in a receiver, criticizing should be done carefully and with tact. Criticizing

- allows you to give feedback and change the direction of another's behaviour,
- allows you to point out someone's weakness and redirect him or her to a more positive action,
- can repair and improve conditions, and
- can promote mutual satisfaction.

**How to criticize**   To criticize,

- describe and specify unacceptable and acceptable behaviour, and the possible consequences,
- avoid blame,
- acknowledge the counterpart's emotions or ideas if necessary and/or if time permits, and
- be certain that the counterpart understands the corrective action and consequences.

*Examples*   Let us consider some examples.

> Hamida, the situational analysis you did was excellent. The bottom-line approach was very helpful. There is some change I'd like, I think the section on marketing strategies lacks explanatory charts and graphs. It would make things clearer to the non-technical audience. Would you add those to the final copy?
>
> Priya, your report doesn't follow the guidelines set by our client. Would you please review Section III of those guidelines and revise it by 3 p.m.?
>
> Karan, you've missed two deadlines on this project. Let's work this out so that the project gets back on schedule. I'd like you to prepare a status report showing where each step actually stands. Set priorities for each point. If conditions warrant, I'll get you extra help.

## NON-VERBAL CUES IN CONVERSATIONS

Non-verbal signals are often more important than the words expressed. Even more than words, non-verbal cues indicate the relationship among the people participating in a conversation. Social psychologist Albert Mehrabian illuminated this matter by describing three dimensions of non-verbal signals that we give off during a conversation. Based on his research, he termed these dimensions immediacy, power, and responsiveness (Fig. 12.2).

### Immediacy

> - Non-verbal signals are often more important than the words expressed.
> - Immediacy is based on the principle that people are attracted to things they like and repelled by things they do not like.

The first dimension, immediacy, relates to spacing among people making conversations. It is based on the principle that people are attracted to things they like and repelled by things they do not like. We move closer to the people and ideas we like. Perhaps we lean towards them and make gestures that intend to bring closer the things we like. When we do not like a person or the ideas we hear, we tend to keep a greater distance and lean away. Also, we may contract our posture with folded arms.

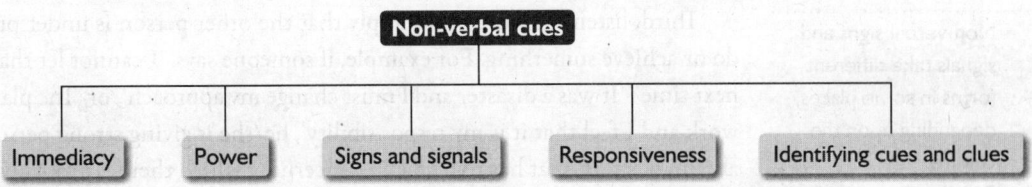

**Fig. 12.2** Non-verbal cues in conversations

### Power

The second dimension—that of power—is characterized by big and expansive movements that symbolically suggest dominance. Standing erect and occupying a lot of space suggests dominance.

### Responsiveness

The third dimension, responsiveness, signals the intensity of our feelings about a person or subject. When we react a lot, we show the strength of our feelings. When we react only a little, we show what might be a lack of concern or indifference. Our facial expressions and body movements provide signals to others that we are following them closely.

Body signals are our unconscious responses to the incoming expressions of others. Sometimes they are incongruent and contradict our words, as when a salesperson prepares a carefully-worded sales pitch but contradicts the words with a meek and unenthusiastic presentation, or when a sports coach, hoping to be seen as the leader, moves timidly and with hesitation.

Many people are afraid of silence because they interpret it as a signal that the communication has gone awry. That is not necessarily so. There are also silences that are golden, such as confident, comfortable, reflective, peaceful, or respectful silences. Such silences can be helpful tools to enhance communication and promote and maintain the existing relationship. Using silence during a conversation has the following advantages:

1. It gives hearers time to think before responding.
2. It shows respect for the speaker.
3. It generate focus and concentration.
4. It conveys deep feelings that words cannot express.

A master conversationalist is one who is able to use silence as a powerful tool.

## How to Identify Cues and Clues

- Responsiveness signals the intensity of our feelings about a person or subject.
- A cue is what you offer someone else if you wish to indicate an area of conversation that is important to you. Clues are what you receive from other people on issues they consider important.

First of all, a *cue* is what you offer someone else if you wish to indicate an area of conversation that is important to you. *Clues* are what you receive from other people on issues they consider important. How do you know when you are being offered conversational clues? First of all, listen carefully when people use the words 'I', 'me', or 'my'. At that point they are speaking about the most important person in the world—themselves.

Second, listen carefully if people follow up comments about themselves with adjectives such as disappointed, annoyed, worried, angry, concerned, unhappy, excited, keen, or enthusiastic. Such words indicate high energy levels.

> - Non-verbal signs and signals take different forms in some places, depending upon the culture.
> - People often give their strongest cues and clues through various signs and signals.

Third, listen for words that imply that the other person is under pressure to do or achieve something. For example, if someone says, 'I cannot let that happen next time', 'It was a disaster and I must change my approach', or 'The plan did not work and I feel that it is my responsibility', he/she is giving strong personal clues about an action that has to be taken concerning which there is probably a critical time element.

Fourth, listen when people express doubts and concerns. If these sorts of clues appear and you want to help, listen to the personal issues expressed. Ask people what they are going to do next, whom they will talk to, what they will say, when they will do it and how. In this way you will help a person talk about a matter, and consider options for action.

### Signs and Signals

Some of the clearest indicators come from people's non-verbal behaviour. A pointed finger to emphasize a point, hands over the mouth to guard against the wrong word, or eyes looking upward for help are signs. Non-verbal signs and signals take different forms in some places depending upon the culture. It is vital, while doing business, to learn what they are in a particular country, as they often speak louder than words.

An important non-verbal clue is how people sit or stand when talking to each other. If they adopt a defensive position with the hands folded or with their body turned away, it could be a signal that they are not necessarily at ease. If, however, they are sitting forward and getting closer to you, it usually indicates that they are willing to give you important information, providing you give them the permission through appropriate questions or reflections.

People often give their strongest cues and clues through various signs and signals. When a person is annoyed, this usually shows instinctively in the way he or she looks. The body will give the key signs and signals. When the persons are relaxed and at ease, they will usually smile more and nod their head.

By recognizing the signs and signals, you can help reduce tension, if any, by opening yourself to a discussion on the matter.

## STRESSFUL CONVERSATIONS

Stressful conversations are unavoidable in life, and in business they can run the gamut from firing a subordinate to, curiously enough, receiving praise. Whatever the context, stressful conversations differ from other conversations because of the emotional loads they carry. These conversations cause embarrassment, confusion, anxiety, anger, pain, or fear—if not to us, then to our counterparts. Stressful conversations cause such anxiety that most people simply avoid them.

Most managers, at some point, might themselves in find conversations that involve unfortunate circumstances.

For example, consider a situation when you suddenly realize that your senior manager is standing at the entrance of your unlocked room wherein you are having a conversation with one of your

> Managers can improve difficult conversations unilaterally if they approach them with greater self-awareness, rehearse them in advance, and apply just certain proven communication techniques.

senior colleagues about the manner in which an employee was fired by the senior manager. Now, your conversation may become stressful because of your fear that the manager might have noticed you and your colleague discussing something about him/her in his/her absence. In another situation, you, as a manager might have to talk to your supervisor about his method of handling the shop floor employees. Such conversations may be stressful and emotions may run high.

Managers can improve difficult conversations unilaterally if they approach them with greater self-awareness, rehearse them in advance, and apply just certain proven communication techniques.

Techniques for handling stressful conversations have within them three simple ingredients needed to make stressful conversations succeed. These are *clarity*, *neutrality*, and *temperance*, and they are the building blocks of all good communication (Fig. 12.3).

Clarity means letting words do the work for us. If a message is given skillfully—even though the news is bad—the content may still be tolerable. When a senior executive, for example, directly tells a subordinate that the promotion has gone to someone else, the news is likely to be highly unpleasant, and the appropriate reaction is disappointment, anger, and anxiety. However, if the content is clear, the listener can begin to process the information. Indeed, bringing clarity to the content eases the burden for the counterpart rather than increases it.

Tone is the non-verbal part of delivery in stressful conversations. It is intonation, facial expressions, or conscious and unconscious body language. Although it is hard to have a neutral tone when overcome by strong feelings, neutrality is the desired norm in crisis communications, including stressful conversations. A neutral tone is the best place to start when a conversation turns stressful.

Temperate phrasing is the final element in this triumvirate of skills. Some phrases are temperate, while others baldly provoke your counterpart to dismiss your words—and your content. In the US, for example, some of the most intemperate phrasing revolves around threats of litigation. 'If you do not get a check to me by 23 April, I will be forced to call my lawyer'—phrases like this turn up the heat in all conversations, particularly in strained ones. Stressful conversations are not a medium to score points or create enemies. The goal is to advance the conversation, hear and be heard accurately, and have a functional exchange between two people.

### Stay Aware and Centred

The primary challenge, when someone seems to be bowling you over with a caustic reaction (or even a verbal/energetic attack), is to stay fully present and centred, so that you can make good choices regarding how to respond.

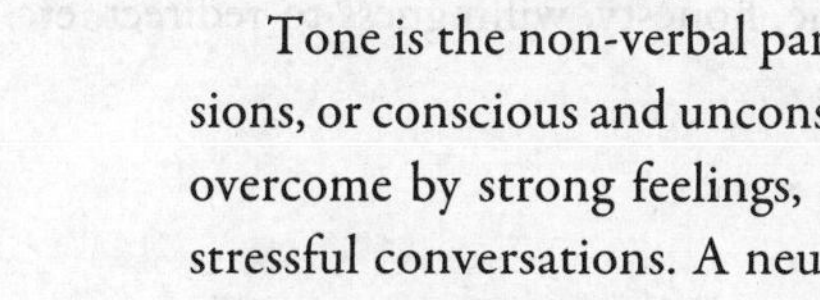

### Respond, Do Not React

Choosing to respond rather than react is to remember that we can be conscious, civil, gracious, and calm in our communications even when someone else chooses differently.

**Tackling stressful conversations**
- Clarity
- Neutrality
- Temperance

**Fig. 12.3** Handling stressful conversations

### Inquire and Validate

> A neutral tone is the best place to start when a conversation turns stressful.

Another potential interpersonal tactic in the face of someone's heated reaction is to inquire and validate the intentions, beliefs, concerns, etc. that are behind the heated words. For example, one inquiry might be, 'It sounds like we've really hit on something that's very important to you. What's most important to you about this?' The person may or may not respond, but the inquiry breaks the escalation in the conversational heat and offers an opportunity for dialogue.

### State Your Intention

Once the pattern of verbal escalation has been broken (e.g., by inquiry and validation), you can begin to reorient the conversation to either a relatively pleasant close (even if temporarily) or shift the focus to the more important priorities of the conversation. One way to reorient is to state your positive intention for the conversation or interaction; for example, you may state, 'My intention for the conversation isn't for us to end up in a screaming match, but to calmly and respectfully exchange ideas so that we can make a decision on this project.' Stating your intention—a positive one—can also serve as one way to break the pattern of escalation to allow for a slight 'cooling off'.

### State Your Appreciation for the Interaction

Regardless of the outcome of any conversation, it is good form—and skillful communication—to express your gratitude and appreciation for the person's time, honesty, willingness to redirect, etc. Doing so allows an open door for continued dialogue.

## Dealing with an Argumentative Communicator

You may be an argumentative talker. There is an effective way to take an opposing view, but it may destroy rapport. There is a way to give your opinion, but it may be received as unwanted advice. When you continue to oppose the comments of your listeners, you run the risk of making them feel wrong, stupid, or uninformed.

An argumentative communicator should be aware that his/her communication efforts may immediately be perceived as a 'fight', regardless of the intention behind it. Following are some tips to deal with an argumentative communicator:

1. Tell the person you do not enjoy arguing, but that you will discuss options and ideas.
2. Tell the person that you respect his/her point of view but disagree.
3. If necessary, tell the person that this subject is something you do not wish to continue discussing because it is personal or volatile.
4. Speak your point of view clearly and what it would take for you to re-evaluate your point of view.
5. Suggest the person to frame his/her comments in a more gentle fashion, for example, 'I know you are not saying that to attack me, it just hurts when you say it that way' or 'Instead of yelling, allow yourself to speak calmly and then I'll be able to listen to you better.'

> Regardless of the outcome of any conversation, state your appreciation for the interaction.

## Communication Tool

**Tips to Prevent You from Becoming an Argumentative Communicator**

- Ask more questions.
- Be aware that not everyone perceives discussion, debate, arguing, and fighting in the same way. Find out what those important to you believe about each of these things.
- Determine why you need to be 'right' or make someone else 'wrong' in heated communications.
- Always think of your intention—if your intention is gentle, speak more quietly because people associate quieter tones with gentler intentions.
- Show people that you care in ways other than verbally so they know you care even when you do argue.
- If you find yourself getting into a heated discussion, ask other persons whether they feel you are arguing or discussing. Ask what the difference would be for them.
- Ask your friends/associates/partners how you can communicate without giving the appearance of arguing.

**Tips for Successful Telephonic Conversations**

- Avoid lengthy conversations.
- Remember the limitations of the instrument. Careful listening, together with direct speech, confined to the topic being discussed, can make up for this limitation.
- Do not talk too fast or too slow.
- The tone of speech is also important. Varied intonations satisfy the listener's need for reinforcement that he/she is involved in a two-way conversation.
- Since you cannot be seen, it is important to insert cues that advise the speaker at the other end that you are there and listening, and that he/she is not on hold.
- Productive conversation, regardless of the purpose of the call, will be facilitated by a positive, upbeat attitude.
- Speak on a clear line and directly into the receiver. Understand the design of your instrument and utilize it according to the instructions for maximum effectiveness.
- Remember the most-prized characteristic of cellular conversations is brevity.

**Tips for Developing Fluency in English for Effective Conversations**

Ask the following questions to yourself and try to answer them:

Do I say umm or aah cause I don't get the right words to continue my statements?

Do I pause a lot when I speak?

Do I use certain expressions such as 'you know', 'I mean', 'actually', etc. during while speaking assignments?

Do I speak very slowly and carefully because I feel that I may commit mistakes?

Do I mumble some words because I'm not very sure about my pronunciation?

Do I feel irritated when a member of the audience interrupts me during my speech?

If your answer is 'yes' to the above questions, then you might have a problem in speaking English fluently.

The fluency with which you speak English depends mostly on your proficiency in English. However even people who have good command over English may be slow or halting while speaking because of lack of preparation or nervousness. But you must realize that gaining good command over a language will pave way for fluency that in turn may enable you to face your audience confidently. However, you may be appreciated only when you speak fluently and accurately. Fluency is nothing but delivering continuous flow of message at an appropriate rate with necessary pauses. Following to be fluent, you may follow the guidelines:

- Aim for clear oral communication devoid of speech errors.
- Write your personal diary in English—what you have done the whole day.
- Make all efforts to develop your proficiency in English which is the key to fluency.
- Listen to good speakers and the news in English. Read newspapers both for content and language, fiction/non-fiction books to understand the use of

- figures of speech such as metaphor, simile, alliteration, etc.
- Expand your vocabulary by learning per day at least five words, their meanings, and usage.
- Try to use only English whenever you speak to your friends and ask them to correct you if you make some mistakes in grammar, vocabulary, or in the use of appropriate pauses.
- Practise correct pronunciation, accent, and tone so that your speech can be impressive
- Learn from your mistakes. For instance, during your initial attempts at speaking, you may use incorrect grammar or vocabulary but make sincere efforts to correct them in subsequent attempts.
- Concentrate on your ideas rather than about your appearance, the impact you are creating, etc.
- Read aloud the passages from books or magazines that you enjoy reading.
- Watch movies to improve your conversational ability.
- Think in English what you have done or are going to do.
- Practise your speaking skills in small talks—on weather, game, hobbies, current affairs, etc.—with your friends or family members.
- Believe in what you're speaking.
- Spare an hour every day for developing your fluency.

Just as we say, 'To learn swimming you need to jump into the pond', we can say that to enhance your fluency in English you need to keep speaking English and continue to learn from your mistakes.

## SUMMARY

Conversation consists of both transmission and reception. There are various types of conversations and conversationalists depending upon the degree of formality and the manner of participation. One should be as good a listener as a speaker to make the conversations effective, fruitful, and meaningful.

It is important to remember that intent matters more than technique. Being clear about the purpose of a conversation and staying true to it, even in the tension or heat of the moment, provides a compass for moving forward. Approaching a difficult conversation with a purpose other than learning is perilous and will undermine your success.

In a good conversation, uncovering assumptions provides the key to greater mutual understanding. Therefore, explore other's views and experience first. Then share your views and experience. Only after the views of both parties are clear does it make sense to solve a problem.

Although it may seem counter-intuitive, the time taken to engage in empathic listening and respectful sharing of divergent perspectives greatly increases the quality and speed of problem-solving. While engaging in difficult conversations often feels risky and challenging, the price of not having them—lost time and productivity and less than optimal results—could cost you and your organization far more than the time and effort of doing so.

Conversing involves far more than a broad knowledge of the language; it has to do not only with words and structures but with the conventions of interactions, involvement of every member, active listening, and not only the understanding of implications but also reflecting upon them. As we all know, practice makes perfect, and the more conversations we are engaged in, the better conversationalists we become. We always need to remember that acquiring conversational skill is the magic key to our professional success and social popularity.

# KEY TERMS

***Acknowledging ideas*** It is the flip-side of 'acknowledging emotion'. You focus on the other person's content—the ideas—rather than the emotion. In acknowledging ideas, you let the other person know that you are paying attention to the content.

***Collective and public conversations*** These are conversations that engage several levels of management across important functions and value-chain activities and in which senior managers keep everyone in-formed about what has been learned, as well as what changes are planned.

***Conversation essentials*** These include Involving everyone, arousing and sustaining interest, shifting from blame to contribution, engaging in empathic listening, developing ideas adequately, moving from certainty to curiosity, separating impact from intent, making effective requests, and using verbal cues appropriately.

***Conversation types*** Depending upon the specific purpose for which conversations are held, these can be categorized into chat, tête-à-tête, dialogue, parley, colloquy, and communion.

***Conversation*** It is a mental occupation and not merely a dribbling into words of casual thoughts. It is an almost imperceptible art whose efforts are more felt than seen. What makes a difference between simple talking and a trained conversation is how best this thought is transmitted, not in isolation but with the assistance of others where cooperation is essentially based on the principle of reciprocity.

***Cues and clues*** A cue is what you offer someone else if you wish to indicate an area of conversation that is important to you. Clues are what you receive from other people on issues they consider important.

***Informing*** It conveys a message to your counterpart. The ability to share information is critical in the business world. Most discussions revolve around giving information and centre on an exchange of messages. The sender states facts, thoughts, feelings, and concerns about the subject.

***Questioning*** It is the single most used category in conversations. Questions can clarify meaning and avoid problems. Insufficient or incorrect information can lead to an improper response or action. The intent of questioning is to seek information.

***Responsiveness*** It signals the intensity of our feelings about the person or subject.

***Stressful conversations*** Stressful conversations are unavoidable. Whatever the context, stressful conversations differ from other conversations because of the emotional load they carry. These conversations cause embarrassment, confusion, anxiety, anger, pain, or fear—if not in us, then to our counterparts.

## Concept Review Questions

1. How does technology narrow down the choice of having business conversations?
2. Discuss briefly some ways to overcome stressful conversations.
3. Explain at least three purposes for which business conversations are held.
4. Discuss the role of non-verbal cues in conversations.
5. How will you manage an argumentative partner in your conversation?
6. Discuss the importance of effective listening in business conversations.
7. Questioning is a step in conversations that requires effective use of language. Discuss.
8. Distinguish between (i) clues and cues and (ii) signs and signals.

## Critical Thinking Questions

1. Paraphrasing skills are essential for those who wish to be effective in their conversations. Do you agree or disagree? Justify your view with adequate examples.

2. Recall any of the conversations in which you participated. Did you reflect your partner's feelings during the conversation? If so, how did you do that? If not, discuss why you did not.
3. Assume that you, as a communication consult-ant, are engaged in a business conversation with one of your customers. The conversation is on how to achieve effectiveness in asking questions during a conflict-resolution process. Prepare a set of guidelines for your customer that would help him/her in enhancing his/her questioning skills.
4. Think of and identify at least 10 situations in which telephonic conversations can be used in business organizations.
5. Critically analyse and bring out the differences between the conversations held for eliciting information from your conversation partners and those for counselling them.

## Projects

1. Visualize the following situations and build a conversation with your friend for each one of these. You can use the given statements as a basis for initiating the conversation.
    (i) You and your colleague are talking in your office. You tell him/her about an interaction you had with Mr Mehra, Corporate Vice-President.
        *Dialogue:* 'After the meeting, I was walking down the hall and Mehra stopped me and said smilingly, "You did really a great job on that account !" I thought so too !'
    (ii) You are reporting to your boss on the status of your group. You know that your boss thinks that the group just has not been pulling its fair weight of late.
        *Dialogue:* 'We finally had a breakthrough in that contract. After all the hours I spent researching the market, I heaved a longish sigh and finally got an idea that he liked. For a while I thought that the group would lose another one.'
    (iii) You are the first and only female member of your audit team. You had hoped that the marked increase in travel would not be a problem because you love the work and do it very well. You are talking to your boss.
        *Dialogue:* 'I know I said I would have no problem with the travel aspects of the job. I thought I would enjoy it. But I find that two to three weeks is too long. I'm not really happy when I'm travelling and my husband is complaining.'
    (iv) You are speaking with an outside consultant, brought in by your boss. The consultant has just delivered a copy of his/her final report.
        *Dialogue:* 'I want to know why I wasn't consulted on that report! You were researching my territory and the decision will have an impact on my people.'
2. Watch at least two conversations on any popular TV talk show, and discuss the techniques the host uses to make the conversation more effective, dynamic, and meaningful.
3. Arrange for the recording of one of your conversations. After the conversation is over, play the recorded version and observe what techniques you and your counterpart used in the conversation. Discuss the various factors that contributed to the effectiveness or ineffectiveness of your conversation.

## REFERENCES

Adair, John 2002, *The Effective Communicator*, Jaico Publishing House, Mumbai, pp. 108–12.

Adler, Ronald B. and Jeanne Marquardt Elmhorst 2002, *Communicating at Work*, Seventh Edition, McGraw Hill Higher Education, New York, pp. 116–18.

Anderson, Paul V. 2003, *Technical Communication*, Fifth

Edition, Thomson Asia Pte Ltd, Singapore, pp. 407–09.

Guffey, Mary Allen 2000, *Business Communication: Process and Product*, Thomson Asia Pte Ltd, Singapore, pp. 107–08.

Lesikar, Raymond V., John D. Pettit, and Marie E. Flately 2002, *Lesikar's Basic Business Communication*, Eighth Edition, Tata McGraw-Hill, New Delhi, pp. 442–44.

Ludlow, Ron and Fergus Panton 1999, *The Essence of Effective Communication*, Prentice-Hall of India, New Delhi.

Madhukar, R.K. 2001, *Business Communication and Customer Relations*, Vikas Publishing House Pvt Ltd, New Delhi, pp. 125–27.

Morris, James A. 1976, *The Art of Conversation*, Simon & Schustor Inc., New York, p. 3.

Robbins, Stephen P. and Mary Coulter 1996, *Management*, Fifth Edition, Prentice-Hall of India Pvt. Ltd, Delhi, pp. 622–25.

Sreevalsan, M.C. 2001, *Spoken English: English Conversation Practice*, Vikas Publishing House Pvt Ltd, New Delhi, pp. 161–63.

## CASE STUDY 1

### Creating a Conversation with Potential Customers

If you owned a store and noticed a customer in the store looking perplexed, would you not go to the customer and ask if there was anything you could help hem/her with? What would you ask at that point? What would be your reply to the customer's response? This, in effect, is a dialogue. You are initiating a dialogue to help the customer at that particular point in the customer's sales cycle, with the goal of moving the customer to the next step in the sales cycle.

In a one-to-one marketing parlance, you are interacting with the customer so as to ascertain more about the customer's needs, to ascertain more about the value of the customer to your business. Based on what you learn, you then tailor the interaction that takes place with that customer so as to provide a unique value to each customer relationship, which in effect is treating customers differently based on their needs and value to your firm.

If you noticed a perplexed customer, would you do nothing and then wait a month or more, collect the names of customers who looked similarly perplexed, and then contact them to ask why they were perplexed? Or would you not even bother to do that and instead simply send them some irrelevant offer?

If a customer needs help, the time to offer assistance is then and there. It can be considered the event that requires action on your behalf. Use the event to interact and solicit more about their current needs and provide a solution for those needs. Then, use the opportunity to follow up to solicit feedback and to ascertain more about future needs and potential value to your firm.

What do you do have to do to create a dialogue? Consider the example of a high-tech company looking to automatically help customers move along the customer lifecycle. The following steps can be used for preparing a dialogue marketing campaign (these steps can also be applied to any other industry):

1. *Review your business and marketing goals* What are the most important business goals of your company, and what is your marketing strategy for accomplishing those goals? What has and has not worked from your existing or prior marketing strategy in accomplishing these goals? For instance, a high-tech company may wish to increase the awareness of a particular line of components, and then increase the sampling and use of its online simulation tool to increase the likelihood that design engineers will incorporate the component in their design.

2. *Identify different segments of customers and their value* All individuals have different needs, and some have more valuable (to you) needs than others. In this case, the company may choose to focus on interacting with segments of engineers that do not normally get exposed to sales representatives (who are typically allocated to the highest revenue accounts).

3. *Identify their needs, starting with the most valuable* Just as your company has its current business needs, so do your customers. What are those needs? You need to identify those customers that have needs that match those that your company can offer. At the same time, you need to be aware of other needs to make

sure you are not missing profitable opportunities. For instance, engineers want to quickly and easily find information on components, request and obtain samples, and test their designs.

4. *Map out the customer lifecycle* How do customers become customers of your company? For example, design engineers conceptualize a design, research component performance information, order and, test the samples, incorporate the sample in a mock-up of the design, and test the design. If the design meets the design specifications, the design engineer can then incorporate the component into the design.

5. *Consider why customers are getting stuck and look to offer assistance* For instance, you track design engineers order datasheets or samples, but then note that they do not return to perform simulations and that no subsequent order for components occurs. Perhaps they are not aware of what more your company can do for them. Or, perhaps they need more help. No automatic follow up occurs after general awareness emails go out, or after engineers request samples, and this contributes to preventing engineers from proceeding further along the sales cycle.

6. *Map out a dialogue relationship to help move customers along the customer lifecycle* In this example, an electronic dialogue can be created that automatically tracks the request for a sample (this becomes the event), and then automatically follows up in a timely manner to inform the design engineer about the benefits of your company's online simulation capabilities. After a short while, you can follow up to solicit feedback on the experience or to inquire if the engineer faced any difficulties. You can also use this opportunity to inquire about the performance of the sample part, inquire about the designs the engineer is working on, to solicit if the engineer would like to have a technical resource call to assist them with their design, as well as ask what more can be done for the engineer. Depending on the stage of the customer lifecycle that the engineer is in and the way that the engineer responds to the questions posed in the email, the dialogue can automatically continue with messages tailored to suit his/her needs.

7. *Define Matrices* Create matrices to track how the dialogue is proceeding. Matrices include email open rates, increases in open rates as the dialogue progresses (showing that customers find the dialogue to be anticipated and relevant to their needs), increases in simulations performed, designs, as well as valuable feedback on what is good and bad about the customer experience and the sampled parts, information on the engineer's current and future designs, and the number of leads passed along to technical sales specialists that can be further tracked to note conversions to sale.

Creating a relationship through dialogues is a significant step above a 'batch-and-blast' approach to interacting with your customers. By using dialogue to ask questions, just as a salesperson would, you can automatically follow up with information the moment it is relevant and anticipated. This enhances the value of the relationship to customers, compresses the sales cycle, and positively affects the ability to retain customers and the growth of a help in business.

## Questions

1. Developing relationships with your customers can be effectively carried out by creating conversations. Discuss with the help of details from the given passage.
2. Discuss any two strategic steps to be adopted to create dialogues with your potential customers.

# CHAPTER 13

# Interviews

## LEARNING OBJECTIVES

After reading the following chapter, you will be able to understand

- the principles of interviewing
- the general preparations required for interviews
- how to achieve success in an interview
- the types of interviewing questions
- importance of non-verbal communication in interviews
- the types of interviews
- the styles of interviewing
- the dos and don'ts of interviews
- case interviewing techniques
- how to master on-site interviews

## INTRODUCTION

An interview is a formal meeting in which a person (or persons) questions, consults, or evaluates another person (or persons). For example, reporters and writers have meetings with eminent persons to ask questions, so that they can gather material for a media story or broadcast. An interview reveals the views, ideas, and attitude of the person being interviewed as well as the skills of the interviewer. Both the interviewer and the interviewee must be well prepared for an interview. This chapter provides you with an understanding of what to expect during interviews and how to prepare for them. First, we describe some ways through which you can learn information about the company you have an interview with. Second, we offer some tips on preparing for the interview by examining different types of interviews and questioning approaches, and by encouraging you to develop answers to the questions while preparing for your interview. Third, we stress that practising for a interview is just as important as preparing for a business presentation or media interview. Finally, we suggest some ideas for mental preparation regarding the interview location and the necessity of creating an excellent first impression, ending with some dos and don'ts to guide you.

> An interview is a formal meeting in which a person or group questions, consults, or evaluates another person or group.

## FUNDAMENTAL PRINCIPLES OF INTERVIEWING

Most employment decisions are based on interviews of applicants (Image 13.1). However, most interviews do not provide us with sufficient information to make an informed decision. As a consequence, most hiring decisions are based on who interviewers like the best. To conduct more effective interviews, apply the following principles:

1. Ask questions that allow the candidate to do at least 70 per cent of the talking. For the most part, avoid questions that can be answered by a 'yes' or a 'no'. The best questions are ones that make the candidates recount their past experience.
2. Phrase your questions so that the desired or 'right' answer is not apparent to the applicant.
3. Ask only one question about one subject at a time.
4. Ask the easy questions first so as to make the applicant feel comfortable.
5. All questions should be directly related to finding out about the applicant's ability to do the job, not about his/her personal life.
6. Spend the entire time writing and recording the candidate's answers and any assumptions you are making.
7. Interviews are generally a poor place to test the candidate's skills, other than the skill of being interviewed. Some interpersonal skills can be tested, however, through the use of role-play.
8. While you are writing, nod occasionally to let the applicant know you are listening.
9. If the applicant does not respond right away to a question, wait. Give him/her time, while you add to your notes.
10. Follow-up—ask the person to tell you more, to give more details.
11. Ask the candidate to describe his/her past behaviour in the kind of situations he/she will encounter on the job.
12. Alternate between easy non-threatening questions and more difficult pointed ones.
13. After you have asked the candidate all your questions, allow him/her time to ask you any questions he/she might have about the job.
14. Close the interview by asking the candidate if there is anything he/she regretted saying, any answer they would like to change, or anything he/she would like to add to his/her previous statements.
15. Spend at least 30 minutes reviewing your notes after the interview and identifying any key qualities that you feel you have not adequately tested. These become objectives for subsequent interviews or assessment experiences.

**Image 13.1** Fundamental principles of interviewing

## GENERAL PREPARATION FOR AN INTERVIEW

> Preparation can make the difference between getting an offer and a rejection.

Understand that interviewing is a skill; and, as with all skills, preparation and practice enhance the quality of that skill. Preparation can make the difference between getting an offer and a rejection. There is no one 'best' way to prepare for an interview. Rather, there are specific and important strategies to enhance one's chances for success in an

# Interviews

interview. Every interview is a learning experience, so learning that takes place during the preparation and actual interview process is useful for future interviews. Initial preparation requires recent assessment of skills, interests, values, and accomplishments; a re-assessment and updating of one's résumé; and research on the targeted company/organization and position. Preparation also includes actual practice of typical and targeted interview questions. Final preparation includes details of dress and appearance, knowledge of the location of the interview, what to expect, and protocols for follow-up.

## Assess Yourself

When one is unemployed or fearing lay-off, the time is right for reassessing current skills, talents, abilities, strengths, weaknesses, interests, and work values. In addition, it is clearly the time to re-examine his/her accomplishments and achievements, particularly those that may be relevant to a prospective employer. Keeping an on-going accomplishments file to maintain items, such as articles, congratulatory letters, kudos from the boss or clients/customers, 360-degree evaluations, and descriptions of successful activities as they occur, is recommended. In the course of daily business life, one often forgets those notable successes.

## Track and Leverage Your Accomplishments

You have been instructed to list your career accomplishments, and you cannot think of any, or you are asked in a job interview, 'What accomplishments are you most proud of?'—and you freeze up. You know you have had accomplishments, but you just cannot dredge them up.

Accomplishments are the points that really help sell you to an employer—much more so than everyday job duties, and you can leverage your accomplishments for success at all stages of the job-search process—résumé, cover letter, and interview.

Use the following prompts to brainstorm all those remarkable things you did. Try to list some accomplishments that set you apart from other job candidates.

In each job, what special things did you do to set yourself apart? How did you do the job better than anyone else did or could have done?

> You can leverage your accomplishments for success at all stages of the job-search process—résumé, cover letter, and interview

How did you take initiative? How did you go above and beyond what was asked of you in your job description?

Were you promoted? (Rapid and/or frequent promotions can be especially noteworthy)

How did you leave your employers better off than before you worked for them?

Did you win any awards, such as 'Employee of the month'?

What are you most proud of in each job?

Is there material you can use from your annual performance reviews? Did you consistently receive high ratings?

Have you received any complimentary memos or letters from employers or customers?

What tangible evidence do you have of accomplishments—publications you have produced, products you have developed, or software applications you have written?

Think of the 'PEP Formula'—profitability, efficiency, and productivity. How did you contribute to profitability, such as through sales increase percentages? How did you contribute to efficiency, such as through cost reduction percentages? How did you contribute to productivity, such as through successfully motivating your team?

### Updating Your Résumé

The accomplishments file serves as a springboard to reassessing your résumé. The file contains content for selective résumé inclusion. If we assume that a résumé must be accomplishment-based rather than descriptive of one's responsibilities, then the file serves to jog one's memory about recent notable activities. Strengthen the résumé by removing all superfluous and/or irrelevant material, all articles (a, an, and the), and work at fitting it all into one page. Use functional headings to help focus the reader on what you have done and what you can do for the prospective employer. Be absolutely certain it is error free.

Let us now assume you have a specific interview lined up. Depending on the available time, use every possible means to learn all you can about the company and position. Refer to books, journals, magazines, newspapers, and any reference materials useful for investors—and job seekers. Visit the company's website as well as competitors' sites. Use investor websites to learn what is happening now in the news with this company and its competitors.

### Re-assessing Your Résumé

A résumé, even your best-yet résumé, needs to be reviewed thoroughly. You need to also know everything that is on it. Be prepared to discuss supplementary experiences that might be important to this employer. Focus on experiences you feel are most relevant and match them to the employer's needs. Practising typical and targeted interview questions is essential. Be able to answer the following basic questions:

- Why are you interested in this field?
- Why are you interested in this company?
- Why are you interested in this position?

Be prepared to discuss anything on your résumé. Be prepared to answer questions/issues you really do not want to answer. For example, consider the following factors:

> - Depending on the available time, use every possible means to learn all you can about the company and position.
> - Be prepared to discuss supplementary experiences that might be important to this employer.

> - As interviewing is a skill, you can only improve your style and acumen with practice.
> - Use the thank-you note to reiterate your interest and emphasize your specific qualifications for the position.

- Your greatest weakness
- Your lack of related experience
- Your lack of leadership experiences
- Your record of job-hopping

How can you improve, enhance, develop, or revise your answers and/or delivery? Because interviewing is a skill, you can only improve your style and acumen with practice.

### Prepare Questions to Ask

The questions you able interviewers, about the company, should reflect your research on the company and position, and should never include questions whose answers are readily available in company literature or website. Do not ask about salary or benefits.

### Follow-up

Send a thank-you note within 24–48 hours of your interview. Send one to every person who interviewed you. Email is acceptable, but follow protocols for formal business correspondence, which is always more formal than a typical email. Use the thank-you note to reiterate your interest and emphasize your specific qualifications for the position. What do you want them to remember about you that is likely to 'sell' you to them as a viable candidate? Everything about the job search should be focused on what you can do for the company, what you bring to the position, and why the employer should hire you.

## SUCCESS IN AN INTERVIEW

Many factors contribute towards success in an interview. Some of these are enumerated as follows:

 You can also refer to the Online Resource Centre for more on interviews.

### Dressing for the Interview

Appearance is very important and good grooming is essential. Your hair should be neat and stylish. Your nails should be clean. Make-up, if applied, should not be heavy. Perfume or cologne should be avoided as some people find certain scents offensive.

### Establishing Rapport

An interviewer's job is to make sure that not only your skill but also your personality is a good match, therefore, you must establish a rapport with the person(s) interviewing you. It begins the instant

---

**Manners, Meals, and Interviews**

Interviews are often stressful—even for job seekers who have been interviewed many times. Interviewing can be even more stressful when you are expected to eat and talk at the same time. One of the reasons employers take job candidates out to lunch or dinner is to evaluate your social skills and to see if you can handle yourself gracefully under pressure. Dining with a prospective employee allows employers to review your communication and interpersonal skills, as well as your table manners, in a more relaxed (for them) environment. Table manners do matter. Good manners may give you an edge over another candidate; so, take some time to brush up your dining etiquette skills.

> You should wait for the interviewer to offer his/her hand first, but be ready to offer your hand immediately.

you walk in to the door. Let the interviewer set the tone. Nothing is as awkward as offering your hand and having the gesture not returned by the other person. Therefore, you should wait for the interviewer to offer his/her hand first, but be ready to offer your hand immediately. Some experts suggest talking at the same rate and tone as the interviewer. For example, if the interviewer is speaking softly, so should you.

### Using Body Language

Body language gives more away about us than speech. Eye contact is very important, but make sure it looks natural. A smiling, relaxed face is always inviting. Hands resting casually in your lap rather than arms folded across your chest also are more inviting. If you normally move your hands around a lot when you speak, tone it down a little. You neither want to look too stiff nor like a bundle of nervous energy.

### Answering Questions

Speak slowly and clearly. Pause before you answer a question. Your answers will seem less rehearsed and it will give you a chance to collect your thoughts. Keep in mind that a very brief pause may seem like an eternity to you. It is not. Prepare answers to some basic questions. Do not memorize the actual answers, rather become familiar with how to answer the questions.

### Asking Questions

Usually towards the end of the interview, the person conducting it will ask you if you have any questions. You should have some. You should ask about what a typical day would entail. You could also ask what special projects you would be working on. As in every other aspect of the job search, you are trying to show the employer how you can fill their needs. By asking about a typical day on the job or special projects, you are putting yourself in the job and showing the employer how you will satisfy the employer's needs. Do not ask about salary, benefits, or vacations, as those all imply, What will you, the employer, do for me?'

## TYPES OF INTERVIEWING QUESTIONS

Skilled interviewers use a variety of questions to draw maximum information from candidates. These are listed, in the approximate order in which they might be asked, as follows:

### Permission Questions

Permission questions demonstrate concern for the other party. They are used at the beginning of the interview to put the other person at ease. Examples include the following:

- Are there any questions you have about the process before we begin the interview?
- Is there anything I can do to make you more comfortable before we begin?
- Okay, should we start with question one?

> Skilled interviewers use a variety of questions to draw the most information from the candidate.

### Factual Questions

Factual questions are low-risk attempts to obtain objective data about an applicant. They are intended to give you a picture of the status of the other party. These

> Factual questions are low-risk attempts to obtain objective data about an applicant.

questions can be used to help make the applicant feel comfortable and are good to use at the beginning of the interview and after a particularly difficult or threatening question. Examples include the following:

What do you do in your present job?
How long have you worked there?
What attracted you to our company?

### 'Tell Me about' Questions

'Tell me about' questions are the most important during a hiring interview. They ask the candidate to describe their past experience. Examples include the following:

Tell me about a recent important decision you made and how you went about it.
Walk me through the first and last half hour of your most recent normal workday. What did you do first, second, etc.?
Tell me about a recent work assignment that made you look forward to going to work.

### 'Feeling' Questions

'Feeling' questions are designed to obtain subjective data on the other party's feelings, values, and beliefs. They are useful as follow-ups to 'tell me about' or factual questions. Make sure that the applicant responds by describing an emotional state, not by describing what they thought. Examples include the following:

How did you feel about that reaction?
What do you like best (least) about your present job?
How would you feel if this were to occur?

### 'Checking' Questions

'Checking' questions allow you to make sure you have understood the other person's answer. They are useful at any point in the interview, but most useful at the end to help you check any assumptions you have made about the applicant. Examples include the following:

Is this what you mean?
As I understand it, your plan of action is this. Am I right?
Are you saying that was a negative experience?

## IMPORTANT NON-VERBAL ASPECTS

Many interviews fail because of lack of proper communication. Communication is more than just what you say. Often it is the non-verbal communication that we are least aware of, yet it speaks the loudest. Following are the top five non-verbal signals, ranked in order of importance, when it comes to interviewing (Fig. 13.1):

**Eye contact** If you have a habit of looking away while listening, it shows lack of interest and a short attention span. If you fail to maintain eye contact while

> - 'Feeling' questions are designed to obtain subjective data on the other party's feelings, values, and beliefs.
> - Many interviews fail because of lack of proper communication.

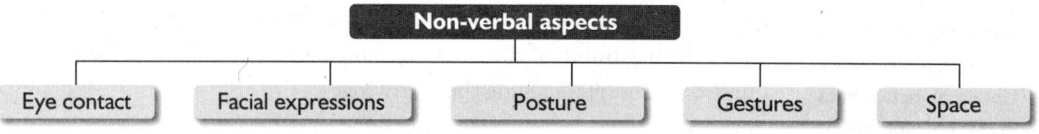

**Fig. 13.1** Important non-verbal aspects in an interview

speaking, it shows lack of confidence in what you are saying; it may also send the subtle indication that you may be lying. Do not just assume you have good eye contact. Ask. Watch. Then practise. Ask others if you ever lack proper eye contact. If they respond that they have noticed, ask if it was during speaking or listening. Take note. Then sit down with a friend and practise until you are comfortable maintaining sincere, continuous eye contact.

**Facial expressions**  Take a good, long, and hard look at yourself in the mirror. Look at yourself as others would. Then modify your facial expressions. First eliminate any negative overall characteristics that might exist, then add a simple feature that nearly every interviewee forgets—a smile, a true and genuine smile that says that you are a happy person and delighted to be interviewed by the company.

**Posture**  Posture sends the signal of your confidence and power potential. Stand, walk, and most of all, sit tall. This statement is not meant to offend short people. Height is not what is important, posture is. When you are seated, make sure you sit at the front edge of the chair, slightly leaning forward, intent on the subject at hand. Your best posture is to always be learning forward slightly.

**Gestures**  Contrary to popular belief, gestures should be very limited during an interview. So, do not use artificial gestures to supposedly heighten the importance of the issue at hand. It will merely come off as theatrical. When you do use gestures, make sure they are sincere and meaningful.

Non-verbal communication plays an important part in any interview

> A job interview is your chance to show an employer what he/she will get if you are hired.

**Space** Recognize the boundaries of your personal space and that of others. For most people, it ranges between 30–36 inches. For most of us, merely the awareness of our personal space is enough to consciously prompt us to stand firm. If you have a smaller than average personal space, make sure you keep your distance so that you do not intimidate someone who possesses a larger personal space.

## TYPES OF INTERVIEWS

A job interview is your chance to show an employer what he/she will get if you are hired. That is why, it is essential to be well prepared for the job interview. Preparing means knowing about the industry, the employer, and yourself. It means paying attention to details, such as personal appearance, punctuality, and demeanour. Knowledge is your best weapon. Before you research the industry and the company and even before you practise answering the questions you might be asked, you should have some general information about job interviews. Let us start by going over the different types of interviews you might face.

### Screening Interview

Your first interview with a particular employer will often be the screening interview. This is usually an interview with someone in human resources. It may take place in person or over the telephone. He/she will have a copy of your résumé in hand and will try to verify the information on it. The human resources representative will want to find out if you meet the minimum qualifications for the job and, if you do, you will be passed on to the next step.

### Selection Interview

The selection interview is a step in the process that makes people the most anxious. The employer knows you are qualified to do the job. While you may have the skills to perform the tasks that are required by the job in question, the employer needs to know if you have the personality necessary to 'fit in'. Someone who cannot interact well with the management and co-workers may disrupt the functioning of the entire department. This can ultimately affect the company's bottomline. Many experts feel that this can be determined within the first several minutes of the interview. However, more than one person being interviewed for a single opening may appear to fit in. Often, job candidates are invited back for several interviews with different people before a final decision is made.

### Group Interview

In a group interview, several job candidates are interviewed at once. Interviewers are trying to separate the leaders from the followers. In any group there is a natural process that takes place where the group stratifies into leaders and followers. The interviewers may also be trying to find out if you are a team player. The type of personality the employer is looking for determines the outcome of this interview. There is nothing more to do than act naturally. Acting like a leader if you are not one may put you into a job for which you are not appropriate.

> Often, job candidates are invited back for several interviews with different people before a final decision is made.

## Stress Interview

A stress interview is not a very pleasant way to be introduced to the company that may end up being your future employer. It is, however, a technique sometimes used to weed out those who cannot handle adversity. The interviewer may try to artificially introduce stress into the interview by asking questions so quickly that the candidate does not have time to answer each one. Another interviewer trying to introduce stress may respond to the candidates answers with silence. The interviewer may also ask offbeat questions, not to determine what the job candidate answers, but how he/she answers.

## Walk-in Interview

A walk-in interview is similar to a traditional interview except that one does not need to pre-schedule an appointment for the interview. Companies generally declare a specific period of the day for interviews on certain days of the week or over a certain period of time. During this period, interested individuals may appear for the interview in that slot as per their convenience along with the necessary documents and credentials. The company conducts an on-the-spot interview to evaluate candidates. While some organizations may hold these interviews at their location, attending job fairs, where a number of organizations gather under the same roof, may also qualify as a walk-in interview.

A candidate prepares for a walk-in interview just as one would for any interview: be well-prepared for the job requirements, be appropriately dressed, and have all necessary documents available and organized. Proper preparation often sets one candidate apart from another. Walk-in interviews are convenient for both the employee and employer. While it gives candidates the benefit of appearing for the interview at a convenient time without hindering their existing job and commitments, companies favor this format as it curtails the amount of time spent in conducting interviews.

## Virtual Interview

A virtual job interview is a simulated conversation between an interviewer and a prospective employee, wherein the interview questions are asked through a video clip. The candidate chooses from a set of responses. The next video clip responds on the basis of the answer selected by the candidate. Several questions are asked and the answers evaluated. The process continues until a decisive conclusion is reached about the candidate's suitability for the role. A virtual interview, although still a relatively new concept, has several advantages.

> It is ideal for job placement in colleges and universities, where a large number of fresh graduates may have to be interviewed at a time, and for workforce and one-stop operations.
> It improves student placement rates and also reduces the amount of time invested on individuals. Once an interview is designed, it can be used repeatedly and consistently.
> It is convenient and designed for the modern learner.
> It is interactive, with multiple learning styles.
> It provides an alternate delivery method for workshop and classroom presentations.

## Campus Interview

Campus interviews are generally conducted by big companies for recruiting fresh graduates. They include career fairs, interviews, internships, etc.

### On-campus Interview

On-campus interviews are conducted, as the name suggests, in the campus of colleges or universities to recruit fresh graduates. It generally takes place from mid-October to mid-March although it is of late turning into a year-round activity. Firms select the most suitable campus and coordinate with the campus placement office for the recruitment process. Firms select the campus based on the number of candidates they intend to hire, campuses that provide fresh graduates best equipped with the knowledge and skills that suit the companies' requirements, and other factors such as location, demographics, competitive environment, general opinion of the school, etc. Often, companies maintain a long-term relation with institutions that produce graduates who would be best suited to the companies' corporate culture.

On-campus interviews allow companies get to select from a huge pool of students under one roof. Generally, there is a preliminary screening based on certain objective criteria such as the overall performance of the student, grades, etc., which allows the companies to short-list the candidates before the interview, further enhancing the efficacy of the hiring process. The actual recruiting may be preceded by several other social activities such as corporate presentations, informal meetings, formal dinner with company representatives, etc.

On-campus interviews hold several benefits for the recruiters as well as students. Companies prefer fresh graduates because it is possible to train and mold them to be most beneficial to the organization, fresh minds bring fresh ideas and are educated in the latest technologies, they are enthusiastic, and also, companies can part with smaller salaries for fresh graduates when compared with an experienced candidate. At the same time, students also gain the opportunity to interview for several organizations within their campus. Students can choose the organization that they wish to start their career with, and many enter big organizations, often even before they complete their graduation. However, as several students are competing for the same opportunities, it is very important to distinguish oneself from the rest. On-campus recruitment remains the most preferred method to hire fresh graduates.

### Off-campus Interview

Off-campus interviews are also aimed at fresh graduates. However, it is conducted at a common location, where students from various institutions may gather to attend the interview. The advantages of an off-campus interview is that a student can research more and look for the exact job profile one wishes to start a career with, and it is easier to distinguish oneself here as a student is competing with a relatively smaller pool of candidates with the same background unlike an on-campus interview. However, it leaves the students with the task of a self-directed search for job interviews, and may be a more prolonged process, which may be tiring and frustrating to the candidate.

### Panel Interview

A panel interview or a committee interview comprises of a panel or a group of interviewers, typically sitting around a conference table, who take turns to ask questions to the candidate (Image 13.2). The set of questions asked may be the same, allowing them to draw comparisons between different candidates on the basis of their responses. The interview may take place with individual candidates separately or with multiple candidates sitting across the interview panel in the same room. The panel of interviewers may often be colleagues at the organization, but from different business functions.

Image 13.2  A panel interview in progress

The number of panel members may vary from two to five. The advantage of this method is that it is less time-consuming for both parties and is more reliable as experts from different functions can evaluate a candidate collectively. However, the process may be stressful and demands more focus from the applicant in responding to the rapid steam of questions. The key to such interviews is to balance eye contact and responses among all the members of the panel and avoid ignoring any member or focusing only on one. Apart from their accomplishments, the candidates are also judged by their responses and questions, their body language, and their ability to be calm and focused under stress.

## Telephonic Interview

Interviews over the telephone are generally conducted for the purpose of pre-screening candidates or for out-of-town candidates as a preliminary step to the in-person interview. It cannot replace an in-person interview, but is used to down size the application pool and to further familiarize the interviewer and the candidate with each other. Like any other interview, telephonic interviews also require adequate planning and preparation. Consider the following factors:

1. It is good to be prepared for a phone interview at any time after the preliminaries, but some employers may schedule a telephone interview. In case of a scheduled call, it is important for one to be available for the call at a place without disturbance and a good network in case using a mobile phone to minimize interruptions. If the employer calls at a time when it is not possible to talk, one may politely explain this and request for an alternate time at the employer's convenience.
2. All the documents made available to the employer must be kept ready and accessible along with a pen and paper to take notes if necessary.
3. As a telephonic interview depends heavily on how one sounds, one has to talk slowly, but audibly and clearly, and use a tone and voice quality that conveys energy and confidence.
4. Eating or smoking during the call must be avoided, although one may have a glass of water reachable if needed.
5. It is important to listen carefully, without interrupting, and keep the answers brief. Having a clock in front helps one to be aware of the time taken to elaborate each answer.
6. One may use a landline to prevent frequent call dropping.
7. Turning off call waiting will help avoid any interruptions during the interview.

## Behavioural Interview

Behavioural interviews are a relatively new and very effective mode of interviewing. The aim is to discern how an individual would react to specific work-related situations on the basis of the individual's past behavior in similar situations. Hence, unlike traditional interviews, which rely on a person's description of hypothetical events, behavioural interviews focus on examples of real incidents, and hence are more reliable and effective. It is based on the basic concept that an individual tends to follow the same pattern of behaviour under identical conditions, and hence, past behaviour is a good indicator of the individual's future performance. These interviews follow a typical pattern of questions, such as some examples mentioned as follows:

> Describe a situation where you achieved a goal against adversities.
> Tell us about a time when you resolved a conflict between team members.
> Give a specific example of how you completed a difficult task within the set deadline.
> Discuss a very difficult problem that you solved successfully.
> Describe how you handled a particularly demanding client and with what results.

The key skills evaluated in these interviews are the individual's leadership qualities, problem-solving skills, ability to handle pressure, communication and interpersonal skills, resourcefulness, initiative, integrity, and individuality.

The candidate is expected to describe a specific situation, what action he/she took, and what were the results. The interviewer may further probe to evaluate the consistency of the answers given. Therefore, it is important for candidates to be honest in their assertions and not exaggerate in order to come across as reliable and worthy. Although it is preferable for a candidate to select and describe situations that portray one's effectiveness, events that did not yield positive results in spite of sincere efforts may also sometimes help highlight a person's capability to handle adversities. However, one has to remember that there are no set correct answers to these questions. The interviewer determines the suitability of the candidate for the job on the basis of the individual's responses, and there may be more than one correct way of dealing with a situation.

Traditional interviews help establish the candidate's technical expertise and knowledge, behavioural interviews help interviewers determine whether the skills and behaviour of the candidate are desirable for a given role in the organization. Behavioural interviews may be challenging to the candidate, and it helps to remember the following basics:

1. As for any other interview, one must be prompt, appropriately dressed, and well prepared.
2. It is important to remain attentive and focused.
3. Brief and complete answers are preferred, but one must be prepared to elaborate.
4. One must convey enthusiasm and confidence.
5. Remember that honesty is a valued quality.
6. It may be helpful to refresh the memory of major work-related situations in the past that one played a key role in.

## Case Interview

A case interview is a job interview where the candidate is expected to resolve a real or hypothetical problem presented to him/her by the interviewer. The challenge may usually be a real problem resolved by the interviewer. These interviews aim at understanding a person's thinking process in the face of an adversity. Therefore, rather than the final answer, the interviewer is focusing on how the candidate approaches the problem, analyzes it, and works out the solution. The logical sequence of actions expected from the candidate is as follows:

1. Ask relevant questions and gather further information about the given situation.
2. Identify the problem.
3. Analyse the problem.
4. Formulate multiple options to resolve the problem with valid reasoning.

The interviewer may guide the candidate through the process with subtle cues, which helps the interviewer understand how the individual uses prior experience and knowledge to identify a problem and develop a structured solution. The key skills evaluated in this process are the individual's problem-solving abilities, resourcefulness, basic intelligence, reasoning, communication and presentation, analytical skills, and general awareness. Case interviews are more commonly used in consulting and investment banking jobs, although it is gradually gaining popularity in other fields.

## STYLES OF INTERVIEWING

The two styles of interviewing used by companies today are traditional and behavioural job interviews.

### Traditional Job Interview

A traditional job interview uses broad-based questions, for example 'Why do you want to work for this company' or 'Tell me about your strengths and weaknesses'. Interviewing success or failure is more often based on the ability of a job seeker to communicate than on the truthfulness or content of his/her answers. Employers are looking for the answer to three questions: does the job seeker have the skills and abilities to perform the job, does the job seeker possess the enthusiasm and work ethic that the employer expects, and will the job seeker be a team player and fit into the organization.

### Behavioural Job Interview

A behavioural job interview is based on the theory that past performance is the best indicator of future behaviour, and uses questions that probe specific past behaviour, for example, 'Tell me about a time where you confronted an unexpected problem', 'Tell me about an experience when you failed to achieve a goal', or 'Give me a specific example of a time when you managed several projects at once'. Job seekers need to prepare for these interviews by recalling scenarios that fit the various types of behavioural interviewing questions. Expect interviewers to have several follow-up questions and probe for details that explore all aspects of a given situation or experience. Recent college graduates with little work experience should focus on class projects and group situations that might lend themselves to these types of questions. Job seekers should frame their answers based on a four-part outline: (i) describe the situation, (ii) discuss the actions you took, (iii) relate the outcomes, and (iv) specify what you learned from it.

#### Behavioural Interviewing Strategies

Behavioural interviewing is a relatively new mode of job interviewing. Employers such as AT&T and Accenture (the former Andersen Consulting) have been using behavioural interviewing for about 15 years now, and because increasing numbers of employers are using behaviour-based methods to screen job candidates, understanding how to excel in this interview environment is becoming a crucial job-hunting skill. The premise behind

> - Interviewing success or failure is more often based on the ability of a job seeker to communicate than on the truthfulness or content of his/her answers.
> - The behavioural job interview is based on the theory that past performance is the best indicator of future behaviour.

behavioural interviewing is that the most accurate predictor of future performance is past performance in similar situations. Behavioural interviewing is said to be 55 per cent predictive of future on-the-job behaviour, while traditional interviewing is only 10 per cent predictive. Behavioural-based interviewing is touted as providing a more objective set of facts to make employment decisions than other interviewing methods. Traditional interview questions ask you general questions, for example, 'Tell me about yourself'. The process of behavioural interviewing is much more probing and works very differently.

Employers use the behavioural interview technique to evaluate a candidate's experiences and behaviour so they can determine the applicant's potential for success. The interviewer identifies job-related experiences, behaviour, knowledge, skills and abilities that the company has decided are desirable in a particular position. For example, some of the characteristics that companies look for include

- critical thinking
- being a self-starter
- willingness to learn
- willingness to travel
- self-confidence
- teamwork
- professionalism

The employer then structures very pointed questions to elicit detailed responses aimed at determining if the candidate possesses the desired characteristics. Many employers use a rating system to evaluate selected criteria during the interview. As a candidate, you should be equipped to answer the questions thoroughly. Obviously, you can prepare better for this type of interview if you know which skills that the employer has predetermined to be necessary for the job you seek. Researching the company and talking to people who work there will enable you to zero in on the kinds of behaviour the company wants. In the interview, your response needs to be specific and detailed. Candidates who tell the interviewer about particular situations that relate to each question will be far more effective and successful than those who respond in general terms. Ideally, you should briefly describe the situation, what specific action you took to have an effect on the situation, and the positive result or outcome.

Frame it in a three-step process, usually called a S-A-R, P-A-R, or S-T-A-R statement, listed as follows:

1. Situation (or task, problem)   2. Action   3. Result/Outcome

The best way to prepare is to arm yourself with small stories that can be adapted to many behavioural questions. Use examples from internships, classes and school projects, activities, team participation, community service, hobbies, and work experience—anything really—as examples of your past behaviour. A good way to prepare for behaviour-based interviews is as follows:

1. Identify six to eight examples from your past experience where you demonstrated top behaviour and skills that employers typically seek. Think in terms of examples that will exploit your top selling points.
2. Half your examples should be totally positive, such as accomplishments or meeting goals.
3. The other half should be situations that started out negatively, but either ended positively or you made the best of the outcome.
4. Vary your examples; do not take them all from just one area of your life.
5. Try to describe examples in story form and/or in a PAR/SAR/STAR statement.

> Employers use the behavioural interview technique to evaluate a candidate's experiences and behaviour so they can determine the applicant's potential for success.

Once you have secured the job, keep a record of achievements and accomplishments so that you will be ready with more great examples the next time you go on a behaviour interview.

### Behavioural Interviewing Technique

The behavioural interview technique is used by employers to evaluate a candidate's experiences and behaviour in order to determine his/her potential for success. The interviewer identifies desired skills and behaviour, and then structures open-ended questions and statements to elicit detailed responses. A rating system is developed and selected criteria are evaluated during the interview. As a candidate, you should be prepared to answer the questions and statements thoroughly. Companies are normally looking for the following skills and traits through behavioural interviews.

**Technical and professional knowledge**  This is the level of your understanding of technical and professional information and your ability to apply technical and professional skills. Typical questions include the following:

> Sometimes it is easy to get in 'over your head'. Describe a situation where you had to request help or assistance on a project or assignment.
> Give an example of how you applied knowledge from a previous coursework to a project in another class.

**Teamwork**  Teamwork is essential for working effectively with others in an organization and outside the formal lines of authority (i.e., peers, other units, senior management, etc.) to accomplish organizational goals and to identify and resolve problems while considering the impact of your decisions on others. Typical questions could include the following:

> Describe a situation where others you were working with on a project disagreed with your ideas. What did you do?
> Describe a situation in which you found that results were not up to your professor's or supervisor's expectations. What happened? What action did you take?
> Tell of a time when you worked with a colleague who was not completing their share of the work. Who, if anyone, did you tell or talk to about it? Did the manager take any steps to correct your colleague? Did you agree or disagree with the manager's actions?
> Describe a situation in which you had to arrive at a compromise or guide others to a compromise.

**Analysis**  Analysis means relating and comparing data from different sources, identifying issues, securing relevant information, and identifying relationships. Typical questions include the following:

> What steps do you follow to study a problem before making a decision?
> We can sometimes identify a small problem and fix it before it becomes a major problem. Give an example of how you have done this.
> Describe a situation in which you had to collect information by asking many questions of several people.
> In a supervisory or group leader role, have you ever had to discipline or counsel an employee or group member? What was the nature

- As a candidate, you should be prepared to answer the questions and statements thoroughly.
- Teamwork is essential for working effectively with others in an organization and outside the formal lines of authority

of the discipline? What steps did you take? How did that make you feel? How did you prepare yourself?

Recall a time from your work experience when your manager or supervisor was unavailable and a problem arose. What was the nature of the problem? How did you handle that situation? How did that make you feel?

Recall a time when you were assigned what you considered to be a complex project. What steps did you take to prepare for and finish the project? Were you happy with the outcome? What one step would you have done differently if given the chance?

What is the most complex assignment you have had? What was your role?

**Adaptability** Adaptability means maintaining effectiveness in varying environments, tasks, and responsibilities, or with various types of people. Typical questions include the following:

How was your transition from high school to college? Did you face any particular problems?

Tell of some situations in which you have had to adjust quickly to changes over which you had no control. What was the impact of the change on you?

**Work standards** Setting high goals or standards of performance for self, subordinates, others, and the organization is vital. Typical questions include the following:

Compare and contrast the times when you did work which was above the standard with times your work was below the standard.

Describe some times when you were not very satisfied or pleased with your performance. What did you do about it?

What are your standards of success in school? What have you done to meet these standards?

How have you differed from your professors in evaluating your performance? How did you handle the situation?

**Job motivation** Sometimes the activities and responsibilities available in the job overlap with activities and responsibilities. These result in personal satisfaction and motivate people to work harder. Typical questions include the following:

Give examples of some satisfying experiences at school or in a job. Give examples of your experiences that were dissatisfying.

What kind of supervisor do you work best for? Provide examples.

**Initiative** Initiative means making active attempts to influence events to achieve goals; self-starting rather than passively accepting; taking action to achieve goals beyond what is necessarily called for, originating action. Typical questions include the following:

Describe some projects or ideas (not necessarily your own) that were implemented, or carried out successfully, primarily because of your efforts.

Describe a situation that required a number of things to be done at the same time. How did you handle it? What was the result?

Have you found any ways to make school or a job easier or more rewarding?

**Ability to learn** Ability to learn help in assimilating and applying new job-related information promptly. Typical questions include the following:

> Planning and organizing helps in establishing a course of action for yourself to accomplish specific goals.

What tricks or techniques have you learned to make school or a job easier, or to make yourself more effective? How did you learn that?

**Planning and organizing** Planning and organizing helps in establishing a course of action for yourself (and/or others) to accomplish specific goals. It also helps in planning proper assignments for personnel and appropriately allocating resources. Typical questions include the following:

How do you determine priorities in scheduling your time? Give examples.

Describe a time during school when you had many projects or assignments due at the same time. What steps did you take to get them all done?

**Communication** Communication involves clearly expressing ideas in writing-including grammar, organization, and structure. Typical questions include the following:

Describe an event where when your active listening skills really paid off for you—maybe also an event where other people missed the key idea being expressed.

What has been your experience in giving presentations to small or large groups? What has been your most successful experience in speech making?

**Customer service orientation** It means making efforts to listen to and understand the customer (both internal and external), anticipating customer needs, and giving high priority to customer satisfaction. Typical questions include the following:

Describe the most difficult customer service experience that you have ever had to handle—perhaps an angry or irate customer. Be specific and tell what you did and what the outcome was.

**Sensitivity** Sensitivity means acting out of consideration for the feelings and needs of others. Typical questions include the following:

Give an example of when you had to work with someone who was difficult to get along with. Why was this person difficult? How did you handle that person?

Describe a situation where you found yourself dealing with someone who did not like you. How did you handle it?

### Sample Behavioural Interview Questions

One of the keys to success in interviewing is practice. Thus, take the time to work out answers to these questions using one of the suggested methods, such as the STAR approach. Be sure not to memorize answers; the key to interviewing success is simply being prepared for the questions and having a mental outline to follow in responding to each question.

A list of sample behavioural interview questions is given as follows:

Describe a situation in which you were able to use persuasion to successfully convince someone to see things your way.

Describe a time when you were faced with a stressful situation that demonstrated your coping skills.

Cite a specific example of a time when you used good judgement and logic in solving a problem.

Tell me about a time when you had to use your presentation skills to influence someone's opinion.

Give me a specific example of a time when you had to conform to a policy with which you did not agree.

Tell me about a time when you had to go beyond the call of duty in order to get a job done.

Give me an example of a time when you had to make a split-second decision.

Give me an example of when you showed initiative and took the lead.

Tell me about a recent situation in which you had to deal with a very upset customer or co-worker.

Tell me about a time when you delegated a project effectively.

Tell me about a time when you missed an obvious solution to a problem.

Describe a time when you anticipated potential problems and developed preventive measures.

Tell me about a time when you were forced to make an unpopular decision.

Describe a time when you set your sights too high (or too low).

**COMMUNICATION TOOL**

**Job Interviewing Dos and Don'ts**

You should be able to achieve success in interviews by following the simple rules provided as follows:

- **Do** take a practice run to the location where you are having the interview—or be sure you know exactly where it is and how long it takes to get there.
- **Do** your research and know the type of job interview you will be encountering. **Do** prepare and practise for the interview, but **don't** memorize or over-rehearse your answers.
- **Do** dress the part for the job, the company, and the industry.
- **Do** plan to arrive about 10 minutes early. Late arrival for a job interview is never excusable.
- If presented with a job application, **do** fill it out neatly, completely, and accurately.
- **Do** bring an extra copy of your résumé to the interview.
- **Do** greet the interviewer(s) by title (Ms, Mr, Dr, etc.) and last name if you are sure of the pronunciation. If you are not sure, **do** ask the receptionist about the pronunciation before going into the interview.
- **Do** make good eye contact with your interviewer(s).
- **Do** show enthusiasm in the position and the company.
- **Don't** be soft-spoken. A forceful voice projects confidence.
- **Do** have a high confidence and energy level, but **don't** be overly aggressive.
- **Don't** say anything negative about former colleagues, supervisors, or employers.
- **Do** make sure that your good points come across to the interviewer in a factual, and sincere manner.
- **Do** stress your achievements. **Don't** offer any negative information about yourself.
- **Do** remember that the interview is also an important time for you to evaluate the interviewer and the company she represents.
- **Don't** inquire about salary, vacations, bonuses, retirement, or other benefits until after you have received an offer.
- **Do** close the interview by telling the interviewer(s) that you want the job and asking about the next step in the process. (Some experts even say you should close the interview by asking for the job.)
- **Do** immediately take down notes after the interview concludes so you **don't** forget crucial details.

## CASE INTERVIEWS

> The case interview is employed primarily by management consulting firms, and is increasingly being used by other types of corporations as part of the job-interviewing process.

A business-school student—at the undergraduate or MBA level—is most likely to know something about how to handle a very specialized kind of job interview—the case interview. Many business-school courses revolve around case analysis, and many business students have become pros at picking business cases apart. Still, the thought of doing so within a tight time frame (usually 15–20 minutes) in the already highly pressured situation of a job interview can be daunting—if not downright terrifying. The case interview is employed primarily by management consulting firms, as well as investment-banking companies, and is increasingly being used by other types of corporations as part of the job-interviewing process. Some firms use case interviews only for MBA-level job candidates, while others use them for undergraduates as well.

Business students who are not totally comfortable with case analysis and liberal arts students with little or no exposure to the case method can take comfort in knowing that a vast collection of resources are available, both on and off the Internet, to tell you everything you need to know about succeeding in a case interview. Here, the purpose is to give you a brief overview of the case-interview process.

Table 13.1 lists certain key behavioural aspects on which a candidate may be evaluated.

### Facing a Case Interview

The case interview, as defined by MIT's Careers Handbook, is an interview in which 'you are introduced to a business dilemma facing a particular company. You are asked to analyse the situation, identify key business issues, and discuss how you would address the problems involved'. Case interviews are designed to scrutinize the skills that are especially important in management consulting and related fields—quantitative skills, analytical skills, problem-solving ability, communications skills, creativity, flexibility, the ability to think quickly under pressure, listening skills, business acumen, keen insight,

**Table 13.1** Various performing skills

| Adaptability | Analysis | Attention to Detail |
|---|---|---|
| Communication—oral | Communication—written | Control |
| Decisiveness | Delegation | Development of subordinates |
| Energy | Entrepreneurial insight | Equipment operation |
| Fact-finding—oral | Financial analytical ability | Flexibility |
| Impact | Independence | Initiative |
| Innovation | Integrity | Judgement |
| Leadership/Influence | Listening | Motivation |
| Negotiation | Organizational sensitivity | Participative management |
| Planning and organizing | Practical learning | Presentation skills |
| Process operation | Rapport building | Resilience |
| Risk taking | Safety awareness | Sales ability/persuasiveness |
| Sensitivity | Strategic analysis | Stress |
| Teamwork | Technical/professional knowledge | Technical/professional proficiency |
| Tenacity | Training | Work standards |

> Case interviews are designed to scrutinize the skills that are especially important in management consulting and related fields

interpersonal skills, the ability to synthesize findings, professional demeanour, and power of persuasion.

Above all, you need to consider that a firm will be looking for someone who can do the real work at hand. Management consulting companies, for example, would want to know whether you are the kind of person who can make a good impression on clients.

### Approaching Case Interviews

Experts agree on many of the fine points of approaching case interviews. Some of these are mentioned as follows:

1. Practise extensively before undergoing a case interview. Use books and websites in resources sections for practice cases. Some companies that use case interviews provide good information on their own websites. Boston Consulting Group, for example, provides an interactive case you can work through for practice, as well as additional cases you can rehearse with friends. Read business magazines and periodicals, such as *The Wall Street Journal*, to get a sense of how companies deal with the kinds of issues likely to be asked about in case interviews.
2. Listen carefully to the question. Paraphrase it back to the interviewer to ensure your understanding. You may also want to take notes; in most cases the interviewer will allow you to do so.
3. Silence—but not too much of it—is golden. The interviewer expects you to take a minute or so to collect your thoughts, so do not be afraid of silence. It is alright to ask the interviewer if it is fine to take a moment to ponder over the case.
4. Remember that there is rarely one 'right' answer for analysing a case. Your process for reaching your conclusions is as important to the interviewer as the conclusion itself.
5. Construct a logical framework to explore the critical issues of the case. Many of the principles you learned in business school can serve as a framework. Examples include Porter's five forces, the SWOT analysis, value chain analysis, and the four Ps of marketing. If you have some business experience, you can also draw on applicable situations that you have encountered. Make sure your conclusion is grounded in action, not just theory. Be able to explain and defend your reasoning.
6. Prioritize the issues and objectives. Do not get bogged down trying to deal with every aspect of the case. As you ask questions, you should be able to pick up clues as to which issues are most important. Some of those clues might be meant to lead you back on track if you have gone astray, so be sure to listen carefully. If direction is not forthcoming, do not be afraid to take control of the conversation, to get to the core of the case.

### Types of Case Questions

The following are some examples of typical cases.

- Calculation/estimation/guesstimate/numerical/market-sizing case
- Problem case
- Probing case
- Business operations case
- Business strategy case

- Résumé case (case based on a company at which you worked)
- Brainteaser/logical puzzle/IQ question case

## MASTERING ON-SITE INTERVIEWS—A GUIDE TO COMPANY VISITS

Most job seekers both eagerly anticipate and dread the invitation to spend a day or two being interviewed at a company's office after an initial interview at a job fair, a screening telephone interview, or on-campus recruiting interview(s). The challenge that lies before you, however, is mastering the informal and formal interviews that await you on the visit. The purpose of the on-site interview is to allow both you and the employer to gain a more in-depth knowledge of each other—to see if there is a 'fit'. The employer, through the multiple interviews, gains a greater understanding of who you are and how you interact with numerous potential co-workers and supervisors. You get firsthand exposure to the company's work environment and corporate culture—and prospective co-workers.

Here are a few critical things you need to know about successfully navigating a company visit. If you master each of these things, you should reasonably expect a job offer.

### Preliminary Arrangements

Once you have received the invitation for the on-site visit, your first test is one of successfully dealing with the travel arrangements and arriving at the employer's office safely—and on time. Every company handles travel arrangements differently, so make sure you clearly understand the procedures and arrangements before you leave for the visit.

### Preparation

You thought you had to know a lot about the company for the initial interview? Well, you now need to become even more of an expert. Spend time researching the company by examining the company's annual reports, the company website, and external sources of information. However, do not stop there. Spend time familiarizing yourself with the key industry (or industries) that the company or division operates within.

### Corporate Culture and Fit

An on-site interview is also a great chance for you to really get a snapshot of the organization's corporate culture. The corporate culture is the environment or personality of an organization; it dictates acceptable business practices, the treatment of employees, and much more.

### Salary

Salary is certainly likely to come up during the on-site visit—just make sure you are not the one to raise the salary issue. However, you need to be prepared with a response when the issue is raised in one or more of the interviews. Try to stay as flexible as possible in any salary discussion.

> The purpose of an on-site interview is to allow both you and the employer to gain a more in-depth knowledge of each other.

### Testing

You may be requested to take one or more aptitude or personality test. The aptitude tests are similar to standardized tests you probably took to get into

> An on-site interview is a great chance for you to really get a snapshot of the organization's corporate culture.

college—and are designed to analyse whether you really have the skills you claim to have. The personality tests are designed to see whether your personality is a fit for whatever personality types of the company is looking for.

### End of the Visit

At the end of the (final) day, when your visit is just about completed, there are several important things you must do before you leave. Presumably, your final meeting of the day will be with the person who has coordinated the visit. If you are excited about the job and feel you had a strong visit, you should ask for the job offer. If you are offered the job, ask about getting a formal, written offer, and ask about when the company needs your decision.

### Follow-up

One of most important things you can do after the on-site visit is to write thank-you notes (or letters) to each person who interviewed you or spent a fair amount of time with you. If you decide to take the offer, your actions will give you an edge as you start on the job—as a courteous and considerate co-worker. Finally, if you did not get a job offer, follow-up with a phone call to the hiring manager.

## SUMMARY

An interview is a formal meeting in which a person questions, consults, or evaluates another persons. An interview reveals the views, ideas, and attitudes of the person being interviewed as well as the skills of the interviewer.

Interviews like any other formal business activity require lot of preparation and it applies both to the interviewer and the interviewee. There is no one 'best' way to prepare for an interview. Rather, there are specific and important strategies to enhance one's chances for interview success.

There are some very simple techniques and tested methods to follow before, during, and after the interview. There are also some very basic interview etiquette to be followed. Similarly, what you say in reply to a question is not so important as how you say it, and what has been your body language while making the response.

Interviews are becoming increasingly complex for both the parties with a growing variety of questions being asked to check the various kinds of skills required for increasingly demanding job profiles. The questions now range from technical to social to behavioural issues and the candidate has to present a balanced picture in almost all of the aspects being tested.

## KEY TERMS

***Behavioural job interview***  It is based on the theory that past performance is the best indicator of future behaviour, and uses questions that probe specific past behaviour—'Tell me about a time where you confronted an unexpected problem', 'Tell me about an experience when you failed to achieve a goal', and 'Give me a specific example of a time when you managed several projects at once'.

***Case interview***  It is one of the most recent techniques used by prospective employers to assess a candidates responses in some actual business situations and try to read his/ her reactions and his/ her assessment of the situation being visualized.

***Interview etiquette***  It involves some simple habits,

gestures, body language, eye contact, and other small things which an interviewee has to keep in mind while facing the interview board.

**Stress Interview** It is a technique sometimes used to weed out those who cannot handle adversity. The interviewer may try to artificially introduce stress into the interview by asking questions so quickly that the candidate does not have time to answer each one.

## Concept Review Questions

1. Why has the interview gradually become a very strategic tool of professional human resources management on the part of the organization. Do you think this change is good? Give reasons.
2. Increased complexities in jobs have also affected the role of interviewers to an extent that their role and linkage to the success of the whole process has become very critical. Discuss.
3. Earlier, Interviews were largely very flexible and had no written rules or principles as such, but nowadays even interviews have some fundamental principles underlying their relevance. Has this transformation been good or bad? Discuss.
4. How important is the résumé in the whole interview process and what are the strategic points in the résumé that require special attention by the candidates?
5. What you speak in an interview is not as important as how you speak; your overall behaviour and body language during the interview have become more important now. Do you agree? Discuss.
6. Behavioural issues have become important in the present context of organizations since most of the employees are supposed to work in teams. Because of this, behavioural interviewing has taken a front seat. What is a behavioural interview and how is the behaviour of a candidate really tested?

## Critical Thinking Questions

1. Imagine yourself as a country manager for a multinational company, about to interview a candidate on the phone. Try framing some questions in your mind before you dial the number. How do you think a telephonic interview will differ from a normal interview in terms of preparation required, choice of questions, etc.?
2. You are just coming out after facing an interview, which you can sense has not gone as per your wish. Is there anything you think, which you can do now to improve your chances and bring yourself back in the contention?
3. Imagine yourself attending an interview where the chief interviewer is not impressed with your ideas and philosophies. How do you prevent the situation from turning worse? Do you indirectly retract some of the statements made earlier to avoid his/her wrath, but in the process expose yourself as an unstable person?

## Projects

1. Visit a few business houses, try and meet some of the people in key positions in the human resources department and try to study their interviewing styles and patterns. Draw comparisons highlighting similarities and dissimilarities in their approaches and styles?
2. Assume you are a general manager (Human Resources) of a large company that is about to recruit a manager (Public Relations). How best you will device your interview, frame questions, and test him/her for the skills needed for a perfect public relations job.

3. Assume your are getting ready for a crucial interview. When you reach the recruiters office, you are asked to wait in a lounge which has four–five more people who have also applied for the same job. If all of you have to spend 30 minutes together, what kind of conversation will you initiate and how would you try to reduce nervousness, etc.?

4. Visit placement/recruitment agencies. Ask for their guidance on how to prepare for interviews in general and any separate preparations required for different kinds of interviews, that is, technical, managerial, etc.

## REFERENCES

Andrews, Patricia and Herschel 1997, *Organizational Com-munication*, Houghton Mifflin Co, Boston, pp. 216–23.

Bouknight, Omari and Scott Shrum, *Your MBA Game Plan: Proven Strategies for Getting Into the Top Business Schools*, Published by Career Press, US.

Department of Speech Communication 2004, *Effective and Ineffective Interpersonal Communication Skills*, Southern Illinois University.

Guffey, Mary Ellen 2002, *Essentials of Business Communication*, Sixth Edition, South-Western Publishing Co, Ohio, pp. 71–83.

Krishna, Murali and K.V.K. Prasad 2002, *Placement and Personality Development*, Environmental Protection Society (NIEE), AP, pp. 47–58.

Ludlow, Ron and Panton Fergus 1999, *The Essence of Effective Communication*, Prentice-Hall Inc., New Jersey, pp. 31–47.

McNamara, Carter 2004, *General Guidelines for Conducting Interviews*, Authenticity Consulting LLC, Toronto, pp. 6.

Penrose, Raseberry, Robert Rasberry, and Bob Mayers 2001, *Advanced Business Communication*, Thomson South Western, Ohio, pp. 124–32.

http://www.scribd.com/doc/51358467/interview-skills, last accessed on 26 April 2010.

http://jobsearch.about.com/od/jobinterviewtypes/g/panelinterview.htm, last accessed on 26 April 2010.

http://www.gfxtra.com/dl/The%20Virtual%20Job%20Interview, last accessed on 10 May 2010.

http://www.wisegeek.com/what-http://en.wikipedia.org/wiki/Case_interview, last accessed on 10 May 2010.

http://job-search-search.com/interviewing/behavioral_interviews, last accessed on 15 May 2010.

http://en.wikipedia.org/wiki/Job_interview, last accessed on 16 May 2010.

http://www.nasrecruitment.com/docs/white_papers/Campus-Recruiting-Trends.pdf, last accessed on 18 June 2010.

http://mbapodcaster.com/2010/01/21/on-campus-versus-off-campus-mba-recruiting/, last accessed on 22 December 2010.

http://www.career.vt.edu/interviewing/TelephoneInterviews.html, last accessed on 22 December 2010.

## CASE STUDY 1

### A True Tale of a Case Interview Gone Bad

**A job seeker's true story** The following is the sad-but-true story of what went wrong in a case interview. The narrator was a liberal arts graduate in political science who worked for a short and unhappy time after graduation as a financial consultant and aspired to a position in management consulting. He was interviewed at McKinsey and Company. The names in the story have been changed.

It was the third week in February on a gloomy gray morning, and I sneaked out of the office and away from the phones, to which I was chained, under the guise of a personal business appointment. I raced to my car, trying perhaps to create a physical excuse for my rapid pulse. Carefully maneuvering around the droop in the ceiling, I shut myself in my dingy red '85 Nissan 200, and with a tentative glance at my leaking sunroof, I was off to be interviewed at what felt like my only salvation from the life-sucking, money-ruled treadmill that had become my existence. I scrambled in the mist from my parking lot to the third tallest building in Atlanta, and headed for the top floor. As I was greeted by the recruiter, I had condensation or perspiration— I'm not sure which— trickling down my temple. She led me back to an area with two sofas already accom-modating three other interviewees. That caught me off guard slightly. For some reason I figured I would be alone since it was the end of recruiting season. Seating myself, I realized I had not really had a chance to contemplate what to expect. I waited there in the morgue.

All three of my companions looked like the antithesis of at-ease. Had I realized at the time that this was the job, I would have been nervous, too, perhaps. I was anxious all right, but it had little to do with the company. If I had been interviewing for a similar paying job at Bob's Wholesale Hardware, I would have felt the same. The Truman scholar from Cali and the Yalie to my left— info I would soon pry out of them—each seemed to be focused on some mental mantra that they were repeating in their heads. Both looked like they were trying to remind themselves that they were brilliant enough and also decide exactly which fine feat they should talk about as their greatest accomplishment, or use for some clever analogy in their interview. I, too, had considered these questions, but not knowing what to expect, I figured I would simply say what I believed. Probably my biggest mistake.

I was surprised at how tight-lipped everyone seemed to be during those few anxious minutes on the couches. I casually sparked up a little conversation and learned that each person was there for a final day-long round of interviews. They kept looking at me with a strange tilt, as if they were sending me telepathic messages saying, 'What are you doing!? Don't you know this is MCKINSEY??!!! They could hold this stuff against us!' One by one, they were led off, leaving me alone on the couch for a few uncertain minutes. Finally, I was greeted by a young woman in her late 20s and pregnant. I will call her Mandy for the sake of this anecdote. She was welcoming, and we chatted as she led me to a narrow little station where we could talk. I found Mandy to be warm, personable, and helpful. She put me at ease in what I realized was a completely unknown environment. She asked me several 'interview-type' questions, but her tone was always helpful and inquisitive.

I think I made three mistakes during this interview: (a) I felt as though I was always trying to give some nebulous right answer and falling short. I had difficulty being concise because my nerves were so shot, and I think my stammering did not help. (b) When she asked a question about where I saw myself in 10 years, I gave a very honest and unusual answer about how people create stress for themselves trying to plan and not being able to be flexible. I instead gave goals but probably was not as concrete as I should have been. I wondered if my honesty was appreciated less than a strong goal-oriented statement. (c) Although I was vaguely familiar with case questions, I was not well versed or practised. When she asked me about how to figure out how many quarters were in a mall, I knew she would want to hear how I structured my analysis, but I probably focused too much on that and also got myself caught in my own thoroughness. Had I been more practised, I could have been more systematic in my approach and then stuck to my answer instead of feeling the need to add something I may have left out.

Walking out of the room back to the sofas, I felt that it had gone fairly well. I had shown some strengths, found some connections with her (she was human). I was not sure whether I had done well or poorly on the case question, but could not think of anything I left out. With hindsight, I could have been a little more efficient and structured but I still think I did all right. Back on the couch we waited, and one by one, my 'friends' were whisked away. Again, I was the last one on the couch and really beginning to believe that I was an afterthought, at best. Maybe, looking back, I should have been flattered, but at the time and under the circumstances, I tried hard to be amused, primarily to keep at bay the doubt that kept creeping in. When my final inquisitor—I will call him Ken—finally arrived, I heard the hammer hit the nail.

Nothing Ken did or said put me at ease or made me feel like the interview was anything other than adversarial. I also knew that the moment I became confrontational, I would lose. He started out with a series of questions that were harmless enough, but sent me scrounging. 'What was your most rewarding leadership experience?' I told him about how I started, at the age of 15, playing ice-hockey, without knowing which way to hold my stick or how to skate backwards, and the next year was chosen captain, and the next again when I led our team to the playoffs. Ken's enthusiastic response, 'That's nice, but how about something *you* did?' Maybe I chose the wrong thing by giving a heartfelt answer as opposed to an ideal answer, or perhaps I just was not clear in my point of leadership by example. Either way, I felt his response to be colder than the February air.

He then asked me a case question: 'How much does a Boeing 757 weigh?' Again, I knew he was less concerned about the number I came up with as opposed to my process, but he was no help. I asked him all sorts of questions, and he just shrugged his shoulders and sat tight-lipped until after the fifth attempt he finally said, 'To answer your one question, you can assume that the seats are empty and the tank is full'. He corrected me a few times, too. 'Now I heard recently that the Concorde that they mounted atop a building near Times Square weighs 25,000 tons....'

'Tons or pounds?' asks Ken.

'I thought tons...right???' I asked as I felt the last bead of self-esteem trickle down the small of my back.

'I don't know,' helped Ken smugly.

'Well I figure the Concorde seats about 300 people, so the 757 probably somewhere around 350–375.'

'Actually, its more like 500,' helped Ken again, 'and you have two more minutes.'

I could barely stand up after our time was up; my legs were weak. Ken started down some stairs, and I mentioned, 'I need to pick up my umbrella and briefcase from the waiting area,' and he said, 'OK, meet me at the door afterwards.' I did not know what to make of it all, but I was scared. I could hardly keep the tears back as I headed for the job I so desperately wanted out of. I had a bad feeling in my stomach. Two weeks later I received a voice message from Ken, and over the next week and a half of phone tag, I could scarcely wonder whether I was nixed, or they wanted to take another look. When we finally connected, he seemed to be friendlier than I remembered. It hurt all the more when he said, 'I've got some bad news...'. I asked why they felt they were not interested, and he said I took too long to answer some questions and seemed to be unsure with numbers. That hurt. All day long, I rapid-fire numbers and calculations on the spot as a financial consultant, always one of the first with an answer. And I have been told time and time again that my biggest strength is being able to communicate a point quickly. Yes, I stumbled in the interview, but it still seemed ironic.

I bombed out in this interview because of (a) innocent naiveté about the big players in consulting and what that *really* meant; (b) unfamiliarity with their process and what it is they look for in a first interview—I just had no clue; (c) emotional turmoil; (d) lack of confidence and certainty about what I was doing and why; and (e) some general bad luck.

## Questions

1. What were the biggest mistakes that the author made? Do you really think that these are mistakes or do you believe that the author is being too under estimative? Discuss.
2. What are some of the necessary mental preparations that the author missed and for which he paid heavily?
3. What are some of the lessons that can be learnt from this case in particular and what can be done to improve upon those lessons?

CHAPTER 14

# Meetings and Conferences

## LEARNING OBJECTIVES

After reading this chapter, you will be able to understand
- the concept of business meetings
- why effective business meetings are so critical in organizational communication
- the basic principles of effective business meetings
- the various steps involved in holding an effective meeting
- how to lead meetings effectively
- the strategic issues related to organizing meetings
- the role of minutes in a business meeting
- how to plan a conference
- the various types of teleconferencing
- the advantages and disadvantages of teleconferencing
- video conferencing and web conferencing, their basic design and use in an organization

## INTRODUCTION

Meetings and conferences play a significant role in international as well as national organizations. On an average, many conferences and meetings are held every year in an organization. These include board meetings, training sessions, and meetings to set priorities and goals. Holding meetings and conferences has become increasingly complex over the past few years.

The Wharton Center for Applied Research published the following findings in *The Wall Street Journal*:

1. The average chief executive officer spends about 17 hours each week in meetings.
2. Senior executives spend an average of 23 hours a week in meetings.
3. Middle managers spend 11 hours in meetings per week.
4. Senior and middle managers said only 56 per cent of the meetings were productive. They added that a phone call or a memo could have replaced over 25 per cent of the meetings they attended.

It is apparent that if managers conduct meetings appropriately, they can reduce the time spent in meetings by one-fourth. Further, the effective management of meetings can reduce the time spent in meetings by an additional 20 per cent. This indicates that conducting meetings effectively results in a reduction of time spent in meetings from an average of 17 to 10 hours per week.

## PURPOSES OF A MEETING

People meet for a variety of reasons. Generally, they meet in order to move group actions forward. This is called task focus. To do this, participants do the following in meetings:

1. They present information to others.
2. They collaborate—review, evaluate, discuss, decide—with each other.

People also meet for social reasons such as the following:

1. They need to belong.
2. They need to achieve and make an impact.
3. They need to communicate, build, and share a common reality.

## PLANNING A MEETING

In planning a meeting, remember that for the task needs to be met, the social needs must be met and for the social needs to be met, the task needs must be met. Is it possible to satisfy both? Yes! Just plan for both the meeting content and process. The meeting content will address task needs while the meeting process attends to social needs. Paying attention to the process ensures that tasks get done.

### BUSINESS COMMUNICATION INSIGHT

**Build Shared Clarity**

Understand the power of clarity and take responsibility for it in your meetings. To do that, consider first what you can do if you are in charge of the meeting. The following steps will help:

1. Consider why you want people to meet. Ask yourself what you will accomplish face-to-face (or via conference call) that you would not accomplish otherwise. This should help you understand the objective of the meeting (but remember that you aren't the only one in need of clarity). Is it for in-formation sharing, relationship building, decision-making, problem-solving, or design?
2. After you know the objective of the meeting, think about the outcomes for the meeting and record at least the following two: (a) What is your perfect outcome? (b) What is your minimum acceptable outcome?
3. Validate the objective and outcomes to the best of your ability. Can you reasonably expect this group to produce your outcome in the time allot-ted? What can be achieved? What preparation is required? Include others in this validation process if it will help you achieve clarity.
4. Start the meeting by clearly stating the objective and outcomes. Make sure all the attendees understand the objective and are willing to work towards it.
5. When it's not 'your' meeting, it is a little trickier to be personally responsible for a clear objective and outcome of the meeting, but you can still do it. If you are a subordinate, guest, or participant in a different capacity, consider some of the following approaches: Ask for the objective and outcomes of the meeting when you are first invited. Let your host know that you take the invitation seriously, that you view meetings as important work and that you wish to be prepared to help produce the desired result.
6. If you show up for a meeting without knowing the objective and outcomes in advance, ask what these are as the meeting gets underway. Doing this in a supportive manner early in the meeting shows that you are there to contribute actively. It will also help the meeting leader because clarity of purpose, shared by all the participants, is the most powerful way to ensure the meeting is successful.
7. Make every meeting 'your' meeting by valuing your time and the contribution you can make.

> - A clear objective provides clear direction for the meeting.
> - An agenda is an outline of things to be discussed at the meeting, along with a time frame for each item.

### Be Specific

Most people agree that a productive meeting will follow an agenda. The most productive meetings, however, are the ones in which, even before considering the items on the agenda, attendees are clear about the overarching objective of the meeting. A clear objective provides clear direction for the meeting. For even greater clarity, the objective can be stated in terms of desired results or outcomes. An outcome is a clear description of what you will deliver by the end of the meeting. Consider the following illustrations of an objective and outcome:

*Objective*   Finalize budget recommendation
*Outcome*   Finalize departmental fiscal year budget for corporate budget review

### Create an Agenda

An agenda is an outline of things to be discussed at the meeting, along with a time frame for each item. To create your agenda, first look to the meeting objective, since your agenda is a path to achieving it. Then look to the participants since they will also have ideas about what is important. Two important tips about the agenda are as follows:

1. Prioritize agenda items in terms of importance to most participants.
2. Assign realistic amounts of time to each agenda item.

### Prepare in Advance

Take the time to prepare for a meeting. This may take only a few minutes to collect your thoughts and jot them down or it may take hours for a formal presentation. Advance preparation allows the meeting to move forward smoothly, eliminating wasted time and the impression that the meeting was unproductive.

## MEETING PROCESS

In this section, the meeting process is discussed (Fig. 14.1).

### Who will Participate?

On a small project team or task force, it will be easy to determine who should participate in meetings. However, in other situations, it is not always a clear choice. The following questions provide a useful filter for choosing participants:

- Whose inputs do we need?
- Who is needed to make a decision?
- Whose consent do we need to move forward?

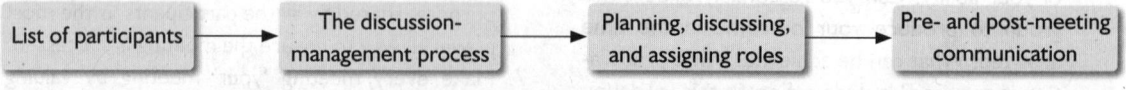

**Fig. 14.1**   The meeting process

> Save time by choosing participants appropriately and scheduling meetings to accommodate key participants' calendars.

Answers to the aforementioned questions will help determine who needs to attend the meeting or even whether the meeting needs to be held or not. Many meetings are held whether or not key participants are available. These meetings have then to be held again when all participants are present. Save time by choosing participants appropriately and scheduling meetings to accommodate key participants' calendars.

### What should be the Discussion-management Process?

Planning for discussion management or facilitation is a critical skill for leaders wishing to conduct great meetings. This is of overwhelming importance for participants' satisfaction. Start with clarity about who is to run the meeting and whether the leader will also act as the facilitator. The default choice—that the group leader or manager runs the meeting and calls on others to talk—is not necessarily the best choice for all meetings. A more participative format allows for the manager or leader to set the meeting objective and then take a seat with the members while another team member actually facilitates the discussion. This format encourages all members to participate.

### Plan, Discuss, and Assign Roles

At least the following four important roles are played in any well-conducted meeting:

- Facilitator
- Recorder
- Leader
- Participant

Some add a fifth role, the timekeeper.

Different individuals can play each of these roles or one person can play all of them. But they all have to be accounted for if the meeting is to flow well and produce results. Planning for these roles can be an ongoing process. Determining role assignments in the beginning engages everybody in the process and validates the expectations and contributions.

### Pre- and Post-meeting Communication

The best way to create commitment to and participation in meetings is to be clear about why you are meeting. Involve as many potential attendees as possible in planning either the content or the process of the meeting. Before the meeting, be sure to consider the following:

- Advance agenda
- Participants
- Time and place
- Preparation of materials
- List of audio/visual equipment available to presenters
- Requests for any special needs

> - Determining role assignments in the beginning engages everybody in the process and validates the expectations and contributions.
> - Capturing and reporting key outcomes of the meeting are critical for follow-up activities.

Capturing and reporting key outcomes of the meeting are critical for follow-up activities. Be sure to capture the following essential and basic items in your meeting notes:

- Decisions
- Action items
- Open issues

Once a meeting is concluded, arrange for the recorder's notes to be posted or distributed to all participants. Post-meeting communication provides form and closure both to participants' contributions and their social needs.

## LEADING EFFECTIVE MEETINGS

> Effective meeting leadership must ensure that a few members of the group do not dominate the discussion at the expense of their less-assertive colleagues.

The leader of the meeting has one basic goal—to accomplish the objectives of the meeting. The following sequential guidelines will be a useful tool if you are presiding over a meeting:

### Starting Time

Start the meeting on time. Nothing says more about the management than starting a meeting at the scheduled time. It has been commonly observed that starting a meeting at the time specified in the agenda immediately serves as an excellent device to catch the participant's attention and sends a right signal about the level of significance of the concerned meeting and the seriousness of the agenda.

### Opening Remarks

Once you have the participants' attention, open the meeting with appropriate remarks and also make some introductory remarks about the objectives of the meeting to set the ball rolling. Keep the following points in mind:

- Establish the right tone—usually serious and positive.
- Be sure to identify any participants unknown to the group so that every member knows each other well.
- Discuss the agenda of the meeting in general, pointing out some background to the situation and the specific objectives of the meeting.
- Identify, if any, time constraints not already expressed in the agenda—for example, when the meeting must end, etc.

### Getting Down to Business

Once you are done with the opening remarks, move to the first item on the agenda. Be extremely careful in not allowing the opening remarks to serve as a springboard to others in the meeting to lose track of the agenda.

**Image 14.1** Balanced participation is important in meetings

### Participation

It is imperative to have a balanced participation in the meeting from all the members (Image 14.1). A common observation has been that some participants talk too much while others talk too little. Effective meeting leadership must ensure that a few members of the group do not dominate the discussion at the expense of their less-assertive colleagues. A practical approach would be to put some direct questions to the quiet ones, specifically soliciting their comments, remarks, or advice instead of trying to prevent the more talkative participants from speaking.

> Close the meeting at an appropriate time once you have covered the items on the agenda.

### Agenda

Use your agenda to keep the discussion on track. If the discussion starts to drift from the item being considered, remind the members of the specific agenda items and try and steer them back to the main issue. If an item in the agenda is taking more time than initially planned, do not try to prematurely stop the discussion, because the participants may feel suffocated. If there is a substantial need for an item to be discussed in detail further, think about holding another meeting addressed to that item.

### Closing

Close the meeting at an appropriate time once you have covered the items on the agenda. Meetings sometimes continue aimlessly after the items have been covered, and it is embarrassing to have someone inquire, 'Is the meeting over?' Before you close the meeting, signal the participants by asking for any final comments or questions. Offer a summary of what has been accomplished at the meeting. Tell the participants that the minutes will be sent to them shortly. Finally, be sure to thank the group members for their time and consideration.

## STRATEGIC ISSUES RELATED TO EFFECTIVE MEETINGS

This section deals with the strategies required to hold effective meetings.

### To Meet or Not to Meet

Meeting when it is not necessary is a waste of time. Many weekly meetings can be eliminated if a decision is taken to meet only when it is absolutely necessary. Some tips for deciding if a meeting is worth your time are given as follows:

**Has a goal been set for the meeting?** Is there a purpose for meeting, or a goal to achieve? Every meeting should have an objective and if the one you have been asked to attend does not, consider recommending that a memo or email be sent instead.

**Has an agenda been created ahead of time?** An agenda is the basis for an effective meeting. Creating and distributing the meeting agenda ahead of the meeting gives participants an opportunity to prepare for it. Having an agenda for a meeting also focuses the discussion and helps the group stay on track.

**Will the appropriate people be attending?** If the appropriate people are not present, important decisions get put on hold. It will also take time to update key individuals on what took place in the meeting they missed. It is better to put the meeting on hold until all the required people are in the room.

**Can the information be covered in an email or memo?** The purpose of most meetings is sharing information and updating others. If possible, make an effort to substitute these types of meetings with an email or memo. Simply send an email to all the people who would have attended the meeting. This will save everyone time; they will still be up-to-date on what is happening and will be grateful for having one less meeting to attend that week.

### Non-verbal Communication in Meetings

Have you ever been to a meeting in which even though the leader said he/she wanted high participation, the leader stood at the head of the table and 'talked at' the participants seated silently down both sides? Chances are you have. It is unfortunate, but true—leaders who do not plan for real participation will not get it, no matter what they say they want. Standing at the end of a long table sends a strong non-verbal message—do not talk, listen. It is a good set-up if you want to discourage participation. Actions speak louder than words. Applying this maxim to management meetings requires that you take careful stock of your meeting room and where people will sit. How much does it matter? In his book *Silent Messages*, Albert Mehrabian reports the percentage of a message communicated through our different communication channels in this way:

- Words we say: 7%
- Tone of voice: 38%
- Body language: 55%

Think of the last time you were with someone who stood with his arms crossed, tapping his foot and looking annoyed, who then huffed, 'I'm fine.' Which clues did you believe—the words or body language and tone of voice? Physical, non-verbal messages often send a much louder message than spoken words.

### Control or Collaboration?

There are ways to deliberately convey non-verbal messages. When you are the leader and you need to maintain control of a meeting, consider the following pointers:

1. Conduct the meeting yourself to signal, 'I am in charge.'
2. Stand while others are sitting to signal, 'I have the floor.'
3. Sit at the head of the table to signal, 'I am in charge.'

If you want a highly participative, collaborative meeting, use the following tips:

1. Ask a team member or facilitator to conduct the meeting to signal, 'Let's share leadership.'
2. Sit while others are sitting to signal, 'I'm with you.'
3. Sit on one side of the table instead of at the head, to signal, 'I'm with you.'

### What if You Expect Confrontation?

The most confrontational position you can assume is to stand or sit directly across from another. You can increase or decrease feelings of confrontation by purposely choosing where to sit in relation to the confronter. If you seek to resolve your differences, try to sit as close as you can to the person. This sends the signal that you want to resolve the conflict.

## Reaching Rapid Consensus in Meetings

Many people believe that the only way to make decisions rapidly in an organization is to resort to the 'chain of command'. According to people with this belief, if the decision has to be made by consensus, it better require the consensus of only a few people because too many people take too much time. The myth these people buy into is that the greater the number of people, the slower the decision-making process. As logical as that may seem, there is evidence that it is not necessarily true. Given the right conditions, large groups can reach consensus rapidly too. The key is whether or not the decision-making environment is politically charged and whether the leader stands for a clear and shared mission. Here are some conditions under which large groups can make decisions rapidly.

> ## ✓ COMMUNICATION TOOL
>
> **Tips for Effective Meetings**
>
> *Don't meet* It's best to avoid meeting if the same information can be covered in a memo, email, or brief report.
>
> *Set objectives for the meeting* Before setting an agenda, determine the goal or the purpose of the meeting. The more substantial your objectives, the more intensive your agenda will be.
>
> *Provide an agenda in advance* The agenda should include a brief description of the meeting objectives, a list of areas to be covered and information stating who will speak on each topic for how long. The agenda should be followed closely during the meeting.
>
> *Allot meeting preparation* Provide each participant with something to prepare for the meeting, and that meeting will take on a new meaning to each group member.
>
> *Allocate action items* Don't finish any dialogue in a meeting without deciding what action can be taken on it.
>
> *Scrutinize your meeting process* Never quit a meeting without evaluating what took place and making a plan to improve the next meeting.

### Clear Focus on Moving Forward Together

The key to rapid consensus among any size group is a clear imperative among all the participants to move forward together. Two things are critical—moving forward and doing it together. In other words, it is in everyone's interest to resolve differences rapidly and take the next step collectively. Thus, any one person's veto is accompanied by a clear responsibility of that person to figure out how to move the group forward.

### Integrate with more Parts of the Organization

Thinking systemically about how a decision affects other departments, divisions, and functions can assist in moving the entire organization forward faster—perhaps not in the case of one decision, but in the case of many decisions over time.

If every department were making decisions by thinking about the impact on other departments, then there would be more communication, information sharing, trust, and alignment among departments. Greater information sharing and alignment can easily lead to faster decisions.

### Consensus with Leader as Time-breaker

Groups that reach a consensus rapidly do so under the pressure of time. Since there is a high value placed on moving forward, the leader should let it be known that if the group does not reach consensus, the leader will make the call and move forward. This usually works because doing something is more important than consensus, even though slightly. A good leader knows how to suspend an issue, allowing the group to decide, all the while letting the group know that if they do not, the leader will.

> - The key to rapid consensus among any size group is a clear imperative among all the participants to move forward together.
> - Greater information sharing and alignment can easily lead to faster decisions.

**Helpful hints** Consider the following tips:

1. To achieve consensus without taking up too much time, have practice group sessions regularly so that members are accustomed to owning decisions together.

> To find out if your meeting was successful you will need to consult both attendees and hosts.

2. To create an environment for achieving consensus fast, first get an agreement that a joint decision must be reached within a certain time. Also develop a consensus that anyone using the veto power has the responsibility to help move the group forward.

## EVALUATING MEETINGS

Meetings are about pleasing two groups—the attendees and the people hosting the meeting. To find out if your meeting was successful you will need to consult both groups. Attendees tell you if they have benefited from the meeting, while stakeholders tell you whether you have accomplished the goals for the event.

### Attendee Evaluations

Ask attendees to fill out anonymous paper surveys after the event or at certain points throughout the event. Ask specific questions like, 'What would you change for next time?' and 'What did you like best and why?' to generate positive and negative feedback. Ask for specific examples of problems or successes and suggestions for how things could be done better. You can also create online surveys, but if people cannot complete them until they get back to their offices, the details of the meeting may not be fresh in their minds or they may forget to fill out the survey.

### Internal Evaluations

When you plan the event, ask the management and the planning team members to list their goals for it. The goals will depend on the purpose of the meeting; however, some possible purposes are generating awareness and media interest for a company, product or cause, providing the tools and space for attendees to make a decision or share ideas and experiences about a specific topic.

You could also create some more specific goals, such as hosting over 200 attendees, building a relationship with a specific group, etc. Ask for anonymous feedback about these goals through a survey or hold a meeting to discuss the positive and negative outcomes of the event and decide if the event goals were met.

## MINUTES

Minutes are one of the most integral part of an effective meeting management process whereby the details of the discussion, who said what, and the final decision is communicated to all the participants. Minutes help in a post-meeting review and act as an official record of the company. These also help participants to understand those points that they may have missed in the meeting. Some tips to help you take better minutes at your next meeting are given as follows:

> Minutes help in a post-meeting review and act as an official record of the company.

1. Carry a copy of the agenda with you. Follow the agenda closely during the meeting and use a stopwatch to note when items begin and end.
2. If the agenda items have been addressed under the allocated time, the speaker should finish. The time that is left over can be used to address any items that could not be covered earlier in the discussion.

3. It is up to the group, with the help of the facilitator, to decide to keep on the issue or move on. For example, the group may want to get through the rest of the agenda and then revisit the extended issue at the end of the meeting. In some groups, the leader may make this decision. If it is important enough, a separate meeting may be scheduled to discuss an issue in more detail. This would also give people time to prepare better for a meaningful discussion.
4. It is the timekeeper's role to let the group know when a speaker's time is up. When one minute remains, signal the group non-verbally (e.g., raise your hand, ring a small bell). This gesture should be determined before the discussion begins. When the speaker's time is up, make the gesture again. Using a non-verbal gesture is comfortable for the timekeeper since he/she does not have to interrupt; it also encourages the speaker to wind up his/her speech.
5. The timekeeper should also alert the facilitator and group members about breaks. You could say, for example, 'I just wanted to let everyone know there are only 10 minutes before our break.' You could also write reminders on cards and hold them up as a reminder.

As follow-up, email an attachment of the meeting notes to each of the participants or save them to the company's network in a meetings folder. This way, all the meeting participants have access to the meeting notes if there is an idea or discussion they would like to revisit. In the email, also summarize the action items assigned during the meeting. Outline what was assigned, to whom it was assigned, the priority level and the due date. When a meeting is adjourned, it is not always clear who is responsible for what, which means action items are not always carried through. By summarizing the action items in an email, you can be certain all the participants understand who is responsible for what.

## PLANNING A CONFERENCE

A conference is a gathering of a particular set of individuals invited to consult with, discuss, and/or present information on a particular topic or set of topics in a related field or subject for the purpose of bettering relations and information exchange between the organizations/markets the individuals represent. Both conferences and meetings serve almost the same purpose, that is, cross-fertilization of ideas, but meetings all more in-house oriented whereas focus of conferences is to invited ideas from outside sources. Both follow almost similar principles and require meticulous planning for their real effectiveness.

The task of planning and coordinating a conference is a high profile but demanding role that can be rewarding at the completion of the event. The following are a few useful tips that will make the task easier. Planning the event is all the groundwork for a successful conference or function. There are two important questions to ask before considering organizing a conference, which are as follows:

1. What is the purpose of the conference?
2. How can the purpose be best achieved?

> Both conferences and meetings follow almost similar principles and require meticulous planning for effectiveness.

### Purpose of the Conference

The purposes of a conference may be diverse. Some of the common purposes are to

- coordinate activities
- build morale
- secure agreement
- brief staff/clients
- solve problems
- exchange information
- initiate policy
- launch products

Keeping the purpose in mind will assist in planning the method to achieve the purpose of the conference. This will also determine how much time allocation is required to achieve the objectives.

## Conducting a Conference

A conference is conducted effectively if the following points are considered carefully:

**Date and time**  Select a date, time, and duration for the conference. These may all be approximates initially, but after reviewing, steps should be taken to enable a much more accurate duration.

When selecting a date, be sure to leave yourself, attendees, and presenters enough time to plan ahead for the conference. Also allow time to be able to find and book a suitable venue. Many conference and function venues get booked well in advance, so you may not have many choices if it is left too late.

**Attendees**  Identify the intended audience of the conference. Consider questions like how many will be attending, and from how far are they required/able to travel to the conference, are there any special requirements of attendees in accessing the conference, for example, wheelchair access, etc.

**Conference content**  Determine the most appropriate topics that will address the conference purpose. Select activities and presenters who can help achieve the conference purpose. The final agenda, order, and content of conference activities will go through many changes until the actual conference is run.

**Venue/Facilities**  Selecting the correct venue may require the most time, as you should always inspect a venue prior to booking it. Preparing a checklist of the conference facilities and requirements will narrow the options. The following points should be decided prior to searching for a conference venue:

*Location*  To help decide the location, ask the following questions:

1. How far are attendees travelling?
2. If attendees are being flown in, how far is it from the nearest airport?
3. How are attendees arriving to the venue? For example, if by car, then is the drive too long?
4. Does the venue need to be close to the workplace or far away?

*Capacity*  Ensure that the venue can provide for the number of intended attendees. Is the conference room layout appropriate for the purpose? The following are a selection of room layouts that can be used (Fig. 14.2):

1. *Theatre*  This arrangement is for briefing a large group, initiating a policy or building morale. Attendees are not required to write anything.
2. *Classroom*  This arrangement is used for briefing groups that are required to take notes and perhaps work in small groups of a maximum of four.
3. *Boardroom*  In this arrangement, all participants can see each other in the conference. It is useful for a group no larger than 20, for securing agreement or solving problems. This arrangement encourages participation of all attendees.
4. *Hollow square*  The participants face each other. Unlike the boardroom arrangement it has more space across from participants.
5. *U-shaped*  This enables group interaction, but the conference is focused around a facilitator in front of the group.

> Boardroom arrangement encourages participation of all attendees.

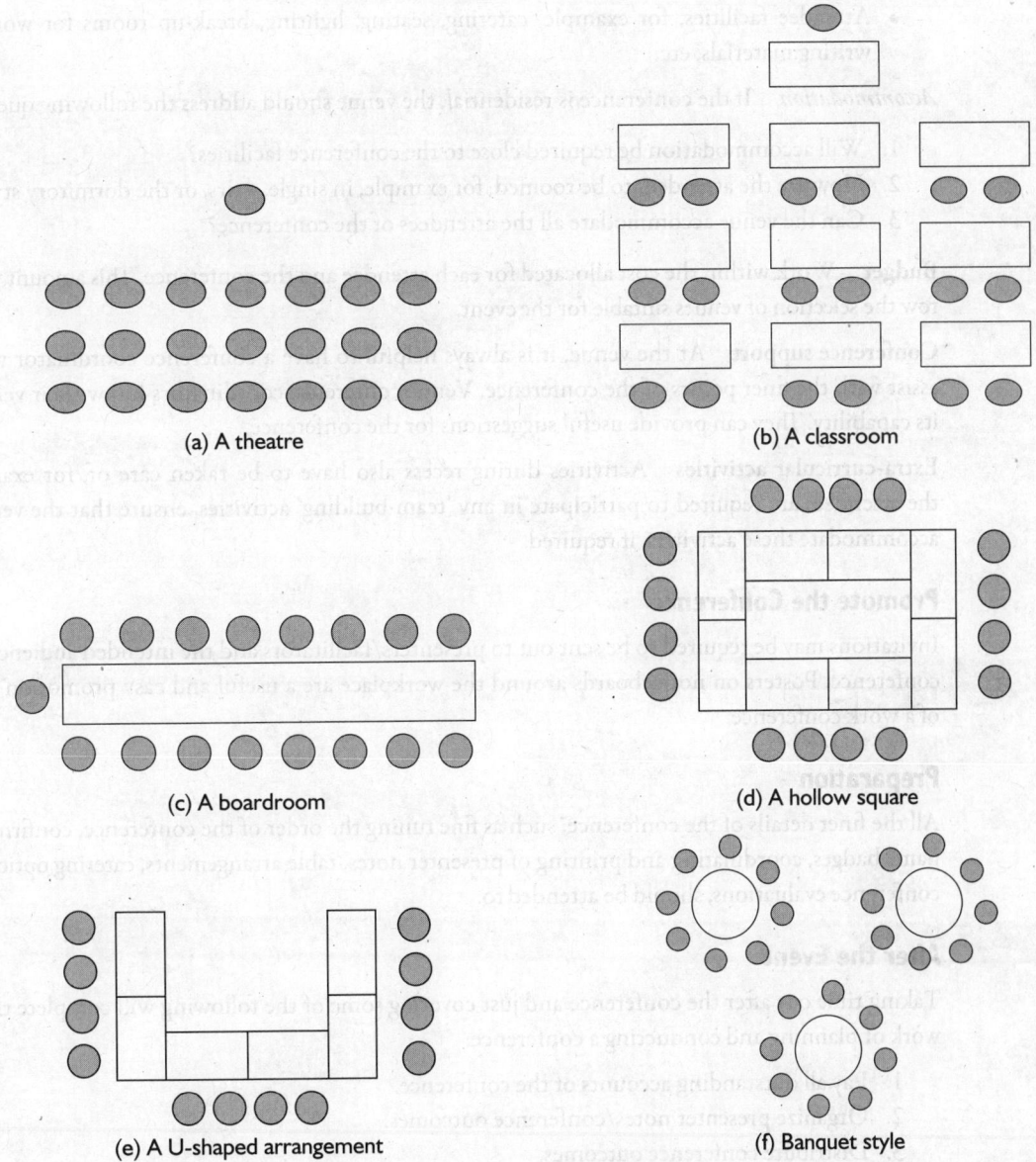

Fig. 14.2 Different types of room layout

5. *Banquet style* This comprises a large conference with smaller groups seated at round or rectangular tables where group and workshop activities can be performed. The banquet style also encourages attendees to network with their immediate group at the conference.

*Facilities* There are a variety of facilities to be considered for a conference which are as follows:

> The banquet style encourages attendees to network with their immediate group at the conference.

- Presenter facilities, for example, speakers, mikes, audio-visual aids, screens, boards, flipcharts, etc.

- Attendee facilities, for example, catering, seating, lighting, break-up rooms for workshops, writing materials, etc.

*Accommodation*   If the conference is residential, the venue should address the following questions:

1. Will accommodation be required close to the conference facilities?
2. How are the attendees to be roomed, for example, in single, pairs, or the dormitory style?
3. Can the venue accommodate all the attendees of the conference?

**Budget**   Work within the cost allocated for each attendee and the conference. This amount will narrow the selection of venues suitable for the event.

**Conference support**   At the venue, it is always helpful to have a conference coordinator who can assist with the finer points of the conference. Venue conference coordinators know their venue and its capability. They can provide useful suggestions for the conference.

**Extra-curricular activities**   Activities during recess also have to be taken care of, for example, if the attendees are required to participate in any 'team-building' activities, ensure that the venue can accommodate these activities, if required.

### Promote the Conference

Invitations may be required to be sent out to presenters/facilitators and the intended audience of the conference. Posters on noticeboards around the workplace are a useful and easy promotion activity of a work conference.

### Preparation

All the finer details of the conference, such as fine tuning the order of the conference, confirmations, name badges, coordinating and printing of presenter notes, table arrangements, catering options, and conference evaluations, should be attended to.

### After the Event

Taking time out after the conference and just covering some of the following will complete the hard work of planning and conducting a conference:

1. Pay all outstanding accounts of the conference.
2. Organize presenter notes/conference outcomes.
3. Distribute conference outcomes.
4. Collect and analyse conference evaluations, if used.
5. Reflect whether the conference reached its objective/purpose.
6. Strengths of the conference.
7. Weaknesses of the conference.
8. Have a team meeting and brief the team about the conference outcomes.

> Posters on noticeboards around the workplace are a useful and easy promotion activity of a work conference.

## TELECONFERENCING

Teleconferencing refers to the exchange of data between geographically separated individuals by means of telecommunication systems such as telephone, computer, radio, or television. With the globalization of businesses, it is increasingly difficult for individuals from different locations to meet for communicating, planning, or brainstorming business ideas frequently. As such, teleconferencing has made it both convenient and cost effective for companies to bring people together for meetings without the need to share a common physical space.

## Types of Teleconference

The three basic types of teleconferencing based on the type of information exchanged are as follows:

- Audio conferencing—allows verbal communication
- Computer conferencing—allows the exchange of printed communication through keyboard terminals
- Video conferencing—allows visual and verbal communication.

### Audio Teleconference

Audio teleconfrence is also known as conference calling. It allows verbal communication over telephone among more than two members. It includes simple home phones with three-way calling to more sophisticated conference call settings used by big firms to connect calls among several large groups of individuals by means of conference bridges. Several software help add additional features to the conference bridges, giving them unique features beyond just being able to answer multiple calls simultaneously. However, since it is a voice-only communication, the necessary documents, written material, and visual aids have to be circulated to the members involved beforehand.

### Audio-graphic Conferences

This is also known as 'electronic whiteboarding' or 'screen sharing' because the computer screen is shared among the participants and used as a whiteboard or an overhead projector. This system allows both voice and visual data exchange in real time. While audio bridges allow verbal communication, lower-band telecommunication channels are generally used to transfer visual data in the form of videos, pictures, documents, graphics, etc. that make the oral communication more effective. This type of conferencing is commonly used in long-distance training and teaching.

### Computer Teleconference

Computer teleconference is a setting that allows multiple users to access a common database. Some examples include instant messaging, chat systems, online courses, etc. It allows the participants to hear and view visual presentations simultaneously and in real time. Online courses are a typical example of such systems wherein the teacher uploads study material, lectures, grades, etc. on a common location accessible to all students. The students can download the material from this site, and in turn upload their assignments and queries into the common files for the teacher to assess/address. This method of coaching has become very common because of its time and cost effectiveness and limited resources required.

### Video Teleconference

Video teleconference allows simultaneous two-way exchange of audio and video, making face-to-face interactions possible between geographically separated individuals. The most important benefit of video conferencing is that along with voice communication, it also allows the participants to see each other's body language and physical cues, which considerably reduces the chances of miscommunication in business interactions. Apart from being used by large organizations for setting up meetings across time zones, video conferencing is also extensively used by many institutes to facilitate distant learning. It allows institutes to effectively conduct courses on unusual subjects that may otherwise not be feasible due to the limited number of students enrolling. Through video conferencing, a tutor can reach out to several groups of students at different sites, making such tutorials not only possible but also more cost-effective and convenient as it reduces travel time and expenses for rural or out-of town students. Although it started as a complicated process requiring several additional devices, video compression technology and Internet advances have simplified video conferences drastically. This technology is now commonly used even at homes, allowing more personalized communication among distantly located family members.

## Advantages of Teleconferences

The advantages of teleconferences are as follows:

- Cuts down significantly on travel costs:  Business representatives from different time zones can still interact effectively at a prescheduled time without having to travel across the globe.
- Saves time:  Not only is travel time reduced, but it also reduces the time spent in socializing in face-to-face meetings, thus allowing shorter and more efficient meetings.
- Makes larger gatherings possible:  With hectic schedules and tight deadlines, it is usually impossible to gather all the involved participants in one place at a given time. Teleconferencing allows people to meet and discuss from their desks, thus making it possible for all the members to be involved in these discussions.
- Improves interaction:  Verbal communication is augmented by body language and physical cues such as confusion, disagreement, satisfaction, or concern in a teleconference, which makes it easier for the team to focus, understand, and collaborate more effectively, and reduces the possibility of miscommunications. The larger number of participants also facilitates a free flow of new ideas and alternatives for faster decision making.
- Facilitates collaboration between home-office and field staff:  With many organizations promoting the work-from-home concept, video conferences allow firms to manage home-office staff as well as field staff efficiently and collaboratively.
- Increases productivity:  Apart from making frequent communication possible, it also increases the involvement of team members and allows urgent meetings to be scheduled on a very short notice, thus improving productivity and efficiency. The decisions and results are more instantaneous and quicker than communication through mails.
- Wider reach of information:  Notices and announcements can be made known to all employees simultaneously and instantaneously.
- Distance education:  Besides business, teleconferencing is also extensively used for distance education by institutes to reach out to students in remote areas and to conduct courses that

may otherwise not be feasible due to the limited number of students enrolling into them. Institutes can now conduct these courses with limited resources, by allowing students from different geographic areas to access the lectures and materials online at a common location, and students can reap the benefits of these courses without the involved travel and associated expenses.

## Disadvantages of Teleconferences

The disadvantages of teleconfrences are as follows:

1. Technical failures may lead to disruptions in the midst of meetings that cause loss of focus and confusion.
2. Effective teleconferencing among large groups requires good acoustics and uninterrupted network services, which might require considerable infrastructural investments.
3. Lack of eye contact between the conversing members may lead to miscommunication or an appearance of disinterest.
4. Participants tend to be more conscious of their appearance when on camera.
5. A lack of familiarity with the equipment and system may be a dissuading factor, especially for older employees.
6. Teleconferencing creates fewer opportunities for socializing among the team members, which results in less rapport among the members.
7. It is not as effective as face-to-face communication for complex interactions such as business negotiations and bargaining.
8. Excessive exchange of data through frequent teleconferences may lead to an information overload, resulting in reduced productivity.

## Applications of Teleconferencing

Teleconferencing has become an integral part of current-day business. Rapid advances in Internet technology, compression algorithms, multimedia hardware and software have made teleconferences an efficient tool in business communication. They only get bigger and more complex when catering to bigger and more demanding business requirements. Today, teleconference is an essential tool used efficiently across businesses, education, health-care government agencies, etc. Some of the common applications of teleconferencing in the various fields are mentioned as follows:

### Home Use

With jobs today often taking youngsters farther away from home than ever before, teleconferencing is increasingly being used by geographically distant family members to communicate with each other. It has made communication a far more efficient, quick, and more satisfying experience.

### Business

All businesses, large or small, depend on this technology to various extents. From cutting down business travelling and associated expenses to facilitating active communication across different time zones, teleconferencing plays a key role in the current global business scenario. It performs the following functions:

1. Saves time.
2. Is cost effective.
3. Reduces business travel drastically.
4. Is more convenient than gathering a set of people in a common physical space.
5. Allows presentations, trainings, meetings, announcements, discussions, and all other forms of business communication.
6. Limits geographical boundaries and time zone issues.

### Employee Training

Teleconferencing is one of the most cost-effective modes of corporate training available, whether it is training large groups of fresh graduates or upgrading latest trends and technologies to existing employees. With various forms of audio and visual aids available to augment the regular classes, it is more productive and effective than the traditional methods of training.

### Distant Learning

One of the major and most useful applications of teleconferencing has been in the area of distance education. This technology has helped institutes reach out to students in remote areas. It has also helped institutes conduct entire courses on unusual subjects that may otherwise not have been possible due to the limited number of students enrolling into these courses. However, with the introduction of teleconferencing, several students from various locations can access lectures and study material at a common location and in turn upload their queries and assignments to be evaluated in the same common location, which has made distant education a convenient and dynamic alternative to classroom teaching.

### Health-care Industry

Teleconferencing has also impacted the health-care industry to some extent by allowing physicians and other paramedical professionals to reach out to patients across vast distances. The data retrieved by medical devices, such as ultrasound imaging devices, microscopes with digital cameras, videoendoscopes, etc., can be transferred effectively with the help of video conferencing equipments to be analysed and discussed by professionals at different locations or between doctor and patient. It has also facilitated better emergency management with the help of real-time telemedicine and telenursing applications, which help patients to gather the necessary information and guidance quickly without spending time in travelling or waiting to see the physician.

### Government/Legal Environment

Government agencies also use teleconferencing for the purpose of internal communication and announcements. In the US, this technology has also been used extensively to conduct legal hearings at remote locations, and sometimes even for testimonies in cases where the legal setting was expected to cause severe psychological stress in the individual.

### Media

The main use of teleconferencing in the media business is for press teleconferencing, wherein journalists from various locations can participate in international press conferences from within their studios. This is also a new and developing trend that is yet to catch up in several countries.

Teleconferencing has several benefits, and at least some, if not all, of the disadvantages may also be addressed to some extent by taking into account the number of participating individuals, their extent of familiarity with the equipments and the technology, their rapport with each other, the purpose of the meeting, and various other factors involved. However, with all its potential, teleconferencing cannot completely replace face-to-face interactions because although it can facilitate the process of setting up a meeting and provide additional aids to enhance communication, it cannot simplify the inherent complexity of group communication. The need of the hour therefore is to strike a balance between the traditional and modern modes of communication for efficient interaction and decision-making.

## EFFECTIVE MEETINGS VIA VIDEO CONFERENCING

People really do not like to video conference. Ask anyone who does it on a regular basis and, at best, the response will be neutral. At worst, the response will be militantly negative. Since the costs of installing and using video conferencing technologies have dropped dramatically over the past five years and the installation base is continuing to grow, the end result is an increased level of dissatisfaction in the video conferencing user community. However, more and more corporations, hospitals, and universities continue to install video conference technology because they see it as an effective way to share limited resources, reduce travel expenses, and increase overall productivity within their organizations. In order to maximize their return on this investment in technology, the end-users need to be trained on how to use the technology effectively.

Let us look at some basic information. When we communicate, 10 per cent of the meaning is contained in the words we choose, 20 per cent is contained in the style of delivery, and 70 per cent is contained in non-verbal cues or body language. That is why video conferencing can be so much more effective than a voice-only conference call. Let us look at some other facts. When we engage in a face-to-face conversation, all parties walk away with an 80 per cent level of common understanding and agreement of what was discussed; in a voice-only meeting, this level drops to 40 per cent; when the meeting is held over video conference, the level rises back up to 60 per cent.

The natural assumption, then, is that meeting over video conference is the next best thing to being there. However, when used properly, video conference can actually be better than being there in person.

Meeting a new team leader can also take place over video conference.

People just need to know how to increase their effectiveness in a video conference. The following tips will help:

**Proper camera placement**  If you are making your presentation from the front of the room, the camera should be placed at eye level with the seated participants (at the end of the conference table or the back of the classroom). That way, when you are looking at the people in your local room, you automatically maintain good eye contact with the people at the far end. You should place a display monitor with the camera so that when you look at the people on the monitor, it appears you are looking them directly in the eye. This keeps people at the far side connected with you and helps them feel as if they are part of the presentation.

**Practise**  Be familiar with the equipment you will be using, including the placement and operation of the cameras, microphones, and remote controls. Make sure there are fresh batteries in all devices, which require them. Practise using the audio visual devices you will be using during the meeting. Be fluent and confident.

**Use your voice and body tools**  Vary the pitch and tone of your voice to add emphasis and meaning. Use appropriate facial expressions and gestures. Remember, the camera does not like rapid or 'throw away' gestures, so hold the gesture a little longer than you may be used to for local presentations. Do not rock or sway. These gestures get amplified over video and become annoying in a short time.

**Make use of slides**  If you are using information from a computerized slide show, such as PowerPoint, the minimum font size is 36–40 points. Anything smaller will be illegible on the far side. Avoid saturated colours, such as deep reds, blues, and greens. They smear and bleed over video. Use graphics to help illustrate your ideas. Minimize the amount of words actually put on the slide. Encapsulate the idea and then expand on it verbally.

**Maintain face-to-face connection**   If you use other sources of visual information, such as a PowerPoint slide show, a whiteboard, or a videotape, remember to switch back to your face as often as possible. Maintaining face-to-face connection is critical for effective communication.

**Light up**   The space used for video conferencing should be lit with indirect light sources. Turn off the downcans. They create inconsistent light levels and will result in raccoon eyes and deep shadows under the chin. A video conference room should have 70 foot-candles of light at the face (not desktop). Indirect lighting (bouncing the light off the ceiling or walls or some other device like half-inch paracube diffusers) will reduce fatigue of the people in the room. Use colour-corrected lamps to achieve a light temperature between 3,200 and 3,400 Kelvin.

**Take breaks**   Remember, video conferencing is very intensive and focused. Plan for a 10-minute break every 50 minutes or so. Let people stretch their legs. Use the 10 minutes to catch your breath and get ready for the next segment.

**Ensure comfort**   Make sure the temperature is set at an appropriate level and the chairs are ergonomically correct.

## WEB CONFERENCING

Web conferencing is a new communication medium, and it is not quite like any other. It may share characteristics with other media, such as teleconferencing and live multimedia presentations, but ultimately it requires specific techniques for maximum effectiveness. Some ideas for creating more successful online events will be discussed here.

**Keep it simple**   It is easy to become enamoured with all the features that today's web conferencing systems offer. Avoid the temptation to try all the features if you are just starting out or if you are trying a new system. Master the basics of slide control, polling and messaging. Once you and your audience are comfortable with these elements, you can gradually introduce more sophisticated features such as streaming audio, whiteboarding, and application sharing.

**Keep it short**   Live events of 60 to 90 minutes are most effective. If your programme requires more time, consider breaking it into segments delivered over days or weeks. Build the presentation around three or four key messages to leave with your audience. Ninety minutes is enough time to interact with the audience—asking them questions for polls and answering their questions.

**Get off to a fast start**   Spend no more than two minutes introducing the event and covering the features of the web conferencing system. Then let the main presenter begin. This will give the event a fast-paced feel that will keep participants tuned in.

> For live events involving more than 20 participants, use one or more specialists in addition to the presenter to answer audience questions.

**Ask good questions**   Do not use a live event to ask pointless demographic questions such as 'From where are you attending?' That kind of information can be determined in pre-event registration. Use the time in front of the audience to ask questions that collect critical feedback and measure the effectiveness of your message.

**Use a specialist**   For live events involving more than 20 participants, use one or more specialists in addition to the presenter to answer audience questions. The barriers to participation are low in an online event, so expect to receive more questions via the instant-messaging feature common to most web conferences than in a typical face-to-face presentation. Using a specialist means that everyone who asks a question will get a personal response while the presenter stays focussed on delivering his/her key points.

**Conduct pre-flight checks**   Pre-flight checks are usually web pages provided by the event service providers that check the participant's computer to ensure it is capable of participating in the programme. All participants should complete one.

**Start with the phone**   To ease people into the technology, first use web conferencing in conjunction with a familiar medium, such as tele-conferencing. Let the teleconference deliver the audio, and let the Web conference offer participants a way to see visual material and ask questions without interrupting the programme. Use the interactive features of the teleconference bridge, such as live question and answer (Q&A) sessions, to simulate a radio 'talk show' format. As the participants become comfortable, you can migrate some of them to Internet-based audio to reduce the teleconference expense.

**Keep slides simple**   Web conferencing works best when slides are formatted with simple designs and a few consistent colours. Do not use full-screen photos in slides. These images will take too long to display for participants. When made 'web ready' for the event, flat colours and simple graphics will display quickly on the screen.

**Plan ahead for software demos**   If a computer application is going to be demonstrated to the audience, select a web conferencing system that supports application broadcasting. This allows the application to be shown directly from a computer. Practise with this a lot before the event to get comfortable with how it works and how it looks from the perspective of the presenters and the audience. Most systems require a plug-in to be downloaded and installed to capture and display what's on the computer screen.

**Hire a professional moderator**   For important events, hiring a professional online moderator, who can conduct interactive polls and talk with a presenter while waiting for results to come from the audience, eliminates awkward dead air. A moderator also can smooth the Q&A process by asking prepared questions and gleaning the best ones from the online audience. Perhaps most importantly, these professionals know how to keep an online event moving when glitches occur and this allows the speakers to focus on their message, rather than worry about which button to click.

**Test and retest**   Once the event is staged and ready to go, make sure to test the links that will be sent to your registered participants. If the correct link is not sent, the audience will not be able to find the event. Also, double-check the phone number for the teleconference for participants and presenters. Problems like these are completely preventable with a minimal due diligence.

**Use both views for the presentation**   On programme day, set up two computers—one with the presenter's view and another logged on as an audience member—for a sense of what the participants are experiencing. Slides that are slow to advance for you may display quickly for the audience. This also will let you check the format and the appearance of the visuals from the participants' perspective.

**Do not go looking for trouble** Glitches can happen during any type of presentation, in person or over the Web. In web-based events, glitches are often an issue only if the presenter acknowledges them. For example, if the presenter clicks a button to advance to the next slide and it is slow to change, he/she gains nothing by telling the audience, 'Gosh, this sure is taking a long time to come up.' Perhaps there is a slower-than-average Internet connection. Just make a mental note to advance slides a little sooner, and no one will be the wiser.

## SUMMARY

A meeting provides a forum for group discussion. The purpose of a meeting is to generate ideas and solutions to a given problem. A meeting is effective when it is able to deliver some solutions to the problems for which the meeting was called for. Every meeting must have an agenda, which contains the information about the items that are going to be discussed in the meeting. Conducting a meeting needs great tact. The chairperson plays a very crucial role in arriving at a constructive decision.

## KEY TERMS

**Conference** It is a meeting with a formal agenda for consultation or exchange of information or discussion.

**Meeting** It is an assembly or gathering of people for a business, social or religious purpose. In a meeting, two or more people come together, to have discussions, often in a formal way.

**Minutes** These are one of the most integral parts of an effective meeting management process whereby the details of what was discussed, who said what, and what was finally decided is recorded and communicated to all the participants.

**Web conferencing** It is a meeting held of participants based at different locations through the Web.

## Concept Review Questions

1. Discuss the role of a leader in a meeting. Why is his/her role so crucial in leading an effective meeting?
2. What are the main contents of the minutes of a meeting? What are some specific principles for effective writing of minutes?
3. What are the effective ways in which a problem participant in a meeting should be dealt with?
4. What are the strategic advantages provided by video conferencing vis-à-vis physical conferencing?
5. How do you deal effectively with a CEO who is a meeting fanatic? How do you explain him/her the cost perspective involved in meetings?
6. Discuss a handy and convenient method of evaluating meetings? Consider both internal as well as external evaluations.

## Critical Thinking Questions

1. You have to hold a condolence meeting on the demise of one of your colleagues of the management committee of your club. Draft the resolution to be adopted at the meeting.
2. Rajeev Rai, owner of a small business employing 25 people, has an appointment with Javed Rehman, vice-president of Metropolitan Bank, to discuss his two-crore business loan. What helpful guidelines

you can give Rajeev regarding his non-verbal behaviour at the conference?
3. Assume that you are a dean at your university, which does not celebrate Ambedkar's birthday with a paid holiday. You are seeking the support of the other four deans for making it a holiday for all college students and employees. Prepare a memorandum, including the agenda for the meeting, for the other deans. Submit the memo and the agenda to your instructor along with responses to the questions likely to be raised by other deans.

## Projects

1. Divide into groups of five, with each member playing the role of the president of one of the five student organizations on the campus. The dean has proposed a plan, whereby all students before going to their Masters' degree programme have to buy a laptop. Your group is also meeting to either support or oppose this proposal. Appoint a group leader and conduct a 15–20 minutes meeting on this topic following parliamentary procedure. Do not adjourn till you have approved a motion, one way or the other. After adjournment, evaluate how effective the meeting was. How was it conducted, how well did each person perform, and were correct parliamentary procedures followed. Write your evaluation in a joint memo to your instructor.
2. Your university is considering a major restructuring exercise in which most of the academic programmes are being revisited and suitable changes are being made in tune with market demands. You have been selected by the administration to chair a committee to present the students' point of view. Decide whom to include in the committee and draft an agenda for the first meeting.

## REFERENCES

Bens, Ingrid 2005, 'How to Discourage Dysfunctional Behavior in a Meeting', web support from www.effectivemeetings.com.

Cook, Charlie 2005, 'Meetings: Vehicles for Achieving Results', Inmind Communications LLC, web support of openthis.com.

Cook, Charlie 2005, 'The Three Most Important Secrets of Successful Meetings', Inmind Communications LLC, web support of www.openthis.com.

Hill, Jenny 2005, 'Managing Meetings', web support of www.learningmatters.com

'How to Conduct a Conference and Planning a Conference', web support of www.TheConferenceGuide.com.

'Logistics for Conference', web support of www.asem3.go.kr.

Kaliouby, Rana El 2004, *Intelligent User Interfaces Conference: Report*, Computer Laboratory, University of Cambridge.

Munter, Seth Daniel 2002, 'Getting Unstuck: Common Problems in Meetings and Some Solutions', *Meeting Resource Guide*.

Raybun, Keith R. 2000, 'Evaluation: Building Strategy and Knowledge in Education Programmes', *IEP - OSI Conference*.

Whinoser, Jay 2003, 'Putting a Price on Meeting Productivity', *The Wharton Center for Applied Research*.

http://en.wikipedia.org/wiki/Videoconferencing, accessed on 15 February 2012.

http://www.joe.org/joe/1984september/a4.php, accessed on 20 January 2012.

## CASE STUDY 1

### A Special Meeting of the Executive Committee

Anand, Vice-President, Systems, ground his cigarette into the ashtray and thought, 'Here go those Save-the-Earth people again.' He had just read a copy of a memo that Savitri, Vice-President, Finance, had sent to Rajiv, CEO, asking that smoking be prohibited throughout the premises of Salient Technologies—both in their Gurgaon and Pune offices. Savitri cited health dangers, reduced productivity, rights of non-smokers, and damage to company property. Anand knew he could cite some arguments also—the rights of smokers, the unfairness of imposing new restrictions that were not in place when workers were hired, the reduced productivity due to stress from not smoking and the fact that other health-related productivity hazards (such as gross obesity) were not banned. He felt that he could easily get the support of Raghu, Vice-President, Marketing, and Vinay, General Manager, Utilities, the two other smokers in the management.

Following these developments, the CEO decides to hold a special meeting of the executive committee, made up of himself and the three vice-presidents (which includes Anand and Savitri) the following week to discuss and resolve the issue. Regular parliamentary procedures were then followed at these meetings.

### Questions

1. Assume the role of Rajiv, the CEO. Compose a memo to the executive committee announcing the meeting and outlining the agenda.
2. Assume the roles of other participants in the meeting and carry on the discussion from your own point. Also write the minutes of the meeting.
3. After the role-play, discuss how each of the participants felt about the meeting? Was anyone arguing from a position he/she did not really agree with? Was the meeting successful? Did anyone lose or win?

CHAPTER 15

# Group Discussions and Team Presentations

## LEARNING OBJECTIVES

After reading this chapter, you will be able to understand

- the concept of group discussions (GDs) and team presentations in organizations
- why effective GDs are so critical in organizational communication
- the basic principles involved in conducting effective GDs
- the various functional and non-functional roles in a GD
- how to improve group performance
- how to assess GDs
- the various benefits and purposes of team presentations
- the execution of a successful team presentation

## INTRODUCTION

A group discussion (GD) is a form of communication in which a small number of people meet face-to-face and exchange ideas through free oral interaction in order to discuss few solutions to a problem and arrive at a consensus. GDs can be conducted at workplaces; they can also serve as an effective tool for an interviewer to assess the various competencies of candidates appearing for a job interview. While in the former case, the participants come prepared for the discussion, in the latter case the candidates may be asked to discuss a topic or a case which they might not have heard of. A GD allows you to exchange information and ideas, and gives you the experience of working in a team. In the workplace, discussions enable the management to draw on the ideas and expertise of its employees, and acknowledge them as valued members of a team. When they discuss in groups, they come out with a number of ideas, thereby developing a variety of solutions to a problem. Moreover, GDs help summarize the ideas, and information that such groups discuss. Each participant can stimulate ideas in the other people present, and through a process of discussion, the collective view becomes greater than the sum of the individual parts.

> A GD allows you to exchange information and ideas, and gives you the experience of working in a team.

A team presentation, which is an offshoot of group dynamics, is another very important management exercise carried out in companies. Instead of a manager making a solo presentation on any organizational issue, a team makes a concerted effort to present its point of view, findings, etc. The fundamental requirement is that the presentation must be a group effort and the audience should get a feel of a unified presentation rather than disjointed small parts presented by three or four members.

> - GDs need to be carefully led by a facilitator or leader who ensures that the group continues discussing the topic of interest and that all participants contribute.
> - Brainstorming is a creative exercise, wherein groups of participants are brought together to explore a common issue and look for possible solutions.

This chapter focuses on the two most useful forms of business communication, namely group discussions and team presentations.

## BENEFITS OF A GD

Any GD entails time and resources, which are both scarce and costly. Therefore, one needs to understand clearly the direct benefits of holding a GD to solve business problems or tackle real-life situations. Some advantages of a GD are as follows:

1. Ideas can be generated, tried out, and exchanged.
2. Group members get an opportunity to respond to each other's ideas.
3. Groups provide a supportive and nurturing environment for academic and professional endeavours when the dynamics are right.
4. GD skills have many professional applications.
5. Working in groups is both fun and fruitful.

**Participants** There are no specific requirements for the participants, apart from them having some knowledge of the discussion area. Also, there is no restriction in the number of participants though generally the maximum number is limited to 10. For complex issues, it is useful to have discussion groups that are multidisciplinary, so that different perspectives and viewpoints can be aired. For other purposes, relatively homogenous groups might be preferred. Whatever the composition, GDs need to be carefully led by a facilitator or leader who ensures that the group continues discussing the topic of interest and that all participants contribute. However, assessment GDs conducted as a part of job interview process do not initially have any appointed leader though one may emerge as and when the discussion proceeds.

**Purpose** GDs can be used to serve a variety of purposes—in identifying problems, in clarifying issues relevant to a particular topic and in the evaluation of products. GDs form a part of brainstorming and focus groups, and are very common in the 'user requirement' stage of product development.

Brainstorming is a creative exercise, wherein groups of participants are brought together to explore a common issue and to look for possible solutions. In a brainstorming exercise, each participant is allowed to be creative and no participant is allowed to criticize another's contributions. Brainstorming is commonly used in the early stages of design in order to explore possible development opportunities. For instance, when a company wishes to bring a change in the existing promotion policy, it can generate innovative ideas from many employees through brainstorming exercise.

Focus groups bring together participants to discuss a particular topic. These differ from brainstorming sessions in that the objective of the meeting in not necessarily to be creative, but rather to come to some agreement regarding a particular topic or issue. For example, focus groups have been used in the assistive technology field to identify the important features that a product should have and to evaluate how successful a particular product is likely to be.

 See the PowerPoint presentation on group discussions in the Online Resource Centre.

## WORKPLACE GD GUIDELINES

> It can be difficult to play both the role of a facilitator and a full participant in a discussion.

This section discusses the basic principles that guide workplace GDs.

### Planning and Preparation

The following factors need to be considered for organizing a GD:

**Purpose** The purpose for which a group is holding the discussion needs to be clear. For instance, a group may want to exchange their views on three proposed new incentive schemes.

**Product** Identify the product or final result you wish to achieve through a GD. For instance, a group discussing the new incentive policies may wish to decide on one to be implemented.

**People** Identify the members who are required to participate in a GD. Keep in mind their role and relevance so as to have a small group.

**Process** Think how to structure a GD. If you wish to have a facilitator you need to select one for the group. Generally in workplace GDs, the facilitator will also contribute to the discussion besides enabling the group to focus on the topic and to have a productive discussion.

**Time and venue** As far as possible try to find out and look into the convenience of the participants regarding the time and venue of the discussion..

### Organizer's Role

It can be difficult for a person who organizes GDs at workplaces to play both the role of a facilitator and that of a full participant in the discussion. However, it usually does not work for someone to only be in the role of facilitator in a GD. Groups often flounder unless at least one person is acting as a facilitator. Explain that your role as a facilitator is to structure, at least initially, the discussion and get it going, but that you also want to participate in the discussion and set the expectation that each person in the discussion should be prepared to step into the facilitator's role. This is easier if you explain what that role entails. A facilitator should do the following:

1. Focus on the process and keep to time. Try to keep the group on its agenda and revising it (with group input), if and when needed.
2. Ensure that the ground rules for the discussion are respected.

**Image 15.1** A GD in progress

### Procedure

How formal or informal you are with a discussion group is for you and the group to decide (Image 15.1). Some guidelines are as follows:

**Ground rules** Even with groups whose members are familiar with each other (and especially with groups that are not so), it is useful to review and post the following set of simple guidelines:

1. Respect opinions that are expressed as an individual's honest perception.

- Respect time limitations and the need to allow sufficient time for all to voice their views
- There is no need to agree (unless you decide otherwise)
- Inquire in order to understand what has led someone to think as they do
- Listen

With groups that work well together, posting ground rules may not be necessary, however, it is a good idea when things get tense.

## FUNCTIONAL AND NON-FUNCTIONAL ROLES IN GROUP DISCUSSIONS

The members of an efficient and productive discussion group must provide for meeting two kinds of needs—what it takes to do the job and what it takes to strengthen and sustain the group. What members do to serve group needs may be called *functional roles*. Statements and behaviours that tend to make the group inefficient or weak may be called *non-functional roles*.

### Functional Roles

A list of the kinds of contributions that are performed by one or several group members is illustrated in Fig. 15.1.

#### Task Roles

Task roles are related to selecting and carrying out a group task.

**Initiating** This includes getting things started, suggesting new ideas, giving new definitions to a given problem, trying a new attack on the problem or introducing new material.

> Hello friends, today we'll be discussing the three proposed new incentive schemes in detail and arrive at the most beneficial and implementable scheme so that we can recommend the same to our VP. I'm sure you might already have gone through the details such as the amount, time of release, entitled employees, etc. in the distributed material. Shall we take up the financial aspect first followed by the time and the category of employees?

**Giving and asking for information** This includes offering facts or generalizations, sharing understanding of a topic, giving information freely, soliciting everyone's input and gathering information.

> In addition to the material I had shared with you yesterday, I would like to add that the amount mentioned in scheme number three includes the incentive for the team performance as well. Does anybody wish to comment on that?

**Giving and asking for reactions** This includes stating opinions and reactions, sharing feelings about what has been said, getting reactions from all group members, and seeking clarification of values, suggestions or ideas.

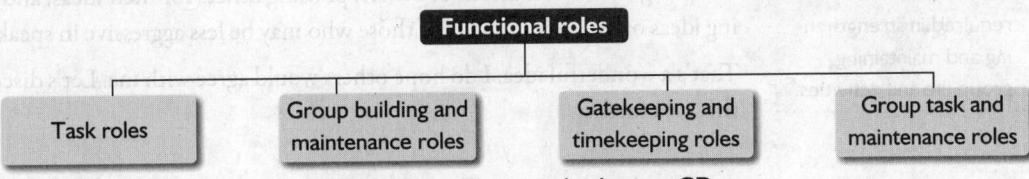

**Fig. 15.1** Functional roles in a GD

I think it's not a good idea to link the team's performance with the incentive as you have just mentioned. I feel so because there may be some disruptive members in the team who may spoil the team performance though the others are dedicated, effective and efficient. Though you may say that it all depends on the team leader, the team may suffer.

**Restating and giving examples**  This results in the presenter of the original idea getting feedback. Restating clarifies ideas. Examples reinforce meaning and aid understanding; they aid in the search for accurate statements and in understanding an idea.

Assume that a member, say X, of the project team is against implementing the solution suggested by another member, Y, because of some personal grievance.. If X happens to be the favourite of the team leader, he may be supported by the leader and the solution brought out by Y may not be considered at all. In such cases, conflicts may arise in a team affecting the quality of team performance.

**Confronting and reality testing**  This includes challenging ideas and information. Often groups allow misinformation and misstatements to pass by out of politeness. Learning takes place when ideas are challenged (politely, of course). Try to envision how a proposal might work and, if adopted, how an idea will work in the real world.

Are you sure your suggestion to implement the performance linked incentive will suit our work environment? Do you foresee any 'heartburns' among fellow colleagues if this scheme is implemented?

**Clarifying, synthesizing, and summarizing**  This includes clarifying ideas and previous statements, and pulling together related ideas or suggestions after the group has discussed them. Clarifying, synthesizing, and summarizing help provide closure.

So, we can clearly see that scheme number two is the most suitable one for our company for the following reasons as put forth during our discussion:

(i) The difference amount among various levels of employees is reasonable.
(ii) The time of releasing the incentive is appropriate as many employees intend to spend more during the reopening of schools.
(iii) The scheme is relatively novel in its approach as compared to the other two.

### Group Building and Maintenance Roles

Group building roles are the functions required in strengthening and maintaining group life and activities. This includes encouraging and supporting, being friendly, warm, and responsive to others, encouraging all members to contribute, agreeing with and accepting the contributions of others, praising others for their ideas, and supporting ideas of others, especially of those who may be less aggressive in speaking out.

> Group building roles are the functions required in strengthening and maintaining group life and activities.

That's a wonderful idea. I do hope others would agree with me. Let's discuss this idea further.

### Gatekeeping and Timekeeping Roles

Gatekeeping and timekeeping roles include trying to make it possible for another member to make a contribution to the group by saying, 'We have not heard from ABC yet', or suggesting limited talking time for everyone so that all will have a chance to be heard, or limiting the discussion on a topic to an agreed-upon time limit.

> Mediating includes harmonizing, conciliating differences in points of view, and making compromise solutions.

**Standard setting** This includes expressing standards for the group to use in choosing its content or procedures or in evaluating its decisions and reminding the group to avoid decisions that conflict with group standards.

**Following** This includes going along with decisions of the group, thoughtfully accepting ideas of others and serving as audience during the GD.

### Group Task and Maintenance Roles

Group task and maintenance roles are required for the following purposes:

**Evaluating** This includes submitting group decisions or accomplishments to compare with group standards or measuring accomplishments against goals.

**Diagnosing** This includes determining the source of difficulties and the appropriate steps to take by analysing the main blocks to progress.

**Testing for consensus** This includes tentatively asking for group opinions in order to find out whether the group is nearing consensus on a decision and sending up trial balloons to test group opinions.

*Example* So, do we all agree that the scheme number two is the best of all because of the financial advantages, suitability of time and ease of implementation?

**Mediating** This includes harmonizing, conciliating differences in points of view, and making compromise solutions.

*Example* Mr XYZ, while you feel that the financial implications are at an advantage in scheme two, Mr ABC feels that the ease of implementation is better in scheme one. However, I am sure all of you will agree with me that the financial implications play a crucial role in our decision making and hence we won't be committing a mistake if we go by XYZ's views.

**Relieving tension** This includes draining off negative feeling by jesting or pouring oil on troubled waters and placing a tense situation in a wider context.

*Example* I guess all of us are exhausted and need some break. Why don't we have a cup of coffee and then resume?

### Non-functional Roles

> Statements and behaviours that tend to make the group inefficient or weak may be called non-functional roles.

Non-functional roles include the following types of behaviour:

**Being aggressive** This includes criticizing or blaming others, showing hostility against the group or some individual and deflating the ego or status of others.

**Blocking** This includes interfering with the progress of the group by going off on a tangent, citing personal experiences unrelated to the problem, arguing too much on a point, and rejecting ideas without consideration.

**Self-confessing** This includes using the group as a sounding board and expressing personal, non-group-oriented feelings or points of view.

**Competing** This includes vying with others to produce the best idea, talk the most, play the most roles, and gain favour with a leader.

**Seeking sympathy** This includes trying to induce other group members to be sympathetic to one's problems or misfortunes, deploring one's own situation or disparaging one's own ideas to gain compliments or support.

**Special pleading** This includes introducing or supporting suggestions related to one's own pet concerns or philosophies and lobbying.

**Horsing around** This includes clowning continually, joking, mimicking, and otherwise disrupting the work and progress of the group.

**Seeking recognition** This includes attempting to call attention to one's self by loud or excessive talking, extreme ideas, and unusual behaviour.

**Withdrawing** This includes acting indifferent or passive, not participating, day-dreaming, and whispering to others.

## IMPROVING GROUP PERFORMANCE

A group's performance can be improved if the following factors are kept in mind:

1. Limit the group to between five and nine members—five is ideal.
2. Seek members with diverse personality traits and backgrounds to gain the benefits of diverse opinions and perspectives.
3. Do not be afraid of conflict—a spirited exchange of opinions is desirable; infighting and personal attacks are counterproductive.

### Criteria for Effective Groups

In this section, the criteria for building effective groups and also the problems that usually hinder a group's effectiveness are discussed. Effective groups

- are action-oriented,
- have a non-threatening group climate,
- accept learning as the *raison d'etre* of the group,
- have participation and interaction by all members,
- cover the agenda efficiently,
- accept evaluation as an integral part of the group operation (i.e., no defensive behaviour), and
- are characterized by regular attendance and thorough preparation by members.

## Problems Hindering Group Effectiveness

The following are the obstacles to the effectiveness of a group:

**Groupthink** Everyone suppresses their real views to maintain group harmony, indicating falsely that the group and all of its ideas are wonderful, and that competitors are stupid.

**Lack of clear goals** No one knows what they are there for.

**Star complexes** Members start vying for the spotlight.

**Wallflowers** Each group has non-contributors.

> Seek members with diverse personality, traits, and backgrounds to gain the benefits of diverse opinions and perspectives.

## ASSESSMENT GROUP DISCUSSIONS

Most compound and business schools use GDs as a selection tool because such discussions provide useful information about a candidate's personality in a very short time. GDs are used to assess certain group skills that cannot be evaluated in an interview situation. Skills such as leadership skills, social skills, listening and articulation skills, situation handling ability and interpersonal ability can be evaluated through GDs. A typical GD involves 8 to 12 participants sitting in a circle or semicircle discussing a topic for a stipulated time, usually for 15 to 20 minutes. Many companies choose to give case studies for analysis with a view to assess a candidates' ability to understand the problem involved, his/her approach to arrive at few alternative solutions, and also his/her ability to convince others with sound arguments. Most GDs follow one of the three formats—structured, unstructured or specialized (Fig. 15.2).

**Structured GDs** Here the time limit and topic is defined. No consensus is expected at the end. No leader is to be selected for facilitating the process. These are easier to handle, as topics chosen are usually general and do not require technical knowledge.

**Unstructured GDs** Here choosing a leader is mandatory and the group has to reach a consensus at the end of the GD. The leader has to direct the group, set the tone for discussion and control the dynamics of the group. Things are sometimes made more complicated by asking the group to propose a topic, discuss it, and reach a consensus.

**Specialized GDs** These include role-plays or scripted GDs where the candidates are given a certain brief about a role that they need to play. For example, a business situation where two companies are negotiating a deal may be used. Candidates are given the profiles of the two CEOs, marketing managers, HR managers, advisors, and a neutral entity, for example, a consultant. Alternatively, candidates could be given the role

> - GDs are used to assess certain group skills that cannot be evaluated in an interview situation.
> - Process includes the manner of expression, communication skills, body language and the attitude of the person.

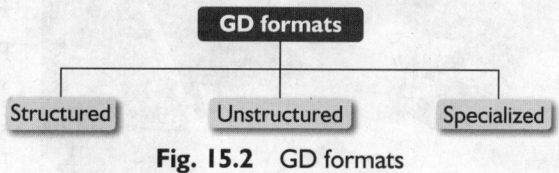

**Fig. 15.2** GD formats

of the five *Pandavas* and the main *Kauravas* negotiating the distribution of their kingdom in a twentieth century setting.

> The key to success in GDs is to be able to effortlessly move from one role to the other depending on what the situation demands.

## Content vs Process in GD

Content refers to things such as the level of preparation and ability to organize thoughts in a logical way, understand the topic in its totality, and innovate. Process includes the manner of expression, communication skills, body language and the attitude of the person. Most candidates are preoccupied with process. Consequently, all vital questions such as 'What should I say?', 'Do I have enough reasoning to sustain my line of argument?', 'Can I think of examples to substantiate my logic?' take a back seat. A preoccupation with process alone is fraught with disastrous results. Akin to 'what' and 'how', both of which are crucial for an effective speech, both content and process are equally important for effective contribution to a GD.

## How does One Ensure Excellence in Both Quantity and Quality of Content?

Excellence in both quality and quantity of content in a GD can be ensured primarily by taking a one minute pause. It is the only way to ensure that you perform above a threshold level of quality. Take your mind off the context for one minute. Utilize this one minute to organize your thoughts and to focus on what you are going to say. All this must be done much before you are swept away in the maelstrom, which will follow.

## What Role should You Specialize in?

Each role has several benefits. However, strong attachment to any single role throughout the GD could limit your chances of success. What is more important is that you demonstrate leadership at every moment. You must be able to move across these roles as the situation demands. Anyone seen to be performing more than three of these roles (see box 'Roles People Play in GDs' on next page) will definitely make a strong impact on the panel. Mobility is the key word in becoming effective in GDs. The key to success in GDs is to be able to effortlessly move from one role to the other depending on what the situation demands (Image 15.2).

**Image 15.2** People play many roles in GDs

## Holding Centre Stage in a GD

There are certain tricks that help you retain centre stage for longer durations and provide you with many chances to speak. However, these should be used with caution and at appropriate moments, like the legendary *Brahmastra* in the Ramayana and Mahabharata. Give data, examples, anecdotes, survey figures, and compelling short stories. You thus avoid facing interjections or arguments. However, be sure of the validity/relevance of your data or story. Use small gestures and hand motions. When you start speaking, use your hands to count the points on your

> ### Roles People Play in GDs
>
> Broadly speaking, participants play the following familiar roles in a GD.
>
> **Mr/Ms Brains/Plan** Mr Brains brings in a lot of substance and comes up with wide interpretations of the topic.
>
> **Downside** It is difficult to stop him/her because he/she is preoccupied with topic discussion as opposed to group discussion. He/she is happily oblivious to simple things like who is sitting next to him/her. At the end of the GD, if you happen to ask him/her whether the person sitting next to him/her was a boy or a girl, the answer would most likely be 'I do not know'.
>
> **Shopkeeper** This is the salesperson, who can sell anything, has the gift of the gab and a very strong ability to relate to people and be at the centre of things.
>
> **Downside** The shopkeeper does not usually come up with original thoughts him/herself. He/she needs Mr/Ms Brains to feed him/her with readymade ideas that he/she can sell.
>
> **Watchman** A watchman's role is to maintain order in the group; usually his/her content contribution is low. Preoccupied with directing the group process, such as controlling the entry and exit of participants' views, he/she is crucial for meeting time commitments made to the panel and in ensuring consensus.
>
> **Critic** The critic criticizes everybody's points without contributing anything new.
>
> **The butcher** The butcher does great service to the group by enhancing the quality of content by not letting participants get away with just about anything. Such a participant is most welcome in a group that has one or two aggressive elements in it.
>
> **The spectator or the passenger** The spectator is involved in the proceedings but plays a limited role. His/her contribution is very limited and does not affect the outcome of the group task.

fingers. However, keep in mind that the quality of feedback as well as the experience of the people who give feedback is important. 'It is like an apprentice chef making a dish in a five-star hotel and the master chef finally tasting it and adding the right amount of salt.'

## Steps in a GD

The following are the steps involved in a GD:

1. Initiate the GD by interpreting the topic and adding points.
2. Facilitate participation by controlling the domination by a few and trying to involve all.
3. Keep the focus of the discussion on the core issue.
4. Provide and ask for information, reaction, and criticism.
5. Discuss and counter-argue each other's interpretation of content.
6. Summarize the points discussed and taking the group into a new direction.
7. Conclude by recapitulating the highlights of discussion and reiterating the overall decision.

## Opening the GD

Depending upon your comfort level with the topic, you may choose to initiate the discussion. Define the topic for others, if necessary. For instance, in a topic such as 'Intervention of media in the personal lives of celebrities should be stopped forthwith', you may wish to define the term 'celebrity' in order to give it a wider scope. You may give examples of celebrities in various fields such as cinema, politics, religion, etc. Otherwise, generally the discussion might focus mainly on Bollywood celebrities only. If

>  **COMMUNICATION TOOL**
>
> **Critical Success Factors in a GD**
>
> **Innovativeness** Ability to have an entirely different perspective
>
> **Quality of content** Indicates the level of preparedness and your knowledge of the topic.
>
> **Logical ability** Ability to reason, think, and debate the pros and cons.
>
> **Behavioural skills** Aggressiveness is negative while assertiveness is positive. Assertiveness is standing on one's own feet, while aggression is trampling on others' feet.
>
> **Communication** Articulation, listening, and body language. Clarity of thought leads to articulate language and frequent and consistent participation. Functional knowledge of language is all one needs.
>
> **Leadership** All the above skills.
>
> More importantly, the fundamental strength that you need to portray to be effective is *mobility*. It is mobility that lets you demonstrate leadership skill as the context demands.

you have a story that you had read recently, you can even start with that. In B-school selection GDs, you may find most of the participants having a desire to broach the topic and hence it is possible that your voice may be left unheard. So, it is better to perform a variety of roles in order to pitch your ideas in a better light.

Make sure that you put up your own points in an emphatic manner and add your comments on the other's arguments thereby contributing significantly to the GD and making your presence felt.

Justify/substantiate your points with some facts or examples. The evaluators look for participants who have some data on the topic or related discussion wherein they can showcase their rational thought process and ability to build arguments.

## Approach to Topics and Case Studies

In a GD, when a topic is presented, take a minute or two to think about the topic with an open mind and note down the major issues that come to mind. Do not jump to any conclusions. Instead, arrive at a stand after examining all the issues in a balanced manner. Only then begin to speak.

Outline the major issues first and then state your stand. That is, give the justification first and the stand later. If we state our stand first, chances are that participants who disagree with our stand will interrupt to contradict before we can elaborate on the reasons. In this situation, the evaluator will only get an impression of what we think and not how we think. The guidelines given here will be helpful to handle topic-based as well as case study-based GDs.

### GDs Based on a Topic

Topic-based GDs are generally more difficult to handle than case study-based ones as there is no starting point for a candidate's thought process, particularly when a topic is unfamiliar. The panel may or may not allow time for thinking. The dynamics in the first couple of minutes are generally chaotic. Ideally, to start with, some ideas have to be generated on the topic. These ideas must then be prioritized so that the presentation is coherent. At this point, there may not be much time to fully develop the ideas.

In order to preempt the possibility of other participants starting off first on the same ideas that we have thought of, we have to start speaking as early as possible. Not only must we develop the idea

> **BUSINESS COMMUNICATION INSIGHT**
>
> **Group Discussions and You**
>
> Group discussions are a central part of the selection process for management-school placements. Business management is principally a group activity and working with groups is an important factor of career success for a manager. There are four main areas tested in a GD: (i) content; (ii) communication skills; (iii) group dynamics; and (iv) leadership skills.
>
> **Content** It is a combination of awareness and the capability to create lucid, rational arguments on the basis of that awareness. Just remembering the facts is useless. You should have a deep understanding of various topics as well as the knack to evaluate the topic and draft arguments.
>
> In-depth knowledge and logical analysis are critical. Since neither of these skills are taught at the school or graduate level, you need to learn and practise them to further your GD preparation.
>
> **Communication skills** The role of the listener is important as communication is a two-way process.
>
> - The listener has his own reading of what you say. If you don't listen to him, you cannot know whether he or she has understood you or not.
> - If you don't listen, your points may not be in sync with the points made by others. An experienced moderator can easily tell if you aren't listening. Other than listening, you also need the skills to
>    - convey your ideas in a clear and crisp manner,
>    - build on others' points, and
>    - summarize the arguments made by the whole group.
>
> **Group dynamics** A GD is a formal peer group interaction that aims to test your conduct as well as your impact on the group. Formal language and mutual respect are a must. In addition, you need to have the following:
>
> 1. *Disposition to listen and discuss various points of view* Do not take tough views in the beginning itself; try to analyse the pros and cons of the issue.
> 2. *Learn to disagree courteously, if required* In fact, it is much better to put your point forward without saying 'I don't agree' or 'You're wrong'.
> 3. *Appreciate the good points made by others* You can make positive inputs by agreeing to and explaining a point made by someone else.
> 4. *Seize the opportunity to make a summary near the end* Although complete agreement is impossible in the timeframe allotted, partial agreement or part consensus is a sign of the group's progress.
>
> **Leadership** A common misapprehension about leadership is that it is all about controlling the group. However, in a GD, a leader's role is to give direction to the group in terms of content. His work is to start the conversation and suggest the path on which the group should continue the discussion.
>
> **How to prepare?** In order to prepare for a GD, both content awareness and practice are vital.
>
> **Content** Consider the following points:
>
> - Improve awareness on current affairs, general knowledge and business trends.
> - Construct opinions on selected topics, considering both sides of the argument.
> - Use brief and lucid points.
>
> **Practice** Consider the following ideas:
>
> - GD skills are not studied from books. Practice in groups.
> - Arrange for experts to observe and give feedbacks.
> - Study each GD performance and plan precise improvements.

as we speak, but also think ahead for subsequent ideas. A weakness in any of these steps will lead to poor presentation.

As a rule of thumb, we should not speak unless we have content for a speech of at least one minute. Also, listening carefully to what the other participants have to say will trigger fresh ideas. A healthy discussion can take place only when there is an exchange of ideas and these ideas are subjected to analysis. Therefore, it is not necessary to keep on generating new ideas for the entire duration. It is also important to carefully examine each word of the topic, noting it down if possible, and checking that there are no words that can have different interpretations. If some ambiguity exists, it makes sense to define the terms first.

### GDs Based on a Case Study

If an individual's analytical skills are good, then case studies are easier to handle than topic-based GDs, because there is a starting point in the form of a particular situation. In business, cases are discussions of situations calling for an appraisal of past action, a decision on future action, or both. Virtually every case calls for both analysis and decision-making. Logical analysis and a firm grasp of the facts are crucial. Judgement is needed to sift through available information and find the relevant facts, and so is imagination for developing an action plan.

A framework for a case analysis is provided here to ensure that the process is as orderly as possible.

1. Understand the situation from different viewpoints.
2. Work out alternative courses of action.
3. Explore the pros and cons of each alternative.
4. Make a decision.
5. Work out an implementation plan.
6. Work out a contingency plan to be used in case the first implementation fails.

In real life, the success or failure of any decision cannot be forecast. What can certainly be done is to have a logical decision-making process and a practical implementation plan.

### Tips for Success in GDs

The following is a list of tips for handling a GD successfully:

1. Be thorough with current issues.
2. Always enter the room with a piece of paper and a pen.
3. Listen to the topic carefully.
4. Jot down as many ideas as possible in the first few minutes.
5. Try to dissect the topic and explore the underlying causes or consequences.
6. Organize the ideas before speaking.
7. Speaking first is a high-risk, high-return strategy. Hence, speak first only if there is something sensible and substantial to say.
8. Try to contribute meaningfully and significantly every time you speak. Do not speak just for the sake of saying something.
9. Identify supporters and opponents and allow the supporters to augment your ideas.
10. Keep track of time and share time fairly.

11. Have an open mind and listen to others' views.
12. Maintain eye contact while speaking and listening.
13. Do not indulge in parallel conversations.
14. Use tact and wit. If you must use humour, do so judiciously so as not to hurt others or deviate from the topic.
15. Display a spirit of cooperation and an accommodative nature.
16. Draw out the silent members and encourage them to speak.
17. If things get chaotic, take the initiative to restore order by providing a fresh direction to the discussion.
18. Attempt to arrive at a consensus although the ultimate aim is to reach a conclusion. Within the specified time, the group may not be able to arrive at a consensus. However, working towards consensus will reveal the individual's capability and inclination towards being a good team player.

## Sample GD topics

A list of some GD topics are listed as follows:

- Borderless worlds—dream or reality?
- Kids today are not what they used to be.
- Indian cinema is neither a source of healthy entertainment nor an agent of social change.
- Materialism—have we sold our souls to the devil?
- Multinational corporations—are they devils in disguise?
- Should youth indulge in politics?
- Business ethics.
- The parliamentary form of democracy has failed in India.
- Consumer satisfaction should be achieved at any cost.
- Managers do not add value to the society
- Profit is the only business of business.
- Growth and integrity are poles apart.
- Government should reduce defence expenditure and spend more on the social sector.
- The UN has not served any purpose in the last decade.
- Religion is a private matter and should be no concern of the state.
- Beauty contests do little to improve the stature of women.
- Can politics be delineated from sports?
- India makes nuclear bombs, but cannot make quake resistant houses.
- Fast changes in Information Technology— excitement or agony?
- Reservation is necessary for social transformation.
- Science and not rhetoric underpins the National Policy.
- Human rights impedes economic programme.
- Subsidies for higher studies should be done away with.
- Virtue has its own reward.
- Is the job of a manager to do the right things or to do things rightly?
- Religious fundamentalism is more dangerous than regionalism.

- 'Tryst with destiny'—has India redeemed its pledge?
- All education should be exclusively provided by the government.
- Money is the sixth sense.
- Capital punishment should be completely abolished from the judicial system

> A successful team is one in which the team members are willing to work together on future projects after the current task is completed.

## TEAM PRESENTATIONS

As we all know, a team consists of two or more individuals who work interdependently towards a common goal. A team presentation is a coordinated effort by its members, who plan, organize, and deliver a unified message aimed at achieving a common purpose with respect to an audience of one or more listeners.

Today, most organizations require employees to collaborate in teams to complete many different tasks. As such, it is important that you learn how to work together as part of a team, and how to work well as part of a team. A successful team is one in which the team members are willing to work together on future projects after the current task is completed. In fact, the necessity for teamwork in the workplace is not a new idea. However, it is becoming commonplace to find that cooperative effort is needed in all the areas of corporate communication. Presentations are no exception.

Team presentations present tremendous opportunities to create something much more than an individual can normally do. It may be easier and quicker to do things on your own, but many of us are more effective as part of a team that combines the knowledge and talent of several people. When you work in a group, there are always varying degrees of 'teamwork' issues that need to be addressed, whether it is developing a consistent presentation style and tone, scheduling team meetings, or determining who will present.

Many of the guidelines that apply to solo presentations stand true for team presentations also. Both follow the same principles. They require the same preparation, structure, audience analysis, and ability to think on your feet. However, team presentations differ in complexity and approach and demand additional attention to certain managerial issues.

The most important aspect about a team presentation is that it has to look like a team presentation—and not a series of loosely-connected parts. Each segment should be integrated with the others to create a sense of seamless communication. The entire team must understand and agree on the overall objective and how their presentations help to achieve it.

### Benefits of Team Presentations

The benefits involved in team presentations are follows:

- Diverse skills or perspectives are built right into the presentation by virtue of having different people presenting it.
- One person can manage audio-visual aids (run the video clip, change the overheads) while one concentrates on talking.
- A long and complex presentation can be made interesting and easy to follow for the listeners by providing a variety of speakers.
- Greater expertise is available.
- Presentation tasks (timing, dealing with questions) can be managed better.

> Each segment should be integrated with the others to create a sense of seamless communication.

- When audience involvement is part of the presentation, the team can mingle and provide leadership.
- Different faces, paces, voices and styles can complement each other.
- Role-play and other creative techniques are more feasible.

Team presentations are very common as teams of experts (engineers, sales people, financial experts, etc.) all present different aspects.

Businesses may lose many sales opportunities when a team presentation is poorly orchestrated and delivered. The client reaction could be, 'If they cannot co-ordinate a team presentation, how can they coordinate the work we need to have done?' Any professional sports coach will tell you that in order to win, you need an effective team. The same can be true of a team presentation. After all, speaking is an audience-centred exercise.

## Purposes of Team Presentations

Team presentations fulfil a variety of purposes.

**Project proposals**   An internal work team or unit solicits approval from the management to begin work on a new product or service that requires commitment of human or capital resources that are not currently in the unit's budget.

**Progress reports**   A team reports periodically on the results of on-going work in carrying out a previously approved plan or contract; such reports may be the basis for decisions to reauthorize continued work or a critical project component (e.g., the design of a more detailed advertising plan).

**Orientation and training programmes**   New employees are inducted into the company through a formal training programme delivered through the coordinated effort of key supervisors, mentors, or exemplary workers who instruct or socialize new team members.

**Contract proposals**   A company solicits business from another firm; those who prepared the bid or are to carry out the contract present the key elements of the proposal and make the case for the capabilities of your firm.

**Venture capital requests**   A company seeks backing from the financial community (banks, venture capital firms, investors) and builds a justification for investment around its business plan, organization, and projections for long-range performance.

**Public agency request/regulatory review**   A firm seeks consideration for tax break, zoning variance, or other significant public action. The firm defends its performance on complying with regulations. The firm also seeks approval to market a product or service that is subject to review.

## Planning and Preparation

Successful team presentations involve various aspects (Fig. 15.3).

### Know the PAL

A team leader is a person who needs to know the presentation's PAL—purpose, audience, and logistics.

**Purpose**   If a team's purpose is to inform the audience, it needs to provide new and useful information. For example, if your team presents to the management the progress of an on-going project, the purpose may be called *informative*. If, however, your team's goal is to persuade the board to grant a

**424** Business Communication

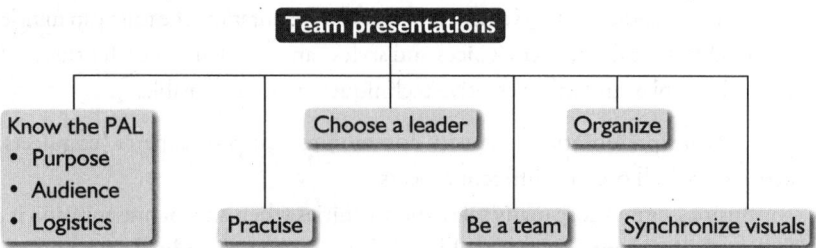

**Fig. 15.3** Elements of a successful team presentation

> A team leader is a person who needs to know the presentation's purpose, audience, and logistics.

proposal, the purpose is *persuasive*. When your team aims at persuading people, it needs to make audience members believe in the message or call participants to action. Your team leader needs to get answers to many questions: Who is in the audience? Are the members of the audience colleagues or prospective clients? Why are they there? What are their demographics (e.g., where they are from or how old they are)? What is their attitude towards your objective? What knowledge do they have and do they need?

**Audience** In order to give an effective presentation, you need to know as much as possible about your audience. Find out key demographics of the audience and determine how familiar they are with the subject of your presentation.

One of the keys to developing effective presentations is learning how to analyse an audience—before you even begin speaking. For example, assume you are speaking to a sales team that has just gone through a rough quarter. If you are aware of this fact before you write your presentation, you can include the type of information that would be most helpful, and avoid the kind of information that would be most harmful.

One goal of your presentation is to meet the expectations of your audience. So, focus on the audience's wants and needs. The success of your presentation depends on your ability to address those wants and needs.

Presenters learn about their audience from a variety of sources. Consider doing the following before a presentation:

1. Interview the organization/company executives in charge of the meeting/event.
2. Interview a sample of the audience members.
3. Review the literature of the company/organization.
4. Search for news of the company/industry via the Internet, magazines, newspapers, etc.
5. Research associates within the industry.

Identify specific audience requirements and how they affect the scope, content, and format of your presentation. It is important to get an idea of the audience size—you do not want the presentation team to outnumber the audience. Even seasoned professional speakers sometimes forget to do all their homework and wind up feeling foolish. Do not let the same thing happen to members of your team.

> - One of the keys to developing effective presentations is learning how to analyse an audience.
> - One goal of your presentation is to meet the expectations of your audience.

**Logistics** Knowing other logistics about the occasion is important too. For example, is your team part of a panel of speakers? Will others be joining your meeting via phone or video hook-up? How much time do you have to make the presentation? What time of the day will you be speaking? What is the room set-up? Will you be seated, or at a podium, or simply standing in a conference room?

The answers to these questions are crucial in helping you tailor your presentation. Once you have determined your PAL, write your overall objective in one sentence or less. This helps you maintain focus during the preparation process.

Answering all PAL questions is critical; it allows the team leader to decide who are the best people to gather for the team. If, for example, the audience is technical, at least one speaker needs to have a technical background. If the audience comprises people from finance, it certainly will not hurt to have an accountant or a person well versed with the financial details on your presentation team.

### Choose Your Leader to Build the Right Team

All members of a team need to work together to achieve the common goal. Before you can do anything, some decisions need to be made—the most important being who will be an effective leader for the team? The leader must be someone who is responsible for all aspects of the presentation—an overseer of sorts. The key role of this person is to develop and implement the proper strategy and preparation.

A team presentation leader should be a SME—subject matter expert. He/she should be organized and dedicated to taking the presentation to its successful conclusion. The team leader needs to be aware of a potential pitfall—delegating too soon. The leader should be hands-on. When the entire presentation is decided and planned, some aspects can be delegated. A good leader is crucial. He/she defines the strategy, sets the tone and explains the message. If the leader simply delegates different segments of the presentation to each team member, the result will be a mishmash of styles and tone.

Job function is a crucial component in selecting a team, however, individual personalities are just as important. Do you have someone who can tell stories and entertain the audience? Do you have someone who is good at moderating in case the Q&A session gets out of hand? Do you have someone who can confidently assure investors if they get skittish? Make sure every person on your team can contribute something to the group.

All members should know how, when, and where team members can communicate with one another both informally and formally.

### Organize

Membes of a tem need to define/refine presentation structure, develop the theme, segments, and speakers, and prepare an executive summary, overview, speaker order and sequencing of other activities. They also need to allocate the time per speaker and activity, keeping in mind the time required for audience questions and where to place Q&A. They should also develop a master outline and segment outlines.

Three small but important details are your introduction, transition, and conclusion. Before you enter the room, make sure you have assigned one person to do the introductions and that everyone is clear how they are going to make the transition to the next speaker.

- All members of a team need to work together to achieve a common goal.
- A team presentation leader should be a subject matter expert.

### Be a Team

It is better if all team members dress similarly. The rule is a level more formal than your audience—it they are in jeans, go for casual slacks. If it suits the occasion, you might all wear corporate or team t-shirts or caps. Never wear your usual clothes for a group presentation. It is a special occasion and your attire should reflect that.

### Synchronize Visuals

A single presentation style (e.g., one PowerPoint show) is required, rather than having each person does his or her own thing. Either one person should do the whole show, or a template should be provided that everyone uses. It should be ensured that every slide has the same look and feel and that type sizes, graphics, and writing style are consistent.

If your preparation time is short, you may want each team member to create his/her own visuals. The key is to ensure the format is standardized. The easiest way to do that is to create a master slide in your presentation software and make sure that everyone follows it to the letter. Your master slide should define the background, font, headings, subheadings, text, and graphics. Once all the segments have been completed, assign one member with the task of putting the whole thing together and checking each slide for consistency.

While visual consistency ensures a professional-looking presentation, a strong, consistent message will really make your presentation stand out. Make sure everyone is clear about the aim of the presentation, the grammatical style, the acceptable amount of jargon, the level of formality and anything else that will influence the final product. When you rehearse the presentation, videotape it so you can pick up any inconsistent messages.

Continuity in visual aids should also carry over into content. Each presentation should use similar vocabulary for common phrases. For example, if the first presenter says 'overheads' to refer to a visual aid and the next person says 'slides' when pointing to the same item, audience may get confused.

### Practise Your Presentation

The ideal is to rehearse in the room you will actually present in with a couple of non-presenters on hand for feedback. Videotaping is highly recommended. It is important to use all the things you will actually use in the presentation. Run that video clip, use the overheads or slides, work with the microphone (if there is one) and do everything exactly as you hope it will go on the day.

Team members, who are not presenting, should make notes of any problems, such as spelling errors in slides, clumsy transitions, and moments of uncertainty.

Recognize the difference between spoken and written language. Unless you are highly skilled as a writer of speeches, your prose will be unsuited for a speech. Learn to work from the bullets on your slides (best) or very short notes.

Individual team members can practise their respective parts, but the whole team needs to practise together too. Practice needs to be coordinated so there is enough time to make any necessary changes.

In addition to team practices, have at least one 'dress rehearsal'.

### Execution

When the day of the presentation arrives, you will not regret one moment of preparation and rehearsal. The following is a checklist:

1. If you can access the room before you present, do so to check that all equipment is present and functional. You can solve many problems with hours to spare. Know where to find technical help.

**Rehearse before Execution!**

2. As you are getting set to present, make sure all systems have been checked. If you are using a data projector, test it and have a slide showing your title at least in the moments before your start. If using videotape, set up the machine so one click is all you need at the right moment.
3. Identify where each person will stand during the presentation so it is easy to move unobtrusively to and from centre stage. Ensure you will not stand in the light from the data projector.
4. Have one person managing the visuals while another presents and ensure they are co-ordinated.
5. At the start of the presentation, introduce your team and topic. Even if the audience knows all the presenters, this is still important as a way of kicking off the presentation. An interesting variation is introducing your agenda and associating each person with a part of that agenda.
6. Present a brief agenda to give an overview and context for the presentation. This also provides a logical transition to the first person.
7. As your teammates make the presentation, give them the same attention you expect from the audience. It is rude to chat among yourselves or to show disinterest in your own presentation. Think of the message you are sending your audience as you observe others in your team presenting.
8. Ensure that two people on the team are closely monitoring your time against expected length. It is important to end on time and allow opportunities for questions, while still getting all of your essential points out. Remember the accordion.
9. For questions following the presentation, have all taking part in the same location. If the entire group will handle questions, all should be centre stage. If one is designated, he or she alone should be up front.

> Team presentations can be a fantastic way to build momentum and interest but they can also be extremely time-consuming.

10. Enjoy the moment. This is the payoff for your hard work.

## Towards Effective Team Presentations

Anyone who has ever been in charge of a team presentation can appreciate the difficulty of synchronizing a group. Team presentations can be a fantastic way to build momentum and interest, especially when you are dealing with a major sale. But they can also be extremely time-consuming. If you decide to deliver a team presentation, consider the following tips to make them more effective:

1. Take the time to build the team. Get to know each other. A cohesive team relies on group dynamics as much as individual efforts. If you cannot work smoothly with one another, your presentation probably will not work well in front of an audience.
2. Appoint a lead person responsible for 'holding' the delivery of the event.
3. Know your audience, their needs, expectations and receptivity, and develop your presentation to satisfy these considerations.
4. Use such tools as formal meetings, contracts and plans to set out what the team hopes to accomplish.
5. Ensure everyone understands the importance of listening.
6. Decide who can deliver best the different messages.
7. Appoint someone to coordinate written and visual materials to ensure professionalism and consistency.

## SUMMARY

Group discussions (GDs) and team presentations are an integral part of business communication. While GDs enable the organizational members to share information, discuss a problem, and arrive at a solution, team presentations facilitate them in presenting a product or idea to win support or gather feedback. Too often, companies do not feel the impact of a meticulous GD or a powerful team presentation until they lose business due to the groups' inability to arrive at a decision or the teams' poor sales presentations. Just like in sports, planning, preparation, and practice prevent poor performance.

When a multi-million dollar project is at stake, your group discussion has to be so focused that it sticks to its goal, and your team presentation needs to be seamless and succinct. Because what you say is just as important as how you say it, begin by forming the right team with the right members. Analyse and organize your message for consistency and influence. Pay special attention to the openings and closings to make sure they are clear and captivating and memorable. Learn how to shift between speaking parts and handle the most challenging questions. Understand the group dynamics and the nuances of teamwork.

GDs are also conducted for assessing the personality of candidates appearing for various interviews. GDs and team presentations pose a special challenge as compared to individual presentations, and there is clearly much more material for your audience to absorb from them than from a solo presentation. By keeping yourself updated with the necessary information and by following certain guidelines, you would be able to master your GDs and team presentations.

## KEY TERMS

**Group discussion** It is a form of communication in which a small number of people meet face-to-face, exchange ideas, and arrive at a consensus.

**Group dynamics** It implies that individual behaviours may differ depending on the individuals' current or prospective connections to a sociological group. Group dynamics is the area of social science that focusses on the nature of groups. Urges to belong or to identify may make for distinctly different attitudes (recognized or unrecognized), and the influence of a group may rapidly become strong, influencing, or overwhelming individual proclivities and actions.

**PAL** It refers to purpose, audience, and logistics.

**Single presentation style** It means having one common mode of presentation. (e.g., one PowerPoint show), rather than having each person does his or her own thing.

**Team leader** He/she is responsible for all aspects of the presentation. The key role of this person is to develop and implement the proper strategy and preparation.

**Team presentation** It is a coordinated effort by team members who plan, organize, and deliver a unified message aimed at achieving a common purpose with respect to an audience of one or more listeners.

**Transitions** These are bridging elements that conclude one section and start another. They are essential for an integrated presentation.

## Concept Review Questions

1. What are some of the basic objectives of companies when they hold a GD on any issue?
2. Why do you think organizations favour GDs over simple brainstorming techniques or meetings?
3. There are different kinds of people involved in a GD, and to solicit participation from everybody requires careful planning. Suggest ways of doing the same.
4. The efficiency of a GD can be improved drastically by using some very simple tools of group dynamics. Discuss some of the tools.
5. How is GD a better technique than interviews, for selecting prospective B-School applicants?
6. Explain the various steps involved in a GD on a (i) topic and (ii) case study
7. How important is audience awareness for your team presentation?
8. Discuss briefly the preparatory steps involved in a team presentation.

## Critical Thinking Questions

1. Which, according to you, is more advantageous—solo presentations or team presentations? Why?
2. A leader is not necessary for creating a team presentation—analyse this statement in about 200 words.
3. How do the transitional devices in a team presentation differ from those used in an individual presentation?
4. Assume that your team has to deliver a presentation on a newly designed product to two audiences—
   (i) The board of directors of your company and
   (ii) prospective clients.
   Will there be a difference in your presentation content, style, and tone? Discuss.
5. Identify some problem areas in the various functional areas of organizations and suggest areas where you think GD will be useful and where they will not? Why?
6. Content is more important than the container. How far do you agree with the above statement with regards to the GD exercise?

## Projects

1. Assume that your employer has asked you to investigate competitors' websites and report your analysis to a committee, comprising many of your senior managers. Team up with two of your friends and select any three companies. Examine their websites and compare their various aspects. Assuming the role of the leader, discuss and prepare a presentation plan for your team. Present your report to another group of your friends. At the end of your team presentation, ask your audience to comment on the aspects such as introduction, organization, conclusion, transition, overall effectiveness, etc.

2. Select a recent technological innovation that is useful for business. Assume that your team has to present this tool to a company's top management and persuade them to procure the same for their company. Discuss with your team the details of this presentation. Prepare the text of your team presentation and also present it to your colleagues/classmates.

3. Conduct some mock GDs in your group on serious topics/issues. Put somebody as a neutral observer. Ask him/her to point out weaknesses and strengths of all the persons in the group. Look into those problem areas identified and try working on them.

## REFERENCES

Bovee, Courtland L. and John V. Thill 2003, *Business Communication Today*, Pearson Education Asia, Delhi, pp. 29–30.

Guffey, Mary Allen 2000, *Business Communication: Process and Product*. Thomson Asia Pvt. Ltd, Singapore, pp. 40–44.

Lesikar, R.V. and M.E. Flatley 2005, *Basic Business Communication*, Tenth Edition, Tata McGraw-Hill Publishing Company Ltd, New Delhi, pp. 444–45.

Ober, S. 2004, *Contemporary Business Communication*, Fifth Edition, New Delhi, Biztantra, pp. 187–94.

Stevenson, S. and Whitmore 2002, *Strategies for Engineering Communication*, John Wiley & Sons, (Asia) Pvt. Ltd, Singapore, pp. 177–84.

http://www.exforsys.com/career-center/group-discussions.html, accessed on 10 December 2005.

### Developing Presentation for a Training Programme

**Project brief** Developing a multimedia presentation for promoting a training programme. The time duration of the presentation was approximately 12 minutes.

**Client** InfoTech company offering comprehensive, end-to-end software solutions and services.

**Project** To develop a multimedia presentation to sell a training programme internally, using tool such as Macromedia Flash, Adobe Photoshop, Sound Forge, Vagas Video Editor, etc.

**Challenge** The concerned company was keen on developing leaders internally. They had developed special training programme for this. Only a few employees underwent this training programme. In turn, the expected number of leaders they could expect in near future was very less. The internal communication the training team was having with employees was limited. Training team was not able to sell this training program internally as the communication was missing a punch.

**Solution** The team wants to be quick in responding. It wants to develop a 15-minute multimedia presentation. The presentation will include inspiring and motivational videos of the leaders of the company. It may also include testimonial videos of some of the employees who had undergone the training programme.

### Question

1. Develop a multimedia presentation incorporating the above mentioned points and also put your own imaginative thinking into it.

## CASE STUDY 2

**Career Couselling**

Participate in a small group (two–three students) discussion that should take place in the presence of an observer, who will give his/her concluding remarks.

Here is a counselling scenario where you will be asked to answer several questions, as a group, based on the information provided and your group discussion. By working with a group, you will have an opportunity to compare notes and to see how others might approach a given counselling situation.

**The case** You have agreed to do career counselling for a 46-year old woman. She is married, and her two children have finished college. She got her college degree in elementary education 25 years ago, taught classes 1 through 3 for two years, then became a housewife when her first child was born. She has always enjoyed art (especially painting and acting), but is not sufficiently talented, and she believes herself to be an artist. Her husband, a secondary school principal, is supportive of her returning to the workforce, but does not want her working at the local fast food chain. They live in a small town, but are within an hour's drive of a large metropolitan area. During your first meeting, you learn that she has held some part-time secretarial/clerical jobs over the years, but her drinking problem has gotten her dismissed twice, most recently three months ago. She is now recovering, and attends a support group two nights per week. She is amenable to retraining, and would like to have an income of ₹10,000 to ₹12,000 per month.

Now, working in your small group, discuss this case and the challenges facing the counselor and the client.

**Questions**

1. What is your first impression of this situation?
2. What more would you want to know and how would you find out more?
3. How would you proceed with this case?
4. What do you envision her tasks to be if she is to obtain and hold a full-time job?
5. What advice and counsel could you give her right now?

CHAPTER 16

# Team Briefing

**LEARNING OBJECTIVES**

After reading this chapter, you will be able to understand

- the term briefing
- the guidelines for effective briefing
- the characteristics of briefing
- the steps involved in briefing
- the benefits of briefing sessions
- different team briefing formats

## INTRODUCTION

Briefing is an essential communication tool that unifies an organization and has several other advantages. This chapter will explain the term briefing, its essential characteristics, the process of briefing in organizations, contents of a briefing, benefits, and tips for effective briefing. The chapter also touches upon why briefing is still not being used in some organizations.

## BRIEFING

Briefing is one of the many means of communicating information. It is also used as a system of communication operated by a management information system that enables leaders and their teams to talk about things that are relevant to their work. It complements the existing methods of communication. If an organization does not brief the teams through group leaders, it is failing to take the first step towards good management communication.

The process of communication pertaining to briefing is similar to that of presentation, conversation, and discussion in as much as the essential components of the communication process remain the same. In other words, all these communication processes have senders, receivers, messages, channels, responses, and feedback.

> Briefing unifies an organization and has several other advantages.

These processes involve subtle differences in the purpose, number of receivers, levels of interaction, use of non-verbal elements, magnitude of the contents, etc. For example, when the production manager of a steel manufacturing company delivers a short

> Briefing can also be defined as a short talk that informs a generally knowledgeable audience about a subject on which they would like to acquire new or additional information.

presentation to all other managers during a weekly meeting, he/she includes very little background to his/her presentation as everybody in the group is almost equally knowledgeable about the context. On the other hand, when the same production manager engages in a discussion with a few of his/her subordinates in order to arrive at a decision on a particular matter, he/she explains the context and content elaborately to avoid any ambiguity.

On yet another occasion, the manager may have to hold a briefing session to a group visiting his production division. There, he/she may have to play a different role as the 'sender' of this communication process, namely this 'briefing'. His/her message would be brief and may be followed by a question-and-answer session, thus, ensuring that the visitors understand the organization well. Hence, although the steps in the communication process involved in briefing are akin to those in other means of communication, briefing differs from others in terms of its purpose, content, audience, structure, and layout.

Briefing can also be defined as a short talk that informs a generally knowledgeable audience about a subject on which they would like to acquire new or additional information. For example, in a pre-placement talk delivered by a company for the campus recruitment at an educational institution, the company official briefs aspirants on the history, progress, major achievements, on-going projects, job prospects, etc. This briefing gives students information about the company.

## BUSINESS COMMUNICATION INSIGHT

**Frequently Asked Questions about Team Briefing**

**How frequently should one hold a team briefing?**

Team briefing meetings should be held on a regular basis as per a set plan. If you're the supervisor who is delivering a team brief, be aware of the team briefing schedule and plan your team briefing sessions around this in association with your line manager or fellow managers.

**What should be the duration of a team briefing?**

Your briefing session should last for a duration of 30 minutes approximately. If there isn't a lot information to convey, then you may decrease the length of the briefing. Always leave ample time for attendees to ask questions—keep in mind that this is a two-way communication.

**How many attendees should there be at a team briefing?**

Ideally, the number of attendees should be between 10 and 20. If you are part of a very big team, look closely at the way you construct team briefings. Perhaps, you could give charge of some duties to deputies/supervisors who could present a brief to a smaller group of team members. Converse with your manager to be sure.

**My team is based at different geographical locations and it would be very tough to get them all together for a 30-minute meeting. What can I do?**

Even if your staff is dispersed geographically, it's still possible to meet with them at least once a month for a team or operational meeting. If this is the case, you should try holding the team briefing at the same time, that is, before the operational team meeting. It's important to make a clear distinction between the team briefing and the operational meeting so that attendees are clear about what is going on. If you cannot get your team together at one location, you could hold the briefing sessions using tele-conferencing or video-conferencing.

**I am liable for front-line staff and it's very difficult to shut down critical services to call a team briefing meeting. What should I do?**

Try to organize your team briefing at a time when it's possible for most of your team members to attend. If, however, some members can't leave their desk (e.g., reception desk), arrange to brief them separately.

**What should I do about briefing the team members absent during the meeting?**

It's important that those who are unable to attend the team briefing still receive the important information discussed during the session and are given the chance to contribute or ask questions. You may need to talk to them separately when they are back at work.

**What should I do with the feedback received?**

It's vital that you use the feedback to make constructive changes—your team members providing feedback will quickly get tired of the system if they sense their assessments are not being taken earnestly. Always give the feedback to your line manager so that it can be communicated to higher management, if required.

### Features

A team briefing has the following features:

- Face-to-face group meetings in teams
- Lasts for around 30 minutes
- Held by team leaders, normally the team's manager or supervisor
- Held at least once a month, with the dates set and notified well in advance

The MD/CEO or the board of directors of a company issue a core management brief (i.e., the written briefing details from the CEO or board, which are passed on to every employee at every briefing) every month, covering main strategic, financial, commercial, policy, and people issues.

Every team leader/manager/supervisor then incorporates these core points into his/her own local brief (i.e., a separate written brief prepared by each team leader, manager, or supervisor, for his or her own team, containing local issues relevant to that team). Team leaders check and agree on their local briefs with their line managers at their own briefing sessions at which they receive the core brief and a local brief from their boss covering subject headings—progress, policy, people, points for action, and general information.

### Process

The process of briefing includes the following key points (Image 16.1)

1. The process is monitored via records and managers attending briefings.
2. Every month the CEO or the board of directors agree on a core brief.
3. The core brief covers subject headings and includes items about financial and statistical performance; organizational policy; strategy, business direction, and market conditions; successes and failures; and changes in senior people's roles and positions.

**Image 16.1** A team briefing in process

4. Line managers of the level of the director and below add local interpretations or explanations to the core brief, where applicable.
5. Line managers and team leaders also prepare their own local brief.
6. Briefings cascade down the organization, each one soon after the briefer's attend, at which they revise and get approval from their bosses for their own local briefs.

## Briefing down the Line

Figures 16.1 and 16.2 illustrate a typical briefing process and a local brief process, respectively.

## Benefits

The benefits of a team briefing are as follows:
1. Facilitates business strategy communication—upward, downward, and lateral.
2. Helps gain acceptance of change.
3. Develops leadership skills.
4. Better alternative to the grapevine.
5. Builds commitment and understanding.
6. Promotes an open communication culture.
7. Helps clear blockages and misunderstandings.

After an effective briefing, people understand what is happening and why their contribution is so important. With energy and enthusiasm flowing from the top, the whole organization is positively charged and united behind a shared vision. Internal relationships are improved, and with a two-way communication process, senior management can assess the needs and expectations of the people and take appropriate action.

Briefing is a powerful method of enabling communications up and down the management structure of any organization. It can act as an important tool in facilitating lateral communication among the various divisions of an organization. For example, the vice-president of a financial company can brief all his/her senior managers on the investments made in the company over the last six months thereby enabling them to gain an overall perspective about the situation. Similarly, a briefing by the personnel manager to all the other managers of a business enterprise on the operations pertaining to its office move will serve as an important communication tool not only to transmit and share the necessary information but also to enable him/her observe others' reactions and get their views.

Briefing provides a consistent and measurable process for conveying strategic and operational information and answering feedback questions throughout an organization. It ensures that the staff at all levels receive information that is relevant to them, which is a mixture of corporate and local issues. The system is capable of being monitored by someone given the responsibility to do so.

> Briefing is a powerful method of enabling communications up and down the management structure of any organization.

In India, where group decision-making plays an important role in most organizations, both private and government, you may find briefing extremely useful. Assuming you are the project leader of a team assigned the task of automating all accounts of XYZ company, you may find it easier to brief your team from time to time rather than meeting them individually to discuss the progress or the related

| Team Briefing—Core Management Brief |||
|---|---|---|
| **Originator:** Deepak Gupta (MD), Lakshmi Textiles Company |||
| Date: 4 December 2011 |||
| **Standing instructions to team briefers:** This is the core brief of the MD concerning corporate goals and objectives which the Heads of Departments can expand on. Please express these points in whichever way you feel is best to help your staff understand. Make notes, action points, and target dates. Please raise queries and get feedback. |||

| **Core brief—important points below:** | **Briefer's notes:** (supplement with the main points below to use in the local brief): |
|---|---|
| **Results** | |
| A large contract for the export of garments has been received from the US worth $10 million. Target date of execution: March 2012. | In-house capacities not adequate to execute the order. Outsourcing activities to commence. |
| Sales to date are up 20%. Profits are up 30% for corresponding period. That is very good news. | |
| Costs are lower than the budget. Results are better than targets and are expected to improve as a consequence of the US order. | |
| **Organization** | |
| The international agreement removes quota controls from April 2012. To exploit the business potential, the marketing department needs strengthening. | The current marketing team cannot focus on all territories. Territory-based marketing executives to be appointed. |
| | Logistics department to be strengthened for timely order executions. |
| **Policy** | |
| All departments to prepare balanced score card performance appraisal system to evaluate employee job performance. | Evaluation should determine training needs and appropriate job allocation based on competencies. |
| Mobile phones with cameras brought in by staff/visitors could pose security problems. Employees should be discouraged to use them. | Make arrangements with security to store mobile phones submitted by employees/visitors. |
| Visitors' car-park spaces should be kept for visitors use only. | Staff on night shift can use visitors' and directors' parking slots while the ongoing drain repair work prevents access to the main car park. |
| **People** | |
| Ajay Srinivasan is joining the company as CIO. | The company is going to implement an ERP system; hence, there is a need to appoint a Chief Information Officer. |
| Sanjay Mathur has resigned and his assistant Rakesh Dua assumes his responsibility. | |
| Jayashree Mani joins the HR Department as Head Trainer. | Jayashree Mani will require a secretary. Hopefully, someone from the company will be recruited. Applicants should have some prior experience in HR. |

**Fig. 16.1** Sample of a typical team briefing

| Team Briefing—Local Brief ||
|---|---|
| **Originator:** Dilip Rao, Logistics Department <br> **Date and Time:** 5 December 2011, 3 pm <br> **Attendees and Absentees:** Initials of the participants in the local briefing to be included. ||
| **Local brief—main points below:** | **Briefer's notes with examples and answers to possible questions:** |
| **Progress** <br> A new packing machine installed which will double the packing capacity of the department | Trained machine operators should ramp up productivity in the new machine to optimum capacity. |
| Productivity should improve to keep pace with the demand. | Winners of cost reduction projects and productivity projects will be sent on an overseas training programme-cum-holiday. |
| **Policy** <br> Mobile phones with cameras not to be allowed into the factory for employees and visitors. | Mobile phones with cameras to be deposited at the security gate by visitors. |
| **People** <br> Rajesh Paltu joins the Logistics Cell as Efficiency Manager. | He will set up teams to be trained to identify areas of idle time and non-productive activities, and thus increase productivity. |
| **Points of action** <br> To develop low weight, compact, and strong cartons. | Identify cross-functional team to work on the project. |
| Objective: reduce freight and insurance costs. | Maybe a day trip to one of the local resorts? Check on transport options. |
| Please give suggestions for the venue of the annual staff picnic. | |
| Team feedback and action point review dates to be fixed. ||

**Fig. 16.2** Sample of a typical local brief

strategies for accelerating the pace of the project. In addition, these briefings will enable you and the members of your team to perceive the exact status and pave the way for modifying strategies because of the very nature of briefings involving questions and feedback.

When a company recruits young graduates and appoints them as management trainees, it initially assumes the responsibility of briefing them all about their place of work. This mode of communication provides a good beginning for both upward and downward communication in the company. Thus, briefing lays the foundation for the development of employees' involvement at work. If the management is unaware of this, there will soon be a general atmosphere of despondency in the organization, because the management seems to be interested in telling, not in listening. Briefing cannot, and should not, be used merely as a method of upward as well as downward communication; it provides an important starting point from which the channels of upward communication can be developed—perhaps through separate meetings.

> Briefing lays the foundation for the development of employees' involvement at work.

**Image 16.2** A supervisor briefing his team member

In the lower echelons of management, junior executives often do not consider themselves as leaders and just consider that their hefty pay packet is merely due to their experience or expertise or both. They forget that they are a part of the management. Briefing their team members about a particular operation makes them realize that they have to act as leaders also. Thus, briefing reinforces management all the way down the line. In some companies, junior executives may show reluctance to the idea of briefing their subordinates thinking that it is not part of their job but it is their job. They may think that 'more money' is the only criterion that differentiates them from their subordinates. However, over a period of time, they may realize that they can help their own team get the best results by appropriate and timely briefing. The briefing that junior executives receive from their superiors may act as a catalyst for the realization that it is not just 'more money' but more responsibility that projects them as leaders among the members of their team.

At this juncture, it would be interesting to note how the briefing sessions differ in organizations having different functions. Let us consider briefing in two types of industries—manufacturing and service. In manufacturing industries, briefing sessions taking place within the industry are of a more technical nature because of the technical operations involved. For example, the briefing given by an executive in HMT, a manufacturing industry, about a newly-introduced manufacturing process may be highly technical and objective in nature. On the other hand, a briefing given by a manager of SBI, a service provider, about the new service introduced by the bank may be highly informative and persuasive in nature. Whatever be the nature of briefing, executives in all business organizations often take recourse to this important tool of communication (Image 16.2).

The grapevine is active in almost every organization and it flows in all directions. Briefing helps control the grapevine, although it does not help an organization get rid of it completely. Of course, people will always listen to the grapevine first—the news is always that much more scandalous—but if there is a briefing system, they will wait to listen to the official version from their managers before coming to any conclusion. In this regard, briefing helps not only the employees but also the managers as they will be better informed during briefing about what their employees think.

In other words, briefing opens up a channel for the grapevine to come up the hierarchical ladder. It certainly does improve the communication of information upwards. Some senior managers find it difficult to understand why people do not seem to have good ideas or even views about what is going on.

Briefing, as a means of communication, helps both team leaders and managers to achieve this goal effectively and efficiently. It promotes openness in communication as it provides scope not only for briefing on project operations,

- Briefing opens up a channel for the grapevine to come up the hierarchical ladder.
- When communication acquires openness in teams, organizations move ahead successfully.

> Timely briefing can help reduce misunderstandings and clear blockages in the communication channels of an organization.

achievement, crisis, etc., but also for inviting opinions, feedback, and questions from the members of the teams. When communication acquires openness in teams, organizations move ahead successfully. As the process of briefing develops a shared sense of mission and vision, it paves way for free interaction among the members of an organization.

Mr Prakash Ramaswamy, the project manager at Honeywell Technology Solutions Ltd, led the project entitled 'Verification and Validation of Flight Management System' for his company. He felt that the periodic briefing sessions he had with his team members enabled him to update them on the progress of the project, which in turn helped them work with more focus towards the collective aim of the project. The sessions also enabled him to answer the queries the team had and obtain feedback from his team.

In many organizations, there exists a communication gap mainly because of the lack of information sharing in the form of timely briefings among the vertical and lateral channels of communication.

Misunderstandings can be costly, time-consuming, and embarrassing, especially in organizational contexts.

Good leaders should always be concerned about the wastage of time and money. For instance, the finance director of a large company unilaterally changed the procedure for signing invoices, and communicated the fact only through memos to the management team. For days, thereafter, people lower down the ladder wasted considerable time trying to find out what the new system was. Often even more time was wasted because someone 'thought' he/she knew the new system but was wrong. In terms of man-hours, the cost was huge; further, the finance director was no longer regarded as an effective leader, which again reduced the company's efficiency. Had he spent a little time on team briefing, he could have avoided the adverse consequences. Timely briefing can help reduce misunderstandings and clear blockages in the communication channels of an organization.

## Techniques

Assuming that briefings are generally used to present information to the target audience on projects, events, or situations, let us try to understand the techniques employed in implementing them. Though these techniques are determined by the purpose of the briefing, the desired response, and the role of the briefer, the underlying steps remain almost the same. To ensure that your briefing turns out to be an effective one, you need to

- be committed
- be clear with the purpose
- determine the audience
- plan and prepare
- structure the briefing
- decide the time
- inform in advance
- deliver
- get opinions and feedback
- encourage questions

Commitment is as crucial for a successful briefing as it is for accomplishing any action. It is essential that you are thoroughly committed to the subject or idea of briefing and are prepared to be involved in its implementation; it helps if the senior management team is committed as well.

Clarity of purpose enables you to decide the contents of your briefing. Only when you are clear regarding the purpose will you be able to brief your team members with adequate focus. As waywardness is undesirable in all types of organizational communication, being focussed on your

> - Clarity of purpose enables you to decide the contents of your briefing.
> - Keeping the purpose and audience in mind, plan and prepare for your briefing.

purpose will prevent you from deviating from the main topic. Look at the following statement of purpose that a manager prepared for his briefing session:

> The purpose of this briefing is to inform my audience about the Internet-based training, which our company is planning to offer. I will invite the audience to share its perceptions with fullness and honesty after listening to this information. In the session, I will ask the audience to come up with any questions, doubts, disagreements, additions, or changes.

It is clear that this manager wants to brief his/her employees about the Internet-based training. Hence, he/she now plans to compile the relevant information which answers why, what, when, and how of this particular training system.

The next step is to decide your target audience. Although you can brief any number of people, your briefing will be effective if the size of the audience is small because it facilitates interaction. For example, when a company visits a university for campus recruitment, the manager gives a briefing only to those students who might have applied for a job in the company and not to all the students of that university. Similarly, when you come out with a new product and wish to brief your colleagues on the same, select the audience in such a way that they critically evaluate the product and come out with suggestions for its betterment. Later on, you can deliver the briefing to a larger audience.

Keeping the purpose and audience in mind, plan and prepare for your briefing. Collect the necessary information for the briefing contents, think about the visual aids to be used, visualize how to introduce and conclude, guess the anticipated questions, etc. Decide the structure and format of your briefing. For example, if your briefing is to provide information, it may have a particular structure; if it is meant for some decision-making, it may have a different structure; if it is meant for providing the present status of a particular project or situation, it may have yet another slightly different structure.

## TEAM BRIEFING FORMATS

Let us look at a few formats that support team briefing.

### Information Briefing

The purpose of an information briefing is to inform the listener. This briefing deals primarily with facts, not conclusions or recommendations, and is used to present high-priority information requiring immediate attention; complex information involving complicated plans, systems, statistics or charts; and controversial information requiring elaboration and explanation. Situation briefings that cover the tactical situation over a period of time usually fall into this category. The following format works well for an information briefing.

#### *Introduction*

The introduction for an information briefing consists of the following points:

- *Greeting*   Address the person(s) receiving the briefing, and identify yourself
- *Purpose*   Explain the purpose and scope
- *Procedure*   Indicate procedure if briefing involves demonstration, display, or tour

### Body

The body includes the following points:

- Arrange main ideas in a logical sequence
- Use visual aids correctly
- Plan effective transitions
- Prepare to answer questions at any time

### Close

The closing paragraph includes the following main points:

- Ask for questions
- Give closing statement
- Announce the next briefing, if applicable

## Decision Briefing

> The purpose of a decision briefing is to obtain an answer or a decision.

The purpose of a decision briefing is to obtain an answer or a decision. Personnel in the major branches of a company use this briefing for most tactical matters requiring command decisions. You can use the following format:

### Introduction

The introduction for a decision briefing includes the following points:

- *Greeting* Address the person(s) receiving the briefing, and identify yourself
- *Purpose* State that the purpose of the briefing is to obtain a decision and announce the problem statement
- *Procedure* Explain any special procedures such as a trip to outlying facilities or the introduction of an additional briefer
- *Coordination* Indicate the accomplishment of any coordination
- *Classification* State the classification of the briefing

### Body

The body includes the following key points:

- *Assumptions* Must be valid, relevant, and necessary
- *Facts bearing on the problem* Must be supportable, relevant, and necessary
- *Discussion* Analyse courses of action and plan for a smooth transition
- *Conclusion* Degree of acceptance or the order of merit of each course of action
- *Recommendation(s)* State action(s) recommended—must be specific, not a solicitation of opinion

### Close

The closing sentences should make use of the following points:

- Ask for questions
- Request a decision

### Follow-up Briefing

If some important official is not present after the briefing is over, the briefer must inform his/her secretary about the decision arrived at. For example, when you want to brief your team about the current status of a project or a situation, you may give a brief background of the earlier status and then proceed. The following format might work for you in this type of briefing:

#### *Introduction*

The introduction for a follow-up briefing includes the following points:

- *Greeting*   Address the person(s) receiving the briefing
- *Identification*   Identify yourself, if appropriate
- *Scope*   Define coverage in terms of time, geographic limits or other applicable specifics

#### *Body*

The body includes the following points:

- Summary of past operations
- Projected operation
- Current operation
- Problems

#### *Close*

The closing sentences include the following main points:

- Solicitation of questions
- Concluding statement and announcement of next briefer, if applicable.

## EFFECTIVE BRIEFING

Effective briefing is an art. It requires alertness, poise, and good judgement. Whether the information you present is in oral, written, or pictorial form, you must be able to think on your feet. There will be times when you will have to come up with precise factual answers to questions that are difficult or even embarrassing. You should avoid verbal ambiguities, vagueness, or misplaced emphasis, which could easily convey a mental picture completely different from the one you have intended.

Timing is another important issue. Team briefings should take place at a set time. All briefings need to take place within a period of 48 hours, to make sure that the grapevine does not pass on the news before the briefings do. It is also a good idea if all people at a particular level are briefed simultaneously, and so you have to think hard about exactly when you can cease all work at that level for half an hour or so. Inform your team well in advance about the date, time, venue, and agenda for your briefing. Always encourage questions and also remember to get opinions and feedback from your team members.

Also, it is highly unlikely that, in any given organization, all the managers and supervisors are communicating effectively to their subordinates. There are always a few who are perennially too busy to get around to it, or who have the

> - Effective briefing requires alertness, poise, and good judgement.
> - Briefing is a management system for communicating information and explaining the message.

## COMMUNICATION TOOL

### Checklist for Preparation, Content, and Presentation of Briefings

**Planning and preparation**

- Be clear with the purpose
- Put items in the briefing folder during the month
- Prepare the rough draft before briefing
- Add the relevant matters, if any, provided by your boss
- Ask yourself questions to ensure, understand and cover the points your audience needs to know

**Content**

- *Progress* Corporate and local performance against target and standards, including financial, commercial and quality issues
- *Policy* Procedures that need introducing, explaining, reinforcing or changing
- *People* Issues concerned with people in the company and the team
- *Points for action* Priorities for the next month for the team and the organization

**Presentation**

- Strive for force and enthusiasm
- Practise the briefing beforehand, when possible, and make sure you have an orderly presentation
- Avoid ambiguous and vague terminology—the terms 'about', 'probably', 'might', etc. convey no useful information, but they do convey an impression of hedging or guessing
- Make the entire briefing a running narrative, and give your information in terms applicable to the situation
- Discuss only the important or essential details, and keep the briefing as simple as possible
- Use examples and make the message relevant to your audience
- Finish briefings forcefully, with a definite closing statement, and always ask, 'Are there any questions?'
- Remember you are briefing the management view

petty-mindedness to think that knowledge is power, or who simply do not enjoy communicating and so do it as rarely as possible, or who do their best but are just bad at communicating. A system ensures that everyone briefs, all the way down the line—not just the people who would brief their subordinates anyway.

Installing a briefing system costs money and takes time. It is, however, an investment towards your organization's future success: once the system has been set up, it will last forever. After the first few months, the only real expenditure is time.

Briefing is a management system for communicating information and explaining the message. In no way does it undercut the role of the unions or of the union representatives—their job is to convey employees' concerns to the management, and they are usually only too glad to be relieved of the unfair burden of explaining the management's concerns to the employees. Also, the better informed the workforce, the easier the task of the union representative, because he she goes to the management with all the pertinent facts on his/her fingertips.

A checklist for the preparation, contents, and presentation of briefings is also given in this chapter. It may be of interest to you in making your briefing sessions more effective and efficient.

## SAMPLE BRIEFINGS

Figures 16.3 and 16.4 illustrate two sample briefings.

In today's technology-driven and highly-competitive marketplace, it is difficult to find skilled workers who can keep their skills constantly updated. Companies must create training curricula designed to both secure their organizational visions and offer learning opportunities continually to their employees so as to add to their personal development. Each employee of an organization has great pressure to perform because of the ever-increasing competition. Training departments have the additional pressure of preparing the employees to adapt to the changes in technology. Unless the employees are familiar with technology, they may not be able to readily accept the changes. There is no doubt that Intranet-based training will be the primary training method in future. Factors driving this opinion include the following:

- Concerns over high costs of traditional classroom training/off-site tuition
- Dissatisfaction with self-paced training programmes
- Complexity of products and services resulting in the need for training both employee and client
- The need to achieve higher productivity and profitability gains with fewer resources
- Corporate knowledge that must be encoded within the organization
- Rapid adoption of the Internet/intranet among entire organizational staff
- Concern over loss of productivity due to on- or off-site classroom training
- Heightened staff expectations for having more and more information; for processes and functions being performed via computer; and for ease of use, convenience, and quality

Learners will have the capability, through several modes of delivery, to receive the training they need, when they need it, wherever they are.

**Web-based Training**

http://www.mindflash.com/pages/home.asp
http://dmoz.org/Computers/Internet/Training/
http://www.emtrain.com/launch_press_release.html
http://www.wbtic.com/default.aspx
http://www.designingwbt.com/
http://www.wbtsystems.com/
http://www.ipan.com/ipan/ipidx.htm

**Fig. 16.3** Sample 1—briefing on 'The Direction of Training'

---

12 September 2011

Mr Navtej Sarna: Good evening, ladies and gentlemen.

His Majesty Jigme Singye Wangchuck, King of Bhutan will pay a State Visit to India from 14–18 September 2011, at the invitation of the Hon'ble President.

During the visit, His Majesty is scheduled to call on the President and have meetings with the Vice-president and Prime Minister. Issues of bilateral interest will be discussed, including the Government of India assistance to the Ninth Five Year Plan of Bhutan. His Majesty will also hold meetings with the Deputy Prime Minister, External Affairs Minister, Finance Minister, and Power Minister.

A Memorandum of Understanding will be signed for the preparation of a Detailed Project Report on Punatsangchhu Hydroelectric Project. The Project, with an estimated generation capacity of 870 MW, has been identified for implementation under the Tenth Five Year Plan of India.

The State visit of His Majesty the King of Bhutan would further reinforce the friendly ties between the two countries.

His Majesty is accompanied by a high-level delegation.

Question: What happened in the CCS meeting?

Answer: CCS reviewed India-China relations in the context of Prime Minister's recent visit to China.

Question: No other issues were discussed?

Answer: This is all I am aware of.

Question: Any particular thing? Because the visit took place long ago.

Answer: Well, they choose today to use the meeting for this purpose of review.

Question: How many MOUs are going to be signed in this visit?

Answer: One.

Question: Many countries have spoken of the recent NATO attacks. What is India's reaction?

Answer: We disapprove of this plan.

Question: Has there been any communication with Pakistan after the foreign minister's visit?

Answer: I am not aware of any such communication.

Thank you

Fig. 16.4 Sample 2—press briefing on 'The Visit of the King of Bhutan'

## SUMMARY

Briefing as one of the means of organizational communication plays a predominant role in the functioning and the progress of an organization. It enables everyone within the organization to share its vision and their roles within it. With its primary objective of ensuring that all employees know and understand what they and others in the organization are doing and why, briefing enables the management to overcome the possible gaps in communication. When briefing is executed in formal establishments, it should not merely be used as a tool to pass on the information from top to bottom. It should be used as far as possible as an interesting means of communication to enrich the audience's knowledge on a particular matter.

Like other forms of group communication, briefing also has its own characteristic features and follows a sequential process involving several steps. A powerful method of enabling communications up and down the management structure of any organization with a number of management levels, briefing can act as an important tool in facilitating communication among the various divisions of an organization.

In today's team-based organizational culture, team briefing assumes an important role in the domain of communication. The job of the manager is to ensure that all teams of the organization are coordinated internally so that the organization's goal is achieved. Hence, it is necessary that both within and outside the team, information is transmitted and comprehended adequately, appropriately, and amicably.

In an ideal briefing, there should be four main subject areas—progress, policy, people, and points for action. All four should be raised during the briefing, although, of course, it is not necessary to be rigid about the presentation.

Briefing sessions are held for different purposes, such as to provide information, to arrive at some decisions, or to convey the progress of a project. Timely briefing can help reduce misunderstandings and clear blocks in the communication channels of an organization.

Day-to-day communication tends to be a somewhat haphazard affair, so, briefing provides you with the scope for putting together all the disparate pieces of news that have amassed during the month and for presenting your team with a coherent overall picture. Another point is that briefing allows you to give the official version. Despite all these advantages, you are likely to hear a number of voices raised in objection to the idea of instituting it in your organization if you do not have such briefings already.

Finally, it is necessary not only to understand the techniques of effective briefing but also the strategies employed in implementing them.

## KEY TERMS

*Briefing* It is a management information system that enables leaders and their teams getting together in groups for a short time to talk about things relevant to their work. It does not replace existing methods of communication, but complements them. The process of communication pertaining to briefing is similar to those related to presentation, conversation, and discussion inasmuch as the essential components of communication process remain the same. In other words, all these communication processes have a sender, receiver, message, channel, response and feedback. And all these processes occur in a communication environment.

*Core management brief* Is a written briefing details from the CEO or board, which is passed on to every employee at every briefing every month. The core brief covers subject headings and will include items about financial and statistical performance; organizational policy; strategy, business direction and market conditions; successes and failings; changes in senior people's roles and positions.

*Decision briefing* It is a briefing held to obtain an answer or a decision. Personnel in the major branches of a company use this briefing for most tactical matters requiring command decisions.

*Effective briefing* Effective briefing is an art that requires alertness, poise, and good judgement. Whether the information you present is in oral, written, or pictorial form, you must be able to think on your feet. There will be times when you will have to come up with precise factual answers to questions that are difficult or even embarrassing. You should avoid verbal ambiguities, vagueness, or misplaced emphasis, which could easily convey a mental picture completely different from the one you have intended.

*Information briefing* It is the briefing held for conveying some important information. The purpose of the information briefing is to inform the listener. This briefing deals primarily with facts, not conclusions or recommendations. Use it to present high priority information requiring immediate attention; complex information involving complicated plans, systems, statistics, or charts; and controversial information requiring elaboration and explanation. Situation briefings that cover the tactical situation over a period of time usually fall into this category.

*Local brief* It is a separate written brief, prepared by each team leader, manager, or supervisor for his/her own team, containing local issues relevant to that team. The organizations that have made briefing a successful tool are those that have introduced a vital element, namely local information.

*Press briefing* It is a briefing given by a spokesperson or an official to the press in order to give some information to the public.

*Project briefing* It is a briefing held to inform the project team about the action plan or progress. When you want to brief your team about the current status of a project or a situation, you may give a brief background of the earlier status, and then proceed.

*Team briefing* It is a briefing given by the team leaders to their members. Briefing, as a means of communication, promotes openness in communication as it provides scope not only for briefing project operation, achievement, crisis, etc., but also for inviting opinions, feedback, and questions from the members of the teams.

## Concept Review Questions

Justify the following statements in about 100 words each, using suitable examples wherever necessary:

(i) Briefing in any organization is better than the grapevine form of communication.
(ii) The essential components of communication process in briefing and meeting are same.
(iii) Briefing not only involves an exposition of the topic but also encourages questions and feedback.
(iv) You can make your briefing sessions more effective only when you plan ahead and make adequate preparation.
(v) During briefing, you are supposed to express the management's view and not your own.
(vi) There are four main aspects that constitute the subject of your briefing—progress, policy, people and points of action.
(vii) The concept of briefing is neither new nor does it solely belong to organizational set-ups.
(viii) Briefing and public speaking differ in their style of presentation.
(ix) Timing is very crucial for effective briefings.
(x) Core brief and local brief are interdependent.

## Critical Thinking Questions

1. Can you think of a few businesses/industries in which briefing is not required at all? Mention at least two such workplaces and discuss why they can do without briefing.
2. Assume that you wish to introduce the concept of briefing in the advertising agency in which you occupy a key position. You face a lot of opposition from your peers for your plan. Keeping the functions of your company in focus, discuss five reasons to convince your opponents.
3. Develop a template for a briefing on project management.

## Projects

1. As the project leader of your team, you need to give a briefing on the latest assignment you have been offered by an external agency to design a scheme for their office automation. Now draft the text of this briefing in about 500 words. Invent the necessary details.
2. Look out in television/reputed journals/newspaper for examples of press briefings given by some officers of the government or public sector companies. Discuss with your friends the effectiveness of these briefings in terms of their content, structure, and style.
3. Hold a 30-minute group discussion on the topic 'Briefing does not serve any purpose in the business organizations'.
4. Visit any nearby industry/business organization, meet some of its executives and find out from them how briefing sessions are conducted in their workplace.

## REFERENCES

Adair, J. 2002, *The Effective Communicator*, Jaico Publishing House, Mumbai, pp. 15–31.

Adler, R.B. and J.M. Elmhorst 2002, *Communicating at Work*, Seventh Edn, McGraw-Hill, New York, pp. 410–11.

'Discover India,' http://www.meadev.nic.in/news/briefing.htm last accessed on 25 May 2004.

Huebsch, J.C. 1986, *Communication 2000*, Butterworths, Durban, pp. 47–56.

'Leadership Briefings,' http://www.centerforexcellence.net/Briefings/brief.html, last accessed on 12 June 2004.

'Management Briefings,' http://www.qm2.org/mbriefs/78.html, last accessed on 18 May 2004.

'Penrose, Rasberry, and Myers 2001, *Advanced Business Communication*, Fourth Edn, Thomson, Singapore, pp. 240–242.

'Project Management Executive Briefing,' http://www.interthink.ca/process/training2a.html, last accessed on 2 June 2004.

Robbins, S.P. and M. Coulter 1996, *Management*, Prentice Hall of India, Delhi, pp. 511–12.

'Team Briefing,' http://www.teamskillstraining.co.uk/, last accessed on 25 May 2004.

## CASE STUDY 1

### Team Briefing

Read the following briefing given by Director, CBI, to his team members about a bank robbery and answer the questions that follow the briefing.

Good morning, ladies and gentlemen,

As some of you would have heard, yesterday afternoon there was a bank robbery in Busy Street. Two people entered the bank and threatened the bank teller with a shotgun. They told the teller to fill two large bags with used money from the till, and to give it to them.

The teller then filled the bags with the cash and gave it to the robbers. The robbers ran out of the bank and jumped into a getaway car that was waiting for them. A witness said the car was a metallic red Mahindra Bolero. The witness also said he thought the registration was CA-R-113 but he was not completely sure about that. Two hours later, we found a Mahindra Bolero abandoned on the main highway out of the city, but the number plates were missing. After investigation, we discovered that the registration plates belonged to a stolen Fiat Uno and we are going to contact the original owner to find out when the car was stolen.

The Bolero was also a stolen vehicle, and we are checking with the Road Transport Office Registration Department to ascertain its owner.

We estimate that the total amount of money stolen was approximately ₹2,500,000. That is all we know at the moment, but we would appreciate any information the public can give. Please note that there is a reward of ₹50,000 if the robbers are caught.

You have just heard the official story. The truth is a little different. Two men entered the Busy Street bank and asked to see the bank manager. One of the employees asked them to wait, and after 15 minutes took them to the manager's office. Five minutes later, one of the men came out of the manager's office and demanded to leave the bank by the back door. The man had a gun, so the assistant manager agreed to the man's demand. When the back door was open, both men left and took the assistant manager and the manager with them. Approximately 25 minutes ago, the bank manager's wife received a phone call from the men saying that if they did not receive ₹5,000,000 within six hours, they would kill the manager and the assistant manager.

This is the reason we have not given the full story to the press because the kidnappers insisted there should be no police involved. The description regarding the car, however, is correct, so please, listen carefully and I will explain what we are going to do.

The men told the manager's wife to go to the local train station tomorrow night and get the 8.30 train to ABC station, which is only 20 minutes away. We will have the money ready by then. The men do not know what the wife looks like, but they told her to carry a blue bag so we are going to send a woman police officer in her place and she will give the cash to the kidnappers when they call her on her mobile phone. We already have 25 police personnel at the ABC station and hope everything will go according to plan.

### Questions

1. As the briefer, frame three questions to find out whether your team members have understood the case thoroughly.

2. As one among the audience, list the important points of the briefing you have just heard.
3. As one of the listeners, write down the steps involved in carrying out the plan suggested by the your Director.
4. Suggest an alternative plan to solve the problem in the case.
5. Brief this case in your own words.

## CASE STUDY 2

**Briefing on 'Maximizing Your Business with Modern Telephone Techniques'**

The following briefing on maximizing your business with modern telephone techniques was given by the Chief Training Officer of an Insurance Company. Read this carefully and answer the questions given at the end.

The phone rings. 'Good evening, Mr John, my name is Krishna with United Insurance. Do you have just a few moments?' Another agent calls. 'Hello, Mr John, how are you? My name is Madhuri Pande, I'm with National Insurance, and I'd like to come by to meet you and tell you about our services. I will be in your area on Tuesday or Wednesday.'

When you think about it, there are literally thousands of agents competing for the ears of the same people, and most use the same tired approaches. Why would prospects choose to listen to your agents over others—if anyone? Why is telephone prospecting so difficult?

Consider some of the challenges facing agents today—challenges that will only increase as we move further into the twenty-first century.

- *Negative perceptions of the insurance industry*
- *Inundation of the marketplace*  Telemarketing magazine tells us that while there were only about half a million people in the telemarketing industry 10 years ago, today more than four-and-a-half-million people are trying to contact the same people that your agents are.
- *Consumers' natural resistance to sales pitches*  You know it well and even understand it. More than likely the last time you were asked by a salesperson if he or she could help you, you reflexively responded, 'No, thanks', even if you were interested in making a purchase!
- *The numbers game or 'If you make enough calls, you'll make enough appointments'*  This fallacy is quite widespread in appointment setting, and can harm the efforts of agents.

It is preparedness and quality presentation—otherwise known as salesmanship—that increases success rates.

*The right approach*  Whether you are prospecting by telephone or face-to-face, the formula for success is the same—50% presentation and 50% delivery. Achieving a powerful telephone voice simply takes work; without it, the delivery will undoubtedly sound 'canned' and hamper results.

The same adage goes for the presentation. Agents must continuously practise their introduction, demonstration, and closing. It is also imperative to be prepared with well-rehearsed rebuttals. It is important to note that the second part of the presentation—demonstration—is usually ignored. Agents introduce themselves and then attempt to close before they have discovered the buying motives of prospects and established a need.

*Introduction*  It is during the introduction segment that agents are most likely to encounter rejection—usually within the first 15 seconds. Therefore, strong introductions are critical. However, if, on hearing the introduction, the prospect immediately begins with 'I'm too busy right now,' the agent must respond simply by saying, 'Great, Mr John, I'll call you back later today. Or would tomorrow morning be better?'

*Demonstration* A critical part of the presentation, demonstration is intended to quickly lower resistance with a series of brief questions—usually between three and six—designed to reveal the prospects' buying motives, open him/her to suggestion, and establish a need with a strong question prior to the close. Rather than telling prospects your purpose outright, you are using questions to give prospects reasons for considering your opportunity. The questions in the demonstration segment aren't being asked just to fill time. They are motivating prospects to answer, and in answering, they are selling themselves on reasons for needing your services.

*Closing* An effective telephone closing has the following 9 steps:

- Suggest a meeting without using the word appointment.
- Ask a question designed to elicit a response to the given suggestion.
- Give the prospect several alternatives for each response, and make sure the prospect writes it down.
- Repeat the prospect's name, then spell it, and again repeat it.
- Repeat the day, date, and time of the scheduled meeting to the prospect.
- Ask for directions, including landmarks and cross streets.
- Offer closing pleasantries.
- Repeat name, day, date, and time.
- Allow the prospect to hang up first.

Every agent should have strong rebuttals to the most common objections at his/her fingertips, and should know them well enough to deliver them without the slightest pause. Statistics prove that 80 per cent of all sales take place between the third and the fifth call. Therefore, agents who are prepared to hang in there have the odds on their side, and will get the appointments they seek with persistence and the proper techniques.

**Practice makes perfect** To develop true experience in rebuttals and make a generally strong, effective presentation, practice is the magic ingredient. Not only must agents practise regularly to refine their skills but managers also must make a commitment to support their agents and spend the time necessary to continually build their skills.

### Questions

1. Write two or three sentences that would serve as a logical conclusion to this briefing.
2. Do you think all the nine steps mentioned under 'closing' are mandatory? Justify your answer.
3. Substitute the introductory paragraph with one prepared in your own words.
4. Mention four other businesses in which telephonic communication plays an important role.
5. As one among the audience in this briefing, prepare two questions to be posed to the briefer.

# PART IV
# UNDERSTANDING SPECIFIC COMMUNICATION NEEDS

17. Communication across Functional Areas
18. Corporate Communication
19. Persuasive Strategies in Business Communication
20. Ethics in Business Communication
21. Business Communication Aids

CHAPTER 17

# Communication across Functional Areas

## LEARNING OBJECTIVES

After reading this chapter, you will be able to understand

- communication within and between functional areas
- integrated marketing communication
- the features of direct and indirect selling
- project management communication
- human resource communication
- financial communication and its constituents
- communication issues in corporate governance
- management information systems as a communication tool

## INTRODUCTION

The concept of communication is shifting in this fast-changing business world. Businesses are seeing the emergence of a new world, a world full of information and complex communication networks, with shifting paradigms for companies and jobs on account of more and more emphasis on quality information and effective information systems. The new communicator's task is to process and channel the right information so that it reaches the right people at the right time and in the right way. In today's organizations, everyone needs to know all the information they need to do their jobs properly. The basic idea is that an organization has various constituents with sometimes conflicting objectives, therefore, the process of the communication system has to be so embedded in the overall organizational system that it binds these various constituents through a common thread, all of them collectively trying to pursue a broader objective as a team.

Organizational communication can be divided into two broad categories—internal and external organizational communication (Fig. 17.1). The former dwells on the various communication techniques and processes being used inside an organization (within the various departments of manufacturing, finance, marketing, human resource, etc.), whereas the latter refers to the interaction of organizations with outside agencies including suppliers, customers, shareholders, the public at large, and various government bodies. In this chapter, each of these functional

> Organizational communication can be divided into internal and external organizational communication.

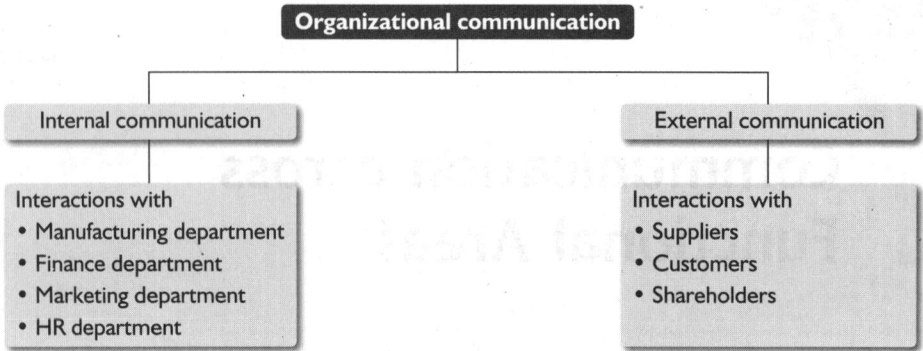

**Fig. 17.1** Types of organizational communication

areas and the communication patterns and standards normally used within these departments are discussed.

## MARKETING COMMUNICATION/INTEGRATED MARKETING COMMUNICATION

Peter Drucker, the legendary management consultant, once said, 'The purpose of business is not to make a sale, but to make and keep a customer.' The customer today has a plethora of choices when it comes to buying products/services. The marketing landscape has changed more in the past five years than in the past 50 years. Consumers have changed beyond recognition. Their behaviour is more complex, their media habits are different, and they are more outspoken. They have a different relationship with brands these days, relationships that are less tolerant, less 'obedient'. Significantly, too, mass media is no longer mass. Communication channels are exploding and fragmenting. Audiences are diminishing; therefore, audiences have more choices and more distractions than ever before.

Marketing communication actually deals with one of the most popular aspects of the five Ps of marketing—promotion. The other four Ps are product, pricing, place, and people. These are loosely connected to marketing communication, but its real relation is with promotion. Several communication channels, which constitute the promotion mix, are available to an organization for carrying out the promotional activity. Effective and efficient coordination of these channels for spreading a consistent customer focused message is the theme of integrated marketing communication.

### Cola Wars

In the summer of 2003, the cola czars, Coca-Cola India and Pepsi Foods Ltd shifted their attention from waging aggressive price wars to integrated marketing plans in order to gain mind share as well as market share. In a bid to pump up consumption volumes, both Pepsi and Coke dropped the price of their 200 ml bottles to just ₹5. To add more fizz to the cola war, Pepsi chose to premiere its third commercial in cyber space—at Yahoo! India—deviating from the traditional route. Meanwhile, Coca-Cola India revamped its website with new technology and features. According to the then Pepsi Foods Executive Director, the company had looked beyond the conventional medium by extending the new campaign to cyber space as an additional medium to reach out to the online community. Meanwhile,

> Marketing communication actually deals with 'promotion', one of the most popular aspects of marketing.

> **BUSINESS COMMUNICATION INSIGHT**
>
> ### 15 Principles of Successful Internal Communication
>
> Effective internal communication is hard work, but research findings and case studies point to some practices and principles which seem crucial to successful internal communications for organizations, employees and members. Here are 15 of them.
>
> **Timeliness and content**
>
> - Providing timely and relevant information to individuals, through channels they use and trust, and in language they understand, remains the basis for successful and strategic internal communications.
> - Communication content should provide context and rationale for changes or new initiatives as they relate to the organization, but especially to the relative performance or requirements of employees in local work units. This underlines the importance of the supervisor's front-line role in communication.
>
> **Channels**
>
> - Face-to-face communication is the richest medium. It should be emphasized in internal communications, especially to resolve conflicts or crises, communicate major changes and celebrate accomplishments.
> - Excellent listening skills reduce errors and misunderstanding, help uncover problems, save time, improve evaluations and facilitate relationship building.
> - Social media are fast and powerful dialogue-creating channels which can empower and engage employees and members. They influence and alter traditional media and their uses, but don't eliminate them. Communicators should blend new and traditional media in ways that help organizations best achieve their goals and enhance relationships with internal and external publics.
>
> **Leadership roles**
>
> - The CEO or senior leader(s) must be a visible and open champion for internal communication. Visibility is the first and most basic form of non-verbal communication for leaders.
> - The communication style of leaders should invite open, ongoing and transparent discussion so that people are willing to voice their opinions and suggestions.
> - The actions of leaders at all levels must match their words. This has everything to do with credibility and the extent to which employees will trust, commit to and follow leaders.
>
> **Professional communicator roles**
>
> - Professional communicators must see themselves as internal experts on communication who serve as facilitators and counselors to executives and managers and provide strategic support for business plans.
> - Communicators must also be organizational experts. They must possess knowledge of the organization's structures, challenges and objectives, as well as understand employee issues and needs and marketplace requirements and realities.
>
> **Participation and recognition**
>
> - Encouraging employee participation in decision-making builds loyalty and commitment and improves the overall climate for communication. Participative decision-making also often improves the quality of decisions.
> - Recognizing and celebrating achievements at all levels helps build shared values and organizational identity. Similar social events, rites, and rituals contribute to and reflect an organization's distinctive culture.
>
> **Measurement**
>
> - Measurement is a key to successful communication in any organization. Through diverse forms and approaches, measurement helps define problems, determine the status quo, record progress, assess value and provide a factual basis for future direction and action. Improving measurement knowledge and practice is an ongoing professional requirement.

### Culture

- Ongoing two-way communication is the foundation for employee motivation and organizational success.
- Two-way (now every-way) communication provides continuous feedback, which is crucial to learning and to processing organizational change.

In addition to achieving specific goals, internal communications should help create and reflect a *culture for communication*, where employees at all levels feel free to openly share ideas, opinions and suggestions. This will enhance employee understanding, build trust, stimulate engagement and encourage greater diversity.

*Source*: Berger, Bruce K., PhD (2008), 'Employee/Organizational Communications', http://www.instituteforpr.org/topics/employee-organizational-communications/, accessed on 2 December 2011. Reproduced with permission.

Coca-Cola India stepped up its mass media advertising to woo cola drinkers across the nation. A new television commercial featuring popular film stars was launched to promote their Coke bottle priced at ₹8.

## Definition of Marketing Communication

Marketing communication integrates humanities, social sciences, and business administration to prepare managers for building realistic strategies in the integrated fields of advertising, public relations, brand communications, direct/database marketing, sales, promotions, and e-commerce. It is all about propagating information related to the organization or its products/services in the outside world. A number of tools are available for the same. A broader view has emerged recently which tries to add some more dimensions to the already existing domains of marketing communication.

The new concept, which is called integrated marketing communication, is the judicious and efficient use of the product promotional tools so that a universal, clear, and effective promotional message is communicated amongst the target audience.

Integrated marketing communication involves the dynamics between the entities of organizations, agencies, and media. The customers are at the center of all this planning. However, some academicians and researchers do not really see any major difference between integrated marketing communication and marketing communication and call this new concept a marketing gimmick.

> Integrated marketing communication aims to use product promotional tools to create a universal, clear, and effective promotional message.

## Medium of Marketing Communication

Marketing communication can take various forms/mediums and companies have a number of choices when it comes to reaching out to a prospec-

### Walmart—Build a Personality

In a densely populated retail industry, most consumers will fall back on brands that command a strong position. The famous discounter, Walmart's brand building revolves around friendly service and the everyday lowest price. The retailer's offer of low prices also includes national brands at a discount. To ensure consistency, the company has developed an information system that interconnects all supply chain participants. The partners are well aware of the inventory position, order status, and the current position in the chain. This is cited as the main reason for the chain's legendary replenishment policies. Employees are motivated to deliver better service every time through a horde of performance-based incentives. By ensuring consistency, Walmart has slowly built its image as a 'friendly and trustworthy partner in a consistently complex world.'

> Demographics are the socio-economic characteristics of prospective buyers pertaining to a geographic unit.

tive customer informing him/her about a particular product or service. Finding advertising medium where your prospects are likely to buy is the key to success in any business. Demographics are the socio-economic characteristics of prospective buyers pertaining to a geographic unit. However, another tool that is sometimes overlooked is psychographics, which pertains to the buyers' lifestyle and attitudes. Specific psychographics could include known fields of interest, patterns of behaviour, purchasing habits, hobbies, etc.

### Efficiency of Medium

The efficient working of any medium requires certain factors to be kept in mind. Efficiency is usually determined by the following factors:

**Cost per exposure** This is a critical factor in determining the rate of profitable response. The cost per exposure also means the cost per amount of selling information that the prospective customer was exposed to.

In a direct marketing medium, a prospective customer can be exposed to a great amount of sales information. However, in a television broadcast, for instance, the maximum amount of time per exposure is usually two minutes. Therefore, the amount of sales information per exposure must be considered. In general, in direct marketing, the more you tell, the more you sell. For example, if you are using the medium of direct marketing to sell a ₹500 retail price product which produces a gross profit of ₹100, and your cost to advertise and sell this product (everything included) is ₹5 per customer, your break-even point would be reaching 20 customers to get one order, or a 5 per cent rate of response. However, if you could cut the cost of that advertising to ₹2.50 per customer, at the same 5 per cent rate of response, you would get a great deal of profit from the advertisement. In fact, you would double your profit each time you advertise.

**Quality of exposure** Exposure can mean many different things, depending upon the medium used. For instance, direct marketing exposure is much more personal and positive than broadcast exposure. When a prospective customer receives a direct marketing piece, it holds that customer's attention to a greater degree than a direct marketing television advertisement. Therefore, even though the cost per exposure in direct marketing may be much higher than the cost per exposure in the broadcast medium, the quality of exposure in direct marketing is usually much greater.

**Density of prospective customers** The greater the density of prospective customers in the medium used, the higher the rate of profitable response you can expect. If you were trying to sell a product using the medium of direct marketing targeted towards the elite apartment dwellers, your density

---

**Integrated Marketing Communication**

Don E. Shultz, who can fairly be described as a principal pioneer and a leading advocate of integrated marketing communication (IMC), defines it thus, 'IMC is the process of managing all sources of information about a product/service to which a customer or prospect is exposed which behaviourally moves the consumer toward a sale and maintains customer loyalty.' According to Philip Kotler, 'Integrated marketing communication is a way of looking at the whole marketing process from the viewpoint of the customer.'

> ### The Original 'Small Car'
>
> Bill Bernbach, founder of the advertising agency, Doyle Dane Bernbach, in New York City, came into prominence during the late 1950s and 1960s with advertising that was outstanding for its insight into psychographics. The advertisements that his agency created were understated, sophisticated, and witty, in keeping with the spirit of the age. At a time when American cars were getting bigger and bigger, and the advertising for them trumpeted that bigger was better, Doyle Dane Bernbach created a magazine advertisement that showed a small picture of the Volkswagen Beetle surrounded by a sea of white space with the headline, 'Think small'.
>
> An equally unconventional advertisement carried the headline 'Lemon' beneath the photograph of an apparently flawed Volkswagen. The advertisements copy explained, 'This Volkswagen missed the boat. The chrome strip on the glove compartment is blemished and must be replaced....We pluck the lemons; you get the plums.' In an era of hype and bombast, the Volkswagen advertisements stood out because they admitted failure in a witty way and gave facts in a believable manner that underlined the car's strengths.

of prospective customers would be very low. However, if you chose a marketing strategy targeted towards suburban homeowners who had purchased your product before, your density of prospective customers would be very high.

Promotion and delivery media can be any of the following:

- Catalogue
- Electronic book
- Newspaper (classified or display)
- Billboards
- Television
- Radio
- Internet
- Telephone

The first step in selecting a medium is to get the best description of the prospective customers you are trying to reach. Do a profile of your prospective customers including age, sex, occupation, education level, interest, income level, and social stature. Now that you have your product and know exactly whom you are trying to reach, you are ready to select your medium.

Online promotional advertisements are growing dramatically and you will find that using the Internet as a promotional medium will be to your advantage. It is less costly and it delivers information at a higher speed and accuracy (Image 17.1). Electronic books, for example, are becoming a popular medium for reaching targeted audiences. They are easily downloadable and your targeted prospects can be reading the advertisement in seconds, after download.

> ### The Great Outdoors
>
> Outdoor advertising is an effective way to reach a highly mobile audience that spends a lot of time on the road, for example, in commuting to and from work or as part of their job. It offers the lowest cost per exposure of any major advertising medium, and it produces a major impact, because it is big, colourful, and hard to ignore. The messages on outdoor boards have to be very brief. So, outdoor advertising primarily serves as a reminder medium and one that can trigger an impulse purchase. For example, Airtel, a leading cellular phone operator in India has a visible presence on national highways, roadside eateries (*dhabas*), bus stops, commercial complexes, and railway and bus stations around the country.

Communication across Functional Areas **459**

**Image 17.1** A noodle brand page on a popular social-networking site

Although a medium does not sell products on its own, it certainly does have a big influence on advertising effectiveness. In large measure, your chosen medium determines who will be exposed to your message, how many people will be exposed to it, and how often. The medium also provides an environment that is favourable or unfavourable.

Let us assume you are selling basmati rice. Visual appeal stimulates taste buds. Prospective customers need to see the steam rising off the rice and peas running off the spoon as you pick them up each time. Because you have a product that requires visualization, you can automatically eliminate radio. Television or a photograph in a print medium would be the best advertising medium.

### How Marketing Communications Works

Marketing communications supports (acts as a hidden supplement to direct selling efforts of the sales team), streamlines (tries to give a concrete direction to the host of marketing activities including marketing communication going on to lure the customer), and mechanizes the selling effort (being simultaneously done by the sales force of the organization) by ensuring the following:

---

**Reality Check**

One question to consider when producing an advertisement is 'How much is the utility I am going to get from this really worth?' It is foolish for a retailer to spend lakhs of rupees producing a television spot for a Diwali sale if the spot is going to run on a local channel in one market. In most cases, the retailer cannot possibly sell enough merchandise to justify that kind of expenditure. But it is equally foolish to try and sell someone a ₹4.6 lakh car or a ₹15,000 vacation with a brochure that costs only a few rupees a copy.

> The medium does have a big influence on advertising effectiveness.

**Making the first sales call**  Even before the sales person reaches the prospective customer and tries to explain to him/her the various features to promote sale, the marketing communication might have already created a desire to know more in the mind of the customers, so much so that they might start 'looking forward' to the sales representatives call.

**Selling when the sales representative is not there**  Either when the sales representative has not reached the customer or when he/she has called, explained the product and left, it is easy for the customers to 'go back' to the marketing communication and learn more or try and recollect some minor details which he/she might have accidentally missed out during the sales call.

**Refuting claims made by competitors and their marketing communications**  Generally, one component of marketing communications could be written pamphlets/information brochures telling the details of the product. These are passed on to the prospective customers by the sales representative during the sales call or otherwise. He/she can also simultaneously verify the credentials of the product vis-à-vis competition.

**Presenting a message about a product that is uniformly correct, concise, and persuasive**  Since this mode of advertising will be done in a standard format, which has been carefully processed and tested, the chances of ambiguity in the messages about the product/service is minimal. It is always easy to refer back to a brochure/pamphlet and be doubly assured before actually purchasing anything.

**Arming the sales representative with supporting documentation and increased credibility**  It is always handy for sales representatives to have detailed brochures about the product to pass on to the prospective customer, which the latter can read and cross-check with what the sales person is saying and the former can refer to during the sales presentation for bringing out any specific technical details without having to remember them.

**Keeping current customers satisfied by reinforcing their buying decision after the sale**  Even after the sale is complete and the prospective customer has bought the product, the various marketing communication tools, like advertisements, help reinforce his/her faith in the product and give a feeling of having made the 'right choice' to him/her.

## DIRECT VS INDIRECT SELLING

A key component of the sales process that comes under extreme scrutiny as internal resources are slashed in the choice between direct and indirect selling. In a direct selling exercise, the product is

---

**Consider the Media Carefully**

If your target audience is very broad, such as the national market for medium-priced automobiles, the media planner will probably select network television, which has a broad reach. If the target is narrower and specialized such as the market for a cosmetic, the media that reaches a more specialized audience, such as women's magazines, would be selected. Moreover, since not all members of the narrow target audience read the same magazines, the media planner might employ a range of magazines to reach a larger percentage of the intended consumer.

> ### The Zing Thing
>
> The case study of Kinetic's launch of their 'scooterette', the Zing, illustrates many of the aspects that are to be considered in choosing an effective medium for positioning a product and the type of promotional activities that ought to be undertaken. 'Kinetic Zing', a smaller and lighter sibling of the full scooter, was positioned as a desirable two-wheeler for buyers in the age group of 16–21. These are essentially urban vehicles, popular in mini metros and cities with large student populations. The Zing was launched in August 2002 and, by March 2003, it had cornered an excellent market share of 20 per cent. But the company needed to do something special for the months of April–July 2003, considered the most crucial months from a sales point of view as the 'pre-college opening' turns large numbers of teenagers into king customers. With this in mind, Kinetic created a special variant of the Zing called the Zing Rockin' series aimed specifically at teenagers such as special attractive dual-tone colour schemes, an under seat charge point, holder for a mobile phone, an FM radio and a cola can holder. Kinetic's research showed that the style-seekers vastly outnumbered the functionality seekers—71–29 per cent. Kinetic created a summer marketing campaign that included a television campaign and a cool event/contest as a good way of creating some interactive buzz. It was found that television and events, rather than the print media were the most effective platforms to talk to the youth.
>
> With its unique features, the Zing completely repositioned other scooterettes as has-beens. Instead of taking a classic brand stand of talking about the product's attributes, the company decided to say that no one else had such-and-such features. The idea used was to create dissonance by saying *Baki sab ki hawa nikaal de*. This was then taken literally—to mean that anyone without a Zing Rockin' would feel deflated. The advertisement was bold and funny, slightly over the top, but definitely entertaining. It really stood out and it worked.

pushed to the customer by giving the customer a live demonstration of the product, for example products like vacuum cleaners and water filters can be demonstrated to an advantage directly. A direct selling exercise is more costly as the company uses its own resources to try and sell its product directly to the prospective customer through direct sales call made by the company's sales representative (Image 17.2).

An indirect selling exercise is normally resorted to by a company in two situations—first, when the product is simple to use and does not require any sales person to give a demonstration, for example, Maggi Noodles; and second, when the product is such that it cannot be carried by the salesperson from door to door like a scooter or car.

An indirect sales effort can normally be made through a marketing communications agent, which at times may be outsourced and can attack the prospective customer indirectly but constantly (not

> ### Testimonials
>
> In industrial and high-end consumer durable marketing areas, buyer confidence is most essential for success and even survival. Most purchases entailing significant risk and/or involvement rely heavily on buyer confidence. Testimonial letters from satisfied dealers and customers are powerful sales tools in this respect and yet few companies give them the incessant attention they deserve. Savvy marketers incorporate letters into their media advertisements and brochures. Service providers mount them on office walls. Sales people tuck them into 'show and tell' brochures. Testimonials have been used by many effectively—in construction, advertising, real estate, and hospitality.

> ### Silence is Golden
>
> The advertising agency Renovision D&R designed a campaign for Deikon air conditioners using unified marketing communication for maximum impact. The ad campaign was fabricated around the note of 'total peace' and was launched across not only print, TV, outdoor, retail, and online media, but was even used by traders and sales staff in the field. Mr Adrias Mendez, the then Vice-President and Executive Creative Director of Renovision D&R, explained, 'Our client manufactures the air conditioners on a technology which single-mindedly transforms into it being more noiseless than other air conditioners.' The results were very promising despite Deikon being about 25 per cent more costly than other air conditioners in the market and not once resorting to promotions, discounts, etc.

**Image 17.2** A popular plastic storage box brand in the direct selling arena

like a sales call, where a representative comes, talks, and goes away and may or may not make an impression). This method is less costly but requires meticulous training and expertise. Before we go any further, let us at the very outset compare and contrast direct selling with indirect marketing communication.

A direct sales call made by a live sales representative almost always has the following features:

**More persuasive and powerful, with the added ability to respond directly to questions and concerns** The biggest advantage with direct sales call is that the sales representative is present as and when the product is being demonstrated which gives the distinct advantage of direct response to any queries and doubts in the mind of the prospective customers. It is more effective in terms of immediate results and carries a bonus of strong possibilities of persuasion.

**More closely and directly related to a sale** As the direct sales team is normally an employee of the organization (except in a few cases, where its is outsourced), the cost of running a direct selling campaign can be easily ascertained and can be then compared with the benefits to conduct a thorough cost benefit analysis.

**An expensive proposition** Any direct selling programme is a huge expenditure for the company, mainly in terms of the labour cost, that is, the salaries of the direct marketing staff. Due of the fact that the amount required is huge and normally not reversible, the company's think tank should think about this option very strategically before actually opting for it.

An indirect sales call made through marketing communications almost always has the following features:

> Direct selling programmes are usually expensive and hence their implementation is a strategic decision.

**Is concise, uniform, and ubiquitous** Since the indirect marketing communication tools like print or electronic media are very costly, the company makes all efforts to see that it is as concise and straight as possible. Also, it is almost omnipresent, for example, as ads in local/national newspapers, on billboards, on television, etc.

### The Urge to Splurge

There was a time not so long ago when the average middle-class Indian had to toil hard for a good number of years to acquire basic amenities like a refrigerator, television, or tape recorder. Possessing an air conditioner, a music system, or a washing machine were seen to be, as a popular television commercial went, 'neighbour's envy, owner's pride'. In the 1990s, this staid scenario changed dramatically with the coming of economic liberalization. A soft interest rate regime and low inflation delivered a double booster dose to consumer spending—they increased the cost of saving and reduced the cost of buying.

A second key factor for the change in spending patterns was the evolving of media. Satellite television and the Internet brought the world into Indian homes. The traditional role of banks, too, underwent a major change. Deregulation and fierce competition, along with rapid strides in information technology redefined the role and structure of banking in India. Banks had to change with the times and become marketing organizations that also sell banking products. Direct selling agents (DSAs) of various banks now go out and sell their products. They make house calls to get application forms filled out and passport photos taken. Telemarketing of personal loan schemes and new banking products are pervasive. Many banks and credit card companies are increasingly targeting India's 14 million cardholders through directly mailed offers of goods and services. Standard Chartered Bank, for instance, with several firsts to its credit, like the first global credit card and the first photocard, was keen to provide incremental value to its customers and continuously increase profitability. Analysing its huge volume of customer data, the bank launched DIVA—a specially designed women's international credit card targeted at the Indian woman who seeks a balance between home and work. The product was bundled with several first time features such as fabulous discounts and 0% interest rates on renowned brands across a wide array of consumer durables, leather products, mobile phones, baby products, travel, airlines, healthcare, etc.

Citibank takes the lead in targeting the youth segment. In mid-2001, it tied up with MTV and the Times group to introduce a primary and an add-on youth credit card, respectively. Citibank's co-branded card was launched in April 2001 with MTV, a youth channel. Offering all the features of Citibank's silver international card, the card offered discounts and freebies at outlets ranging from discotheques to restaurants. The following year, the MTV Citibank card co-opted more partners ranging from bowling alleys to Internet cafes to give youngsters the discounts they were looking for.

A direct sales call is persuasive and powerful.

**Gets an entry where sales reps sometimes cannot** Many of the sales calls fail to materialize at the very first stage because sales representatives fail to get appointments with prospective customers due to the latter's busy schedules and other engagements. It is here that marketing communication manages to escape through this barrier and targets the customer even if he/she is preoccupied and does not have time to actually meet the sales representative for a detailed discussion.

**Has a relationship to sales that is difficult to document** The efforts of marketing communications cannot be isolated from other

> ### Selling a Chain Reaction
>
> Some companies recruit selling agents rather than employing people directly. Take a look at Tupperware, the company that has turned direct selling into an art form around the world. At first glance, it is tough to understand how Tupperware has carved out a niche for itself. It makes premium plastic containers used for storing or serving food and it has to compete against thousands of unbranded competitors that are sold at dirt-cheap prices. But Tupperware has been a hit even in India, partly because it has a direct selling army that is excellently trained and motivated. Kanwar S. Bhutani (Previously part of Tupperware) had stated, 'Our products are much more expensive than the plastic products available in the market. But then they have their benefits, which need to be explained. This cannot be done in an off-the-shelf approach.'
>
> Samir Modi, Modicare Ltd, which sells an extraordinary range of products from cosmetics to water-purifiers and agricultural products, stated, 'The retail environment in India is very poor. The customer does not always enjoy the shopping experience. Direct selling overcomes that.'
>
> How does it work? People who want to become distributors buy a starter kit from the company which costs between ₹1,000 and ₹5,000 depending on the company and its products. The kit contains literature on the company and five or six of its top products. The distributor then tries to sell its products. Most people drop out of the business almost immediately when they discover how tough selling can be. But for those who stay on, there are rewards. The distributor earns a generous margin of between 20 to 25 per cent on all sales. More importantly, he or she must recruit more people to become distributors. The recruiter gets a percentage on sales by people he/she has recruited.
>
> Why do companies choose the direct selling route? The general wisdom is that any product that needs an explanation or a demonstration is best sold through direct selling. Moreover, the product must have a distinguishing factor and should be different from the products available in the market.

marketing efforts, being simultaneously made by the company, and analysed independently. It is a grey area in terms of budgeting because the company would always like to see how much has the company gained by the marketing communication campaign.

**Costs only a few rupees** The cost of indirect selling through an integrated marketing communication is very low as compared to the cost incurred in direct selling. Moreover, the investments made in any marketing communication plan is a one time investment, the fruits of which will keep on coming to the company for a longer period.

## PROJECT MANAGEMENT COMMUNICATION

In a fast-changing business environment, more and more businesses are moving away from the traditional set-up of functioning and moving towards a network kind of organizational structure where each new work is treated as a separate project and all functional areas of marketing, finance, production, etc. play their own roles in these projects.

> The cost of indirect selling through an integrated marketing communication is very low as compared to the cost incurred in direct selling.

Project communication refers to all systems and techniques used by organizations to effectively monitor the status of projects through various kinds of status reports, etc. and also to see that there is sufficient communication within the functional areas involved in a particular project. Properly communicating on a project is a critical success factor for managing the expectations of the sponsor

> - Project communication refers to all systems and techniques used by organizations to effectively monitor the status of projects through various kinds of status reports.
> - It is very important for a company to identify the various stakeholders that are to be communicated to and the kind of information that will interest them.

and the stakeholders. If these people are not kept well informed of the project progress, there is a greater chance of facing problems due to differing levels of expectations. In fact, in many cases where conflicts arise, it is not because of the actual problem, but because the client or manager was surprised.

## Managing Project Communication

All projects should communicate status. This includes the project team reporting to the project manager and the project manager reporting to the sponsor and stakeholders. Two typical forums for communicating status are through status meetings and status reports. Larger projects need to be more sophisticated in how they communicate to various stakeholders. This multifaceted approach is defined in a communications plan.

### Communication Needs for Each Stakeholder

A lot of communication takes place as and when a project is analysed, implemented, and completed. To develop an effective communication system, it is very important for a company to identify the various parties or groups that are to be communicated to and the kind of information that will interest them more.

It is quite obvious that in any project in an organization, not all communication regarding the project has to be communicated; also every level and, moreover, the significance of this communication also varies. It is important to carefully determine the communication needs for each stakeholder. The stakeholders could be the clients or customers, shareholders, financers, the media, or society at large. Usually this kind of communication breaks down into three general areas—mandatory, informational, and marketing.

**Mandatory** This kind of communication generally includes project status reports, legal requirements, financial reporting, etc. This information is sent out to the recipients. There are various types of communications required by a company, an industry, or law. These could be as follows:

---

### Mera Gaon, Mera Des—Indirect Selling in Villages

Today, the ultra bright shine of Colgate or some other international brand of toothpaste holds more appeal than the traditional methods of cleaning teeth. Charcoal-cleaned teeth are a rare sight; same is the case with the twigs of *neem* and *babul* trees. Consumerism and globalization are invading parts of India where, as some would venture to say, time seemed to have ceased for centuries. These villages and small towns, which were once inconsequential dots on maps, are now getting the attention of global marketing giants and media planners. Rural marketing is gaining new heights in addition to rural advertising. Approximately 80 per cent of India lives in over half a million villages, generating more than half of the national income. The challenges of reaching this magnitude of the rural masses where scores of languages or rural dialects are spoken are formidable. To achieve their goal, marketers must perforce use both conventional and original forms of indirect selling techniques. In addition to rural market discourse, media forms such as wall paintings, calendar, outdoor, print, radio, and television advertising are used. Messages must be crafted to meet rural tastes and sensibilities. A uniquely Indian media form is van technology, which has changed the face of not only marketing but also political campaigning.

*Project status report*   This is nothing but a report in a structured format mentioning the details of the progress related to the various activities involved in a project. This report is, more or less, an attempt to look at the budget estimates and, with a particular time elapsed, the project manager can check the cost incurred and how well he/she is doing as compared to the budget estimates.

*Status meeting*   Every week or so, the project team can hold a meeting to assess the progress and make changes, if required. This meeting should be attended by all concerned and there should be no hiding of facts in these meetings. Any delays and cost overruns should be exactly reported and carefully looked into during the meeting.

*Meeting with a steering committee*   Normally, a project is overseen or supervised by a steering committee, which has members from almost all the functional areas of the business involved in the project. The steering committee should also conduct regular meetings to update everyone, discuss issues, and analyse any anomalies present.

*Reporting details to shareholders or the board of directors*   Shareholders and the board of directors usually closely watch the progress of a project as a company's prospects are normally tied up in these projects. The company should make all available information about the project public to the shareholders so that they are not kept in dark. Suppressed information about the company may lead to a large scale manipulation of share prices through insider information which is not good for any professional and respectable company.

*Financial report like budget vs actuals, or any other required financial information*   All financial information related to a project has to be prepared as and when required and send to all parties interested including the management, financers, etc., for their independent and objective assessment of the project by comparing the actual results achieved with the projected figures in the budget.

**Informational**   This kind of communication refers to any information people want or need to know. This information is usually made available for people outside the company but interested in the project. It requires them to take the initiative, or 'pull the communication'. Informational communication could be any one of the following:

*Awareness building sessions that people are invited to attend*   Awareness building sessions are not held as training sessions but held to build awareness. For example, awareness building sessions can be held by an environmentally-sensitive organization to dispel fears about possible imbalance to the ecological system, being perceived by the local community, where a civil project is being undertaken. The organization can try and explain some of the doubts in the minds of the locals and try to develop a good corporate image by fostering a healthy relationship with the local community.

*Project deliverables placed in a common repository*   A company can place project information in a directory or library that people can access and can also bring out some publications or articles in journals or magazines to convey information about an ongoing project and its possible benefits to society. A feature in a newspaper highlighting the broad objectives of the project could also be helpful.

> Informational communication refers to any information people want or need to know.

*Project information on a website*   With the growing proliferation of computers and the advent of the Internet, it will be a cost-effective exercise for a company to share details of a project on the company's website so that busy people

> Marketing is designed to build buy-in and enthusiasm for the project and its deliverables/benefits.

can browse through these details while working, and make their own objective assessments about the project.

**Marketing** Marketing is designed to build buy-in and enthusiasm for the project and its deliverables/benefits. Many a time, there is some negative publicity about a project in the society due to various reasons like political and social factors, etc. even before the project kicks off. By effectively marketing their project, a company can lessen this negative feeling to an extent because without the support of society and the locals in particular, it is very difficult for organizations to succeed in a project. This type of information is sent out by the company to the appropriate people/groups through a one-on-one communication channel.

Typical examples include the following:

- Project newsletters with a positive marketing spin
- Meeting one-on-one with key stakeholders on an ongoing basis
- Travelling road shows to various locations and departments to explain projects and benefits
- Testimonials from others that describe how the project deliverables provided value
- Contests with simple prizes to build excitement
- Project acronyms and slogans to portray positive images of the project
- Project countdown till live date
- Informal (but purposeful) walking around to initiate discussions about all the good things the project is accomplishing.
- Celebrations to bring visibility to the completion of major milestones
- Project memorabilia with project name or image portrayed on things such as pens, frisbees, cups, t-shirts, etc.

## Ideal Project Communication Mix

As already discussed, there are various kinds of project communication tools available. Therefore, it is important for a company to devise a suitable mix of these tools for a project. The mix is largely dependent on the organizational culture, the size of the project, and the expectancy levels of the stakeholders. Let us try and lay down an optimum project communication mix for small, medium, and large projects.

### Small Projects

Small projects usually do not need more than basic status reporting. If the project manager is doing any hands-on work on the project, he/she will probably have a very good idea of the overall status. However, if he/she is not working on the project details, he/she may need a formal status reporting process. The following process would be typical:

1. Project team members should send a status update to the project manager on a weekly basis.
2. The project manager should send a status update to the project sponsor and stakeholders on a fortnightly or monthly basis.
3. The entire project team should attend project status meetings. The meetings should focus on the status against the project work-plan, uncovering any current issues, scan change requests, or potential risks.

### Medium Projects

> In medium-sized projects, communication should include formal status meetings and status reports.

In medium-sized projects, communications should include formal status meetings and status reports. In a smaller project, these could be fairly informal. For a medium project, the following activities should be formalized:

1. The team should attend status meetings on a weekly or fortnightly basis. The client should definitely have representation at the status meeting. If the project manager prefers, there could be status meetings for the project team and a separate meeting with the client.
2. The project manager should send status reports to all stakeholders on a fortnightly or monthly basis.
3. The project team members should send a weekly or fortnightly status report to the project manager detailing their progress during the reporting period. This information is used by the project manager to update each assigned activity in the work-plan.
4. On a monthly basis, usually after the financial systems close, the project manager should issue a formal monthly status report to all the stakeholders, including financial information about the project.

### Large Projects

In a large project, all the communication takes place in context of an overall communications strategy and plan. Status meetings and status reporting are required, just as for a medium size project. In addition, there are many other types of proactive communication that need to be considered. This creative and proactive communication is laid out in a communication plan, which is created as follows:

1. Project stakeholders should be determined.
2. For each stakeholder, how to fulfil communication needs should be brainstormed. What information stakeholders need to know, how often they need an update, and what would be the best manner to deliver the information should be determined. A quarterly newsletter should go out to the entire client organization for informational and marketing purposes.
3. The communication options that were established above should be prioritized. The communication options that provide high value and require low effort from the project team should be implemented.

## Branding a Project/Marketing Communication in a Project

Usually, project communication does not have a marketing angle to it. However, with increasing social awareness and growing media sensitivity, organizations are not taking any chances and are attempting to educate society and other parties not directly involved in the project through marketing communication. For example, the Delhi Metro project being carried out in the National Capital Region (NCR) puts in a good amount of effort focused on building market reputation as a world-class commutation service. Investments in these kinds of campaigns do not bring any monetary benefits, but bring in fringe benefits, like greater acceptance and a good corporate citizen image, which pays in the end. Most projects have no requirements for this type of communication and it is more appropriate in some than others.

Branding is a more sophisticated form of marketing communication. The purpose of branding a project is to establish an identity that conjures up a positive image and goodwill. This is exactly what

> The purpose of branding a project is to establish an identity that conjures up a positive image and goodwill.

the marketing people try to do when they brand a product. Your purpose is to associate a positive image and emotion when a person hears of your project. This is not something most projects need to be concerned about. However, ask yourself the following questions regarding the implications that your project will have on the organization:

1. Does it affect a large number of people or maybe the entire company?
2. Will it require a culture change or a change in the way people do their job?
3. Will the project make people nervous? For instance, will it result in efficiencies so that less people are required to do the same function?

These are the types of projects that would require branding. The people being affected would wonder if they should think of the company as responding to competitive challenges or if the project could cost them their jobs. Most large projects have an image associated with them. Branding helps you to proactively build the image you want to portray rather than have one thrust upon you. Of course, branding takes time, so you also need to have a project with a long time span.

There are certain activities that a project team can perform to help with the branding campaign. If possible, they should consider meeting with the marketing department to gather more ideas and get help on how to establish a brand and how to successfully implement it. Examples of activities include the following:

**Establish a positive project name**   For instance, a project called MarketForce probably gives more of a positive image than one called Marketing Process Improvement Initiative. A similar idea is a catchy acronym. You can build a positive image with an easy to remember acronym as well.

**Establish an image/logo**   The project should have an image or logo associated with it. The image must be positive and it should be included on all written communication coming from the team.

**Buy trinkets**   Put your project name or logo on mugs, t-shirts, pencils, frisbees, etc. Reward people with a token that contains the project logo when they do something good.

**Hold face-to-face meetings**   Spend time seeing as many people as possible in person-to-person meetings or small group meetings, especially at the beginning of the project. No one wants to get all the information about an important project through email. It lowers the project's importance.

Other ideas include lunch and learns, a series of simple words to associate with the project logo, gathering testimonials of satisfied customers, ongoing personal communications, etc. Find ways to keep your project and your positive message in front of people.

All this is contingent on including a steady stream of informational content such as building awareness through mass contact programmes, posting information on a website, etc. A steady stream of information, combined with positive project branding should help the project be successful and overcome any negative perceptions about the project and its purpose.

> Human resource communication refers to the techniques and processes used by organizations across the world to communicate with their employees.

## HUMAN RESOURCE COMMUNICATION

Human resource (HR) communication refers to the techniques and processes used by organizations across the world to communicate with their employees about issues related to employee appointments, promotions, compensation packages, training, personalized counselling, retirement benefits, and other employee benefit programmes run by the organizations.

Human resource communication is more than the art and technique of effectively imparting thoughts, information, and ideas. It has become the single most important element in helping organizations share their vision and galvanize their employees to action in moving the organization forward. This is because clear, concise, and consistent communications educate employees, enabling them to appreciate the value of their organizations' programmes. It also keeps employees focused, informed, productive, and committed. Businesses had come to realize the importance of human resource a long time back, and with growing employee turnover rates, they have come to realize that it is not only the various kinds of employee benefits which are important, but that it is equally important to educate employees about these benefits.

Organizations are spending lots of money on recruitment and employee training and cannot afford to lose a manager who is strategically placed in the organizational structure. Losing a key manager to a competitor is a very painful experience for corporations because it puts them on a back-foot by severely affecting the company's fortunes. Therefore, HR managers are willing to do anything to prevent such an incidence from recurring.

Human resource communication has become a very important strategic input to all business plans since more and more companies are going all out to communicate with their employees about the various HR initiatives being taken up by the company including training, compensation schemes, retirement benefits, organizational changes, etc.

### Kaizen—Nissan Motors UK

In the fiercely competitive automobile market, it is vital to train people to work in a hi-tech industry with sophisticated quality systems. Nissan Motors UK's training department conducts a training needs analysis to assess individual employee needs and to organize training programmes. The department concentrates on the following five main areas:

1. Technical development—teaching skills related to robotics and electrics, plus the required knowledge such as wiring rules and regulations
2. People development—identifying employee needs and ambitions; providing courses to help personal development such as in team building and communication skills
3. Understanding processes—workshops covering safety, production operations, etc.
4. Computer skills and graduate training—from basic to highly technical
5. Trainee development—courses for graduate trainees ranging from accountancy to team building

Nissan is famously associated with *Kaizen* or continuous quality improvement. Nissan believes in not restricting the company to the existing ways of doing things, but in continuously seeking improvements in all its actions. *Kaizen* can involve the smallest change in everyday working practice as well as a major change in production technology. Typically, these improvements are initiated by teams of employees sitting down together and sharing ideas for improvements. Small steady changes are maintained to make sure that they actually work. *Kaizen* improvements save money, time, materials, and labour effort as well as improving quality, safety, job satisfaction, and productivity. *Kaizen* permeates the Nissan Motors UK suggestion scheme, which offers not financial or individual rewards but items that benefit the whole team such as a microwave for the staff kitchen or pool table for the canteen.

Companies that are seeing a high rate of employee turnover and that are conducting exit interviews have come to this realization that many of the employees leaving the organization were actually not aware of the various employee benefits schemes available to them. There are lots of benefits and schemes for employees provided by the employers besides regular salary and common allowances, such as, housing allowance, of which employees are not even aware. Following are some of the benefits:

- Compensation programmes—executive compensations, salary administrations, incentive pay programmes, deferred compensations, and performance management programmes
- Stock related long-term incentive programmes and other fringe benefits, including health insurance
- Civil enforcement and remedies and laws effecting employee benefits plans
- Organizational change communications
- Reductions in workforce and early retirement windows, including messaging to those who remain in the workforce
- Expectation and crisis management
- Transition communications
- New organization communications strategy development
- Executive coaching and consulting
- Leadership performance and rewards
- Employee effectiveness

 You can refer to the Online Resource Centre for various formats used in human resource communication.

### Human Resource Communication in Indian Industries

Indian companies have been slow to respond to the global developments in the field of HR communication. Part of the reason could be that until recently Indian companies, barring a few, did not attach

---

**Incubating Innovation**

Every employee possesses the power to innovate. The challenge, believes Bernand Martyris, Senior Vice-President (HR), Indian Hotels Co. Ltd, is to create an encouraging environment that allows and recognizes this. This is one of the key elements of the company's Stars or Special Thanks and Recognition Systems programme. This globally acclaimed model has triggered soaring employee satisfaction scores, besides numerous employee suggestions and innovations, many of which are the best practices today. 'Whether it's an indigenously manufactured bathroom mat or a new chemical for the laundry, every idea is big and shared across the hotel chain,' says Mr Martyris. 'It has shattered the myth that only people at the top are creatively inclined.

> ### Ultimatix—Managing the Future
>
> With offices in various geographical locations, IT leader Tata Consultancy Services needed to deploy employees in a seamless and integrated manner. The innovative solution it engineered to meet these challenges was called Ultimatix. Designed in-house, it digitized the whole organization in real time through the Web. Every single employee was connected through this platform across the globe. Ultimatix was also very successful in cutting through layers of decision-making within Tata Consultancy Services. Ultimatix became the company's single employee-service window. It ensured that employees got their services without much difficulty. They could log in with their claims, loans, or even leave applications for processing. Approvals would be given online. This system or virtual human resources proved a godsend to a population that was highly mobile. Besides its HR policies, the organization has taken its appraisals and employee satisfaction surveys online. It does not end here. The survey findings, along with implemented suggestions, are also posted online. Rising employee satisfaction scores endorse the popularity of these initiatives.

much significance to human resources. The employee turnover was high and till such time that the company was able to push its top line and maintain a reasonable bottom line, the top management hardly bothered about high attrition rates.

In the 1990s, with the entry of multinational corporations (MNCs), came the professional approach to human resources for the first time. Increasingly, Indian companies are now trying to go all out to woo their employees in more than one way and the employees are also more aware of their basic rights and privileges. However, HR communication in India is still in a very nascent stage and a lot of work is still to be done. Most of the efforts undertaken by companies in this area pertain to retirement benefits, medical benefits, training, etc.

Training is one area wherein many Indian companies are investing money. This requires a very thorough communication from the top management to the personnel who are supposed to benefit from these training programmes. The HR department sees to it that the message is clearly passed on and that there are no doubts and inhibitions about a training programme. For example, when engineers from Hindustan Zinc Ltd, Udaipur, came for a month long refresher course to BITS, Pilani, Mr Pradeep Bhattacharya, General Manager—HR, spent close to a day briefing the participants on the benefits of the programme and how this training would help them in moving up the hierarchy faster. He and his team have been actually doing this for almost a month, both formally and informally. The participants were from a middle-aged group and the motivation levels had to be perked up before they went for the actual course.

There are plenty of examples like this in professional Indian companies. However, there are still many grey areas wherein the companies have to work hard and become more transparent. One of the grey areas commonly sighted by employees is the compensation package statement. Upon joining an organization, many new employees fail to interpret the statement of compensation offered along with the appointment letter. Some companies make the figures so ambiguous and misleading that an employee cannot figure out his/her actual salary in hand. For example, many companies include the subsidized lunch, breakfast, tea, etc. offered to the employees during the office hours (at the original cost) as a part of total salary. This helps in inflating the gross salary, but it does not affect the take-home salary, which matters most. Similarly, knowledge-based

> Training programmes require very thorough communication from the top management to the employees.

companies offer employee stock options (ESOPs) without mentioning the clause of lock-in and the conversion ratio embedded in the options. At the end of the day, what is required is effort from the industry bosses to come clean on their salary offers and make them transparent and easy to comprehend.

## Business Process Outsourcing in India—Victim of Poor HR Communication

The information technology (IT) enabled services business process outsourcing (BPO) industry is being looked upon as the next big employment generator. It is, however, no easy task for an HR manager in this sector to bridge the ever-increasing demand and supply gap of professionals. Unlike the software industry counterpart, the BPO HR manager is not only required to fulfil this responsibility, but also to find the right kind of people who can keep pace with the unique work patterns in this industry.

Adding to this is the issue of maintaining consistency in performance and keeping the motivation levels high, despite the monotonous work. The toughest concern for an HR manager is the ever the

### Human Resources—Brand Building for Success

The early years of this century saw an increasing number of companies focusing on creating their own unique 'HR brands'. Traditionally viewed as a powerful marketing tool to manage customer perception, 'branding' is being increasingly used by a HR department as a tool to recruit new people and establish its position in the organization. This is a reflection of the changing role of HR department—from recruiting entities to business partners, internal consultants, and operational, as well as administrative experts. The past few years have seen corporate leaders dramatically change their perception of human resources. From being looked at as a support functionary, human resources today is viewed as a key player in promoting corporate success and customer satisfaction. The role of an HR manager is now that of public relations expert with strong problem-solving skills. While HR branding has been an established phenomenon in the West, it is still to catch up with Indian organizations. However, there are a few companies like Tata Consultancy Services (TCS), Infosys, IBM, Cadence, HP, Sun Microsystems, Wipro, Daksh, Satyam, Tata Telecom, Texas Instruments, Polaris Software, and Birlasoft that have successfully established their HR brands both in India and abroad. Among the Indian companies, Wipro and Infosys are the leaders in branding. In the case of MNCs, Microsoft, IBM, Intel, Oracle, HP, and Accenture are the leaders. TCS, while it had successfully implemented its HR policies, was lacking in effective communication with its employees across the globe. 'We decided to bring about a significant change in our communication processes, the way things were communicated. In addition, we also decided to align the HR and corporate communication relation to make an impact on our internal customers', says Atul Takle, Vice-President of corporate communications at TCS.

Understanding the importance of communication, the human resource department adopted different public relations related activities to reach out to its employees. Things like changing the tone of the communication, encouraging Friday dressing, evolving a separate human resource logo or sending employees calendars listing monthly human resource activities has helped TCS score high on the employee satisfaction surveys. Talking about future success stories, Martin Apple, Vice-President for human resources at IBM India Ltd, says, AQ 'Organizations which invest in hiring the best and developing their skills, can provide a high performance culture that will be the frontrunner. HR plays an important role in partnering, supporting and sometimes leading the business in these areas. It won't be easy, but ongoing communication, and actually meeting the organization's real and expressed needs, will help HR earn respect.'

## Indian Top 10

'It is not the cash that fuels the journey to the future, but the emotional and intellectual energy of every employee,' commented Gary Hamel and C. K. Prahalad in *Competing for the Future Business Today* (BT).

Noble & Hewitt conducted a 'best employer' study among Indian companies with the objective of finding out which of them had really charged the 'emotional and intellectual energy' of their managerial employees and how they had done it. The honours list of 10 companies was selected out of 155 companies that had responded to the request for data. It may be noted that the performance of these companies was significantly better than that of other companies in the same industry. The common characteristics that stood out among the winners were high employee satisfaction levels, HR practices, and the CEOs' commitment to people.

**The honours list**

1. Infosys
2. Procter & Gamble
3. Hewlett-Packard
4. ICICI Bank
5. Hughes
6. LG
7. Hindustan Unilever Ltd
8. Compaq
9. Asian Paints
10. BPCL

The rankings show that it does not matter what industry you are in as long as you care for people and realize that they are your most critical resources. It is worth noting that one winning characteristic alone will not create a great workplace; what is required is a combination of practices and their alignment with business processes. Some highlights of these characteristics are as follows:

**Pride in the company** Employees of these companies take tremendous pride in their company's operations and achievements, and have faith in its future prospects. Few have negative things to say.

**Faith in leadership** Employees admire their leaders for making them feel 'safe and well-led'. Leadership in these companies tends to have a key impact on the corporate culture. The leaders of these companies respond faster to employee needs. In some cases, they actually know most people by name.

**Living their values** The culture at these companies is developed because of well thought out processes and through the selection of specific policies and procedures. 'Best employers' also inculcate and reinforce desired behaviour through training and recognition.

**Open house** The prevailing spirit in these companies is one of openness. Employees are free to voice opinions and feel valued. Everybody is accessible regardless of seniority, level, function, or 'aura'.

**Holistic approach to life and thoughtful perks** Money is not everything. 'Best employers' accept that their employees have a life outside of the office. They also value long-term relationships with their workers. Hence they provide for considerable benefits over and above pay. For instance, employees could require child support and day care facilities during working hours. Many of these companies facilitate holiday travel and accommodation. Employees like to have fun with their families, so 'best employers' include the family while celebrating organizational events.

---

high attrition rate. In India, the average attrition rate in the BPO sector is approximately 30–35 per cent. If a person leaves after the training, it costs the company about ₹60,000. For a 300-seater call centre facing the normal 30 per cent attrition, this translates into ₹60,00,000 per annum. It is true that this is far less than the prevalent attrition rate in the US market (around 70 per cent), but the challenge continues to be greater considering the recent growth of the industry (read the less time span) in the country.

One reason that partially explains this scenario is the poor HR communication undertaken by these companies, both at the time of inducting new employees and also subsequently. Keeping low attrition levels is a major challenge if the salary growth plan for each employee is not well defined. All this only encourages poaching by other companies who can offer a higher salary. The

**Image 17.3** A call centre

much-hyped 'work for fun' tag normally associated with the industry has in fact backfired, as many individuals (mostly fresh graduates) take it as pastime. Once they join the sector and understand its requirements, they are taken aback by the long working hours and, later, the monotony of the job starts setting in (Image 17.3).

The reason for the high attrition rate is that many individuals are not able to take the pressures of work. The demands of the job and the odd timings are not adequately conveyed. Besides the induction and project training, not much investment has been done to evolve a 'continuous training programme' for the agents.

> Poor HR communication can lead to employee attrition.

Motivational training has to evolve in this industry. Though the industry has taken many initiatives in conducting training for new entrants and agents, it is the development of the skills of the middle management (comprising of the team leaders and supervisors) that needs to be taken care of. Due to the vertical movement in the industry, most individuals get promoted a rank or two above their current position. However, since they do not have any management background, things start becoming difficult for them (considering that mostly it is fresh graduates who join this industry). All this not only affects the scale, service, and quality of the company but also the personality of the individual who feels at a loss. According to most industry experts, with technologies, techniques, processes, and methodologies being redefined and reinvented by the day, the contact centre manager needs to constantly handle changes in management philosophy and operational practice to successfully and consistently deliver customer goals.

In spite of so many initiatives, the major concern of the industry experts is that nobody has really taken it as a 'career choice' but rather as a 'pastime' or 'time-gap employment'. If a mature industry has to evolve, the picture needs to be changed wherein it becomes 'the' choice industry, like its software counterpart.

## FINANCIAL COMMUNICATION

Financial communication is all about conveying all financially sensitive information and data of the previous year including the company's overall performance, major capital expenditures undertaken, profitability performance, stock market performance, etc. to financial stakeholders, such as shareholders, financial institutions, and financial analysts.

> Financial communication is aimed at conveying financially sensitive information and data of the previous year.

The majority of economic activity in Western democracies is conducted through private sector corporations, with the result that the ultimate ownership of capital is derived from the executives who decide how capital is to be deployed. Corporate financial communication forms part of the governance structure whereby corporate executives are made accountable for their decisions, and is, therefore, an important area of academic research.

### The Cool Thing is OK—But the Solid Stuff is Critical

Good employers offer birthday cards and free coffee at the workplace only as additions to more fundamental benefits such as advancement opportunities, development programmes, and financial security. Mere feel-good policies, such as casual-dress every day, do not subsitute for poor leadership and lack of communication.

**Engaging work opportunities and rewards** Good employers provide significant responsibility early on. They believe in giving their people the freedom to take decisions. They treat mistakes as opportunities to learn. They encourage individuality and proactive thought. They also encourage and reward employees. A performance-based pay is, more often than not, the norm.

**Equality** Good employers recognize that every employee—regardless of her or his level—needs housing and medical benefits. Their workers are provided equal access to these requirements or access as per need that is not based on the employees' position in the company. Gender equality is consciously practised, as is equal opportunity for all.

**Work environment** They boast of great work environments with facilities for training, conference rooms, gyms, green areas, ATMs, and travel desks readily provided to all. Harassment and discrimination are taken seriously—some have articulated policies to deal with these issues.

**Share and learn** These companies are confident—but not complacent. They are always looking to learn from others. They often work with academic institutions or consulting firms to keep abreast of knowledge and new practices.

**HR policies** Employees drive the HR policies at these companies. Senior management and HR departments are the facilitators. Employee needs dictate policies and practices.

**The good citizen** There companies encourage employees to participate in community activities. And environmental conservation is something that all of them are concerned about.

**When the 'fit' is not right** Sanchita Singh, Senior Manager—HR, Techbooks, India, points out how things can go wrong if the HR department of an organization does not do its job thoroughly. The example she cites is of a manufacturing organization, where the average employee age was above 35 years and employees were rigid and stagnant in their style of working. The management hired an achiever from the software industry (which was at its boom then) to introduce a new style in keeping with the times. He was known to have introduced drastic changes in the software companies he had worked with. He was very aggressive in his working style and had also worked in the manufacturing industry earlier. The organization did not check the 'cultural fit' of the individual, that is, whether he would fit in with the unique characteristics of the company. He took charge as the head of operations and started introducing major changes. It led to a lot of opposition, which ultimately affected production, and, finally, he was asked to leave.

Harish Govind, General Manager—HR, Blue Star Infotech, gives another example of an organization where, after the appointment of a senior person in the commercial function to deal with internal and external customers, complaints started coming in from existing customers about the products. This was a new phenomenon as earlier there had been no complaints. It was later that they realized that the functionary was not behaving properly with the customers as per his position, and was not sympathetic to their problems; therefore, the consumers became upset and decided to protest by lodging product complaints. The company tried to salvage the situation by having counselling sessions with the individual, but it did not help and he ultimately left the organization. Had a temperament check taken place either, through a structured process or a reference check, the company could have saved a bit of its money, time, and reputation.

Today's business environment is characterized by rapid change. The intense competition for media and investor attention makes it difficult to reach out with important messages. When a company comes under scrutiny due to rumours of impending issues the intense focus from the markets and the media may cause problems. The objective of financial communication is to protect and enhance shareholder value.

The tactics found within investor relations (IR) are used to build close relationships with investors, analysts, and the financial media. Most investor relations activities are linked to the financial calendar and can be planned beforehand. However, acute situations may arise such as initial public offerings, takeovers, mergers, and new share issues.

CEOs, CFOs, vice-presidents, directors of investor relations, and other management team members are called upon every day to report their company's current financial position and prospects for the future. How shareholders and analysts receive this information can have a serious impact—negative or positive—on the company's stock market performance and bottom line. Indeed, a company's very stability can hang in the balance with financial reporting. Individuals charged with disseminating financial information must possess sharp communication skills or else the slightest slip can cause a drop of several points on the stock market.

## Constituents of Financial Communication

As more and more stress is laid on full disclosure of performance by corporations across the globe, it has become a highly sensitive and eagerly awaited piece of information.

 See the Online Resource Centre for an example of financial communication.

Organizations are trying their best to bring out as much information as possible, to send a clear and distinct message to the investing community at large. Transparent financial communication has come to be recognized as a key element for professional organizations in the West. Barring a few cases like IPOs, etc., financial communication is more or less structured, both in terms of timing as well as the content. Financial communication provides information on the following topics:

- Company at a glance
- Chairman's message
- Outlook
- Key figures
- Share price information
- Balance sheets, income statements, and other price-sensitive financial data
- Investor relation releases
- Finance calendar
- Tradings worldwide
- Stockholder structure
- Mergers and initial public offerings
- IPO road shows
- Corporate governance

**Company at a glance** This talks about the board of directors (including the chairman)—their tenure, their compensation, and other dealings. It also details a company's memorandum and article of corporation, the present and proposed line of business, major brands and products, worldwide locations, major image campaigns, major innovations, social responsibilities and obligations, and environmental sensitivity.

**Chairman's message** It is through this that the chairman addresses the shareholders directly and gives a brief snapshot of the company's performance in the last financial year including the sales, profits, and other details. He/she also talks about other major achievements of the company such as any tie ups, strategic alliances, mergers, etc. and also proposes a dividend which then has to be endorsed by the shareholders.

**Outlook**  This report contains forward-looking statements that reflect the management's current views with respect to future events. Such statements are subject to risk and uncertainties including economic downturn, change is currency exchange rates and interest rates, introduction of competing products, increased sales incentives, etc. If any of these risks or uncertainties occur or if the assumptions underlying these statements prove incorrect, then actual results may be materially different from those expressed or implied by such statements. The company does not normally assume any obligation to update these statements, which speaks only as of the date on which it is made.

---

### A Sample Chairman's Message

**Ladies and Gentlemen, My Shareholders**

In 2001, Gorbet Group's profits improved for the fifth successive year. The market of contrast media (X-ray and MRI) for medical imaging in which Gorbet specializes continues to be driven by scientific advances supported by an emerging installed base of imaging equipment. Indispensable for the analysis and therapeutic monitoring of major pathologies (notably cardiovascular illnesses and cancer), contrast products are substantial contributors to public well-being and measures to limit health costs. These encouraging factors assure this market's long-term growth projections on a worldwide basis. The Group's flagship x-ray and MRI products, **Rexetix**® and **Poqarem**®, representing more than 60% of total sales, grew respectively 5.7% and 15% at constant exchange rates. The group achieved further market share gains in Europe, adding 6.7% as compared to the prior year. Despite the rise in the value of Euro in relation to US dollar and Asian and South American currencies, Gorbet Group's sales remained stable in relation to 1999 at 300 million. At constant exchange rates, the Group's sales increased 3.7% in relation to 1999.

As in 1999, Gorbet Group's operating profit grew 20%, representing 10% of the sales for the last financial year compared with 8.3% in prior year, in answer to better margins and tight control over costs. Also, in this period, the Group's net income pitched 43.5% to 9.09 million, enhancing the net profit to 4% compared with a net income of 6.33 million and a net margin of 2.8% in 1999. At the same time, the Group produced a free cash flow of 13 million for the period under review, further decreasing net debt, at 31 December 2001, to 48.7 million indicating a gearing of 48% compared with 61.1 million and a gearing of 65% at 1999 year-end. These enhanced margins will provide the Group with means to continue to dedicate significant efforts to MRI R&D (magnetic resonance imaging and research and development) and pursue its work on **Soanm**® and **Vienm**®, at the end and beginning of phase III trials.

Additional growth accelerators being realized by the Group include strengthening of its operations in all key markets, product innovations, notably in MRI, continued profits in industrial and marketable efficiencies, and competitiveness. Accordingly, following the introduction of **Ailom**® in Paris and Zurich in 2001, in early 2002, the Group successfully launched **Pogarem**® in Berlin, Europe's largest market. For 2002, we forecast increase in sales driven by the performance of **Pogarem**® and **Rexetix**®, accompanied by further gains in margins and a stronger balance sheet. On this basis, the Board of directors will ask the General Meeting to approve a net dividend of 0.75 demonstrating a rise of 25%.

Jigyasa Bhatia
Gorbet Group

**Share price information**  This provides all the stock market data related to the company's stock, including price and volume date, short and long positions, daily close and open positions, market capitalization, historical highs and lows, and other technical analysis data. It also has some chart analysis done for the investor community.

**Balance sheet, income statement, and other price sensitive financial data**  This is the backbone of all financial communication, whereby the company puts in the total financial statements for the investor community including the income statement and the balance sheet in a standard format for easy understanding.

**Investor relation releases**  In some countries, like Germany, the law requires an issuer of a publicly-listed stock to release important news about the company, which is not in public knowledge, immediately, if—due to its effects on the financial situation or the general business development of the company—the news might have a substantial influence on the share price.

---

### A Sample Outlook Report of Daimler Chrysler

(Updated outlook as of 29 April 2012)

- We expect global economic prospects to improve during the year, and we believe the positive trend will gradually include the economies of the euro zone.
- As the year progresses, gradual improvements in economic conditions should also have a positive effect on the international demand for automobiles. For the US, Western Europe, and Japan, little growth in sales of passenger cars is expected. We see signs of continuing improvements in the North American truck market, and also expect slightly higher sales of trucks in Europe compared with last year.
- For the full year, the Mercedes Car Group expects that unit sales, revenues, and earnings will be similar to the high levels of the prior year. As the year moves forward, the decrease in unit sales in the first quarter should be compensated for by the model changeover for the SLK and the A-Class, the facelift of the C-Class and the launch of the smart for four and the CLS. (smart CLS-Class)
- The Chrysler Group expects its markets to remain highly competitive in the year 2012, with a continuation of high price incentives in the United States. Despite the expenditure for the launch of nine new products, Chrysler Group is expected to end the year with considerable positive earnings as a result of the efficiency improvements that it has achieved.
- The commercial vehicles division will profit in the year 2012 from the continuous improvement of its internal processes, economies of scale, and an attractive product range. For the full year, the division anticipates a further improvement in its operating profit.
- The services division should benefit from the stable underlying business trend and continued favourable refinancing conditions in 2012. We anticipate another good result for the full year, which might however be lower than in 2011 as a result of the Toll Collect charge.
- For the full year, EADS (European Aeronautic Defence and Space Company) assumes stable revenues and an increase in its profitability. EADS' contribution to the Group's operating profit should therefore be higher than last year. The effects on earnings of our investment in MMC (Mitshubishi Motors Corporation) could not yet be conclusively assessed when this report went to press (April 29). However, the impact will be significantly lower than if we participate in a capital increase for MMC.
- On the basis of our divisions' expectations and our decision as regards MMC, Daimler Chrysler expects to achieve an improvement in operating profit for the full year compared with 2011 results (excluding restructuring expenditures at the Chrysler Group and excluding the capital gain realized on the disposal of MTU Aero Engines).

> A financial calendar reflects a company's professional approach and open attitude towards financial disclosures.

This is intended to prevent that news, with relevance to the share price, being known only to 'insiders', who might use this knowledge to their advantage. These are called *investor relation releases*.

06 February 2012   DaimlerChrysler US Sales increase 1% in May 2012
06 February 2012   Chrysler Group May 2012 sales improve 5%

**Financial calendar**  The finance calendar is the whole year planner for the company, wherein the company tries to share some important future events, with regard to financial communication, with the shareholders, analysts, bankers, etc. It merely talks about dates for financial disclosures, like when will the full annual report be presented, when is the interim report likely to be presented, the annual press conference, and investors and analysts meets, etc.

The exercise is primarily undertaken to reflect a company's professional approach and open attitude towards the disclosure of financial data. It also helps the parties interested in the information to schedule their engagements accordingly, so that they do not miss any of these important dates of disclosure of financial information necessary for their subsequent analysis about the performance of the company.

**Tradings worldwide**  This gives us the information about where all the company's stocks are traded in different stock markets in the world and what composition it has in the major stock market indices. With the integration of global financial markets, it is a common sight today to see major companies getting listed in almost all major stock exchanges of the world.

Since most of the multinational companies are doing businesses in most of the countries where they are listed, they might have shareholders in those countries also. Therefore, most of these companies share information about where in the world are their shares listed and how much importance is being given to the company's stock as reflected in the weightage in the market index. Shareholders nowadays form a big global community and it is important for them to know how their company is being perceived in other corners of the world.

**Stockholder structure**  This provides the break up of the share holding patterns, both geographical region-wise and also investor groups-wise. It also gives details about major shareholders and their holdings and information on floating stocks. The data is normally presented in percentage terms. This is a very important piece of information for the shareholders as they come to know about the major shareholders and also holding patterns of other big players like financial institutions, mutual funds, investment banks, etc. It also gives an idea about the retail investors and their total stake in the company. The promoters holdings also give lot of information. For example, if the company is, by and large, dominated by the big players like financial institutions, etc. and (besides the promoter who hold a good percentage again) the retail investors hold a very small portion of the stocks, it gives a negative impression about the company's attitude as such companies are considered to be open to more manipulations and malpractices. The reverse holds true for a company where the percentage of retail investors is on the higher side.

**Mergers and initial public offerings**  Periodic pieces of information about the company often appear when mergers happen. A merger or an initial public offering (IPO) is a big change for a company and, therefore, has to be dealt with separately. The investor community views mergers, etc. with a cautious mindset and, therefore, is satisfied only when this issue is detailed out separately by the company in the financial communication. A merger normally brings with it a new company in the

### Merger Communication

In any merger or acquisition, the management must focus on communication as a priority for maintaining productivity and stakeholder confidence, both inside the company and out in the marketplace. This requires starting early on a merger-communication plan. In fact, when it seems imminent that the merger will go through, it is important that a company brings in internal or external resources on a confidential basis to plan key messages and how they will be delivered to all the different audiences.

The plan should take into consideration the following:

*Be quick about communicating* The company must ensure that all material pertaining to communication is completed in advance and distributed to everyone simultaneously. At the same time, the plan must be flexible enough to support last minute changes. Public companies have to follow their own release policies.

*Share the excitement* From the beginning, the company should ideally communicate the benefits of the merger to its employees, customers, and other key audiences. Share your thinking as openly as possible with as many specifics as possible. It pays to be honest. If the benefits plan is not strong, this should be plainly stated. But other areas where employees do stand to gain should be identified and highlighted.

*Take time to be visible* Although print and electronic media are effective in merger communications, face-to-face meetings, small group chats, or one-on-one discussions have greater impact.

### Merger without Tears

A global leader in telecommunications equipment systems and services had announced its intention to acquire another large player in the industry. Having acquired other firms in the past and having learnt from past mistakes, it needed help in coordinating communications to employees, customers, investors, analysts, and suppliers prior to closing the deal and during the integration period.

The telecom company hired Persona 3.0, a US-based brand consulting firm which helps companies build strong identities through strategic development, writing, and design. In tandem with another company, Fifth Floor Consulting, Persona 3.0 was able to help the two companies involved in the merger by

- developing an integration communications team made up of key people from both companies,
- establishing guidelines and principles for all communications during the deal
- creating a process for communicating to all audiences prior to deal close and throughout the integration process,
- creating an 'audience message matrix' to make sure communications were coordinated to all employees in over 20 offices around the world,
- identifying content for weekly communication newsletters, and
- surveying all key audiences to gauge their perception of the impending deal and identify communication needs.

As a result of these measures, Persona 3.0 was able to lead the client integration managers successfully to implement a communication programme that simplified a complex communication challenge, leading to an easier integration.

fold, a new capital structure, and maybe a new business philosophy all together. Therefore, mergers are a very strategic landmarks in the life of an organization and professional companies are expected to come out with all information related to a merger including the motives behind the merger, the basis of the merger, the calculation of merger ratio, projected effects on profitability, EPS, share price, etc.

Similarly, when a company is comes out with an initial public offering, many changes take place and existing shareholders expect complete transparency in the pre-IPO and post-IPO scenarios. An IPO does not only bring in fresh capital, it also has an effect on the earnings per share, market prices, current shareholders stakes, capital structures, etc. As far as possible, the current shareholders must be informed about the reasons behind opting for an IPO—the pricing, the timing, and the size. The company should also share information on possible financial effects after the IPO is complete.

## CORPORATE GOVERNANCE

Corporate governance issues are, quite rightly, receiving ever more attention and are being increasingly discussed by the general public. It has become a norm to report all the information about a company, which could be price sensitive or otherwise. The annual consolidated financial statements as well as the interim consolidated financial statements (quarterly financial statements) of the company and subsidiaries are prepared in accordance with the generally accepted accounting principles in the country concerned. A company should try and make all efforts to ensure that shareholders exercise their rights at the general meeting and participate in voting. The rights and obligations of the board of directors of the company should be clearly spelt out.

Moreover, companies are now supposed to report even non-profitable activities, in which they are engaged, which otherwise bring credibility to the company's corporate image. Activities like environmental protection, child care, education, etc. are being actively taken up by these 'corporate citizens' and it will be good for the company if they can share all this information with the shareholders, etc. Corporate governance is a buzz word in the industry and more and more organizations are trying to outsmart each other by bringing out as much information for disclosure as possible. For example, companies like Infosys have started putting their HR management under the assets category of the balance sheet to put in the value of their employees in monetary terms. Indirectly, they are trying to send out the message that even this information is being shared, and simultaneously boost the goodwill between the employees and the company.

## MANAGEMENT INFORMATION SYSTEMS—A COMMUNICATION TOOL

Organizations today are faced with a problem of 'plenty' when it comes to information; to manage this information so that it is communicated to the right person at the right time is a daunting task. It is here, where information technology comes handy and provides a robust communication network in the organization. More over, the transformation of business caused by the Internet-related technologies and e-business demonstrates that information systems and information technology are essential ingredients for business survival and success. An information system can be any organized combination of people, hardware, software, communications networks, and data resources that collect, transform, and disseminate information in an organization.

As a consumer, one has to deal regularly with the information systems that support business operations at the many retail stores where one shops. For example, most retail stores now use computer-based information systems to help them record customer purchase, keep track of inventory, pay employees, buy new merchandise, and evaluate sales trends. Store operations would grind to a halt without the support of such information systems. They also help managers make better decisions and gain competitive advantage, about issues such as decisions on what product to discontinue or add that are typically made after an analysis provided by computer-based information systems.

> Management information systems are being used extensively in all business functions for effective information management.

Management information systems (MIS) are being used extensively in all business functions including sales and marketing, finance, human resources, and operations. Marketing teams are using MIS to develop effective interfaces with the market, get superior feedback from customers, develop a product according to customer's tastes and likes, and improve demand forecasting. Finance departments use MIS to do accounting, develop accounting reports, and to prepare balance sheets and other income statements. Similarly, HR divisions use MIS to develop HR inventories and for effective manpower planning. Production departments are using MIS to streamline the whole process starting from the purchase of raw materials from suppliers to the point where the final product is shipped to the market.

The business application of an information system has changed and expanded significantly over the years. From the role of accounting and record keeping in 1960s to that of MIS and decision support system (DSS) in 1970s, it has come to a stage where it is now a knowledge system, thus becoming an integral component of business processes, products, and services that help a company gain a competitive advantage in the global marketplace.

## The E-business Enterprise

Businesses are becoming e-business enterprises. The Internet and Internet-like networks inside an enterprise (intranets), and between an enterprise and its trading partners (extranets) have become the primary information technology infrastructures that support the business operations of many companies. Enterprises rely on such technologies to revitalize internal business processes, implement electronic commerce systems among business customers and suppliers, and promote enterprise collaboration among business teams and workgroups. Figure 17.2 shows how an e-business enterprise depends on the Internet, intranets, extranets, and other information technologies to implement and manage e-business operations and collaboration.

The enterprise collaboration system involves the use of groupware tools to support communication, coordination, and collaboration among the members of networked teams and workgroups. It depends largely on the intranets, extranets, and other networks to support such systems. For example, employees and external consultants may form a virtual team that uses corporate intranet and an extranet for electronic mail, video conferencing, electronic discussion groups, and web pages of work-in-progress information to collaborate on business projects.

## Communication between Functional Areas

Having discussed communications in specific functional areas, we now take a look at some of the more important cross-functional communications commonly taking place in organizations. No department can function in a vacuum and there has to be an efficient communication system within departments to help in the effective growth of the company. The more the functional departments communicate, the more they trust each other and the more the 'wall' between the departments gets dented. Modern-day professional organizations practise a high degree of transparency within business units and expect all the functional departments to share every piece of information that is vital and affects them as a whole.

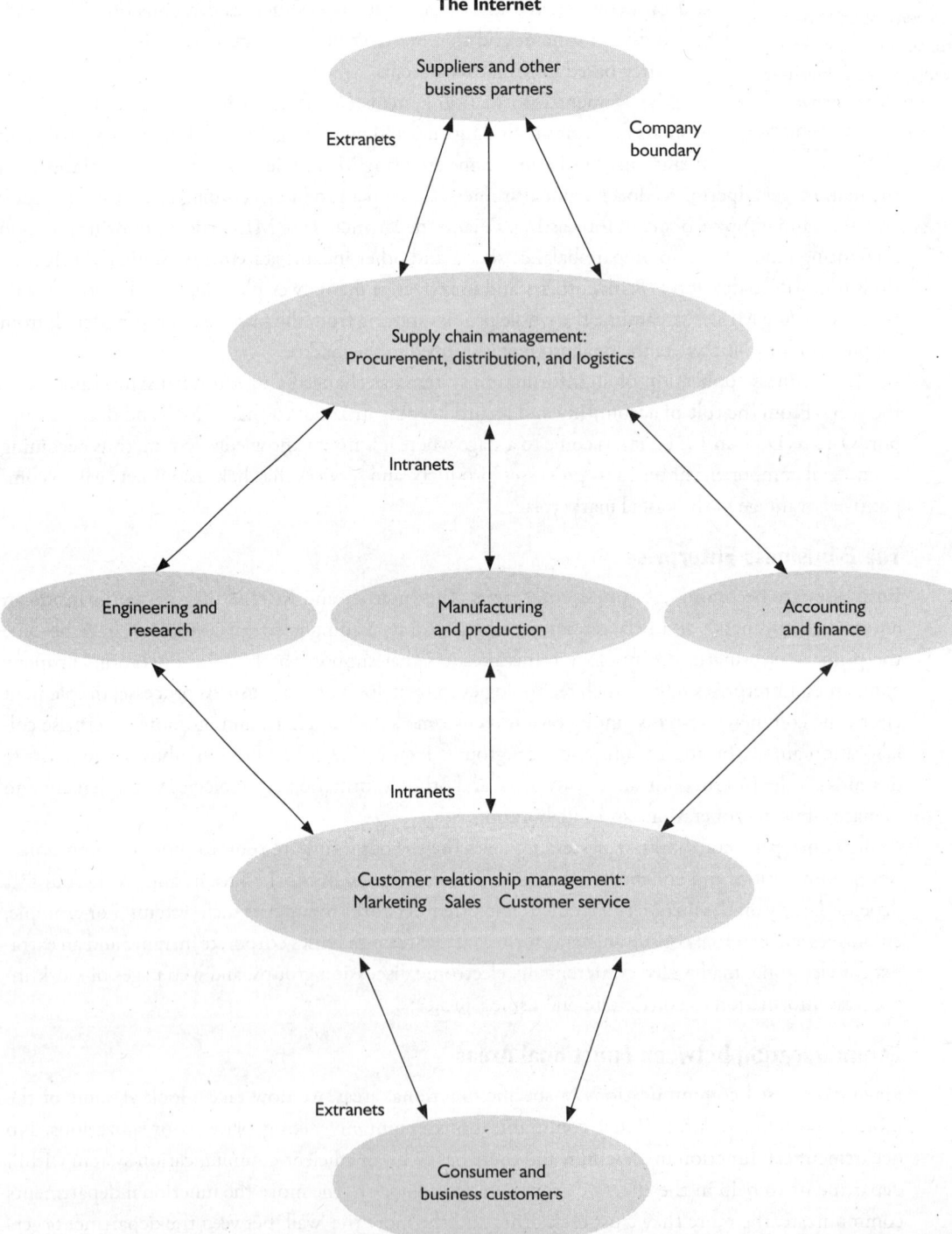

**Fig. 17.2** E-businesses implementing and managing e-business operation and collaboration

> **Communications Meet Operations**
>
> Angela Sinickas, President of Sinickas Corporations, Inc., a communication consultancy specializing in helping corporations achieve business goals, exhorts her colleagues to dig deeper into their organizations. Many companies, she says, spend a great deal of money researching customer satisfaction through focus groups and surveys. Yet, they rarely share this information with the employees who could improve customer perceptions through their own actions—if they knew what customers did and did not like about the way they do business. The reason given for this withholding of information is that by informing employees of the problems causing customer dissatisfaction, the competition may gain access to the information and use it against them. In the meantime, employees complacently keep doing the same things the same way—and keep losing more customers to the competition.

## Marketing and Production

By far, the most debated issues in a corporate set-up normally pertain to the objectives clash between the marketing and production departments. The marketing team usually likes to see the company offering more and more models, quickly with shorter lifespan. The production department is more concerned about the quality and performance of the product rather than offering more variants/models. This is where an effective communication system is highly desirable. Both the functional units must trust each other, share facts, and try to respect each other's constraints and think strategically so that the overall organizational goals are not undermined.

### Product Development Process

Product development process is the most competitive area in organizations nowadays, because of the short life of products due to fast changing customer tastes and habits. Designing new products and getting them to market quickly is the challenge facing manufacturers in industries as diverse as computer chips and potato chips. Customers of computer chip manufacturers need ever more powerful super computers for their evolving product lines. Food producers need to provide their grocery store customers new taste sensations to sustain or enlarge their retail market share. Although the potential opportunities to be realized in developing new products are exciting, making them happen is a challenge. New product development entails a complex set of activities that cuts across most functions in a business. Needless to say, an efficient and effective communication system within the organization is the minimum requisite for the product development process to be smooth and successful.

The product development process starts from the market where customers give their choice of preferences, tastes, likes, and dislikes. Now, it is important for the marketing team to keep their eyes and ears open when communicating with customers. A customer, being aware of his/her desires, will spell out his/her needs, price, and quality expectations very clearly. The company's marketing team must have a sensor mechanism in place to effectively read that message and communicate it back to the company. If this is done properly, more than half of the battle is already won. If this is done badly, no matter how well you design your product and place it in the market with best promotion schemes, it is bound to fail, simply because the homework was not done properly. Then, once the company's top brass agrees to the idea of developing such a product as desired by the sales team, extensive consultations take place between the finance,

> An efficient and effective communication system within the organization is an important aspect of the product development process.

production, and marketing departments. The finance department looks into the cost aspects of the product, the investments to be made, and the final pricing. The production department is concerned about the quality standards, production process, time required, etc. All these three parties have genuine concerns and complete transparency in communication is required at this stage so that the whole company stands behind the product and it (the product) is put forward in the market after thorough cost and other analyses (Fig. 17.3).

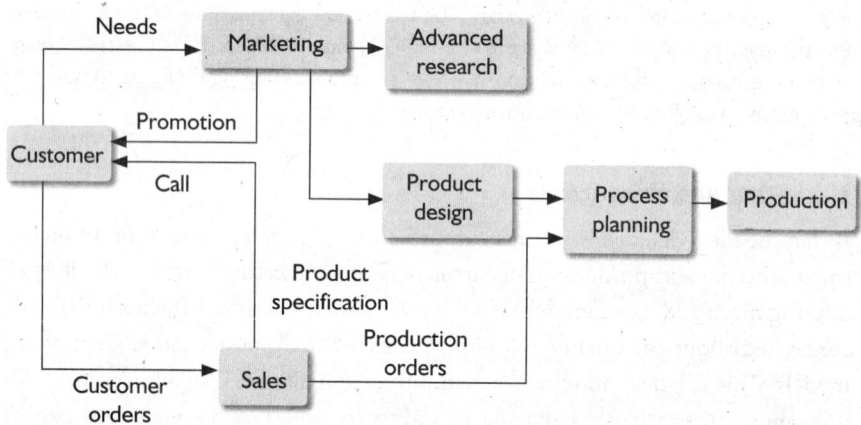

**Figure 17.3** Major business functions involved in the product development process

## Finance and Other Functional Areas

Finance is rightly considered the lifeblood of an organization. However great an idea might be, it remains to be seen whether that idea can be translated into a product or service that is economically viable. All product development activities discussed above have to necessarily come through the finance department, which looks into the cost, pricing, and future revenue expectations of that idea before giving it a green signal. It is, therefore, very important to communicate with the finance department on a continuous basis and involve it at each stage by constantly sharing all strategic information through a proper communication system.

Many managers make the serious mistake of bringing in the finance department at later stages of product development, which may result into a wonderful idea going down the drain. The finance aspect is an almost undetectable component of any process initiated in an organization and it is better to be as transparent with them as possible and regularly communicate with them on all issues. It has been commonly observed that marketing departments will always push for more funds to be released for marketing communication and will always love to have more and more variants, improved versions of products to be launched quickly in the market. It is here where their objectives may sometimes go in a different direction from that of the finance and production departments. It should be appreciated by a marketing division that there is a limit on the company's spending on advertising and sales promotion and, similarly, there is a limit on how many models of the product can be produced and launched. Both these divisions require continuous communication at all levels so that these kinds of differences can be smoothened out.

> ### Culture Fit
>
> Knowledgeable managers realize the critical importance of hiring the right candidate who can be a 'cultural fit' in their existing teams. While many organizations conduct 'cultural tests' (to find out the character, aptitude, and communication styles), there are others who hold negative interviews (pressure/no-win situations) to observe how candidates hold up under stress. The aim is to avoid the mistake of hiring someone who does not fit into the company's culture. Pramode Sadarjoshi, Director and Head of HR at Cognizant Technology Solutions, says, 'Organizational culture is akin to the DNA of a human organism, which is unique and specific. These are characteristics that have made the organization what it is. Each organization's culture has its own strengths and weaknesses. So, when an organization recruits people, it decidedly wants those who are talented and competitive notwithstanding and "fit" into its culture.' He adds that organizations do not want any outsider to come and disturb their cultural fabric—values and ethics, work style, leadership patterns, philosophy of running the business, and managing people. In fact, they are always looking for people who can enhance their culture. Cognizant, he asserts, is very conscious of this issue and consequently recruits 60 per cent of employees from campuses so that they can be groomed and nurtured into the company's culture.

### HR and Other Functional Areas

*Communication to the HR division should be as specific as possible.*

It is the HR department's function to bring in the right people in the organization as and when required and to give the right kind of training to the right person. It becomes imperative for all the other departments of the organization to have good communications with the HR department and pass on the information about their personnel requirement and the specific knowledge/skills required. The HR department then tries to match the desired skill levels through its recruitment and training process. Selecting a wrong person for a job means a huge loss to the company and it should be avoided by timely and specific communication between the HR department and other functional areas. For example, if the marketing department requires a marketing manager for its western division, it should specifically communicate the exact profile of the persons it is looking for so that the HR team recruits the right person.

Communication to the HR division should be as specific as possible; therefore, organizations are trying to bring in more accurate job specifications as the jobs are becoming increasingly specialized. Gone are the days when you could find a recruitment advertisement specifying only broad qualifications and background. Companies are coming out with job advertisements, which clearly spell out specialized qualification and work experience so that only persons with the exactly matching profile may apply. Recruitment is a costly business nowadays and effective HR communication can reduce the cost to a great extent, if only the HR department works in a more transparent manner and regularly communicates with other functional areas.

## SUMMARY

Communication within the functional areas of an organization is a very strategic issue and needs to be carefully looked into by the employer and the employee both. It is only when the functional areas communicate within themselves and with each other through a formal structured communication system, that there can be transparency in dealings. With transparency, an element of trust and goodwill is created within an organization.

Marketing communication forms the backbone of all sales efforts being done by the marketing staff and can effectively supplement the various sales promotions and advertising techniques being used by the organization.

Human resource communication provides detailed knowledge about the various policies of the organization with regard to employee compensation and other benefits including training programmes, etc. to employees, which otherwise may have gone unnoticed.

Project communication is important for organizations, like software companies, which treat every project/assignment as a profit centre. It becomes vital for such organizations to keep track of various projects for smooth resource allocation and to avoid unnecessary delays.

Financial communication is all about providing financial data pertaining to the company's performance to the investor community at large. Organizations must try to bring in a complete disclosure policy revealing all substantial and price sensitive information to the parties interested.

Operations communication is primarily more visible in the material requirement planning stage whereby the department sees to it that there is no shortage of any kind of material in any of the functional areas thus ensuring smooth product cycles.

Communication between the various functional areas within an organization is also very important and may require two or more departments, at a time, to come into the picture for a strategic decision like product development, recruitment, capital investment, etc. Effective communication across the functional areas then becomes the key to the success of any strategy.

## KEY TERMS

*Cross-functional communication* It refers to the situations where various functional areas are supposed to maintain to proper communication, not only within themselves but also with other functional areas, and work as a team, for example, product development.

*Financial communication* It is the structured communiqué sent out at defined time-periods, normally to investor communities informing them about the company's financial performance in the previous year.

*Human resource (HR) communication* It is the communication sent out by an employer to an employee telling him/her about the various HR policies including compensation, etc.

*Marketing communication* It is the judicious and efficient use of the product promotional tools so that a universal, clear, and effective promotional message is communicated amongst the target audience.

*Operations communication* It refers to the communication patterns and styles unique to a manufacturing division, normally related to material planning, production scheduling, and to the total supply chain.

*Project communication* It refers to properly communicating details on a project, including the status, to all the stakeholders and sponsors.

## Concept Review Questions

1. If an organization expects a clear and transparent communication network with its trading partners, it should first try and bring its own house in order. Discuss.
2. The more time you 'invest' in cross-functional communication, the lesser are the chances of failure. Discuss this statement in light of a proposed implementation of an ERP system in an organization.
3. Communication across functional areas will involve not only some cosmetic efforts but also a paradigm shift in the attitudes of the employees. Discuss.
4. For any supply chain to be successful and fully integrated, each and every member of the value chain has to show the willingness and effort to share and mutually benefit. Explain this in the context of some failure stories.

5. Financial figures and data can be easily manipulated and experience shows that this has been quite rampant in all corners of the world. Build a case for full disclosure and complete transparency of financial results by an organization.
6. MIS has become an integral part of organizational communication architecture and reduces a lot of personal prejudices and inhibitions. Discuss.
7. The marketing team of a company always prefers products with shorter product life cycles, whereas the production team prefers just the opposite. Why?
8. Human resources has become one of the most important assets of an organization and organizations are trying their best to retain their employees. Effective HR communication can help here. Discuss this statement in light of the huge employee turnover in software companies.

## Critical Thinking Questions

1. Think of two common organizational problems/situations that can arise because of lack of communication between the functional areas of marketing and finance in an organization. How can these be avoided?
2. Suppose you are working with an advertising agency, which is being approached by a very large business house that has never advertised in the past. Make a case for effective marketing communication.
3. As a vice president of finance, you want to practise a very high level of corporate governance by going for full and complete disclosure of financial information. You are at loggerheads with your CEO, who believes that not all information has to be passed on to the shareholders. Defend your opinion.

## Projects

1. Visit a business house, and try to meet some of the people in key positions in the HR department and study their communication styles and patterns with their counterparts in the other functional areas of the company.
2. Assume that you are the project manager of a company involved in civil construction. What kind of mechanisms would you use to be updated about the status of the project? Develop a cost effective feedback tool.
3. Identify a company, which you believe is spending heavily on advertising. Try to study their advertising strategies with respect to a particular television advertisement, in context of target audience identification, message delivery styles, choice of endorsers, etc.
4. Look out for recruitment advertisements appearing in newspapers. Identify an advertisement, which you think is very specific, and another, which is not. Discuss your choice. Why do you think the company opted for that particular kind of advertisement?

## REFERENCES

Arora, Shipra, 'The Challenge of Retaining New Hires'.
Austin, Mark and Jim Aitchison 2002, *The New Blueprint for Marketing Communications in the 21st Century*, J Wiley & Sons (Asia) Pte Ltd, Singapore, pp. 27–44.
Betts, Mike 1999, 'Brand Competence: A Value-led Framework that Integrates Marketing, HR and PR and Enables your Employees to Deliver your Brand to Customers more Effectively', *Strategic Communication Management*, Volume 3, Issue 4, pp. 28–34.
Clegg, Carrie, 2002, 'Documents as Prototypes: Designing Written Drafts for Communication across Cross-Functional Teams', *Society for Technical Communication*, Vol. 4, pp. 38–43.
Dovitsu, Wayne 1997, 'The Economics of Corporate Financial Communication', *ACCA Occasional Research Paper*, No. 19, United Kingdom, Glasgow, pp. 44–56.
Drucker, Peter F. 1977, *People and Performance*, Harper College Press, Palatine, Illinois, p. 90.

Hamel, Gary and C. K. Prahalad 1994, *Competing for the Future Business Today (BT) Noble & Hewitt*, Harvard Business School Press, Harvard, p. 22.

Jasrotia, Punita, 'Brand Building to Attract and Retain the Best Talent'.

Kotler Philip 2005, *Marketing Management*, Pearson, New York, pp. 518–20.

Markus, Will, 2001, 'A Typology of Enterpreneurial Communicators—Findings From an Empirical Study in E-Business', *The International Journal on Media Management*, Vol. 3, Issue 3-Autumn, pp. 17–27.

McNamara, Carter 2004, *Basics in Internal Organizational Communications*, Authenticity Consulting, LLC.

McNamara, Carter 2004, *Field Guide to Leadership and Supervision for Business*, Authenticity Consulting, LLC.

'NYSE Bell Tolls for Grasso'.

Online Resources 2001, *Tips and Techniques: The Communications Audit*, The Public Relations Society of America, 33 Maiden Lane, 11th Fl., New York, pp. 14–16.

Shultz, Don E., 2003, *The Next Generation: Five Steps For Delivering Value and Measuring Financial Returns*, McGraw-Hill, New York; p.101.

Singh, Sanchita, 'Why Organisations Need to Campaign for E-learning Among Employees'.

Sukowski Oliver, and Martin J. Eppler 2002, *Knowledge Management Case Studies. Project Experiences, Implementation Insights*, Net Academy Press, St. Gallen, Switzerland, pp. 24–32.

Tripathi, Smita, 'Selling a Chain Reaction'.

Ramswamy, Shobha, 'All in a Day's Work'.

Wreden, Nick 2003, *Fusion Branding: How to Forge Your Brand for the Future*, J Wiley & Sons, Canada, pp. 37–46.

http://www.authenticityconsulting.com/pubs/SP_gdes/SP_pubs.htm, last accessed on 24 October 2005.

http://www.authenticityconsulting.com/pubs/SP_gdes/SP_pubs.htm, last accessed on 24 October 2005.

http://www.expressitpeople.com/20040329/cover.shtml, last accessed on 24 October 2005.

http://www.expressitpeople.com/20031027/cover.shtml, last accessed on, 24 October 2005.

rediff.com India Ltd, last accessed on 05 July 2003.

www.expressitpeople.com/20030512/cover.shtml, last accessed on 24 October 2005.

www.forbes.com/2003/09/18/cx_da_0918topnews.html, last accessed on 24 October 2005.

www.tata.com, last accessed on 3 September 2003.

### The Pentagon

In the wake of continued accounting scandals, insider trading deals, CEOs at the trough, and other unpleasant business revelations, how do we begin to change the atmosphere of mistrust and dishonesty that permeates the US's perception of corporations? One answer may lie embedded in the US military's latest experiment with the media. During the Iraq conflict, the Pentagon embarked on a press programme that will no doubt go down in history as one of the greatest military public relations coups of all time—the embed programme. After a quarter century of mutual animosity between the press and the Pentagon, generated largely by the Vietnam War, it was a radical and unconventional idea. You can bet virtually every member of the Pentagon brass initially opposed this idea hands down, for the same reasons most corporate executives would. However, under the insistence and guidance of Pentagon spokesperson, Torie Clarke, and others, journalists were embraced by the US military and actually encouraged to do their jobs. 'Many in the media worked hard with us on the principles and guidelines by which the program was run', says Clarke. 'It was very much a collaborative effort with them, and we were all very transparent about intent, concerns, and problems in advance of the war starting'.

Virtually every member of the Pentagon brass now concedes it was the best idea ever devised for turning around press preconceptions and negative coverage. The old way of doing business with the press is no longer the best way. It is essential in our media-saturated culture to have a solid relationship with the press before you need it. Welcoming journalists into your corporation is the best way to make them sympathetic to your situation. The more journalists get to know you, your company and employees, the more they come to appreciate what your company is about and what you are trying to accomplish. This is not about friendship and camaraderie. It is about honest discourse and mutual understanding. The general consensus is that the embed programme produced exactly what the military had hoped for lots of positive, complimentary, and supportive stories as both sides got used to the idea of mutual access after so many years of suspicion and cynicism.

Mark Strassman, a CBS News correspondent just returned from the war, stated, 'It was a leap of faith. There was a lot of demystification to this process. Here you had two institutions who didn't like or trust each other and they had to learn to work and live together. My view of the US military was so much higher than before this programme. Odds are if I were immersed in a some corporate culture the same way, I would have the chance of being similarly impressed.'

Forging a closer relationship with the press is not without some risk. You will have to be prepared to weather the occasional unflattering report, as was the case with the military. But it is better to shine the light on yourself. Small mistakes are often overlooked or excused by reporters if they are allowed 'inside'. Those same mistakes are often exaggerated if reporters are kept out. The vast majority of journalists are not after you or your company. But when you avoid, ignore, ridicule, fear, or otherwise limit press access to your company and your business dealings, you are inviting the very scrutiny you are trying to avoid. American Airlines' their CEO Don Carty's choice to avoid bad publicity by keeping quiet on his company's questionable pension plan almost sent AA into bankruptcy, and it ultimately cost Carty his job. The bottom line is if you have nothing to hide, then do not hide it. Cultivate a strong and healthy relationship with the press. As Strassman points out, 'More mistakes in reporting are made through ignorance, than intent.' If you have something to hide, the story will inevitably get out. If you have a relationship with the press, you may not be able to control it, but you can shape it. Clarke agrees there are lessons for corporate US in the Pentagon's success. Her advice to CEOs: 'Make communications an integral part of your entire business plan.' For that to succeed, Clarke notes, 'Leadership needs to be involved from start to finish'. There will be much discussion and review of the Pentagon's embed programme in the months to come, but this is a certainty: it will change, for at least a generation, the context of editorial discussions about the US military. Every single editorial meeting will now include journalists who will defend the military instead of just those who criticize it. Is not that change of perception alone, worth embedding a reporter or two in your company?

### Questions

1. Discuss the underlying theme of the above situation/case and make your own assessment of US military's communication strategies based on the case.
2. Why do you think organizations, like the Pentagon that are normally very secretive in their style of working, are suddenly talking about transparency and trust?
3. What do you think Clarke means by the statement, 'Leadership needs to be involved from start to finish'.
4. Do you think that the Pentagon's strategy of being media friendly will work? Discuss.

## CASE STUDY 2

### Merrill Lynch

Merrill Lynch is one of the world's leading financial management and advisory companies, with offices in 36 countries and total client assets of approximately $1.3 trillion. Through Merrill Lynch's investment managers, the company is one of the world's largest money managers.

**The challenge** Merrill Lynch wanted to improve the effectiveness of in client communications and increase its efficiency in cross-selling various products and services to existing clients. However, it was experiencing strategic and operational issues with its client communications. When a prospect signed up for a new client relationship, such as a cash management account or individual retirement account, that individual would receive multiple pieces of mail within the first 60 days, which could pertain to product and service confirmations for the features the client had selected for their relationship. Thus, clients were often overwhelmed with communications, and, in some instances, received multiple pieces of mail from Merrill Lynch in a single day. Some of these mailings were handled directly by Merrill Lynch, while others were outsourced through numerous contractors, resulting in communications that failed to reinforce the

Merrill Lynch brand. Many of these mailings involved manual, pick-and-pack fulfillment, allowing for a margin of error. This was particularly troubling when compliance documents were involved.

As the result of a Six Sigma review, a methodology used by Merrill Lynch to evaluate and make business enhancements, Merrill Lynch determined that its client communications needed to be improved. It was agreed that a new, more effective method of communicating with their clients was needed to reinforce the post purchase experience. Armed with data that indicated that the first 90 days of the 'client experience' for new accounts were critical, Merrill Lynch sought experienced business partners that could work closely with them to design and develop a customized, automated, one-to-one client communication solution. Merrill Lynch was looking for a solution that would

- help it streamline, personalize, and customize its communications to individual clients,
- help it effectively cross-sell its products and services to its existing client base,
- allow it to more effectively manage its brand,
- improve the effectiveness of its client communications, resulting in operational efficiencies and quicker time to market,
- deliver more revenue, a higher degree of customer satisfaction and higher customer retention,
- reduce the frequency and length of calls to its help desk,
- eliminate spoilage and waste due to document obsolescence,
- increase document and kit integrity,
- allow it to track the results of the solution's implementation,
- meet its aggressive internal solution announcements and rollout dates, and
- enable it to launch a new beyond banking offer.

Merrill Lynch was looking for a high-value solutions provider that would empower its client communications through

- a consultative approach to develop an effective solution to its business problems,
- a full array of integrated services that would enable it to use one provider, and
- superior customer service, utilizing new technologies, while ensuring confidentiality and integrity.

**The solution** Merrill Lynch asked Addison, a marketing com-munications agency with a specialization in simplified communications, to partner with it in analysing and clarifying the data-capture and disclosure documents for the basic brokerage and retirement accounts. The review also covered multiple pieces of client correspondence related to the account-opening process. Addison explored the existing account-opening process with financial advisors, marketing and product managers, information systems, production staff, print-on-demand experts, and legal and compliance officers. The information gathered during discovery, coupled with Addison's unique approach to content analysis and disposition, helped drive the recommendations for a simplified account-opening process and output. In conjunction with Merrill Lynch's legal team, Addison rewrote all disclosures and programme descriptions in plain English, reducing word counts by about 50 per cent. It created the final designs for the kit and worked closely with IT personnel at Merrill Lynch as they programmed the new outputs. Merrill Lynch engaged Bowne Enterprise Solutions, a premier provider of digital printing and electronic delivery of client communications, to improve the effective-ness of its client communications. Specifically, it asked Bowne to

- evaluate the design approach selected by Merrill Lynch,
- develop an automated and personalized marketing communications solution utilizing print on-demand, intelligent variable binding, fulfillment, quality control procedures, and point-to-point database tracking and release, and
- implement this automated solution to produce, print, and distribute new account welcome kits on demand.

Bowne implemented a customized, data-driven, and print-on-demand solution. The manufacturing process utilizes leading-edge intelligent binding equipment that ensures the integrity of a secured document consisting of personalized pages and a matching personalized cover. 'We were extremely impressed with Bowne Enterprise Solutions' consultative approach and their ability to develop a solution', said Madeleine Yates, Director of Global Private Client Marketing, Merrill Lynch. 'The BES solutions management, development, printing services and client services organizations worked closely with our marketing, operations, and systems organizations, as well as our external communications design firm, to conduct a business process analysis of our data and operations. This led to the development of an integrated, end-to-end solution that consolidated multiple client communications documents into one perfect-bound book. The entire process is automated, dramatically reducing our error rates.'

What is more, the solution was delivered to Merrill Lynch within some very aggressive deadlines that had been set for the internal announcement and rollout. Timing was particularly important to the client because of commitments they had made to announce the programme via a closed-circuit video cast to their sales force of over 20,000 financial advisors and client associates in support of a major product launch.

The Bowne solution combines many different elements, such as a welcome letter, disclosure documents, privacy pledges, forms, and a customer reply envelope in one booklet. This eliminates the use of loose pieces that can be misplaced or lost. This complete, turnkey solution enables Bowne to receive a direct data feed from Merrill Lynch when a new account signs up. When Bowne receives data from the client, it goes through an acknowledgement process. Next, the data is validated through business rules embedded in a 'rules engine'. Then a customized, personalized booklet is compiled, including different content, documents, and mailing instructions. A report is then automatically issued to the client who decides to process or not. When the client authorizes a kit, Bowne compiles and delivers a highly-personalized and customized kit to the recipient within 24 to 48 hours. The kit features a personalized welcome letter from the financial advisor who established the new Merrill Lynch relationship with the client, thanking him/her for becoming client. It also includes an overview of the services he/she signed up for and any additional forms he/she needs to fill out and return. Using programming logic, the forms are pre-populated with contact information and other relevant fields of information, thus simplifying their completion by the recipient, facilitating increases in return rates and a reduction in return times. 'The end result was truly a collaborative effort between all members of our solution implementation team, of which Bowne was a key member. One example of this close teamwork was Bowne's working with us to meet our requirement to include a customer reply envelope with each individual book,' said Yates.

Other examples of Bowne's consultative approach are as follows:

- Working with the client's external design firm to both agree to and test for what was best for the production process (e.g., design, layout, and paper specifications)
- Facilitating and managing Merrill Lynch's business process for defining business rules and exception criteria. Bowne business analysts and software engineers collaborated with the Merrill Lynch team to map systems data to a rules engine, critical to the compilation of the welcome kit. Bowne also worked closely with the clients to test and validate the solution.
- Using a bundled approach to services, Bowne managed the paper procurement, typeset cover proofs, and inventory management of stock shells for the pre-printed work. To meet the internal business needs of clients, Bowne provides fortnightly management reports, as well as daily reports, outlining service commitments met and inventory usage.
- Bowne's service level performance has been exceptional since the solution was first rolled-out.
- Bowne's quality control capabilities are state-of-the-art, thus ensuring high levels of quality.
- In addition to fortnightly and daily reports to the client, the Bowne solution allows for real-time reporting.

**The benefits** 'This solution has helped us deliver customized, personalized communications to our clients that are targeted, timely, and easy to read, understand and respond to. That translates into a greatly improved client experience, greater brand integrity, higher customer retention and new revenues. This solution also allows us to demonstrate our ability to deliver on the promise of Total Merrill,' Yates concluded.

## Questions

1. What, according to you, is the problem with Merrill Lynch and do you think the problem is serious?
2. How exactly did Addison, the marketing communication agency helped solve Merrill Lynch's problem partially?
3. How did Bowne help Merrill Lynch in the development of an integrated, end-to-end solution that consolidated multiple client communication documents into one perfect-bound book'?
4. In light of the above case, discuss the importance of 'improved client experience, higher customer retention and cross selling' in the financial services industries the world over.

CHAPTER 18

# Corporate Communication

## LEARNING OBJECTIVES

After reading this chapter, you will be able to understand

- corporate communication functions
- corporate communication strategies and tactics, reviewing the ingredients of a comprehensive corporate communication plan
- the responsibilities and duties of professional corporate communicators
- crisis communication and how organizations need to have a crisis communication plan

## INTRODUCTION

Corporate communication is a relatively new arrival in the workplace and in the field of business education. Organizations are now striving to develop internal managerial expertise in corporate communication and learn how to use the outside expertise of public relations (PR) agencies wisely. Corporate communication should be part of every manager's essential toolkit, as a set of mental habits, shared by the leadership and understood at every level of management.

The purpose of this chapter is to address the importance of corporate communication. You need to pay attention to corporate communication because missed opportunities and serious threats to a business are the rather costly alternatives. A variety of constituencies, including employees, customers, competitors, current and potential partners, special interest groups, governments, and the media, are hounding today's businesses. These keep organizations on their toes and see to it that anything interesting (which is not ordinary) happening within the company is brought to public knowledge. In this process, most of the organizations have become extremely sensitive towards society at large and see corporate communication as a very strong tool to effectively build their reputation and image in the society and to, eventually, sell more.

Following are some facts about how companies have reacted to specific corporate communication situations:

> Organizations see corporate communication as a strong tool towards brand building.

1. Television images of defective tires exploding damaged the reputation of both Ford and Bridgestone.

2. Drug maker Eli Lilly faced lawsuits for failing to warn patients that an unscrupulous pharmacist may have diluted the company's cancer drugs.
3. The US Justice Department and individual states in the US continue to scrutinize Microsoft for unfair monopolistic trade practices.
4. The share prices of Reliance Industries, India, took a major blow during the ongoing fight between the Ambani brothers despite repeated clarifications by both the brothers.

Successful corporate management in the new millennium is essentially about managing the accelerated pace of change. When companies develop strategies for responding to changes, manage-ments, particularly in the developing world, often overlook the importance of communicating the change initiatives to employees. In most Indian companies, employee communication often means a monthly or a quarterly newsletter. In most cases, the standard contents are the CEO's inauguration of some irrelevant internal function, coverage of employee picnics, or family events and other material, which have little impact on equipping the employees to understand and adapt to a company's strategic initiatives. If a strategy must succeed, it is imperative that the entire organization understands it and works in tandem for achieving corporate goals.

## WHAT IS CORPORATE COMMUNICATION?

By corporate communication, we mean a corporation's voice and the image it projects of itself to the world. Included in this field are areas such as corporate reputation, corporate advertising and advocacy, employee communication, investor relations, government relations, media management, and crisis communication. We look at corporate communication from several vantage points. It is most visibly a *function* that may be centralized or dispersed across a company's units. A majority of the companies have corporate communication departments that appear on their organizational charts along with traditional functions like marketing or accounting. In addition, corporate communication is also the *process* a company uses to communicate all its messages to key constituencies a combination of meetings, interviews, speeches, reports, image advertising, and online communication. Ideally corporate communication is an attitude towards communication or a set of mental habits that employees internalize. The result is good communication practices that permeate an organization and are present in all its communication with its constituencies.

Corporate communication is defined as the product of communication, it could be memos, letters, reports, websites, emails, speeches, or news releases. The aggregate of these messages is what a company sends to its constituencies, whether internal or external.

Thus, corporate communication encodes and promotes

> Memos, letters, reports, websites, emails, speeches, and news releases are common corporate communication tools.

- a strong corporate culture,
- a coherent corporate identity,
- a reasonable corporate philosophy,
- a genuine sense of corporate citizenship,
- an appropriate and professional relationship with the press,
- quick and responsible ways of communicating in a crisis,
- an understanding of communication tools and technologies, and
- sophisticated approaches to global communication.

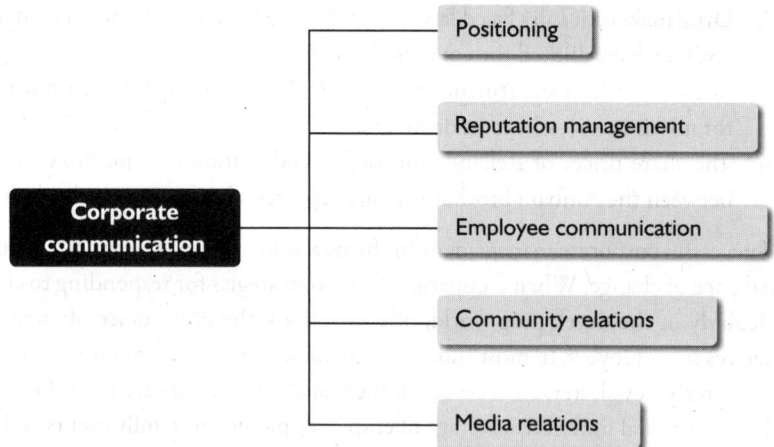

**Fig. 18.1** Aspects of corporate communication

## Practice Areas

Following are aspects of corporate communication (Fig. 18.1).

### Corporate Positioning

Every industry is witnessing unprecedented competition. As competition intensifies, companies must work hard to differentiate themselves from their peers. They must carve out a unique position in the minds of their key stakeholders based on their visions, values, unique strengths, and the value that they bring to the lives of customers, shareholders, and the communities that they serve. Maximizing shareholder value alone is not enough. Each company must identify and consistently project the unique value that it brings to the marketplace. As the pace of change intensifies, and as managements respond to these changes with newer products and services, the companies have to redefine themselves for their present and future stakeholders.

### Reputation Management

Nowadays, perception is reality, and a company's reputation capital is perhaps its most important asset. If the reputation of a well-known company is damaged, it can wither and die in a matter of months, destroying shareholder value and hurting the interests of virtually every category of stakeholders. Conversely, even a lesser-known company, which builds a solid reputation, can thrive and grow by competing effectively in the marketplace for customers, employees, vendors, desirable business partners, and capital. In the process, the company is able to deliver sustained shareholder value.

Every action of a company has a bearing on its reputation. In such an environment, active and deliberate corporate reputation management is a necessary extension of traditional brand management. After all, the primary brand is the overall corporate brand.

### Employee Communication

Successful corporate management is essentially about managing the accelerated pace of change. When companies develop strategies for responding to changes, managements, particularly in the developing world, often overlook the importance of communicating the change initiatives to employees. In most Indian companies, employee communication often means a monthly or a quarterly newsletter.

If strategy must succeed, it is imperative that the entire organization understands it and works in tandem for achieving corporate goals.

## Community Relations

> Media relations is vital to the success of any organization's overall communication strategy.

Issues affect communities where they live and work, and especially when their day-to-day conveniences are at stake. The affected people expect, and have a right to, up-to-date and correct information and access to company spokespersons who can effectively address their concerns. A little sensitivity and effort on the part of the corporate managements can help build effective community relations in locations where their plants operate.

## Media Relations

An effective media relation is vital to the success of any corporation's overall communication strategy. A sound media relations programme can deliver huge benefits to a corporation. Companies must place emphasis on deploying superior media relations skills and developing strategic media relations programmes that effectively deliver the client's key messages through the relevant media to their target audiences. Managers should be trained on how individual media will treat a particular piece of information and must have the expertise in matching the client's messages to the right media vehicles.

# CORPORATE CITIZENSHIP AND SOCIAL RESPONSIBILITY

An organization's corporate values and how it behaves as a corporate citizen have a direct relationship with its business performance and financial success. A study conducted by a US public relations agency, Golin Harris, 'Doing Well by Doing Good', showed that corporate citizenship translated to the bottom line. The study, undertaken in April 2005, showed that 40 per cent of the 3,500 respondents said that good corporate citizenship made them more willing to do business with a company. Investing in corporate citizenship is a positive brand-building strategy, not merely a defensive brand-protection strategy. Progressive brands realize that corporate citizenship is more than a 'nice to have'—it is a 'must have' to achieve success. The survey found that corporate citizenship could influence consumer opinion and behaviour, and essentially turn consumers into brand champions. Respondents indicated that good corporate citizenship by a company would inspire them to consider the following actions (in ranking order):

1. Be willing to try the company's products for the first time.
2. Welcome the company into their community.
3. Recommend the company's products and services to friends and family.
4. Improve the overall trust for the company, its people, and its products.
5. Improve the overall opinion of the company's reputation.

## Corporate Social Responsibility

In its simplest terms, many equate corporate social responsibility (CSR) with being a good corporate citizen by supporting worthwhile community causes.

As per the European Union, 'CSR is a concept whereby companies integrate social and environmental concerns in their business operations and in their interactions with their stakeholders on a voluntary basis.'

In its earliest days, CSR was often seen as simply reacting to criticism of corporate behaviour (i.e., Nike's issues over sweatshops and Exxon's problems over oil spillage from Exxon Valdez) by attempting to 'do good'. As a result, critics accused some companies of using CSR in an opportunistic manner in order to 'buy' goodwill. Many early CSR initiatives were also environmentally focused. In the late 1990s, activist groups, such as Greenpeace and Amnesty, emerged. They focused on specific causes, were well organized, and knew how to galvanize media and public opinion across international borders. Businesses felt they had to respond as reputations and sales were at stake. Corporate codes of conduct were developed, and CSR became a formal 'must do' core business principle instead of a 'would like to do' or 'maybe we have to do' activity. As a result, today CSR is a major corporate discipline, with its own body of knowledge. For larger organizations, especially multinationals, it is no longer optional; it is linked to core business objectives.

> Corporate social responsibility is being increasingly linked to core business objectives.

### How does CSR Fit with PR?

In its earliest days, CSR was essentially a PR initiative, because it was PR that often played a key role in defending questionable corporate practices. Also, it was PR, in the absence of any other advocate, that often made recommendations about the proactive steps corporations should take to avoid future risks. However, PR often found itself condemned because, in the early days, it was seen as helping corporations to communicate that they were 'doing the right thing', and this was often perceived as 'buying goodwill'. It was a classic case of shooting the messenger (although in retrospect some of the communication was rather 'over the top' and somewhat self congratulatory).

Today, much CSR strategy is developed and driven by specialists who integrate it into the business. And in its purest sense it has evolved to encompass environmental and social impacts, workplace practices, and corporate governance. This is clearly beyond the PR function. However, PR continues to have a role in the communication of the chosen CSR initiatives to various stakeholders. It is currently more fashionable to appear to be reticent and circumspect about CSR initiatives to avoid being labeled as 'trumpeting' the good work being done. Nevertheless, at the end of the day, an organization that embraces CSR still needs its stakeholders to be aware of its stance and activities so communication (albeit more subtle) is still a key ingredient.

 Please refer to the Online Resource Centre for a sample of SAIL's CSR brochure.

### Reasons for a Business being More Socially Responsible

Some of the reasons for a business to be socially responsible are as follows:

1. Taking a leadership position through CSR can help differentiate the business and give it a competitive advantage.
2. Community involvement can help bring more unity to a business, win the support of staff, and help foster a better corporate culture.
3. Adopting a CSR-driven philosophy can lead to efficiencies in energy and materials use and often lower costs.
4. Government and key stakeholders can often view more sympathetically a company that incorporates CSR into its everyday business.
5. Evidence of a company that abides by CSR principles can help attract employees.

## Corporate Reputation—A Benefit to Organizations

> - Corporate reputation is a definable attribute or asset.
> - Building relationships that preserve company reputation in both good and bad times requires proactive communication.

Reputation is no longer a 'nice thing to have'. It is now a definable business attribute or even asset. This is because, increasingly, organizations have begun to appreciate that there are tangible benefits from having a good reputation and often dire consequences if you do not. Reputation equals rational expectations (based on product and performance) and emotional expectations (based on behaviour and perception). Business experience and research has demonstrated time and again that a good reputation helps a company sell its products, recruit the best and the brightest, and attract the most desirable business partners. Communication and relationships have taken on a new importance as intangible assets represent more and more of a companies' total worth. Not just reputation, but intellectual capital, employee commitment, public trust, and corporate brands are corporate assets that must be developed and preserved for success in business. The reputation management challenge is to build, maintain, enhance, and defend an organization's reputation in perpetuity. Building relationships that preserve company reputation in good times and bad requires proactive communication.

### Benefits of a Better Reputation

Companies with a good corporate reputation enjoy benefits such as word-of-mouth endorsement, market dominance, and the ability to charge premium prices; for example, Armani, Rolls-Royce, or Microsoft. In the case of Microsoft, it can be argued that the early work the company put into building a reputation for innovation and functionality sustained it through its period of litigation and 'rushed-to-market' products.

Specifically, a better reputation is likely to

- increase the likelihood of products or services being recommended or bought,
- assist in obtaining premium prices for products or services,
- help attract and retain better employees and management,
- make it easier to do business with suppliers, retailers, or joint venture partners,
- help you attract investors or raise capital, and
- protect from unfair criticism if the organization should come under any pressure.

The communication specialist helps build a reputation by

- getting management to agree to standard messages that reflect the vision, values, and actuality of the organization,
- identifying and using key and influential channels of communication to reach stakeholders, and
- ensuring that communication to key stakeholders and audiences is not haphazard but is planned and committed throughout the year.

## CORPORATE COMMUNICATION STRATEGY

Corporate communication strategy is the strategic management of the issues and relationships between an organization and its various audiences. It has to have the following traits embedded into it:

- Macro-level orientation
- Goal setting
- Anticipating other's reactions
- Serving as a basis for action
- Links to organizational goals
- Legitimizing some issues/de-legitimizing others
- Shaping memory
- Making sense out of the confusing and ambiguous
- Providing point of identity
- Evolving

## CRISIS MANAGEMENT/COMMUNICATION

Crisis is a never-ending part of human life. In everyday life, we face many crises individually and collectively, even as a nation. In the recent past, we have been facing several crises created by terrorists, anti-social elements, nature, etc. If we look, retrospectively, at the way we have dealt with them, there may be different opinions and criticisms. Any collective crisis situation is handled only by three establishments—the government, media (i.e., electronic, print, and new media), and politicians. Take, for example, the crises on account of the hijacking of a plane to Kandahar a few years back, kidnapping of Rajkumar by Veerappan, the Kargil war, the Gujarat earthquake, the Agra Summit, etc.

- In almost all of the above cases, there was criticism that the government was neither proactive nor not effectively communicative.
- There were accusations that the media, particularly visual media, sensationalized the events.
- Politicians were blamed for taking political advantage of the difficult situations.

Informally, the government, media, and politicians blamed each other. The government felt that the media and politicians were sensationalizing the issues; the media accused the government for not being proactive and blamed politicians for taking advantage of the situations; the politicians accused the government for not taking them into confidence and not revealing all the information to them. Ultimately, this led to the three establishments acting independently without addressing the core issues of crises. Only the peripherals were addressed.

There was more criticism about the way the Kandhahar episode was handled. People were of the opinion that the government was not proactive in communication and was unprepared/unwilling to give authentic information to the public; the media, more particularly the visual media, was accused of televising the emotions of the family members; politicians were accused of taking political advantage during the critical hour instead of supporting the government. Whatever the reasons, ultimately the government was forced to surrender before the terrorists and release a dreaded terrorist. There were also expert opinions that had the situation been handled collectively, the country would not have succumbed to the pressure of terrorists.

On the other hand, during the critical time in the US, after the 11 September 2001 attacks on the World Trade Center, the mayor of New York came out with periodical statements of position; television media created a conducive atmosphere and prepared

Aah! The crisis is over! We handled it just great!

the public to fight against terrorism and did not sensationalize the event; the political personae and parties, including Bill Clinton, rallied behind President Bush to fight the root cause of the crisis, namely cross-border terrorism. However, it must be noted here that not all reactions in the US at the time or later were justifiable. Still the coordination among the government, media, and politicians is of significance from the point of crisis management.

> A crisis is any situation that threatens the integrity or reputation of a company, usually brought on by adverse or negative media attention.

The above discussion would certainly help find some strategies in handling such crises in the future, bringing together the three systems, namely the government, media, and politicians. It involves prevention as well as preparation exercises to identify crises (e.g., in case of the Bhopal gas tragedy, the magnitude of crisis, perhaps, could have been reduced had the crisis been identified beforehand.). It includes both crisis planning and response, including a well-planned response team with spokes person(s), manuals that outline guidelines during a crisis, etc.

A crisis in a business scenario is any situation that threatens the integrity or reputation of a company, usually brought on by adverse or negative media attention. These situations can involve any kind of legal dispute, theft, accident, fire, flood, or man-made disaster that could be attributed to a company. It can also be a situation where, in the eyes of the media or public, a company did not react to one of the above situations in the appropriate manner. This definition is not all encompassing but is designed to give an idea for the types of situations that might possibly arise. If handled correctly, the damage can be minimized. One crucial thing to remember in a crisis is to tell it all, tell it fast, and tell the truth. If you do this you will have done all you can to minimize the repercussions. When a situation arises that may be a crisis, the first thing to do is contact the CEO and the chief of the public relations department. The sooner these two organizations get involved, the sooner the plan can be implemented.

In crisis situations, the pace of the conflict accelerates dramatically. This means that the parties have to react very quickly to changing conditions or risk having their ability to protect their interests substantially reduced. Crises are further complicated by increased levels of fear, anger, and hostility that are likely to be present. Often in crises, communication is distorted or cut off entirely. As a result, rumours often supplant real facts, and worst-case assumptions spiral upwards fast. In addition, parties often try to keep their real interests, strategies, and tactics secret and use deceptive strategies to try to increase their relative power. In these difficult situations, the parties' ability to make rapid and sound decisions is largely dependent on their ability to quickly obtain reliable information. Thus, communication needs to be increased during crises, not cut off. To prevent uncontrolled escalation, disputants must be able to effectively communicate with adversaries, intermediaries, and other parties effectively, even under urgent and highly emotional conditions. In the most serious situations, crisis communication involves efforts to prevent or halt violent confrontations. 'Hotlines', rumour control teams, and crisis control centres offer related approaches for dealing with such problems (Ref. No. 11, Conflict Research Consortium, University of Colorado.).

> - Communication needs to be increased during crises.
> - Corporate crises can be precipitated by a variety of situations like product defects.

## Crisis Preparedness

Corporations are vulnerable to a crisis that can hurt their business, damage consumers, investor, and employee confidence, and in worst cases, even threaten their very

> **BUSINESS COMMUNICATION INSIGHT**
>
> **Five Steps to Better Crisis Communication**
>
> We get upset at any company that has appeared to take potentially damaging shortcuts in its quest to make money. When a crisis hits your industry, your customers will be quick to believe the worst about you. Committing to the following five steps will help you survive the crisis:
>
> 1. **Express genuine empathy** If your industry is affected by a crisis—whether or not it's your company's fault—you must acknowledge the tragedy and express your feelings early and often. Deflecting blame or failing to express sympathy appears callous and unconcerned, two qualities that must not be associated with your brand if you hope to keep your customers' confidence. Getting your facts straight before making any kind of public statement is important, but expressing genuine empathy for anyone harmed, injured, or killed must be your first response.
>
> 2. **Own the message quickly** In the first few hours after a crisis, a huge amount of misinformation spreads online. Too many bloggers simply copy and paste. It takes a leap of courage to be assertive and react quickly. Get your facts straight, reach out directly to principle stakeholders first, and, once everyone is on the same page with the message, start talking.
>
> 3. **Commit to full transparency** Being transparent demonstrates confidence in your product and your manufacturing and distribution methods. Very few companies or industries have the courage to be fully transparent. After a crisis, it might be the only way to rebuild your reputation.
>
> 4. **Put a face on the industry** The media abhors a vacuum. If you don't put a face on the industry, others will, and it might not be the face you want to show the public. All too often during a crisis, an industry will turn to one official spokesperson. But people want to hear from those in the field, those who do the work. It's critical to offer a group of individuals who are prepared to speak on the topic.
>
> 5. **Train the industry's spokespeople** It can be quite damaging for an untrained spokesperson to speak to the media directly. Not because he or she has something to hide, but because that person might not realize how easy it is to be misinterpreted or misquoted. Everyone must speak from the same playbook to create a coherent message.
>
> Source: Gallo, Carmine, 'Five Steps to Better Crisis Communications', http://www.businessweek.com/smallbiz/content/aug2010/sb20100831_024818.htm, accessed on 2 December 2011. Reproduced with permission.

existence. The actions of a modern-day corporation are also subject to intense scrutiny from a variety of interest groups and the media. Corporate crisis can be precipitated by a variety of situations including product defects or contamination, as the recent cases in India involving mineral water, cola, and chocolates brands have amply demonstrated. These crises have had crippling effects on brand reputations and consumer confidence. Crises can also result from disputes in industrial relations, accidents, takeover bids, boardroom battles, family separations, litigation, government investigations, or major disasters. The best strategy is to be prepared for potential crisis situations.

There are two important requirements for successfully managing crises. First, the company must work towards resolving the issues that created the crisis. Second, it must act fast to manage the perceptions of the problem amongst its key stakeholders in order to salvage and sustain its reputation and business. Knee-jerk responses to crises or wishful thinking that the crisis will blow over can only further complicate situations. It is also not enough to identify the production problem or recall the products, rescue survivors, settle the labor dispute, or win the lawsuit. A company must simultaneously reach out to win the hearts and minds of the public in general and its direct stakeholders in particular. It must act decisively to maintain its credibility and sustain the loyalty of its customers, the morale of its employees, and the commitment of its investors. Companies involved in litigation and investigations by government and regulatory bodies face special communication challenges. The development of messages and their delivery require skilled and experienced professionals. Communication is often constrained by legal considerations, which require complex decision-making processes.

## Crisis Communication Planning—Organizing and Completing a Plan that Works

This section discusses the need for an effective communication plan to help tide a company over during a crisis and also lists various crises that should be part of a crisis plan.

### Need for a Crisis Communication Plan

Whether big or small, no organization should be without a crisis communication plan. Crises happen all the time—it could be a fire, robbery, high-profile sexual harassment case, or major safety issue with one of the products. Whatever it is, it is highly likely that some kind of crisis is going to hit each company sometime in the next few years. There are many aspects to being prepared for a crisis, many of which are not worth preparing for in advance, either because of their low probability of occurrence (e.g., an alien abduction of your entire management team), or the fact that many crises require more real-time attention than a crisis plan can prepare for in advance. However, almost all crises have a consistent element, which can, and must, be planned for in advance—how a company will communicate with the media during and after the crisis.

How well a company manages the media during a crisis could determine whether the company gets hurt or grows as a result. Many companies that do not handle these issues suffer the ultimate fate—the death or reorganization of the company. Think about various corporate scandals—Worldcom, Enron, Martha Stewart—and how those companys' bottom lines were affected. And while you are at it, think of the ultimate example of excellent crisis management—the original poisoned Tylenol case, where J&J came out more strongly positioned with the public than they were before the crisis happened. Another great example of how excellent crisis management can build, rather than destroy, is the success that former New York Mayor Rudi Giulaini has enjoyed since his excellent handling of the press (and many other factors) during the 9/11 attacks on the World Trade Center. Much of this success came as a result of their relationships with the press during the crises.

The two key elements of any crisis plan are as follows:

1. The crisis plan itself (i.e., how a company will deal with the issue at hand, to minimize loss and downtime)
2. The crisis communication plan (i.e., how to communicate with the press and public about the crisis that is occurring)

> It is important for organizations to have a crisis communication plan in place.

Many companies prepare one without the other. Unfortunately, both are important. Keep in mind that most company crises never get reported in the press. Sometimes that happens because the story was not newsworthy, but oftentimes it happens because the company handled the situation so skillfully that it never became visible to the press. Other times, a crisis may be significant enough that it is both newsworthy and gets attention in the press. But that attention either lasts for a very short period of time, or it is so well handled that the company grows as people see how well they handled the crisis. A key element in making sure that this happens is the development of a crisis communication plan in your organization. Even if you do not elect to create a crisis plan (not recommended, but most companies do not have one), it is vitally important that you put together a plan to effectively communicate with the press and public when the inevitable crisis occurs.

In other words, an effective crisis communication plan may be the most important part of your crisis planning process. A list of crises that could happen and should be a viable part of a crisis plan are as follows:

- Government investigation
- Controversial law suit
- Accusation of discrimination based on race, sexual preference, or gender
- Product recall
- Serious injury to someone within or outside of the organization
- Protest
- Strike
- Physical violence between co-workers
- Insider trading scandal
- Theft by an outsider (ideas or physical assets)
- Embezzlement
- Hostile takeover
- Outbreak of food poisoning caused by a company (maybe even at a company picnic)
- Death of top executive
- CEO gets arrested for drunk driving
- Natural disaster
- Plane crash
- Congressional hearings make something that was legal illegal, and a company is used as an example
- Plummeting stock price
- Major interruptions in service
- Computer system crash, causing loss of all data
- One of the employees is accused of a high profile crime
- Sexual harassment case
- Fire
- Explosion
- Rape on a company's premises
- Dramatic downsizing, causing significant job loss in a geographic region
- Chemical spill
- Radiation leak
- A major competitor has a huge crisis, throwing attention on a company
- Caught in a lie

- False advertising accusation
- Celebrity spokesperson embroiled in personal scandal
- Oil spill
- Closing of a facility
- Production sourcing internationally or at a non-union facility
- Union grievance

## Media Release in Crisis Situations

In all kinds of crisis, it is important to understand the value of effective communication with respect to the media. The following issues, therefore, need to be kept in mind.

### Designated Spokesperson

In a crisis, one individual should be designated as the primary spokesperson to represent the company, make official statements, and answer media questions throughout the crisis. A backup to the designated spokesperson should also be identified to fill the position in the event that the primary spokesperson is unavailable. In addition to the primary spokesperson and the backup spokesperson, individuals who will serve as technical experts or advisors should be designated. These resources might include a financial expert, an engineer, a leader in the community or anyone your company deems necessary during a specific kind of crisis. This will take some brainstorming by the crisis communication team since what is needed may not always be apparent. There should be an authority or technical expert in the concerned field who should be available to supplement the knowledge of the spokesperson.

The criteria for the spokesperson, backup spokesperson, and crisis communication expert are that he/she should be comfortable in front of a camera and with reporters, preferably he/she should be skilled in handling media, in directing responses to another topic, in identifying key points, able to speak without using jargon, respectful of the role of the reporter, and knowledgeable about the organization and the crisis at hand. He/she should also be able to establish credibility with the media, able to project confidence to the audience, suitable in regard to diction, appearance, and charisma, accessible to the media and internal communication personnel who will facilitate media interviews, able to remain calm in stressful situations and, sincere, straightforward, and believable. In addition to the designated spokesperson and backup, if other parties involved in the crisis, that is, police, fire department, health officials, etc. also have spokespersons, it is important to obtain the identity of those individuals as early as possible, so that all statements and contacts with the media can be co-ordinated between those individuals and their organizations/interests, whenever possible.

### Media Policies and Procedures

Locations for interviews and press briefings should be decided by the crisis communication team. A place to be used as a media centre should be selected. It should be some distance from the office of the crisis communication team, company spokesperson, and emergency operations centre to ensure that the media is not in the middle of the action if they happen to take the wrong turn or have to pass by those offices or areas on the way to the restrooms. If there is a visual (e.g., a fire or rescue operation), do not make the media centre in such a remote site that they cannot see what is going on because they may not show up and if they do, you will lose their confidence as it may appear that you are hiding something. Do not change the rules that you already have established for the media. For example, normally if media persons are required to be escorted, then even during a crisis they should still be escorted. Various alternatives should be considered and early preparations should be made to find people who can escort the media during a crisis. If there are special circumstances that would require media persons to be escorted, such as a safety hazard, they should be advised of this up front. Any change in the way the media is dealt with during a crisis may change the views of reporters. It is important that the media feel that you are not trying to hide anything.

Reporters may ask to talk to the staff or faculty or students of a school who were involved with or have been affected by a crisis. It is best to restrict all interviews to the primary or backup spokesperson or technical expert. Controlling the interview process is the key to managing a crisis. However, remember that reporters have the right to interview anyone they want to and if they do not get the answers they want from you, they will get them somewhere else. They are usually after a scoop and want a different angle than the reporter standing next to them. If the possibility is there to provide them with what they want, consider it very carefully. All media should be treated equally. What is given to one reporter (such as access to an area effected by a crisis) should be available to all.

### Practising Tough Questions

A crisis situation is always difficult when dealing with the media. Therefore, tough questions and rehearsals are necessary to help a spokesperson prepare. It is important, at the onset of a crisis, that the primary and backup spokespersons, and advisors spend some time rehearsing prepared statements and answers to possible 'tough' questions that may be asked by reporters. If possible, similar rehearsals should be conducted prior to each media interview, briefing, or news conference. It is also important to anticipate and practise new questions as the story evolves. It is better to be prepared than surprised by the depth of questioning by the media. The communication/public relations staff should prepare questions and answers for the practice sessions. These questions and answers should be for internal use only and not for distribution outside the organization. Do not volunteer information unless it is a point that the company wants to make and the question has not yet been asked. Do not talk off the record.

### Prepared Statements

It is important to communicate immediately in times of crisis and failure to do so may lead to loss of the greatest opportunity to control events. A fill-in-the-blanks news release can be used with little or no preparation as the first news release. The first news release should include at a minimum the who, what, when, and where of the crisis situation. Give facts that have been gathered from reliable sources and confirmed. Do not overreach yourself or speculate. There is a limit to your role, to exceed that limit is a mistake. If you do nothing more than show concern for the public and for your employees in your first press interaction, you are already on the right track. The corollary of expressing concern and generating goodwill at the consumer level is securing the loyalty of your customers and employees by taking the initiative to share information with them. You must have a prepared statement on hand that can be used to make an initial general response to the media when knowledge about the crisis first becomes known on a widespread basis or by reporters. As the crisis progresses and new information and facts become available,

> A spokesperson should provide definitive and not speculative information.

> ### Sample News Release
>
> A .............................. at .............................. involving .............................. occurred today at .................. . The incident is under investigation and more information is forthcoming.
>
> A (what happened) at (location) involving (who) occurred today at (time). The incident is under investigation and more information is forthcoming.
>
> For instance:
>
> An explosion at 1210 Tilak Street, the main plant for the Indian Toy Company occurred today at 3 p.m. The incident is under investigation and more information is forthcoming.

it is also advisable to develop prepared statements to be made by the spokesperson at the onset of any media interview, briefing, or news conference. These prepared statements also can be read over the telephone to reporters who call to request information but are not represented at news conferences or briefings. The statement can also be sent by fax or email upon request.

You could put down a definitive time for the next news conference or release of information if you have fixed upon it but that is not necessary. This will not solve your problems, but may buy you enough time to prepare for the next news conference or release. You could also add information, if it is available, such as, how many casualty's there are known up to this point or any other pertinent information available. Once again, this information should be definitive and not speculative, verify everything you say. This will help your credibility in the long run.

## Key Audience

In a crisis situation, consider what the most effective method of communication would be for each group of people. Ensure that you communicate with each group that is part of your audience. A list of people served by public affairs or communication departments is as follows:

- Employees—management, hourly/prospective/salaried employees, families, union members, and retirees
- Community where employees live, neighbourhood coalitions, community organizations, plant locations, chambers of commerce
- Customers
- Geographical groups
- Local, regional, national, and international groups
- Distributors, jobbers, wholesalers, retailers, and consumers
- Industrial/business groups
  - Suppliers, teaming partners, competitors, professional societies, sub-contractors, joint ventures, and trade associations
- Media
- General, local, national and international groups; foreign trade and specialized groups
- Academia
- Trustees, regents, directors, financial supporters, students, prospects, administration, faculty/staff, and alumni

> It is important to communicate with each group that is part of the audience.

- Investment/financial groups
- Analysts—institutional holders, shareholders, bankers (commercial and investment), stockbrokers, portfolio managers, and potential investors
- Government
- Legislative, regulatory, executive, and judicial groups
- Special interest groups
- Environmental, safety, handicapped/disabled, minority, expert, consumer, health, senior citizens, and religious groups

## SUMMARY

Corporate communication is an attitude towards communication or a set of mental habits that employees internalize. The result is good communication practices that permeate an organization and are present in its communication with all its constituencies.

Reputation equals rational expectations (based on product and performance) plus emotional expectations (based on behaviour and perception). Corporate social responsibility is achieving commercial success in ways that honour ethical values and have respect for communities and the natural environment.

A crisis is any situation that threatens the integrity or reputation of a company, usually brought on by adverse or negative media attention.

## KEY TERMS

***Corporate communication*** It refers to a corporation's voice and the image it projects of itself. Included are areas such as corporate reputation, corporate advertising and advocacy, employee communication, investor relations, government relations, media management, and crisis communication.

***Corporate reputation*** It equals rational expectations (based on product and performance) plus emotional expectations (based on behaviour and perception). Business experience and research has demonstrated that a good reputation helps a company sell its products, recruit the best and the brightest, and attract the most desirable business partners.

***Corporate social responsibility*** It refers to, in its simplest terms, being a good corporate citizen by supporting worthwhile community causes.

***Crisis management*** It refers to the actions taken by a company to tackle any crisis that threatens the integrity or reputation of the company.

## Concept Review Questions

1. In the current environment, why do you think corporations have to practise social responsibility more and practise it seriously?
2. What exactly could lead to a business crisis? Why do you think a plan for handling crisis situations is a must for companies?
3. What is effective investor relations management? How has a normal investor become a very important stake holder in the recent past?

## Critical Thinking Questions

1. Repeatedly, we have witnessed very poor PR skills when it comes to government organizations in India. A crisis is generally blown out of proportions by the media, primarily because of lack of credible information and by the time organizations try to do some damage control, it is too late. Why do you think such things happen? Suggest a suitable strategic plan to manage such situations.

2. Organizations like ITC are spending crores of rupees in the social responsibility sector by opening schools, hospitals, etc. in rural India. Critics argue that it is merely eyewash on their misdeeds (read sale of tobacco) and more of business diplomacy. Discuss.

## REFERENCES

Bahal, Madan 2005, *Knowledge Driven Communications*, Adfactors PR Pvt Ltd, p. 2.

Balsubramanian, N. 1998, 'Changing Perceptions of Corporate Governance in India', *ASCI Journal of Management*, p. 16.

Blomquist, Bob 2004, *Web-based Communication for Corporate Communication*, Interactive Video Tech.

Derry R. 1991, 'Institutionalizing Ethics Motivation' in Freeman's *Business Ethics*, Revised Edition, Oxford University Press.

Dolenga, H.E. 1990, 'An Iconoclast Looks at Business Ethics', *Advanced Management Journal*, Vol. 55, No. 4.

Goodman, Michael B. 2002, 'Current Trends in Corporate Communication', ANA Corporate Communication Committee Meeting, PowerPoint Presentation, 2002.

Harrison, J. and E. Freeman, 1999, 'Stakeholders Social Responsibil-ity and Performance—Empirical Evidence and Theoretical Perspectives', *Academy of Management Journal*, Vol. 42. p. 6.

Jacquelyn Ottman 2003, 'Eco-Innovation and Green Marketing: Antidote to Corporate Reputation Blues', J. Ottman Consulting, Inc., Vol. 10, No. 2.

Karnad, Amol 2000, 'The Socially Responsible Corporation in India—The Value of Readership' *Management Review*, IIM Bangalore, p. 10.

Parker, Martin (Ed) 1998, *Ethics and Organisation*, Sage, pp. 24.

Schanzenbaecher, Bernd 2001, *Sustainability—A Growing Challenge for Corporate Communication*, Credit Suisse Group, Madison, NJ.

Thomson, Ian, and Alistair MacDonald 2001, *Corporate Communication: Standards, Practice and Issues—Access to Information: A Key to Building Trust*, International Institute for Environment and Development, Vancouver, Canada, p. 10.

http://www.greenmarketing.com/articles/Ottman_Report v10i2.html, 27 October 2005.

http://prnewswatch.com/ 2005/09/, last accessed on 27 October 2005.

www.corporate comm.org/archive.html, last accessed on 27 October 2005.

www. corporatecomm.org/archive.html, last accessed on 27 October 2005.

## CASE STUDY 1

### How to Repair the Reliance Image*

In this case study, two approaches—from a PR head's and a consultant's perspectives—to handle a spate of controversies faced by Reliance will be discussed.

**Mr X, Head, Public Relations** The flight path for the Ambani brotherhood version 2.0 that I would prescribe would have at least two distinct aspects to start with. The brothers, once they decide on the Kamath formula, its money modalities and on finally going their separate ways, will simply have to find a clever method by which they will each become truly independent entities on and

---

* The case has been adapted from *Business Standard*, http://www.business-standard.com/india/mws/repairing-reliance/207912/, accessed on 5 May 2005.

of their own. They would inevitably have to then derive independent and coherent image structures. Only one of them will, in image terms, be actually able to inherit the so-called Reliance brand. Therefore, the other, will have to abandon that precious brand, at some stage, which is not so far in the future. This could be a serious issue. It could even be the basis of some rather hard bargaining at this stage, and with good reason. The Reliance Brand, after all, has a substantial and exploitable value of its own. This image advantage will be one that both parties will seek to retain. But they cannot. In the end, only one will be able to appropriate the benefits. If both do, both lose.

(Wicked thought: the other brand available to inherit is the underlying and latent brand Ambani. Could one be traded off against the other? Do both have the same value? Can this be the basis of an equal image bifurcation?)

The next step would be to take stock of the course after the embankments have been breached by the torrent. This would happen by measuring perception and reputation year on year through stakeholder research. It is imperative to professionalize communication for a strategic plan to reverse the damage and rebuild reputation. Focused outreach programmes would need to be built to address key editors, bureaucrats, and analysts separately. Accessibility, honesty, and transparency would need to take the place of closed-door mystique. Shareholders are looking for comfort from the idea that systems are being put into place for corporate governance. So, they will need to set up advisory boards that comprise large customers, respected industrialists, and/or economists who will give independent advice to the management on key issues of importance to the market place. These boards must comprise fiercely independent people. An endeavour to seek counsel from people who have squeaky-clean reputations would help the perception that there is a single-minded focus on restoring Dhirubhai's legacy.

But what has been outlined so far is only step two. Substantively, there is step one before that. Even before this bifurcation of images takes place, the brothers would be well advised to spend a considerable portion of their communication energies drawing attention to the reorganizing of their new corporations. To take attention away from the minutiae of disconnect, both will also have to do big-ticket announcements that will occupy the space that hostilities had previously gobbled. Unless there is the unleashing of fresh corporate energy of the gigantic variety, there will be temptation to return to the battlefield stories. It involves the re-establishment of corporate governance and the refurbishment of credible management talent at the top levels in both companies. Basic, mundane, and boring, but it gives confidence. The Reliance image is like Humpty Dumpty: all the king's horses and all the king's men can never put the original image together the way it was. But an image makeover is certainly possible.

**Mr Y, Consultant** Reliance is a brand. It is a thought that lives in the minds of three distinct segments of people with whom a brand typically communicates—the B2B, B2C, and C2C segments. But brand Reliance has a problem—a big one. It is a sullied brand today. The needs and aspirations of each of these segments are different. But everyone has a worry. In the B2B segment, vendors are worrying about the state of the agreements they have signed with the group. In the B2C segment, the image of Reliance as a squabbling entity is one consumers love to talk about. Apart from shareholders, there are also the actual users of Reliance facilities, be it in power, telecom, or petroleum. Add to this, the circuit of the fringe set who are not business partners, vendors, or consumers. These are the potential consumers. Most brand communicators ignore them. I would look at them keenly.

I would address each of these segments with care and sensitivity. First of all, I would urge an immediate cessation of hostility before this communication task begins. The rules are simple: all dirty linen must be washed in private; and keep politics out of the issue. It adds a different dimension altogether. What is done is done. Do not add any more negative baggage to the brand. I believe communication is not a single piece of work. It is a cascade. Crisis management communication needs to be a quick and efficient cascade that addresses all the segments that have been delineated.

A brand communication cascade is a set of repeat experiences, each different, but each engineered to result in a series of thoughts. This is a corporate issue. The role of PR is clearly dominant compared to the role of advertising. I would use the tool of systemic PR to advantage, but with sensitivity. PR is like an onion. The first layer is 'pink paper' PR—messaging that will appeal mainly to corporate readers. Then there is deeper, 'white paper' PR, which appeals to the lay reader as well. That is followed by 'pink' and 'white' television. The final layer is the core—the larger mass of people. I would address each as a separate package, but not make the mistake of restricting the communication cascade to the elite. The brand is a much deeper entity.

**Questions**

1. Do you see any fundamental difference between the approaches suggested by the two people above? One is a PR head and other is a freelance consultant.
2. How serious, according to you, would be the option of dropping the 'Reliance' brand by one of the brothers, in both the short and the long run?
3. What, according to the PR head, are the few very important steps to be taken to build the already badly dented corporate image?
4. 'To take attention away from the minutiae of disconnect, both will also have to do big-ticket announcements.' What is this strategy all about and will it work in this case?
5. How does the consultant compares a PR exercise to an onion? Discuss the comparisons made and the relationships at each layer in detail.
6. Identify a few more incidents from Indian corporate history where organizational reputations have suffered badly because of family or internal problems. How have they reacted to it and how many of them have successfully restored their credibility?

CHAPTER 19

# Persuasive Strategies in Business Communication

## LEARNING OBJECTIVES

After reading this chapter, you will be able to understand

- the importance of persuasive communication in business
- the AIDA model
- the various elements of an effective online advertisement
- the various strategies involved in conflict resolution process
- the role of a mediator in conflict management
- the effective use of language in conflict resolution
- negotiation and its two basic approaches
- the guidelines for successful negotiation
- the nuances of intercultural negotiation

## INTRODUCTION

Let us consider the following examples:

> Two partners are convinced that they have a winning idea for a new restaurant. They meet with a commercial loan officer from a local bank to seek financing for their project.
> Faced with a wave of injuries, a foreman of a construction crew convinces his/her team members that they need to observe safety practices more carefully.
> A local real-estate brokerage has merged with a nationwide chain. Ever since the news became public, rumours have swept the office about how the changes will affect pay, policies, and even job security. The owner has called a company-wide meeting to reassure employees that the changes will benefit them.
> A group of employees has grown increasingly disgruntled with the boss's policy on vacation scheduling. They have chosen a three-person delegation to present their grievances.

These examples show us how common persuasion is on the job. At one time or another, everyone in an organization needs to influence the thinking or actions of others. When an issue is especially important, persuasion frequently takes place in a presentation.

The outcome of any kind of persuasion depends largely on the reasonableness of your request, credibility, and ability to make your request attractive to the receiver.

Executives presenting the profile of their company at a pre-placement talk should be persuasive so that they can attract good candidates for their organization. Copywriters designing an advertisement for a business should be persuasive so that their advertisements immediately catch the attention of their audience, thereby turning them into customers. Managers negotiating for a deal need to be persuasive so that they can accomplish their goals.

Persuasion enables business enterprises to achieve their goals, thereby paving the way for their success in the business arena. There are various tasks in business that require the art of persuasion. This chapter discusses the three major and most commonly used business strategies, namely advertising, negotiation, and conflict resolution that require the art of persuasion. All these three business tasks are discussed with special reference to communication that forms an integral part of any business strategy.

> Persuasion enables business enterprises to achieve their goals, thereby paving the way for their success in the business arena.

## Business Communication Insight

### Four Steps in Persuasive Communication at Work

Effective workplace persuasion was studied closely by Professor Jay Conger, Professor of organisational behaviour at the University of Southern California. He reviewed the characteristics of successful business leaders and change agents, and studied the academic literature on persuasion and rhetoric. Conger's research indicated that effective persuasion comprises the following four distinct and necessary steps:

1. *Establish your credibility* In the workplace, credibility comes from expertise and relationships. People are considered to have high levels of expertise if they have a history of sound judgement or have proven themselves knowledgeable and well informed about their proposals. They have demonstrated over time that they can be trusted to listen and to work in the best interests of others.

2. *Frame your goals in a way that identifies common ground with those you intend to persuade* The best persuaders closely study the issues that matter to their colleagues. They use conversations, meetings, and other forms of dialogue to collect essential information. They are good at listening. They test their ideas with trusted contacts and question the people they will later be persuading. Often this process causes them to alter or compromise their own plans before they even start persuading.

3. *Reinforce your positions using vivid language and compelling evidence* Persuasive people supplement data with examples, stories, metaphors, and analogies to make their positions come alive. Vivid word pictures lend a compelling and tangible quality to the persuader's point of view.

4. *Connect emotionally with your audience* Good persuaders are aware of the primacy of emotions and are responsive to them in two important ways. Firstly, they show their own emotional commitment to the position they are advocating (without overdoing it, which would be counterproductive). Secondly, they have a strong and accurate sense of their audience's emotional state, and they adjust their tone and the intensity of their arguments accordingly.

*Source:* Harrison, Kim, 'Four Steps in Persuasive Communication at Work', http://www.cuttingedgepr.com/articles/empcomm_foursteps.asp, accessed on 9 December 2011. Reproduced with permission.

>  **COMMUNICATION TOOL**
>
> **Four Big Mistakes in Major Persuasion Projects**
>
> From his painstaking research, Professor Jay Conger concluded that the big four mistakes in major persuasion projects are as follows:
>
> 1. *Attempting to make your case with an upfront hard sell* Setting out a strong position at the outset actually gives potential opponents something to grab on to and to fight against. It's far better not to give opponents a clear target at the start.
> 2. *Resisting compromise* Too many people see compromise as surrender, but compromise is essential to constructive persuasion. Before people buy into a proposal they want to see that the persuader is flexible enough to respond to their concerns. Compromises can often lead to better, more sustainable, shared solutions.
> 3. *Thinking the secret of persuasion lies in presenting great arguments* Great arguments matter, but they are only one component. Other factors matter just as much, such as the persuader's credibility and their ability to create a mutually beneficial position for themselves and their audience (a win-win situation), connect on the right emotional level, and communicate through vivid language that makes arguments come alive.
> 4. *Assuming persuasion is a one-time effort* Persuasion is a process, not an event. Shared solutions are rarely reached on the first try.
>
> *Source:* Harrison, Kim, 'Four Steps in Persuasive Communication at Work', http://www.cuttingedgepr.com/articles/empcomm_foursteps.asp, accessed on 9 December 2011. Reproduced with permission.

## ADVERTISING

In today's competitive business world, advertising has become an integral part of every organization. No organization can survive without advertising, whether it is consumer advertising or political persuasion, charity appeals, or public safety campaigns.

### Definition

Advertising can be defined as a communication, a marketing, an economic, a social, a public relations, or an information and persuasion process. It is a non-personal communication of information, usually paid for and usually persuasive in nature, about products (goods and services) or ideas by identified sponsors through various media.

Advertising is directed to groups of people rather than to individuals and is, therefore, non-personal. These groups might be consumers or business people (Image 19.1).

Most advertising is paid for by sponsors. Bajaj, Coco-Cola, Videocon, and your local fitness salon pay the newspaper, radio or television station to carry the advertisements we read, see, and hear. However, some sponsors do not have to pay for their advertisements. There are some national organizations, such as the Red Cross Society and the Society for Prevention of Cruelty to Animals (SPCA), whose public service messages are carried at no charge. Most advertising is intended to be persuasive—to push consumers to buy products; however, some advertisements, such as legal announcements, are intended merely to inform, not to persuade.

- Advertising is directed to groups of people rather than to individuals and is, therefore, non-personal.
- Advertising reaches us through a channel of communication referred to as a medium.

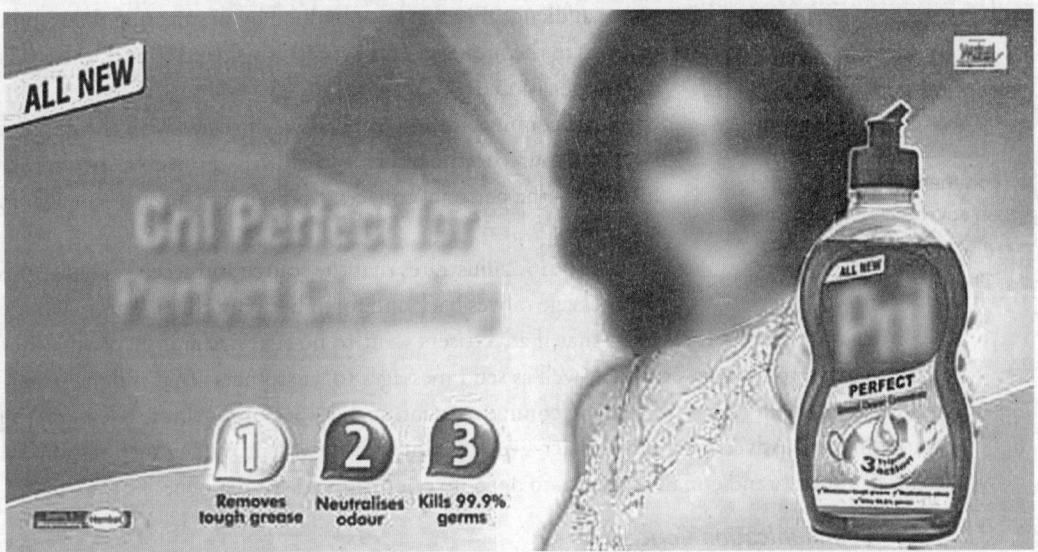

**Image 19.1** A utensil cleaner's ad targets homemakers

In addition to promoting tangible goods, such as soaps, soft drinks, and detergents, advertising helps publicize the intangible services of bankers, beauticians, telephone companies, and auto repair shops. Increasingly, advertising is used to advocate a wide variety of ideas, economic, political, religious, and social. The term 'product' encompasses goods, services, and ideas.

An advertisement identifies its sponsors and they pay for the advertisement. Advertising reaches us through a channel of communication referred to as a medium.

In addition to the traditional mass media—radio, television, newspapers, magazines, and billboards—advertising uses other media such as direct mail, brochures, e-advertising, and videocassettes also. First and foremost, advertising is another form of communication. Successful advertisers—and the advertising specialists they employ—work to apply the elements of the communication process in the marketplace.

## Advertising as a Form of Communication

In a sense, advertising is a conversation with consumers about a product. It gets attention, provides information (and a little bit of entertainment), and tries to create some kind of response, such as a sale. Most advertising, however, is not as personal as a conversation because it relies on mass communication, which is more indirect—and complex—than a simple conversation. Mass communication is usually thought of as a process, which is depicted here in a communication model that outlines the important players and steps.

### Basic Communication Model

The process of mass communication begins with a source (S), who is a sender who encodes a message (M)—puts it in words and pictures. The model explains how communication works—the message is presented through channels of communication (C), such as a newspaper, radio, or television. The message is decoded or interpreted by the receiver (R) who, in advertising, is a member of the

- Mass communication is a one-way process with the message moving from the source to the receiver.
- The working tools of a communicator are called signs.
- An advertisement, regardless of the medium in which it appears, is a collection of signs.

target audience. Feedback is obtained by monitoring the response of the receiver to the message. This process is referred to as the SMRC model of communication.

Mass communication is a one-way process with the message moving from the source to the receiver (Fig. 19.1). However, interactive communication—the personal conversation—is a two-way form of communication (Fig. 19.2).

Figure 19.2 illustrates that the source and receiver change positions as the message moves back and forth between them. This is a model of how a conversation works. It suggests that if advertisers want to be effective and successful, they need to learn to listen to messages from, as well as send messages to, customers. That is done partly by using more interactive forms of marketing communication such as personal selling, telemarketing, online marketing, etc. Advertising can also achieve more interactivity by providing such response devices as toll free numbers and e-mail addresses to open up opportunities for dialogue.

### Three Communication Concepts

To understand advertising as a form of communication, it is necessary to understand the three basic communication concepts—signs, fields of experience, and meanings.

**Signs** The working tools of the communicator are called signs. Signs are the visual, verbal, or audio elements that are exchanged between the participants in a communication relationship—the elements that stand for something in the mind of one participant and, if accepted, will come to stand for something in the mind of the other. For example, if an advertisement for a two-wheeler uses the picture of the two-wheeler itself, it refers to literal association, whereas, if it uses a galloping race horse, it refers to a subjective association.

An advertisement, regardless of the medium in which it appears, is a collection of signs—words, pictures, and sounds. As communicators, advertising people work as sign manipulators; their job is to

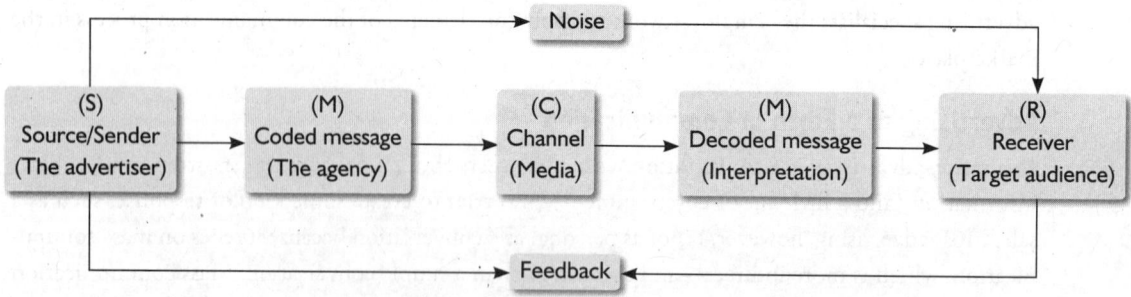

**Fig. 19.1** A basic communication model

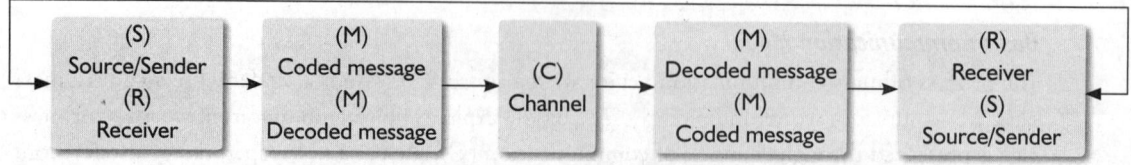

**Fig. 19.2** Interactive communication model

select signs based on their personal experience and reach results that will be interpreted by the consumer as desired by the advertiser.

**Field of experience** Advertisers manipulate signs based on their knowledge of the consumer's field of experience that is the total of his/her life experiences. The more the overlap in the field of experience between the consumer and the advertiser, the greater and more accurate the sharing of thought, that is, more communication takes place. If an advertiser for foam pillows uses a feather as a sign, it is because he/she shares the experience of the prospective consumers who want their pillows to be as soft as feathers.

**Meanings not transmitted in the communication** Signs are manipulated in advertisements to produce shared thought. Meaning results only when signs are shared by advertisers and consumers—that is, when they both interpret the message to mean the same thing. Communication often breaks down because signs in advertisements do not have the same meaning for the two parties due to their diverse fields of experience.

## Advertising Communication Elements

The eight elements of the communication process are as follows:

- Source
- Receiver
- Encoding
- Decoding
- Message
- Feedback
- Channel
- Noise

The source and receiver are the principal participants in the process; the message and channel are the objects employed by the participants to communicate; encoding, decoding, and feedback are functions of the process; and noise is the element that inhibits effective communication. Each of these eight elements has a fundamental role in understanding advertising as communication.

The basic process remains the same for all forms of communication, however, advertising stands out in terms of source, message, and receiver dimensions because of the number of people and complex processes involved. The discussion that follows may facilitate your understanding of these dimensions.

### Source

In advertising, who is really the source of the communication? The sponsor named in the advertisement? Certainly, the sponsor is legally responsible for the communication, but usually he/she does not actually produce the message. That is done by the sponsor's advertising agency. So, the author of the communication is actually a copywriter, an art director, or, most often, a group at the agency—people outside the text of the message. To the customer, this persona is the source of the within-text message.

Consider the well-known advertisement for Colgate toothpaste in which the dentist addresses a group of children. If we have to arrive at the source dimensions of this advertisement, we may find that the sponsor is the product company, the author is the copywriter, and the persona is the person who plays the role of the dentist.

> In the marketing communication process, a source encodes a message that is sent through a channel to be decoded by a receiver.

### Encoding

In the marketing communication process, a source encodes a message that is sent through a channel to be decoded by a receiver. The source is multidimensional, comprising a sponsor, an author, and a persona. In advertising, the encoding of messages—the conversion of mental concepts into symbols—is the responsibility of the creative team. Together, they work under the supervision of a creative director (often a former copywriter) who is ultimately responsible for the creative product—the final form the advertisement takes.

> Advertisers use media to convey commercial messages to their target audiences.

### Message

The heart of advertising communication is the message. In advertising, one of the most important decisions is the kind of persona and message to use. In the encoding process, the advertising professional usually begins by studying the emotions, attitudes, and the concepts that drive particular types of customers. Once those are identified, symbols are developed. These symbols, in the form of images and text, are then placed in the most suitable format for the message dimension and the medium in which they are to appear.

### Media/Channel

In advertising, the term media refers to communication vehicles, such as newspapers, magazines, radios, televisions, billboards, direct mails, and the Internet. Advertisers use media to convey commercial messages to their target audiences, and the media depends (to different degrees) on advertising revenues to cover the cost of their operations. The media are usually classified into either mass or niche media. Newspapers, magazines, television, and radio are considered mass media because they deliver messages to a widespread and anonymous audience Advertising media such as cable television and direct mail are often viewed as 'niche' media because they reach a narrowly defined audience with unique demographic characteristics or special interests.

The media is composed of channels of communication that carry messages from advertisers to the audience. Advertisers may require a different media mix to reach different target audiences. For instance, Jet Airways may use a prime-time commercial about its services when it wants to attract new users. However, when Jet Airways wants to prompt these potential new customers to subscribe to its service, it may use a direct mail campaign.

### Receivers and Decoding

In advertising, receivers are also multidimensional. The first line of consumers is the group of decision-makers at the sponsor's company or organization. These sponsor consumers are the gatekeepers who decide if the advertisement will run or not. Therefore, before an advertisement even gets a chance to persuade the real consumers, it must first persuade the sponsor's agents. The actual consumers are people in the real world who comprise the advertisement's target audience.

### Feedback

Feedback is important as it completes the cycle, verifying that the message was received. Feedback employs the same sender–message–receiver pattern, except that it is directed from the receiver back to the source. In advertising, feedback may take a variety of forms—redeemed coupons, telephone inquiries, visits to stores, requests for more information, sales, or responses to a survey.

Feedback tells the source how much was actually communicated. In effect it reverses the communication flow so that the receiver becomes the encoder and the source becomes the receiver. Feedback can be immediate, as in face-to-face interpersonal communication, or delayed, as in advertising.

> Noise is anything that interferes with the encoding and decoding of messages between the source and the sender.

### Noise

Noise is anything that interferes with the encoding and decoding of messages between source and sender. In general noise falls into three categories—environmental, mechanical, and psychological.

*Environmental noise* refers to interference that is external to the message exchange between source and receiver. For example, the drowning out of your television set (while you are watching an advertisement) by a neighbor's barking dog is an environmental noise.

*Mechanical noise* is interference that is caused by machine-assisted problems in communication. Poor colour reproduction in the latest issue of your favourite photography magazine is an example of mechanical noise.

*Psychological noise*, also called semantic noise, is interference that is caused by source encoding or receiver decoding mistakes or problems. The incorrect use of signs in a television commercial is psychological noise, for example, thinking about your upcoming interview while watching television.

In advertising communication pitfalls arising due to these three categories of noise—environmental, mechanical, and psychological—cannot be eliminated entirely in actual practice. However they can be anticipated and planned for, especially psychological noise. Encoding and decoding problems can be reduced if advertisers make message and media decisions based on research that allows them to consider the consumer's perspective.

## AIDA—MASTER FORMULA

One of the oldest models that advertising experts rely on, to assess the general appropriateness of a print advertisement, is known as AIDA. This acronym stands for *attention* (e.g., are you talking to me?), *interest* (e.g., why are you talking to me?), *desire* (e.g., nice idea, but do I really need it?), and *action* (e.g., what will I have to do to?). If your message can grab the reader's attention, create an interest in the firm, produce a desire to learn more about the services, and compel people to 'act' by attending a seminar, asking to be placed on your mailing list, or by calling one of your partners, you have probably created an effective and persuasive message.

### Attention

Good advertisements should grab the attention of your target consumers. An advertisement or commercial is a stimulus. It must break through consumers' physiological screens to create the kind of attention that leads to perception. Attention, therefore, is the first objective of any advertisement and its fundamental building block. An artist may spend as much time and energy figuring out how to express the big idea in an interesting, attention-getting way as searching for the big idea itself.

Print advertisements often use the headline as the major attention-getting device. A copywriter's goal is to write a headline that expresses the big idea with verve. Usually designed to appear in the largest and boldest type in the advertisement, the headline is often the strongest focal point conceptually as well as visually.

> The AIDA model stands for attention, interest, desire, and action.

An attention-getting device should create drama, power, impact, and intensity, and it must be appropriate—relate to the product, tone of the advertisement, and

**Image 19.2** Effective advertising generates interest

needs or interests of the intended audience. This is especially true for business-to-business advertising, where rational appeals and fact-based thinking dominate.

### Interest

Effective advertising helps to generate interest in your product or service amongst the right people (Image 19.2). Interest, the second step in the advertisement process, is extremely important. It carries the prospective customer—now paying attention—to the body of the advertisement. It must keep the prospect excited as the information becomes more detailed.

There are many effective ways to stimulate interest—dramatic situations, stories, cartoons, or charts. In radio, copywriters use sound effects or catchy dialogues. Television frequently uses quick cuts to maintain interest.

### Desire

An advertisement should create, in the audience, a desire to purchase the product or service that is being promoted. This step establishes credibility for the product or service and creates a desire for it.

### Action

The advertisement should also provide a call to action and tell the customers exactly how and where they can buy the promoted product or service. The purpose of an action step is to motivate people to do something—send in a coupon, call the number on the screen, or visit the store—or at least to agree with the advertiser.

The call to action may be explicit such as—'Call for additional information' or implicit such as: 'Fly the friendly skies'. Designers cue customers to take action by placing dotted lines around coupons to suggest cutting and by highlighting the company's telephone number with large type or a bright colour.

## PLANNING ADVERTISEMENTS FOR RESULTS

Certain things are basic to planning advertisements whose results can be measured. The pointers that may help plan advertisements so that they make the company stand out consistently when people read or hear about it are as follows:

> An advertisement should create, in the audience, a desire to purchase the product or service that is being promoted.

1. Plan the advertisement around one idea. Each advertisement should have a single message. If the message needs reinforcing with other ideas, keep them in the background. If you have several important things to say, use a different advertisement for each one and run the advertisements on succeeding days or weeks.

2. Establish the objective. For example, 'Is the advertisement meant to sell the total company image or a product?' or 'Is it a new product or an old one?'.
3. Identify stores fully and clearly. Make sure your advertisements identify your sponsorship as fully and frequently as possible without interfering with the message. Logotypes and signatures in visual advertisements should be clean-lined, uncluttered, and prominently displayed. Give your address and telephone number. It is possible to use a musical or sound effect signature identified with your store to create a 'logo' on radio too.
4. The headline and illustration must support each other and establish the subject of the advertisement. The reader should know at a glance what is being advertised. Pick illustrations, which are similar in character. Graphics—drawings, photos, borders, and layouts—that are similar in character help people to recognize an advertising immediately.
5. Pick one audio format or typeface and stick to it. Using the same typeface or the same audio format for radio or television helps people to recognize advertisements quickly. Using the same format, type, and illustration also allows one to concentrate on the message when checking advertisement response changes.
6. Make the copy easy to understand. Printed messages should be broken up with white space to allow the reader to see the lines quickly. Broadcast messages should be written conversationally.
7. Tell the listeners how what is being advertised will help them. Consumers buy benefits, not products; therefore, emphasize benefits, not facts.
8. Get the main message in the first sentence, if possible. Sentences should be short and direct. Get straight to the point and catch the audiences' attention in the first five seconds of the radio or television commercial.
9. Try out the script on somebody else or read it into a tape recorder. When the tape is played back, it is easy to spot phrases that are hard to understand (or believe). Ears are better than eyes for judging the broadcast advertisements.
10. Facts are static pieces of information that only describe a product/service. Benefits are dynamic interpretations of what the facts will do for the product/service user. Therefore, an advertisement should stress on the benefits.
11. Illustrate the product in use. The reader must be able to relate to the product and its use through the illustration.
12. Repeat a successful advertisement and drop a low-scoring advertisement. Stay with a winner. A good advertisement does not wear out as fast as the advertiser thinks.

## EFFECTIVE ONLINE ADVERTISING

> The Internet has emerged as a medium for marketing and advertising since the 1990s.

The Internet has emerged as a medium for marketing and advertising since the 1990s. The Internet is different from conventional advertising media in several respects. First, it can serve as not only a communication channel but also as a transaction and distribution channel. Consumers can get information and make purchases and payments all through the Internet. No other medium can accomplish these marketing functions instantly, without resorting to other means.

Second, the Internet is by nature interactive. Users can initiate a shopping process by visiting a website and then clicking on hyperlinked text for more information. It is a two-way communication, with the Internet serving as a provider of customized content that meets an individual's needs.

Third, it has the capacity for multimedia content. It can carry not only text and graphics but also audio and video content. The multimedia nature of the Internet is suitable for high-impact advertising. It has become an integral part of the media mix for many advertisers, and new forms of advertising have filled the Internet landscape. These new forms include animated banner advertisements, sponsor logos, interstitials (a browser window entirely filled by pop-ups), advertorials (advertisements written in the form of editorial copy in a printed publication), advertainment (a combination of advertising and entertainment), and 3-D visualization.

When creating online advertisements, one needs to focus and consider several factors in order to come up with a winning advertisement. Clear goals will help you select the necessary requirements, from several options available, when actually creating the advertisement. Use these goals to identify your customer base and the sites that best satisfy their requirements. Study these sites and find out why they click. Identify the reasons that would compel users to visit these sites and convert them from casual information gatherers to repeated customers. A few essentials of online advertising are as follows:

1. Recognize the top sites where it will be profitable to place the advertisement.
2. Focus an advertisement by understanding your clients and knowing precisely what they want. Utilize this knowledge in creating effective content for advertisements. While a picture is worth a thousand words, steer clear of insensitive graphics. Come up with catchy phrases that clearly communicate the business goals and expertise.
3. Define the goal of the advertising campaign. The goal may be to produce 100 transactions, generate 1,000 visitor sessions, or produce 500 leads. Whatever it is, clearly define the objective.
4. Identify the most likely sites for achieving these goals. Sites that are most relevant to the product or service will, most probably, be the best bet; but also consider larger sites or networks that can target the audience you are trying to reach. They can be very cost effective. If there are multiple products or services that appeal to various target markets, consider sites that reach all those various segments.
5. Formulate specific promotional messages that correspond to the goals. Those promotional messages should concentrate on the major selling points of the product or service and have a strong call-to-action. For instance, 'Get a FREE Trial Issue to Entrepreneur Magazine. Sign-Up Today and Download Our FREE Report', 23 Tips for Closing a Sale. Click here for your FREE Trial Issue!'
6. Design the advertisement so that it looks like it belongs on the sites where you are advertising. For instance, you may want to use the site's font faces in your text, colour schemes in your background, font colour choices overall, and emulate images where appropriate. Try to conform to the environment so potential customers visiting the site do not gasp in shock when they see your advertisement.

## CONFLICT MANAGEMENT

> Conflicts occur when two or more competing responses or courses of action are considered for a single event.

All relationships, personal and professional, experience some kind of conflict. Conflicts occur when two or more competing responses or courses of action are considered for a single event. Conflicts are normal, natural, and sometimes even necessary for continued growth and development. Some people feel it is best to avoid conflict. While this may be appropriated at times, it is not always recommended. The main issue with conflict is not so much that it occurs, but how you manage it when it does.

My sword is sharper and stronger ... accept defeat!

Organizational conflicts arise when two or more parties, with perceived incompatible goals, seek to undermine each other's goal-seeking capability. An organizational conflict involves varied issues—sometimes it involves work-related issues such as scheduling, funds, and work assignments; at other times, it focuses on personal issues such as the amount of socialization during work hours, sexual harassment, or whether appointed consultants are doing their job efficiently. The dispute may be loud and argumentative, calm and rational, or so indirect that it is never mentioned outright.

A poorly-handled conflict can certainly be dangerous as relationships suffer and productivity declines. On the contrary, a skilfully-handled conflict can result in several benefits. It can function as a safety valve, letting people ventilate frustrations that block their effective functioning. It can lead to solving troublesome problems. It is the responsibility of the upper management, department heads, and supervisors not only to resolve conflicts but also to minimize the effects of their sources through responsible communication with each other and with their employees. Overcoming conflicts successfully often makes people feel that together they have made progress towards their mutual goals.

When teams bicker, organizations quarrel, or nations war, the predictable remedy prescribed by the voices of reason is communication. The prevailing view is that, faced with conflict, communicating is always the right thing to do.

The good news about this is that communication skills can be learned, applied, and enhanced. Those who work as conflict resolvers believe that they are effective communicators, and most of them are able to articulate the essentials of good communication. The communication process poses not only the biggest challenge to their effectiveness as conflict resolvers but also the greatest opportunity to enhance their effectiveness.

The following attitudinal principles are the basis of successful communication for everyone, particularly when dealing with conflict:

- A poorly handled conflict can certainly be dangerous as relationships suffer and productivity declines.
- Communication skills can be learned, applied, and enhanced.

1. Caring about what others are saying is the key to good communication.
2. There is always new information to learn from a communication.
3. Good communication requires focused energy.

4. Effective communication demands joint effort between speaker and the listener.
5. Communication is different from persuading, evaluating, and problem solving.
6. One should understand other people's difficulty in communicating.
7. The best communication occurs when people are genuine and natural.

It is also necessary to remember that communication is a necessary but not a sufficient condition for the resolution of complex conflicts.

## Organizational Conflicts

**Image 19.3**  Conflicts are common in organizations

Organizational teams may experience two kinds of conflicts—cognitive and affective (Image 19.3). Cognitive conflicts centre on issues and are considered healthy and functional. They force discussions and stimulate creative thinking. They make team members get involved as they examine, compare, and reconcile their differences. In addition, these conflicts also promote the acceptance of a team decision. Research shows that the best decisions are made by teams that experience healthy differences of opinion but are able to keep their conflicts aimed at issues.

### Sources of Organizational Conflicts

Organizational conflicts are not based on personal value systems; they are by-products of changing dynamics within a structure. When left unattended, these dynamics cause conflict within an organization. If these forces clash with personal values, then interpersonal conflicts can also occur.

Let us look at some common sources of conflicts in the workplace.

**Change**  It is normal, and expected, for organizations to undergo some changes. New policies, changes in operational procedures, and a certain amount of employee turnover are common internal changes all organizations experience. Externally, municipal, state, or central legislation can also require an organization to make specific changes. Other forms of change are more drastic. Reorganizations and 'rightsizing' can wreak havoc in organizations, threatening everyone's job security. Even growth can cause conflict. Although growth is normally seen as good for an organization, communication breakdown is sure to occur, responsibilities change, and reporting relationships may be shuffled. Changes within an organization definitely cause conflict.

**Conflicting goals and objectives**  Usually this is the result of poor communication and planning. The goals and objectives of one department may clash with those of another department. Better communication between department heads can usually resolve these issues.

> Organizational teams may experience two kinds of conflicts—cognitive and affective.

**Limited resources**  Limited resources can mean practically anything—not enough employees, lack of space, shortage of finances, outdated equipment, and so on. These and similar problems can cause organizational conflict by limiting expected performance of individuals, departments, and perhaps even the organization as a whole.

> Today, organizational conflicts are seen as normal and natural.

## STRATEGIES FOR MANAGING CONFLICT

A conflict in the workplace, some time back, used to be perceived as negative—something to be avoided at all costs. Associated with undesirable behaviour, it was viewed, as a characteristic of individuals who could not get along with others, were not team players, or simply did not fit in. The best way to deal with it was to avoid it. Today, conflict is viewed differently. Organizational experts tell us that conflict is normal and natural. In addition, it is viewed as an interpersonal dynamic that, when handled well, can at least be managed, often resolved, and potentially has very creative results. Today, it is critical that we recognize the importance of dealing with conflict rather than adopting the traditional response of avoiding it. Without the ability to deal with conflict, we cannot be successful in our work. Whatever our position—staff, faculty, or management—our ability to effectively manage differences is a critical factor for our personal and professional success.

How can you manage disagreements in ways that build, rather than harm, personal and collegial relationships? Such disagreements or conflicts can occur between individuals or between groups of people. Five strategies for managing conflicts or stressful situations are as follows:

- Collaborating
- Compromising
- Competing
- Accommodating
- Avoiding

**Collaborating (win–win)** Collaborative communicators are committed to working together to resolve conflicts. Collaboration is based on the assumption that it is possible to meet one's needs and those of the other person. It assumes that conflict is a natural part of life and that working with the other person will produce the best possible solution. The benefits of collaboration are clear—not only can the issue at hand be resolved, but the relationship between the parties can also be improved.

Teamwork and cooperation help everyone achieve their goals while also maintaining relationships. The process of working through differences will lead to creative solutions that will satisfy both parties' concerns.

*When to use*  Collaborations should be used when

- there is a high level of trust
- you do not want to have full responsibility
- you want others to also have 'ownership' of solutions
- the people involved are willing to change their thinking as more information is found and new options are suggested
- you need to work through animosity and hard feelings

*Drawbacks*  Collaborations have the following drawbacks:

- The process takes a lot of time and energy
- Some may take advantage of other people's trust and openness

> Teamwork and cooperation help everyone achieve their goals while also maintaining relationships.

*Example*  The management of a company announces a new policy involving the change in timings. One particular department does not agree with the management on this new policy while all others do agree. Here, a collaborative effort is one of the ways to manage the disagreement.

**Compromising (win/lose–win/lose)**   In this strategy, each party sacrifices something he/she is seeking to reach an agreement. While this approach does not give any one of the parties, in a dispute, everything he/she seeks, it provides an outcome that, by definition, everyone involved can live with.

Both ends are placed against the middle in an attempt to serve the 'common good' while ensuring that each person can maintain something of his/her original position.

*When to use*   Compromises should be worked out when

- people of equal status are equally committed to goals
- time can be saved by reaching intermediate settlements on individual parts of complex issues
- goals are moderately important
- collaboration is unsuccessful, as a backup

*Drawbacks*   This strategy has the following drawbacks:

- important values and long-term objectives can be derailed in the process
- may not work if initial demands are too great
- can spawn cynicism, especially if there is no commitment to honour the compromise solutions

*Example*   The employee union of an industry goes on strike, as the management does not accede to their request for more benefits. A compromise between the two sides might be a solution.

**Accommodating (lose–win)**   Accommodators give ground as a way of maintaining harmony. In many cases, accommodating is hard to defend. It can be equivalent to appeasement, sacrificing one's principles, and putting harmony above dealing with important issues. You could appease others by downplaying conflict, thus protecting a relationship.

*When to use*   This strategy should be used when

- an issue is not as important to you as it is to the other person
- you know you cannot win
- it is not the right time
- harmony is extremely important
- what the parties have in common is a good deal more important than their differences

*Drawbacks*   It has the following drawbacks:

- one's own ideas do not get attention
- credibility and influence can be lost

*Example*   Despite the hint from the market survey conducted by the marketing department, the production department of an organization did not change the design. Above all, the marketing division also accommodated this negligence and launched the product that turned out to be a failure. It is easy to imagine that a less accommodating approach might have caused the production department to take the survey seriously and redesign the product.

> A competitive approach is also known as the zero-sum approach.

**Competing (win–lose)**   A competitive approach to conflicts is based on the assumption that the only way for one party to reach its goals is to overcome the other. Termed also as the zero-sum approach, this approach is common in resolving many conflicts.

When goals are extremely important, one must sometimes use power to win.

*When to use* This strategy should be used when

- you know you are right
- quick decision is needed
- a strong personality is trying to steamroller you
- you need to stand up for your rights

*Drawbacks* It could have the following impact:

- Conflict may get escalated
- Losers may retaliate

*Example* An employer might find that the cost of providing on-site equipment is more than offset by reduced absenteeism and greater appeal when recruiting new employees and hence decides in favour of it. Unsympathetic management turns a deaf ear to the request of employees to make provisions for on-site exercise facilities, implying—or even stating outright—that the physical condition of employees is not the concern of the employers and that providing easy access to exercise would require a cash outlay and reduce time spent on the job. Therefore, a competitive approach seems the only way.

**Avoiding (lose—lose)** One way to deal with the conflicts is to avoid them whenever possible and withdraw when confronted. Avoid conflict by withdrawing, sidestepping, or postponing.

*When to use* This strategy should be used when

- the conflict is small and relationships are at stake
- more important issues are pressing and you feel you do not have time to deal with this particular one
- you see no chance of having your concerns met
- you are too emotionally involved and others around you can solve the conflict more successfully
- more information is needed

*Drawbacks* It has the following drawbacks:

- Important decisions may be made by default
- People may take advantage of a person who constantly avoids confrontation

*Example* In the workplace, a communicator who avoids conflicts might accept constant schedule delays or poor-quality work from a supplier to avoid confrontation or might cover up for a coworker's frequent absences even if it means doing the other person's work. Avoidance may have the short-term benefit of preventing confrontation, but there are usually long-term costs, especially in ongoing relationships.

### Role of Mediation in Conflict Resolution

> Mediation is an informal process where disputing parties discuss their situation with the goal of reaching a mutually satisfactory agreement.

Mediation is one of the most popular dispute resolution processes. It is used by corporations as an approach to conflict resolution in which a third party helps disputants arrive at a resolution to a conflict. In other words, mediation is an informal process in which disputing parties discuss their situation with the goal of reaching a mutually satisfactory agreement or gaining new perceptions about the situation, with the help of a neutral third party that serves as an intermediary

Mediation through meditation

between the disputing parties to help them reach their own agreement or resolution.

A mediator does not make a decision or impose a solution, but assists the disputants as they attempt to find their own way through the conflict. Under the right circumstances, mediation makes a big difference to how well people handle conflicts. Disputes involving business-to-business rifts are best suited for mediation.

**Attributes of successful mediators** Following are some attributes required to be a successful mediator:

*Experienced* Those with previous experience of the mediation process and conflict-management communication make the best mediators.

*Ethical* Honest and principled people make the best mediators.

*Creative* Mediators must be masters at teaching creativity because they want the disputing parties to come up with as many ideas as possible. The mediator must be creative in all stages of mediation.

*Flexible* A mediator models behaviour that he/she wishes the parties to emulate. Being flexible is an important skill when working with people. If one way of getting people to work together fails, another might succeed.

*Engaged in ongoing mediation training* A good mediator is always learning new methodologies and skills so that he/she does not get stuck doing things one way.

*Empowering* Good mediators empower the disputing parties to reach their own resolution.

**Stages of mediation** The stages of mediation are as follows:

1. Stage one—Introduction (initial statement of intentions)
2. Stage two—Problem determination (parties' statements)
3. Stage three—Problem identification (clarification of presentation and underlying problems and statement of parties' intent to resolve conflict)
4. Stage four—Generation and evaluation of objects (creative thinking/brainstorming/idea generation)
5. Stage five—Selection of options (testing for workability)
6. Stage six—Agreement/no agreement/partial agreement

> Good mediators empower the disputing parties to reach their own resolution.

*Introduction* The mediator's introductory statement is important. It sets the stage for the mediation. Mediation is often called a 50–50 proposition—50 per cent of the role is the mediator's, by keeping the structure and guiding process; 50 per cent of the role is the parties', by taking responsibility for the substance of the dispute. During the introduction, the mediator.

- helps empower the parties by emphasizing the major roles that they will play in the mediation
- establishes an informal environment and states how much time is available for the mediation
- determines whether the parties are ready and able to begin the mediation.

*Problem determination*   In this stage, each of the parties has the opportunity to make a statement, fully describing his/her perspectives of the situation. Often the person who brought the complaint begins. The mediator may ask neutral, open-ended questions to clarify the issues and terms. The mediator also may reframe or restate, if necessary, in order to defuse any negative words or phrases. While each party is talking, the mediator listens intently, using active listening techniques. He/she takes notes to facilitate recall and tracking; pays attention to the body language and other non-verbal communication of both parties. He/she then summarizes each party's perspective.

*Problem identification*   This stage involves clarification of the presenting or underlying problems and a statement of the parties' intent to resolve the conflict. After the summary in stage two, the mediator requests each party to clarify the presenting problem or issue (e.g., 'What would you like to accomplish during this mediation?', 'What are your issues?', etc.). If the parties have several issues, the mediator assists them in assigning priorities to these issues. He/she then assists the parties in discerning whether there are any underlying issues, which often centre on longstanding difficulties that have festered into an overt conflict.

*Generation and evaluation of options*   The mediator helps the parties discuss relevant contract clauses, regulations, methods of conduct, or what, if any, restrictions there might be on creating the best solution. He/she then assists the parties to think creatively and search for remedies and potential solutions.

*Agreement/no agreement/partial agreement*   During this final stage of mediation, the mediator helps parties to clarify the selected option and work out the details that may include exploring all identifiable 'what ifs'. He/she then helps the parties summarize the agreement and drafts the agreement. The mediator congratulates the parties on their success and arranges for any follow-up. If there is no agreement, the mediator refers the case back to the sponsoring agency or court.

Successful mediators require skills in questioning because the questions that they pose to the parties involved in conflict are vital, not only for eliciting relevant information or for clarifying some issues, but for a number of varied reasons.

*Questioning skills*   Communication is composed of a sender, receiver, and message. Effective communication takes place when the receiver understands the message the way the sender intended. Questioning is a communication skill that is used to help a receiver understand a message better. If a question is to be effective, there needs to be a purpose for asking the question. Legitimate purposes include the following:

- Gathering needed information
- Understanding facts of past events that led to the present situation
- Understanding the consequences or results of the situation
- Focusing attention on a particular angle or topic
- Directing the path of the conversation
- Encouraging someone to think about an issue in a different way
- Concluding a communication

> Effective communication takes place when the receiver understands the message the way the sender intended.

Two examples of questions related to concluding a communication are as follows:

1. Are we clear about this situation?
2. Is there anything more we need to talk about related to this issue?

> Effective questioning skills elicit information that might not otherwise be revealed.

Effective questioning skills elicit information that might not otherwise be revealed. It clarifies things, identifies issues and facts, and provides new insights or meanings. Effective questioning is part of good listening skills. It lets speakers know that they are heard and that the listeners want to understand. On the other hand, ineffective questions may place the receiver on the defensive, thus hindering communication. Questions should not make any one uncomfortable or irritated. Some general rules for asking questions are as follows:

1. Ask only essential or necessary questions.
2. Have a reason beyond curiosity to ask a question.
3. Be aware of how many questions are asked.
4. Avoid questions beginning with 'why'.
5. Avoid double or multiple questions in order to allow the receiver to respond to one question at a time.
6. Avoid leading questions.
7. Be aware of the tone of voice in which the question is asked.
8. Phrase questions so that the answer you want is easy for the respondent to give.

### Words and Phrases in Conflict Resolution

We often use words and phrases that cause the receiver to react negatively. For instance, some receivers cringe when they hear a sentence that starts with the phrase 'by the way'. This is because the phrase appears to convey a secondary thought or afterthought as in, 'By the way, we would not have put on the fund-raising drive if it had not been for your organizational skills'. Used this way, the phrase 'by the way' diminishes what follows. It is also used to make something that is being sneaked into the conversation appear offhand or casual, as in, 'By the way, I will not be at the meeting tomorrow'.

There are a variety of target words and phrases that arise while mediating. Some of them are as follows:

**Apology** When a request for an apology becomes an impediment to the conflict-resolution process, it can be helpful to reframe or refocus the discussion. When one party is fixated on an apology, sometimes asking the person to reframe his or her desire is helpful. The person may say that he/she just wants to hear the other party say that he/she regrets what has happened.

**Compromise** The word 'compromise' sometimes is a volatile term in mediation. Parties often state, 'I will not compromise my principles.'

**Threat** Any phrase such as 'or else', or sentence, such as, 'You will be sorry', that is perceived as a threat is a definite block to communication and mediation.

> In conflict-resolution communication, it is usually best to keep one's communication as neutral as possible.

**Side, story, facts, and truth** Consider this opening used by a mediator: 'Each of you will have an opportunity to tell your side of the story. I want to know the facts and what you consider to be the truth in this case.' This opening is loaded with explosive words—'side', 'story', 'facts', and 'truth'. Any of these can block communication. The parties involved believe that they are not telling a story and that there are no sides, only the truth and facts. The mediator should rather say: 'Each of you will have an opportunity to voice your perspective or view of the situation.'

> The key non-verbal elements play a major role in conflict-resolution process.

In conflict-resolution communication, it is usually best to keep one's communication as neutral as possible. Practicing the art of positive or neutral communication is not easy, and it may take a great deal of time to effect a change in one's habits.

A few sample words that are used in positive and negative connotations are as follows:

**Positive/neutral words**   Full, curiosity, spontaneity, habit, calm, active, pleasure, life, energy, enthusiasm, ready

**Negative words**   Anger, forgiveness, closure, complain, compromise, criticism, cynicism, pride, superior, skeptic, tough

### Non-verbal Elements

An understanding of non-verbal communication is vital when you are mediating or trying to resolve a conflict with your disputant by yourself. Moreover, using positive non-verbal communication yourself will make you a better person in the process.

Among the various non-verbal elements that we have discussed in this book, the four key elements—posture, facial expression, tone of voice, and limb position—play a major role in conflict-resolution process. Of these, the tone of voice is the most easily disguised and should not be the only element on which a judgement is based.

During the process of conflict resolution, when the other side is speaking, reassure it by using positive body language—make a lot of eye contact, smile, nod in agreement with their major points, and generally act as though you are persuaded by their arguments. This tends to draw the other side out by making it feel that you are easier to negotiate with.

## NEGOTIATION

Negotiation is, undoubtedly, a part of our everyday life. You need to negotiate with people around you when you are

- deciding on a date for the next meeting of your project group,
- agreeing on realistic project deadlines,
- deciding on a strategic alliance with another firm,
- agreeing about a change of work rules with the union,
- getting a raise in pay,
- deciding the new work timings for shop floor employees, and/or
- choosing a new location for the office.

The stakes may be different in each of the above cases, but the common thread running through them is the need for negotiation skills. Negotiating is an activity that all managers engage in to some degree, perhaps dozens of times every day. The aim of negotiation is to explore a situation to find a solution that is acceptable to both parties.

Negotiation is the process in which two or more individuals or groups, having both common and conflicting goals, state and discuss proposals for specific terms of a possible agreement. It normally

> Good negotiation skills are essential for the smooth running of any business.

occurs between companies, groups, or individuals because one has something the other wants and is willing to bargain to get it. Negotiation is one of the key skills of conflict resolution or dispute resolution and is central to success because it combines communication, persuasion, and resolution. It is usually regarded as a form of alternative dispute resolution.

Good negotiation skills are essential for the smooth running of any business. One should be able to negotiate in many different situations to get the results that are wanted and needed every time.

## Communication and Effective Negotiation

Clear communication is the key to effective negotiation. All the three important skills—listening, understanding, and speaking—that are encompassed in communication are vital for negotiating effectively. You cannot have one skill work without the others—for instance, you cannot have good understanding without good listening and speaking. Negotiation is most effective when people are able to clearly identify and discuss their sources of disagreement and misunderstanding.

### Listening

The best listeners almost always turn out to be the best negotiators (Image 19.4). Why? Invariably, the best negotiators observe the communication skills (both verbal and non-verbal) of their counterparts, they note how other negotiators use word choice and sentence structure for effect; and they study vocal skills like pitch, tonal quality, and rate of speech.

As an active process of concentrating all of one's attention on the other person, listening enables you to encourage the other person to share thoughts and feelings.

**Image 19.4** Good negotiators are good listeners

### Speaking

Negotiation processes are often most effective when the disputing parties take time to think through what to say. When possible, both parties should plan ahead to meet at a time and place convenient to both. The negotiation begins with a clear and concise explanation of the problem as each party sees it. For instance, when you negotiate for a price with a consultant, you may find your communication smoother when you say, 'I become very upset when you quote an exorbitant price', rather than saying, 'You make me mad when you quote an exorbitant price,' as the latter appears to be an aggressive statement.

### Understanding

If two negotiating parties do not understand each other's problems and concerns, then the process of negotiation will either be broken off or will end with solutions that do not work. Hence, a common understanding must be reached before the two parties can look for solutions. To ensure proper understanding of your negotiating partner's statements and feelings, avoid assuming things. Rather, develop the practice of asking questions such as 'Did I hear you correctly?', 'I sense you are under pressure. Do you want to talk

> Clear communication is the key to effective negotiation.

about this?', or 'I'd like to hear from you about how you are feeling on this aspect'. These questions or statements encourage communication and better understanding between the negotiating parties.

## Basic Approaches to Negotiation

'In a co-operative situation, the goals are so linked that everybody "sinks or swims" together, while in the competitive situation, if one swims, the other must sink,' says Morton Deutsch E.L. Thorndike, Professor and Director Emeritus of the International Center for Cooperation and Conflict Resolution at Teachers College, Columbia University.

The basic approaches to negotiation or bargaining are as follows:

- Integrative (collaborative or win–win)
- Distributive (competitive or win–lose)
- Mixed

The differences between an integrative and a distributive negotiation ar given in Table 19.1.

### The Win–Win or Integrative Approach

In these negotiations, the prospects for both side's gains are encouraging. Both sides attempt to reconcile their positions so that the end result is an agreement which will benefit both—therefore, the resultant agreement tends to be stable. Win/win negotiations are characterized by open and empathetic communications and are commonly referred to as partnership agreements.

### The Win–Lose or Distributive Approach

The second is called the distributive or win/lose approach. In these negotiations, each of the parties seeks maximum gains and, therefore, seeks to impose maximum losses on the other side. This approach often produces agreements that are inherently unstable, as represented by the triangle balanced on its apex.

### The Mixed Approach

In real life negotiations, both of these processes tend to be at work together. It needs to be emphasized that many situations contain elements of both distributive and integrative negotiating. For example, in negotiating a price with a customer, to some degree your interests oppose the customer's (you want a higher price; he/she wants a lower one) but to some degree your interests coincide (you want both you and your customer to be happy).

## Six Basic Steps of Negotiations

It is now time to look at the six basic steps involved in the negotiating process. Each step, regardless of the time it takes, is important. Once you understand the steps and their purpose, you will be able to effectively meet any negotiating challenge. The following discussion through an example would facilitate your understanding of these six steps (Fig. 19.3):

### Getting to Know One Another

Negotiating is like any other social situation that has a business purpose. It moves more smoothly when the parties take time to get to know one another. It is helpful to assess those involved before negotiations begin.

**Table 19.1** Differences between integrated and distributive negotiations

| Integrated Negotiation | Distributive Negotiation |
|---|---|
| • Both sides can win. | • One side wins and the other loses. |
| • Promotes effective communication where ideas are verbalized, group members pay attention to one another, accept ideas, and are influenced by them. These groups have less problems communicating with and understanding others. | • Communication is obstructed as the conflicting parties try to gain advantage by misleading each other through false promises and misinformation. Communication is ultimately reduced as the parties realize they cannot trust each another to be honest and informative. |
| • There are a variable amount of resources to be divided. | • There are fixed resources to be divided so that the more one gets, the less the other gets. |
| • One person's interests coincide with the other's. | • One person's interests oppose the others. |
| • The dominant concern here is to maximize joint outcomes. | • The dominant concern in this type of bargaining is usually maximizing one's own interests. |
| • Dominant strategies include cooperation, sharing information, and mutual problem solving. | • Dominant strategies include manipulation, forcing, and withholding information. |
| • This type is called 'creating values' since the goal here is to have both sides leave the negotiating feeling that they have greater value than before. | • This type is also called 'claiming value' since the strategies involved deteriorate the value and relationships become bitter. |

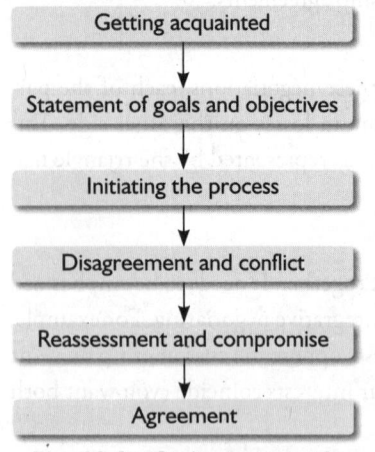

**Fig. 19.3** Six basic steps of negotiation

### Statement of Goals and Objectives

Negotiating normally flows after the opening, into a general statement of goals and objectives by the involved parties. Specific issues may not be raised at this time because the parties are just beginning to explore the needs of the other. You need to build an atmosphere of cooperation and mutual trust. For example, as a salesperson offers to show Neha the available refrigerators, she comments, 'I hope I can find a model I like at a fair price. I was attracted to this store because you seem to be able to make a profit and give the customer a good buy at the same time. I feel both are important.'

### Starting the Process

Some negotiations are complex and have many issues to be resolved. Others may only have a few. Also, individual issues may vary greatly in complexity. No one can predict the direction negotiations will take until both parties have presented the issues. There may be hidden needs that neither party has raised, but these will surface as talks proceed. A skilled negotiator will study the issues closely before negotiations begin in order to determine where the advantages lie, in so far as splitting or combining issues.

> Some negotiations are complex and have many issues to be resolved.

### Expressions of Disagreement and Conflict

Once the issues have been defined, disagreement and conflict will often occur. Good negotiators never try to avoid this phase because they realize that this process of give and take is where successful deals are made.

### Keys to Integrative Bargaining

- Orient yourself towards a win-win approach: your attitude when going into negotiation plays a huge role in the outcome
- Plan and have a concrete strategy and be clear on what is important to you and why it is important
- Know your BATNA (Best Alternative to a Negotiated Agreement)
- Separate people from the problem
- Focus on interests, not positions; consider the other party's situation
- Create options for mutual gain
- Generate a variety of possibilities before deciding what to do
- Aim for an outcome based on some objective standard
- Pay a lot of attention to the flow of negotiation
- Take the intangibles into account; communicate carefully
- Use active listening skills; rephrase, ask questions, and then ask some more

> Conflict has a way of bringing out different points of view.

Disagreement and conflict, handled properly, will eventually bring the negotiators together. If handled poorly, it will widen the differences. Conflict has a way of bringing out different points of view.

### Reassessment and Compromise

At some point, normally, one party will move towards compromise (Image 19.5). Statements reflecting this often begin with words like 'Suppose that ...?', 'What if ...?', or 'How would you feel about ...?' When these statements begin, the other negotiator should listen carefully to see if an attempt to compromise is being offered. The response should be carefully stated.

### Agreement in Principle or Settlement

When an agreement is reached, it will be necessary to affirm it. This normally means placing the agreed terms in writing. If possible, this should be done while the parties are together so they can agree on the language.

Since agreement is the ultimate objective of any negotiation, it is important to determine the level of authority of the party you are negotiating with at the outset. Remember that when you have the authority to make an agreement, always strive to negotiate with a person who has the same level of authority.

### Planning and Preparation

Successful negotiation comes from the skilful execution of a plan. Here are certain guidelines for effectively planning your negotiation process:

### Begin by Thinking through Your Objectives

Once your objectives are established, concentrate on the issues and categorize them

**Image 19.5** Compromise is a part of negotiation

> **Complex Negotiations**
>
> Neha is interested in buying a new refrigerator. She has studied advertisements in the newspapers and selected an appliance shop that seems to have good prices. She has done enough homework to know exactly what she wants and has a good idea of what she should pay. On entering the store, she introduces herself to a salesperson, learns his/her name, and tells him/her she would like to have someone who knows refrigerators show her different models. She is careful to clearly establish her purpose and a business-like tone. She observes the salesperson's attitude and approach to the sale closely to pick up clues to the stores sales policies, willingness to bargain, and desire to satisfy new customers.
>
> The salesperson responds to Neha's statement by asking her what she wants in a refrigerator in terms of size, accessories, and efficiency of operation. He/she also asks her for a price range. Neha outlines her needs and the salesperson acknowledges they can be met by most of the manufacturers he/she represents. He/she does tell her, however, that she has selected some expensive options that will take her above her expressed price range. Neha replies, 'I do not see why they should.'
>
> Neha determines the model she wants and asks the price. The salesperson says, '₹17,999.' Neha is shocked because, by her understanding of the advertisements, it should not be more than ₹15,500 and she says so. The salesperson points out that this particular model has two features not included in the sales models. Neha acknowledges this but still questions the added cost.
>
> After some discussion, Neha says, 'I just can't pay that much. I will look elsewhere.' The salesperson suggests a cheaper model, but Neha stands firm. The salesperson then says, 'Could you handle ₹17,000? Neha echoes, '₹17,000?' The salesperson adds, 'That includes transportation and connection'. Neha answers, 'I cannot exceed ₹15,500.'
>
> The salesperson responds to Neha's offer of ₹15,500 by saying , 'I just could not do that but I will let you have it for ₹16,500.' Neha replies, 'Well, okay. If that includes delivery and installation you can write up the order.'

as major or minor concerns. Do this not only for your issues but also for those issues that you anticipate the other party will be concerned about.

Assume that a company based in India and another based in the US want to merge. People keep focusing too much on the money. When it is a merger, you might have noticed that the two chairmen will talk about what money is going to change hands and who is going to be the chairman. All the other issues of getting the two companies to work together—different cultures, pay scales, titles, etc.—do not get proper attention. They have not thought through implementing the agreement. They have not thought through all the concerns of who gets laid off. How do you merge two departments that are geographically and financially different?

### Develop a Time Perspective

After being satisfied with the study of objectives and issues and gathering information to support one's position, decide how much time to devote to the effort, and also estimate the time factors for your opponent. Time is often a pressure point that can force concessions that one would prefer not to make.

> Successful negotiation comes from the skilful execution of the plan.

### Identify Sources of Power

The relative power of the parties is another key factor to consider during your preparation. Power, in this instance, is not defined as the ability to force an action; but rather to influence an outcome by logic, validity, or legitimacy of a position. Following are some positive sources of power:

**Persistence**   Do not concede or back off at the first sign of resistance. Give the other party time to think and consider alternatives. Then try again.

**Competition**   There is always competition for what you have, whether it is money, ideas, or products. Never forget that people always have options.

**Expertise**   Use what you have. You will receive more consideration from people who believe that you have more knowledge, skill, or expertise than they do.

**Legitimacy**   Give your position and yourself legitimacy by using supportive documentation. This often has great influence whether deserved or not.

**Involvement**   Get everyone involved. Personal involvement often will cause those participating in negotiation to work hard to ensure it does not fail.

**Attitude**   Do not relieve tension on the other negotiator. If you need time to reduce stress, take a break. Try to maintain a win-win attitude.

## Guidelines for Successful Negotiation

In the business world, you must negotiate constantly with clients, suppliers, colleagues, and even supervisors. Consider the following pointers, and you will be able to successfully use your decision-making skills during negotiations and come to sound solutions and business decisions.

### Set Up Your Goals and Plan Your Negotiation Time

Be sure that you go into negotiations with concrete goals in mind, some of which are as follows:

1. What is the most important goal for me?
2. What is actually negotiable?
3. What are the alternatives?
4. What do I want as compensation if we come to a concession?
5. Where is the compromise threshold, where should I lay down the line?

For example, if you go in to see your boss for a raise, and you cannot give rational reasons for the raise, then you do not even need to bother walking into the negotiations—you will not accomplish anything.

Also, be sure that you do not just keep your own goals in mind. A successful negotiation is one where the needs of all concerned are taken into account.

### Genuinely Communicate Your Own Strengths

Make sure that strengths are communicated, regardless of whether others have the same strengths or not. Today's negotiation coaches recommend 'saying what you really think'. Honesty and trustworthiness are most important because the others can see any discrepancy between verbal and non-verbal communication.

### Pick the Right Moment

When preparing for negotiations, do not just think about which arguments to use, but think about when, during the negotiation process, would it be the best time to use them. By planning this way, arguments are made more potent. A serious and executable decision can seldom be made when negotiations are hurried.

### Be Fair and Objective

When negotiating, keep cool and do not let your emotions get the best of you. If you feel provoked or insulted by the others, change the subject and address the negotiation climate rather than the subject matter. Wait for a little while, start at a new and uncontroversial point in the argument, and act as if nothing had happened.

### Listen Attentively, Ask Questions, Repeat, and Summarize

> - Hurried negotiations do not lead to executable decisions.
> - Concentrate on the message that the others are trying to get across to you.

In order to avoid misunderstandings and vagueness, and to effectively navigate the others through the negotiations, keep the following pointers in mind:

1. Concentrate on the message that the others are trying to get across to you. Be patient, talk less, and wait to succeed in a negotiation. Your silence allows the others to express their ideas, which makes them feel that they are being taken seriously and gives you time to get an overall grasp on things. When negotiating, stamina and endurance usually count the most.
2. Do not interpret statements according to your understanding of them; instead, ask questions to clear any doubtful issue. Skilfully formed questions show that you are listening attentively and are trying to figure out the motives and the background behind the other's argument.
3. When negotiating, use the question, 'What would you suggest?' as often as possible. This will not only make the others happy, but later on, nobody would be able to say that they did not have the chance to state their opinions.
4. Repeat basic statements throughout the negotiation process—by saying, 'Have I correctly understood that …?' you let others know that you are paying attention to what is being discussed and that you want to ensure that you understood it correctly. Avoid making your own interpretations, judgements, or assumptions.

### 'Visualize' Your Arguments

During negotiations, do not just make claims, but make ideas clear with easy-to-follow steps. You can do this by using charts, graphs, diagrams, charts, or overheads. These visual aids make arguments and calculations easier to understand and accept.

### Use Clever Phrases

To keep the negotiations from running headlong into a brick wall, do not always reply directly, but form your arguments wisely.

**Transform the argument**   Instead of saying, 'I see this differently,' you are better off saying, 'You are talking about a problem that can be seen from many different angles. In this case, the most important thing is ….'

**Reinterpret**   Instead of saying, 'I am of a completely different opinion …,' you should say, 'That is a good point, but I think we should also take into consideration ….'

**Ignore**   Instead of saying, 'No, that will never work,' you should say, 'Yes, that is an important problem, but let us concentrate on the following situation for now.'

**Forward an argument**   Instead of saying, 'We will not come to a solution that way,' you should say, 'Before we come to a conclusion, we have to consider ….'

### Dealing with Defeat

Be aware that a negotiation is a constant game of give and take. Do not automatically consider a compromise as a defeat.

### Confirmation and Summary

Never leave a negotiation without summarizing what you believe has been agreed upon. This gives both sides the chance to clear up any misunderstandings. For example, you many say, 'So, let us just summarize what we have agreed today—you are going to reduce your delivery period by two weeks, and we are going to pay immediately on receipt of the goods. Is that correct?' Points that are mentioned at the end usually stick best in people's minds and both parties can walk away with the knowledge that they have reached a solution.

## INTERCULTURAL NEGOTIATION

There is so much international business these days that we seldom give much thought to the pitfalls of negotiations with prospective business partners or customers from a different cultural background. The most critical phase for an international venture is the first negotiation. Consider the following example:

> An American executive flew to Tokyo to land a contract with a Japanese company. He told his boss that he would be back in a week with the contract in hand. On Monday, his first day in Tokyo, his Japanese counterpart invited him to play golf. They played, and the American won the game by a couple of strokes. The next day, the American expected to have a business meeting, but his counterpart wanted to play golf again. They did, and the American won again. When his host suggested another game the next day, the American blurted out in frustration, 'But when are we going to start doing business?' His host, taken aback, responded, 'But we have been doing business!' Since the American did not realize what was going on, he probably did not make the best business use of those golf outings. At the very least, he could have tried to lose on the second day (although his host, not wanting a guest to lose face, might have made it difficult for him to do so). As it turned out, they started meetings on the third day and a contract was signed on Saturday, but the American was in such a hurry to conclude the contract within the week that he conceded a number of points as his self-imposed deadline approached.

The story illustrates conflicting culture-based business practices that can cripple a deal before it even starts.

First, the two concerned individuals had different objectives in mind. The Japanese executive did not care much about signing a contract. His culture is strongly collective, in which life in general depends on close relationships, beginning with one's immediate family. In business, a contract is merely a guideline pertaining to one small transaction of a larger relationship between the parties. What he wanted was to get to know the American, to determine whether this was someone on whom he could depend in the future, and to build a relationship that would lead to not just one contract but many.

The American's primary objective was to get a signature on that particular contract. His culture is strongly individualistic, one that emphasizes self-reliance and individual accomplishment. He had promised that he would return home with a signed contract for this transaction, not with some vague understanding for unknown deals that might or might not ever come to pass.

> As the world becomes increasingly connected, people must consider the important issue of intercultural negotiation.

Second, the two executives had very different concepts of time. For the Japanese executive, time is important but it takes a back seat to getting things right. For him, the relationship needed to get off to a good start. This would take as much time as needed. Then, in discussing the terms of the contract, everything had to be fully understood. This, too, would take as much time as needed. For the American, time is a precious commodity, not to be wasted on golf or 'nit-picking' the terms of a standard contract that was comprehensible only to lawyers. The bottom line for him was that the contract needed to be signed by the end of the week. Some international businesspeople take advantage of the cultural ignorance of their counterparts. They sacrifice long-term success for short-term gain. For an Asian, plans for the first business negotiation might include suggesting that the negotiating schedule build in more time for social events and longer negotiating sessions. For a Westerner, it might require developing proposals for a more extensive relationship between their two companies. A party to an international business negotiation, long before its first negotiating session with someone from another culture or country, needs to develop a negotiating plan that will minimize potential conflicts and augment the chances of reaching an agreement—and a business relationship—that will stand the tests of time.

As the world becomes increasingly connected, people, both at home and while travelling abroad, must consider the important issue of intercultural negotiation.

### The Intercultural Dimension

All cultures have their own preferred styles and strategies for dealing with and managing conflict. Yet, it is quite difficult to be culture-specific when discussing about how to deal effectively with cross-cultural conflicts. Nevertheless, there are some general skills involved in cross-cultural negotiation and conflict management that can be highlighted. A basic requirement for effective conflict management and negotiation is to know as much as possible about the other culture(s). Although experiential knowledge is preferable, research of the culture, norms, values, history, society, etc. can be very helpful. The most significant feature of good cross-cultural relations, as most cross-cultural sources will indicate, involves avoiding stereotypes. Although certain generalizations may be fairly assessed with regard to how certain cultures deal with conflict, individual differences should always be considered paramount. In fact, some cultural specialists suggest that all conflicts are intercultural to an extent, since each individual person has her/his own personal history and experience, own set of beliefs, values and assumptions, and, ultimately, own set of 'survival skills'.

### Five Intercultural Negotiation Skills

Proficient intercultural negotiation involves learning from the experiences of others and avoiding major mistakes. Business negotiations, for example, particularly those involving investment decisions, require a deep understanding of the socio-economic and political situation of the host country. There may also be considerations involving political or cultural sensitivity. Five fundamental skills that are essential for successful intercultural negotiations are as follows:

> Proficient intercultural negotiation involves learning from the experiences of others and avoiding major mistakes.

- The ability to empathize with others. So as to be able to see the world as other people see it and to understand the behaviour of others from their perspective

- The ability to demonstrate the advantages of what one proposes so that counterparts in the negotiation will be willing to change their positions
- The ability to manage stress and cope with ambiguity as well as unpredictable demands that are often part of intercultural negotiations
- The ability to express one's own ideas in ways that will help the people with whom one negotiates to objectively and fully understand the objectives and intentions at stake
- Sensitivity to the cultural backgrounds of others, along with an ability to adjust one's objectives and intentions in accordance with existing constraints and limitations

### COMMUNICATION TOOL

**Mistakes to be Avoided during Intercultural Negotiations**

1. Avoid looking at everything from your own definition of what is 'rational', 'logical', and 'scientific'.
2. Avoid pressuring the other party with a point that he/she is not readily prepared to accept; wait for a more favourable time.
3. Avoid looking at issues from the narrow perspective of self-interest.
4. Avoid asking for concessions or compromises which are politically or culturally sensitive; you will not succeed with this kind of approach.
5. Avoid adhering to your agenda if the other party appears to have a different set of priorities.
6. Avoid speaking in jargon (i.e., using colloquialisms), which can confuse the other party and even create a feeling of mistrust.
7. Avoid passing over levels of authority in matters that affect the interest of middle level officials. The top tier of hierarchy may have the power to commit the organization or governing entity, but implementation will require the support of people at intermediate and lower levels.
8. Avoid asking for a decision when you know that the other party is not able to commit.

## SUMMARY

Many business people at many levels are greatly concerned about their relationships with other people on the job. Persuasive communication includes skills, methods, and techniques to achieve a positive outcome from one-on-one and group communication.

One of the most important goals of language and communication is persuasion. A great deal of the communication that is directed towards us seeks to change our minds about issues and objects, to change our feelings about things, to change our tastes, and to change the way we behave. And much of the communication we direct towards others also seeks to achieve such changes. We may attempt to persuade others through a variety of means, consciously or unconsciously, for example, by highlighting the positive aspects, being economical with the truth, using humour, waiting till the other person seems to be in the right mood, reeling off facts and figures, or trying to make the other person feel anxious about the consequences of not complying.

The three major forms of persuasive communication, namely advertising, conflict management and negotiation, testify to the fact that persuasion plays a significant role in business. It enables business enterprises to achieve their goals, thereby paving the way for their success in the business arena. The effective strategies used in these three forms enable businesspeople to achieve success in their respective activities. Hence, it is important for businesspersons to develop the skills of persuasion while creating an advertisement, managing a conflict, or negotiating a deal for their businesses.

## KEY TERMS

***Advertising*** It can be defined as an impersonal communication of information, usually paid for and usually persuasive in nature, about products (goods and services) or ideas by identified sponsors through various media.

***Advertising communication*** It refers to the process through which the message of an advertisement is communicated to the target audience and the effectiveness of the advertisement is observed by the source.

***AIDA*** It refers to the master formula to create an effective advertisement or to assess the general appropriateness of a print advertisement. This acronym stands for attention, interest, desire, and action.

***Conflict management strategies*** These fall under five categories—collaborating, compromising, accommodating, competing, and avoiding.

***Dimensions*** Multiple dimensions are involved in advertising communication. The source dimensions are the sponsor, the author, and the persona; the message dimensions are autobiography, narrative, and drama; and the receiver dimensions are the implied, sponsors, and actual consumers.

***Feedback*** It may take a variety of forms in advertising—redeemed coupons, telephone inquiries, visits to stores, requests for more information, sales, or responses to a survey.

***Media*** It refers to, in advertising, communication vehicles such as newspapers, magazines, radios, television sets, billboards, direct mails, and the Internet. Advertisers use media to convey commercial messages to their target audiences, and media depend, to different degrees, on advertising revenues to cover the cost of their operations.

***Mediation*** It is one of the most popular dispute-resolution processes. It is an approach to conflict resolution in which a third party helps disputants arrive at a resolution to a conflict. In other words, mediation is an informal process in which disputing parties discuss their situation with the goal of reaching a mutually satisfactory agreement or gaining new perceptions about a situation, with the help of a neutral third party who serves as an intermediary between the disputing parties.

***Negotiation*** It is the process whereby interested parties resolve disputes, agree upon courses of action, bargain for individual or collective advantage, and/or attempt to craft outcomes which serve their mutual interests. Negotiation is a universal human activity and is needed in every relationship that we form.

***Noise*** It is anything that interferes with the encoding and decoding of messages between the source and the sender. In general, noise falls into three categories—environmental, mechanical, and psychological.

***Online advertising*** It refers to the method of advertising through the Internet that can carry not only text and graphics but also audio and visual content. The multimedia nature of the Internet is suitable for high-impact advertising. Companies can advertise their products on the sites that best suit their customers' needs.

***Organizational conflicts*** These are situations that arise when two or more parties, with perceived incompatible goals, seek to undermine each other's goal-seeking capability. Organizational teams may experience two kinds of conflicts—cognitive and affective. Cognitive conflicts centre on issues and are considered healthy and functional. On the other hand, affective conflicts aim, not at issues but, at feelings and personalities. They are disruptive and dysfunctional.

***Sources of organizational conflict*** These refer to changes, limited resources, conflicting goals and objectives, and a domino effect.

***Stages of mediation*** These are introduction (initial statement of intentions), problem determination (parties' statements), problem identification (clarification of presentation and underlying problems and statement of parties' intent to resolve conflict), generation and evaluation of objects (creative thinking/ brainstorming/idea generation), selection of options (testing for workability), and agreement/no agreement/partial agreement.

***Three basic communication concepts*** These are signs, field of experience, and meaning. Signs are the working tools of the communicator and are visual, verbal, or audio elements that stand separate and alone between the participants in the communication. Field of experience refers to the consumer's experiences, the knowledge of which the advertisers use to manipulate signs. Meaning results only when signs are shared by advertisers and consumers, that is, when they both interpret the message to mean the same thing.

**Win–lose or distributive approach** In the win–lose or distributive approach to negotiations, each of the parties seeks maximum gains and, therefore, usually seeks to impose maximum losses on the other side. This approach often produces inherently unstable agreements.

**Win–win or integrative approach** In the win–win or integrative approach to negotiations, the prospects for both side's gains are encouraging. Both sides attempt to reconcile their positions so that the end result is an agreement under which both will benefit, therefore the resultant agreement tends to be stable. Win/win negotiations are characterized by open and empathetic communications and are commonly referred to as partnership agreements.

## Concept Review Questions

1. Discuss the multiple dimensions that the components of advertising communication process acquire as compared to the single dimension they have in a general purpose communication.
2. Explain any five essentials of online advertisements.
3. What is the role of a mediator in a conflict resolution process?
4. Discuss the two types of organizational conflicts with suitable examples.
5. Explain the various stages of mediation in resolving a conflict.
6. Distinguish between the collaborating and accommodating strategies of conflict resolution.

## Critical Thinking Questions

1. Analyse the format elements of any two advertisements and discuss their effectiveness with reference to the AIDA formula.
2. Creative without strategy is 'art'. Creative with strategy is 'advertising'. – by Jeff Richards, Professor and Chairman of the University of Texas Advertising Department
Elaborate on this statement using any two advertisements of your choice.
3. Assume that you are the project manager of a company. Among the five strategies of conflict resolution process, which one would you use to resolve a dispute between two members of your team? Invent the necessary details.
4. The managing director of a large industrial corporation is thinking of a strategy to resolve a conflict that has come up between two of his managers—manager—marketing and manager—HR. The main point of dispute is whether the market survey that the marketing manager is proposing should include issues related to the personal habits of the respondent. Assuming the role of the MD, explain how you would proceed to solve this tussle and what specific questions you would ask as a mediator. Also, list at least 10 positive words that you would use and 10 negative words you would like to avoid during this process.

## Projects

1. Form two groups consisting of three members each. Design a print advertisement for creating awareness among the public on water conservation. Compare and contrast the effectiveness of the advertisement each group has created.
2. Visit a village in your neighbourhood and conduct a survey to find out the types of conflicts that arise in that village. You can talk to the village officers or people of that village to gather information. Also find out how they resolve the conflicts. You can also

visit any business organization to conduct the same survey. Analyse both the data to find out how the types and strategies of conflict resolution differ in these two cases.
3. Consider two companies that wish to have an agreement on their merger proposal. Before signing the MoU (memorandum of understanding), both the parties negotiate on various issues. Form two parties consisting of two members each. Assume that each party represents the top executives such as chairman and vice-chairman of some industries. Make seating arrangements with a table and two chairs on either side. Identify the relevant issues and start the negotiation process. Ask a group of people to evaluate your negotiation strategies.

## REFERENCES

Arens, William F. 1996, *Contemporary Advertising*, Sixth Edn, Irwin Publishing, Chicago, pp. 6–13.

Deutch, Morton and Peter T. Coleman 2000, ed. Jossey Bass, *The Handbook of Conflict Resolution*, Wiley & Sons, San Fransico, pp. 132–39.

Dicker, Laurie 2004, *Making Conflict Resolution Happen*, Jaico Publishing House, Mumbai, pp. 90–95.

Kestner, Prudence Bowman and Larry Ray 2002, *The Conflict Resolution Training Program: Leaders Manual*, San Francisco: Wiley Company, pp. 206–18.

Krugman, Dean M., Dunn, Barban, and Reid 1994, *Advertising*, Eighth Edn, The Dryden Press, USA, pp. 51–65.

Wells, William, Burnett, and Moriaety 2002, *Advertising: Principles and Practice*, Sixth Edn, Pearson Education, Delhi, pp. 154–58.

**Creating the New Identity of Mezen: An Information Technology Services Corporation**

The process of relaunching carved out a unique brand identity for Mezen. The Mezen 'assurance of applying ideas' and the values that govern Mezen, cut out a unique character for the brand.

Mezen is a dependable, humane, and prosperous corporation focused on consumer needs, offering a range of products, solutions, and services that fulfil those needs, bearing in mind the socio-economic actualities of the country. Mezen is also a skilled, honest, and important business partner and employer, that places emphasis on long-term, mutually favourable relationships, and offers solid development opportunities with a stimulating work and business atmosphere.

**Internal communication** An enormous challenge by itself, as the organization had a strength of 10,000 people, spread across various places. At first, only the top management, consisting of about 20 people, knew the details. Hence, 60 members of the senior management of Mezen were informed in February 1998. In April 1998, the announcement began reaching out to all locations starting with Pune in Maharashtra (where Mezen had started setup). Maximum people liked the change. As A. Mathur put it, 'You may like the new identity or dislike it but you cannot ignore it. We have done a lot of exploration and due diligence on the modification. We are assured that it will be well-received. Now only the market and time will tell us whether we have made the right judgement.'

An identity handbook was made to communicate the new identity and values inside the organization. Guidelines for product packaging, stationery, visiting cards, car stickers, and signage internally and externally were circulated. Advertising guidelines were also developed. This created a whole new persona of the organization. The vendors and internal people were taught about the usage of the new identity handbook. Signage, visiting cards, and stationery had the new lively appearance.

**Advertising** This was a massive task. There were various issues—What should be communicated? Who was the intended audience? Will it grow sales? How would growth be measured? Would an individual division/product get suitable representation? After a lot of consideration, it was decided that the values and vision would be communicated. Advertising was to be evaluated by how well the values gained the attention of the customers (and not how sales have improved). An 'as is' research was led in December 1997 to form the baseline. The focus was on the male segment living in the top ten cosmopolitan cities that formed the bulk of Mezen's customers.

The advertising broadcasted how Mezen understood the requirements of the customer and how it had crafted innovative products and services to satisfy them. Uprightness and value for money was to be recognized as a result of the experience an individual had with the organization and its members. Six advertisements were produced showcasing 'applying ideas' in software, hardware, and the lighting business. The tag line 'We think of you' was constant in all the commercials.

**The result** The result is for everyone to see. Mezen radically became a well-known corporation. It wouldn't be right to give all the credit to the identity or the advertising. The vast success was a result of a big orchestration of the launch. The identity had high visibility as outdoors gave it a grand image, corporate communication helped Mezen to showcase itself on the cover of leading magazines, stationery was changed, new product packaging was introduced, and then advertising reached daily and weekly press. However, the ultimate stimulus came because of external changes. The IT industry was recognized as the future, leading to huge increases in Mezen Stock prices. The CEO, A. Mathur, became the richest Indian in April 1998. With this and with the knowledge economy getting more recognition, his success proved that one does not have to come from old business clans to become the richest Indian.

It is said that fortune favours the brave. The environmental factor proved lucky for Mezen. The new brand personality got an impeccable launch platform. The brand has been evaluated on how it has performed on the values through both qualitative and quantitative exploration with customers. Mezen is now perceived by the customers as an earnest, caring, and dependable organization.

### Questions

1. What was the task that challenged Mezen?
2. Discuss the approaches that Mezen undertook to establish its new brand identity.
3. How did Mezen use its advertising campaign effectively to meet the new challenge?
4. What assured Mezen of the success of its advertisement campaign?

# CHAPTER 20

# Ethics in Business Communication

## LEARNING OBJECTIVES

After reading this chapter, you will be able to understand:
- the term ethical communication
- the importance of values and ethics in organizational communication
- how ethical codes work in communication
- ethical issues involved in organizational communication
- ethical dilemmas that managers face at the workplace
- strategic approaches to ethical communication
- ethical communication on the Internet
- ethical implications of communication using electronic mail
- ethical issues involved in advertising

## INTRODUCTION

Communication is central to human experience. Through communication, we cultivate relationships and come to understand ourselves, others, and the world in which we live. To live well, we must communicate well, and to communicate well, we must understand both the visible and the subtle issues related to communication. Ethical issues related to business communication are one such issue. Understanding the ethics of communication helps us communicate effectively.

Traditional notions of organizational communication have framed ethical questions as largely frivolous, and ethics in organizational communication played a limited role. There were two fundamental factors which contributed to this thought: (i) There was an inherent confusion over the responsibility and accountability issues related to ethical communications in organizations. It was difficult to hold a manager (division) responsible for an unethical communication practice and employees were often seen pointing fingers at each other when it came to taking responsibility for a wrong done. The issue was about who takes the responsibility to practise ethics and why. (ii) There were serious limitations on discussions regarding ethical questions in organizations.

Ethical leaders set the standard of truth for every employee they lead. The moment people take leadership positions, they have an opportunity to place the highest premium on truthfulness. Cases of fiscal malpractices at Enron, WorldCom, and Arthur Andersen illustrate the need for every form of communication put forth by leaders to be an accurate representation. Yet, leading by example cannot be the only process by which this standard is relayed. It must become a company slogan, from the accounting office to the shop floor, that 'truth is job 1'. Truthful information is quality information to the CEO, board of directors, and investors. This chapter discusses one of the most important components of ethical leadership—ethical communication.

## ETHICAL COMMUNICATION

What does it mean to be an ethical communicator? Some important characteristics of ethical communication are discussed as follows:

**Getting your point across without offending the audience** One of the most important issues that should be kept in mind while communicating is that to get the desired response from the target audience, one needs to get his/her point across in an effective manner. For example, executives and managers in a PR team could easily be offended with a message that is conveyed in a crude manner. There are other subtle ways to tell them exactly the same thing; such that the message is loud and clear for managers to interpret and, yet is not offensive.

Managers must always remember that when they are communicating, they are not just communicating the message to be conveyed—they are also indirectly communicating the rules, policies, and principles the company follows.

**Maintaining and sustaining a relationship with your audience** It is always very important for a communicator to maintain the same wavelength with the target audience so that the target audience feels 'at home'. Master communicators strike a chord with the audience immediately and develop a relationship which is based on trust. Great orators such as Gandhi and Churchill did not have any problem in developing a sustainable relationship with their audience primarily because of their ability to strike a one-to-one relationship within minutes, and the audience experienced a feeling of comfort and security in their presence.

**Presenting information to the audience without deliberately withholding vital information** In the modern world, when information is such an important input to all strategic decisions, it becomes essential for organizations to be careful when communicating with the outside world. They should see to it that the information being communicated is complete, and that no vital information is being withheld on purpose. With more and more accounting scandals coming to light in recent corporate history, the importance of corporate information is even more critical now. Professional organizations are trying to practise 'corporate governance' by sharing each and every piece of information which could be price sensitive with the investors' community at large. Companies are becoming increasingly aware that while filing prospectus for listing in stock exchanges for an IPO, all material information must be disclosed, and that such an attempt will actually result in a better corporate image in the long run. All major accounting scandals in the past, such as that of Enron, are prima facie cases of information concealment on the part of organization, resulting in heavy losses to investors and the investor confidence taking a huge dip. All relevant parties involved in the process must be fully informed about the facts in any decision making process within the organization.

> When managers communicate, they indirectly communicate the rules, policies, and principles of the company.

> **I'm OK, You're OK**
>
> Rahul, a senior manager at an automobile piston manufacturing plant, is responsible for planning an overseas trip for his company's top-performing dealers in piston rings and sleeves. His assistants are all doing their work satisfactorily, except for Raj, who did not turn up for the last two meetings, and is yet to check with some dealers about their plans for joining the group. His slow pace could lead to the cancellation of the trip if airline seats were not available.
>
> Rahul is thoroughly frustrated and would love to give vent to his feelings about Raj's poor work. That would certainly ease his tension. However, if he is an ethical communicator, he will think over the consequences of his communication with Raj.
>
> If Raj has been going slow due to health problems, an outburst could well leave him feeling resentful. He might even slow down on his work further, increasing the chances of the whole trip falling through. Since Rahul's priority is ensuring a good holiday for the company's dealers, the best option would be to approach Raj with a cool head and encourage him to feel that his contribution is vital to the successful implementation of the trip. In this way, the chances of conflict can be averted.

**Understanding that ethics are related to values and may differ for the audience** For this concept to be successfully understood and practised in an organization, there should be a conscious effort by the top management to have a well-defined value system perpetuating throughout the organization—a value system cherished by each employee. It is only when the organization is functioning on some common, shared value systems that the employees will respect each other and take into cognizance each other's ethical stances. A sound and robust value system imbibed in the corporate culture is a guarantee for ethical employees and ethical communication. Once that is done, employees tend to have mutual respect for each other and the way they communicate within the organization and with outsiders. Respect for each other comes naturally.

**Making sure all information is accurate and researched** Information passed on during any kind of communication has not only to be complete but also correct and true, that is, valid. It is pointless to share information that is actually false or based upon premises that are not tested. The information should be tested, source identity must be verified, and only then should information be communicated formally. For example, a major product-launch exercise for a company could go wrong and lead to huge losses for the company if the sales force, which is a part of the market research team, gives a false feedback that a similar product offering by a rival has been very successful. This sales force information could be primarily based on market rumours, gossip, hearsay, and not facts. Information which is not true is even worse than no information at all.

- All relevant parties must be fully informed about the facts in any decision-making process within the organization.
- Information that is not true is worse than no information at all.

Complexities in post-modern information societies driven by media and communication technology have led to an increased interest in values and principles that provide a platform for decision making. The study of ethics within communications and the communication of ethical ideas represent such a platform. All forms of communication are inextricably linked to ethical reasoning through the common principles of truth and honesty, trust and relationships, reputation and integrity, conduct and justice. A fast developing field of research recognizes the deep connection of the act and the process of communication with ethical reasoning. People, through their relationships and values, engage in

## Whose Problem is it, Anyway?

The accident at a nuclear power plant in Three Mile Island, Pennsylvania, in 1978, is a chilling example of how badly things can go wrong because of thoughtless, non-ethical ways of communicating. During the government investigations that followed the incident, a document written by an engineer who had observed a somewhat similar problem at another plant in South Carolina was found. His report, written in a standard format, contained—on page three—his observation of the problem at the South Carolina plant and the similar circumstances prevailing at Three Mile Island. He had also made a strong case for measures to be undertaken to fix the underlying problem. Unfortunately, no one ever read this crucial part of the report. Those to whom the report had been addressed testified that they rarely ever read such standard reports.

In this case, while it is difficult to lay the entire blame for the accident on the engineer, it is obvious that if he had been more conscientious about his communication, the accident could have been averted. The main thrust of his communication should have appeared, well highlighted, right at the beginning of the report. He could also have spoken up and tried to impress upon the appropriate people, the need for urgent action.

communication in order to establish common agreements and to identify areas of dispute. Communication ethics offers a perspective and focus that may address many intractable human issues.

> Ethical issues are bound to arise because communication plays a significant role in influencing others.

Ethical issues are bound to arise because communication plays a significant role in influencing others. The way a person communicates in the organization is largely affected by the way he/she wants to be perceived by others, and also how he/she would like others to behave. A manager behaving in an autocratic manner and practising, by and large, one-way communication will largely have negative effects on the receiver, and it is quite possible that the receiver may also start behaving in a similar fashion if exposed to such a communication style for long.

The intent is as important as motivation. The speaker brings in his/her intention in his/her style of communication. If the intention is clear and strong, it will be easily reflected in the way the message is being communicated. Professional managers will always use different communication styles to bring out their real intention to their subordinates.

We consciously choose to use a specific type of communication to get what we want. This is again a conscious style of communication delivery used by smart managers to get to the desired results, and therefore, it is very useful for driving home a point to the employees in the organization.

## Why Ethics in Organizational Communication?

There are some fundamental assumptions that shape the discussion on communication ethics.

Would you like to fly business class to Hawaii?

> Every communication decision has some ethical dimension to it.

Every communication decision has some ethical dimension to it, whether acknowledged or not. Starting from the time when an individual joins an organization to the time he/she retires, there are many landmark events in his/her career where communication has ethical dimensions attached to it. For example, at the time of joining, an organization communicates an employee's work profile, job responsibilities, salary, and perks through an appointment letter, which is a very interesting piece of document, and organizations believing in ethical communication try to be as objective and transparent as possible. There are countless complexities involved in the communication process, but the communicator is initially faced with only three simple choices—to speak, listen, or remain silent. In each choice, there is an ethical decision. In speaking, a communicator chooses to disclose information, motives, or feelings to someone. Judging whether or not this communication should take place is partly an ethical decision. For instance, should one share a rumour about an organizational change with a colleague?

### Look before You Leap

Few would doubt that ethical concerns are inherent to the act of speech, but what about the act of listening? In the modern world, because instant and credible information has to be given, it becomes necessary to resort to guess work, rumours, and assumptions to fill in the voids.

Remaining silent may seem like the safest way to avoid ethical dilemmas. However, even here, there is no safe harbour, because remaining silent in the face of unlawful behaviour or a potentially harmful situation is a serious ethical decision. In sum, whether communicators choose to speak, listen, or remain silent are ethical considerations. For example if the marketing head of an organization chooses to remain silent regarding the reports given by the sales team that a particular product is suffering because of its poor quality, which is probably because of the substandard raw material supplied by a particular supplier, it is a direct indication of some unethical behaviour on part of the marketing head, and his/her behaviour comes under the ethical scanner.

Communication ethics inevitably involves both motives and impact. It is easy to condemn people who lie to pull off swindles. Their motive is deceit, and the results are immoral. But what happens when the motives are good but the impact is bad? For instance, a manager wanting to boost contribution in his/her unit tries something strange, but with good intention. He/she proceeds to attain salary information about each employee from the personnel department. On each employee's cheque, he/she attaches a note suggesting a 'fair percentage gift'. Certainly, the means used to attain this 'noble' goal are, at best, questionable. Indeed, most of the employees would feel that this action is a violation of their privacy. A well-intended communication would be wrongly interpreted, and the impact would be entirely different from what was originally thought of.

Ethics are often seen as irrelevant to the fundamental purpose of business. Do ethics have an impact on the bottom line? It would be nice to say that ethical behaviour always results in increased profits or productivity. But that is simply not the case. Many corporations with high ethical standards have been overwhelmed by unscrupulous competitors. Employees who altruistically 'blow the whistle' on unethical corporate practices frequently suffer from financial strain, social ostracism, and harassment.

> Communication ethics inevitably involves both motives and impacts.

### Ethical Code in Communication

Ethical communication does not entail any defined set of codes. However, corporate houses around the globe tend to follow some basic principles when it comes to ethical communication. Some of these will be discussed here:

### Who Decides What Ethics to Follow?

Many people believe that discussing ethics will inevitably lead to imposing one's morality on others. The heritage of western civilization is one that seeks to give people the widest possible freedom and individual discretion in forming moral opinions. Hence, even seeking to persuade someone of the rightness or wrongness of a particular decision can be seen as a first step on the sacred ground of individual discretion and responsibility. Thus, it is often assumed that the safest course is to avoid the discussion altogether. While philosophers may enjoy debating the question, 'Do we have the right to impose our values on others?', managers do not have that luxury. They must ask, 'In this instance, is it right to impose our ethics on others?' The fundamental point is that, to avoid ethical discussions so that one does not impose one's view on others is, ironically, an unethical 'cop-out'.

In the Indian context, the interplay of many opposing cultural forces make communication even more complex. For instance, in advertising, American companies often run campaigns that compare their products with those of competitors. Traditionally, disparaging a rival company's products was considered unethical in India, and hence, was never practised. However, this situation has gradually changed over the years with the entry of multinational companies and overseas advertisement agencies, and we now see such advertisement campaigns on a limited scale. When Cartoon Network, a popular television channel, began dubbing its popular cartoon serials into Indian languages so as to attract a larger audience of Indian children, and thereby increase their market share of TV viewership, it failed to take into account the repercussions of simply translating American colloquialisms into the vernacular. A character, addressing another in jest as, 'You dirty dog!' might translate into *Arrey, kuttey!*, much to the consternation of parents and public watchdog organizations who protested vociferously against the promotion of bad language among small children. The channel was perforce made to realize the implications of operating in a culture different from its own and began to pay more attention to the nuances of regional languages. TV channels in their pursuit of market-driven objectives, perhaps end up communicating politically incorrect statements, and can become insensitive to the ethical norms of communication in a specific cultural context.

1. Truthfulness, accuracy, honesty, and reason are essential to the integrity of communication. Endorse freedom of expression, diversity of perspective, and tolerance of dissent to achieve the informed and responsible decision making fundamental to a civil society.
2. Strive to understand and respect other communicators before evaluating and responding to their messages.
3. Promote communication climates of caring and mutual understanding that respect the unique needs and characteristics of individual communicators.
4. Condemn communication that degrades individuals and humanity through distortion, intolerance, intimidation, coercion, hatred, and violence.
5. Commit to the courageous expression of personal convictions in pursuit of fairness and justice.
6. Access to communication resources and opportunities are necessary for fulfilling human potential and contributing to the well being of families, communities, and society. Advocate the sharing of information, opinions, and feelings when facing significant choices, while also respecting privacy and confidentiality.
7. Unethical communication threatens the quality of all communication, and consequently, the well being of individuals and the society in which we live. Accept responsibility for the short- and long-term consequences of our own communication and expect the same of others.

> Truthfulness, accuracy, honesty, and reason are essential to the integrity of communication.

> **BUSINESS COMMUNICATION INSIGHT**
>
> **Business Ethics**
>
> Based on how it is construed and applied within a small business, business ethics as a subject can vary significantly from one business to the next. What seems ethical to one organization may not appear ethical to the next—and the same goes for personnel. Hence, it is essential to plainly communicate the ethical position of the business to all personnel. Employees should act in an ethical manner with full understanding of the ethical stance of the business.
>
> **Significance of ethical communication** Ethical practices of a business should be communicated effectively to employees for their understanding. Employees who act in appropriate ethical manner should be appreciated and ethical behaviour should be communicated to all employees on a regular basis. This aids in setting ethical standards for other workers in the organization.
>
> **Ethics policy** All businesses must have a well-drafted ethics policy that specifies what is expected of employees within the business. It should list the company's ethical standards and beliefs such as always being truthful in business communications, dealing with clients and other employees impartially and reporting ethical violations, if noticed. This policy should be thoroughly read and signed by all employees upon their acceptance of employment and this process should be carried out on annual basis.
>
> **Ethics training** It's essential that the business conducts ethics training for all employees because everyone's perception of ethics can differ. Some people may perceive taking business supplies for personal use as unethical, whereas they might not believe that taking an office pen home with them is the same. The business should teach the employees about its ethical values through role play as well as hypothetical settings. This can help employees recognize what the business considers as ethical and unethical.
>
> **Management role** A manager's role in implementing ethical practices in a business is to always exhibit ethical behaviour in verbal and non-verbal form. Management should strengthen ethical behaviour in others with appreciation and use unethical behaviour as a tool for educating other employees. In addition, managers should realize that they are role models for the business and must act appropriately. If they believe their employees should act in an ethical way, they must also do the same and lead by example.
>
> **Considerations** In periodic employee meetings, use news stories to reinstate the business stand on ethics. Circulate the story to employees to read and review before the meeting. During meetings, describe the news article and have workers identify the ethical and unethical behaviours revealed in the story. Also, question the employees what should have happened and how they should handle if they come across a similar situation in the business.

In reading over these principles, one can note the two ethical communication themes of caring and responsibility. Some are obvious, while other principles are not as obvious in their representation of these themes, yet the importance of the ethics of care and responsibility are still clear. For example, 'access to communication resources and opportunities is necessary to fulfil human potential and contribute to the well being of families, communities, and society,' emphasizes an ethic of caring and 'commit to the courageous expression of personal convictions in pursuit of fairness and justice,' stresses an ethic of responsibility. Others integrate both caring and responsibility, such as, 'advocate the sharing of information, opinions, and feelings when facing significant choices, while also respecting privacy and

> Unethical communication threatens the quality of all communication.

> ### The Tylenol Tale—Cure the Headache
>
> The story of Tylenol—Johnson & Johnson's popular analgesic—is a well-known example of how ethical behaviour on the part of the company helped turn a potential disaster into triumph. In 1986, an individual succeeded in lacing the drug with cyanide, leading to widespread panic about the extent of the contamination. The company, which had faced a similar situation a few years ago, acted speedily to recall the drug from every outlet in the US. Also, the company did not start selling the product again until it had developed more protective packaging that would be much harder to tamper with. Johnson & Johnson's quick and responsible actions communicated a positive, reassuring image of the company as a champion of consumers, so much so that the company went on to recover 70 per cent of its market share of the drug.

confidentiality'. In following this last principle, communicators must take responsibility for encouraging all participants to share information, and at the same time, communicators must care for others by respecting others' wishes.

## VALUES, ETHICS, AND COMMUNICATION

At the foundation of ethical behaviour is a value system that serves as a guide for judging one's own as well as others' behaviour, and, above all, for resisting changes. Values are amongst the most

> ### Corporate Ethics—Why an Asset?
>
> Organizational ethics and moral standards have gained more prominence in the corporate culture of today, as 'enlightened' companies recognize that commercial success means much more than the profit margin. The realization has dawned that it is the image of the company, and the goodwill it generates in the market that determines its success in the truest sense of the word. It is also a known fact that only those companies which portray a 'clean' image can attract the brightest and the best talent. They consider it a matter of pride to be associated with the organization and have a greater sense of belonging. Studies have also proved that there is a direct correlation between ethical conduct and job satisfaction. It is one of the greatest motivating factors and induces strong feelings of loyalty.
>
> A strong sense of values and familial culture at the workplace are needs as strong as a good remuneration package. IT companies have been amongst the first to recognize these needs, and have been at the forefront of training in corporate and customer ethics. Hema Ravichander, the then Senior Vice-President, Human Resource Development, Infosys Technologies, said, 'We at Infosys have a distinctive work culture and value system. Our value system, anagrammed as C-LIFE, places a great deal of importance on customer delight, leadership, integrity, transparency, fairness and pursuit of excellence.' At Infosys, all new employees go through 'values workshops' led by senior Infoscions. Case studies, artifacts, and standardized presentations are used at these sessions. Additionally, the company has an email address where employees can send their queries and seek clarifications on values and their practice. A senior Infoscion responds to these queries. Adds Ravichander, 'We believe that it is very important to identify values, articulate them, and strongly reinforce them through action.'
>
> High ethical standards are now recognized as an asset for a company, and unethical behaviour as a liability. A company often incurs financial losses on account of additional expenses incurred to stay on the right side of the law. However, it is increasingly being recognized that, in the long run, such losses are suitably balanced by non-financial advantages, such as a good company reputation.

> **COMMUNICATION TOOL**
>
> **Seven Signs of an Ethical Business**
>
> 1. Teach employees how to behave ethically by demonstrating, recognizing, and rewarding ethical behavior.
> 2. Tell the truth. Fully reveal relevant information to stakeholders and authorities.
> 3. Consider the interests of everyone who will be affected by their business decisions.
> 4. Treat all individuals and groups with dignity and respect.
> 5. Maintain honest and complete communication with employees, customers, and the community.
> 6. Avoid conflicts of interest.
> 7. Demonstrate, encourage, and support active involvement in their communities.
>
> Source: Weiss, Laurie, '7 Signs of an Ethical Business', http://daretosayit.com/blog/2007/03/7-signs-of-an-ethical-business/, accessed on 2 December 2011. Reproduced with permission.

stable and enduring characteristics of individuals, and are the basis upon which attitudes and personal preferences are formed, as well as the basis for crucial decisions, life direction, and personal tastes. Organizations, too, have value systems, and are perhaps the most critical components of the organizational culture. Increasing number of scholars and managers are stressing the importance of an organization's values and culture in building a strong, creative, and productive work force. What are the most important values an organization can stress? Managers at all levels place the highest value on integrity and competence in their superiors, peers, and subordinates. Moreover, individuals thrive in an organization that stands for values they can embrace in their personal lives. Excellent companies have clearly stated values that make sense to their employees, and they reinforce these values through everything they do.

Almost every important issue discussed, assessed, and acted upon in an organization relates, directly or indirectly, to ethics. Ethical issues are those that focus on value judgments concerning right and wrong, and goodness and badness in human conduct. Ethics go beyond simple questions of legality or illegality. The field of ethics considers what our relationships are and ought to be with our employers, coworkers, subordinates, customers, stockholders, suppliers, distributors, and all other members of the communities in which we operate. Ethics is the awareness that one is an intrinsic part of a social order in which the interest of others and one's own interests are inevitably intertwined.

From a communication perspective, ethical communication facilitates the individual's ability to make sound choices. Ethical communication may include providing complete and accurate information upon which others can base their choices. It may involve establishing a supportive environment in which others feel comfortable making informed choices. In general, those who aspire to communicate ethically and supportively should espouse the following kinds of behaviour:

> - Values are the bases on which attitudes and personal preferences are formed.
> - Ethical communication facilitates the individual's ability to make sound choices.

**Descriptive (rather than evaluative)** Being non-judgemental, slow to question others' standards and values, and willing to seek additional information.

**Problem-oriented** Interested in defining mutual problems and cooperatively seeking solutions, rather than pointing at people who can be blamed for problems.

> A person's approaches and communicative interactions depend on his/her ethical perspective.

**Spontaneous** Straight forward, honest, and tactfully direct; unwilling to deal with others in manipulative ways.

**Respectful** Demonstrating and seeking mutual trust and respect, encouraging participative planning while de-emphasizing status, power, and formal role relationships.

**Empathic** Attempting to see issues and problems from others' perspectives; identifying with others' needs, interests, and values.

**Provisional** Willing to admit that one could be wrong, open to new ways of doing things, tentative in one's views.

## Ethical Perspectives

The way a person approaches decision-making and communicative interactions depends largely on the ethical perspective from which he/she is operating. Ethics can be viewed from several different vantage points, each of which provides a different foundation for making moral judgements. The 'best' approach or solution to a given ethical dilemma will vary, depending upon the ethical perspective embraced. Among those commonly sited are religious, economic, legal, utilitarian, universalistic, humanistic, dialogic, and situational perspectives (Fig. 20.1).

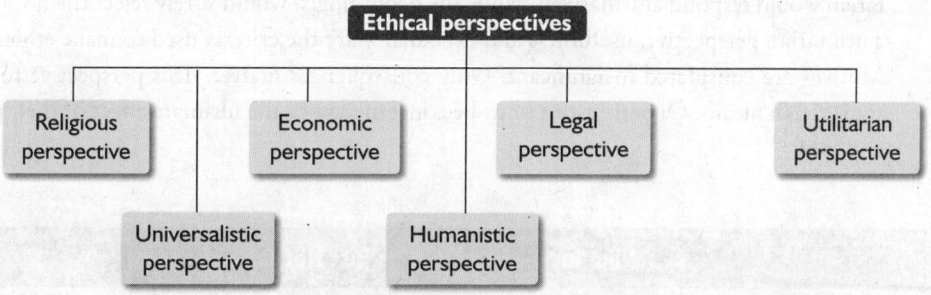

**Fig. 20.1** Ethical perspectives

### Honesty is the Best Policy

A CEO from an engineering firm decided to pay a surprise visit to a customer, as she had spare time due to a delayed flight. Her company had recently installed a pasteurizing plant for the customer. At the dairy plant, the CEO was dismayed at the welding work on the stainless steel frame assembly. It was poorly finished and 'raw', which meant residual milk could collect in the crevices and lead to breeding of germs, which was totally unacceptable from the hygiene point of view in a dairy milk pasteurization unit. Pointing out the defect, the CEO apologized to the customer and promised to get the fault rectified by her company's engineers. The customer, who had neither noticed the defect, nor complained about it, was amazed at the CEO's commitment to high standards and dedication to customer service. People working for the company as well as other customers still talk about this incident. Unsurprisingly, the company continues to be the leader in its field.

> - Legal analysis reduces ethical judgements to a matter of law.
> - The utilitarian perspective focuses on ends rather than means.

### Religious Perspective

The religious perspective teaches that behaviour such as lying, stealing, murder, or treating others with disrespect is wrong. For example, Christianity teaches us to treat others as we would like to be treated ourselves.

### Economic Perspective

The economic perspective bases ethical judgements on impersonal market forces. This school of thought holds that managers should consistently act to maximize revenues and minimize costs, and that this strategy will itself assure society of the greatest long-term benefits.

### Legal Perspective

Legal analysis reduces ethical judgements to a matter of law. Anything that is legal is ethical. Anything illegal is unethical. This approach has the advantage of facilitating simple ethical decisions—one has to only investigate the law, rule, or behavioural code governing a particular practice.

### Utilitarian Perspective

One of the classic cases of ethical tension exists between those who are concerned with the moral quality of an action, independent of its consequences (deontologists), and those who believe that any action is right if it produces the greatest good for the greatest number of people (utilitarians). 'Would you be willing to murder an innocent person if it would end hunger in the world?' The utilitarian would respond affirmatively, while the deontologist would surely reject the notion. Thus, from a utilitarian perspective, usefulness and expediency are the criteria used to make ethical judgements. Motives are considered insignificant. Only consequences matter. This perspective focuses on ends rather than means. Organizations must be concerned with the ultimate effect of their plans, policies, and rules.

---

#### Nike Inc.—'Just Do It' is Just Not Enough

Nike Inc., a global brand leader in footwear, clothing, equipment, and other accessories for sports and athletics in several countries, has been prominently targeted by a broad range of social activists and journalists as a symbol of how big business, in its quest for maximizing profits and minimizing costs, ignores human rights and the working conditions of employees in developing countries, particularly in South Asia. The list of allegations against certain franchisee factory outlets of Nike are those of payment of poor wages, pathetic working conditions, sexual harassment, and use of child labour. Nike shares factory locations with independent third parties where approximately 20 per cent of the employees work on Nike products, claiming that this system enables them to monitor their supply chain efficiently. However, it keeps the names of these factories confidential, and does not allow independent inspections, claiming that this would be unfairly used by activists to make further attacks rather than start a dialogue to help the company address and resolve the existing problems. Given the uncovering of certain malpractices among franchisee factory outlets, Nike has since devised and implemented a code of conduct for its contract factories. It also works with Global Alliance to review conditions in 21 of these factories and to resolve issues as they develop. However, it is difficult to recover a tarnished image, and, notwithstanding all their remedial actions, criticism of Nike's policies continues unabated.

> ### The Merchant of Venice
>
> Shakespeare's famous play *The Merchant of Venice* is one of the earliest examples of the distinction between strictly commercial values and more generally understood moral values such as compassion and mercy. Briefly, the merchant, Antonio, enters into a contract with Shylock, the moneylender, to give a pound of his flesh if he reneges on his loan repayment. Unfortunately, his luck takes a bad turn when his fortunes are shipwrecked, and Shylock (who hates the merchant) insists on extracting his pound of flesh. Antonio is saved by the beautiful and clever heiress, Portia, who, disguised as a lawyer, pleads his case before the court. When Shylock insists on the terms of the contract being honoured, Portia wins the case by arguing that, while the bond concerns a pound of flesh, there is no mention of shedding blood. Shylock may have his pound of flesh, on the condition that no blood is shed and not more than an exact pound of flesh is removed. Stymied, Shylock retracts and settles for money instead. The real value of this tale, however, lies in Portia's speech on the qualities of mercy and her plea for considering the human predicament of the merchant who was in debt due to no fault of his.

### Universalistic Perspective

Whereas the utilitarian perspective considers the outcome of an action, the universalist perspective maintains that, because outcomes are too difficult to predict or control, the more appropriate focus is on intention. At the heart of the universalistic perspective is the belief that people have certain duties or responsibilities in their dealings with one another, such as telling the truth and adhering to agreements.

### Humanistic Perspective

The humanistic perspective actually makes an attempt to make ethical judgements philosophically, isolating certain unique characteristics of human nature that would be valued and enhanced. It then takes a look at a particular technique, rule, policy, strategy, or behaviour and attempts to determine the extent to which it either furthers or hampers these uniquely human attributes.

### Dialogic Perspective

According to the dialogic perspective, the attitude that individuals in any communication transaction have towards one another is an index of the ethical level of that communication. When people communicate from a dialogic perspective, their attitudes are characterized by honesty, trust, concern for others, open-mindedness, empathy, humility, sincerity, and directness. The dialogic perspective is unique in its focus on communication as the primary means of examining the ethical level of human behaviour.

### Situational Perspective

> The dialogic perspective is unique in its focus on communication as the primary means of examining the ethical level of human behaviour.

Ethical criteria might vary as variables in the organizational situation change. In an organizational crisis involving genuine danger to human lives, the leader who uses emotional appeals or behaves autocratically might well not be judged to be harsh from a situational perspective, although the same behaviour in ordinary circumstances would more likely be viewed as unethical. The major advantage of the situational perspective is its flexibility and the extent to which it encourages thoughtful consideration of the particular context of each act of human behaviour.

> - Communication among organizations or individuals within organizations should reflect the ethics of the organization.
> - Directive communications explain to someone what needs to be done and, sometimes, how to do it.

However, the ethical judgement must be grounded in one or more of the general ethical perspectives discussed above; otherwise, problems of inconsistency and unfairness may result. For example, a manager fires a first-line supervisor immediately, when presented with decisive evidence that he/she was behaving badly with his/her subordinates. In this situation, the dialogic perspective was sacrificed so that the utilitarian principle of the greatest good for the greatest number could be upheld.

## Ethical Issues Involved in Business Communications

Business communications can either be among organizations, people within an organization, or among an organization and the public. Communications within and among organizations or individuals within organizations should also reflect the ethics of the organization. The same basic rules of ethical communication apply to all three: and (i) be honest; (ii) be respectful; and (iii) show sensitivity to cultural differences. These basic rules have been discussed as follows (Fig. 20.2).

### Honesty

Communications can convey the truth or create impressions that are misleading and disguise reality. Organizations that value their reputations avoid communications that knowingly contain falsehoods, deceptive statements, or incorrect conclusions or data. To choose deliberately to mislead may be tempting because the truth sometimes casts an individual or an organization in less than stellar light.

### Respect

Business communications, whether are directive, comparative, explanatory, or promotional, need to be respectful of the readers' intelligence and their desire for accurate, useful information. Directive communications explain to someone what needs to be done and, sometimes, how to do it. Proving a sufficient level of details to understand what needs to be done, how it should be done, and why it should be done helps avoid ethical pitfalls that result from misunderstanding and simultaneously show respect to the recipient of the communication. Explanatory communications are closely related to directive communications, and the same standards for showing respect apply.

### Sensitivity to Cultural Differences

With globalization comes an expansion of the role ethics plays in communication as well as an increased level of difficulty in communicating ethically. In a national setting, corporations deal with a more homogeneous culture, and it is easier to convey honesty and respect when people use the same language with only regional differences or differences based on diversity. In a global setting, there are multiple cultures to accommodate. In a national setting, we see one set of rules and ethical expectations, but globalization also means multi-nationalism and multiculturalism, thus, multiple sets of rules and expectations apply. There are far more opportunities to miscommunicate than to communicate effectively. For example, people in Japan and the US both believe in respect and compassion. Yet, when it comes to dealing with ailing parents, people in these two countries act out their commitment to

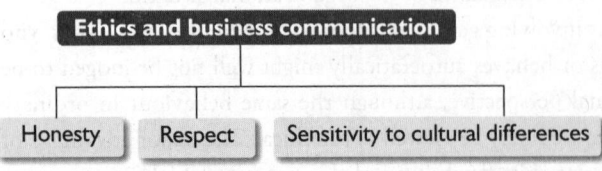

**Fig. 20.2** Ethical issues in business communication

> ### Fair and Square
>
> Business and ethics need not necessarily be at variance with each other, as the ethical consumption movement in the West has demonstrated. A new breed of activists, who have entered the marketplace with the ultimate aim that all products should be produced fairly, have discovered that ethical products, developed carefully, have increasingly valuable marketing assets. One success story of a coffee producer is that of Cafedirect, which as its name implies, procures coffee and tea directly from growers. In a sector that has experienced overall decline, Cafedirect 5065, a freeze-dried coffee product in the UK has been the fastest growing brand of its kind. The company's speciality and ground products also contributed to its robust annual growth rate of 20%. The secret of Cafedirect's success? Paying satisfactory prices on the one hand to coffee growers, who feel that their long heritage of expertise in producing a quality product is valued by the company, and on the other, marketing the coffee and tea as 'ethical' to a public that is increasingly concerned about these issues.

> ### Test the Ethics of a Message
>
> - Does the message comply with the law?
> - Is it balanced? Is it fair to all concerned?
> - Who will it benefit or harm?
> - If you were receiving the message, how would you feel?
> - Have you checked it out with others?
> - Would you be embarrassed if others found out about the message?
> - Does the message make you feel good about yourself?

respect and compassion differently—in ways that reflect their cultural differences. In the US, it is common for families to be geographically dispersed and ailing parents to reside in 'care facilities' where they can get the needed attention. In Japan, such facilities are not consistent with a culture that expresses respect for parents by ensuring that they stay with their own children, who give them personal care. This is less about 'right and wrong', rather it is about being 'different'. Different cultures express care and respect differently.

## WHAT DOES A PROFESSIONAL COMMUNICATOR DO?

Professional communicators engage in the following practices and behaviour:

1. Professional communicators uphold the credibility and dignity of their profession by practising honest, candid, and timely communication, and fostering the free flow of essential information in accord with the public interest.
2. Professional communicators disseminate accurate information and promptly correct any erroneous communication for which they may be responsible.
3. Professional communicators are sensitive to cultural values and beliefs, and engage in fair and balanced communication activities that foster and encourage mutual understanding.
4. They refrain from taking part in any undertaking, which they consider to be unethical.
5. Professional communicators protect confidential information and, at the same time, comply with all legal requirements for the disclosure of information affecting the welfare of others.

> Professional communicators are sensitive to cultural values and beliefs.

> **✓ COMMUNICATION TOOL**
>
> **Commandments of Ethical Communication**
>
> Your commitment to professional excellence and ethical behaviour means that you should
>
> - use language and visuals with precision,
> - prefer simple, direct expression of ideas,
> - satisfy the audience's need for information, not my own need for self-expression,
> - hold myself responsible for how well my audience understands my message,
> - respect the work of colleagues, knowing that a communication problem may have more than one solution,
> - strive continually to improve my professional competence, and
> - promote a climate that encourages the exercise of professional judgement and that attracts talented individuals to careers in business communication.

6. They do not guarantee results that are beyond the power of the practitioner to deliver.
7. Professional communicators are honest not only with others but also, and most importantly, with themselves as individuals, for they seek the truth.

## ETHICAL DILEMMAS FACING MANAGERS

There are many ethical dilemmas facing a manager. Some of the more vexing ones are as follows:

### Secrecy

'Vijay, don't worry! You can count on me to get you that promotion.'

Secrets are held for honourable and dishonourable reasons. Secrecy is best defined as 'intentional concealment'. There is no moral judgement implied in the definition. Herein lies the challenge for a manager—to determine when secrets are justifiable and when they are not. For example, an engineer who remains silent about potentially catastrophic failures in a product has, in some way, abrogated moral responsibility. Employees and managers should not take such a duty lightly. Secrets have a clear and detrimental impact on decision-making and consumer safety.

On the other hand, in some situations, secrecy may be essential in order to make successful decisions or to encourage innovation. There is a need for the concerned manager to discuss the projected promotional prospects or even the salary projections of employees with the personnel manager, but not with the employees. The employees may not live up to expectations; leeway is needed. The fact that employees are not always privy to all corporate information does not imply an intention to deceive.

- Secrets can also be defined as intentional concealment.
- Corporations also have a legitimate need to protect certain information from competitors.

Corporations also have a legitimate need to protect certain information from competitors. Many corporations invest millions of dollars for research

> ### Snow Brand Milk Products—Not so White
>
> Snow Brand was Japan's premier dairy foods company until the year 2000, when around 15,000 people were affected due to bacterial contamination on a production line of one of the company's factories. Snow Brand's reaction was to try and cover up information about what had actually happened. The company also dragged its feet on recalling its products, until forced to do so by the city authorities. Snow Brand also tried to fudge details about the valve where the contamination was found, claiming that it was rarely used. It later transpired that it was, in fact, used every day.
>
> There were other such half-truths, all of which conveyed the impression that the company was more concerned about its reputation rather than the well being of its customers.
>
> Snow Brand's image and its sales plummeted dramatically, and the company had to close five of its factories. Its downfall was a result of its poor communication with the public, its slow response to the crisis, and the huge mistake it made in covering up its faults. It had lost the trust of its customers.

to develop new products or procedures. If other companies gain access to that information, they can produce the product for a much lower net cost because they do not have to pay for the research and development costs. The net effect is that there is no incentive for the corporation to be innovative. Trade secrecy has implications not only for individual corporations but also for the general technological advancement of the society. Yet, there must be limits even to trade secrecy. Too much secrecy about trade practices creates more problems than solving them. One of the most vital aspects of the innovative process is having access to new ideas. When the clamp of secrecy is too tight, interactions are too few and too restricted. The net result—lack of innovation—is all too predictable.

Thus, problems are evident at either end of the spectrum. Too much secrecy bogs down the creative process. Too little secrecy removes incentives. There is a middle ground of sorts. Patents and copyrights allow for information to be used and generally circulated while providing a modicum of protection for researchers and authors; but even with these devices, there may be problems. Changing some minor aspect of a product may be enough to circumvent a patent infringement lawsuit. Therefore, one of the continuing dilemmas for the business society is to work out ways to avoid the stifling effects of either extreme of the secrecy continuum.

## Whistle-blowing

An employee who goes public with information about corporate abuses or negligence is known as a whistle-blower. The most important issue for the manager is to find ways to make whistle-blowing unnecessary. Corporations and managers legitimately expect employee loyalty. Only under extraor-

> ### Whistle-blowers
>
> In 2002, *Time Magazine* named three courageous women as persons of the year, for their role in exposing misconduct in US corporations. Sherron Watkins at Enron and Cynthia Cooper at WorldCom exposed massive accounting frauds, while Colleen Rowley sent detailed evidence to the FBI to alert the agency about the 11 September 2001 terrorist attacks. The best-known recent example in India is that of engineer Satyendra Dubey, who paid with his life for blowing the whistle on corruption in the Golden Quadrilateral project.

> - A leak is a kind of anonymous whistle-blowing.
> - Rumours tend to focus on events and information, while gossip focuses on people.

dinary circumstances should such obligations be cast aside. Some whistle-blowers are motivated by greed, jealousy, and revenge. That does not mean that they are necessarily wrong, but it does cast doubt about such a person. Some such employees are simply misinformed, while others confuse public interest with private interest. Certainly, the community has a right to know about corporate practices that are potentially hazardous. Yet, an over-ambitious courtship of the whistle-blower can be problematic. Stifling criticism through autocratic managers may work in the short run, but is disastrous in the long run. The objective then for the organization is not to squash dissent, but to have some procedures whereby complaints, concerns, and criticism can be handled internally rather than externally. The 'open door' policy is the typical approach taken. This policy allows the employees to take a grievance to their supervisor first and then up through the chain of command until they get satisfaction.

Some employees choose to 'swallow the whistle' rather than discuss the matter with a manager who may be part of the problem in the first place. The result is the loss of potentially valuable information by the organization and the public at large. While the open door policy is useful in many situations, it does not really meet the needs of the potential whistle-blower. That is, the grievances tend to be considered in the context of how they affect the chain of command rather than on the proprietary of the individual case. Hence, appeals are rarely investigated, or impartially considered. In short, either 'swallowing the whistle' or 'blowing it' can be problematic. Therefore, the central challenge for organizations is to plan how to properly channel employee dissent.

## Leaks

A leak is a kind of anonymous whistle-blowing. The accused does not know who chose to release certain information or why they have done so. Employees also leak information to the press for honourable or dishonourable reasons. Leaks may cause organizational plans to be altered or abandoned. Leaks can be a form of political manoeuvring in the organization or a way to sabotage the career of a colleague competing for a job. Are leaks ethical? In one sense, the ethics of leaking information is the same as that of whistle blowing. Indeed, the preventive measures are about the same. However, there is one distinction between the two that casts a dark shadow over the propriety of the leak, namely the person who leaks information cannot be cross-examined, whereas a whistle-blower can be. Using a leak is dubious in nature and should be undertaken in the rarest of circumstances.

**Image 20.1** Information through the grapevine travels fast

## Rumours and Gossip

Rumours and gossip seem to be an inevitable part of everyday corporate life (Image 20.1). Even though rumours and gossip often travel through the same networks, there is a distinction between the terms. Rumours tend to focus on events and information, while gossip focuses on people. To the manager the ethical dilemma is twofold: (i) Should gossip about other employees be listened to? (ii) What should be done about rumours in the organization? Managers appear to be on slippery ethical ground when they listen to gossip about fellow employees. Even though the information is often treated as 'yet to be confirmed', there is often a tendency for the gossip to cloud judgements about that person. The information has a way of creeping into performance evaluations and promotion decisions, even if it happens unintentionally. Moreover, the information may be completely inaccurate.

Rumours can have a disastrous effect on corporations. Proctor & Gamble spent years and thousands of dollars fighting a rumour that their corporate symbol represented a devil. Rumours that McDonald's added worms to its meat in order to increase protein content lowered sales in some states. Both the rumours were unequivocally false. But clearly, the impact was great.

## Lying

Of all the ethical dilemmas discussed so far, lying would appear to be the least morally perplexing. Most would agree that one ought not tell a lie. A lie is a false statement intended to deceive. Yet, lies in business are more common than many would care to admit. One of the most frequent justifica-

### The Spin

'A spin is such a radical misuse of language that it eludes proper definition,' says Raymond N. Mackenzie, Professor of English, University of Saint Thomas, in a study on language and business ethics. When we spin a fact, we put the best possible light on it, a light that shows it in the way most advantageous to ourselves. The very word *spin* is vivid, lively, and jaunty; it suggests that a sort of game is being played, and ideally, it is being played expertly. Thus, the word itself invites us to lay aside questions of ethics: in a game, one is supposed to play hard and cunningly, not to be concerned with issues of morality. The point of spin is to hide unpleasant realities and to create an impression of good news when the truth is bad.

Political discourse led the way in spin, and the Vietnam war was an especially fertile period for its practice, as bombing raids were called *protective reaction strikes* and the practice of burning down villages was called *pacification*. But business learned quickly too, and it is a rare manager today who will speak of laying people off (which itself was originally a gentle euphemism for firing them) rather than *downsizing, restructuring,* or *outsourcing.* But spin is more insidious than the mere use of euphemisms, which most people can see through pretty quickly. Spin has, in many environments, become expected and even being demanded—a manager ought to sound 'managerial', and a politician ought to sound political. For example, a manager should never refer to a situation as a *problem* but always ought to spin it into an *opportunity* or, at the very worst, a *challenge.*

Business and political leaders are expected to swim, as it were, in the warm, comforting waters of euphemism and jargon. So, if a leader tells us hard, painful facts, he or she is somehow appearing unprofessional, and if a politician expresses pessimism about a situation, he or she is somehow not quite right for the job. US presidential aspirant Bob Dole's 1996 presidential campaign was certainly damaged by his tendency to put things starkly, which led many to see him as gloomy and sarcastic—as if one ought only to trust and elect an upbeat, continually cheerful person. The problem is not so much spin itself, as it is the culture it spawns through its sheer pervasiveness. On the one hand, as shareholders or employees or voters, we detest being lied to; but, on the other hand, we demand it. The spin culture has not so much undone community as it has created a parody of community, a community of continual mistrust, one in which we must assume that a leader is lying to us, and one in which we likewise feel we are expected to lie to any superior.

> Lying breaks down trust between individuals, thus hampering organizational effectiveness.

tions for duplicity is that the intent was good. The 'white lies' that are uttered to flatter or to avoid hurting someone's feelings are of this kind. Some people even argue that certain 'little lies' are inconsequential and have 'little' actual impact. However, the very people who vigorously defend a falsehood on such grounds are rarely comfortable with others telling them 'white lies'. Moreover, there can be some long-term unintended consequences of lying.

One of the greatest harms of a lie is that potentially valuable information is not made available to change a policy, alter a procedure, or mitigate potentially serious situations. For example, when an employee lies about various actions during a crisis, the true cause of the disaster may never be known; thus the potential for recurrence is high. The bottom line is that lying should be resisted. Lying breaks down trust between individuals, shaking the very foundation upon which discourse between people is based.

### Gobbledygook

George Orwell, in his 1946 essay, 'Politics and the English Language' dubbed such language as 'doublespeak', 'makes the bad seem good, the negative appear positive, the unpleasant appear attractive or at least tolerable'. It is the intentional use of vague and unclear language in order to avoid responsibility. Here is an example of a recall notice sent by an American auto manufacturer.

'A defect which involves the possible failure of a *frame support plate* may exist on your vehicle. This plate (*front suspension pivot bar support plate*) connects a portion of the front suspension to the vehicle frame, and its failure could affect *vehicle directional control*, particularly during heavy brake application. In addition, your vehicle may require adjustment service to the *hood secondary catch system*.... Sudden *hood fly-up* beyond the *secondary catch* while driving could impair driver visibility....'

The writer's use of technical jargon and ambiguous terms such as 'vehicle directional control' and 'adjustment service' cloak a potentially life-threatening condition. The average reader may not even care to finish reading the entire letter. Legally, the company has done its bit to keep customers informed of serious problems with their cars. This is a prime example of how it is possible to deliberately cover up a problem that may cost the company money by using evasive and misleading language. An ethical communicator must be committed in his/her intention to get the message across to his/her audience. His/her message would therefore be conveyed in language that is straightforward, clear, and simple. The notice that follows exemplifies this, in stark contrast to the previous one:

'We have enclosed a letter from the Administrator of the National Highway Traffic Safety Administration (NHTSA), which provides very important information and precautions to help avoid injury from an inflating air bag. Please read this letter carefully to ensure that you fully understand the precautions listed. We have also enclosed two warning labels, which list these important precautions.

We encourage you to attach these warning labels over the existing air bag warnings on the sun visors in your dual air bag car...We urge you to leave the labels in place for any subsequent owners of the vehicle.

Remember the ABCs for: Air bag safety, Buckle everyone, with Children in the back seat...

You can rest assured that we at Subaru are committed to your safety and satisfaction with your Subaru product.'

In sharp contrast to the previous notice, this notice is a good example of ethical communication. It shows concern for its customers, has a personal tone, and offers helpful information in easily understood terms. It goes one step further in offering help even to future owners.

## Ambiguity

> Ethical organizations must have a culture that symbolically signals its commitment.

Since all language contains some degree of vagueness, there might be some question as to why the topic is even discussed in a chapter on ethics. Yet, ambiguity, like secrecy, can be used for ethical or unethical purposes. For example, when an employee asks his/her supervisor about the possibility of promotion and is told, 'We have the very best in mind but we cannot discuss it now,' the supervisor implies that the subordinate would in fact be promoted. That is at least one possible interpretation. But what the manager actually mean is that he/she has 'the best' in mind for the company, which meant that the employee would eventually be fired. That, of course, is another possible interpretation. There can be no doubt that only the most cynical of employees would come away with the latter interpretation. Was such a statement an ethical way to stall further discussion? In a lie, the onus of responsibility for veracity clearly is with the sender of the message but with ambiguity, who is actually responsible, is not altogether clear. There can be no question that in the example above, deception was the obvious intent and indeed the effect. In this sense, the manager's actions were unethical. Moreover, there were legitimate alternatives open to the manager. If he/she wanted no further discussion, he/she could have simply said, 'We will have to discuss it later'. Such an expression implies no commitment and does not lead the employee astray.

## STRATEGIC APPROACHES TO CORPORATE ETHICS

There is probably no way to guarantee that a corporation or its employees will behave ethically. Yet acknowledgement of occasional failures does not reduce our fundamental ethical responsibility.

---

### Exxon—Corporate Irresponsibility

The Exxon Valdez oil tanker made international headlines in 1989 when it ran aground and spilled a significant quantity of its cargo of 1,260,000 barrels of oil into the sea. It was later established that the crew member steering the ship at the time was not certified to do so. In addition, the captain and many of the crew had been drinking heavily. What followed was worse. Not only did Exxon react extremely slowly to the crisis, it failed completely in communicating any concern over the accident. The then Exxon Chairman, Lawrence Rawl, refused television interviews. A week passed by with the media clamouring for more information about the company's remedial actions to contain the spillage. Finally, Frank Larossi, the then director of Exxon Shipping, held a press conference at Valdez. He was obviously not well-prepared, for even small bits of good news were promptly contradicted by journalists and fishermen who had personally witnessed the disastrous effects of the spill. The eventual television appearance of the chairman was the last straw. Questioned live about the company's latest plans for cleaning up the oil spill, Rawl revealed that he had no idea about these and stated that it was not his job to read such reports. The repercussions for Exxon, of the oil spill and consequent environmental disaster, along with the damage caused to its image by its dismal management of the crisis were enormous. The company not only had to pay the largest ever fine levied for corporate irresponsibility—a total of $7 billion—it lost market share and its position as the largest oil company in the world. The name 'Exxon Valdez' is now synonymous with corporate irresponsibility and arrogance.

Organizations, like people, should strive for ethical behaviour. This is as much a philosophical position as a moral one. Moreover, like all great philosophical statements, it implies certain actions. For organizations, it implies action on three basic levels: (i) cultural, (ii) policy based, and (iii) personal. Ethical organizations are created and sustained by individuals of personal integrity, operating in a culture of principle, and governed by ethical policies.

## Corporate Culture

There is little consensus on the nature of information ethics. In short, there are few agreed upon cultural values for how information is to be treated. Building consensus on informational values may be one of the greatest cultural challenges facing CEOs in the future. For example, only in the last few years has an ethic about copy protected software started to emerge. Indeed, the ethical organizations must have a culture that symbolically signals its commitment. There are varieties of ways to do this, including the development of a set of fundamental operating principles that are widely circulated in organizations. But principles are not enough; they must be translated into policies.

### *Which Detergent Washes the Whitest?*

Would you stop using your favourite detergent if you knew that it was a 'non-ethical' product? In order to cater to the passion of Indians for whiter clothes, detergent companies offer products that pollute rivers and kill fish. Ecologically safe, 'bio-wash' detergents that are available in the West, have still not found a place in the Indian market. However, the world is changing rapidly. Customer awareness about ethics in corporate culture is considerably more and affects their buying decisions. Organizations, that are in tune with these trends, have realized that it is now good business to think of society's interests when the organization makes certain decisions. Johnson & Johnson, for example, decided to stop manufacturing feeding bottles to promote the concept of breastfeeding.

### *The Delighted Customer*

Here is a quote from N.L. Mirchandani, former personnel head and currently an HRD advisor to Crompton Greaves and a prominent name in the Indian industry, regarding the concept of corporate ethics, 'We at Crompton Greaves call this concept Customer Delight. Since our products are highly technical in nature, we adopt the concept in the following manner. We believe that our customer should be happy; should come back to buy our products, and at the same time we also keep in mind that any of our products do not harm the society. With adequate market research we find both the positive as well as negative features of our product. The necessary changes, if required, are conveyed to the engineers, design team who can thus make the correct product that the society desires. That is why every Crompton product is environment friendly. Every Crompton product is easier for the consumer to use and has a good shelf life with no break downs.'

## Organizational Policy

There are three critical policy issues that every organization must face. First, what information should be gathered? Second, how should that information be gathered? Third, how should the information be used?

## Policy Issue I—What Information should be Gathered?

- A proper information policy should consider the often-conflicting needs and desires of the three fundamental groups.
- Organizations need to respect employees' freedom of speech while simultaneously protecting vital information.

There are important ethical considerations when one gathers information, and organizations need to carefully consider the implications of their procedures. One way to capture the perplexities facing an organization is to examine the tension between one who controls access to the information and one who desires the information. In particular, three fundamental parties are involved—individual/potential employees, the organization, and the community at large. A proper information policy should consider the often-conflicting needs and desires of each of these three groups (Table 20.1).

**Sector 1** Organizations routinely collect such information. Employee files need to be structured in such a way that managers have access only to the information necessary to make proper decisions. The guiding principle in making such decisions should be relevancy to the decisions that need to be made. Many of these changes can be easily implemented by changing the forms used to collect employee information. Gathering more information is not always better; it can be intrusive.

**Sector 2** It represents the quandary often faced by employees in resolving their respective responsibilities to the community at large and to the company. Employees need to have a clear sense of what they can and cannot discuss with members of the community at large. Organizations need to respect employees' freedom of speech while simultaneously protecting vital information. Employees should be aware that trade secrets, marketing plans, and the like are out of bounds. Making the community privy to internal policy disputes is another questionable activity, although employees of public agencies are allowed a little more leeway in publicly criticizing policies. On the other hand, employees are

**Table 20.1** Dilemmas in gathering information

| | By From | Information Desired By | | |
|---|---|---|---|---|
| | | Individual | Organization | Community |
| Information Controlled | Individual | | Sector 1<br>Medical Records<br>Employment of Spouse<br>Marital Status<br>Off-job behaviors<br>Personality tests | Sector 2<br>Corporate misconduct<br>Trade secrets<br>Corporate strategy<br>Policy disputes |
| | Organization | Sector 3<br>Performance appraisals<br>Personal files<br>Salary projections<br>Private management files | | Sector 4<br>Recommendation letters<br>Product information<br>Employees names, phone numbers |
| | Community | Sector 5<br>Affirmative action<br>Professional standards<br>Legal rights | Sector 6<br>Competitor strategy<br>Government policies<br>Forthcoming media stories | |

ethically obligated to report corporate misconduct and consumer safety concerns if the corporation proves unresponsive.

**Sector 3**   It addresses the issue of what degree of access employee should have to files about themselves. As suggested above, there are a few areas in which the company rightfully restricts employees access to their records, like projected promotion prospects or salary plans. IBM has an exemplary policy on this point. Employees are allowed to see almost all job-related and non-job-related information in their files. If they feel an error has been made, they can insert explanatory material. This policy of open employee files may sound burdensome to some organizations but few companies have utilized it well.

**Sector 4**   It represents the information that a community desires about an organization. Publicly held corporations have a legal responsibility to provide certain information to their stockholders, like earnings, assets, and liabilities. Product information is another area of concern about which corporations need to have a policy. Balancing the legitimate need for trade secrecy and the public's need for information is tricky. Certainly, clear warning of potential hazards must be provided by the company. The precise shape of the warning and the extent of the warning is an ethical issue that is being hotly debated at present. Another issue of concern is how much information about an employee can be released to outsiders without the employee's knowledge.

**Sector 5**   It represents information primarily under the control of the community that is desired by employees. Corporations have some limited responsibilities to insure that individuals are aware of laws and government policies that affect their well-being. Corporate newsletters often serve this function. Organizations also have a vested interest in allowing their employees access to professional organizations and societies. Organizations quite legitimately seek information about the community at large. The environment has a tremendous impact on the corporation.

**Sector 6**   It lays out some of the ethical decision points for the organization. How far should the organization go in trying to gather information about a competitor, the government's future plans, and the press? The issues here are particularly fuzzy because the restrictions often are more in terms of *how* the information is gathered rather than *what* information is gathered.

### Policy Issue 2—How is the Information Gathered?

If information objectives are legitimate but the means used to gather the information are not, then the entire process is deemed unethical. Managers, therefore, must not only be concerned with what information they gather but also the means by which it is gathered. Organizations must have some kind of policy on what methods can be used to gather information about employees. Should an organization carry on investigations about employees without their knowledge? These vexing issues not only raise questions about employee privacy but also send powerful messages about the degree of trust the management has in its employee.

> Organizations must have some kind of policy on what methods can be used to gather information about employees.

Fundamentally, the issue comes to fairness. Most of the information needed about competitors can be legitimately obtained from published sources that are widely available.

Organizations would be well advised to set up 'due process' procedures to air employee grievances. Corporate due process is a dispute resolution pro-cedure whereby a neutral agency or person has the power to investigate,

> Communicators should take care that their remarks are pertinent to the purpose at hand.

adjudicate, and rectify. Employees have a vehicle for dealing with grievances outside the normal chain of command. Corporate due process is a kind of organizational safety valve for employees. It is needed because some problems cannot be resolved fairly through the normal open-door policies. Grievance review boards typically disregard rank and status issues and focus on the merits of an employee's case.

### Policy Issue 3—How is the Information Used?

Information, unlike property, can be lost without you knowing it. Unlike a thief who steals jewellery, someone could read a personnel file and leave no clue that a theft has even taken place. In this sense, providing security for information is more difficult than protecting property. Once information is released, it is no longer under your control. For instance, mailing in a donation to a worthy cause often means that your name is placed on dozens of mailing lists for other charities, which freely send you their literature and solicitations. Therefore, organizations need to carefully consider a few fundamental questions.

Who is allowed access to information? As already suggested, employee files should be classified in such a way that managers have access only to information they really need to make decisions. Also, organizations need to have restrictions on the type of channel that can be used to request certain information. It is far too easy for an unauthorized person to pick up the phone and gather classified information. In a crisis or time of uncertainty, employees feel more secure if there are guidelines about when information will be forthcoming.

Organizations should consider when information should be destroyed. Negative information in a personnel file often tags along with a person for years. This may unfairly influence decision-making. For example, one executive was not given a promotion because his personnel file contained a note about 'larcenous tendencies'. It turns out that characterization referred to a teenage prank. How long should performance appraisals be kept on record? Is there really any need to keep an appraisal form 10 years old?

### Relevancy

Communication should be structured around the norm of relevancy, that is, communicators should take care that their remarks are pertinent to the purpose at hand. Private confidential discussions have no place in external decisions. In this context, relevancy means that only information relevant

---

**William LeMessurier—Standing Tall**

William LeMessurier worked as the design and construction consultant on Citicorp's headquarters (a tower) in New York, which was constructed during the late 1970s. In 1978, a college student who had studied the innovative design of the tower with 59 storeys called LeMessurier to bring to his notice a possible deficiency. Rather than dismissing the student's observation, LeMessurier took up the matter in great detail and discovered that the student had been correct. Faced with a problem involving professional responsibility, LeMessurier managed the difficult task of communicating with a broad group of people and getting them to cooperate in repairing the structural deficiencies before a hurricane could collapse the building. Corporate culture and organizational policy are powerful forces that can mold the ethical spirit of an organization, but they are not substitutes for the character of an individual employee.

> Even accurate information can be useless if communicated in an untimely fashion.

to a specific purpose is collected. It means that when the information is no longer pertinent, it is disposed of. The norm of relevancy means that all relevant facts be brought to bear on a decision.

### Accuracy

A healthy respect for truth is the foundation of communication. Only when information is reliable can we be free to make choices. Lies and half-truths rob people of fundamental choices. If an employees lies about the true cause of accident, it prevents the organization from protecting others from harm. Information is sketchy enough in these situations; intended deception not only compounds the difficulty but may also point investigations in precisely the wrong direction. Therefore, all employees must be committed to the ethic of accuracy, even when the implications prove personally painful.

### Timing

Even accurate information can be useless if communicated in an untimely fashion. Why? Just as with a lie, choice can be restricted. Everyday an employee who sits on the news of impending lay-offs may deprive some employee of another job opportunity that comes his/her way. By timing communication properly, one communicates respect for the individual. Truth is not the only criteria by which communication is judged. Information may well be accurate and even timely but fail to be used with discretion.

## ETHICAL COMMUNICATION ON THE INTERNET

Communication technology has changed so radically in the past 10 years that we no longer even know what is ethical, let alone legal. Since communication has changed, a workable framework is needed that defines ethical communication in the Internet era.

The Internet is the latest and in many respects most powerful in a line of media—telegraph, telephone, radio, and television. It has enormous consequences for individuals, nations, and the world. Use of the new information technology and the Internet needs to be informed and guided by a resolute commitment to the practice of solidarity in the service of the common good, within and among nations. This technology can be a means for solving human problems, promoting the integral development of persons, and creating a world governed by justice, peace, and love. The spread of the Internet also raises a number of other ethical questions about matters like privacy, security and confidentiality of data, copyright and intellectual property law, pornography, hate sites, dissemination of rumours and character assassination under the guise of news, and so on.

### The Internet

> Digital divide refers to the discrimination dividing people on the basis of access to information technology.

The Internet has a number of striking features. It is instantaneous, worldwide, decentralized, interactive, endlessly expandable in contents and outreach, flexible, and adaptable to a remarkable degree. It is egalitarian, in the sense that anyone with the necessary equipment and modest technical skills can be an active presence in cyberspace, declare his or her message to the world, and demand a hearing. It allows individuals to indulge in anonymity, role playing, and fantasizing and

> Cultural domination is a problem when a dominant culture carries false values inimical to the true good of individuals and groups.

also to enter into community with others and engage in sharing. The technological configuration underlying the Internet has a considerable bearing on its ethical aspects—people have tended to use it according to the way it was designed, and to design it to suit that kind of use.

## Some Areas of Concern

Let us now consider some areas of concern regarding ethical communication on the Net.

### Digital Divide

One of the most important of areas of concern involves what today is called the digital divide—a form of discrimination dividing the rich from the poor, both within and among nations, on the basis of access, or lack of access, to the new information technology. In this sense, it is an updated version of an older gap between the 'information rich' and 'information poor'. The expression 'digital divide' underlines the fact that individuals, groups, and nations must have access to the new technology in order to share in the promised benefits of globalization and development and not fall further behind. It is imperative 'that the gap between the beneficiaries of the new means of information and expression and those who do not have access to them ... not become another intractable source of inequity and discrimination.' Ways need to be found to make the Internet accessible to less advantaged groups, either directly or at least by linking it with lower-cost traditional media. Cyberspace ought to be a resource of comprehensive information and services available without charge to all, and in a wide range of languages. Public institutions have a particular responsibility to establish and maintain sites of this kind. In this connection it should be borne in mind that the causes and consequences of the divide are not only economic but also technical, social, and cultural.

### Cultural Domination

There is also a growing concern about the cultural dimensions of what is now taking place. Precisely as powerful tools of the globalization process, the new information technology and the Internet transmit and help instil a set of cultural values—ways of thinking about social relationships, family, religion, the human condition—whose novelty and glamour can challenge and overwhelm traditional cultures. Intercultural dialogue and enrichment are, of course, highly desirable. Indeed, dialogue between cultures is especially needed today because of the impact of new communications technology on the lives of individuals and peoples' but this has to be a two-way street. Cultures have much to learn from one another, and merely imposing the worldview, values, and even language of one culture upon another is not dialogue but cultural imperialism.

Cultural domination is an especially serious problem when a dominant culture carries false values inimical to the true good of individuals and groups. As matters stand, the Internet, along with the other media of social communication, is transmitting the value-laden message of western secular culture to people and societies that are, in many cases, ill-prepared to evaluate and cope with it. Many serious problems result, for example, in regard to marriage and family life, which is experiencing 'a radical and widespread crisis' in many parts of the world. Cultural sensitivity and respect for other people's values and beliefs are imperative in these circumstances. Intercultural dialogue that 'protects the distinctiveness of cultures as historical and creative expressions of the underlying unity of the human family, and ... sustains understanding and communion between them' is needed to build and maintain the sense of international solidarity.

### *Freedom of Expression*

The question of freedom of expression on the Internet is complex and gives rise to another set of concerns. Freedom of expression and the free exchange of ideas must be upheld, as freedom to seek and know the truth is a fundamental human right, and freedom of expression is a cornerstone of democracy. Authoritarian regimes are by far the worst offenders in this regard; but the problem also exists in liberal democracies, where access to media for political expression often depends on wealth, and politicians and their advisors violate truthfulness and fairness by misrepresenting opponents and shrinking issues to sound-bite dimensions.

### *Internet Journalism*

The Internet is a highly effective instrument for bringing news and information rapidly to people. But the economic competitiveness and round-the-clock nature of Internet journalism also contributes to sensationalism and spreading of rumours; to a merging of news, advertising, and entertainment; and to an apparent decline in serious reporting and commentary. Honest journalism is essential to the common good of nations and the international community. Problems visible in the practice of journalism on the Internet call for speedy correction by journalists themselves. The sheer overwhelming quantity of information on the Internet, much of it unevaluated as to accuracy and relevance, is a problem for many. But, we are also concerned lest people make use of the medium's technological capacity for customizing information simply to raise electronic barriers against unfamiliar ideas. That would be an unhealthy development in a pluralistic world where people need to grow mutual understanding. While Internet users have a duty to be selective and self-disciplined, that should not be carried to the extreme of walling themselves off from others. The medium's implications for psychological development and health likewise need continued study, including the possibility that prolonged immersion in the virtual world of cyberspace may be damaging to some. Although there are many advantages in the capacity technology gives to people to 'assemble packages of information and services uniquely designed for them', this also 'raises an inescapable question: Will the audience of the future be a multitude of audiences of one? ... What would become of solidarity—what would become of love—in a world like that?'

Regulation of the Internet is desirable, and in principle, industry self-regulation is best. 'The solution to problems arising from unregulated commercialization and privatization does not lie in state control of media but in more regulation according to criteria of public service and in greater public accountability.' Industry codes of ethics can play a useful role, provided they are seriously intended,

> - The sheer overwhelming quantity of information on the Internet is a problem for many.
> - Determined action in the private and public sectors is needed to close and eventually eliminate the digital divide.

involve representatives of the public in their formulation and enforcement, and, along with giving encouragement to responsible communicators, carry appropriate penalties for violations, including public censure. Circumstances may sometimes require state intervention, for example, by setting up media advisory boards representing the range of opinion in the community. The Internet's transnational, boundary-bridging character and its role in globalization require international co-operation in setting standards and establishing mechanisms to promote and protect the international common good. In regard to media technology, as in regard to other issues, 'there is a pressing need for equity at the international level'. Determined action in the private and public sectors is needed to close and eventually eliminate the digital divide.

Many difficult Internet-related questions call for international consensus, for example, how to guarantee the privacy of law-abiding individuals and groups without keeping law enforcement and security officials from exercising surveillance over criminals and terrorists; how to protect copyright and intellectual property rights without limiting access to material in the public domain and how to define the 'public domain' itself, how to establish and maintain broad-based Internet repositories of information freely available to all Internet users in a variety of languages, and how to protect women's rights with regard to Internet access and other aspects of the new information technology. In particular, the question of how to close the digital divide between the information rich and the information poor requires urgent attention in its technical, educational, and cultural aspects.

## Ethical Implications of Privacy in Electronic Mail

Cyberspace, the electronic frontier, may be perceived as a lattice of communities; some linked, some isolated. Communities (users of electronic mail) have shared the commonality of a hierarchy of virtues, intra-group civility, loyalty, tolerance, and common pursuits. However the current online community, as a whole, does not share a hierarchy of virtues, though some localized segments do. Among such segments, the people with whom one interacts most strongly will be selected more by commonality of interests and goals than by accidents of proximity, and as such will share some values. This online community as a whole does place a great stock in words in order to communicate ideas and concepts through the virtual world (Image 20.2).

### The Community

In the Internet community, one's identity is defined by his/her electronic mail (email) address. This transient assemblage of letters and digits provides a non-physical basis of identity. This virtual self may act as a proxy of the physical being holding a similar name, or it may not. This metaphysical puzzle is created by the technology and networks employed to gain access to this community. The technology offers its own conceptual, ethical, and technical challenges. Therefore, the cyberspace community exhibits an inherent basic ethical dilemma of what one (individual cyberistic community member) has a right to do versus what is right to do.

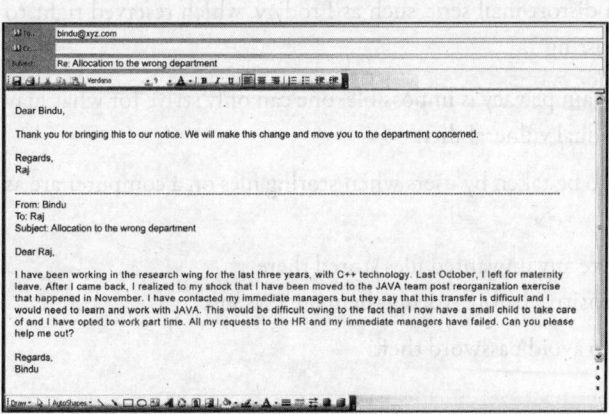

**Image 20.2** Email is a significant mechanism of communication transfer

### Identity

Once one has entered the Internet community and received an identity (unlike other communities where one originally arrives with some appearance of an identity), individuality and inherent personal rights within the community become an issue. One such right would be the right to privacy, generally thought of as being free from unnecessary intrusion into one's private affairs. Since the most common denominator of the online community is communication among the members as defined by their email addresses, email is the most significant mechanism of communication transfer and, therefore, group interaction.

### Privacy

This discussion of privacy with email will be explored as a personal rather than a technical issue, in order to identify potential ethical implications. The attempt of the discourse would be to blend existing ethics into today's technologies, aided by the concepts of computer ethics. Ethics, as such, are not to be viewed as prescriptive, but as preferable to prevent problems prior to presentation rather than punishment after unethical acts have been committed. The concept of individual privacy with email would suggest users' expectations of an exclusive access and account usage. Personal problems with email transmission arising from the technology employed and current legal framework include the following:

**Received mail**  It can

- be from anyone other than the account holder ('spoofing')
- be from hackers forging the 'From' field
- be from someone with access to the account
- arrive via anonymous remailer
- arrive due to mailing lists, where the e-mail address of everyone on the list is accessible

**Sent mail**  The following situations may arise:

- Computer systems may crash and may not resolve names into addresses
- Computer and domain names at destination sites frequently change
- Anonymous remailers may not be secure

In general, consider the following factors:

- Bounced mail may be seen by an unscrupulous person
- System administrators and operators can read messages in spool files at local sites—source or destination
- Many companies consider individual emails as corporate property
- Service provider specifications can distort mail sent, such as Prodigy, which reserved right to edit any public messages prior to posting

Therefore, since absolute security to maintain privacy is impossible, one can only strive for what may be considered an acceptable level of individual vulnerability.

**Storing files**  Common technical steps to be taken by users when storing files on a computer are as follows:

- Note system backup times and delete any unwanted files stored there.
- Encrypt messages that are reader sensitive before storing them on a system.

**Password**  Consider the following tips to avoid password theft:

- Choose a secure password
- Do not let anyone see it being entered
- Change it frequently

## Communication Tool

**Computer ethics**

The ten commandments of computer ethics are as follows:

1. Thou shalt not use a computer to harm other people.
2. Thou shalt not interfere with other people's computer work.
3. Thou shalt not snoop around in other people's computer files.
4. Thou shalt not use a computer to steal.
5. Thou shalt not use a computer to bear false witness.
6. Thou shalt not copy or use proprietary software for which thou hast not paid.
7. Thou shalt not use other people's computer resources without authorization or proper compensation.
8. Thou shalt not appropriate other people's intellectual output.
9. Thou shalt think about the social consequences of the program thou art writing or the system thou art designing.
10. Thou shalt always use a computer in ways that insure consideration and respect for thine fellow humans.

- Never mention passwords in emails
- Always logout completely
- Do not leave online account unattended, or use 'xlock' if it is not inconvenient to others
- Check host file

### Need for Better Protocol

While the forerunner of today's Internet, ARPANET may be viewed as a social construct for those early users (defense department sponsored researchers), the modern Internet is definitely shaping society. While this technology will continue to shape society, it need not exhibit technological determinism. The destiny and perception of the users' experience need not be led simply by the available technology, and the minority segment able to master it. While those for whom the project was a social construct are a majority of those able to master the technology, the majority of the new users exhibit more aspects of popular culture and inherent desires and interests.

**The 10 commandments and email**   The commandments (in the box above) are readily applicable to the topic of privacy in email. Some general examples and illustrations are listed as follows:

*Respect confidentiality (commandments 1, 2, and 8)*   If you desire to forward or otherwise share received mail, check with the sender to make sure it is permissible. If that is somehow impossible, strip off all personal and identifying information including routing.

*Do not 'flame' (commandments 1 and 10)*   To send an inflammatory remark or message can cause great harm to another individual. Such words delivered electronically are experienced differently than any other type of media, with potential for long lasting effects.

*Do not use anonymous remailers (commandments 1, 5, and 10)*   Do not use these services, unless whistle blowing or otherwise fear of recrimination for telling the truth. This would be a teleological decision, based on the extrinsic value of the action.

*Do not look at other's messages (commandment 3)*   Gaining access to another's account is not justifiable unless expressly acting as their agent. Looking at someone's printed out mail is equally incorrect.

*Do not misrepresent or lie (commandment 5)*   Given the issue of the lack of privacy with email transmission, the potential exists for a misrepresentation or falsehood to revisit the sender. While the old adage of 'what goes around comes around' may not be universally true with positive energies and deeds, it often is realized via negative actions and perspectives.

*Follow guidelines (commandment 7)*   Check to see if the service provider or company has an electronic messaging privacy policy. If one exists, learn what is delineated. If not, follow guidelines for development summarized below. Anything transmitted may be publicly aired if a privacy policy is not in effect.

*Consider the presentation of a message (commandment 10)*   Evaluate the physical appearance of the message to be sent. Consider starting with a blank line, do not shout (all caps) and eliminate sexist language from emails by using gender-neutral pronouns and titles. Try to be aware of cultural differences or other issues that may affect the reader adversely.

## Application of Computer Ethics to Problems Identified

What can one do, within this framework, about problems identified earlier? Let us consider a few options.

### Receiving Mail

The following tips would come in handy:

- Do not be on a mailing list if do not want the world to know your email address—this may 'conceal' but will not avoid the general problems noted previously.
- Try not to become a 'lurker', instead be a contributory participant as a member of the community.

### Sending Mail

The following pointers should be kept in mind when sending emails:

- Be aware of and respect the comfort level of recipient(s) with your words.
- If involved as a mailing list editor, recognize the significance of the role as a publisher with the acquisition, use, and dissemination of information.

In general, the following guidelines are important:

- In an organization that has, or is considering, email usage, develop and distribute an email privacy policy.
- Follow the relevant EMA guidelines for formulating a privacy policy for corporate electronic messaging.
- Upon discovery of uncomfortable situations specific to a service provider, such as Prodigy, encourage ethical competition.
- If a company does not have an email privacy policy, it should establish privacy solutions that deal with all methods of employee communication media.

### Additional Concerns

The following questions will help settle upon an email privacy policy:

1. Who has a stake in establishing a responsible policy regarding access to and disclosure of company electronic mail? How will the policy affect the employer, employee, third parties, law enforcement authorities, and electronic communications service providers?
2. What baseline legal rights and duties constrain any policy?
3. What operational features of electronic communications systems should affect any policy on access, use, and disclosure?
4. What analogies can be used to help formulate a consistent set of policies?
5. What criteria should be used to evaluate a proposed policy?
6. Has your policy been disclosed in advance by all concerned?
7. Who from the organization should participate in the development of the policy?
8. What corporate assets should be considered when formulating overall workplace privacy policies?
9. What information will you want to gather in advance or during the course of formulating your policy?

Here, some of the ethical implications of privacy with email have been identified and explored, however, the uncontrollable communication and, therefore, information flow will continue to pass and grow through the Internet backbone as a form of media. The value of, and right to, privacy will continue to compete with other values in our global society within the virtual community. The clash of old inherent freedoms and new emergent technologies will continue to generate ethical issues for discussion, reflection, and action.

## ETHICS IN ADVERTISING

The importance of advertising is steadily on the increase in modern society. Advertising, using media as its vehicle, is a pervasive and powerful force shaping attitudes and behaviour in today's world. In today's society, advertising has a profound impact on how people understand life, the world, and themselves, especially in regard to their values and their ways of choosing and behaving.

The field of advertising is extremely broad and diverse. In general terms, an advertisement is simply a public notice meant to convey information and invite patronage or some other response. As that suggests, advertising has two basic purposes—to inform and persuade, and—while these purposes are distinguishable—both very often are simultaneously present. Advertising is not the same as marketing (the complex of commercial functions involved in transferring goods from producers and consumers) or public relations (the systematic effort to create a favourable public impression or 'image' of some person, group, or entity). In many cases, though, it is a technique or instrument employed by one or both of these. Advertising can be very simple—a local, even 'neighbourhood', phenomenon—or it can be very complex, involving sophisticated research and multimedia campaigns that span the globe. It differs according to its intended audience, so that, for example, advertising aimed at children raises some technical and moral issues significantly different from those raised by advertising aimed at competent adults. Not only are

> Advertising has two basic purposes—to inform and to persuade.

many different media and techniques employed in advertising; advertising itself is of several different kinds: commercial advertising for products and services; public service advertising on behalf of various institutions, programmes, and causes; and—a phenomenon of growing importance today—political advertising in the interests of parties and candidates. Making allowance for the differences among the different kinds and methods of advertising, we intend what follows to be applicable to them all.

Advertisers are selective about the values and attitudes to be fostered and encouraged, promoting some while ignoring others. This selectivity gives the lie to the notion that advertising does no more than reflect the surrounding culture. For example, the absence from advertising of certain racial and ethnic groups in some multiracial or multi-ethnic societies can help to create problems of image and identity. Advertising also has an indirect but powerful impact on society through its influence on media. Many publications and broadcasting operations depend on advertising revenue for survival. This often is true of religious media as well as commercial media. For their part, advertisers naturally seek to reach audiences; and the media, striving to deliver audiences to advertisers, must shape their content so to attract audiences of the size and demographic composition sought. This economic dependency of media and the power it confers upon advertisers carries with it serious responsibilities for both.

## Benefits of Advertising

Enormous human and material resources are devoted to advertising. Even people who are not themselves exposed to particular forms of advertising confront a society, a culture—other people—affected for good or ill by advertising messages and techniques of every sort. Advertising also has significant potential for good, and sometimes it is realized. Some of the ways that happens are as follows:

### *Economic Benefits of Advertising*

Advertising can play an important role in the process by which an economic system, guided by moral norms and responsive to the common good, contributes to human development. It is a necessary part of the functioning of modern market economies, which today either exist or are emerging in many parts of the world and which—provided they conform to moral standards based upon integral human development and the common good—currently seem to be 'the most efficient instrument for utilizing resources and effectively responding to needs' of a socio-economic kind. In such a system, advertising can be a useful tool for sustaining honest and ethically responsible competition that contributes to economic growth in the service of authentic human development. Advertising does this, among other ways, by informing people about the availability of rationally desirable new products and services and improvements in existing ones, helping them to make informed and prudent consumer decisions, contributing to efficiency and the lowering of prices, and stimulating economic progress through the expansion of business and trade. All of these can contribute to the creation of new jobs, higher incomes, and a more decent and humane way of life for all.

### *Cultural Benefits of Advertising*

Because of the impact advertising has on media that depend on it for revenue, advertisers have an opportunity to exert a positive influence on decisions about media content. This they do by supporting material of excellent intellectual, aesthetic, and moral quality presented with the public interest

**Image 20.3** Effective advertising—a cola ad
© Oxford University Press ANZ

in view, and particularly by encouraging and making possible media presentations which are oriented to minorities whose needs might otherwise go unserved. Moreover, advertising can itself contribute to the betterment of society by uplifting and inspiring people and motivating them to act in ways that benefit themselves and others.

### Moral and Religious Benefits of Advertising

In many cases, too, benevolent social institutions, including those of a religious nature, use advertising to communicate their messages—messages of faith, patriotism, tolerance, compassion and neighbourly service, charity toward the needy, messages concerning health and education, and constructive and helpful messages that educate and motivate people in a variety of beneficial ways.

### Harms Done by Advertising

There is nothing intrinsically good or evil about advertising. It is a tool, an instrument that can be used well. It can also have a negative, harmful impact on individuals and the society at large. If harmful or utterly useless goods are touted to the public, false assertions are made about goods for sale, and less than admirable human tendencies are exploited, those responsible for such advertising harm society and forfeit their good name and credibility. More than this, unremitting pressure to buy articles of luxury can arouse false wants that hurt both individuals and families by making them ignore what they really need.

### Economic Harms of Advertising

Advertising can betray its role as a source of information by misrepresentation and withholding relevant facts. Sometimes, the information function of media can be subverted by advertisers' pressure upon publications, etc. to not treat questions that might prove embarrassing or inconvenient. More often, though, advertising is used not simply to inform but to persuade and motivate—to convince people to act in certain ways—buy certain products or services, patronize certain institutions, and the like. This is where particular abuses can occur. The practice of brand-related advertising can raise serious problems. Often there are only negligible differences among similar products of different brands, and advertising may attempt to move people to act on the basis of irrational motives (e.g., brand loyalty, status, fashion, sex appeal, etc.) instead of presenting differences in product quality and price as bases for rational choice. Sometimes advertisers speak of it as part of their task to 'create' needs for products and services, that is, to cause people to feel and act upon cravings for items and services they do not need.

Serious harm can be done if advertising and commercial pressure become so irresponsible that communities seeking to rise from poverty to a reasonable standard of living are persuaded to seek this progress by satisfying wants that have been artificially created. The result of this is that they waste their resources and neglect their real needs, and genuine development falls behind. Similarly, the task of countries attempting to develop types of market economies that serve human needs and interests after decades under centralized, state-controlled systems is made more difficult by advertising that promotes consumerist attitudes and values offensive to human dignity and the common good.

### *Cultural Harms of Advertising*
Advertising also can have a corrupting influence upon culture and cultural values. We have spoken of the economic harm that can be done to developing nations by advertising that fosters consumerism and destructive patterns of consumption. Consider, also, the cultural injury done to these nations and their people by advertising whose content and methods, reflecting those prevalent in the first world, are at war with sound traditional values in indigenous cultures. Today this kind of 'domination and manipulation' via media is rightly a concern of developing nations in relation to developed ones, as well as a 'concern of minorities within particular nations'.

Communicators also can find themselves tempted to ignore the educational and social needs of certain segments of the audience—the very young, very old, poor—who do not match the demographic patterns (i.e., age, education, income, habits of buying, and consuming, etc.) of the kind of audience advertisers want to reach. In this way the tone and the level of moral responsibility of the communications media in general are lowered.

All too often, advertising contributes to the invidious stereotyping of particular groups that places them at a disadvantage in relation to others. This often is true of the way advertising treats women; and the exploitation of women, both in and by advertising, is a frequent, deplorable abuse.

### *Moral and Religious Harms of Advertising*
Advertising can be tasteful and in conformity with high moral standards, and occasionally even morally uplifting, but it also can be vulgar and morally degrading. Frequently, it deliberately appeals to such motives as envy, status seeking, and lust. Today, too, some advertisers consciously seek to shock and titillate by exploiting content of a morbid, perverse, and pornographic nature accessible to a vastly expanded audience, including young people and even children, and a problem, which at one time was confined mainly to wealthy countries has now begun, via the communications media, to corrupt moral values in developing nations.

Even today, some advertising is simply and deliberately untrue. To be sure, advertising, like other forms of expression, has its own conventions and forms of stylization, and these must be taken into account when discussing truthfulness. People take for granted some rhetorical and symbolic exaggeration in advertising; within the limits of recognized and accepted practice, this can be allowable.

Much advertising directed at children apparently tries to exploit their credulity and suggestibility, in the hope that they will put pressure on their parents to buy products of no real benefit to them. Advertising like this offends against the dignity and rights of both children and parents; it intrudes upon the parent-child relationship and seeks to manipulate it to its own base ends.

### Advertising and Social Responsibility

Social responsibility is such a broad concept that we can note here only a few of the many issues and concerns relevant under this heading to the question of advertising. The ecological issue is one. Advertising that fosters a lavish life style that wastes resources and despoils the environment offends important ecological concerns.

Something more fundamental is at issue here: authentic and integral human development. Advertising that reduces human progress to acquiring material goods and cultivating a lavish life style expresses a false, destructive vision of the human person harmful to individuals and society alike. Advertisers, like people engaged in other forms of social communication, have a serious duty to express and foster an authentic vision of human development in its material, cultural, and spiritual dimensions. Communication that meets this standard is, among other things, a true expression of solidarity.

In the final analysis, however, where freedom of speech and communication exists, it is largely up to advertisers themselves to ensure ethically responsible practices in their profession. Besides avoiding abuses, advertisers should also undertake to repair the harm sometimes done by advertising, by publishing corrective notices, compensating injured parties, increasing the quantity of public service advertising, and the like. This question of 'reparations' is a matter of legitimate involvement not only by industry self-regulatory bodies and public interest groups, but also by public authorities.

Moreover, for the reasons and in the ways sketched here, we believe advertising can, and often does, play a constructive role in economic growth, exchange of information and ideas, and fostering solidarity among individuals and groups. Yet it also can do, and often does, grave harm to individuals and to the common good. In light of these reflections, therefore, we call upon advertising professionals and upon all those involved in the process of commissioning and disseminating advertising to eliminate its socially harmful aspects and observe high ethical standards in regard to truthfulness, human dignity, and social responsibility. In this way, they will make a special and significant contribution to human progress and to the common good.

## SUMMARY

Effective communication in organizations is always embedded with the ethical aspect of communication. With growing complexity in businesses, it has become imperative for organizations to have a sound value system and to try to instil a reasonable level of ethics in the employees. Ethical communication calls for some very simple practices. The communication partners should have a high element of trust, must share full and correct information without any prejudices, and above all, try to respect the audiences or the receiver's value systems.

Ethical issues in communication could be related to secrecy, whistle blowing, rumours and gossips, leaks, and ambiguity. Organizations should make efforts to contain these ethical dilemmas or, if at all they appear, should handle them professionally. Communication over the Internet adds more ethical issues to the already existing loopholes. Emails have become the most popular means of communication in modern organizations, and with their increased popularity comes the added responsibility of practising high level of ethics while transferring messages over the computer.

Ethical issues assume a very high level of significance when a company is using mass communication, like an advertisement, to tell about a product or service. Advertisements should be carefully drafted so that they do not impinge upon the target audiences' value systems.

## KEY TERMS

***Advertising ethics***   These refer to all ethical issues related to advertising. Advertising has an indirect but powerful impact on society through its influence on media and, therefore, advertisers should be very careful in exercising their roles and ethical stances.

***Computer ethics***   These refer to all ethical issues related to the use/misuse of systems, use of pirated software, and unwarranted invasion of privacy, etc.

***Ethical code***   These are the unwritten and implicit level of ethics every employee is supposed to maintain when working in an organization.

***Ethical communication***   It is basically communicating with an eye on the ethical issue involved in communication. It involves sharing full and correct information, respect for the target audience, and maintaining a good degree of healthy relationships based on mutual trust and respect for each others value systems

***Ethical leader***   They set the standard of truth for every employee, as they lead by following all the ethical practices.

***Organizational communication***   It refers to communication, which in various forms, primarily involves managers in an organization.

***Social responsibility***   It is a long-term commitment to the betterment of society imbibed in the strategic goals of an organization. Organizations have a more vital role to play in the modern context with growing linkages between what they do as business entities and what society expects from them.

***Utilitarian theories***   These hold that the moral worth of actions or practices are determined solely by their consequences

***Value systems***   These are among the most stable and enduring characteristics of individuals. They are the basis upon which attitudes and personal preferences are formed, as well as the basis for crucial decisions, life directions, and personal tastes.

***Whistle-blower***   It refers to an employee who goes public with information about corporate abuses or negligence.

## Concept Review Questions

1. What is the basic nature of ethics? Who decides what is ethical? How does culture influence ethics? Are ethics just standards agreed upon by members of a culture?
2. How do you think multicultural awareness relates to effective and ethical communication? Provide an example to illustrate your answer.
3. Is effective communication and ethical communication the same thing?
4. How can technological advances help make communication more effective? How do you think technology affects the ethics of communication?
5. Discuss whether or not communication must be intentional. Do you think intentionality of communication

relates to communication effectiveness or communication ethics?
6. Why do you thinks students at undergraduate level should have a compulsorily course on cyber ethics?
7. Is it ethical to tell a lie if someone else gave you permission to? For example, the phone rings, you pick it up, and your father tells you, 'If it is for me, tell them I am not home.' Else, your boss may instruct you, 'Tell the customer it has been back ordered,' when in reality, he/she forgot to order the part.
8. When does the public's right to know go too far in violating an individual's right to privacy?
9. What ethics/morals are best applied to the business world? Is it ethical for corporations to use psychological research to manipulate people through a message? What is the most appropriate way to handle ethical issues when they arise?
10. Is it morally correct to advertise to young children? For example, is it ethical to use cartoons to promote a product or target children who are too young to understand that they are being targeted?

## Critical Thinking Questions

### 1. Body Image

Do girls think they are overweight because they are getting the wrong idea of the perfect body from fashion magazines? A 1991 study conducted by a Boston hospital and published in *Pediatrics* shows that more than two-thirds of the girls in grades 5–12 said that their idea of the perfect figure was influenced by magazine photos. Forty seven per cent said that, because of the pictures, they wanted to lose weight. However, only 29 per cent of the 548 girls in the study were actually considered to be overweight. The girls reported that they regularly read magazines such as *Seventeen*, *Glamour*, and *Jet*. About one-third of the respondents were in elementary school and half of those reported reading fashion magazines two to five times a month.

*Source*: Associated Press report, 2 March 1999.

(a) Are fashion magazines, particularly those aimed specifically at young girls, acting responsibly when they publish photos of models with perfect figures?
(b) What ethical principles support your answer to this question?
(c) Whose responsibility is it to take the lead on the issue raised by this case study, and how might this issue be properly addressed?

### 2. Magazines

Advertisers know that young people are a rich market. Even very young children can be influenced enough to get their parents at purchase a desired product. A new, slick 200-page magazine *Toy Wishes* bills itself as 'the ultimate holiday buying guide'.

Some observers see the magazine as a helpful tool for busy parents who can now study the new toys and make purchase decisions, while, at the same time, avoiding the crowded aisles at toy stores. Other observers, however, see the publication as a thinly veiled marketing ploy directed at the children themselves. What child could resist paging through the magazine while squealing, 'I want that! I want that!'? The magazine's publisher notes that the publication is targeted at both kids and parents and that it will make shopping a pleasant and less-stressful experience. The magazine includes 'wish list' cards which kids can fill out and send to relatives. What better way to get the toys they want?

*Source*: Baltimore Sun, October 1999.

1. What ethical principles should govern advertisements (and publications) that target young children?
2. Is it ethical to make sales pitches to very young children who may not understand the advertising's purpose and often lack the cognitive skills to make discriminating choices?
3. Is it a parent's responsibility to shield a child from intrusive advertising messages?
4. Does the publication in which an advertisement appears have any responsibility in this situation?

3. **War and National Security**
   (a) With war and national security issues, how much should the media tell the public and how much should be kept secret?
   (b) How much does the public need to know and how much should the media tell us? We have seen instances when too much information, given by the media to the public, has resulted in mayhem and other instances where information given has stopped govern-ments from taking extreme and unwise steps.
4. **Television—Reality and News**
   (a) How much accuracy is expected in television depictions of reality?
   (b) What are the ethics that are associated with news reporting?

**Ethical issues in everyday personal interactions**
   (a) When is it ethical to lie?
   (b) What are the downfalls of honesty?
   (c) Is leaving out details considered lying? How bad is not disclosing all the information you have. What justifies a lie? Is it okay to lie if there is a crisis?
   (d) Is there a point when ethics should be put aside? Is it always necessary to be ethical?

## Projects

1. Pick an event that has ethical implications (e.g., problems and/or controversy). Pick an event with a specific set of individuals associated with it rather than a generalized problem. Divide yourselves into groups and focus on the issues keeping in mind public relations, broadcasting, or human communication related to your selection.

   Investigate the event such that you can answer the following questions:

   (i) What are the facts of the event? What actually happened? Note that there may be more than one account of the facts and you may have to sort them out and note any differences of opinion as to what the facts are.
   (ii) What is the 'rhetoric' that surrounds the event? What attributions are being made, whether justified or not, and are they based on fact, rumour, supposition, or opinion? Specifically, what judgements are being made, by who, and where? How are those judgements or attributions being presented?
   (iii) Thinking outward in layers, what are the ethical issues associated with the event? Think about the issues from the perspective of the participants, observers, family, friends, reporters, editors, public relations professionals, and others. Every event that has ethical issues will generally have a series of ethical problems/decisions that grow outward from the core. What are they?

2. Pick a medium of communication. A medium of communication, broadly defined, is a system/process that enables people to communicate with one another. This includes mass media, like television, radio, newspapers, and magazines. It also includes art media like oil paintings and films, correspondence media, like letters and memos, telephonic media, like cell phones, family radio, and intercoms, and media like face-to-face interaction, intimacy, classes, and live speeches. Having selected a medium, identify the roles associated with that medium of communication. What ethical responsibilities, options, and choices exist for each role?

## REFERENCES

Allyn and Bacon 2001, *Human Communication*, Pearson Education, pp. 44–72.

Benatar, D. 2002, *Ethics For Everyday*, Mcgraw-Hill, Boston, pp. 64–75.

Bowers, Jeremy 2003, *The Ethics of Modern Communication*, Scotia Press, Canada, pp. 24–31.

Castells, M. 1996, 'The Rise of the Network Society', *The Information Age: Economy, Society and Culture*, Blackwell, Cambridge, MA, Oxford, UK, Vol. I, pp. 556.

Coopman, Stephanie J. and James L. Applegate March 2000, 'Social-Cognitive Influences on the Use of Persuasive Message Strategies among Health Care Team Members', *American Communication Journal*, Volume 3, Issue 2, pp. 11–16.

Edgar, Andrew 2000, 'The "Fourth Estate" and Moral Responsibilities', *Ethics and Media Culture: Practices And Representations*, Berry, David (Ed), Focal Press, Oxford, pp. 73–88.

Iggers, Jeremy 1999, *Good News, Bad News: Journalism Ethics and the Public Interest*, Westview Press, Oxford, pp. 22–26.

Johannesen, R. L. 2002, *Ethics In Human Communication*, Fifth Edn, Waveland Press Inc., Prospect Heights, pp. 27–35.

Lepoire, B., J. Burgoon, and R. Parrott 1992, 'Status and Privacy Restoring Communication in the Workplace, *Journal of Applied Communication Research*, pp. 419–35.

Matheson, Donald 2005, 'Gadamer and Elements of a Communicative Ethics in News Practice', http://www.troubador.co.uk/journals/buy_journals. asp?journal=es 27 October.

Ruben, Brent and L. Stewart 1998, *Communication and Human Behavior*, Allyn-Bacon Boston.

Seeger, M.W. 1997, *Ethics and Organizational Communication*, Hampton Press, Cresskill, NJ, pp. 41–56.

Seeger, Matthew W. Fall 2001, 'Ethics and Communication in Organizational Contexts: Moving from the Fringe to the Center', *American Communication Journal*, Volume 5, Issue 1, pp. 22–24.

## CASE STUDY 1

### Electronic Mailing and Ethics

One communication technology rapidly growing in popularity is email, the system whereby individuals send one another messages over a computer network. The email recipient can, at his/her leisure, display the contents of his/her email box (which typically lists the sender of each message and some indication of each message's content), and then decide which of those messages to read. This method of communication can be extremely convenient. The sender can transmit messages whenever he/she wishes; the recipient can read messages and write responses as time allows. However, the privacy of such messages has become a source of some controversy. In 1993, for example, *Macworld* published a survey showing widespread eavesdropping by employers. Based on responses from 301 businesses employing over 1 million workers, the magazine estimated that as many as 20 million Americans might be subject to electronic monitoring on the job. The *Macworld* survey found that more than 21 per cent of the respondents had searched their employees' computer files, electronic mail, voicemail, or other networking communications. Of those who admitted to snooping, 74 per cent had searched computer work files, 42 per cent had searched electronic mail, and 15 per cent had searched voicemail. Why had those searches been conducted? To monitor workflow, investigate thefts, or prevent industrial espionage, some said. But, whatever the purpose, there are no legal limits placed on employers 'spying' on their employees in their workplace. They are free to view employees on closed circuit televisions, tap their telephones, search their email and network communications, and rummage through their computer files with or without employee knowledge or consent, twenty four hours a day.

Georgia Jones learned this lesson the hard way. An email expert, she was hired by a high-tech computer software firm in California to assist with the installation of a new email system and to provide training to the company's 350 employees concerning how that system should be used. After she had taken the job, she met with officials of the company to plan email installation and training. Among the many questions she asked was, 'Will employees' email messages be confidential?' 'Absolutely,' she was assured. During the training sessions, she repeated this information for the company's employees; she had been told that email messages would be kept confidential, so employees need not worry about the information they sent to one another. A few months after the email system had been installed and all employed had been trained, two first-line supervisors were fired by management. The rumour mill said they had been fired for being 'insubordinates', and that the email messages they had sent one another strongly criticizing the management had somehow ended up 'in the wrong hands'. Because she was concerned about this rumour, Georgia decided she should meet with the company's president. When she entered the president's office to keep their appointment, she noticed a stack of computer printouts on the credenza located along one wall of his office. A closer look revealed the contents of these printouts—employees' email messages. When she asked, 'What are those?,' the president answered, 'None of your business!'

**Questions**

1. If you were Georgia, what would you do?
2. What breaches of ethics, if any, occurred in this case?
3. In your opinion, should employees have the right to inspect employees' e-mail files, voice mail messages, computer files, and so on? Why or why not?
4. If you were going to develop a code of ethics to address this issue, what rules and guidelines might you include?

CHAPTER 21

# Business Communication Aids

### LEARNING OBJECTIVES

After reading this chapter, you will be able to understand

- the elements of effective English
- the essentials of effective paragraphs
- the power of reading
- the rules regarding punctuation and capitalization
- referencing styles
- email etiquette and related acronyms
- various business terms

## INTRODUCTION

Business communication in today's global business environment is dominated by technological aids. However, the importance of traditional skills in using the elements of standard English can never be ignored. For example, as a user of email, you have to be precise, direct, and free from errors, and also know the expected etiquettes; as a manager using video conferencing for communicating with your counterparts in other locations, it would benefit you if you are well versed with all the business terms and acronyms; as a writer or reader of business documents, you may have to keep yourself updated on the various referencing styles used in business reports and proposals. You must have acquired adequate English language skills in your academic life. Nevertheless, reviewing certain basic business communication aids will give you an edge over others by adding effectiveness to your business communication. This chapter illustrates certain rules of grammar, syntax, punctuation, paragraph writing, and referencing styles, and also provides a list of business terms, email etiquettes, and acronym.

> Reviewing basic business communication aids will aid in effective business communication.

## ELEMENTS OF EFFECTIVE ENGLISH

This section describes certain rules of grammar that would be helpful in business communication.

## Grammar and Syntax

Grammar refers to the rules used for combining words into sentences. This section will serve as a review of certain fundamental grammar rules that may help you avoid any communication barrier you may wish to avoid or overcome. By doing so, you can speak or write grammatically correct sentences.

### Correct Form of Verbs to Denote Correct Tenses

Consider the verb forms in the following examples.

>**Incorrect:** If he had *came* earlier, he could have met the CEO.
>**Correct:** If he had *come* earlier, he could have met the CEO.
>**Incorrect:** Despite the manager's orders, the employees have not *began* the operations.
>**Correct:** Despite the manager's orders, the employees have not *begun* the operations.

### Matching Subjects Agree with Verbs Despite Intervening Phrases and Clauses

A singular verb or pronoun is used with a singular subject and a plural verb or pronoun agrees with a plural subject. Some examples are as follows:

> The four *workers have* a photocopy of *their* assignments.
> Rohan's wife *was* quite late for *her* appointment.
> *Mr Thomas and Mrs Thomas plan* to forgo *their* bonuses.
> Included in this envelope *are a contract and an affidavit*.
> The tellers or the *clerks have* to balance *their* cash drawers before leaving.

Locate the subjects correctly. Do not be deceived by prepositional phrases and parenthetic words that often disguise the true subject.

>**Incorrect:** The report, despite its faulty analysis, illogical conclusions, and impractical recommendations *remain* as submitted.
>**Correct:** The report, despite its faulty analysis, illogical conclusions, and impractical recommendations *remains* as submitted.
>**Incorrect:** The manager and one of his secretaries *wishes* to attend the function.
>**Correct:** The manager and one of his secretaries *wish* to attend the function.
>**Incorrect:** Either the printer or the software *are* causing the glitch.
>**Correct:** Either the printer or the software *is* causing the glitch.

### Subject Nearer to Verb

Two subjects when joined by correlative conjunctions (or, either/or, nor, neither/nor, or not only/but also), the verb and any pronoun should agree with the subject that is nearer to the verb. The first noun in this type of construction may be disregarded when determining whether the verb should be singular or plural. Pay special attention to using the correct pronoun; do not use the plural pronoun *their* unless the subject and verb are plural. Note that subjects joined by *and* or *both/and* are always plural. Let us look at the following examples:

> If two subjects are joined by correlative conjunctions, the verb and any pronoun should agree with the subject that is nearer to the verb.

Either Robert or Ramesh *is* at *his* desk.
Either the manufacturers or the *distributors are* responsible.

> An expletive is an expression that comes at the beginning of a clause or sentence.

Neither the manager nor the employees were at fault.
Neither the receptionists nor the *operators were* able to finish *their* tasks.
Not only the actress but also the *dancer has* to practice *her* routine.
Both *the employer and the employee have* to practise *their* routines.

### Singular Verbs for Most Indefinite Pronouns

Consider the following examples:

*Each* of the employees *is* being interviewed.
*Anybody* flouting these rules *is* subject to disciplinary action.

Note that anyone, anybody, anything, each, either, everyone, everybody, everything, neither, nobody, nothing, someone, something, and somebody take singular verbs.

### Singular or Plural Verbs for Collective Nouns

A singular verb is used when the members of the group operate as a unit and a plural verb when the members operate as individuals of that group. Consider the following examples:

**Correct:** The organizing committee is working effectively.
**Incorrect:** The finance committee were divided in their opinion.

Note: Since there is considerable range for individual choice in the use of collective nouns, it is important to be consistent. Once the noun is assumed as a single unit, it cannot be, without some explanation, referred to in the plural.

### Treating Company Names as Singular

Consider the following examples.

**Incorrect:** Malik and Brothers *has* paid for *its* last order. *They* are ready to reorder.
**Correct:** Malik and Brothers *has* paid for *its* past order. *It* is now ready to reorder.

### Expletives

An expletive is an expression, such as *there is, there are, here is,* and *here are*, that comes at the beginning of a clause or sentence. Because the topic of a sentence that begins with an expletive is not immediately apparent, such sentences should be used sparingly in business writing.

In sentences that begin with an expletive, the true subject follows the verb. Use *is* or *are*, as appropriate.

There *is* no *reason* for his behaviour.
There *are* many *reasons* for his behaviour.

### Intervening Words

Any word that comes between the subject and the verb is disregarded when establishing agreement. First determine the subject, then make the verb agree. Some intervening words that do not affect the verb are *together with, rather than, accompanied by, in addition to,* and *except*. Let us consider a few sentences.

Only *one* of the mechanics *guarantees his/her* work. (not *their* work)
The *appearance* of the workers, not their competence, *was* being questioned.
The *secretary*, together with the clerks, *was* filing *her/his* form. (not *their* forms)

### Pronouns

> Case refers to the form of a pronoun and indicates its use in a sentence.

Some pronouns (*anybody, each, either, everybody, everyone, much, neither, no one, nobody*, and *one*) are always singular. Other pronouns (*all, any, more, most, none,* and *some*) may be singular or plural, depending on the noun to which they refer. Consider the following examples:

*Each* of the labourers *has* a different view of *his/her* job.
*Neither* of the models *is* doing *his/her* job well.
*Everybody* is required to take *his/her* turn at the booth. (not *their turn*)
*All* the *pie has* been eaten.
*All* the *cookies have* been eaten.
*None* of the *work is* finished.
*None* of the *workers have* finished the work.

**Case** Case refers to the form of a noun, an adjective, or a pronoun that shows its relationship to another word. There are three cases, namely nominative, accusative, and genitive.

Here, only the pronoun form cases have been discussed.

*Nominative case* Nominative pronouns (*I, he, she, we, they, who, whoever*) are used as subjects of sentences. Consider the following examples:

They are furnishing the figures.
Mrs Meera asked if *Rohan and I* were ready to begin.
*We* old-timers can provide some background.
It was *she* who agreed to the proposal.
*Who* is chairing the meeting?
Mr Lorenz wanted to know *who* can be depended upon.

*Objective case* Objective pronouns (*me, him, her, us, them, whom, whomever*) are used as objects of verbs, sentences, clause, or phrase.

For who/whom constructions, if he or she can be substituted, who is the correct choice; if him or her can be substituted, whom is the correct choice remember: *who-he, whom-him*. The difference is apparent in example 5 shown under the nominative case—who can be depended upon versus whom we can depend upon. Now, consider the following examples:

Thomas sent *me* a fax.
Please wait for *her.*
John asked *us* to provide some background.
The work was assigned to *me.*
To *whom* shall we mail the specifications?
Anne is the type of person *whom* we can depend upon. (Whom is the object of the verbs *depend*)

*Possessive case* Possessive pronouns (*my, mine, his, her, hers, our, their, whose, your*) are used to show possession or close connective between two things. Consider the following examples:

Tripti sings *her* own songs.
Samir has lost *his* job.

> Use reflexive pronouns to refer to or emphasize a noun or pronoun that has already been named.

You and I should share half *our* income with the poor.
They have lost *their* senses.
I am unable to find *my* book.
*Your* files are missing.
He is a friend of *hers*.

**Reflexive pronouns**  Reflexive pronouns, which end in *–self* or *–selves*, refer to nouns or other pronouns. Reflexive pronouns (*myself, yourself, himself, herself, itself, ourselves, yourselves,* or *themselves*) refer to or emphasize a noun or pronoun that has already been named. Do not use reflexive pronouns to substitute for nominative or objective pronouns.

I *myself* have some doubts about the proposal.
You should see the exhibit *yourself*.

In the following cases, note the incorrect/correct usage of reflexive pronouns:

**Incorrect:**  Veena and *myself* will take care of the details.
**Correct:**    Veena and *I* will take care of the details.
**Incorrect:**  Mary administered the test to Thomas and *myself*.
**Correct:**    Mary administered the test to Thomas and *me*.

## Subjunctive Mood

Verbs in the subjunctive mood refer to conditions that are impossible or improbable. For example, in the following examples, 'were' is in subjunctive mood.

I wish the situation *were* reserved.
If I *were* you, I would not mention the matter.

## Modals

Modals are used in the following cases:

1. *Asking/giving for permission:*  May (formal and polite); *can* (informal and friendly); *could* (very polite).

   May I come in Sir?
   Can I assist you in this work?
   Could I use your computer for a few minutes?

2. *Asking for things:*  Can, could, will. Consider the following examples:

   Can I have your book please? (friendly)
   Could you lend me your car for an urgent work? ( polite)
   Will you do me a favour, please? ( less polite)

3. *Ability*:  *Can* (present ability); *could* (past ability); *be able to* (ability at any time). Some examples are as follows:

   Our president can handle any situation.
   Our president could give suggestions immediately three years ago.
   Our manager *is/was/will be able to* complete the project on time.

4. *Possibility:* May (a good possibility); *might* (a weak possibility); *could* (a very weak possibility).

   As the reaction of our customers is good, we *may* sell our entire stock.
   I hope you *might* have received my letter posted last week.
   The sales *could* pick up in the next few days.

5. *Suggestion, advice, duty:* Should, ought to, could

   We *should* recruit more chemical engineers in our company. (Suggestion)
   We *should* ask a professional consultant for such problems. (Advice)
   We *ought to* seek a professional consultant's advice. (Strong advice/the right thing to do)
   We *could* write to the production department to produce more quantity next month. (Suggestion put forward rather tentatively)

6. *Necessity, obligation, compulsion, prohibition:* Must, have to, had to, have got to, must not.

   We *must* air-condition the entire building. (Necessity)
   I *have to* seek our manager's approval before proceeding further. (Obligation)
   All employees *have to* produce their identification cards at the gate. (Compulsion)
   Employees *must not* smoke within the company premises. (Prohibition)
   You *must* carry this file with you for the meeting. (Insistence)
   You *have to* carry this file with you for the meeting. (Compulsion)

Note that *must* suggests the *desire/insistence* of the speaker and *have to* suggests *external compulsion*.

## Infinitives, Gerunds, and Participles

An infinitive is the basic form (*to-form*) of a verb such as to sell and to make. (Let us look at a few examples:)

   Radha needs *to sell* her wares.
   Shyam must work *to make* money.

A gerund is a *noun* formed by adding –ing to the verb, such as selling and making.

   *Selling* is an art.
   *Making* error-free documents is a difficult task.

A participle is a word made by adding –ing (present participle) or –ed, –en, etc. (past participle) to a verb, such as selling, reducing, turned, broken, etc.

   We can achieve our target by *selling* more products.
   We can make this scheme more successful by *reducing* the risks involved.

The following verbs are followed by infinitives: *agree, decide, fail, forget, hope, want, learn, offer, plan, promise, refuse, manage, choose.*

> A gerund is a *noun* formed by adding *ing* to the verb.

   Several members *failed to turn* up for the meeting.
   Our vice-president has *promised to take* up this matter.

The following verbs are followed by gerunds and not by infinitives: *avoid, continue, suggest, mind, deny, finish, keep, miss, dislike, enjoy, delay, go on, give up, put off, can't help,* etc.

Mr Singh is busy in the meeting. Do you *mind waiting* for a while?
Our manager *avoids working* late in the evenings.

The following sentences illustrate that certain verbs can be followed either by an infinitive or by a gerund but with different meanings:

I *stopped supervising* the staff. (I was supervising—then I stopped)
I *stopped to supervise* the staff. (I stopped whatever I was doing and supervised the staff)

## Conditionals

**Probable**   The condition is likely to/can be fulfilled

If we engage a few more programmers, our job will be over in two days.
If you need our services, call us at our office next week.
If you wish to complete this report by tomorrow, you should work at least five more hours.

**Improbable**   In this case, a condition is hypothetical.

If their approach were unbiased, they would accept our proposal.
If you forced me further, I would rusticate you.

**Impossible**   In this case, a condition cannot be fulfilled as the time is already past.

If I had found the stock of raw material satisfactory, I would have placed a bulk order.
*or*
Had I found the stock of raw material satisfactory, I would have placed a bulk order.
If you would have written the complete address, the letter would have reached us.
*or*
Had you written the complete address, the letter would have reached us.

## Modifiers (Adjectives and Adverbs)

An adjective modifies a noun or pronoun; an adverb modifies a verb, an adjective, or another adverb.

Use a comparative adjective or adverb (*-er, more,* or *less*) to refer to two persons, places, or things, and a superlative adjective or adverb (*-est, most,* or *least*) refers to more than two.

The Datascan is the fast*er* of the two machines.
The XR-75 is the slow*est* of all the machines.
Rose Marie is the *less* qualified of the two applicants.
Rose Marie is the *least* qualified of the three applicants.

> An adjective modifies a noun or pronoun; an adverb modifies a verb, an adjective, or another adverb.

Note that double comparisons such as 'more faster' are not used. The position of a modifier in a sentence is important. Look at the following sentences to learn how the position of *only* changes the meaning:

We are obliged only to supply those items specified in your contract.
We are obliged to supply only those items specified in your contract.

Only we are obliged to supply those items specified in your contract.

We are obliged to supply those items specified only in your contract.

> A fragment is a part of a sentence that is incorrectly punctuated as a complete sentence.

Note that in any particular context, only one of the above sentences would be correct. The others would very likely cause problems.

To avoid ambiguity, place modifiers as close as possible to the noun or verb they modify. If the modifiers are long phrases, they also should be placed near the right noun or verb. Otherwise, mistakes in their position may create ludicrous meanings; consider the following examples:

*Ambiguous*   Being built on solid rocks, the engineers of Elite Constructions Ltd, thought that the building would not settle. (Who was built on solid rocks—the engineers or the building?)

*Clear*   The engineers of Elite Constructions Ltd, thought that the building would not settle as it was built on solid rocks.

### Avoid Fragments

Ideas must always be expressed in complete sentences. Avoid sentence fragments. A fragment is a part of a sentence that is incorrectly punctuated as a complete sentence. Each sentence must contain a complete thought.

*Fragment*   He had always wanted to be a marketing representative. Because he liked to interact with people.

*Complete*   He had always wanted to be a marketing representative *because* he liked to interact with people.

### Avoid Run-on or Fused Sentences

A run-on sentence refers to two independent clauses running together without any punctuation between them or with only a comma between them (the latter error is called a *comma splice*). A sentence with two independent clauses must be connected by a coordinating conjunction (*and, or, nor, but, yet, so,* etc.) or by a semicolon (;).

*Run-on*   Katherine is a hard worker she even frequently works through lunch.

*Complete*   Katherine is a hard worker; she even frequently works through lunch.

*Comma-splice*   Katherine is a hard worker, she even frequently works through lunch.

*Complete*   Katherine is a hard worker. She even frequently works through lunch.

### Word Order—Emphatic Beginning and Ending

In speech, you emphasize certain ideas and de-emphasize others with facial expressions, gestures, and by raising or lowering your voice. In writing, you convey your emphasis—the relative importance of your ideas—through the selection and arrangement of words. Where you place words, phrases, and clauses within a sentence conveys your emphasis to readers. Readers tend to focus on the beginning and the end of a sentence, expecting to find key information there.

> A colon or a dash can add emphasis by isolating an important word or phrase at the end of a sentence.

**Beginning with important ideas** Placing key ideas at the beginning of a sentence stresses their importance. The following sentence places emphasis on the study, not on those who conducted it or participated in it:

> In a landmark study of mental stress at workplaces, Dr Sooraj Modi of AIIMS, New Delhi, followed 200 middle-level managers and 400 inner-city working-class men from the northern region.

Situations that demand a straightforward presentation—laboratory reports, memos, technical papers, business correspondence, and the like—call for sentences that present vital information first and qualify ideas later. Consider the following sentences:

> Dividends will be paid if the stockholders agree. (Emphasizes the dividends, not the stockholders)
> Treating cancer with interferon has been the subject of a good deal of research. (Treatment, not research)

An empty phrase such as *there is* or *there are* at the beginning of a sentence generally weakens the sentence. Consider the following examples:

> *Unemphatic* There is heavy emphasis placed on the development of computational skills at this institute.
> *Emphatic* Heavy emphasis is placed on the development of computational skills at this institute.

**Ending with important ideas** Placing key elements at the end of a sentence is another way to convey their importance. A colon or dash can add emphasis by isolating an important word or phrase at the end of a sentence. Consider the following examples:

> Benazir had always dreamed of owning one company: a company like L&T.
> The new recruits need a good deal of special attention—and they deserve that attention.

At the end of a sentence, qualifiers such as conjunctive adverbs or other transitional expressions lose their power to indicate the relationship between ideas. Place transitional words and phrases earlier, where they can fulfil their purpose and also add emphasis. Consider the following examples:

> *Less emphatic* Smokers do have rights; they should not try to impose their habit on others, however.
> *More emphatic* Smokers do have rights; however, they should not try to impose their habit on others.

**Using climactic word order** Climactic word order is the arrangement of a series of items from the least to the most important. When you use climactic word order, the momentum of the sentence places emphasis on the key idea at the end. Consider the following sentence:

> The nation's most prominent businesses all boast large annual budgets, locations in important cities, and the most committed managers and employees. (Commitment is the key idea)

> Climactic word order is the arrangement of a series of items from the least important to the most important.

**Conveying emphasis through sentence structure** As you write, you can construct sentences that emphasize more important ideas and de-emphasize less important ones.

A cumulative sentence begins with an independent clause, followed by additional words, phrases, or clauses that expand or develop it. As it presents its main idea first, a cumulative sentence tends to be clear and straightforward (most English sentences are cumulative)

> The company depends on its President, who has had a vision, anticipated and solved several problems, and nurtured young managers.

**Using periodic sentences** A periodic sentence places the main idea at the end of the sentence. It moves from supporting details, expressed in modifying phrases and dependent clauses, to the main idea, which is placed in the independent clause. Consider the following example:

> After a tough day at work that involved preparing several important technical documents, the manager could not concentrate at the meeting that went on for a long time.

> *A periodic sentence places the main idea at the end of the sentence.*

In the preceding sentence, the writer adds emphasis to the main idea not only by placing it in the independent clause but also by keeping readers waiting for it.

Note that in some periodic sentences, the modifying phrase or dependent clause comes between subject and predicate. Consider the following example:

> The company, after several discouraging and unsuccessful ventures, finally reached its pinnacle of success.

Periodic sentences are generally more emphatic than cumulative sentences, but the most emphatic sentence is not always the best choice. Since the periodic structure forces readers to wait—or even search—for the delayed main idea, periodic sentences tend not to be as straightforward as cumulative ones.

**Conveying emphasis through parallelism and balance** By highlighting corresponding grammatical elements, parallelism helps writers convey information clearly, quickly, and emphatically.

A good writer uses parallel structure; that is, he or she puts nouns, verbs, phrases, thoughts, and so on into a similar form. This is done primarily for style—it makes the writing easier to read and in turn, easier for the reader to understand. Often, sentences that seem to be correct but just sound wrong have a lack of parallelism at the core of their problem.

> *Non-parallel* We seek an individual who is a self-starter, who *owns* a late-model automobile and who *has the willingness* to work.
>
> *Parallel* We seek an individual who *is* a self-starter, *owns* a late-model automobile, and is *willing* to work.
>
> *Non-parallel* The production manager was asked to write his report *quickly, accurately,* and *in a detailed manner.*
>
> *Parallel* The production manager was asked to write his report *quickly, accurately,* and *thoroughly.*

**Conveying emphasis through repetition** Unnecessary repetition makes sentences dull and monotonous as well as wordy. Consider the following example:

> *Unnecessary repetition makes sentences dull and monotonous as well as rambling.*

> We got three estimates, and the one we got from the Johnson Brothers seemed more reasonable than the one we got from Country Carpenters.

Effective repetition, however, can place emphasis on key words or ideas. Consider the following examples:

> They decided to begin again: to begin hoping, to begin trying to change, to begin working towards a goal.
>
> If ever two groups were opposed, surely those two groups are runners and smokers.

Words may be effectively repeated within a sentence or paragraph.

**Conveying emphasis through active voice** Active voice is generally more emphatic and concise than passive voice.

> *Passive* The prediction that oil prices will rise is being made by economists.
>
> *Active* Economists now predict that oil prices will rise.

Passive voice tends to focus readers' attention on the action or its receiver rather than the actor. The receiver of the action is the subject of a passive sentence, so the actor fades into the background ('by economists') or is omitted ('the prediction is now being made'). Sometimes, of course, you want to stress the action rather than the actor. If so, it makes sense to use the passive voice. Consider the following examples:

> Cheques are written in English.
>
> Good quality mobiles are bought and sold at this shop.
>
> All relevant data of our branch offices is collected and analysed; then a head office account is prepared.

## EFFECTIVE PARAGRAPHS

Developing well-structured and adequately-developed paragraphs is essential for effective business communication. Paragraphs tell the readers where the topics begin and end, thus assisting them to organize the content in their mind. Once they organize the information, they may be able to comprehend the text with ease. There are many business documents such as reports, proposals and letters, which contain several units of information. Well-structured and adequately-developed paragraphs enable the readers not only demarcate the units of information but also grasp them without much difficulty. There are some other *central components of paragraph development* that help to make this formula work. These components are often overlooked, but developing the sentences that complete the steps of the paragraph development process is not possible without the following components:

- Topic sentence
- Coherence
- Unity
- Adequate development

### Topic Sentence

> Developing well-structured and adequately developed paragraphs is essential for effective business communication.

A topic sentence is a sentence that expresses the main idea of a paragraph. This sentence is also known as key sentence or theme sentence. Everything in the paragraph must explain or illustrate the topic sentence. Look at the following examples—paragraphs with topic sentences in the beginning and at the end, respectively:

> **BUSINESS COMMUNICATION INSIGHT**
>
> ### Master English Vocabulary and Grammar
>
> To learn the English language effectively, it's important that you know the rules of grammar and at the same time, expand your vocabulary. Vocabulary is defined as a list of words you should know to help you communicate in English with others.
>
> The two major features of any language are grammar and vocabulary, and you can study them using traditional methods or through innovative easy methods. You need to study the rules, read books on miscellaneous topics in the language, pay attention to the instructions and signs on products of everyday use.
>
> **Read a grammar book** A grammar book will familiarize you with the rules of the language and enhance your vocabulary. These books are available online or in stores and explain the basic doctrines of sentence construction, subject-verb agreement and help you learn useful words which reappear in the language.
>
> By going through the rules carefully, you can attain a basic understanding of the language and then apply it in everyday situations.
>
> **Pick up new words everyday** If you wish to learn new words and enhance your English vocabulary, pick out a new English word each day, find its meaning and remember it so that you may use it later on. You may focus on verbs, or adjectives, nouns, and so on.
>
> **Read books** The best way to learn is through reading. Experts in the language are often proficient readers. Reading English books is a unique way of increasing your stock of words. Reading novels (fiction or nonfiction) and short stories or magazines can help teach you about the rules of correct grammar and usage.
>
> Observe the way in which words are used in a sentence and how they have been applied. It is also a way to get acquainted with the ways in which the words are chosen and used. It's a good idea to keep a list of new words you have come across and write their meanings so that it can be referred when required.
>
> If you come across a word which you don't know while reading, look it up in the dictionary. As you get into the habit of reading, the list will start emerging and consequently, you will learn more words.
>
> **Act like an editor** To get a thorough idea of words and their usage, you can correct your writing as well as the writings of others. If you are drafting an essay or composition, get your friend or colleague to review your work and make grammatical corrections, if any. This practice can help you increase your aptitude and master the language. Group communication can profit you to get a better understanding of grammar and vocabulary.

In order to minimize conflicts and increase efficiency, work must be divided equitably among team members. Overburdening one individual will quickly lead to resentment and conflict. In addition, when assigning tasks to various team members, the team must consider not only the quantity of work to be undertaken by an individual but also the nature of the work. For example, editing a document is rarely as interesting as drafting it. If someone is consistently assigned the task of editing, he/she is liable to become bored (and thus, ineffective). Where feasible, team members should rotate through both the less challenging and more interesting tasks.

> A topic sentence is a sentence that expresses the main idea of a paragraph.

When assigning tasks to various team members, the team must consider not only the quantity of work to be undertaken by an individual but also the nature of the work. For example, editing a document is rarely as interesting as drafting it. If someone is consistently assigned the task of editing, he/she is liable to become bored (and thus, ineffective). Where feasible, team members should rotate through both the less challenging and more interesting tasks. But overburdening one individual will quickly lead to resentment and conflict. *Hence, in order to minimize conflicts and increase efficiency, work must be divided equitably among team members.*

## Coherence

Coherence in a text implies that each sentence of a paragraph should be well linked with the sentence that precedes and follows it. You can provide transitions between sentences/ideas by using the following:

- Pronouns
- Transitional tags
- Repetition of key words or phrases
- Parallel grammatical structure

### Use of Pronouns

An example illustrating the use of pronouns is given as follows:

> Copying machine operators are responsible for keeping *their* machines in good working condition. If *they* detect any problem, *they* must notify *their* supervisor immediately. The supervisor will inspect the machine and determine whether *they* can continue to use *it*.

### Transitional Tags

Let us now consider examples showing both inadequate and adequate use of transitional tags (also see Table 21.1).

*Inadequate use of transitional tags* Stress can have many side effects. A supervisor feeling pressure to complete a difficult project may become irritable, develop ulcer, or succumb to illness such as cold, flu, or more serious diseases. A student preparing for exams just the day before may feel nervous, frustrated and may even develop exam fever.

*Effective use of transitional tags* Stress can have many side effects. For instance, a supervisor feeling pressure to complete a difficult project may become irritable, develop ulcer, or possibly even succumb to illness such as cold, flu, or a more serious disease. Similarly, a student preparing for exams just the day before may feel nervous, frustrated and may even develop exam fever.

### Repetition of Key Words and Phrases

> Each sentence of a paragraph should be well linked with the sentence that precedes and follows it.

The following example illustrates the repetition of key words and phrases in sentences to emphasize on coherence.

*Ego strength* is a personality measure of the strength of a person's *conviction*. People who score high on *ego strength* are likely to resist impulses and follow their *convictions* more than those who are low on *ego strength*. That

**Table 21.1** Some useful words/phrases that can serve as transitions in paragraph/essay writing

| Intention | Transitional Words/Phrases |
|---|---|
| Addition | and, or, nor, moreover, again, first, secondly, thirdly, next, last, lastly, finally, even more important, furthermore, also, in addition, further, besides |
| Time | while, after, when, meanwhile, during, next, then, in the past, immediately, later, soon, in the meantime, afterwards, following at length, after a few days, never, always, whenever, sometimes, now, once, simultaneously |
| Place | here, there, nearby, beyond, wherever, opposite to, adjacent to, neighbouring on, bordering |
| Examples | for example, as an illustration, to demonstrate, specifically, for instance, to illustrate, again, such as |
| Similarity | in the same way, by the same token, similarly, in like manner, likewise, in similar fashion |
| Contrast | on the contrary, in contrast, nevertheless, but at the same time, although that may be true, nonetheless, on the other hand, yet, and yet, notwithstanding, otherwise, however, after all, though, despite this fact |
| Clarification | that is to say, in other words, to put it another way, to explain, to clarify, to rephrase it, still, conversely, instead, even so, for all that, namely |
| Cause | because, on account of, for that reason, due to the fact that |
| Effect | therefore, consequently, as a result |
| Purpose | thus, hence, accordingly, in order to, for this purpose |
| Qualification | so that, to that end |
| Intensification | indeed, to repeat, by all means, undoubtedly, to be sure |
| Summary | to summarize, in sum, in short, to sum up, in brief, in summary |
| Conclusion | to conclude, in conclusion, finally, therefore, thus, it is now obvious that, with this object, with that in mind, thereupon, then, so, on the whole, as I have said |
| Concession | admittedly, granted, it is true, to be sure, almost, nearly, probably, perhaps, maybe, although, in fact, without doubt, doubtlessly, obviously, unquestionably, inescapably, certainly, surely, of course, nobody denies, clearly, even though, in a manner of speaking, to be more precise, of course, needless to say |
| Spatial order | above, below, in the distance, nearby, beyond, opposite to/adjacent to, in front/in back, to the right/ to the left |
| Numerical order | first, second, third, etc., in the first place, secondly, thirdly, etc, to begin with, next, finally |
| Emphasis | again, for this reason, indeed, most compelling evidence, on the negative side, significant that, to emphasize, truly, another key point, frequently, in fact, most important information, on the positive side, surprising, to point out, with this in mind, first thing to remember, important to realize, key point, must be remembered, point often overlooked, surprisingly enough, to repeat |

is, individuals high in *ego strength* are more likely to do what they think is right. We would expect managers with high *ego strength* to demonstrate more consistency between moral judgement and moral action than those with low *ego strength*.

### *Parallel Grammatical Structure*

The following example illustrates the use of both non-parallel and parallel grammatical structures:

*Non-parallel* Even the best communicators learn as much as possible about their listeners and tailor their remarks to their interests, attitudes, *and what their values are.*

*Parallel* Even the best communicators learn as much as possible about their listeners and tailor their remarks to their *interests, attitudes, and values*.

## Unity

Unity refers to the extent to which all of the ideas contained within a given paragraph 'hang together' in a way that is easy for the reader to understand. When the writer changes to a new idea—one which is not consistent with the topic sentence of the paragraph—he/she should begin a new paragraph. Unity is important because it aids the reader in going along with the writer's ideas. The reader can expect that a given paragraph will deal only with one main topic. Consider the following example:

> Employees' attitudes at National Electric Company should be improved. The workers do not feel that they are a working team instead of just individuals. If people felt they were a part of a team, they would not misuse the tools, or deliberately undermine the work of others. Management's attitude towards its employees should also be improved. Managers at National Electric act as though their employees are incapable of taking decisions or doing their own work. Managers treat workers like objects, not human beings.

Note that two main ideas are presented in this paragraph. The topic sentence indicates that the paragraph will deal with the subject of 'employees' attitudes', but halfway through, the paragraph shifts unexpectedly to the topic of 'management's attitudes'. To achieve unity in this paragraph, the writer should begin a new paragraph when the switch is made from writing about employees to writing about managers.

---

 **COMMUNICATION TOOL**

### Tips for Improving Your Reading Speed

1. Look at groups of two to three words instead of focusing on every word. For example,
   - The finance manager/has promised/to complete the task/before noon.
2. Try to strengthen your vocabulary. Familiarize yourself with new words so you do not get stuck on them when you read them again.
3. Avoid moving your lips when reading. Force yourself to read faster so that you can no longer move your lips.
4. Read more. 15 minutes a day of reading an average size novel equals 18 books a year at an average reading speed!
5. Determine your purpose before reading. If you only need main ideas, then allow yourself to skim the material. Do not feel you must read very word.
6. Spend a few minutes every day reading at a faster than comfortable rate (about two to three times faster than your normal speed). Use your hand or an index card to guide your eyes down the page. Then time yourself reading a few pages at your normal speed. You will find that often your normal reading speed will increase after your skimming practice.
7. If you have poor concentration when reading, practise reading for only 5–10 minutes at a time and gradually increase this time.
8. Use different reading speeds for different purposes. For example, you may have to use a lesser reading speed if your business document consists of a huge amount of statistics, whereas you can use a higher reading speed when you read the summary of a business report.

If you have the desire to improve, the willingness to try new techniques, and the motivation to practise, you are sure to improve your reading speed.

### Adequate Development

A paragraph is adequately developed when it describes, explains, and supports the topic sentence. If the topic sentence is not developed fully, or if the reader is left with questions after reading the paragraph, the paragraph has not been adequately developed. In general, a paragraph that consists of only two to three sentences is underdeveloped. A good rule of thumb is to make sure that a paragraph contains at least four sentences that explain and elaborate on the topic sentence. Consider the following paragraph:

> The topics of leadership and management are both similar to and different from one another in several important ways. To be effective, a manager should be a good leader. And good leaders know how to manage people effectively.

The topic sentence promises to discuss 'several' points of comparison and contrast between leadership and management, but the remainder of the paragraph falls short of fulfilling this promise. Only one point of comparison is raised, and this point is left unexplained. Several questions remain unanswered. How are leaders different from managers? In what specific ways are the two alike? Why must a manager be a good leader to be effective? Why must good leaders know how to manage people effectively? To achieve adequate development in this paragraph, these questions should be addressed.

## POWER OF READING

Let us consider the time generally spent by professionals on communication activities. We often observe that the time they spend on receiving information (listening and reading) is more than that they spend on sending (speaking and writing) information. Reading is one of the most important academic tasks faced by students and a very important communication task performed by professionals. To be able to read over 300 words per minute, comprehend what you have read, and remember the reading material is essential in today's world. Information is bombarding our personal and professional lives through email, the Internet, magazines, and work-related materials.

An average college student reads between 250 and 350 words per minute (wmp) on fiction and non-technical materials, however, 'good' reading speed is around 500 to 700 wpm. The various reading speeds are discussed in Table 21.2. By becoming more and more aware of these rates and practising everyday, you can become effective and efficient in your reading:

## PUNCTUATION AND CAPITALIZATION

Correct punctuation marks are required to bring clarity in your business writing. As these marks can affect meaning, you need to use them judiciously. Periods, commas, colons, etc. tell your reader when to pause, or how to relate two ideas. Take, for example, the following sentence—by punctuating this sentence differently, you can give different meanings to this sentence, as shown below:

> Correct punctuation marks are required to bring clarity to business writing.

*A woman without her man is nothing.*

This implies that any woman who does not have a man is incomplete.

*A woman: without her, man is nothing.*

By adding a colon and a comma, we have changed the meaning in the

**Table 21.2** Various reading speeds

| | |
|---|---|
| Upto 100 wpm | Elementary reading ability. Little reading experience with low level of understanding. Max. levels of regression, sub-vocalization and mind-riff. At this rate, reading is tough. |
| 100–200 wpm | 6 and 12 year old readers, or someone deliberately avoiding reading throughout life, wherever possible. High levels of regression, sub-vocalization and attention problems. Understanding is about 50% or less of what is read. |
| 200–250 wpm | Average reading speed which includes the majority of world's readers for a good part of their lives. Regression is 10% of all words read with full sub-vocalization. Intermittent attention problems. Usually understanding more than 50% of what is read. |
| 250–350 wpm | Slightly above-average reading speed typically in post-high school graduates, or eager casual readers with decent reading experience. Occasional regressions with marginally reduced sub-vocalization. No problem in comprehending more than 50% what is read. |
| 350–500 wpm | Much above average and approaching good comprehension. Reading is a pleasurable activity. Occasional regressions to recompense mind drift and improved recognition without full sub-vocalization. |
| 500–800 wpm | A suitable reading speed that helps excellent comprehension (75% and above). Reading is enjoyable and there is decent control over daily reading commitments for personal and office purposes. |
| 800–1000 wpm | Exceptionally efficient reading speed with low sub-vocalization and no regressions. Word recognition is outstanding and understanding is optimum. No reading pressure or time problems associated with managing large amounts of information. A first-class scholar or highly successful business person or someone who has completed a high-level reading development programme. |
| over 1000 wpm | A born swift reader or trained speed reader who retains skills by consistent practice. Characterized by high understanding and full control over reading requirements. Reading is an important part of the individual's routine, easily reads two or more books per week. |

second example. The clause reads like a definition. Now the sentence implies that men are incomplete without women.

To make sure that the meaning you intend to express and the meaning your reader receives are one and the same, you need to use the right punctuation marks in the correct places, and to do this, you need to know all the punctuation marks and what they can and cannot do.

Some professions and businesses have their own style of punctuation. A journalist, for example, may omit some punctuation marks that are normally included in a business letter. A lawyer, on the other hand, uses many more punctuation marks when preparing a legal form than are essential for most types of business writing.

You also need to know what to and what not to capitalize. It is difficult to give rules that will cover every conceivable problem in capitalization. In fact, what is capitalized is mostly a matter of editorial style and preference rather than a matter of generally accepted rules. Moreover, although there is a clearly recognized rule requiring capitalization of proper nouns and adjectives, opinions differ concerning what a proper noun is.

The important goal should be consistency within a particular document. Certain rules concerning punctuation and capitalization given in this section may guide you not only in your technical writing but also in all other types of writing.

## Punctuation

This section describes when to use a comma, a semicolon, a colon, a dash, quotation marks, a hyphen, parentheses, and an apostrophe.

### *Comma*

A comma performs the following functions.

1. *Separates a series of words or phrases*   When a conjunction joins the last two elements in a series, use a comma before the conjunction.

   Managers hire and train new employees, offer them encouragement and direction, and evaluate them once a year.
   The administration formed a committee to determine the need for additional personnel in the department, create job descriptions for approved positions, and advertise those approved positions.

2. *Sets off items in a date or address*   No comma is, usually, necessary when only the month and year are written.

   The committee met on August 20, 2003, to discuss the plan.
   The study was conducted from January 15, 1975, to February 1, 1979.
   The committee met in August 2003 to discuss the plan.
   The study was conducted from January 1975 to February 1979.
   These instruments were carried on commercial airliners en route from New Delhi, India, to London, England.
   The computer program is available from COSMIC, 112 Alexander Hall, University of Mumbai, India.

3. *Separates a short question from a statement*   When a question is dependent upon the statement for its meaning, comma is used to separate the two.

   It was Mohan who bought the radio, wasn't it?
   You had planned to start early, hadn't you?

4. *Sets off words of direct address*   See the following examples:

   Alice, can you type this paper?
   No, John, someone else will have to type it.

5. *Sets off the direct speech from the rest of the sentence*   See the following examples:

   'Ms Leela,' said the office superintendent, 'you have been rather careless in your work.'
   'Congratulations,' said the chairman, 'you have produced an excellent report on pollution control.'

> A comma is used to set off an adverb clause also at the beginning of a sentence.

6. *Separates two adjectives modifying the same noun*   Rather than joining the adjectives by a conjunction, a comma is used instead.

   A persuasive, well-documented research proposal was submitted by the department of Biology.
   An informative, intelligent report is expected to be presented today.

7. *Sets off introductory verbal phrases modifying the subject of the sentence.*

   Observing carefully all the reactions, we finally arrived at the results of our experiment. (Participle)
   After unpacking the car, we took it to the garage. (Prepositional phrase)
   To advance in the profession, one must work hard. (Infinitive)

8. *Separates the main clauses in a compound sentence*

   We finished our aptitude tests, and the teachers started preparing for our interviews.
   The experiment was over, and we were ready to do the calculations.

9. *Sets off an adverb clause at the start of a sentence*

   When I finished the assignment, I met the manager to present the highlights.
   Although I had arrived late for the inaugural ceremony, it hardly seemed to have begun.

   Note that adverb clauses appearing at the end of the sentence do not need commas unless they begin with *though*, *although*, and sometimes, *because*.

10. *Sets off introductory prepositional phrases*   A comma is used to introduce such phrases if they are lengthy, or several phrases are used together, or for clarity. A single prepositional phrase at the beginning of a sentence does not usually require a comma.

    At the beginning of the year 1950, they set off for their trip. (Required)
    In 1950 they set off for their trip. (Not required)

11. *Sets off parenthetical expressions*

    This group has, we understand, been very successful.
    You are, however, very fortunate to secure the position.
    Mr Kumar is, to tell the truth, unable to meet the obligation.

12. *Sets off adjectives that follow the noun they modify*

    The resume, neat and crisp, attracted the attention of the recipient.
    Your behaviour, cordial and humble, suits this job.

13. *Sets off contrasting expressions from the rest of the sentence*

    It was John's attitude, not his qualifications, that fetched him the job.
    They found out the mistake by a thorough audit, not by mere interrogation.

14. *Sets off an appositive from the rest of the sentence*

    Ms Johnson, the company president, will present the award at our annual dinner.
    George Powers, a former football star, gave a talk.

15. *Sets off non-restrictive adjective clauses from the rest of the sentence*

>The boy, who is my friend, will come to visit us.
>The acid, which is pungent, will corrode the pipes.

## Semicolon

A semicolon is used in the following situations.

1. *Before words and expressions such as however, then, thus, so, hence, in fact, in truth, that is, therefore, etc. when these expressions are preceded and followed by independent clauses.*

   >Our M.D. has lived many years in the West; therefore, I understand his attitude.
   >The auditors made six recommendations; however, only one has been adopted so far.

   Note that a comma is used to set off these words at the beginning of a sentence.

2. *Between two independent clauses when the conjunction is not expressed.* Semicolons should join only those independent clauses that are closely related in meaning.

   >Abdominal exercises help prevent back pain; proper posture is also important.
   >Alice looked at the letter for a long time; it was illegible.

   Note that generally, you should not place a semicolon before a coordinating conjunction that links two independent clauses. The only exception to this guideline is if the two independent clauses are very long and already contain a number of commas.

   >**Incorrect** The economy has been sluggish for four years now; but some signs of improvement are finally beginning to show.
   >**Correct** The economy has been sluggish for four years now, but some signs of improvement are finally beginning to show.

It may be useful to remember that, for the most part, you should use a semicolon only where you could also use a full stop. There is one exception to this guideline. When punctuating a list or series of elements in which one or more of the elements contain an internal comma, you should use semicolons instead of commas to separate the elements from one another, as follows:

>The study has brought to light three things—that the water situation, no matter how grim, will be easily resolved; all suggestions can be easily implemented; and people of the campus will be satisfied.

## Colon

A colon can be used in the following ways:

1. *To introduce lists.* Such lists are often, but not always, introduced by words such as *these, as follows*, and *the following*.

   >You are asked to bring the following: the budget records, the committee report, and the schedule for the intensive course.

2. *After the salutation in a business letter.*

   >Dear Mr Andrews:

Note that after the salutation in a letter, usually a comma is used.

3. *To introduce a quotation.*

He quoted this proverb: 'The rain falls on the just and the unjust'.
This was her favourite quotation: 'Mend your speech a little; lest it may mar your fortune'.

## Dash

A dash may be used as follows:

1. *To set off a series of appositives.*

A number functions—HR, Marketing, Production, and Finance—are essential in businesses.

2. *Before a summary of preceding details in a sentence.*

June, July, August—these are the usual vacation months.

3. *To show an unexpected or abrupt change in thought or structure of a sentence.*

The procession ended up in violence—at least that is what we heard from a reliable source.

4. *To make an appositive more emphatic.*

There was only one possible means of entrance—the window in the back room.

## Italics

Italics perform the following functions:

1. *Indicate complete publications*   Titles of books, magazines, plays, newspapers, movies, ships, planes, trains, etc. are italicized.

We saw *Gone With the Wind* yesterday.
*The Queen Mary* just docked.

2. *Designate words when spoken of as words.*

The word *iron* has an unusual history.

3. *Emphasize a word or phrase.*   This aspect of italics is used sparingly.

I am betting *she* is going to be somebody.

## Quotation Marks

Quotation marks perform the following functions:

1. *Enclose a direct quotation*

'You can't do that', he shouted.

2. *Sets off titles*   The titles of stories, articles, chapters, poems, essays, works of art, radio and television programmes, etc. are enclosed within quotation marks.

We were asked to read 'You can Win' on the very first day we joined this job.
Did you watch 'All in the Family' last night?

3. *Draw special attention to or set off a word or expression.*

She described him as being 'generous'.

## Hyphen

A hyphen is used as follows:

1. *In writing fractions and in all numbers from 21 to 99.*

    two-thirds, forty-five

2. *To separate the parts of a compound word.*

    self-control, one-third, well-dressed

3. *Between the words of a group of words* In case a group of words take the place of a single adjective before a noun, a hyphen is used.

    The student consulted an up-to-date dictionary.
    It was a well-documented report.

    Note that compound words used as adjectives, preceding the words they modify, and acting as a single idea are often hyphenated; whereas, they are often not hyphenated when they follow the words they modify.

    Don't touch those red-hot coals. (Hyphenation)
    The coals will be red hot soon. (No hyphenation)

4. *Between a prefix and proper noun or adjective*

    She is neither anti-American nor pro-German.

5. *With the prefixes* All-, self-, ex- (when it means 'former'), and sometimes between a prefix ending in a vowel and a root beginning with the same vowel make use of hphens.

    God is all-knowing and all-powerful.
    They liked the candidate's self-possession.
    The ex-champ was dining with her ex-husband.
    He entered the contest as the anti-intellectual candidate.

6. *To unify single capital letters joined to nouns or participles*

    A-flat, I-beam, U-turn, H-bomb, T-square, X-ray, V-neck, C-span, etc.

7. *Between a numbered figure and its unit of measurement*

    2-litre bottle, 8-foot board, 42-hour week, 10-day vacation, 500-mg dose, etc.

## Parantheses

Consider the following points when using parantheses:

1. Parentheses are used to enclose a side remark, explanation, translation, or comment. Sometimes this is an appositive.

    Beside this stream (we were camping here at the time), we unearthed an Indian skeleton.
    My typewriter (a Remington portable) has been restored.

2. When using parentheses with other punctuation marks, punctuate the main part of the sentence as if the parenthetical portion was not there.

> Parentheses are used to enclose a side remark, explanation, translation, or comment.

A punctuation mark comes *after* the second parenthesis if the punctuation mark applies to the whole sentence and not just to the parenthetical portion.

> Although Suzanne has three pets (two birds and a dog), she left them with her boyfriend when she went home for Christmas.
> Did they buy that big house (the one with the two-car garage)?

Place the punctuation mark *inside* the second parenthesis if the punctuation mark applies only to material within the parenthetical portion.

> I heard that it was an emergency. (Did they get there in time?) He should have been more careful.

3. Use parentheses to enclose a number, letter, or symbol when used as an appositive, which defines or identifies another word or group of words.

> There were eight (8) new rules added to the club's bylaws at the last meeting.
> The Greek letter delta (δ) is often used in mathematics to indicate an infinitesimal change in values of variables.
> Be sure to include a copyright (©) symbol in that statement.

## Apostrophe

An apostrophe is used to indicate the following:

1. *Possession* If a noun is singular, add an apostrophe and s.

   > A teacher—teacher's book, a company's employees, etc.

   If the noun is a plural one ending in s, add only an apostrophe.

   > The teachers—teachers' book, students' manuals, etc.

   If the noun is plural but does not end in s, add an apostrophe and s.

   > Children's books, women's rights, etc.

2. *The omission of a word, letters, or numerals.*

   > Couldn't, I've, he's, 'n', doesn't, it's, let's, I was born in '53, etc.

## Capitalization

The following points should be kept in mind when beginning a word with a capital letter:

1. *The first word of every sentence, line of poetry, or direct quotation*

   > James said, 'My lawn doesn't need mowing.'

2. *Proper nouns, proper adjectives, and titles which precede a name*

   > Judge Jones, Uncle James, Chinese food, etc.

3. *All sacred names* The Bible, names of all religious sects, names of churches, etc. are capitalized.

   > We found the quotation in the Old Testament in the 'Book of Job.'
   > 'Follow the Christ, the King...'
   > Sikhism, Hinduism, etc.
   > St James Lutheran Church

4. *The months, days of the week, and all holidays*

    Memorial Day, Monday, the fourth of June, Republic Day, etc.

    Note that the seasons are not capitalized.

5. *The words north, south, east, and west when they refer to a part of the country, but not when they refer to a direction*

    The company feels that the Northwest offers greater opportunities than the East.
    We were driving east.

6. *Special events, historical eras, and geographical areas*

    The War of Indian Independence, the Louisiana Purchase, the Boston Tea Party, the Victorian Era, etc.

7. *Names of special buildings, organizations, and companies*

    Life Insurance Corporation, the Woolworth Building, Rotary Club, etc.

8. *Titles of books, documents, stories, poems, musical works, art works, and plays*   Capitalize all words in titles except prepositions, conjunctions, and the articles *a*, *an*, and *the*.

    *Chicken Soup for the Soul*, *A Passage to India*

    Note that prepositions of more than four letters are frequently capitalized.

    'Journey Through the East is a great article.'

9. *The word president when it refers to the President of a nation.*

    The President vetoed the bill.

10. *Abbreviations of educational degrees.*

    M.Sc., B.A., etc.

11. *The names of all races and nationalities.*

    Indian costumes, French soldiers, Mexican food, etc.

12. *Mother and father, unless they are preceded by such words as my, his, your, etc.*

    I knew Father would coach the team.
    I knew that my father would coach the team.

13. *All languages.*

    Spanish, English, Latin, Russian, Hindi, etc.

14. *School subjects that are languages or have numbers after them*

    He is taking Russian.
    I plan to take algebra and art.
    I plan to take Algebra I and Art I.

15. *Titles that precede names*   Stand-alone titles or those that follow names are not capitalized. This, however, applies to text, not necessarily to lists.

    Dean James R. Sturdivant, Vice-President Smith

> James R. Sturdivant, dean of the College of Medicine
> Catherine Smith, vice-president for Academic Affairs
> The dean of the college, the vice-president of the university

16. *Complete and proper names*   These include names of universities and colleges, governmental units, companies, *and their major subdivisions, but not partial forms*. etc.

    > Delhi University
    > The university will comply with the rules and regulations of the Immigration and Naturalization Service.
    > Department of Mathematics
    > Courses offered by the department are listed in the schedule.
    > College of Liberal Arts and Sciences
    > The college has 21 departments.
    > Alumni Association
    > The programmes of the association are usually well supported.

**Do not capitalize**   The following points indicate when not to capitalize.

1. *Names of curricula, programmes, majors, or minors*   Names of specific courses should be capitalized, however.

   > Students may major in sculpture or graphic design.
   > Advisors encourage students to take courses in computer science.
   > Advisors encourage students to take Introduction to Computer Science I.

2. *First or second semester, or summer session*

   > What was first semester total enrollment?
   > Did the professor give you any assignment during the summer session?

3. *The words figure, table, or page unless they occur at the beginning of a sentence or are followed by a number*

   > This form is illustrated in the figure on page 162.
   > Characteristics of this chemical compound are listed in the table given below.
   > This is illustrated in Figure 1.2.

4. *The words state and government unless they are part of a proper name*

   > The project obtained government funding.
   > All employees of the State of Gujarat are included.
   > The officials of the Indian Government are expected to arrive tonight.

5. *Academic degrees*   These should not be capitalized when they are referred to in general terms in text, but their abbreviations should be capitalized.

   > Our Chairman holds a master's degree in business administration and a doctorate in finance.
   > Our Chairman holds an MBA and a PhD in finance.

## REFERENCING STYLES

Referencing (or citing sources) is the important process of acknowledging another person's ideas, specific language, graphic illustrations, and other materials borrowed for constructing your own academic or professional documents/assignments.

Business writers document material borrowed from the work of others because

- appropriate citation adds credibility to the writer's assertions,
- it helps the writer avoid plagiarism, and
- guides the reader to sources for further reading or investigation about a topic.

The three common referencing styles are as follows:

- Modern Language Association (MLA)
- American Psychological Association (APA)
- Chicago Manual Style (CMS)

Conventions about documentation styles become institutionalized over time as communities of scholars, publishers, and professional organizations work together to develop citation models that efficiently and gracefully refer readers to sources. In fact, there is no one particular referencing style that is followed in all business writing. Many businesses have developed their own hybrid systems. These companies generally supply guidelines illustrating their in-house style to employees. Before starting any research project on job, you may have to find out about your organization's preferred referencing style or refer to the some previous reports, proposals, etc. Although there are several styles for documenting the sources, all of them include the following information:

- Name of the author(s)/editor(s)
- Title, edition, and volume number of the work
- Place of publication and name of publisher
- Year
- Relevant page numbers

These styles differ mainly in their layout as the details are presented in different sequences using different punctuation marks.

Citing resources is a two-step process. The *first step* is to cite sources in the body of the paper where the material appears. The *second step* is to include the sources and publication information in a list of references at the end of the document. Sample entries to facilitate your understanding of citing and listing references in MLA, APA, and CMS styles are as follows:

### MLA Style

Let us now discuss the MLA style in some depth.

#### *In-text Citation*

At the end of a quotation or reference, the author's last name and relevant page numbers appear in parentheses as follows:

> 'With the improved access to the global business, several multinational companies have found their market in India.' (O'Brien 192)

## Works Cited

In MLA style, a bibliography called 'Works Cited' lists all references cited in your document. Some writers also include all works consulted. The entries are arranged alphabetically.

**Annual report**   National Petroleum Industries. *Annual Report 2002–2003,* Mumbai: NPI. 2003.

**Book with one author**   J.O'Brien. *Wall Street on Trial: A Corrupted state,* Hoboken: Wiley, 2003.

**Book with two authors**   Adams Ramon and Seymour Stevens. *Personnel Management.* Cambridge, MA: All-State. 1999.

**Book with organization as author**   Corporate Libraries Association. *Directory of Business and Financial Service.* New Delhi: Corporate Libraries Association. 2000.

**Journal article**   Allison, G.W. The Implications of Experimental Design for Biodiversity Manipulations. *American Naturalist* 153 (1) 1999: 26–45.

**Periodical article**   Ganguly Sumit. India's Pathway to Pokhran II. *International Security* Vol. 23, No. 4 (Spring 1999), 148–177.

**Online magazine article**   Murthy Anand, 'Saturn's Orbit Still High With Consumers,' Marketing News Online, 4 March 1997, Retrieved 13 May 1999 http://www.aaa.org/pubs/mn/c715/n1.htm

**Newspaper article**   'Let Employees Determine their own Benefits.' *The Hindu*. 31 July 1999.

**Newspaper article from an electronic database**   Sally Satel. 'OxyContin Half-truths Can Cause Suffering.' *USA Today*, 27 October 2003, final edition. Lexis-Nexis, via Galileo, Retrieved 28 October 2003 < http://www.galileo.usg.edu>

**Interview**   Ramaswamy Prakash. Personal Interview.17 May 2005.

**World Wide Web**   Quincy, Dinah J. 'Maxwell Announces New Health Benefit,' Maxwell Corp. Home Page. 13 November 2001. (Retrieved 14 January 2002) http://www.max_corp.com/NEWS/2001/f92500.html

**Government document**   Centre for Monitoring the Indian Economy (CMIE), *Monthly Review of the Economy*, October 1997.

**Case studies**   Kanter, R.M. 'FCB and Publicis (A): Forming the Alliance,' Harvard Business School Case No. 9-393-099 (Boston: Harvard Business School Publishing, 1993).

## APA Style

The APA style is discussed as follows:

### In-text Citation

The author's last name, year of publication, and relevant page numbers follow the quotation or reference in parentheses as shown below:

'With the improved access to the global business, several multinational companies have found their market in India.' ( O'Brein, 2003, p. 192)

**Annual report**   1. National Petroleum Industries. (2003). *Annual Report 2002–2003*. Mumbai: NPI.

**Book with one author**  O'Brien, J. (2003). *Wall Street on Trial: A Corrupted State,* Hoboken: Wiley, 192.

**Book with two authors**  Adams, Ramon, and Seymour Stevens. (1999). *Personnel Management.* Cambridge, MA: All-State, 203–06.

**Book with organization as Author**  Corporate Libraries Association. (2000). *Directory of Business and Financial Services,* New Delhi: Corporate Libraries Association, 345.

**Journal article**  Allison, G.W. (1999). The Implications of Experimental Design for Biodiversity Manipulations. *American Naturalist* 153 (1): 26–45.

**Periodical article**  Ganguly Sumit. India's Pathway to Pokhran II. (Spring 1999). *International Security* Vol. 23, No. 4, 148–77.

**Online magazine article**  Murthy Anand (1997, March 4). 'Saturn's Orbit Still High with Consumers,' Marketing News Online, Retrieved 13 May 1999 from <http://www.aaa.org/pubs/mn/c715/n1.htm>

**Newspaper article**  *The Hindu*. (1999, July 31), 'Let Employees determine Their Own Benefits.'

**Newspaper article from an electronic database**  Satel, Sally. (2003, October 27), 'OxyContin Half-truths can Cause Suffering.' *USA Today*, final edition. Lexis-Nexis, via Galileo, http://www.galileo.usg.edu

**Interview**  Ramaswamy Prakash. (2005, May 17). Personal Interview.

**World Wide Web**  Quincy, Dinah J. (2001, November13). 'Maxwell Announces New Health Benefit,' Maxwell Corp. Home Page. http://www.max_corp.com/NEWS/2001/f92500.html (Retrieved 14 January 2002).

**Government document**  Centre for Monitoring the Indian Economy (CMIE), *Monthly Review of the Economy*, October 1997.

**Case studies**  Kanter, R.M. (1993). 'FCB and Publicis (A): Forming the Alliance,' Harvard Business School Case No. 9-393-099. Boston: Harvard Business School Publishing.

## Chicago Manual Style

The Chicago Manual style is discussed in this section.

### In-text Citation

At the end of a quotation or reference, a superscript number as shown below marks the reference. This guides your readers to a complete reference at the bottom of the page or to a list at the end of your document:

> 'With the improved access to the global business, several multinational companies have found their market in India.'[2]

**Annual report**  National Petroleum Industries, 2003 , *Annual Report 2002–2003,* Mumbai: NPI.

**Book with one author**  J.O'Brien. 2003, *Wall Street on Trial: A Corrupted State,* Hoboken: Wiley, 192.

**Book with two authors**   Ramon Adams and Seymour Stevens. 1999. *Personnel Management*. Cambridge, MA: All-State, 203–06.

**Book with organization as author**   Corporate Libraries Association, 2000, *Directory of Business and Financial Services,* New Delhi: Corporate Libraries Association, 345.

**Journal article**   G.W. Allison. 1999. The Implications of Experimental Design for Biodiversity Manipulations. *American Naturalist* 153 (1): 26–45.

**Periodical article**   Sumit Ganguly. India's Pathway to Pokhran II. *International Security* Vol. 23, No. 4 (Spring 1999), 148–77.

**On line magazine article**   Anand Murthy, 'Saturn's Orbit Still High with Consumers,' Marketing News Online, 4 March 1997 http://www.aaa.org/pubs/mn/c715/n1.htm (Retrieved 13 May 1999)

**Newspaper article**   *The Hindu.* 'Let Employees Determine their own Benefits.' 31 July 1999.

**Newspaper article from an electronic database**   Sally Satel. 'OxyContin Half-truths can Cause Suffering.' *USA Today*, 27 October 2003, final edition. Lexis-Nexis, via Galileo, http://www.galileo.usg.edu

**Interview**   Prakash Ramaswamy, project manager, Honeywell Technology Solutions, 17 May 2005. Interview by author. Bangalore, India.

**World Wide Web**   Dinah, J Quincy, 'Maxwell Announces New Health Benefit,' Maxwell Corp. Home Page. 13 Nov 2001. http://www.max_corp.com/NEWS/2001/f92500.html (Retrieved 14 January 2002)

**Government document**   Centre for Monitoring the Indian Economy (CMIE), *Monthly Review of the Economy*, October 1997, 180.

**Case studies**   R.M. Kanter, 'FCB and Publicis (A): Forming the Alliance,' Harvard Business School Case No. 9-393-099 (Boston: Harvard Business School Publishing, 1993).

## EMAIL ETIQUETTE

Email is rapidly becoming the communication medium of choice in businesses. Most email messages inform employees, request data, supply responses, confirm decisions, and give directions. As an effective alternative to phone and courier, email enables you to contact, at the same time, a large number of people spread over wide geographical areas. Be it the Outlook Express, or Yahoo! Mail, Gmail, or any other mail server, you can reach milestones in building new business relationships, keeping alive the existing ones, interacting with acquaintances or just bridging gaps in communication. Some basic features of email etiquette apply while mailing people worldwide.

**No caps**   Look at the key marked Caps Lock on your keyboard—keep it off while typing an email—except for the normal use of capitals, proper nouns, to start a sentence, etc. Use Lower case as it is considered polite and easier to read. Capitals are considered extremely rude in electronic media and are a kin to shouting in a verbal conversation. Use proper fonts and avoid the colourful designs and tables if the email adopts a business approach.

> Most email messages inform employees, request data, supply responses, confirm decisions, and give directions.

**Signatures**   Attach a signature to the end of each message you send via email—name of business, contact information, url, and marketing slogan. Try to be simple.

>  **COMMUNICATION TOOL**
>
> **Quick Tips**
>
> - Be concise and to the point.
> - Answer all questions and preempt further questions.
> - Use proper spelling, grammar, and punctuation, where needed.
> - Make it personal.
> - Use templates for frequently used responses.
> - Answer swiftly.
> - Do not attach unnecessary files.
> - Do not overuse the high priority option.
> - Do not write in capital letters.
> - Read the e-mail before you send.
> - Do not overuse 'Reply to all'.
> - Be careful with formatting and HTML.
> - Do not forward chain letters without requesting delivery and read receipts.
> - Do not ask to recall a message or attach a message without prior permission.
> - Never use email to discuss confidential issues.
> - Use meaningful subject avoid 'Urgent' or 'Important'.
> - Use active voice instead of passive.
> - Do not ever forward any junk mail related to offence or obscene remarks.
> - Do not reply to spam mail.
> - Know your cyber laws.

**Grammar and punctuation** Do not type in a big mass of text. Divide in paragraphs and use applicable punctuation, commas, etc. Check spellings too.

**Quoting** Most email programmes make it easy to include text from the message your are responding to. This is useful because it puts your reply into context and gives the recipient an idea of what you are talking about. Observe the guidelines—set up your programme to insert 'Quote Headers' so that the original message can be clearly distinguished from the reply message. Leave a blank line between quotes and replies. Quote only to relevant portion of the message you are replying to. Avoid quotes of more than 10 lines.

**Chat language and humour** Do not use chat word such as 'Neways', 'b4', or 'kewl', as they seem irritating in regular business emails. In friendship mails, all is fine as far as the reader understands the right meaning. Go easy on humour. Add a joke at the end to add humour, but avoid sarcasm.

**Use subject line** Use the subject line intelligently. It should introduce the reader to the topic of the email.

**Limit the length of the message** Disk quota is alloted to each user, and so, limit the length of the message instead of prolonging the email. Do not assume everyone wants to receive your five MB files on jokes.

**Circulation of forwards** Do not send each and every forwards to 'all'. The long emailed list forwarded jokes or pictures are especially irritating and are especially not welcome.

**Spamming** Spamming is the electronic equivalent of junk mail. It refers to sending information about yourself/services you offer to people, who have not interest in it. In the online world, it is a taboo and can result in no-use mail junks.

**Chain letters** These are forbidden on the electronic mail networks as they unnecessarily load the system and interfere with the delivery of other messages. If chain letters are received, they can be sent to service providers who can suspend the offender's account. One can also report to abuse for unwanted mails, like harassing, filthy talk, etc. Know the relevant spam rules.

### Acronyms

Acronyms are so common that they regularly receive critical comments. Apart from technical acronyms such as BBS (bulletin board system), BCC (blind carbon copy), DNS (domain name system), FAQ (frequently asked question), HTML (hypertext Mark-up language), URL (uniform resource location), ISP (Internet service provider), chat groups and virtual worlds have their abbreviations, some of which turn up on email and in personal web pages.

## BUSINESS TERMS

In business communication, using business terms appropriate to the context enhances your professional image and enables you to comprehend your superiors using such terms while conducting meetings or conversing with you. A list containing business terms that you may find useful in your professional career is given as follows:

**Absenteeism:** A situation relating to habitual absence of the workforce from the work place

**Abstract:** A short written statement that contains the most important details of a longer piece of writing, such as a newspaper article, a report or a speech

**Accountability:** A management term referring to specified obligation of an employee for identified function or result

**Across the board:** Something embracing all without exceptions

**Ad hoc committee:** A one-time committee set up for a specific purpose

**Advertisement:** An announcement made recurrently over mass media regarding some service/product by the concerned organization for inviting public attention

**Agenda:** List of businesses to be transacted at a meeting; usually a formal meeting

**AIDA:** An acronym in marketing management, it stands for awareness, interest, desire and action defining the four psychological stages of the buyer of a product

**Annual general meeting (AGM):** The statutory annual meeting of the shareholders of a company in which the annual accounts are accepted, together with any proposals that require the approval by the general body of the shareholders

**Anti-trust laws:** Laws aimed at preventing monopoly

**Attitude:** A person's inherent or characteristic tendency to respond to or conduct in the environmental and external stimuli

**Attribute:** A distinctive feature of some person or of an organization

**Audit:** To make a review of books of accounts and financial statements for accuracy, truth, and fairness

**Authority:** The power conferred upon a position/post in an organization

**Bankrupt:** A firm is declared bankrupt when it fails to pay its creditors, and its assets must be liquidated for partial disposition of the liabilities.

**Bar code:** A series of lines of different width, printed on a product or package that an optical scanner can read to ascertain prices, etc.

**Bargaining:** A compromise position in organizational conflict; the purpose is conflict resolution/containment

**Bench marking:** An approach aimed at improvement of a process; makes an attempt to perceive an activity or process that is existing and then to select an external point of reference by which the activity can be evaluated.

**Board (management):** An appointed group of persons for the purpose of management of a corporate entity

**Bootlegging:** Illegal transfer and trade of goods

**Bottleneck:** Anything that impedes movement and progress

**Brand:** The name and symbol of particular merchandise

**Briefing:** Act of providing verbal information or instruction

**Brochure:** A small unbound booklet or leaflet that promotes a company's products or services

**Business ethics:** A set of code of conduct that governs business practices

**Business plan:** A business proposal put forward by any businessman ready for investments

**Buzzwords:** A technical jargon adopted for popular use

**Cartel:** A term in economics, which means an arrangement when a few sellers combine to wield monopoly powers over pricing of the products

**Case study:** An appraisal of an individual or a group or a community of any social unit or of any business situation

**Censor:** Ban on objectionable materials

**Chain of command:** The way through which the authority flows from the employees of lowest rank to higher up officials

**Channel of communication:** The medium by which a message is sent from the sender to receiver, that is, telephone, telex, fax, letter, etc.

**Communication:** The act of transmitting information

**Competition:** A state or symptom of the economy where many buyers and sellers freely compete for the same or similar goods and commodities

**Connotation:** When a word implies some other meaning over and above its literal meaning

**Contract:** Any agreement (written or oral) enforceable by law

**Conventional wisdom:** The generally accepted view

**Copyright:** The exclusive legal right allowed to the originator to produce and sell any work of art for a specified period

**Creditworthiness:** A creditor's measure of a consumer's past and future ability and willingness to repay debts

**.com:** One of the major Internet domains, usually representing for-profit business entities—other major Internet domains include .net, .org, .gov, .info, .biz, and .edu

**Customer:** Someone who has bought or made the decision to buy a product or service

**Chief executive officer:** The highest ranking executive officer within a company or corporation, responsibile for the overall management of its day-to-day affairs under the supervision of the board of directors

**Chief financial officer:** The officer of the organization responsible for handling finds, signing cheques, the keeping of financial records, and financial planning of the company

**Database:** A computer program that helps users organize information; databases range from simple collections of rows and columns (similar to a spreadsheet) to complex systems that process and manipulate millions of records in a variety of ways

**Debt:** Borrowed funds that are generally secured by collateral or a co-signer

**Direct marketing:** The process of sending promotional messages directly to individual consumers, rather than via a mass medium; includes methods such as direct mail and telemarketing

**Deflation:** A reduction in the general level of prices sustained over several months; usually accompanied by declining employment and output

**Domain name:** The text-based URL or address of a website; Domain names usually consist of several different segments. The name www.allbusiness.com, for example, includes the generic 'www' and '.com' identifiers, along with the unique name 'allbusiness'.

**Discount:** A deduction from the stated or list price of a product or service in relation to the standard price; A discount is a selling technique to encourage customers to buy and is offered for a variety of reasons: for buying in quantity or for repeat buying; as a special offer to move a slow-moving line or for paying by cash, etc.

**Distribution channel:** The route a product follows as it moves from the original grower, producer, or importer to the ultimate consumer

**Downsize:** Term used to indicate employee reassignment, layoffs, and restructuring in order to make a business more competitive, efficient, and/or cost-effective.

**Electronic data interchange (EDI):** The exchange of standardized document forms between computers for business use; traditionally been a very complex and expensive undertaking (as more companies build inexpensive, standards-based networks around the Internet, however, EDI systems are becoming cheaper and easier to use)

**E-business:** The conduct of business on the Internet, including the electronic purchasing and selling of goods and services, servicing customers, and communications with business partners

**Employee stock ownership plan (ESOP):** A retirement-type plan in which a trust holds stock in the employees' names; employees receive cash from the stock only when they leave the company or when the company is sold

**Entrepreneur:** An innovator of business enterprise who recognizes opportunities to introduce a new product, a new process or an improved organization, and raises the necessary money, assembles the factors for production and organizes an operation to exploit the opportunity

**Ergonomics:** The study of workplace design and the physical and psychological impact it has on workers; it is about the fit between people, their work activities, equipment, work systems, and environment to ensure that workplaces are safe, comfortable, and efficient, and that productivity is not compromised

**Exit interview:** An interview conducted at the end of an employee's term of employment to obtain employment feedback and to remind the employee of his/her confidentiality obligations

**Expenses:** Personal costs incurred by an employee in carrying out activities for an organization that are reimbursed by the employer

**FAQs:** Frequently asked questions

**Feasibility study:** An investigation into a proposed plan or project to determine whether and how it can be successfully and profitably carried out

**Flow chart:** A graphical representation for the definition, analysis, or solution of a problem, in which symbols are used to represent operations, data, flow, equipment, etc.

**Franchising:** A relationship in which the franchisor provides a licensed privilege to the franchisee to do business, and offers assistance in organizing, training, merchandising, marketing, and managing in return for a consideration.

**Freebie:** A product or service that is given away, often as a business promotion

**Free market:** A market in which supply and demand are unregulated, except by the country's competition policy, and rights in physical and intellectual property are upheld

**File transfer protocol (FTP):** The most common way to download and upload files over the Internet; FTP operations require special software that is built into the most popular web browsers and that is also available in a number of stand-alone applications website builders use FTP to upload files to a web host computer

**Fulfilment:** The process of responding to customer inquiries, orders, or sales promotion offers

**Guarantee:** A promise to step in and perform another's obligation should the first person fail or default

**Globalization:** The process of tailoring products or services to different local markets around the world

**Gross domestic product (GDP):** The total flow of goods and services produced by an economy over a year, measured by the aggregate value of goods and services at market prices

**Gross national product (GNP):** GDP plus domestic resident's income from investment abroad less income earned in the domestic market accruing to non-citizens abroad

**Growth rate:** The rate of an economy's growth as measured by its technical progress, the growth of its labour, and the increase in its capital stock

**Guerilla marketing:** A marketing technique, the aim of which is to damage the market share of competitors

**HyperText Mark-up Language (HTML):** One of the foundations of the Web, HTML is a text-based language used to describe the structure and layout of a document

**HyperText Transfer Protocol (HTTP):** The set of standards that lets web servers and browsers communicate with each other

**Hard sell:** A heavily-persuasive and highly-pressured approach used to sell a product or service

**Horizontal integration:** The merging of functions or organizations that operate on a similar level; Horizontal integration involves the union of companies producing the same kinds of goods or operating at the same stage of the supply chain.

**Hyperinflation:** Very rapid growth in the rate of inflation so that money loses value and physical goods replace currency as a medium of exchange

**Infringement (of copyright):** Any unauthorized use of a copyrighted work other than fair use

**Income statement:** A financial document that shows how much money came in (revenue) and how much money was paid out (expense)

**Inflation:** A sustained increase in a country's general level of prices that devalues its currency, often caused by excess demand in the economy

**Internet:** The vast collection in interconnected networks that provide electronic mail and access to the World Wide Web.

**Intellectual property:** The ownership of rights to ideas, designs, and inventions, including copyright, patents, and trademarks; protected by law in most countries, and the World Intellectual Property Organization (WIPO) is responsible for harmonizing the law across different countries and promoting protection of intellectual property rights

**Invoice:** A bill prepared by the seller of goods or services telling purchasers how much they owe

**Internet service provider (ISP):** Companies that provide access to the Internet, via either dial-up access numbers or a dedicated service such as DSL; many ISPs also offer Web hosting, domain name registration, and other like services.

**Joint photographic experts group (JPEG):** One of the two most common image types used on the Web, GIF being the other; used mostly for photographic reproductions and also referred to as jpg.

**Local area network (LAN):** A geographically-limited communications network linking computers, printers, and other devices; Ethernet is the most common means of creating a LAN

**Letter of credit:** A document issued by a bank guaranteeing payment of a customer's debt up to a set amount over a set period of time, used extensively in international trade

**Leverage:** A method of corporate funding in which a higher proportion of funds is raised through borrowing than share issue

**License:** A contractual arrangement, or a document representing this, in which one organization gives another the rights to produce, sell, or use something in return for payment

**Market:** A set of potential or real buyers or a place in which there is a demand for products or services

**Marketing communications (marcom):** The process and techniques involved in marketing, promoting, or selling products or services through creative, visual, or written communications

**Medium:** A type of publication or communications method (such as newspapers, television magazine, radio, billboard, and the Internet) that conveys news, entertainment, and advertising to an audience

**Multimedia:** Information that combines different types of content, such as text, images, animation, video, and audio

**Market niche:** A well-defined group of customers for which what you have to offer is particularly suitable

**Market positioning:** Finding a market niche that emphasizes the strengths of a product or service in relation to the weaknesses of the competition

**Marketing mix:** The set of product, place, promotion, price, and packaging variables, which a marketing manager controls and orchestrates to bring a product or service into the marketplace

**Netiquette:** A code of conduct that governs behaviour on the Internet; requires Internet users not to send unsolicited commercial email, or spam, to large numbers of other users—many ISPs and discussion groups ban users who consistently violate these rules

**Negotiation:** A discussion with the aim of resolving a difference of opinion, or dispute, or to settle the terms of an agreement or transaction

**Net worth:** The total value of a business in financial terms; net worth is calculated by subtracting total liabilities from total assets.

**Original equipment manufacturer (OEM):** A company that produces the equipment that bears another company's label

**Objective:** An end toward which effort is directed and on which resources are focused, usually to achieve an organization's strategy

**Outsourcing:** Term used in business to identify the process of sub-contracting work to outside vendors; the transfer of the provision of services previously carried out by in-house personnel to an external organization, usually under a contract with agreed standards, costs, and conditions.

**Overhead:** A general term for costs of materials and services not directly adding to or readily identifiable with the product or service being sold

**Patent:** Secures to an inventor the exclusive right to make, use and sell an invention for a designated period of time

**Performance appraisal:** A face-to-face discussion in which one employee's work is discussed, reviewed, and appraised by another, using an agreed and understood framework

**Price discrimination:** The practice of selling of the same product to different buyers at different prices

**Press release:** A document that communicates information to the press

**PLC (Product life cycle):** The stages of development and decline through which a successful product typically moves

**Proforma:** A projection or estimate of what may result in the future from actions in the present; A pro forma financial statement is one that shows how the actual operations of the business will turn out if certain assumptions are achieved; a document issued before all relevant details are known, usually followed by a final version

**Promotion:** A form of communication that calls attention to products and services, typically by adding extra value to the purchase, and includes temporary discounts, allowances, premium offers, coupons, contests, and rebates

**Psychographics:** The system of explaining market behaviour in terms of attitudes and life styles.

**Publicity:** Any non-paid, news-oriented presentation of a product, service, or business entity in a mass media format

**Public domain:** A copyright term that means a particular work is free for all to use without permission; Works in the public domain include those that were never copyrighted, those for which the copyright has expired, and public documents.

**Public relations:** Communication with various sectors of the public to influence their attitudes and opinions in the interest of promoting a person, product or idea

**Questionnaire:** A data-gathering form used to collect information by a personal interview, with a telephone survey, or through mail

**Return on investment (ROI):** The amount of profit (return) based on the amount of resources (funds) used to produce it; also, the ability of a given investment to earn a return for its use

**Recession:** A stage of the business cycle in which economic activity is in slow decline; usually follows a boom, and precedes a depression; and characterized by rising unemployment and falling levels of output and investment

**Redundancy:** Dismissal from work because the relevant job ceases to exist; occurs most frequently when an employer goes out of business necessitating a cutback in the workforce, or relocates part, or all, of the company

**Response marketing:** In e-marketing, the process of managing responses or leads from the time they are received through to conversion to sale

**Retailing:** Businesses and individuals engaged in the activity of selling products to final consumers

**Sales channel:** A means of distributing products to the marketplace, either directly to the end costumer, or indirectly through intermediaries, such as retailers or dealers.

**Sales force:** A group of sales people or sales representatives responsible for the sales of either a single product or the entire range of an organization's products

**Sales forecast:** A prediction of future sales, based on past sales performance; takes into account the economic climate, current sales trends, company capacity for production, company policy, and market research

**Sales promotion:** Activities, usually short term, designed to attract attention to a particular product and to increase its sales using advertising and publicity

**Shareware:** Software that anyone may download for free and pass along to others; the creators of shareware programs usually ask users to pay a small fee if they use the product after a specified period of time

**Sarbanes–Oxley Act:** A comprehensive federal law aimed at corporate governance and fraudulent financial transactions

**Secure electronic transactions (SET):** A standard for transmitting credit card data securely over the Internet; uses a series of digital certificate exchanges to verify the identities of consumers, merchants, and banks (although most major e-commerce players endorse SET, the standard's cost and complexity have hindered its progress; for now, the simpler SSL standard secures most e-commerce transactions)

**Soft sell:** The technique of using low-pressure appeals in sales

**Spam:** Slang for unsolicited commercial email; 'spamming' people with unwanted commercial email solicitations is considered unethical and now illegal in several US states (most ISPs terminate a user's account if he/she uses it to send spam).

**Survey:** A research method in which people are asked questions.

**Teleconferencing:** A meeting conducted by telephone among people in different locations.

**Telemarketing:** Using the telephone to sell, promote, or solicit products and services.

**Trademark:** A name, phrase, logo, image, or combination of images used to identify and distinguish a business from others in the marketplace; often used to include service marks that apply to businesses providing services as opposed to selling products (can be either registered or unregistered, with different levels of protection).

**Voicemail:** An automated service that answers phone calls and records incoming messages; enhanced voicemail services add features such as personalized greetings, longer recording times, and more saved messages.

**Warranty:** A guarantee about the performance of a product, or a promise to perform a specific act, such as repairing or replacing a defective or broken product.

**Workgroup:** Two or more networked computers that share files or other resources; a large network may consist of several smaller workgroups, each having different levels of access to various types of data

**What you see is what you get (WYSIWYG):** Used to describe any computer program that displays content, as it will appear in its finished form; many applications promise WYSIWYG features, but differences in output devices and screen displays make it nearly impossible to meet this goal every time

# Interview Questions

APPENDIX **A**

## 50 Standard Interview Questions

Listed below are commonly asked questions in interviews. Prepare the answers and rehearse them.

1. Tell me about yourself.
2. Why should we hire you?
3. Do you have any actual work experience?
4. How would you describe your ideal job?
5. Why did you choose this career?
6. When did you decide on this career?
7. What goals do you have in your career?
8. How do you plan to achieve these goals?
9. How do you evaluate success?
10. Describe a situation in which you were successful.
11. What do you think it takes to be successful in this career?
12. What accomplishments have given you the most satisfaction in your life?
13. If you had to live your life over again, what would you change?
14. Would you rather work with information or people?
15. Are you a team player?
16. What motivates you?
17. Tell me one quality in you that your friends admire the most.
18. Are you a goal-oriented person?
19. Tell me about some of your recent goals and what you did to achieve them?
20. What are your short-term goals?
21. What is your long-range objective?
22. What do you see yourself doing five years from now?
23. Where do you want to be ten years from now?
24. Do you handle conflict well?
25. Have you ever had a conflict with a boss or professor? How did you resolve it?
26. What major problem have you had to deal with recently?
27. Do you handle pressure well?
28. What is your greatest strength?
29. What is your greatest weakness?
30. If I were to ask one of your professors to describe you, what would he or she say?
31. Why did you choose to attend your college?
32. What changes would you make at your college?
33. How has your education prepared you for your career?
34. What were your favourite classes? Why?

35. Do you enjoy doing independent research?
36. Who were your favourite professors? Why?
37. Why is your grade point average (GPA) low?
38. Do you have any plans for further education?
39. How much training do you think you will need to become a productive employee?
40. What qualities do you feel a successful manager should have?
41. Why do you want to work in the industry?
42. What do you know about our company?
43. Why are you interested in our company?
44. Do you have any location preferences?
45. How familiar are you with the community that we are located in?
46. Will you relocate? Are you open to relocating in the future?
47. Are you willing to travel? How much?
48. Is money important to you?
49. How much money do you need to be happy?
50. What kind of salary are you looking for?

## Sample Answers to Some FAQs

This section provides answers to some frequently asked and rather tough interview questions. You can use them as the basic structure for formulating your own answers, but do not memorize these answers. Answer the questions with specific examples that show clear evidence for what you are saying about yourself. Always provide information that shows that you want to offer your very best to the company and have specifically prepared yourself for that.

Q. Tell me about yourself/introduce yourself.
A. (1) My background to date has been centred on preparing myself to become the very best manager/marketing professional/fund manager that I can. Let me tell you specifically how I have prepared myself to be one of the best fund managers ...
(Note: If you are interested in a very specific domain/profession, you can answer like this.)
A. (2) I am a person with passion to learn more and carry out my responsibilities with effectiveness and efficiency. During the course of my academic career at my university, I have learnt a lot from my friends and professors on both academic and non-academic matters. As a result of this, I have been able to enhance my knowledge and skills in various domains. I am an amiable person, and therefore, I can easily move in a large circle of friends and work in teams very well. I am looking forward to applying my knowledge and skills in my job, thereby contributing to my organization and at the same time enriching my experience.
(Note: If you do not have any particular area of expertise, you can answer like this.)

Q. Why should we hire you?
A. Because I sincerely believe that I am the best person for the job. I realize that there are many other students who have the potential to do this job. However, not only do I have the ability, but I also bring an additional quality—my attitude for excellence. My project experience in marketing research also gives me an edge over others. In 2010 and 2011, I won the best project award because of my passion for excellence. I can continue my efforts and make the projects successful in your company as well.

Q. **Where do you see yourself 10 or 15 years from now?**
A. Although it is certainly difficult to predict things far into the future, I know the general direction I want to progress towards. Within five years, I would like to become the best HR manager/chief technology officer/operations manager your company has. In fact, my personal career mission statement is to become a world-class marketing professional. I will work towards becoming the expert that others rely upon. And in doing so, I feel I will be fully prepared to take on any greater responsibilities that might be presented in the long run.

Q. **What is your greatest weakness?**
A. I would say my greatest weakness has been my lack of proper planning in the past. I would over-commit myself with too many variant tasks, then not be able to fully accomplish each as I would like. However, since I have come to recognize that weakness, I have taken steps to correct it. For example, I now organize everything on my smart phone so that I can plan all my appointments and 'to do' items.

Q. **What qualities do you feel a successful manager should have?**
A. The key quality should be leadership—the ability to be a visionary for the people who are working under him or her. A manager should be one who can set the right course and direction for the subordinates. He/she should also be a positive role model for others to follow. As a leader, he/she should be able to inspire and motivate others to reach the highest of their abilities. I would like to tell you about a person whom I consider to be a true leader ....

Q. **If you had to live your life again, what would you change?**
A. That is an interesting question. I realize that it can be very easy to continually look back and wish that things had been different in the past. But I also realize that things in the past cannot be changed, only future matters. That is why I always strive to improve myself each and every day and am working hard to increase my knowledge in the ... field.

That is also the reason why I want to become the very best ... your company has ever had. And all of that is still in the future. So to answer your question, there is nothing in my past that I would want to change. I look only to the future to make changes in my life.

If you are truly interested in the job, one thing you should do at the end of the interview is recap: (a) why you feel you are the best candidate for the job (give two or three of your strongest attributes and/or qualifications) and (b) why you are interested in the position on offer. Do not expect employers to make the first move. Let them know of your interest and desire to work for them.

# Impact Words

**APPENDIX B**

Here are 100 impact words that can possibly be used during job interviews or other professional presentations in order to create a positive impression in the minds of your audience.

1. accomplished, accommodate, achieve, active, adapt, aptitude, attain, assure, awarded
2. balanced, build, boost, brilliant
3. challenge, commitment, competent, composed, confident
4. dedicated, dependable, determined, deliver, demonstrate, dependable, diligent, dynamic
5. earned, energetic, engineered, enhance, enterprising, enthusiastic, established, excellence, exceptional, explore
6. facilitate, flexible, focused, fulfil
7. generate, goal
8. harmonious, honest
9. inspired, integrity, intense
10. keen
11. level-headed, logical, loyal
12. maintained, managed, methodical, mobilized, motivated
13. open-minded, opportunity, optimize, optimistic, organized, outstanding
14. passionate, perform, perseverance, poised, productive, proved
15. resilient, respect, responsibility
16. satisfy, secured, self-confidence, self-reliant, skilled, spearheaded, splendid, strength, strive, structured, succeed, surpassed, systematic
17. talent, timely, tracked
18. uncovered, undertook, united, updated
19. validated, verbalized, versatile, vitality
20. widened, won, wonderful

### Examples showing the use of impact words in sentences

| Don't Use | Use This |
|---|---|
| I **like** this work very much. | I am **passionate** about doing this work. |
| The method we had adopted **yielded good results.** | Our method was found to be very **productive.** |
| I **feel good** about my future. | I am very **optimistic** about my future. |
| The manager is a very **calm and cool** person. | The manager is a **level-headed** person. |
| The director **led** the team for the particular project. | The director **spearheaded** the team for the particular project. |
| The rise of the Internet **has contributed to** the growth of business on a global scale. | The rise of the Internet has **facilitated** the growth of business on a global scale. |

(Contd)

| Don't Use | Use This |
|---|---|
| We **tried our best** to reach a consensus on the issue. | We **strived** to reach a consensus on the issue. |
| It was a **very good** attempt. | It was a **brilliant** attempt. |
| My strength is that **I am good at many things.** | My strength lies in my **versatility.** |
| My team members were **interested in trying out new ways of doing the task.** | My team members were very **enterprising.** |

# Transitions

APPENDIX C

Providing transitions between ideas is largely a matter of attitude. We must never make any assumption about our readers' knowledge. In fact, it is a good idea to assume not only that the readers need all the information we have and need to know how we arrived at it, but also that they are not quite as quick as we are. We might be able to leap from one side of the stream to the other; however, we must consider that the readers might need a few stepping stones, and be sure to place them in readily accessible and visible spots.

Transitional tags range from the most simple—the little conjunctions *and, but, nor, for, yet, or, so*—to the more complex signals, including conjunctive adverbs and transitional expressions such as *however, moreover, nevertheless,* and *on the other hand*. The use of the little conjunctions, especially *and* and *but*, comes naturally to most writers. However, often a question arises whether one can begin a sentence with a small conjunction. Is not the conjunction at the beginning of the sentence a sign that the sentence should have been connected to the prior sentence? Well, sometimes, yes. However, often the initial conjunction calls attention to the sentence in an effective way. Look at the following sentences:

- Thus, a new form of energy has to be developed in a big way. And nuclear energy could very well be the solution.
- First, they assumed that water could be supplied by a centralized system. But, the cost was too high.

Beginning a sentence with a conjunction too often can be distracting, so this should be done only occasionally to vary sentence pattern or speed of the narrative flow of your text.

Transitional tags play a major role in providing a smooth flow to paragraphs. Transitions may be in the form of single words, phrases, sentences, and even whole paragraphs. They help to establish relationships and a logical progression among the ideas in a paragraph. A list of transitional words/phrases indicating the purpose for which they are used is given below.

### Transitional words and phrases

| Intention | Transitional Words/Phrases |
| --- | --- |
| Addition | and, or, nor, moreover, again, first, secondly, thirdly, next, last, lastly, finally, even more important, furthermore, also, in addition, further, besides |
| Time | while, after, when, meanwhile, during, next, then, in the past, immediately, later, soon, in the meantime, afterwards, following, at length, after a few days, never, always, whenever, sometimes, now, once, simultaneously |
| Place | here, there, nearby, beyond, wherever, opposite to, adjacent to, neighbouring on, bordering |
| Examples | for example, as an illustration, to demonstrate, specifically, for instance, to illustrate, again, such as |
| Similarity | in the same way, by the same token, similarly, in like manner, likewise, in similar Fashion |
| Contrast | on the contrary, in contrast, nevertheless, but, at the same time, although that may be true, nonetheless, on the other hand, yet, and yet, notwithstanding, otherwise, however, after all, though, despite this fact |

(Contd)

| Intention | Transitional Words/Phrases |
|---|---|
| Clarification | that is to say, in other words, to put it another way, to explain, to clarify, to rephrase it, i.e. (means 'in other words'), still, conversely, instead, even so, for all that, namely |
| Cause | because, on account of, for that reason, due to the fact that |
| Effect | therefore, consequently, as a result |
| Purpose | thus, hence, accordingly, in order to, for this purpose |
| Qualification | so that, to that end |
| Intensification | indeed, to repeat, by all means, undoubtedly, to be sure |
| Summary | to summarize, in sum, in short, to sum up, in brief, in summary |
| Conclusion | to conclude, in conclusion, finally, therefore, thus, it is now obvious that, with this object, with that in mind, thereupon, then, so, on the whole, as I have said |
| Concession | Admittedly, granted, it is true, to be sure, almost, nearly, probably, perhaps, maybe, although, in fact, without doubt, doubtlessly, obviously, unquestionably, inescapably, certainly, surely, of course, nobody denies, clearly, even though, in a manner of speaking, to be more precise, of course, needless to say |
| Spatial order | above, below, in the distance, nearby, beyond, opposite to/adjacent to, in front/ in back, to the right/to the left |
| Numerical order | first, second, third, etc.; in the first place, secondly, thirdly, etc.; to begin with; next; finally |
| Emphasis | again, for this reason, indeed, most compelling evidence, on the negative side, significant that, to emphasize, truly, another key point, frequently, in fact, most important information, on the positive side, surprising, to point out, with this in mind, first thing to remember, important to realize, key point, must be remembered, point often overlooked, surprisingly enough, to repeat |

# British and American Vocabulary

APPENDIX D

| British Words | American Equivalent |
|---|---|
| Accumulator, battery | Battery |
| Aerial | Antenna |
| Angry | Mad |
| Anywhere | Anyplace |
| Aubergine | Eggplant |
| Autumn, fall | Fall |
| Banknote (note) | Bill |
| Barrister | Attorney |
| Bill | Check |
| Bin/dustbin | Trash can |
| Biscuit/bickie | Cookie |
| Bonnet (car) | Hood |
| Boot, trunk | Trunk |
| Bottom of the street, end of the street | End of street |
| Braces | Suspenders |
| Bun, muffin | Muffin |
| Car park | Parking lot |
| Caretaker | Janitor |
| Cashier | Teller |
| Charge sheet, police record | Rap sheet |
| Chemist's | Drugstore |
| Chips | French fries |
| Cinema | Movie theater |
| Clothes peg | Clothespin |
| Comforter, quilt, blanket, duvet | Quilt, blanket |
| Condom | Rubber |
| Constable | Patrolman |
| Cooker | Stove |

| British Words | American Equivalent |
|---|---|
| Cot | Crib |
| Cotton | Thread |
| Couch/sofa/settee | Sofa |
| Crash | Wreck |
| Crisps | Potato chips |
| Crossroads | Intersection |
| Curriculum vitae (CV) | Résumé |
| Curtains | Drapes |
| Diversion | Detour |
| Draughts | Checkers |
| Drawing pins | Pushpins/thumbtacks |
| Dressing gown | Robe |
| Dual carriageway | Divided highway |
| Dummy | Pacifier |
| Dustman | Garbage man |
| Engine | Motor |
| Engine driver | Engineer (train) |
| Estate agent | Realtor |
| Exhaust pipe (exhaust) | Tailpipe |
| Fairy cake | Cupcake |
| Film | Movie |
| Fire engine | Fire truck |
| Flagpole, flagstaff | Flagstaff |
| Flat | Apartment |
| Flyover | Overpass |
| Football, soccer | Soccer |
| Fortnight | Two weeks |
| Garage, gas station | Gas station |
| Garden | Yard |

| British Words | American Equivalent | British Words | American Equivalent |
|---|---|---|---|
| Gear-lever | Gear-shift | Nowhere | No place |
| Glue | Gum | Number plate | License plate |
| Gone off, spoiled | Spoiled | Nursing home | Private hospital |
| Graduate | Alumnus | Oculist, optician | Optometrist |
| Grill | Broiler | Off-licence | Liquor store |
| Ground floor | First floor | Off you go, go ahead | Go ahead |
| Gumshoes, Wellington boots | Rubbers | Paraffin | Kerosene |
| Gym shoes, pumps | Gym shoes | Parcel, package | Package |
| Handbasin/sink | Sink | Pavement | Sidewalk |
| Handbag | Purse | Peep | Peek |
| Headmaster/headmistress, principal | Principal | Petrol | Gas/gasoline |
| | | Petrol station | Gas station |
| Hoarding | Billboard | Phone box | Telephone booth |
| Holiday | Vacation | Plaster, band-aid | Band-aid |
| Hoover | Vacuum cleaner | Play time/break time | Recess |
| Ill | Sick | Plimsolls | Gym shoes |
| Interval | Intermission | Polo neck, turtle neck | Turtle neck |
| Jam, jelly | Jelly | Post | Mail |
| Jersey, jumper, pullover, sweater | Sweater | Post box | Mail box |
| | | Post man | Mailman, mail carrier |
| Jug | Pitcher | Postal code | Zip code |
| Lift | Elevator | Pram | Baby carriage |
| Lorry | Truck | Pub | Bar |
| Macintosh, raincoat | Raincoat | Public school | Private school |
| Mad | Crazy | Public toilet | Rest room |
| Maize | Corn | Pudding/afters/dessert/sweet | Dessert |
| Mason | Stoneworker | | |
| Maths | Math | Puncture | blow-out |
| Mean | Stingy | Push-chair | Stroller |
| Motorway | Freeway | Queue, line | Line |
| Moulting, shedding | Shedding | Railway | Railroad |
| Mum/mummy | Mom | Reel of cotton | Spool of thread |
| Nappy | Diaper | Return | Round trip |
| Nasty, vicious | Mean | Reversing lights | Back-up lights |
| Nick, steal | Steal | | |

| British Words | American Equivalent | British Words | American Equivalent |
|---|---|---|---|
| Rise (in salary) | Raise | Tap | Faucet |
| Roll/bap, bun | Bum | Tap (outdoors) | Spigot |
| Roundabout | Traffic circle | Taxi | Cab |
| Rounders, baseball | Baseball | Tea towel | Dishtowel |
| Rubber | Eraser | Term | Semester |
| Rubbish | Trash | Tights | Pantyhose |
| Run the bath | Fill the bath | Timetable, schedule | Schedule |
| Saloon (car) | Sedan | Toilet/loo/bog | Bathroom/restroom |
| Sellotape (sticky tape) | Scotch tape | Torch | Flash light |
| Shoelace, shoestring | Shoestring | Tramp | Hobo |
| Shop | Store | Trousers | Pants |
| Silencer, muffler | Muffler | Trunk road | Highway |
| Single | One-way | Turn-ups | Cuffs |
| Somewhere | Someplace | Underground railway | Subway |
| Spanner | Wrench | Underpants | Shorts |
| Spanner, wrench | Wrench | Verge (of road) | Shoulder (of road) |
| Staff (of a university) | Faculty | Vest | Undershirt |
| Starter | Appetizer | Waistcoat | Vest |
| State school | Public school | Wardrobe | Closet |
| Subway | Underground walking passage/underpass/ pedestrian tunnel | Wash your hands | Wash up |
| | | Wellington boots/wellies | Galsohes |
| | | Windscreen, winshield | Windshield |
| | | Wing | Fender |
| Sump | Oil pan | Zebra crossing/pedestrian crossing | Crosswalk |
| Sweets | Candy | | |
| Swimming costume/ cozy | Bathing unit | Zip | Zipper |

# Common Usage Errors

APPENDIX E

- Adverbial Expressions: very, much. No definite rule can be given as to which adjectives are usually preceded by 'very' and which by 'much'. You can learn the correct usage only by constant observation and practice:
  Avoid – I am very much tired after my walk.
  I am very much pleased to see you.
  Grain has become very much dear owing to the war.
  Prefer – I am very tired after my walk.
  I am very pleased to see you.
  Grain has become very dear owing to the war.
  But the following are correct:
  I am very much afraid she will miss the train.
  I am very much happier now than I was last month.
  I was very much distressed when I heard of his death.
  Note: 'Very' can be omitted in each of these four sentences, without softening the superlative.
  Also study the following:
  We were much (or very much) surprised at your attitude.
  I am much (or very much) concerned about it.
  The Labour Opposition was much (or very much) surprised at your attitude.
  I am very tired.
  He was very drunk.
  The seating accommodation was very limited.
  I was much afraid of being ill.
- Fruit is more often used in the singular form than in the plural, even when it implies more than one fruit:
  I have brought you some fruits as present. (Say fruit.)
  But it is used in the plural when we mean that the fruits are of different kinds:
  What fruits grow in Kashmir? Cherries, gooseberries, apples.
- Vegetable, on the other hand, is always used in the plural.
  Note the following:
  Please get some fruit and vegetables from the bazaar.
  In the hot weather vegetables are a better food than rice.
  Note also: There is a fruit stall here, but not vegetable stall.
  He lives only on vegetable diet.
- Clothes, meaning articles of dress (i.e., garments), is always used in the plural:
  She went to the well to wash her clothes.
  I had a new suit of clothes made by the tailor.
  Be careful of the wet paint or you will spoil your clothes.
- Cloths means pieces of cloth not made up into garments:
  I gave the servant two clean cloths (i.e., pieces of cloth) and told him to polish the spoons and the table.

- For/to. The mistaken use of for in place of to:
  Avoid – This water is good for drinking.
  He went to the field for playing cricket.
  She went to the well for washing her clothes.
  Prefer – This water is good to drink.
  He went to the field to play cricket.
  She went to the well to wash her clothes.
- In case and if. In case must be carefully distinguished from if. It must not be used as equivalent to if. 'I shall take my umbrella in case it rains' is perfectly correct, but 'I shall take my umbrella if it rains' does not convey the same meaning. The first sentence implies that there is no rain at the time of starting.
- Compromise. He was compromised does not mean the same thing as He had made a compromise or consented to a compromise. He was compromised really means that he was placed in a compromising situation, i.e., a false position in which his interests were endangered.
- Dangerous(ly). I saw when her state was dangerous. The word dangerous is used in this sentence in the sense of dangerously ill, a construction which it will not bear.
- What do I do? is not permissible in English. We should say What am I to do?
- Emergent. To talk of an emergent case in the sense of a case which requires urgent or immediate attention is erroneous. In English emergent means emerging from.
- Enjoy. I enjoyed thoroughly. 'Enjoy' must have an object, and therefore, this expression is incorrect. I enjoyed myself thoroughly or I enjoyed the morning thoroughly would be correct.
- Fear for. Fear for is often misused for afraid of. I fear for you means that I am anxious on your behalf. It does not mean that I am afraid of you.
- Female/Woman. Females is often misused for women. The word female merely indicates sex. A human being belongs either to the male or female sex. To talk of the females in one's house or one's family, or female inmates, is indecorous; say women.
- Follow. I will follow you is often used by students in the sense of go with you, but this is wrong. Follow implies coming after (at a definite distance or definite interval), not go in with.
- Leave of/from. To take leave of means to part from or say goodbye to a person. But take leave from is used in the sense of obtaining permission from one's employer to stop work for a time. The following sentences are wrong: Sadly, he took leave from his wife (say, took leave of). I took leave of my employer for a month (say, took leave from).
- Part from/with. One parts from people, but with things. It is, therefore, incorrect to say: She parted with her friends (say, parted from). She was forced to part from her money (say, to part with).
- With a view to. With a view to is always followed by a gerund: 'He went there with a view to finding out the facts of the case.' 'With a view to studying the most modern books, he joined the local library.'
- Go/Come. It is the commonest thing to say, 'I hope to go over to your place next week'. 'I will go to you tomorrow.' The word come should be used in such contexts; e.g., 'I hope to come over next month'; 'I hope to come to Delhi next week; I will come over tomorrow; or 'I will come and see you tomorrow'.
- Healthy expressions. (a) I hope you are keeping good health is not good English. (Say enjoying good health, or still better, I hope you are well, or keeping fit.)
  (b) She seems very much reduced. Say, She looks much thinner, or merely, She looks very thin (not lean).
  (c) I have been in (or on) sick bed. Say, I have been ill in bed, or I have been in bed with cholera (etc.).

- High time implies the urgent necessity of doing something, owing to delay in the past which has brought matters to a head; e.g., It is high time to do something in the matter. But it is wrong to say, As it was high time, he left for college without taking his food. The meaning attached (quite wrongly) to the expression here is that it was getting late.
- Hope implies pleasurable anticipation. In any other sense the use of the word 'hope' would be wrong; e.g., I hope to get fever soon. I fear I am going to have fever would of course be the proper way of putting it.
- Leave should not be used in the sense of holidays. What are you going to do during the leave? is wrong. It should be, What are you going to do during the holidays?
- Noun clauses are often misused after like and want:
  
  Avoid –   I like that you come and see me.
  
               I want that you come and see me.
  
  Prefer –  I should like you to come and see me.
  
               I want you to come and see me.
- Male member is very often misused for male or man. The use of family members is incorrect: say members of the family. It is also wrong to say syndicate members, council members, etc.
  
  Avoid –   The male members of my family did not agree to this.
  
               His family members are not here.
  
  Prefer –  The men in my family did not agree to this.
  
               The members of his family are not here.
- May is frequently misused for could or might. May implies that permission is granted. It should not be used by a subordinate to a superior, e.g., a lecturer advising the Principal: You may ask them to prepare their essays at home. (You might tell....or You could tell....would, of course, be the proper way of putting it.)
- Be precise and concise. He failed to go there is wrong. In general use, say He did not go there. For the past one week is wrong. Say, For the past week.
- On the contrary/on the other hand. When two statements or ideas are directly opposed to each other, and attention is to be drawn to this opposition, the second of these statements needs to be introduced by on the contrary. On the other hand merely implies contrast. An expressed or understood on one hand goes before when on the other hand is used. The following examples illustrate their correct use:
  
  I intended no offence; on the contrary, I meant to compliment you.
  
  He is not my friend; on the contrary, he is my worst enemy.
  
  She has not finished her essay; on the contrary, she has just begun it.
  
  Failure on the one hand, and poverty on the other, pained him much.
  
  Duty required her to obey her father; on the other hand, love dictated a different course of action.
- Addicted to. Addicted to is never used in a good sense. We can never say, 'He is addicted to singing'. It is always used in a bad sense; e.g., 'He is addicted to gambling'. Or, 'He is addicted to alcohol'.
- All right. These words should always be written as two separate words and never as alright.
- Pulling on well. They are pulling on well. Say, pulling well together. Pulling together means working in harmony. Pulling on in the sense of getting on somehow is rarely used in English.
- Purchase is rarely used in English in the sense of buy. It is so used only figuratively, e.g., 'He purchased victory by sacrifice'.
- Rather and very, when used together, do not strengthen each other. Actually they cancel each other out. Rather means not very, a little, somewhat. He was rather very tired = He was somewhat very tired. This is

meaningless. The meaning intended is that the person was extremely tired. Rather very does not convey this meaning.
- Reading. I am reading in the sixth class. Say, I am in the sixth class. But I am reading for Honours is correct.
- Plurals such as sceneries, drainages, advices, and meats should be avoided. If a plural is wanted, say, bits of scenery, or better, scenes; drainage systems; pieces of advice, or better, much advice.
- Sick should not be used in the sense of some bodily disorder. It is wrong to say I am sick, or my brother fell sick. Say, I am ill; my brother fell ill. Sick is now only used to mean vomiting, or to be ready to vomit, or to denote 'the mental state of weariness, boredom, or disgust'; e.g., 'I am half sick of shadows,' said the Lady of Shallott. 'He is sick of this life.'
- Soon is often misused for quickly; soon is a question of time, quickly of pace or speed.
  Avoid –  He walked soon. He ate soon.
  Prefer –  He walked quickly. He ate quickly.
- Used to is frequently used wrongly as an auxi-liary to form a present tense denoting habitual action. We used to take our meals at ten. Say: We generally dine at ten. Used to implies a habit which once prevailed, but has been discontinued.
- Study the following.
  He is a boy of seven years old. (Say, He is a boy seven years old.)
  He disposed it off. (Say, He disposed of it.)
  I had been to Delhi last week. (Say, I went to Delhi last week.)
  I hope you would do it. (Say, I hoped you would do it, or I hope you will do it. But I wish you would do it is correct.)
  Do you know swimming? (Say, Do you know how to swim, or Can you swim?)
  When do you go to your bed? (Say, When do you go to bed?)
  They worked whole the day. (Say, the whole day, or all the day.)
  I have consented for attending a funeral. (Say, to attend).
  We go for walking. (Say, we are going for walk.)
  They played fairly. (Say, played fair.)
  The rose smells sweetly. (Say, smells sweet.)
- The same. The use of the same for a pronoun (it, them, they, etc.) is common in business letters, but is undesirable; such as, "When you have examined the samples, please return the same to us with your remarks." It would be better to use 'them' for 'the same.'
- What if? Say, why not? Or What does it matter? Similarly, Why not we go? is not good English. Say, Why not go? Or Why should we not go? Why shouldn't we go?
- Study the following.
  (a) I failed to get a job and so I am keeping quiet. (Say, I am nothing or I am unemployed.)
  (b) Have you taken your meals? (Say, Have you had your food? Or Have you had your dinner?)
  (c) Please do the needful. (Say, Please do what is necessary.)
- Be careful in the use of etc. When written in full, this is etcetera, meaning 'and other things'. If you want to begin with such as, you must not end with etc.
  Avoid making a statement such as:
  Many kinds of fruits grow in Kashmir, such as apples, peaches, plums, pears. etc.

Why not? Because such as means that you are going to mention some but not all. To put etc. is to say the same thing twice. You may use either of these forms:

(i) Many kinds of fruits, such as apples, peaches, plums, pears, grow in Kashmir.

(ii) Many kinds of fruits—apples, peaches, plums, pears, etc.—grow in Kashmir.

Do not confuse the two constructions.

- As follows. The verb is invariable in number: never 'as follow'. 'His argument is as follows.' 'The rules and regulations are as follows.'
- Broadcast. We never say 'broadcasted.' 'Pandit Nehru's speech was broadcast (not broadcasted) from the A.I.R. Station, Dehli.'
- Aggravate. The word aggravate means 'to add to some hurt which already exists'. A sentence such as 'The noise aggravated him' is wrong because aggravated is not used in its proper sense. We can however say, 'The noise aggravated his trouble'. His trouble already exists; the noise makes it worse. Instead of aggravate, one should use annoy, trouble, etc., according to the context.
- Kindly requested. "Applications are 'kindly requested' to enclose a stamped envelope for reply." The sentence, as it stands, means that the request is made in a kindly spirit.

  But this is not the idea here. Applicants must act in a kind way by sending a stamped envelope. We should amend the sentence thus: 'Applicants are requested to be so kind as to send a stamped envelope for reply'.
- Transpire. 'What transpired between the two lovers.' Transpire is often wrongly used in the sense of happen, occur, come to pass. It really means to look out, to become known.

  The sentence above ought to read, 'What occurred (or went on)...'. The following sentence has the correct use: 'It has transpired that the lovers are parted'.
- Individual. Individual is often used wrongly for the more usual person, man, etc. and individuals is used instead of people, persons. The sentence An individual who has been of very great assistance to the police, should read 'A person (or a man) who ...'.

  Individual(s) may be used only when there is some idea of comparison with a crowd or body of people: 'The morality of a crowd as a whole is said to be lower than the average morality of the individuals composing the crowd.'

  'The fruits of this labour will benefit the nation and not an individual.'
- Claim. Modern English usage stigmatizes the use of claim in the sense of assert. Claim may be followed by the infinitive only when (a) it is in the active voice and (b) the infinitive represents an action done by the subject: 'He claimed to have discovered a new planet'. But the following sentences are unacceptable: 'The car was claimed to do fifty miles to the gallon'; 'The examination was claimed to be just and fair'. (A.B.C. of English Usage.)
- Dare. 'He dare not do it.' 'Dare he go?' 'He dare do anything.' In negative and interrogative sentences and wherever the dependent infinitive has no 'to', dare is used for the normal dares in the third person singular present tense.
- Due. A. B. C. of English Usage says: 'unlike owing to, due (to) has never become a compound preposition, that is, due retains its adjectival function and must be properly related to the noun or pronoun it qualifies'. Thus in the sentence Due to the bed weather, he cannot come, 'due' obviously does not qualify 'he', and therefore has nothing left to qualify. If due is to be used, the only way is to provide it with an actual noun: 'His inability to come was due to the bad weather,' where 'due' qualifies 'inability'. But the obvious and idiomatic construction is, 'Owing to the bad weather, he cannot come.' It is a good rule to use due only as a

predicative adjective (as in the sentence above—that is, not like a participle, as the first word, or as a phrase). It is incorrect to say: 'Some articles have increased in price due to the increasing demand'. We should say 'owing to'.
- Equally. Equally is never followed by as in Modern English. In such sentences as 'I am interested in detective stories equally as you', as should be replaced with with. In such a sentence as 'The Opposition are equally as guilty as the Government', equally is tautological. If as is omitted, the correct idiom with equally is: 'The Opposition and the Government are equally guilty'.
- A failed B.A. Avoid such expressions, for it is no honour to fail in an examination. You may say, 'I tried to get my B.A., but unhappily was not successful.'
- An England-returned gentleman. Such an expression will provoke an Englishman's smile, for it is meaningless. You may say, 'He has been to England'.
- Half. Half of them is or are ? The rule is that when the noun or pronoun following of is singular, half is considered singular: 'Half of our heavy task was done'. When the noun or pronoun following of is plural, half is considered plural: 'Half of the apples were rotten'. The same rule applies to lots of and heaps of.
- In possession of is active, equivalent to 'holding'; in the possession of is passive, equivalent to 'held by'. 'The thief was found in possession of the papers.' 'The papers were found in the possession of the thief.'
- Probable. When probable is used as a predicate adjective after an anticipatory it, it has to be followed by a 'that ...' noun clause: 'It is probable that it will happen,' not 'It is probable to happen'.
- 'Providing that ...' should not be used in writing, though the construction is by no means un-common in colloquial and business English.
- Reason. "At least three warnings are necessary in connection with the word reason:
    (i) 'The reason is because' is a type of tautological expression that defies both grammar and logic. The correct idiom is 'The reason (why etc.) is that ....' So the sentence 'The reason why I am dealing with so many pictures tonight is because I happen to have seen them all just, recently' may be recast in two ways:
        (a) 'The reason .... is that I happen ....'
        (b) 'I am dealing with so many pictures tonight because I happen ....'
Equally bad, and almost equally common are: 'The reason ... is due to', and 'The reason ... is on account of'.
    (ii) 'Because of that reason' is a near relative of the error dealt with under(i). You act not because of but for that reason. Reason itself indicates cause.
    (iii) 'The reason for the increase may be attributed to the rapid development of science during the past two centuries.' The increase may be attributed, not the reason; the reason is the rapid development.
In all three types of sentences cited, the trouble arises from a confusion of ideas that leads to a double statement of cause." (Adapted).

# Commonly Misspelt Words

APPENDIX F

Here is a list of some commonly misspelt words:

| | | | |
|---|---|---|---|
| abandon | acclamation | adjourn | agree |
| abbey | accommodate | administrator | agreeable |
| abbreviate | accompaniment | admirable | agreement |
| abduct | accompany | admission | agriculture |
| abeyance | accomplice | adopt (adapt) | aide-de-camp |
| abhor | accomplish | adulterate | alcohol |
| abhorrent | accord | advantageous | alert |
| abject | accordance | adventure | alien |
| abolish | accredited | adventurous | alienate |
| abolition | accrue | adversary | allege |
| abominable | accumulate | advertisement | allegory |
| absence | accurate | advice | alliance |
| absolutely | accusation | advisable | alliteration |
| absorb | accuse | aerial | allot |
| absorption | accused | aerie (or aery) | allowance |
| abstain | accustomed | aero plane | allude |
| abstemious | achieve | aeronaut | allusion |
| abstinence | acknowledgement | aesthetic | almighty |
| abstract | acquaint | affectionate | almost |
| absurd | acquaintance | affiliate | alms |
| absurdity | acquiesce | affirmation | aloof |
| abundance | acquire | affix | aloud |
| abundant | acquisition | afflict | already |
| abyss | acquit | affluence | altogether |
| academic | across | affray | amass |
| academy | actuality | afraid | ambassador |
| accede | actually | against | ambiguity |
| acceleration | acute | agape | ambiguous |
| accent | additional | agency | ambitious |
| accept | address | aggravate | amenity |
| acceptance | addressee | aggregate | amiable |
| access | adequacy | aggression | ammunition |
| accessible | adequate | aggrieved | analysis |
| accident | adhere | agitator | anarchy |
| accidentally | adhere | agony | ancestor |

| | | | |
|---|---|---|---|
| anchor | assignation | brunette | cipher |
| ancient | attendance | buffet | circular |
| anecdote | audience | bungalow | circumstantial |
| anger | autobiography | buoyant | coalesce |
| angle | autumn | bureaucracy | coerce |
| angry | avenue | business | coffee |
| anguish | awe | butcher | coincide |
| annihilate | bailiff | cadence | collaborate |
| announce | balcony | cadre | collapse |
| annual | balloon | café | colleague |
| annually | balm | calendar | commemorate |
| anoint | banana | caliber | commission |
| anonymous | bankruptcy | callous | committee |
| antidote | banquet | calumny | communication |
| antique | barbarous | can dour | comparable |
| antiquity | barrier | canoe | comparison |
| antiseptic | bazaar | canonize | competition |
| antithesis | beauteous | cantonment | complement |
| anxiety | beautify | canvass | compliment |
| anxious | beguile | capacious | comprehension |
| apologize | behavior | cap-a-pie | condolence |
| apology | believe | caprice | conference |
| apostle | benediction | carcass | conscious |
| apparatus | beneficent | career | consecutive |
| apparent | beneficial | caricature | contemporary |
| appearance | besiege | carriage | contemptible |
| appetite | bestow | casualty | correspondence |
| application | bewitch | catalogue | countenance |
| appreciate | bias | caterpillar | creature |
| apprentice | bicycle | celebrate | cubicle |
| approach | bier | celestial | curiosity |
| appropriate | binocular | cemetery | cylinder |
| approval | biography | censure | cypress |
| approve | biscuit | centenary | daffodil |
| approximate | bivouac | ceremonial | damn |
| aptitude | bizarre | ceremony | daunt |
| aquatic | blasphemy | certain | dearth |
| architecture | bosom | chafe | deceased |
| armature | bough | champion | deceit |
| ascetic | bounteous | character | decency |
| assemblage | bouquet | charismas | decision |
| assent | breathe | chronicle | declaration |

| | | | |
|---|---|---|---|
| deference | eczema | feign | grieve |
| defiance | effeminate | felicitous | guarantee |
| deficiency | efficacious | fever | guardian |
| defy | effrontery | fibre | guild |
| deity | eighty | field | guise |
| deliberate | elapse | fiend | gymnasium |
| delineate | elegance | fierce | half-caste |
| delirious | elegiac | fiery | hammock |
| deliverance | elementary | flourish | handiwork |
| demoniac | eligible | foible | handkerchief |
| demurrage | emancipation | forebode | harangue |
| dependence | embarrassed | forecast | harass |
| dependent | embroidery | foreign | hasten |
| depression | empyrean | foretell | heinous |
| derision | enamel | foreword | hereditary |
| descend | enamour | forfeit | heroes |
| descent | endeavour | forgo | heroine |
| despot | endow | forty | heterogeneous |
| develop | enfranchise | forward | hideous |
| devour | ennoble | fourteen | hindrance |
| diagnosis | enthusiasm | fraud | holiday |
| diarrhea | entreaty | freer | horde |
| dictionary | envisage | freight | horizon |
| difference | equilibrium | fruition | humorist |
| digression | ethereal | fulfill | hurricane |
| dilemma | etiquette | fullness (fulness) | hygiene |
| discern | evaporate | furlong | hypocrisy |
| disciplinarian | exaltation | furlough | hypocrite |
| discipline | exasperate | furniture | ideal |
| discreet | excellence | galloping | idiom |
| disguise | exception | gardener | idiosyncrasy |
| dissolution | exclamation | gaudy | idolatry |
| donor | exhilarate | gauge | ignominy |
| doughty | explanation | gauging | illiteracy |
| drudgery | explosion | genealogy | illiterate |
| dubious | extinguish | genius | illusion |
| dwelling | extraordinary | glutton | immanent |
| dynasty | extravagance | gnaw | immeasurable |
| dysentery | fascinate | goddess | immediate |
| earnest | fashion | good-bye | imminent |
| eccentricity | feature | gorgeous | necessary |
| ecstasy | February | grammar | negotiate |

| | | | |
|---|---|---|---|
| negro | opposite | jealous | literary |
| negroes | oppress | jeopardize | litigant |
| neighbour | ordinary | jersey | litigious |
| nestling | original | jess amine | livable |
| niche | ounce | jovial | livelihood |
| niece | immovable | judgement | lottery |
| night | impartial | jugglery | lovable |
| ninth | impassable | juice | luxurious |
| notable | impenetrable | jungle | lyre |
| noticeable | impiety | kaleidoscope | magnificent |
| notified | impostor | key | magnify |
| notifying | impoverish | kitchen | magnifying |
| novice | inaccessible | knack | maintenance |
| noxious | inadequate | kneel | majority |
| nutriment | inalienable | knowledge | manageable |
| nutriment | inappropriate | knuckle | maneuver |
| nutrition | incandescent | laboratory | manifesto |
| nymph | inclement | laborious | mantelshelf |
| oasis | inconsolable | labyrinth | manufactory |
| obedience | inconvenient | lacerate | manufacture |
| obituary | incredulous | language | marketed |
| oblique | indefatigable | languid | marriage |
| obliterate | independence | laudation | marshaled |
| obnoxious | indigenous | launder | martial |
| obscure | indiscretion | laurel | marveled |
| obsequies | indispensable | league | marvelous |
| obsequious | indomitable | ledger | masquerade |
| observance | infallible | legitimate | masterpiece |
| occasion | infinitesimal | leopard | mattress |
| occurred | inflammation | leper | mayoralty |
| occurrence | influential | lever | measuring |
| odour | ingenious | liaison | medicinal |
| offence | ingenuity | liberate | mediocre |
| offensive | ingenuous | library | memorandum |
| Olympic | ingratiate | licence | mercenary |
| omelet (omelette) | ingredient | license | mileage |
| omen | inoculation | licentiate | millennium |
| omission | inquisitor | lieutenant | millionaire |
| omniscient | insurrection | lineage | miniature |
| onomatopoeia | irresistible | lineament | minstrel |
| opium | itch | liquefy | miscellaneous |
| opportunity | itinerant | liquidate | mischief |

| | | | |
|---|---|---|---|
| mischievous | panegyric | phthisis | pyorrhea |
| misjudgement | panorama | physician | pyre |
| modeled | pantaloon | physique | quack |
| modified | pantheism | picnic | quaint |
| modifying | parade | picturesque | quarrel |
| moisten | parallel | pier | quarreled |
| moneyed | paralyses | pigeon | quarrelsome |
| monitor | paralysis | pillage | quarterly |
| monologue | parchment | piquant | quell |
| mortal | parliament | pique | querulous |
| mosquito | paroxysm | pistol | question |
| motto | partition | pitiful | quiescent |
| mottoes | passionate | plausible | quiet |
| mountainous | pastoral | plea | quinine |
| moustache | pastry | pleasant | Quixote |
| movable | pasture | plebian | quorum |
| murkiness | patronage | pledge | quota |
| murky | pavilion | pneumonia | quote |
| muscular | peak | politician | raciness |
| musician | peasant | pollute | radiance |
| myriad | peculiar | populace | raillery |
| mystery | pecuniary | portray | rarefy |
| navigable | pedestal | position | raspberry |
| outcast | peevish | précis | ratable |
| ovation | penance | precocious | rating |
| overawe | penitence | predicament | ravenous |
| overhaul | penitent | predilection | razor |
| overwhelming | penury | preference | realm |
| owner | pepper | premium | recede |
| oyster | perceptible | presumptuous | receipt |
| pacify | perennial | pretentious | receivable |
| paddle | permanence | preventive | receive |
| pageant | permissible | procrastinate | receptacle |
| palace | persecute | profession | recompense |
| paladin | personal | prohibit | reconcilable |
| palanquin | personnel | proprietor | reconciliatory |
| palatial | perspire | psalm | recurred |
| palmy | persuasion | pseudonym | recurrence |
| palsy | perturbation | pudding | reducible |
| paltry | perversion | pungent | referee |
| pamphlet | pharmacy | purse | reference |
| panacea | philosophy | pursuit | regiment |

## Appendix F: Commonly Misspelt Words

regrettable
rehearsal
relief
religious
relive
remedy
reminiscence
remitted
removable
remuneration
repelling
repetition
replaceable
repository
reprehensible
reproducible
reprovable
repudiator
reputable
requital
resistance
resolvable
respite
resplendent
responsible
restaurant
resumption
resurrection
retraceable
retractable
retrievable
retrieve
revel
reveled
revenue
reverie
reversible
revival
rhapsody
rheumatism
rhyme
rhythm

ribald
ridiculous
righteous
rigorous
rogue
symbol
symmetrical
symphony
symptom
synonymous
synopsis
syntax
syrup
tacit
taciturnity
tactician
talisman
tamable
tambourine
tangible
tapestry
tariff
tattoo
tawdry
teachable
teasel
technique
tedious
teetotaler
telegram
telephone
telescope
temerity
temperament
temperance
tempestuous
temporary
tenable
tenacious
tenancy
tendency
tenement

tenor
tenuity
termagant
terrestrial
tertiary
testament
testimonial
theatre
therapeutics
thermometer
thief
roguery
roseate
routine
ruling
ruling
rum our
Sabbath
sacrifice
sacrificial
sacrilege
sacrilegious
sagacious
sagacity
salutary
salutary
satchel
sate less
satellite
saucer
sauciness
sausage
saviour
scabbard
scenery
sceptic
schedule
scheme
scholar
schooner
science
scientific

scintillate
scissors
scurrilous
scythe
secede
secrecy
sedentary
seize
seizure
sensibility
sensitive
separable
separate
sepulcher
serviceable
several
sewer
shabbiness
sheriff
shield
shoeing
shriek
shyly
shyness
siege
sieve
signatory
silkiness
similar
similarly
simultaneous
sincere
sincerity
sinecure
siphon
siren (not syren)
sixtieth
sizable
skein
skilful
slyly
smoky

| | | | |
|---|---|---|---|
| smoulder | suicide | tolerance | unanimous |
| solecism | suitor | tomato | unassuming |
| solemnize | summary | tomatoes | unconscionable |
| soliloquize | sumptuous | tongue | uncouth |
| soliloquy | supercilious | torpor | undersigned |
| somber | superfluous | tortuous | undoubtedly |
| somersault | superintendent | tournament | undulatory |
| sootiness | supersede | traceable | unfledged |
| sorcery | superstition | tragedy | ungrudging |
| souvenir | supervise | traitorous | unguent |
| spasm | suppressor | tranquility | unintelligible |
| specify | supremacy | transcend | unique |
| spectre | surfeit | transference | unison |
| sphere | surliness | transferred | unitary |
| splendour | surname (not | transgressor | unmistakable |
| sponge | sir-name) | transient | unnatural |
| spontaneous | surveyor | treasurer | unsavoury |
| sprightly | survivor | treatise | unspeakable |
| squalid | susceptible | treble | unthinkable |
| squalor | suspender | tremendous | until |
| squeak | suspense | tremor | unwieldy |
| squire | suspensor | tremulous | upbraid |
| stalwart | suspicious | trespass | urine |
| statutory | suzerainty | tributary | usable |
| staunch | swerving | tricycle | useful |
| stillness | sycamore | triennial | usually |
| stratagem | sycophant | trifling | usurp |
| strategy | syllable | trousers | utilitarian |
| stupefy (not stupify) | sylvan | tuberculosis | utterance |
| stylish | thieving | Tuesday | uxorious |
| subduing | thigh | tuition | vacancy |
| subservience | thistle | turbulence | vaccinate |
| subsistence | thorough | twelfth | vacillate |
| subterranean | threatening | twentieth | vacuum |
| subtle | threshold | typing | valedictory |
| succeed | through | tyrant | valiant |
| successful | ticklish | ulterior | valleys |
| succour | tincture | ultra vires | valuable |
| succumb | tiring | umbrage | variegated |
| sufferer | tithe | umbrella | Vaseline |
| sufficient | tocsin | umpire | vegetable |
| suffrage | toilet | unalloyed | vehement |

## Appendix F: Commonly Misspelt Words

veiled
veneer
vengeance
venison
venomous
ventilator
venturesome
venturous
veracious
veracity
verandah
verify
vestige
veteran
veterinary
vicinity

vicissitude
victuals
vigorous
vigour
village
villain
villainous
vinegar
visible
visitor
vitiate
vivacity
vivify
vocabulary
volleys
volunteer

votary
wag (g) on
waif
walnut
waltz
warily
wary
wasteful
weasel
Wednesday
weird
welcome
welfare
whirl
wholesome
wield

wilful
wilfulness
withhold
witticism
woollen
worshipped
wreak
wrought
yacht
yeoman
yield
zodiac
zoology

# Index

AIDA 519

Business correspondence 154
   Basic principles 155
   Components 156
   Kinds 161
   Letters 161
   Memo report 172
   Memos 171
   Strategies 158
Business presentations 296
   Conclusion 325
   Controlling 331
   Delivery 304
   Introduction 319
   Main body 323
   Organizing/Outlining 303
   Sales presentations 327
   Stage fright 331
   Structuring 302
Business proposals 205
   Components 207
   Format 211
   Formula 216
   Key elements of winning 217
   Layout and design 216
   Types 206
Business reports 195
   Characteristics 197
   Kinds 197
   Parts 201
   Purpose 199
   Steps in writing 199
Business writing 133

Careers 222
   Career goal 224
   Job search 224
   Preparing résumé 225
Communication 3
   Benefits 8
   Business 5
   Characteristics 7
   Components 12
   Effectiveness 4
   Facts 14
   Features 7
   Functions 9
   Importance 8
   Process 12
   Strategies to improve 36
   Telephonic 5
Communication aids 587
   Business terms 617
   Effective paragraphs 597
   Elements of effective English 587
   Email etiquette 615
   Punctuation and capitalization 602
   Reading 602
   Referencing styles 612
Communication barriers 25
   Closed communication 27
   Difference in status 27
   Incorrect medium 28
   Information overload 28
   Lack of trust 27
   Message competition 29
   Message complexity 29
   Organizational structure 26
   Physical distraction 30
   Unethical communication 30

Communication media 104
   Conferencing 114
   Effectiveness 126
   Emails 119
   Groupware 121
   Instant messaging 117
   Internet 110
   Negative impact 123
   Positive impact 122
   Selection 124
   Technologies 104
   Tools 105
Communication network 14
   Upward communication 15
   Downward communication 16
   Horizontal communication 16
   Spiral/Diagonal communication 17
Conferences 384, 393
   Conduction 394
   Planning 393
   Preparation 396
   Promoting 396
Conversations 336
   Essentials 337
   Management 340
   Non-verbal cues 346
   Stressful conversations 348
Corporate communication 494
   Corporate citizenship 497
   Crisis 500
   Media release 505
   Practice areas 496
   Strategy 499
Cross-cultural communication 88
   Communication styles 90

# Index

Ethical communication 546
  Code 550
  Dilemmas 560
  Ethics in advertising 577
  Internet 570
  Issues 558
  Perspectives 555
  Privacy 573
  Strategic approaches 565
  Values 553

Follow-up letter 249
  Rejection 250
Functional areas 453
  Financial communication 475
  Human resource 469
  Management information systems 482
  Marketing communication 454
  Project management communication 464

Group discussions 408
  Approach 418
  Assessment group discussions 415
  Benefits 409
  Functional roles 411
  Improvement 414
  Non-functional roles 413
  Performance 414
  Sample GD topics 421
  Steps 417
  Tips for success 420
  Workplace GD 410

Informal communication 18
  Grapevine 18
  Contacts with outsiders 20
Instructions 178

Audience 186
Format 183
Graphics 182
How to write 180
Oral 185
Written 179
Internal communication 20
  Tips 20
Interpersonal communication 23
  Stages 23
  Styles 24
Interviews 357
  Case interviews 376
  Mastering 378
  Non-verbal aspects 363
  Preparation 358
  Principles 358
  Questions 362
  Styles 370
  Success 361
  Types of interviews 365
  Types of questions 362

Listening 261
  Advantages 264
  Barriers 270
  Common myths 265
  Listening in leadership 274
  Motivational benefits 281
  Pay-offs 290
  Poor listening 284
  Process 263
  Strategies 288
  Three managerial levels 279
  Types 265

Manager, roles 10
  Decisional 11
  Informational 11
  Interpersonal 10
Meetings 384

Evaluating 392
Leading effective meetings 388
Minutes 392
Planning 385
Process 386
Purposes of meetings 385
Strategic issues 389
Teleconferencing 396
Video conferencing 401
Web conferencing 403

Non-verbal cues 73
  Appearance 80
  Chronemics 47
  Definition 55
  Facial expressions 61
  Gestures 68
  Haptics 80
  Interpreting 54
  Kinesics 66
  Oculesics 59
  Posture 70
  Proxemics 48
  Significance 82
  Tips 75

Online recruitment 251
  Advantages 251
  Techniques 251

Persuasive communication 512
  Advertising 514
  Advertising communication 517
  AIDA 519
  Basic approaches 533
  Communication 532
  Conflict management 523
  Guidelines 537
  Intercultural 539
  Negotiation 531
  Online advertising 521

Organizational conflicts 524
Planning advertisements 520
Public speaking 296

Résumé 222
Arrangements 227
Electronic résumé 233
Mistakes 231
Scannable résumé 233
Sending résumé 246
Résumé format 230
Chronological 232
Combination 232
Functional 232
Mini 232
Targeted 232

Team briefing 432
Benefits 435
Features 434
Formats 440
Process 434
Samples 443
Techniques 439
Team presentation 408, 422
Benefits 422
Effective 428
Execution 426
Planning and presentation 423
Purpose 423
Teleconferencing 396
Advantages 398
Applications 399
Disadvantages 399
Types 397

Video conferencing 401

Web conferencing 403

# About the Authors

**Meenakshi Raman** was formerly Professor and Head, Department of Humanities and Social Sciences, at the Birla Institute of Technology and Science (BITS) Pilani, KK Birla Goa Campus. She has several years of teaching experience and has taught English and communication at various levels. Dr Raman is a co-author of three other books in the area of communication published by OUP and has several articles to her credit.

**Prakash Singh** is Associate Professor and Area Chairman, Finance and Accounting, Indian Institute of Management, Lucknow. Dr Singh has over seven years of experience in teaching courses at the postgraduate level and also conducts training programmes for managers and other professionals.

# Related Titles

### STRATEGIC MANAGEMENT
### [9780198070795]

**N. Chandrasekaran**, *Vice President, Corporate Affairs, Take Solutions and Director, Centre for Logistics and Supply Chain Management, Loyola Institute of Business Administration (LIBA), Chennai*, and **P.S. Ananthanarayanan**, *Consultant and Visiting Faculty, Bharathidasan Institute of Management (BIM), Trichi, LIBA, and University of Madras, Chennai*

This is a comprehensive textbook designed to meet the requirements of postgraduate management students. Written in a student-friendly style, it includes discussions on concepts and research in the field, and provides a balanced approach to the subject.

### Key Features
- Contains extensive discussion on the importance of governance and corporate social responsibility
- Provides a brief to readers on how to overcome risk-based challenges when applying new strategies
- Discusses the process of strategic cost management to help readers understand how the expenses of a project can be monitored

### PRODUCTION AND OPERATIONS MANAGEMENT, 2/e
### [9780195690873]

**Kanishka Bedi**, *Vice President (Executive Education) and Associate Professor, U21 Global Graduate School, Singapore*

This completely revised edition adopts an application-oriented approach to the subject.

### Key Features
- Includes detailed coverage on Bureau of Indian Standards (BIS), Agmark grading, ISO 9000, ISO 14000 and COPC-2000 in the chapter on quality management
- Provides hands-on applications of various models, such as the transportation model, using MS Excel, MS Project, and SPSS

### HUMAN RESOURCE MANAGEMENT
### [9780198076681]

**Uday Kumar Haldar**, *Principal, Swami Vivekananda Institute of Management and Computer Science, Kolkata*, and **Juthika Sarkar**, *HR practitioner*

This book explains the core concepts and theories of human resource management and uses a large number of examples, exhibits, images, figures, and cases.

### Key Features
- Covers various facets of HR systems including acquiring, retaining, and developing talent
- Dedicates a chapter exclusively to the contemporary research findings in the field of HRM
- Discusses HR strategies in different sectors, such as manufacturing, services, and knowledge industry

### FINANCIAL MANAGEMENT, 2/e
### [9780198072072]

**Rajiv Srivastava**, *Professor, Indian Institute of Foreign Trade, New Delhi* and **Anil Misra**, *Associate Professor, Management Development Institute, Gurgaon*

This new edition provides a detailed coverage of the core concepts of financial management and has been updated thoroughly with additional sections and improved explanations.

### Key Features
- New sections on corporate debt restructuring and regulation of working capital finance
- Revised content related to corporate governance, economic value added, venture capital and private equity, and long-term and short-term sources of funds
- Improved explanations of existing topics

## Other Related Titles

- 9780198066460   *Organizational Change and Development* by Bhattacharyya
- 9780198063025   *Supply Chain Management* by Chandrasekaran
- 9780198064145   *IT for Management* by Muthukumaran
- 9780195669855   *Management Information Systems* by Jaiswal and Mittal

Visit us at www.oup.co.in and www.oupinheonline.com